THE MGM
STOCK COMPANY:
The Golden Era

James Robert Parish
and
Ronald L. Bowers

Editor T. Allan Taylor
Research Associates John Robert Cocchi
Florence Solomon
Photo Associate Gene Andrewski

Arlington House   New Rochelle, N.Y.

DEDICATED TO

The Artistic, Technical, Administrative,
and Sales Talent
who made the MGM product possible

PN
1998
.A2
P394

"CIRC" — VGC

ACKNOWLEDGMENTS

Research Consultant: Doug McClelland

Mrs. Loraine Burdick; Bruco Enterprises; Cinemabilia Book Shop (Ernest Burns); *Filmfacts* Ernest Parmentier); *Film Fan Monthly* (Leonard Maltin); *Films in Review* (Charles Reilly); Ray Gain; Pierre Guinle; Mrs. R. F. Hastings; Charles Hoyt; Richard M. Hudson; Ken D. Jones; Albert B. Manski; Mrs. Earl Meisinger; Jim Meyer; Peter Miglierini; Norman Miller; Movie Poster Service (Bob Smith); Jeanne Passalacqua; Michael R. Pitts; Mrs. Peter Smith; Don Stanke; Charles K. Stumpf; John S. Spano; Leon Van Dyke

Fourth Printing, January 1975

Library of Congress Catalog Number 73-154412

ISBN 0-87000-128-0

MANUFACTURED IN THE UNITED STATES OF AMERICA

CONTENTS

June Allyson

"She's skinny; she's a little bowlegged; she can't sing much or dance much. She's certainly no raving beauty, and she's got a speaking voice that seems to be crying for cough drops after every syllable." That's how one plain-speaking friend described June Allyson, who, for filmgoers since the 1940s, has always been the wistful girl next door, wearing Peter Pan collars and starched skirts. It was an image which fit neatly into the "family" of MGM stars. She fortuitously began in motion pictures in the middle of America's involvement in World War II, a time when the public held high in esteem the wholesome, virtuous girl friend or wife left behind by a soldier going to war. June projected this wholesomeness convincingly and the public eagerly went to see her films, particularly when she was teamed with bobby-soxers' delight Van Johnson.

Within a few short years after the war had ended, however, June's screen career rapidly declined and despite another decade of film work and later a television series, she has been unable to revive her movie career successfully. While the June Allyson of the screen may have been part of the American dream, her personal life has been shatteringly a series of deprivations, hard work, and misfortune.

Her real name is Ella Geisman and she was born in a Bronx tenement on October 7, 1917 (MGM publicity releases took as many as ten years off her age). When she was six months old her father, a building superintendent, deserted his wife, taking their small son with him. Mrs. Geisman took baby Ella to live with her parents and got a job in a printing plant at $20 per week. When she could afford it, she and her daughter would rent an apartment, always without a bathroom, as June recalls, and when things would be going badly, they would move back with her grandparents.

At the age of eight, while playing with a neighborhood boy, a tree limb fell on both of them. Her friend was killed and she was hurt so badly she had to wear a brace for four years. While the brace and swimming for therapy helped her regain her strength, she began escaping the deprivation of her world in movie theatres, watching the dancing of Fred Astaire and Ginger Rogers. She saw some of their pictures eighteen times and began telling her schoolmates that she was better than Rogers and was going to set out to prove

9

it. She entered Amateur Night contests in the Bronx, and even though she never won, she kept on dancing. Things were a little better at home, now an apartment at 1975 Bryant Avenue, since her mother had remarried. After high school June began to seek jobs as a dancer. There was a $50 a week play date at the Club Lido in Montreal and then appearances in several movie shorts for Vitaphone and Educational Films.

When June was twenty, she got a part in the chorus line of a Broadway musical, *Sing Out The News*. When that flopped, she joined the chorus line of the Copacabana nightclub until she was hired for the chorus of Jerome Kern–Oscar Hammerstein II's musical *Very Warm For May*. That show opened in 1939, and one of her colleagues in the chorus was Vera-Ellen. This role got June into Rodgers and Hart's *Higher And Higher*, playing Nellie. She recalls: "I've been in more flops than you can imagine. I couldn't dance, and Lord knows I couldn't sing, but I got by somehow. It was Richard Rodgers who was always keeping them from firing me, as every dance director wanted to do." It was that kind of grit that kept her working. After *Higher And Higher*, she understudied Betty Hutton in Cole Porter's *Panama Hattie*, which starred Ethel Merman. When Hutton was felled by measles, understudy June took over and, lo and behold, there was a famous director in the audience. The director was George Abbott, and he put her in his *Best Foot Forward* at $125 weekly, and when he went to Hollywood to direct that film he took her along, as he did Desi Arnaz.

The film version of *Best Foot Forward* (1943), which starred Lucille Ball, was being produced by MGM and June found herself under contract to Metro. According to June, it was MGM producer Joe Pasternak who persuaded Louis B. Mayer to look at her screen test by pleading to the studio kingpin: "Please look at this test and do just two things. Look at her eyes and listen to her voice. Don't pay any attention to anything else about her. These are distractions we can iron out." Thus was born the celluloid June Allyson, the diminutive redhead with the surprisingly husky voice (caused by chronic bronchitis and enlarged vocal cords—in 1961 she underwent a throat operation which for a spell caused her voice to return to a high soprano).

MGM next gave her a specialty number in *Girl Crazy* (1943) treating Mickey Rooney roughly in a Manhattan nightclub number, then a guest spot in the revue, *Thousands Cheer* (1943), and a small role in *Meet The People* (1944). The stars of the latter were Lucille Ball and Dick Powell. Powell and his then wife, Joan Blondell, were finding marriage rough going, and June and the actor–crooner soon became a "thing." (They married on August 19,1945 with Louis B. Mayer smiling as they cut their wedding cake.)

By now, MGM had decided she was right for them and gave June a starring part opposite Van Johnson (he had been in *Best Foot Forward* on Broadway) and the public responded to the two "typically" American young actors. They each became what one critic termed the "improbable distillation of the nonexistent thing we call 'average.'" The picture was *Two Girls and a Sailor* (1944) with pert starlet Gloria DeHaven as June's sister. MGM was

With Van Johnson in *High Barbaree* (1947)

With Dick Powell and David Wayne in *The Reformer and the Redhead* (1950)

pleased with the public's reception to June and cast her as the lady cellist with a husband at war in *Music For Millions* (1945) starring Margaret O'Brien, the only girl on the lot who cried on screen more often than June. June's teary specialty came to the fore in *Her Highness and the Bellboy* (1945) in which she plays an invalid who loves bellhop Robert Walker, who cannot see straight because of the dazzling beauty of visiting royalty Hedy Lamarr. She and Kathryn Grayson are sisters who desert Boston for cabaret lights in *Two Girls from Boston* (1946). The same year she was showstopping with "Cleopatterer" in *Till The Clouds Roll By*, but curiously adrift as Claudette Colbert's neurotic daughter in *The Secret Heart*.

High Barbaree (1947) was badly conceived fantasy drama, with June playing the loyal wife of flyer Van Johnson, downed in the World War II Pacific. *Good News* (1947) was a 1920s college musical with Peter Lawford, and she and Johnson were together again in the slapstick *The Bride Goes Wild* (1948). After performing the memorable "Thou Swell" in *Words and Music* (1948), she was Jo in the remake of *Little Women* (1949) and despite the unavoidable comparisons to Katharine Hepburn's 1933 version, she was quite believable. Her next picture she was reluctant to make, but it contains her best performance. That was *The Stratton Story* (1949) a very good biopic starring James Stewart as the baseball player who loses his leg in a hunting accident. June's husband Powell had persuaded her to accept the assignment as the typical wife-next-door, because he was perceptive enough to know she had far more competition in glamorous musical roles. *The Stratton Story* displays her beautifully in her screen synthesis as an unsophisticated Margaret Sullavan type of screen star.

Although June was now in her prime, MGM was not. She was given less and less rewarding roles, because, she claims, the studio felt any picture with her in it would make money, and it would be ridiculous to waste time tailor-making vehicles for her. Two costarring pictures with Powell were not boxoffice hits: *The Reformer and the Redhead* (1950) and *Right Cross* (1950). Nor was another with Van Johnson, *Too Young To Kiss* (1951), much better. She played a doctor in *The Girl in White* (1952), a nurse who loves Humphrey Bogart in *Battle Circus* (1953), and ended her MGM contract with Van Johnson in *Remains to Be Seen* (1953), which played on the wrong half of a double bill. The final straw for June was when the promised role in *The Long, Long Trailer* (1954) was handed to ex-MGM player Lucille Ball.

June was reluctant to leave MGM which she explains, "had been mother and father, mentor and guide, my all-powerful and benevolent crutch. When I left them, it was like walking into space." However, she went immediately into the top-grossing *The Glenn Miller Story* (1954) at Universal at the special request of James Stewart who played her bandleader husband in this smartly sentimental biography. More noble wife roles followed: *Executive Suite* (1954) back at MGM; *Woman's World* (1954) at Twentieth Century-Fox; *Strategic Air Command* (1955), again with Stewart and in VistaVision; and *The McConnell Story* (1955) with somnambulant Alan Ladd. It was against her

With Peter Lawford, Ray McDonald, Joan McCracken, Loren Tindall, and Pat Marshall in *Good News* (1947)

husband's advice that June accepted the lead opposite José Ferrer in *The Shrike* (1955), but an opportunity to play an onscreen shrew intrigued her, not to mention the possibility of an Oscar for her meaty dramatic assignment. She was strident in *The Shrike* and rightly received no Oscar nomination.

The mid-1950s found June as the "remake queen" in a trio of indifferent rehashes of past successes. *The Opposite Sex* (1956) at MGM was a musical rendition of *The Women* with June in the Norma Shearer part. *You Can't Run Away From It* (1956) was a jazzed-up version of *It Happened One Night*, but Columbia's earlier, unofficial remake *Eve Knew Her Apples* (1945) was far more felicitious. *My Man Godfrey* (1957), with David Niven, only proved that June was no reincarnation of the late Carole Lombard. Her swan song as a leading lady in motion pictures was *Stranger in My Arms* (1959), as the widow who defies her mother-in-law (Mary Astor) in running after Jeff Chandler.

In 1960, Powell persuaded June to undertake a video series, in a format similar to *The Loretta Young Show* but it lasted only one season. That same year she and Powell separated and she began divorce proceedings, because his television work never allowed him time at home. In 1961 she underwent a kidney operation and throat surgery, and during her recuperation she and Powell reconciled. Shortly thereafter, Powell discovered he had cancer and he died on January 2, 1963. She and Powell have a daughter Pamela, whom they adopted in 1948, and a son Richard Jr., born in 1950. Powell left an estate estimated at $2 million. Ten months after Powell's death, June married Glenn Maxwell, owner of two barber shops in California (he had been Powell's barber). They divorced in 1965, remarried in 1966, and divorced a second time, but still live together. The second divorce was prompted by the terms of Powell's will: She gets $700 monthly if married, $4,000 monthly if unmarried. She was quoted as saying that Maxwell is "the nicest man I've ever known—besides Richard."

Throughout the early 1960s June was professionally inactive. She was a guest on Judy Garland's television series in 1963 and did a summer of stock with a pre-Broadway show that fell apart. She attempted a nightclub act in 1967 in Las Vegas with Donald O'Connor, and three years later, returned to Broadway to take over Julie Harris' role in *Forty Carats*. Her reviews were respectable, but more often than not she was out of the show due to "illness," the same problem that has befallen her in 1972 while touring in the national company of *No, No Nanette* with Judy Canova and Dennis Day. She has been more effective in small guest starring roles on television, such as an episode of *Name of the Game* which reteamed her with Van Johnson, and a 1971 telefeature, *See the Man Run*, in which she was the distraught wife of Eddie Albert—their daughter had been kidnapped. She was also among those who adorned the nostalgia-bent *The Twentieth Century Follies* (1972), a special on which she sang-and-danced "Ballin' The Jack." Besides a guest-starring assignment on television's *Sixth Sense* series, June took time to return to her alma mater for a brief cameo in Metro's *They Only Kill Their Masters* (1972), reunited with such fellow alumni as Ann Rutherford and Peter Lawford.

Looking back on her career, June recently reflected: "I never did feel quite right about the roles I was called upon to portray—the gentle, kind, loving, perfect wife, who will stand by her man through 'anything.' In real life I'm a poor dressmaker and a terrible cook; in fact, anything but the perfect wife."

When asked if there were any of her movies she would like destroyed, June quickly replied: "Yes. *The Three Musketeers*." Two movies she wishes she had been asked to appear in: *All About Eve* and *The Three Faces Of Eve*.

JUNE ALLYSON

Best Foot Forward (MGM, 1943)
Girl Crazy (MGM, 1943)
Thousands Cheer (MGM, 1943)
Two Girls and a Sailor (MGM, 1944)
Meet the People (MGM, 1944)
Music for Millions (MGM, 1945)
Her Highness and the Bellboy (MGM, 1945)
The Sailor Takes a Wife (MGM, 1945)
Two Sisters from Boston (MGM, 1946)
Till the Clouds Roll By (MGM, 1946)
The Secret Heart (MGM, 1946)
High Barbaree (MGM, 1947)
Good News (MGM, 1947)
The Bride Goes Wild (MGM, 1948)
The Three Musketeers (MGM, 1948)
Words and Music (MGM, 1948)
Little Women (MGM, 1949)
The Stratton Story (MGM, 1949)
The Reformer and the Redhead (MGM, 1950)
Right Cross (MGM, 1950)
Too Young to Kiss (MGM, 1951)
The Girl in White (MGM, 1952)
Battle Circus (MGM, 1953)
Remains to Be Seen (MGM, 1953)
The Glenn Miller Story (Universal, 1954)
Executive Suite (MGM, 1954)
Woman's World (20th-Fox, 1954)
Strategic Air Command (Paramount, 1955)
The McConnell Story (WB, 1955)
The Shrike (Universal, 1955)
The Opposite Sex (MGM, 1956)
You Can't Run Away from It (Columbia, 1956)
Interlude (Universal, 1957)
My Man Godfrey (Universal, 1957)
Stranger in My Arms (Universal, 1959)
They Only Kill Their Masters (MGM, 1972)

With Humphrey Bogart in *Battle Circus* (1953)

15

Leon Ames

" I held all the great beauties on my knee. And the hell of it was, they were all thirteen," Leon Ames said recently regarding his 1940s years at MGM where he was best noted for his screen father characterizations. Almost from the start of his professional career, Ames realized he was not leading man material, and settled down to a busy schedule of minor and then supporting player parts in a long string of movies, ranging from poverty row quickies to A productions at the major studios. Having served a long stage and screen apprenticeship, his Metro tenure represented his gravy years. He worked just as hard, or harder, at that studio, emoting in an average of four pictures per year, but he was receiving a decent if mild $500 weekly salary and had the benefit of appearing in well-mounted screen fare. *Meet Me In St. Louis* (1944) proved a fortuitous casting assignment. Although it typed him as the epitome of the old-fashioned screen dad, it led to starring parts in two teleseries.

Ames was born Leon Wycoff in Portland, Indiana on January 20, 1903, where his father was a furniture manufacturer and farmer. Always stagestruck, in 1925 Ames wangled a job with the Charles K. Champlin Company then playing Lansford, Pennsylvania. He was first a general business man, then took on bit acting parts. Three years later he was in the road company of *The Cat and the Canary*, then *Love 'Em and Leave 'Em*, and next *Broadway* (1929). When *Tomorrow and Tomorrow* (1931) with Kay Johnson was playing Los Angeles, he was signed by Universal to do the romantic hero in their *Murders in the Rue Morgue* (1932), starring Bela Lugosi and Sidney Fox. Then he slipped back into playing very minor characters in several pictures before he was cast as Preston Foster's brother in Fox's *The Man Who Dared* (1933), a fictionalized biography of the late mayor Anton Cermak of Chicago. In 1934–1936 he toured with *Tobacco Road* and made his Broadway debut in *Bright Honor* (1936) but managed to sandwich in such pictures as *Strangers All* (1935) with May Robson, the first film in which he was billed as Leon Ames.

Ames continued to work steadily in Hollywood, but he could find no niche to make his mark. He was a gangster chief in *Charlie Chan on Broadway* (1937), and a suspect in *Mysterious Mr. Moto* (1938). He had his first real screen lead in Grand National's *Cipher Bureau* (1938) as a government counterespionage agent, followed by a similar role in the same company's

Panama Patrol (1939). Meanwhile he was popping up on screen as Louis Napoleon in *Suez* (1938), as an unsavory character in Don Barry's *Calling All Marines* (1939), and as a man suspected of murdering his mother (Blanche Yurka) in *Ellery Queen and the Murder Ring* (1941).

Ames had met actress Christine Gossett on a Hollywood soundstage, and they were wed in 1938. Their daughter Shelley was born in 1941 and a son, Leon, Jr., was born in 1944.

Ames returned to Broadway in 1940 to play the former football hero in *The Male Animal* and then was seen in *The Land Is Bright* (1941), *The Russian People* (1942), and *Guest In The House* (1942). He then went back to the West Coast, played Captain Wheeler in the initial *Crime Doctor* (1943) entry, and Pat O'Brien's lifelong friend in RKO's *The Iron Major* (1943). He was performing in a tour of *Silk Hat Harry* in 1943 when MGM signed him to a seven-year contract. His first role was as the head of the Smith household in *Meet Me in St. Louis*. As the harassed breadwinner in a house full of women, he almost uproots his family to move to New York, but changes his mind much to everyone's relief, both on and off screen. He is the one who sings (actually producer–composer Arthur Freed dubbed his voice) "You and I" with his film wife Mary Astor. If he seemed confounded by the antics of his screen children in this Technicolor musical, he had no allusions about child performers. He later would say about professional juveniles: "All as sweet as sugar until the director says 'action.' And then they'll cut your throat with a dull saw."

In *Thirty Seconds Over Tokyo* (1944) he was Lt. Jurika, a dapper crook in *The Thin Man Goes Home* (1944), and a Major in *They Were Expendable* (1945). He had a would-be comic role as the heavenly guardian angel in *Yolanda And The Thief* (1946) but his best Metro work came later that year in *The Postman Always Rings Twice*. He was the shrewd prosecuting attorney who nails John Garfield for the crime. As a change of pace he played the hammy 1920s-style matinee idol in *Merton Of The Movies* (1947), was Elizabeth Taylor's dad in *A Date With Judy* (1948), and Rosalind Russell's jealous producer–lover in RKO's *The Velvet Touch* (1948). He inherited Samuel Hinds' role of Mr. March in the remake of *Little Women* (1949) and ended his Metro stay as a secret service agent in *It's a Big Country* (1951). For Warners he was most effective as Doris Day's homey, small town father, to Rosemary De Camp's on-tune wife and mother, in the Booth Tarkington-derived *On Moonlight Bay* (1951) and the followup *By the Light of the Silvery Moon* (1953).

On November 22, 1953 the video series *Life with Father* debuted on CBS-TV with Ames as the senior Clarence Day in turn-of-the-century New York. His favorite remark was an exasperated "Oh, no!" Lureen Tuttle was his patient wife. The series ran until July 5, 1955. Ames would later appear in stock versions of the play.

In 1957, he was president of the Screen Actors Guild and in 1958 was back on Broadway in the short-lasting comedy *Howie*. Also he had done a road tour of *The Moon Is Blue* in 1952. He returned to the screen as the mercenary father of Rodney Harrington (Barry Coe) in *Peyton Place* (1957) and gave an incisive performance as Paul Newman's industrialist father, who is incapable of coping with his own alcoholic wife (Myrna Loy), in *From the Terrace* (1960).

Ames was again a television series star in 1962 when he took over Spencer Tracy's film role in the teleseries *Father of the Bride*, filmed at MGM. His daughter Shelley had a small role as the office receptionist.

After playing the college president to professor Fred MacMurray in Walt Disney's *The Absent-Minded Professor* (1961) and the sequel *Son of Flubber* (1963), he did two more Disney movies and then retired for five years. He still had his longtime business venture, Studio City Ford Company, to keep him busy, but he grew tired of the professional inactivity and accepted cameo roles in *On a Clear Day You Can See Forever* and *Tora! Tora! Tora!*, both done in 1970. Then he played the old sheep rancher in *Toklat* (1971), about a grizzly bear on the rampage. He was unbilled as the pediatrician in the almost all-black actor remake of *The Asphalt Jungle* called *Cool Breeze* (1972), had a bit in Elizabeth Taylor's *Hammersmith Is Out* (1972), and lately starred in Alaska Pictures' *The Timber Tramp* (1973). Active as he has always been, he now wants to remain in harness as an actor.

LEON AMES

Murders in the Rue Morgue (Universal, 1932)
13 Women (RKO, 1932)
The Famous Ferguson Case (FN, 1932)
State's Attorney (RKO, 1932)
A Successful Calamity (WB, 1932)
Silver Dollar (FN, 1932)
Cannonball Express (World-Wide, 1932)
Uptown New York (World-Wide, 1932)
Parachute Jumper (WB, 1933)
Alimony Madness (Mayfair, 1933)
The Man Who Dared (Fox, 1933)
Forgotten (Invincible, 1933)
Ship of Wanted Men (Showmen's Pictures, 1933)
The Count of Monte Cristo (UA, 1934)
I'll Tell the World (Universal, 1934)
Now I'll Tell You (Fox, 1934)
Reckless (MGM, 1935)
Strangers All (RKO, 1935)
Mutiny Ahead (Majestic, 1935)
Get That Man (Empire, 1935)
Stowaway (20th-Fox, 1936)
Dangerously Yours (20th-Fox, 1937)
Death in the Air (Puritan, 1937)
Murder in Greenwich Village (Columbia, 1937)
Charlie Chan on Broadway (20th-Fox, 1937)
45 Fathers (20th-Fox, 1937)
International Settlement (20th-Fox, 1938)

Bluebeard's Eighth Wife (Paramount, 1938)
Walking Down Broadway (20th-Fox, 1938)
The Spy Ring (Universal, 1938)
Island in the Sky (20th-Fox, 1938)
Come On Leathernecks (Republic, 1938)
Mysterious Mr. Moto (20th-Fox, 1938)
Strange Faces (Universal, 1938)
Cipher Bureau (Grand National, 1938)
Suez (20th-Fox, 1938)
Secrets of a Nurse (Universal, 1938)
Risky Business (Universal, 1939)
I Was a Convict (Republic, 1939)
Pack Up Your Troubles (20th-Fox, 1939)
Mr. Moto in Danger Island (20th-Fox, 1939)
Panama Patrol (Grand National, 1939)
Man of Conquest (Republic, 1939)
Fugitive at Large (Columbia, 1939)
Code of the Streets (Universal, 1939)
Legion of Lost Flyers (Universal, 1939)
Calling All Marines (Republic, 1939)
Thunder Afloat (MGM, 1939)
East Side Kids (Monogram, 1940)
Marshal of Mesa City (RKO, 1940)
No Greater Sin (University Film Products, 1941)
Ellery Queen and the Murder Ring (Columbia, 1941)
Crime Doctor (Columbia, 1943)

The Iron Major (RKO, 1943)
Meet Me in St. Louis (MGM, 1944)
Thirty Seconds over Tokyo (MGM, 1944)
The Thin Man Goes Home (MGM, 1944)
Son of Lassie (MGM, 1945)
Weekend at the Waldorf (MGM, 1945)
They Were Expendable (MGM, 1945)
Yolanda and the Thief (MGM, 1946)
The Postman Always Rings Twice (MGM, 1946)
Lady in the Lake (MGM, 1946)
No Leave, No Love (MGM, 1946)
The Show-Off (MGM, 1946)
The Cockeyed Miracle (MGM, 1946)
Undercover Maisie (MGM, 1947)
Song of the Thin Man (MGM, 1947)
Merton of the Movies (MGM, 1947)
Alias a Gentleman (MGM, 1948)
On an Island with You (MGM, 1948)
A Date with Judy (MGM, 1948)
The Velvet Touch (RKO, 1948)
Little Women (MGM, 1949)
Any Number Can Play (MGM, 1949)
Scene of the Crime (MGM, 1949)
Battleground (MGM, 1949)
Ambush (MGM, 1949)
The Big Hangover (MGM, 1950)

Dial 1119 (MGM, 1950)
Watch the Birdie (MGM, 1950)
The Skipper Surprised His Wife (MGM, 1950)
The Happy Years (MGM, 1950)
Crisis (MGM, 1950)
Cattle Drive (Universal, 1951)
On Moonlight Bay (WB, 1951)
It's a Big Country (MGM, 1951)
Angel Face (RKO, 1952)
By the Light of the Silvery Moon (WB, 1953)
Let's Do It Again (Columbia, 1953)
Sabre Jet (UA, 1953)
Peyton Place (20th-Fox, 1957)
From the Terrace (20th-Fox, 1960)
The Absent-Minded Professor (BV, 1961)
Son of Flubber (BV, 1963)
The Misadventures of Merlin Jones (BV, 1964)
The Monkey's Uncle (BV, 1965)
On a Clear Day You Can See Forever (Paramount, 1970)
Tora! Tora! Tora! (20th-Fox, 1970)
Toklat (Sun International, 1971)
Cool Breeze (MGM, 1972)
Hammersmith Is Out (Cinerama, 1972)
The Timber Tramp (Alaska Pictures, 1973)
Brother of the Wind (Narrator: Sun International, 1973)

With Margalo Gillmore and Jacqueline de Wit in *The Happy Years* (1950)

Pier Angeli

Pier Angeli was brought to Hollywood in 1951 as part of MGM's attempt to meet the demands of the new international cinema in which Continental screen types were becoming highly desirable. Her ethereal beauty soon tagged Pier as a new Ingrid Bergman. Fred Zinnemann, who directed her in her first American film, MGM's *Teresa* (1951), exclaimed that: "This girl can climb to the absolute top and become one of the outstanding stars of her generation." The demure Italian beauty with a luminous sensitivity seemed headed for cinema stardom when everything went awry. Her emotional involvements and marital difficulties forced her to rue the day she decided to pursue an acting career against her father's wishes.

She was born Anna Maria Pierangeli on the island of Sardinia on June 19, 1932, twenty minutes before her twin sister, Maria Luisa, who would likewise become an actress under the screen name of Marisa Pavan. Signor Pierangeli was a construction engineer and in 1935 moved the family to Rome where he became an architect. His wife had been an amateur actress before she married him, and she encouraged the lovely twin girls to become actresses. (Pier's husband Vic Damone would later state that she was "carefully and almost savagely trained for the stage from the day she was five years old.") Pier was discovered by French director Leonide Moguy who costarred her with Vittorio De Sica in *Domani È Troppo Tardi* (1950), later released in the United States as *Tomorrow Is Too Late* (1952). After a second Italian feature for Moguy, Pier was put under MGM contract when Zinnemann and producer Arthur Lowe selected her as the soulful Italian bride of G.I. John Ericson in *Teresa*.

It was while filming *Teresa* in Italy that she met singer Vic Damone, also under MGM contract, who was then doing his Army service. Damone was an Italian Brooklynite named Vito Farinola, and he induced her to join him in performing for the G.I.s. He sang "September Song" while holding Pier in his arms. After her father, who had vehemently objected to his daughters' show business careers, had died, Pier moved to Hollywood with her mother and sister, and MGM gave her the advantage of its publicity machinery. She was soon a popular cover girl and named a Star of Tomorrow. She was starred with Stewart Granger in *The Light Touch* (1951) and with Gene Kelly in *The*

Devil Makes Three (1952). In the *Equilibrium* segment of *The Story of Three Loves* (1953), she played the young trapeze artist with Kirk Douglas. Then she starred with Ricardo Montalban in *Sombrero* (1953). They were all forgettable pictures, but the public liked her and studio executives expected her to become a star. Her best friend on the studio lot was Debbie Reynolds, who taught her American slang, and her frequent escorts were James Dean and Kirk Douglas. The press did not see a serious romance with Dean, but it did hint at an engagement with Douglas. All this speculation ended with her front page wedding on November 24, 1954 to Vic Damone, who had returned to Hollywood to complete his MGM contract.

On the following February 25th, Pier fell while aboard an airplane and broke her pelvis. She was pregnant at the time, and she sued the airline for $200,000. The case was settled for $45,000, and her son, Perry Rocco Luigi, named in honor of singer Perry Como, was born a healthy child on August 21st. That same year her hotel room was robbed of $28,000 in jewelry while she and Damone were visiting London; and in 1956, she suffered a miscarriage and broke her ankle. When she had recuperated, she played the wife of boxer Rocky Graziano (Paul Newman) in *Somebody up There Likes Me* (1956) and received the best notices of her career: "In a movie that bursts with violence and fear, she is gentle and courageous and proves herself a fine and lovely actress."

Her marriage to Damone had been a series of much-publicized emotional separations and reconciliations, with Damone blaming his "meddlesome" mother-in-law for most of their difficulties. In 1957, they separated and Pier went to Paris to star in *The Vintage* (1957) with Mel Ferrer and Michele Morgan. Then she did her last role under her MGM contract, playing the circus girl who marries Danny Kaye in *Merry Andrew* (1958).

She received her divorce from Damone in 1959, but would spend the next six years in endless court battles with her former husband over custody of their son, each accusing the other of kidnapping the boy, each time either one traveled with him. Since she had no movie contract, she appeared instead in a television production, *Bernadette* (1958), based on the miracles of Lourdes, recorded an album of Italian songs for Roulette Records in a "warm and surprisingly rich" singing voice, and gave an impressive performance as the Tahitian girl opposite Laurence Olivier in the television production of *The Moon and Sixpence* (1959).

These ventures did little to promote her career, however, and she returned to Italy. In between court battles, she and Damone talked of another reconciliation and of even having another child. But then Damone called one of her escorts, Italian actor Maurizio Arena, a "bum," and the fight was on again. She exchanged slaps with playboy Marchese Gianfranco in a nightclub in 1961, and the following year, in London, married Italian bandleader Armando Travajoli. He was fifteen years older than Pier. Their son Howard Andrea (called Popino) was born in 1963. They separated after a short time. In 1964 a lonely and nearly forgotten Pier said, "I am still in love, deeply and eternally, with Jimmy Dean," verifying a romance that had not really been exploited by the press and had ended several years before Dean's untimely death. The court battles over Perry's custody resumed and finally the boy went to live with his father in 1965, while spending summers with his mother in London.

Pier made several more motion pictures. She was in *The Battle of the Bulge* (1965) and assorted European coproductions made on the cheap. There were rumors of tax problems and poverty, with her sister, Marisa Pavan, and Marisa's husband, Jean Pierre Aumont, coming to Pier's rescue. Presumably penniless and alone in 1971, she told the press: "It would be better if I was already dead. I can't go on anymore." A few months later she arrived in Hollywood and was feted at a party cohosted by her friend Debbie Reynolds and Debbie's best friend, Agnes Moorehead. Reynolds set out to help Pier secure work and with a renewed optimism, Pier told reporters: "Life is beautiful. I am very happy to be back. Maybe I'll be before the cameras soon or I'll put on my own show in Las Vegas."

On September 10, 1971, without her knowing she had been accepted for a guest-starring role on the television series *Bonanza*, Pier died from an overdose of barbituates. She was living with drama coach Helen Sorell, and had been under a physician's care for a stomach disorder. In a gallant gesture, Debbie Reynolds offered to adopt Pier's younger son, then a ward of the British court and in private school in London. The answer came from Pier's mother, an angry refusal. She said: "The boy is mine. I was made his legal guardian by the British court in 1968."

Immediately before her death, Pier was part of a newspaper controversy over an exploitive picture she had made in Italy, called *Addio Alexandra* (also known as *Love Me, Love My Wife*). She had appeared in the (near) nude for a *ménage à trois* love scene in the film, allegedly with the stipulation that it not be released in the United States unless that scene was removed. Matt Cimber, former husband of Jayne Mansfield, owned the rights to the picture and had planned to release it over Pier's protests. The last picture she made before dying was *Octaman* (1972), a monster–suspense feature with Kerwin Mathews and Jeff Morrow. For the little girl who lost the role of *Lili* to Leslie Caron and the role of Rima the Bird Girl in *Green Mansions* to Audrey Hepburn—two MGM assignments she wanted badly to play—these exploitation features were a sad denouement to a career that held so much unfulfilled promise.

PIER ANGELI

Domani È Troppo Tardi (Italian, 1950)
Domani è Un Altro Giorno (Excelsa, 1951)
Teresa (MGM, 1951)
The Light Touch (MGM, 1951)
The Devil Makes Three (MGM, 1952)

The Story of Three Loves (MGM, 1953)
Sombrero (MGM, 1953)
The Flame and the Flesh (MGM, 1954)
The Silver Chalice (WB, 1954)
Santarella (French–Italian, 1954)

With John Ericson in *Teresa* (1951)

Somebody up There Likes Me (MGM, 1956)
Port Afrique (Columbia, 1956)
The Vintage (MGM, 1957)
Merry Andrew (MGM, 1958)
S. O. S. Pacific (Universal, 1960)
The Angry Silence (Valiant, 1960)
Musketeers of the Sea (Italian–French, 1962)
White Slave Ship (AIP, 1962)
Sodom and Gomorrah (20th-Fox, 1963)
Battle of the Bulge (WB, 1965)
Spy in Your Eye (AIP, 1966)
MMM 83-Missione Morte Molo 83 (Italian, 1966)

Per Mille Dollari Al Giorno (Spanish–Italian, 1966)
Shadow of Evil (7 Arts, 1967)
Rose Rosse Per Il Führer (Italian, 1968)
One Step to Hell (NTA, 1968)
Vive America (Spanish–Italian, 1969)
Les Enemoniades (Spanish–Italian, 1970)
Every Bastard a King (Continental, 1970)
Addio, Alexandra (International Arts, 1971)
Nelle Pieghe Della Carne (Italian–Spanish, 1971)
Octaman (Heritage Enterprises, 1972)

Edward Arnold

Portly Edward Arnold was one of the screen's most polished and well-liked character players, specializing in public officials who were often a little shady in their ethics. As the stereotyped version of the screen politician (congressman, senator, mayor, and judge), he gave credibility to his characterization that strengthened any picture enormously. He was not as talented a biographical actor as George Arliss, Charles Laughton, or Paul Muni, but his Diamond Jim Brady is a respectable try. For eighteen of his twenty-five years on the screen, Arnold was a staple of the MGM lot. In his way he did as much for the productions he graced as such disparate, but equally essential, studio stock players as Una Merkel or Keenan Wynn.

Arnold was born Guenther Schneider, of German ancestry, on February 18, 1890, in a tenement in New York City's poverty-stricken Lower East Side. His father died, leaving Arnold, his four brothers and sisters, and his broken-spirited mother to make do as best they could. At age eleven, Arnold began working as a newsboy, an errand boy, a bellhop, and then as the attendant to the boiler system in the sub-basements of Columbia University. At age fourteen, the year in which his mother died, he played Lorenzo in *The Merchant of Venice*, a production sponsored by an East Side settlement house. The experience made such an impression on him that from that time on he pursued an acting career. When he wrote a book of memoirs in 1940, he entitled it *Lorenzo Goes to Hollywood*, harking back to his first days as a thespian.

Arnold made his professional debut in New Jersey on March 1, 1905, as a bit player with the Ben Greet Players, a Shakespearean repertory company. He earned a $25 weekly salary. Maxine Elliott doubled his pay when she hired him as a juvenile lead and assistant stage manager with her acting company. Later after a brief tour with Ethel Barrymore, he was hired by Essanay Studio in Chicago to play a Western hero, replacing Francis X. Bushman, who had "gone Hollywood." Essanay paid Arnold $125 a week and during his several years there he played in over forty two-reelers. But he craved the excitement of a live audience and returned to Broadway where he earned good notices playing the virile Burr Winton in *The Storm* in 1919. With considerable work and energy, he developed a good professional reputation on

Broadway, leading to such contrasting assignments as the millionaire in *Easy Come, Easy Go* (1925), Beatrice Lillie's leading man in *The Third Little Show* (1931), and the gangster in *Whistling in the Dark* (1932). The latter show proved to be his most famous stage role. While on tour with that production, Universal Pictures took an interest in his screen potential and signed him to a nonexclusive contract in December 1932. His ample 200-pound physique made him a formidable screen personage and he debuted in *Okay, America* (1932), a film which also featured MGM's Maureen O'Sullivan.

MGM first used Arnold in the role of the doctor in *Rasputin and the Empress* (1932), and the following year they had their new contractee repeat his stage part in *Whistling in the Dark* (1933), which proved to be more a vehicle for Ernest Truex and Una Merkel than Arnold. He was sincere as the priest in Helen Hayes' *The White Sister* (1933), but much more effective on loanout to Paramount as the senator who seduces laundry girl Sylvia Sidney in *Jennie Gerhardt* (1933). He demonstrated his flair for reasonable hamming as Emperor Valerius in Eddie Cantor's *Roman Scandals* (1933), but it was in Metro's *Sadie McKee* (1934) that audiences took real note of the performer. Cast as the alcoholic millionaire who weds down-and-out Joan Crawford, he gave credence to an assignment that could easily have been a hackneyed portrayal. Arnold's Mr. Brennan in that film is an unstable man who knows that money cannot buy his wife's love, and all the capering he can manage will not turn him into a dashing playboy. His soul and physical appearance clash, and in the materialistic world the surface look always grabs the prize. Arnold would play many variations on this essentially tragic type in his films to come.

It was as Louis XIII in George Arliss' *Cardinal Richelieu* (1935) that Arnold first essayed a screen biographical portrait. Later the same year he would star as *Diamond Jim* (1935) in Universal's flashy production of the nineteenth-century millionaire who loved money, food, and Lillian Russell (Binnie Barnes). Universal was so pleased with that picture that they cast Arnold as the lead in *Sutter's Gold* (1936) directed by James Cruze. It was an extremely well-mounted and costly film by Universal standards, but burdened with a sluggish script. When it failed at the boxoffice, the blame was laid at Arnold's feet and the lack of his marquee appeal. He played the title role in the now forgotten *Meet Nero Wolfe* (1936), which should have led to a continuation of the Rex Stout detective character, but Arnold, unlike the later and similar Sydney Greenstreet, lacked a sufficently eccentric image to garner a huge filmgoing following in such a series of films.

By 1938, in *You Can't Take It with You* done for Frank Capra at Columbia, Arnold was cast as the grasping tycoon and found himself in a lucrative rut. Metro used him on the home lot as the sinister munitions king in *Idiot's Delight* (1939), while Capra borrowed him again for a corrupt politician's role in *Mr. Smith Goes To Washington* (1939). Fox utilized Arnold in 1940 to essay a crooked financier in *Johnny Apollo,* and to repeat his Diamond Jim Brady role in Alice Faye's *Lillian Russell.* During the 1940s, MGM used him more and more on the home lot, usually in stock assignments, whether it was a gangster film, *Johnny Eager* (1941); a costume yarn, *Kismet* (1944); or a lush revue, *The Ziegfeld Follies* (1946). On loan to RKO, he had performed well as Daniel Webster arguing with the crafty Devil (Walter Huston) in *All That Money Can Buy* (1941). When Warner Brothers borrowed Arnold to portray a harassed father in *Janie* (1944), he was pushed into a new screen type for him that would sustain him throughout the 1940s. In Warner's sequel *Janie Gets Married* (1946) and the Paramount trilogy *Dear Ruth* (1947), *Dear Wife* (1949), and *Dear Brat* (1950), in which he was the suburban judge who finds no peace at home with two such bothersome daughters as Joan Caulfield and Mona Freeman, he played with smoothness and expertise the domestic comedy film father who has some bark to his bite and eventually restores order to any chaotic situation.

Arnold concluded his MGM tenure in 1950 as Pawnee Bill in *Annie Get Your Gun*, and as the excitable admiral in the would-be comedy, *The Skipper Surprised His Wife*. His 1950s free-lance film assignments were of little consequence, his last role being in the flimsy *Miami Expose* (1956) for Columbia, released shortly before he died of a cerebral hemorrhage on April 26, 1956.

Throughout his screen career, Arnold was a public-spirited Hollywood citizen, having been an officer of the Academy of Motion Picture Arts and Sciences, and onetime president of the Screen Actors' Guild. It was announced in 1950 that he would run for Republican Senator from California, but it was too early in the 1950s for an actor to be taken very seriously in the political arena. Despite his large real estate holdings, he always remembered his humble beginnings, and was known for his professional and personal modesty. He was married three times: to Harriet Marshall, by whom he had three children; to Olive Emerson; and to Cleo McClain.

EDWARD ARNOLD

Okay America! (Universal, 1932)
Rasputin and the Empress (MGM, 1932)
Three on a Match (WB, 1932)
Afraid to Talk (Universal, 1932)
Whistling in the Dark (MGM, 1933)
The White Sister (MGM, 1933)
The Barbarian (MGM, 1933)
Jennie Gerhardt (Paramount, 1933)
Her Bodyguard (Paramount, 1933)
Secret of the Blue Room (Universal, 1933)
I'm No Angel (Paramount, 1933)
Roman Scandals (UA, 1933)
Madame Spy (Universal, 1934)
Sadie McKee (MGM, 1934)
Thirty Day Princess (Paramount, 1934)
Unknown Blonde (Majestic, 1934)
Hide-Out (MGM, 1934)

Million Dollar Ransom (Universal, 1934)
The President Vanishes (Paramount, 1934)
Wednesday's Child (RKO, 1934)
Biography of a Bachelor Girl (MGM, 1935)
Cardinal Richelieu (UA, 1935)
The Glass Key (Paramount, 1935)
Diamond Jim (Universal, 1935)
Crime and Punishment (Columbia, 1935)
Remember Last Night? (Universal, 1935)
Sutter's Gold (Universal, 1936)
Meet Nero Wolfe (Columbia, 1936)
Come and Get It (UA, 1936)
John Meade's Woman (Paramount, 1937)
Easy Living (Paramount, 1937)
The Toast of New York (RKO, 1937)
Blossoms on Broadway (Paramount, 1937)
The Crowd Roars (MGM, 1938)

You Can't Take it With You (Columbia, 1938)
Let Freedom Ring (MGM, 1939)
Idiot's Delight (MGM, 1939)
Man About Town (Paramount, 1939)
Mr. Smith Goes to Washington (Columbia, 1939)
Slightly Honorable (UA, 1940)
The Earl of Chicago (MGM, 1940)
Johnny Apollo (20th-Fox, 1940)
Lillian Russell (20th-Fox, 1940)
The Penalty (MGM, 1941)
The Lady from Cheyenne (Universal, 1941)
Meet John Doe (WB, 1941)
Nothing But the Truth (Paramount, 1941)
Unholy Partners (MGM, 1941)
Design for Scandal (MGM, 1941)
Johnny Eager (MGM, 1941)
All That Money Can Buy (RKO, 1941)
The War Against Mrs. Hadley (MGM, 1942)
Eyes in the Night (MGM, 1942)
The Youngest Profession (MGM, 1943)
Standing Room Only (Paramount, 1944)
Janie (WB, 1944)
Kismet (MGM, 1944)
Mrs. Parkington (MGM, 1944)
Main Street After Dark (MGM, 1944)
Weekend at the Waldorf (MGM, 1945)
The Hidden Eye (MGM, 1945)

The Ziegfeld Follies (MGM, 1946)
Janie Gets Married (WB, 1946)
Three Wise Fools (MGM, 1946)
No Leave, No Love (MGM, 1946)
The Mighty McGurk (MGM, 1946)
My Brother Talks to Horses (MGM, 1946)
Dear Ruth (Paramount, 1947)
The Hucksters (MGM, 1947)
Three Daring Daughters (MGM, 1948)
Big City (MGM, 1948)
Wallflower (WB, 1948)
Command Decision (MGM, 1948)
John Loves Mary (WB, 1949)
Take Me Out to the Ball Game (MGM, 1949)
Big Jack (MGM, 1949)
Dear Wife (Paramount, 1949)
The Yellow Cabman (MGM, 1950)
Annie Get Your Gun (MGM, 1950)
The Skipper Surprised His Wife (MGM, 1950)
Dear Brat (Paramount, 1951)
Belles on Their Toes (20th-Fox, 1952)
The City That Never Sleeps (Republic, 1953)
Man of Conflict (Atlas, 1953)
Living It Up (Paramount, 1954)
The Houston Story (Columbia, 1956)
The Ambassador's Daughter (UA, 1956)
Miami Expose (Columbia, 1956)

With Ronald Colman in *Kismet* (1944)

Fred Astaire

Fred Astaire has achieved screen immortality for bringing to every aspect of his work his unique charm, gentlemanly manners, and elegance. While his charm may have been innate, his success as a dancer–singer–actor was the result of much-admired, hardworking professionalism. He may not have been the greatest dancer in the world, but he was by far the most memorable screen performer in that category because of his endless endeavors to make all that he did on camera appear so simple. Again, while he was not the most innovative of movie dancers, his contribution was still indelible because he was responsible for disposing of the proscenium as the ultimate background for dance routines in cinema. He just danced wherever the plot took him: on a staircase, in a park, on a street, or in a toy shop. For his "unique artistry and his contributions to the technique of musical pictures," he was presented with a special Oscar in 1949. Astaire was not a singer and yet aside from Ethel Merman, no establishment singer has had more songs written especially for him. While he never gave any major actor competition in the Best Actor race, his screen portrayals were always ebullient with a pleasing sense of humor that made audiences happy. Most of all, the long-legged, bony-faced star had *class*. For nearly ten years (1945–1954) he was under contract to MGM, where even without his famed screen partner, Ginger Rogers, he did some of his best movie work.

He was born Frederic Austerlitz on May 10,1899 in Omaha, Nebraska. His father was a beer salesman, and when his sister, Adele, eighteen months older than Fred, began taking dancing lessons, Astaire was sent along to keep her company. Soon they were performing for school and parish hall programs. In 1906 their mother took them to New York City and enrolled her children in the Ned Wayburn School of Dance. During the next decade they played a three-a-day vaudeville circuit as the team of Fred and Adele Astaire, the surname they legally adopted for professional purposes. Their schooling was garnered mainly from their mother's tutoring. They were booked into New York in 1916 where their notices were so good that Astaire took out a full page advertisement in *Variety*, quoting from their review. This ploy earned them a spot in the Broadway musical, *Over the Top* (1917). For the next fifteen years they appeared in ten shows, becoming the darlings of New York and London.

With Lucille Bremer in *Ziegfeld Follies* (1946)

For Goodness Sake was especially written for the performing duo in 1922, and George Gershwin wrote two of his best musicals for the couple: *Lady Be Good* (1924) and *Funny Face* (1927).

The Astaires starred in *The Band Wagon* in 1931 and during that period made a Vitaphone short subject as a screen test for a proposed cinema version of *Funny Face. Funny Face* was shelved for many years and the short subject was the only screen work in which Adele ever appeared. During the run of *The Band Wagon*, she informed her brother that she was retiring to marry Lord Charles Cavendish, the second son of the Duke of Devonshire. Dubious about the prospects of performing on Broadway as a single dancer, Astaire signed a movie contract with RKO Pictures. Before RKO readied a vehicle for him, he appeared at MGM in *Dancing Lady* (1933) in a Alpine dance number with star Joan Crawford. Later that year, on July 12th, he wed Phyllis Baker Potter, a divorced New York socialite whom he had met at a luncheon given by Mrs. Graham Fair Vanderbilt.

The project RKO lined up for Astaire was *Flying Down to Rio* (1933) and his dancing partner was to be the sassy Ginger Rogers, who had scored so successfully as the grasping show girl "Anytime Annie" in Warner Brothers' *42nd Street* (1933). Although Dolores Del Rio and Gene Raymond were theoretically the leads of *Flying Down To Rio*, it was Astaire and Rogers dancing the "Carioca" who were the hit of that film. The next year RKO paired them again in *The Gay Divorcee*, in which they performed the classic "Continental." RKO had an obvious boxoffice smash hit in the dancing duo and continued to team them in lightweight, sophisticated, diverting musicals, paying them each $150,000 per film. In 1935, it was *Roberta,* which also boasted Irene Dunne in the cast for added audience lure. *Top Hat* (1935) had their "Cheek to Cheek" number, and *Follow The Fleet* (1936) had "Let's Face the Music and Dance." For that dance number Ginger wore a heavily beaded gown, which she insisted on wearing, despite the bruises Astaire incurred from it as they whirled around the dance floor. This was the beginning of the end, due to Astaire's temper and Ginger's eye-diverting beads. *Swing Time* (1936), then *Shall We Dance* (1937), *Carefree* (1938), and *The Story Of Irene and Vernon Castle* (1939), and their partnership ended, as did Astaire's contract with RKO. His only non–Ginger Rogers costarring vehicle at RKO was *A Damsel In Distress* (1937), which utilized the more aristocratic, but less agile, Joan Fontaine as Astaire's *vis-à-vis.*

Without a partner again, Astaire chose the screen's best tap dancer, Eleanor Powell, for his next partner. They had fun making *Broadway Melody of 1940* at MGM. He said, "She 'put 'em down' like a man, no ricky-ticky sissy stuff with Ellie. She really knocked out a tap dance in a class by herself." Paulette Goddard did her effervescent best to keep up with him for one number in *Second Chorus* (1940), after which he got his first "natural" dancing partner since Adele, in Rita Hayworth for *You'll Never Get Rich* (1941). Astaire liked working with Rita and agreed to Columbia teaming them again in *You Were Never Lovelier* (1942). Then came *Holiday Inn* (1942) which, despite Astaire's agility, was still a Bing Crosby vehicle.

MGM hired Astaire to perform a couple of turns in *Ziegfeld Follies* (1946), in which he danced with newcomer Lucille Bremer in the balletic "Limehouse Blues" and did the excellent "The Babbitt and the Bromide" with Gene Kelly. MGM next paired him with Bremer in *Yolanda and the Thief* (1945) which was released before *Follies*. Their dancing was way above par in this fantasy story, but the film was not popular. At the conclusion of Paramount's *Blue Skies* (1946), Astaire announced his retirement. MGM agreed only after he promised them that he world return to them if and when he decided to resume his career. When Gene Kelly broke his ankle while preparing for *Easter Parade* (1948), MGM coaxed Astaire to replace him. Astaire loved working with Judy Garland and says that he had more fun making this picture than any other. Their "A Couple of Swells" routine was the film's highlight.

Astaire's intended retirement was short-lived as MGM wooed him into making additional films. He and Garland were assigned to *The Barkeleys of Broadway* (1949), but when she was physically unable to complete the picture, they called in Ginger Rogers and played up the publicity about the two stars being reunited. The Technicolor movie was boxoffice, but the Astaire–Rogers team never appeared in another film together. Vera-Ellen partnered him in *Three Little Words* (1950). When Garland proved too sick to replace a pregnant June Allyson in *Royal Wedding* (1951), MGM boosted their own Jane Powell to the vacant part. *The Belle of New York* (1952) had also been planned for Garland, but it was Twentieth Century-Fox's Vera-Ellen who danced with Astaire instead. With *The Band Wagon* (1954) Astaire reached the zenith of his screen dancing, admirably partnered in this case by Cyd Charisse. *Daddy Long Legs* (1955), *Funny Face* (1957), and *Silk Stockings* (1957), the latter again with Charisse, found a charmingly mature Astaire still exuding his professional style with great charm and ease.

He played his first straight dramatic role in *On the Beach* (1959) as the playboy sports car driver who prefers his own brand of death. His *déjà vu* attitude was quite appropriate for the role. His last good movie part was the dapper socialite father in *The Pleasure of His Company* (1961), in which he displayed a whimsical comedy style in the proper Cyril Ritchard tradition. At age sixty-nine he was seen as the old "musical" Astaire in the unsuccessful musical *Finian's Rainbow* (1968). The following year he played in a dismal European-filmed caper entry, *Midas Run* (1969).

The first of four Astaire television specials appeared in 1959, with Barrie Chase as his new dance partner. He won Emmys for three of his four outings. During the 1970 television season Robert Wagner induced him to play his oncamera sleuth father in a semiregular role on the ABC teleseries, *It Takes a Thief*. That same year he was seen in the telefeature *The Over the Hill Gang Rides Again*, playing a bewhiskered old drunk.

He has two children, Fred, Jr. (born in 1941) and Ava (born in 1942). On September 13, 1954, he suffered a tragedy from which he was a long time recovering: the death from cancer of his wife Phyllis. It was Astaire's only marriage. Joan Crawford, with whom he had made his feature film debut, says that the Astaire's marriage was "one of the most perfect I'd ever known." As she grew to know them over the years, she said, "I made a mental note. It was good for me to know that a marriage like theirs could happen in show business."

The performing Fred Astaire with "the face of a comedian and the figure of a jockey" is a far cry from the offcamera shy but warmhearted individual. It is estimated that Astaire, whose legs were once insured by RKO for $1 million, provided over $200 million in grosses in the course of his thirty-plus feature film career. Modest about his successful career, his one seeming vanity is to be thought too elderly to perform. Although now in his seventies, he does not contemplate retirement.

FRED ASTAIRE

Dancing Lady (MGM, 1933)
Flying Down to Rio (RKO, 1933)
The Gay Divorcee (RKO, 1934)
Roberta (RKO, 1935)

Top Hat (RKO, 1935)
Follow the Fleet (RKO, 1936)
Swing Time (RKO, 1936)
Shall We Dance (RKO, 1937)

With Vera-Ellen in *Three Little Words* (1950)

A Damsel in Distress (RKO, 1937)
Carefree (RKO, 1938)
The Story of Vernon and Irene Castle (RKO, 1939)
Broadway Melody of 1940 (MGM, 1940)
Second Chorus (Paramount, 1940)
You'll Never Get Rich (Columbia, 1941)
Holiday Inn (Paramount, 1942)
You Were Never Lovelier (Columbia, 1942)
The Sky's the Limit (RKO, 1943)
Yolanda and the Thief (MGM, 1945)
Ziegfeld Follies (MGM, 1946)
Blue Skies (Paramount, 1946)
Easter Parade (MGM, 1948)
The Barkeleys of Broadway (MGM, 1949)

Three Little Words (MGM, 1950)
Let's Dance (Paramount, 1950)
Royal Wedding (MGM, 1951)
The Belle of New York (MGM, 1952)
The Band Wagon (MGM, 1953)
Daddy Long Legs (20th-Fox, 1955)
Funny Face (Paramount, 1957)
Silk Stockings (MGM, 1957)
On the Beach (UA, 1959)
The Pleasure of His Company (Paramount, 1961)
The Notorious Landlady (Columbia, 1962)
Finian's Rainbow (WB–7 Arts, 1968)
Midas Run (Cinerama, 1969)
Imagine (Joko, 1973)

Mary Astor

"I was never totally involved in movies. I was making someone else's dream come true," says Mary Astor. That "someone else" was her megalomaniac father, Otto Ludwig Wilhelm Langhanke, who had pushed his daughter into a motion picture career at the age of twelve. She spent years trying to please him and live up to his expectations and then years overcoming the resultant emotional problems: a combination of fear, hatred, and lack of confidence. Her father's influence was such that in 1925, in the middle of her affair with John Barrymore, the nineteen-year-old could not muster the courage to accept Barrymore's proposal that she divert her career to the stage, when he said: "I could make it happen, baby, I really could! I could teach you things that make an audience want to wrap you in their arms. I could make you a truly great actress." Whether or not that speech was from the heart or merely an effusion in the heat of *amour*, Mary did have a spark, a delicate beauty, and an incisive histrionic technique that never seemed to have blossomed fully on the screen; and during a film career that spanned forty-three years, audiences always knew she was capable of more. Her career was a series of what she calls "changes": silent pictures while still a teenager, then talkies, a love-diary scandal, an Academy Award, alcoholism, and finally a moderately successful writing career. For seven of those years, 1942–1948, she was under contract to MGM where, despite the publicity that announced that studio's desire to promote her as a "star," she ended up being the studio's high class "Mom." As Mary put it "my *femme fatale* image of the Diary days went down the Culver City drain."

She was born Lucile Vasconcells Langhanke on May 3, 1906 in Quincy, Illinois, where her father taught German in the local schools. As a small child she had begun taking piano lessons and it was her father's desire that she be a concert pianist. That was until, at the age of twelve, she entered her photograph in a Fame and Fortune contest sponsored by *Motion Picture* magazine. Six months later she received a notice in the mail that she had placed among the group from which, at the end of the year, the winner would be selected. But her father chose not to wait and took her to the Chicago office of Brewster Publications so they could get a look at her in person. Yes, they thought her beautiful but too young and suggested she try again next year. She

34

did and this time she placed again. Determined that she should be noticed, the Langhankes moved to New York, where Mary was finally photographed with a group of girls who had entered the contest. That was in June of 1920, and although she did not win the contest, she did strike the eye of photographer Charles Albin who received her father's permission to use the "Madonna-child" as his model.

While posing at Albin's studio at Columbus Avenue and 66th Street, Mary met Lillian Gish, who was then working for D. W. Griffith in silent pictures being made in suburban Mamaroneck. Otto Langhanke stepped in and Gish arranged for Mary to test for Griffith. Griffith complied and said the girl was indeed beautiful but told Langhanke that he thought her too delicate to handle the grind of making films. However, years later, Gish told Mary that Griffith's real reason was that he could immediately see that her father was "a walking cash register" and said: "I could never mold this child into an actress with him on my neck all the time."

Undaunted, Langhanke managed to get her into a few two-reelers and then a six-month contract with Famous Players-Lasky at $60 weekly. She did bits in three films, after which Lewis J. Selznick (David O.'s father) used her in *John Smith* (1922). That prompted Famous Players-Lasky to give her a second offer, this time one year at $500 weekly. She arrived in Hollywood in April 1923, where not long thereafter Jesse Lasky, along with Louella Parsons and Walter Wanger, decided her professional name should be Mary Astor. That year John Barrymore was preparing *Beau Brummel* (1924) at Warners. When he saw her photograph, he requested she be tested as his lead in that film. During the test Mary recalls he whispered in her ear: "You are so goddamned beautiful, you make me feel faint."

She was signed for the picture at $1,100 per week, and to the consternation of her protective parents began a romance with the forty-one-year-old matinee idol. Warners put her under contract and during the next four years she appeared in over twenty features, what she referred to as a "treadmill of trash." While the roles may have been trash, her father was happy to be taking her weekly checks, and he purchased for the family an "ornate and showy" home on Temple Hill Drive. Among those films was another with Barrymore, *Don Juan* (1926), but by this time their romance had cooled, because Barrymore's roving eye had turned to beauteous blonde Dolores Costello. On loan to Fox, she did *Dressed to Kill* (1928) with Edmund Lowe, a part she jumped at because it cast her as a gun moll.

Mary left Warners in 1928, married director Kenneth Hawks, and signed a contract with Fox for $3,750 a week. After four pictures, that studio, in its transition-to-sound scare, offered to keep her on at half salary, but she refused and made her stage debut with Florence Eldridge (Mrs. Fredric March) in Vincent Lawrence's *Among the Married*. The play was produced in Los Angeles and her salary was $150 a week. During the run of that play, on January 2, 1930, Hawks was killed in a airplane crash. He had been working on a film at the time. A year and a half later she remarried, to Dr. Franklyn

Thorpe, the physician who had attended her illnesses after her husband's death.

She made her talking film debut successfully in Paramount's *Ladies Love Brutes* (1930) and then signed a one-year contract with RKO. Her films there were a string of "Bs" except for *Holiday* (1930) with studio star Ann Harding. In this, Mary was impressive as the ambitious, materialistic sister. When RKO offered to give her a new starring contract, she refused, supposedly because she did not wish to be typed and because she was afraid of the responsibility that comes "once your name is above the title."

Free of her contract, she went to MGM and played the second lead in *Red Dust* (1932), giving a sensitive portrayal of the wife who is tempted by the virile Gable. Her new husband insisted Mary demand of her father that she now receive her own salary checks. She was twenty-six years old, a wife and a mother (a daughter, Marylyn, born in 1932). The suggestion created such a row that her parents sued her for nonsupport, and while she did begin receiving her newly won checks, she had to continue to contribute to her family's life style, therefore, reluctantly she signed another contract with Warners to insure her weekly salary.

Her assignments were more "Bs" and she went on to another contract, with Columbia. The year was 1936 and all hell broke loose when her husband sued her for divorce and demanded custody of their daughter. He used a "diary" she had kept between 1929 and 1934 as evidence that she was an unfit mother. The diary's most revealing contents were alleged accounts of sexual intimacies with numerous Hollywood actors, as well as an affair with playwright George S. Kaufman which began when Mary took a three-week vacation to New York in 1933. This was the biggest publicized scandal in Hollywood up to that time, and during the summer of 1936, Mary and the diary were headline news. The diary was impounded by the court but never actually used as evidence. What were supposedly authentic pages from the diary revealed no more provocative a content than Mary's opinion about motion pictures: "I don't like the work and I hate Hollywood." And most of the "facts" that appeared in the newspapers were no more than rumors. The court's decision was that each parent would share equal custody of the child. Nevertheless, the diary was not forgotten for years to come. Although Mary once said she thought the diary had been burned in 1952 by court order, it still reposes in the managing editor's confidential file in a vault three levels under 42nd Street in New York City, in the *Daily News* building.

According to Mary, her career was not really hurt by the scandal, and one role that certainly helped her image was the beautifully played, sympathetic widow, Edith Cortwright, in Samuel Goldwyn's production of Sinclair Lewis' *Dodsworth* (1936). That assignment had been on loan from Columbia, and after a forgettable *Lady From Nowhere* (1936) with Charles Quigley, she free-lanced. She was Antoinette de Mauban in *The Prisoner of Zenda* (1937) with Ronald Colman, and the disillusioned wife of Raymond Massey in *The Hurricane* (1937). In a good comedy, *Midnight* (1939), starring

Claudette Colbert, Mary played the wife of John Barrymore, and found him to be a "politely quiet, sick old man." He was only fifty-seven years old but would die two years later.

Her greatest personal success came when Bette Davis asked for her to be cast as the selfish, career-minded concert pianist in *The Great Lie* (1941). Mary was better than good, and used her own piano background to finger properly the Tschaikovsky Piano Concerto No. 1 in B-Flat Minor (the off-screen pianist was Max Rabinovitch), and she received the Academy Award as the best actress in a supporting role. Warners then gave her the best role of her film career: the lethal, deceitful murderess, Brigid O'Shaughnessy, in the well-remembered *The Maltese Falcon* (1941) with Humphrey Bogart. They used her with Bogart again in *Across the Pacific* (1942).

In 1942 she did not wish to be tied down to a studio contract, but the wartime economy squeeze made free-lancing precarious, so she signed a seven-year agreement with MGM and settled in as the lot's personification of the homey but beautiful screen mom. She was also known as "one-take" Astor. She was Kathryn Grayson's mother in *Thousands Cheer* (1943) and Judy Garland's parent in *Meet Me in St. Louis* (1944). On loan to Twentieth Century-Fox, she was Dorothy McGuire's glamorous friend in *Claudia and David* (1946), enjoying the chance to wear chic clothes. She mothered Elizabeth Taylor in *Cynthia* (1947), both Esther Williams and Ricardo Montalban in *Fiesta* (1947), and at Paramount was the tough mater of equally strong-willed Lizabeth Scott in *Desert Fury* (1947). She had a good character role as the aging whore in Fred Zinnemann's *Act of Violence* (1948), starring Van Heflin. While working on that film she was also playing Marmie in the remake of *Little Women* (1949).

She recalls working on *Little Women* as a very unpleasant experience where everyone but her was having a good time. The reason for Mary's lack of enthusiasm was a personal problem that had started as early as 1937 —alcoholism. She refused MGM's offer to renew her contract (her drinking had seemingly never interfered with her work) and left the studio and entered a sanitarium for several months. Over the next two years there was a suicide attempt, and a plea to the Motion Picture Relief Fund for financial aid.

In 1952 she felt ready to resume her career, and her first venture was a tour in the play *Time of the Cuckoo*, which had been played on Broadway by Shirley Booth. Once in New York, she spent the next four years working steadily in theatre and television. On television she appeared in such vehicles as *The Star, Sunset Boulevard,* and *The Women.* There was a Broadway flop, *The Starcross Story,* with Eva Le Gallienne, and a fairly successful tour of *Don Juan in Hell* with Kurt Kasznar, Ricardo Montalban, and Reginald Denny as directed by Agnes Moorehead, who had played Mary's role of Dona Aña in the original production.

Her last film appearances to date were a very mixed bag. She was June Allyson's strangely obsessed mother-in-law in *Stranger in My Arms* (1959), she had a meaty role (much cut up in the final release print) in *Return to Peyton*

Place (1961), cavalierly directed by José Ferrer; and she was a very attractive seasoned Broadway star in *Youngblood Hawke* (1964). For her cinema swan song, she chose to do a cameo role in Bette Davis' *Hush, Hush, Sweet Charlotte* (1964) as the murderous dying old lady (she looked much aged).

In 1936, Mary had married actor Manuel del Compos by whom she had a son, Anthony, before they divorced in 1941. Four years later she married Thomas Wheelock, and after being separated for several years, they divorced in 1955. During the 1950s, Mary's drinking problem was still evident. After a conversion to Catholicism and some very meager years financially, she consulted a priest-psychoanalyst who suggested, as part of her therapy, that she write out her problems. The result of this therapeutic device was a book of memoirs published in 1959 as *My Story*. Considering the time in which it was published, it was very revealing. Its success and the regeneration of her personal life led her to a moderately lucrative career in fiction writing (five novels). A second book of memoirs, *A Life in Film*, was published in 1971.

Mary now lives in Fountain Valley, a retirement community south of Los Angeles. Although she has not acted in nearly a decade, she retains her Screen Actors' Guild membership card and says: "I can always be reached by mail." She recently was contacted by the Academy of Motion Pictures Arts and Sciences. Thirty years after the fact, they were prompted by a statement in *A Life on Film* ("I would dearly love to have a real Oscar") to correct an oversight and present Mary with an actual Oscar for her *Maltese Falcon* victory. It happened that, during World War II, plaques were used for awards with the understanding that substitutes would later be replaced by Oscars.

MARY ASTOR

John Smith (Lewis Selznick, 1922)
The Man Who Played God (UA, 1922)
Second Fiddle (W. W. Hodkinson, 1923)
Success (Metro, 1923)
The Bright Shawl (FN-Inspiration, 1923)
The Rapids (W. W. Hodkinson, 1923)
Puritan Passions (W. W. Hodkinson, 1923)
The Marriage Maker (Paramount, 1923)
Hollywood (Paramount, 1923)
Woman Proof (Paramount, 1923)
The Fighting Coward (Paramount, 1924)
Beau Brummell (WB, 1924)
The Fighting American (Universal, 1924)
Unguarded Woman (Paramount, 1924)
The Price of a Party (Howard Estabrook, 1924)
Inez from Hollywood (FN, 1924)
Oh, Doctor (Universal, 1925)
Enticement (FN, 1925)
Playing with Souls (FN, 1925)
Don Q, Son of Zorro (UA, 1925)

The Pace that Thrills (FN, 1925)
The Scarlet Saint (FN, 1925)
The Wise Guy (FN, 1926)
Don Juan (WB, 1926)
Forever After (FN, 1926)
High Steppers (FN, 1926)
The Rough Riders (Paramount, 1927)
The Sea Tiger (FN, 1927)
Sunset Derby (FN, 1927)
Rose of the Golden West (FN, 1927)
Two Arabian Knights (UA, 1927)
No Place to Go (FN, 1927)
Sailors' Wives (FN, 1928)
Dressed to Kill (Fox, 1928)
Heart to Heart (FN, 1928)
Three-Ring Marriage (FN, 1928)
Dry Martini (Fox, 1928)
Romance of the Underworld (Fox, 1929)
New Year's Eve (Fox, 1929)
Woman from Hell (Fox, 1929)

With Freddie Bartholomew and Walter Pidgeon in *Listen, Darling* (1938)

With Van Heflin in *Act of Violence* (1948)

Ladies Love Brutes (Paramount, 1930)
The Runaway Bride (RKO, 1930)
Holiday (RKO, 1930)
The Lash (FN, 1931)
The Royal Bed (RKO, 1931)
Behind Office Doors (RKO, 1931)
Sin Ship (RKO, 1931)
Other Men's Women (WB, 1931)
White Shoulders (RKO, 1931)
Smart Woman (RKO, 1931)
Men of Chance (RKO, 1932)
The Lost Squadron (RKO, 1932)
A Successful Calamity (WB, 1932)
Those We Love (World Wide, 1932)
Red Dust (MGM, 1932)
The Little Giant (FN, 1933)
Jennie Gerhardt (Paramount, 1933)
The World Changes (FN, 1933)
The Kennel Murder Case (WB, 1933)
Convention City (FN, 1933)
Easy to Love (WB, 1934)
Upperworld (WB, 1934)
Return of the Terror (FN-WB, 1934)
Man with Two Faces (FN, 1934)
The Case of the Howling Dog (WB, 1934)
I Am a Thief (WB, 1935)
Straight from the Heart (Universal, 1935)
Dinky (WB, 1935)
Page Miss Glory (WB, 1935)
Red Hot Tires (WB, 1935)
Man of Iron (WB, 1935)
The Murder of Dr. Harrigan (FN, 1936)
And So They Were Married (Columbia, 1936)
Trapped by Television (Columbia, 1936)
Dodsworth (UA, 1936)

Lady from Nowhere (Columbia, 1936)
The Prisoner of Zenda (UA, 1937)
The Hurricane (UA, 1937)
Paradise for Three (MGM, 1938)
No Time to Marry (Columbia, 1938)
There's Always a Woman (Columbia, 1938)
Woman Against Woman (MGM, 1938)
Listen, Darling (MGM, 1938)
Midnight (Paramount, 1939)
Turnabout (UA, 1940)
Brigham Young—Frontiersman (20th-Fox, 1940)
The Great Lie (WB, 1941)
The Maltese Falcon (WB, 1941)
Across the Pacific (WB, 1942)
The Palm Beach Story (Paramount, 1942)
Young Ideas (MGM, 1943)
Thousands Cheer (MGM, 1943)
Meet Me in St. Louis (MGM, 1944)
Blonde Fever (MGM, 1944)
Claudia and David (20th-Fox, 1946)
Cynthia (MGM, 1947)
Fiesta (MGM, 1947)
Desert Fury (Paramount, 1947)
Cass Timberlane (MGM, 1947)
Act of Violence (MGM, 1948)
Little Women (MGM, 1949)
Any Number Can Play (MGM, 1949)
A Kiss Before Dying (UA, 1956)
The Power and the Prize (MGM, 1956)
The Devil's Hairpin (Paramount, 1957)
This Happy Feeling (Universal, 1958)
Stranger in My Arms (Universal, 1959)
Return to Peyton Place (20th-Fox, 1961)
Youngblood Hawke (WB, 1964)
Hush, Hush, Sweet Charlotte (20th-Fox, 1964)

Lew Ayres

As early as 1932 Hollywood fan magazines were describing the new, young, handsome actor Lew Ayres as a dreamer, a thinker who lived in an unpretentious, sparsely furnished home in the Hollywood Hills. They described him further as an amateur geologist who enjoyed music and collecting books and who hated to grant interviews. Incongruous as this existence was to the clichéd view of movie stars' lives, it was only a prelude to the enigmatic life of this actor. For ten years later, at the height of his popularity as the idealistic physician in the *Dr. Kildare* series, he was sent to a labor camp as the most famous conscientious objector of World War II. Today the same adherence to principle would have made him a hero, but in the superpatriotic 1940s, it ruined his career, with the press almost unanimously denigrating him for his beliefs.

Ayres was born in Minneapolis, Minnesota, on December 28, 1908. While attending the University of Arizona and studying medicine, he played the banjo, guitar, and piano in the college orchestra. After graduation he joined first Henry Halstead's orchestra and then Ray West's band. While appearing with West at the Coconut Grove club in Los Angeles, Ayres was spotted by movie talent scout Ivan Kahn and signed to a six-month contract with Pathé. His only assignment at the studio was a bit in a silent called *The Sophomore* (1929). Nevertheless, Paul Bern, Irving G. Thalberg's MGM associate, decided he would be right as the young lover of Greta Garbo in her last silent picture, *The Kiss* (1929). Ayres and Garbo worked well together and the critics hailed him as a new find. In its transition to sound, however, MGM failed to sign him to a contract. Universal did sign him, and his first picture for them was the now classic *All Quiet on the Western Front* (1930). Ayres played the idealistic young German soldier who goes to war believing it to be ennobling, only to find it a brutal, inhuman experience. His famous death scene showed him in the trenches, reaching out to touch a butterfly and exposing himself to the bullet of a sniper. The audience watched in shock and disbelief as his hand "goes slack with his fingers dangling." Ayres' performance in this picture is still highly regarded today. His other Universal assignments, including *Iron Man* (1931) with Jean Harlow, were strictly a lot of B-grade pictures. When Fox borrowed him to play the news reporter with

41

whom Janet Gaynor falls in love in *State Fair* (1933), he decided to move to that studio the following year. Fox ended up doing no better for him than had Universal. Reviewers began to say he had better find a good role or his career would be over soon.

He talked Republic into allowing him to direct some pictures. They agreed, only on condition that he star in the first one as well, which was *The Leathernecks Have Landed* (1936). But after its release Republic reneged on its promise of more directing. Ayres then signed on at Paramount, but was only featured in several programmers, such as *Last Train from Madrid* (1937) which topcast relative newcomer Dorothy Lamour. It was Columbia who found just the right role to give Ayres' career that necessary resuscitation. They signed him to play in Hepburn's *Holiday* (1938), as Katharine Hepburn's brother, a hard-drinking rich youth who has succumbed to the ennui of the money-oriented society in which he lives. He and Hepburn had a marvelous drinking scene together. In fact, director George Cukor got the best performance of Ayres' career from this shy actor.

His performance in *Holiday* impressed MGM, and they signed him to a contract. They used him in several romantic vehicles as courtier to their stellar ladies: Joan Crawford in *Ice Follies Of 1939,* Jeanette MacDonald in *Broadway Serenade* (1939), Lana Turner in *These Glamour Girls* (1939) and Greer Garson in *Remember?* (1939). But Ayres' claim to fame at MGM was his role as the warm, good-natured Dr. James Kildare in nine *Dr. Kildare* pictures made between 1938 and 1942, following in the footsteps of Joel McCrea, who had played the character in the kickoff entry of the series, *Interns Can't Take Money* (1938), made at Paramount. As an occasional break from his Kildare filmmaking, Metro used him to support Ann Sothern in her series work, *Maisie Was a Lady* (1941), or paired with Laraine Day in an economy murder mystery, *Fingers at the Window* (1942).

In 1941, Ayres announced himself as a conscientious objector because of his religious beliefs and refused to take up arms in World War II. He stated he would "praise the Lord, but *not* pass the ammunition." The press and the film colony blasted him for his original stand. *Variety* editorialized that he was a "disgrace to the industry." MGM's Nicholas Schenck said he was "washed up with this studio." In March 1942 he entered a labor camp at Cascade Locks, Oregon, but two months later was assigned as an assistant chaplain at Ft. Lewis, Washington. The Army Medical Corps took him on as an orderly and for twenty-two months he energetically served at three Pacific beachhead invasions: Hollandia, Leyte, Luzon. General Carlos P. Romulo, writing in *I See the Philippines Rise,* said: "He risked everything rather than violate his faith in the divinity of man. He had made that protest bravely and it had won the respect of all."

When Ayres was discharged in 1945 he said: "The war has altered my attitude toward life. The world faces a great crisis. I want to help the people of the world to get better acquainted, to live in peace, to be friendly toward one another. Hatred is the real cause of the war. If we want to stop wars, we must destroy hatred first." There was talk of his entering the ministry when he first resumed civilian life, but he chose to take up his acting career instead. Parts were not easy to obtain in post–World War II Hollywood, particularly for an actor approaching forty years of age and having no studio tie. Universal did use him as the psychiatrist in *The Dark Mirror* (1946), and the mature Ayres projected an interesting characterization. Perhaps his best screen work was done for Warner Brothers, first in the loose remake of *The Letter*, entitled *The Unfaithful* (1947), and then as the kindly doctor in the touching yet saccharine *Johnny Belinda* (1948). Jane Wyman received an Oscar for that picture. Ayres was nominated for one, but he was far outdistanced by Laurence Olivier's performance in *Hamlet*.

A few more economy features followed, including yet another version of *Donovan's Brain* (1953), and then Ayres retired from screen work to devote his time to his major interest of studying philosophy and comparative religions. He made a recording of Bible stories and in 1955 released a beautifully intelligent film entitled *Altars of the East*, which depicted many of the religions of the East. He wrote, produced, directed, and financed the film with several years of research that took him over 40,000 miles. The following year he published a book of the same title, and signed for the musical stage version of *Lost Horizon*, entitled *Shangri-La*. However, he walked out of this show over script change. He also starred with Nanette Fabray in a *Playhouse 90* program called *The Family Nobody Wants*.

In 1957 Secretary of State John Foster Dulles appointed Ayres to a three-year term on the U.S. National Committee for UNESCO. In 1958 he hosted the CBS-TV summer series, *Frontier Justice*. That same year his home and his collection of books were destroyed by a California forest fire. In 1959 he organized CURE, the Congress for Universal Religious Exchange. He returned to motion pictures to play the vice-president in *Advise and Consent* (1962), giving one of the better performances in that Otto Preminger production.* In the remake of *The Biscuit Eater* (1972) Ayres had the small role of Earl Holliman's employer. Ayres occasionally turns up as a television guest star, and in 1971 made an appearance on *The Interns*. (Shades of type-casting!)

He has been married three times. First to lively Lola Lane of the Lane sisters on September 15, 1931. They were divorced in 1933 and the same year he wed the most vivacious Hollywood female of them all, Ginger Rogers. But their respective careers prevented that marriage from working and they separated on May 4, 1936. However, Ginger was so busy making movies that she did not pick up her final divorce until 1940. On February 14, 1964, at age fifty-six, Ayres married airline stewardess Diana Hall.

Ayres' career as an actor reveals a man who really chose the wrong vocation, because his acting was largely a matter of trading on his pleasantly

---

*In Irving Wallace's *The Man* (1972), a telefeature released initially to theatres, Ayres again portrayed the vice-president, but in this puerile production he was wheelchair-bound and merely had one small scene, which he dignified with more sincerity than the script required.

earnest personality. Besides his well-remembered performance in *All Quiet on the Western Front,* he never gave another screen characterization which delved inside the part.

LEW AYRES

The Sophomore (Pathé, 1929)
The Kiss (MGM, 1929)
All Quiet on the Western Front (Universal, 1930)
Common Clay (Fox, 1930)
Doorway to Hell (WB, 1930)
East Is West (Universal, 1930)
Iron Man (Universal, 1931)
Up For Murder (Universal, 1931)
Many a Slip (Universal, 1931)
Spirit of Notre Dame (Universal, 1931)
Heaven on Earth (Universal, 1931)
Impatient Maiden (Universal, 1932)
Night World (Universal, 1932)
Okay America! (Universal, 1932)
State Fair (Fox, 1933)
Don't Bet on Love (Universal, 1933)
My Weakness (Fox, 1933)
Cross Country Cruise (Universal, 1934)
Let's Be Ritzy (Universal, 1934)
She Learned about Sailors (Fox, 1934)
Servants' Entrance (Fox, 1934)
Lottery Lover (Fox, 1935)
Silk Hat Kid (Fox, 1935)
The Leathernecks Have Landed (Republic, 1936)
Panic on the Air (Columbia, 1936)
Shakedown (Columbia, 1936)
Murder with Pictures (Paramount, 1936)
The Crime Nobody Saw (Paramount, 1937)
Lady Be Careful (Paramount, 1937)

Last Train from Madrid (Paramount, 1937)
Hold 'Em Navy (Paramount, 1937)
King of the Newsboys (Republic, 1938)
Scandal Street (Paramount, 1938)
Holiday (Columbia, 1938)
Rich Man—Poor Girl (MGM, 1938)
Young Dr. Kildare (MGM, 1938)
Spring Madness (MGM, 1938)
Ice Follies of 1939 (MGM, 1939)
Broadway Serenade (MGM, 1939)
Calling Dr. Kildare (MGM, 1939)
These Glamour Girls (MGM, 1939)
Remember? (MGM, 1939)
Secret of Dr. Kildare (MGM, 1939)
Dr. Kildare's Strange Case (MGM, 1940)
The Golden Fleecing (MGM, 1940)
Dr. Kildare Goes Home (MGM, 1940)
Dr. Kildare's Crisis (MGM, 1940)
Maisie was a Lady (MGM, 1941)
The People vs. Dr. Kildare (MGM, 1941)
Dr. Kildare's Wedding Day (MGM, 1942)
Dr. Kildare's Victory (MGM, 1942)
Fingers at the Window (MGM, 1942)
The Dark Mirror (Universal, 1946)
The Unfaithful (WB, 1947)
Johnny Belinda (WB, 1948)
The Capture (RKO, 1950)
New Mexico (UA, 1951)
No Escape (UA, 1953)
Donovan's Brain (UA, 1953)
Advise and Consent (Columbia, 1962)
The Carpetbaggers (Paramount, 1964)
The Man (Paramount, 1972)
The Biscuit Eater (BV, 1972)
Battle for the Planet of the Apes (20th-Fox, 1973)

With Holmes Herbert in *The Kiss* (1929)

With Nell Craig and Lionel Barrymore in *Young Dr. Kildare* (1938)

With Edgar Dearing, Ann Morriss, Burgess Meredith, Joyce Compton, and Ed Gargan in *Spring Madness* (1938)

Fay Bainter

"Her contribution to the film and to my performance was immeasurable. It just wouldn't have been the same picture without her," wrote Bette Davis in her autobiography, *The Lonely Life*, in reference to Fay Bainter's stellar portrayal of kindly Auntie Belle in *Jezebel* (1938). Not only did Fay win a supporting actress Academy Award for that role, but in the same Oscar race she was also competing with costar Bette Davis in the best actress category —Davis for *Jezebel* and Fay for *White Banners* (1938). Davis received her second Oscar that year, but Fay proved repeatedly that she was able to hold her own against some of Hollywood's biggest powerhouse talents, beauties, and salty characters—two Hepburns, Kate and Audrey; Joan Crawford; Walter Brennan; Judy Garland; and that teenaged scene stealer Mickey Rooney.

Before entering motion pictures at the late age of forty-one, Fay had a lengthy theatrical experience behind her, from child actress to ingenue to leading lady, and when she began in the cinema, she was wise enough to realize that character roles were right for her. "There comes a day when the flush of youth disappears from every woman's face. Most women dread it. I did. Like so many things, however, it is worse in anticipation than in actual fact." During her twenty-eight years on the screen, she performed with a naturalness in character parts which made audiences not only believe in her and trust her, but admire her as well. For four of those years during the 1940s, she was one of the best exponents of MGM's stable of valorous mothers.

Fay was born in Los Angeles on December 7, 1892, making her stage debut at age six in Oliver Morosco's production of *The Jewess*. Morosco kept her on for child parts in *The Little Princess, Little Lord Fauntleroy*, and *The Prince and the Pauper*. She left that professional company when she was fourteen and began playing ingenues in a variety of stock troupes. Her Broadway debut came in 1912 in *The Rose of Panama*. It lasted three weeks and it was back to stock where her most important opportunity came playing in Minnie Maddern Fiske's touring company of *Mrs. Bumpstead Leigh*. She learned a great many acting techniques from Madame Fiske, and in 1916, Fay decided to return to Broadway. For the next two decades she became one of its most admired actresses—*East Is West, Jealousy, Caprice, Lysistrata, For*

Services Rendered, *Uncle Tom's Cabin* (she was Topsy), and her noteworthy interpretation of Grace, the bitch wife in Sinclair Lewis' *Dodsworth*.

Dodsworth opened in 1935, and by that time she had already made her motion picture debut, playing Lionel Barrymore's wife in MGM's *This Side of Heaven* (1934).* She did not think she was very good in that picture and told the press she did not care for motion pictures. But, like many theatre-trained actors, once she got her feet wet she changed her mind. In her second picture, James M. Barrie's *Quality Street* (1937), she easily outacted Katharine Hepburn. Critics chastised Hepburn for her screen mannerisms and called Fay's portrayal as the wistful sister the "triumph of the production." The same year she was even better as the daughter-in-law of Beulah Bondi, who resents her mother-in-law's meddling, in Leo McCarey's poignant tearjerker about old age, *Make Way for Tomorrow*.

The next year she reached the height of her work in motion pictures in the aforementioned *Jezebel* and *White Banners*, and played her first unsympathetic screen role as the vindictive spinster who hates Joan Crawford in *The Shining Hour* (1938). At Warners, she again played opposite Claude Rains in *Daughters Courageous* (1939), which, when not focusing on John Garfield and the Lane Sisters, allowed Fay to radiate that special maternal warmth which would be so typical of her 1940s film work.

In 1940, she joined MGM's stellar lineup to compete with Mary Astor, Spring Byington, and Selena Royle as that studio's most American, apple-pie mother image. She mothered Mickey Rooney in *Young Tom Edison* (1940), was the wise Mrs. Gibbs in United Artists' cloying *Our Town* (1940), had her favorite role as John Payne's strict mother in *Maryland* (1940) at Twentieth Century-Fox, and shepherded Judy Garland and Rooney through *Babes on Broadway* (1941). She continued in more of the same: *Journey for Margaret* (1942), *The Human Comedy* (1943), and *Presenting Lily Mars* (1943). Then, after playing the captain of a group of nurses in *Cry Havoc* (1943) and Hedy Lamarr's astrologer in *The Heavenly Body* (1943), she ended her MGM contract.

Following World War II, she was on the screen less frequently, but was at her professional best in *State Fair* (1945) and *The Virginian* (1946). She returned to Broadway in two minor vehicles, *The Next Half Hour* and *Gayden*, made successful touring appearances in *The Glass Menagerie* and *Long Day's Journey into Night*, and was a guest on many television shows.

In 1962, after nine years' absence from the screen, she returned as the grandmother in William Wyler's *The Children's Hour*. She had performed the same role on tour, and it was Wyler who had directed her in her award-winning *Jezebel*. Again, twenty-four years later, she received an Oscar nomination and should have won. It was her last screen performance. She died on April 16, 1968 after a long illness, survived only by her son. She was buried

*She had been a strong contender for the female lead in RKO's *Cimarron* (1931) but both studio producer William LeBaron and star Richard Dix convinced director Wesley Ruggles to allow RKO newcomer Irene Dunne to play the part of Sabra.

in Arlington National Cemetery beside her husband of forty-two years, Lt. Comdr. Reginald Venable.

FAY BAINTER

This Side of Heaven (MGM, 1934)
Quality Street (RKO, 1937)
The Soldier and the Lady (RKO, 1937)
Make Way for Tomorrow (Paramount, 1937)
Jezebel (WB, 1938)
White Banners (WB, 1938)
Mother Carey's Chickens (RKO, 1938)
The Arkansas Traveler (Paramount, 1938)
The Shining Hour (MGM, 1938)
Yes, My Darling Daughter (WB, 1939)
The Lady and the Mob (Columbia, 1939)
Daughters Courageous (WB, 1939)
Our Neighbors, the Carters (Paramount, 1939)
Young Tom Edison (MGM, 1940)
A Bill of Divorcement (RKO, 1940)
Our Town (UA, 1940)
Maryland (20th-Fox, 1940)
Babes on Broadway (MGM, 1941)
Woman of the Year (MGM, 1942)
The War Against Mrs. Hadley (MGM, 1942)
Mrs. Wiggs of the Cabbage Patch (Paramount, 1942)
Journey for Margaret (MGM, 1942)
The Human Comedy (MGM, 1943)
Presenting Lily Mars (MGM, 1943)
Salute to the Marines (MGM, 1943)
Cry Havoc (MGM, 1943)
The Heavenly Body (MGM, 1943)
Dark Waters (UA, 1944)
Three Is a Family (UA, 1944)
State Fair (20th-Fox, 1945)
The Kid from Brooklyn (RKO, 1946)
The Virginian (Paramount, 1946)
Deep Valley (WB, 1947)
The Secret Life of Walter Mitty (RKO, 1947)
Give My Regards to Broadway (20th-Fox, 1948)
June Bride (WB, 1948)
Close to My Heart (WB, 1951)
The President's Lady (20th-Fox, 1953)
The Children's Hour (UA, 1962)

With Melvyn Douglas in *The Shining Hour* (1938)

Lucille Ball

For many years, Lucille Ball obscured the biographical details surrounding her beginnings by perpetrating the myth of her being born in Butte, Montana, and by using the nickname "Montana." Press agents continued this game in her early career. But Lucy was actually born in Jamestown, New York (August 6, 1911), and the Butte story is significant only inasmuch as that was where her father, a telephone lineman, died when she was four years old.

During her adolescence Lucy recalls she was big for her age with an inferiority complex to match, but at fifteen, she willfully set out for New York City and the *theatre*. She enrolled in the John Murray Anderson–Robert Milton Drama School where she was spellbound by the star pupil, Bette Davis. So spellbound in fact that Anderson sent her home with a note saying: "She's too shy and reticent to put her best foot forward."

But Lucy was not about to give up so easily, and she set out auditioning for chorus jobs. After being fired from three shows, she took a job as a model for Hattie Carnegie at $35 a week. Several years later, as a result of being the model used by Liggett and Myers for their Chesterfield Girl, she was selected as a Goldwyn Girl to be used in *Roman Scandals* (1933), starring Eddie Cantor. She had already had an unbilled bit in *Broadway Through a Keyhole* (1933). Sam Goldwyn was not personally impressed with Lucy but his dance director Busby Berkeley was, and she was hired. Goldwyn used her in two more films, *Nana* (1934) and *Kid Millions* (1934), before she joined Columbia's stock company at $75 weekly, appearing in walkons, bits, and as a foil for the Three Stooges. She finally received billing as a nurse in *Carnival* (1935) but was fired shortly thereafter in a Columbia economy move.

RKO picked up her contract the very same day and it was back to more unbilled bits—*Roberta* (1935), *Old Man Rhythm* (1935), *Top Hat* (1935), and *The Three Musketeers* (1935). After the latter, she complained to the front office, so they began assigning her small speaking roles: *I Dream Too Much* (1935), *Chatterbox* (1936), *Follow the Fleet* (1936). The parts were not very rewarding and the disillusioned young actress decided to try the stage in a musical called *Hey Diddle Diddle*. It was a disaster, closing in Philadelphia, and she was back at RKO. This time Ginger Rogers (one of RKO's prize talents whose mother was that studio's drama coach) suggested that Lucy be given the role of the tough, aspiring actress in *Stage Door* (1937). Despite the competition of a cast which included Rogers, Katharine Hepburn, and Eve Arden, Lucy was able to demonstrate her flair for comedy in a sizeable role.

The studio took note and gave her bigger roles, rushing her through twenty-one pictures in the next four years. But quantity did not guarantee quality. If the pictures were melodrama, they were second-rate. If they were comedy, it was the stereotyped, wisecracking variety of which she recalls: "Eve Arden and I competed for years—one of us would be the lady executive and the other would be 'the other woman.' They were the same roles, for we'd walk through a room, drop a smart remark, and exit. I called us 'the drop-gag girls.' I didn't dig it at all, for in such parts you lose your femininity. That was one of the reasons I wasn't too fond of staying in pictures."

However, a few pictures were noteworthy: In *Five Came Back* (1939), a little melodrama with Chester Morris, she was good as the thick-skinned dame, and as the golddigging chorine in *Dance, Girl, Dance* (1940), she caused producer Erich Pommer to hail her as "a new find." She got top billing and met Desi Arnaz in *Too Many Girls* (1940) and gave a knockout performance as the vixenish nightclub singer in *The Big Street* (1941). The latter was a Damon Runyon fable and Lucy won the role when her friend Carole Lombard introduced her to Runyon, who in turn recommended her for the part. Her performance induced James Agee to write: "Pretty Lucille Ball, who was born for the parts Ginger Rogers sweats over, tackles her 'emotional role' as if it were sirloin and she didn't care who was looking."

The Big Street was also the picture which brought her to MGM's attention. They could not decide on an actress for the Ethel Merman stage role in *Dubarry Was a Lady* (1943), so they signed Lucy, cast her in the role, and announced their intention to build her into an MGM "star." They gave her the dressing room vacated by Norma Shearer, assigned their best technicians to glamorize her, dyed her hair to the strawberry pink which has now become her trademark, but the build-up never quite clicked. She did prove she could handle musical comedy in *Dubarry* even if it was Red Skelton's picture, and when the glamorous Lana Turner became pregnant, MGM cast Lucy in her stead, as the movie star in *Best Foot Forward* (1943).

In the studio's all-star revue, *Thousands Cheer* (1943), Lucy, Ann Sothern, and Marsha Hunt had an amusing scene as prospective WAVES being medically examined by Frank Morgan. Nevertheless, MGM gave neither her nor Dick Powell any help in a wartime message musical, *Meet the People* (1944). A stint in *The Ziegfeld Follies* (not released until 1946) had her as a whipcracking tamer of female cat dancers in a surrealistic setting, and she was relegated to the supporting cast of *Without Love* (1945) as the wisecracking real estate agent, but she walked away with every scene in which she played. Finally Metro did justice to her by casting her in *Easy To Wed* (1946). This was a musical remake of *Libeled Lady* which had starred Jean Harlow and Spencer Tracy, and the remake was better than the original. Cast opposite Keenan Wynn, Lucy had the best role of her career.

51

With Red Skelton in *Dubarry Was a Lady* (1943)

Despite this success, Lucy and MGM could not come to terms, and she began sitting out her contract. Two loanouts resulted and the relationship was dissolved. "At Metro, I kept being held back by show-girl-glamour typing. I wanted to do comedy." She recalls that the only thing she learned during her four years with MGM was how to use props, and this she learned on the sidelines from another MGM contractee, Buster Keaton. Her timing and use of props has since become one of the fortes of her television success.

Following her breakup with MGM, she signed a limited contract with Columbia, at $85,000 per picture and did two middling comedies, *Miss Grant Takes Richmond* (1949) with William Holden, and *The Fuller Brush Girl* (1950) opposite Eddie Albert. For Paramount she made two more comedies, and these were two of her best: *Sorrowful Jones* (1949) and *Fancy Pants* (1950), both remakes and both with Bob Hope. She broke her contract at Columbia over differences with Harry Cohn, by playing a harem girl in a lousy picture called *The Magic Carpet* (1951). She lost the prize role of the elephant girl played by Gloria Grahame in Cecil B. De Mille's *The Greatest Show on Earth* (1952) when she became pregnant (she had wed actor–band leader Desi Arnaz in 1940).

Having performed successfully in radio's *My Favorite Husband* since the mid-1940s, Lucy decided to embark upon a television series—*I Love Lucy* in 1951—with her husband and made television history. It afforded her an opportunity to work in front of a live audience as a feminine clown, and she has remained the most popular video funny girl for the past twenty years. She and Arnaz extended their television involvement in the late 1950s when they purchased RKO studios and turned its sound stages into a television production facility named Desilu. Lucy and Arnaz were divorced in 1960 and sold Desilu for many millions of dollars, and the following year she wed nightclub comedian Gary Morton. Besides her daughter, Lucie Desiree, Lucy is the mother of Desi IV.

Her post-1950 film career has been spotty. MGM, under Dore Schary, wooed her and Arnaz back to make two comedies for them, the nifty *The Long, Long Trailer* (1954) and the strained fantasy *Forever, Darling* (1956). Bob Hope, whose own cinema career was fading, paired with her in the adultery comedy *The Facts of Life* (1960) and the more plush but less spontaneous *Critic's Choice* (1963). A much middle-aged Lucy did a cameo in *A Guide for the Married Man* (1967) and teamed with Henry Fonda and Van Johnson in the lively *Yours, Mine and Ours* (1968). At present, she has finished the film version of *Mame* for Warner Brothers, having proven in her 1960 Broadway-starring vehicle *Wildcat* that she could talk, sing, and mug her way through a full-bodied musical comedy performance.

Ironically, Lucy, who was always a lesser light at each film studio she worked for, has ended up as one of the top attractions of the movie industry's nemesis, television, and is today one of Hollywood's wealthiest citizens.

Broadway Thru a Keyhole (UA, 1933)
Blood Money (UA, 1933)
Roman Scandals (UA, 1933)
Moulin Rouge (UA, 1934)
Nana (UA, 1934)
Bottoms Up (Fox, 1934)
Hold That Girl (Fox, 1934)
Bulldog Drummond Strikes Back (UA, 1934)
The Affairs of Cellini (UA, 1934)
Kid Millions (UA, 1934)
Broadway Bill (Columbia, 1934)
Jealousy (Columbia, 1934)
Men of the Night (Columbia, 1934)
The Fugitive Lady (Columbia, 1934)
Carnival (Columbia, 1935)
Roberta (RKO, 1935)
Old Man Rhythm (RKO, 1935)
Top Hat (RKO, 1935)
The Three Musketeers (RKO, 1935)
I Dream Too Much (RKO, 1935)
Chatterbox (RKO, 1936)
Follow the Fleet (RKO, 1936)
The Farmer in the Dell (RKO, 1936)
Bunker Bean (RKO, 1936)
That Girl from Paris (RKO, 1936)
Winterset (RKO, 1936)
Don't Tell the Wife (RKO, 1937)
Stage Door (RKO, 1937)
The Joy of Living (RKO, 1938)
Go Chase Yourself (RKO, 1938)
Having Wonderful Time (RKO, 1938)
The Affairs of Annabel (RKO, 1938)
Room Service (RKO, 1938)
The Next Time I Marry (RKO, 1938)
Annabel Takes a Tour (RKO, 1938)
Beauty for the Asking (RKO, 1939)
Twelve Crowded Hours (RKO, 1939)
Panama Lady (RKO, 1939)
Five Came Back (RKO, 1939)

That's Right, You're Wrong (RKO, 1939)
The Marines Fly High (RKO, 1940)
You Can't Fool Your Wife (RKO, 1940)
Dance, Girl, Dance (RKO, 1940)
Too Many Girls (RKO, 1940)
A Girl, a Guy, and a Gob (RKO, 1941)
Look Who's Laughing (RKO, 1941)
Valley of the Sun (RKO, 1942)
The Big Street (RKO, 1942)
Seven Days' Leave (RKO, 1942)
Dubarry Was a Lady (MGM, 1943)
Best Foot Forward (MGM, 1943)
Thousands Cheer (MGM, 1943)
Meet the People (MGM, 1944)
Without Love (MGM, 1945)
Abbott and Costello in Hollywood (MGM, 1945)
The Ziegfeld Follies (MGM, 1946)
The Dark Corner (20th-Fox, 1946)
Easy to Wed (MGM, 1946)
Two Smart People (MGM, 1946)
Lover Come Back (Universal, 1946)
Lured (UA, 1947)
Her Husband's Affairs (Columbia, 1947)
Sorrowful Jones (Paramount, 1949)
Easy Living (RKO, 1949)
Miss Grant Takes Richmond (Columbia, 1949)
A Woman of Distinction (Columbia, 1950)*
Fancy Pants (Paramount, 1950)
The Fuller Brush Girl (Columbia, 1950)
The Magic Carpet (Columbia, 1951)
The Long, Long Trailer (MGM, 1954)
Forever, Darling (MGM, 1956)
The Facts of Life (UA, 1960)
Critic's Choice (WB, 1963)
A Guide for the Married Man (20th-Fox, 1967)
Yours, Mine and Ours (UA, 1968)
Mame (WB, 1973)

*Unbilled Appearance

With Desi Arnaz in *The Long, Long Trailer* (1954)

Ethel Barrymore

Ethel Barrymore was the epitome of post-Victorian beauty for many Americans and Londoners during the first three decades of this century. She was a tall, 5' 7", slender, dark-haired patrician beauty with elegant posture and a husky voice for which critic Ashton Stevens dubbed her Ethel Barrytone. Women copied the Ethel Barrymore walk and the Ethel Barrymore voice. Winston Churchill proposed marriage to her but she turned him down. She had hoped to be a concert pianist (and played the piano very well for many years), but her family heritage dictated a career as an actress. Her grandmother was Louise Lane Drew; her mother, Georgiana Drew; her father Maurice Barrymore; and her uncle, John Drew. They were all members of America's royal acting family. Likewise, Ethel and her two brothers, Lionel and John, carried on this tradition. Ethel not only followed in her family's tradition but enhanced it for many years as the First Lady of the American theatre, especially with her performance as Mrs. Mott in *The Corn Is Green* (1940), which she played for three years. She made a few silent pictures circa 1915–1919, most of them for the original Metro Company, and one of which—*Life's Whirlpool* (1917)—was directed by her brother Lionel. Irving Thalberg convinced her to costar with her two brothers in MGM's *Rasputin and the Empress* (1932), but the body of her film work was between 1944 and 1957. For five of those years, 1949–1953, she was under contract to MGM as their grand dame in residence, offering her prestigious presence to generally inferior product.

She was born Ethel Mae Barrymore on August 15, 1879 in Philadelphia. Her childhood years were spent surrounded by the theatrical elite of the day. By her teens she was destined to become an actress. She later said, "We became actors not because we wanted to go on the stage, but because it was the thing we could do best." She was determined not to be just a star, or the niece of so-and-so, and set out to learn her craft to the utmost of her abilities. Her first success was as Madame Tretoni, the opera diva in Clyde Fitch's *Captain Jinks of the Horse Marines* which opened in New York on February 4, 1901. Three days later her name was in lights on the marquee and thereafter it was a series of successes on Broadway and in London. It was at this time that she starred in *Sunny* and ad-libbed a line at the end of the play, which became her trademark: "That's all there is. There isn't any more." Her London debut was on May 15, 1904 in the comedy *Cynthia*. She proved her versatility a year later playing Nora in *A Doll's House*. On December 20, 1928 she opened in New York City in *The Kingdom Of God* and the name of the theatre in which she played was the Ethel Barrymore Theatre.

Always a champion of her brother, John, whom she adored, she agreed to play the Czarina in *Rasputin and the Empress* (1932), a rather static account of the Russian scene, more noteworthy for gathering together the Barrymore clan in one spot at one time than for its entertainment value. Ethel was just as happy to return to the stage, where she was still a queen and master of her own destiny, uninhibited by telling closeups which did disservice to the middle-aged star. But after her sojourn with *The Corn Is Green* she turned to motion pictures as a lucrative refuge. By then, in 1944, she was sixty-five and quite ready to reign supreme as a matriarch screen type with a heart of gold. She won a best supporting actress Oscar for playing Gary Grant's Cockney mother in the stark *None But the Lonely Heart* (1944). She garnered three more Academy Award nominations for her emoting in *The Spiral Staircase* (1946), *The Paradine Case* (1947), and *Pinky* (1949). In the latter picture, she was particularly memorable as the generous grand old lady who bequeaths her property to Jeanne Crain.

Ethel signed with MGM in 1948 and three of her four releases the next year were for that studio. She seemingly took up at Metro where the late Dame May Whitty left off, although Ethel was considered a far more prestigious commodity and was flagrantly used to bolster the "artistic" value of any major motion picture at hand into which she could be interwoven—suitably or not. Whether as the elderly aristocrat who dies at the gaming tables in *The Great Sinner*, the patron of the arts in Mario Lanza's *That Midnight Kiss*, or as the benevolent Mother Superior in *The Red Danube*, she was Ethel Barrymore, dignifying scantily written roles with her decades of know-how. Her biggest assignment at MGM was in *Kind Lady* (1951), portraying the house owner who is imprisoned by the crafty Maurice Evans and his accomplices, Angela Lansbury and Keenan Wynn. But the studio did not promote that vehicle, and it came and went quickly. Her final studio venture was in the multiguest-star effort *Main Street to Broadway* (1953) in which she shared scenes with invalid brother Lionel.

She celebrated her seventy-fifth birthday on the Warner Brothers soundstages playing in *Young At Heart* (1954), and three years later made her final film, *Johnny Trouble* (1957). It was a tender but badly paced remake of *Someone to Remember* (1943) which had starred that wonderful character player, Mabel Paige. Ethel was an occasional television performer in the 1950s, appearing on such diverse shows as *Climax*, the *All Star Revue* with Tallulah Bankhead, and clowning with Jimmy Durante on his video variety program.

On June 18, 1959, at age eighty, Ethel died of a heart attack in her Beverly Hills home and was buried beside her brothers in the Calvary

Cemetery Mausoleum in Los Angeles. She had been married only once, to New York socialite–stockbroker, Russell Griswold Colt from 1905–1923, by whom she had three children: Samuel Peabody Colt, John Drew Colt, and Ethel Barrymore Colt. The failure of that marriage was a lifelong tragedy to Ethel. Colt was a *bon vivant* and playboy, and their union was doomed from the beginning. When she informed a Roman Catholic cardinal of her plans for a divorce, he cautioned her against remarriage. Ethel said, "I remember that I found no difficulty in reassuring him. It never entered my head to marry again. My divorce is merely legal. It was granted in Rhode Island, quietly and without opposition, on the grounds of desertion and nonsupport."

Ethel was an avid baseball fan, with a nonpartisan, encyclopedic knowledge of the game. One of Ethel's staunchest admirers and imitators was the younger Tallulah Bankhead. Tallulah likewise became a baseball fan, but Ethel always considered her a novice in her enthusiasm because she could never remain impartial. Ethel and Tallulah remained friends for years, but Tallulah's habit of impersonating the great actress was not without mishap. At a party hosted by Condé Nast's Frank Crowninshield, where Ethel was a guest, the host had Tallulah perform her impersonation. Afterwards, Ethel remarked, "But your impersonation makes me look so fat." Tallulah replied, "It's not my fault. I was imitating you, Miss Barrymore." Whereupon the elder actress briskly slapped Tallulah across the face.

Ethel was well-known for her wit and sharp tongue, and once upon mention of the name of the Broadway columnist, Walter Winchell, Ethel acidly quipped, "I don't see why Walter Winchell is allowed to live!"

With Walter Huston in *The Great Sinner* (1949)

ETHEL BARRYMORE

The Nightingale (Alco, 1915)
The Final Judgment (Metro, 1915)
The Kiss of Hate (Metro, 1916)
The Awakening of Helen Richie (Metro, 1916)
The White Raven (Metro, 1917)
The Lifted Veil (Metro, 1917)
The Eternal Mother (Metro, 1917)
An American Widow (Metro, 1917)
The Call of Her People (Metro, 1917)
Life's Whirlpool (Metro, 1917)
Our Mrs. McChesney (Metro, 1918)
The Divorcee (Metro, 1919)
Rasputin And the Empress (MGM, 1932)
None But the Lonely Heart (RKO, 1944)
The Spiral Staircase (RKO, 1946)
The Farmer's Daughter (RKO, 1947)
Moss Rose (20th-Fox, 1947)

Night Song (RKO, 1947)
The Paradine Case (Selznick, 1948)
Moonrise (Republic, 1948)
Portrait of Jennie (Selznick, 1948)
The Great Sinner (MGM, 1949)
That Midnight Kiss (MGM, 1949)
The Red Danube (MGM, 1949)
Pinky (20th-Fox, 1949)
Kind Lady (MGM, 1951)
The Secret of Convict Lake (20th-Fox, 1951)
It's a Big Country (MGM, 1952)
Deadline, U. S. A. (20th-Fox, 1952)
Just for You (Paramount, 1952)
The Story of Three Loves (MGM, 1953)
Main Street to Broadway (MGM, 1953)
Young at Heart (WB, 1954)
Johnny Trouble (WB, 1957)

John Barrymore

Of the Barrymores, America's Royal Family of Actors, John was the real actor. His sister Ethel called him a genius, as did many critics, and Helen Hayes recently said that to John, acting was a duty. He always maintained that he had become an actor only because it was expected of him. Indeed, his grandmother, Mrs. John Drew, urged her three grandchildren to learn to act before they did anything else. And yet, even if his vocation was not entirely of his own choosing, his stage and screen performances, before the effects of alcohol became overpowering, were fired by far more than just technique. He could and often did turn in inspired performances.

John Sidney Blythe Barrymore was born on February 15, 1882, in Philadelphia. Although he grew up in the shadow of the stage footlights, his first vocational thoughts were directed toward journalism and painting. For a time he created the illustrations for the Ella Wheeler Wilcox poems which were published by the N.Y. *Evening Journal*. He made his acting debut, of sorts, when he replaced an actor for one night in sister Ethel's vehicle, *Captain Jinks of the Horse Marines*, in Philadelphia in 1902. He walked on stage, forgot his lines, and adlibbed, "I've blown up, old chap. Where do we go from here?" The following year he appeared in a Chicago production of Sudermann's *Magda* and made his New York debut on December 28, 1903 in Clyde Fitch's *Glad of It*. His performance earned him acceptable notices as a comedian and he soon became one of the New York stage's favorite comedic actors.

Barrymore did not take his profession too seriously, preferring his life of drinking and romancing. He presumably had earned his manhood at the age of fourteen at the instigation of his stepmother, Mamie Floyd. True or not, his offstage reputation as Broadway Lothario soon outdistanced most of his histrionic efforts. One of his most famous affairs was the much-talked-about romance with Evelyn Nesbitt, the protégé of architect Stanford White. On September 1, 1910 Barrymore married a socialite ten years younger than himself, Katherine Corri Harris, but they divorced when Katherine chose to be always in the theatrical limelight, while he demanded a quiet domestic life when not in front of the footlights. The marriage ended in 1917.

He signed a contract in 1913 with Famous Players-Lasky and made his screen debut in an adaptation of one of his stage successes, *An American*

Citizen (1914). He was so impressed with the new medium that he exclaimed, "The film determines an actor's ability, absolutely, conclusively. It is the surest test of an actor's qualities. Mental impressions can be conveyed by the screen more quickly than vocally. The moving picture is not a business, it is an art."

He continued to work in motion pictures but his stage career took on more prominence when it verged to dramatic roles under the guidance of his friend, playwright Edward Sheldon. It was the latter who suggested that Barrymore star in a stage version of John Galsworthy's *Justice*, the story of a bank clerk who is driven to suicide. The play opened in 1915 and the *N.Y. Times* reported: "For Barrymore the first night of *Justice* was a milestone. By his simple, eloquent, deeply touching performance as young Falder, he arrested the attention of the city and gained overnight a prestige which is priceless in the theatre, a prestige all his work in trivial entertainment would not give him. It is what the theater can bestow on those who serve it loyally. This comes now to a player whose years in the theatre have been lackadaisical." Years of stage greatness for John followed as a result of that production: *Kick-In, Peter Ibbetson* with brother Lionel, *Redemption, The Jest*, to name just a few.

His film career had continued sporadically during this period. He had made *Raffles, the Amateur Cracksman* (1917) for an independent company and then in 1918 signed another contract with Famous Players. In a dramatic excursion away from the romantic-adventure film for which he had become noted, Barrymore persuaded the studio to cast him in *Dr. Jekyll and Mr. Hyde* (1920), the film which brought him international acclaim. Other film actors would later play the dual role in this Robert Louis Stevenson tale, but Barrymore's screen performance remains the best regarded. It was the peak of his silent screen career and occurred in the same year that he performed his notable stage characterization of Shakespeare's *Richard III*.

Also in that year, on August 5th, he wed poetess Michael Strange. Her real name was Blanche Oelrichs, the ex-Mrs. Leonard M. Thomas. The mother of two sons by her first marriage, she bore Barrymore a daughter, Diana, on March 3, 1921. After starring in a play written by his wife, *Claire de Lune*, one of his rare flops, Barrymore opened on November 6, 1922 in *Hamlet*, which is regarded generally as the best performance of his entire career. He played the role for 101 performances, thereby breaking the 100-performance record set by Edwin Booth. Following his success with *Hamlet*, which he also took to London, he turned full time to the screen. He starred in *Sherlock Holmes* for Sam Goldwyn in 1922, and played the title role in Warner Brothers' *Beau Brummel* (1924). His performance in the latter was sometimes ludicrous and sometimes inspired, but it nonetheless induced that studio to sign him to a lucrative contract at $76,250, plus a hefty overtime fee if the production went beyond seven weeks, and a liberal expense account. His costar in *Beau Brummel* had been the nubile Mary Astor, with whom he had had an affair for several years. His marriage to Michael Strange had been on the wane for some time, although he actually did not divorce her until 1928.

61

He starred for Warners in *The Sea Beast* (1926), a romanticized version of Herman Melville's *Moby Dick*, and he fell in love with his 21-year-old costar, Dolores Costello, whom he described as "preposterously beautiful." *Don Juan* (1926), which boasted synchronized music, reteamed him with Mary Astor. Warner publicized the production as starring "The World's Greatest Actor as the Greatest Lover of All Ages." Because of Barrymore's established screen reputation and the new gimmick of a soundtrack, this romantic malarkey did very well at the boxoffice, but cinema reviewers were carping already that the 44-year-old Barrymore was just a remnant of his former self and only filled with posturing and mechanical gestures. Barrymore's name was still a marketable commodity, however, and United Artists offered him $100,000 per film plus a percentage to work under their aegis. The potentially higher salary enticed Barrymore, who was finding it difficult to pay for his real-life efforts to be the great lover. For after all, there was always the alimony to pay. As he later said, "Alimony is the most exorbitant of all stud fees and the worst of it is, you pay it retroactively. A man must properly pay the fiddler, but in my case it so happened that a whole symphony orchestra had to be subsidized." Not deterred, he married Dolores Costello on November 24, 1928, and they had two children: Dolores Ethel Mae (April 8, 1930) and John Blythe Barrymore, Jr. (June 4, 1932).

After starring in three United Artists' pictures, *The Beloved Rogue* (1927), *Tempest* (1928), and *Eternal Love* (1929), the latter directed by Ernst Lubitsch, Barrymore signed again with Warner Brothers at $30,000 a week, plus a percentage of the profits. The talkies were in their first flush of success and the studios were eager for actors with proven stage voices. Barrymore played a be-wigged dandy in *General Crack* (1929), reprised *Moby Dick* (1930) with Joan Bennett as his *vis-à-vis*, and then turned to a bizarre character role as the bearded *Svengali* (1931). The latter picture was popular enough to have him and his female lead, Marion Marsh, reteamed in a very similar property, *The Mad Genius* (1931).

It was at this critical juncture that Irving Thalberg brought the fifty-year-old Barrymore to MGM under a nonexclusive contract at $150,000 per picture. He was teamed with his brother Lionel, already a Metro studio fixture, in *Arsene Lupin* (1932) which found its own audience, but certainly not to the same degree as the glittering *Grand Hotel* (1932) in which John shone as the aging jewel thief who almost finds a new life with ballerina Greta Garbo. That same year he made *State's Attorney* at RKO, and, at that same studio, performed his memorable role of Katharine Hepburn's demented father in *A Bill of Divorcement*. This was a role close to his heart, for Barrymore had for years been haunted by the memory of his own father's mental breakdown and death in a sanitarium. It is said that part of Barrymore's drinking problem was a result of this tragedy, and Barrymore himself remarked about his alcoholic intake, "It helps me not to worry about the future too much."

Metro thought it a brilliant boxoffice coup to join the three Barrymores in one feature, and wooed Ethel from the Broadway stage to play the female lead in *Rasputin and the Empress* (1932). The final results were not worth the trouble involved, particularly when Prince Felix Youssoupoff, upon whose character John's role was based, sued MGM and won a liberal libel case. *Reunion in Vienna* (1933) with Diana Wynyard, who had played Barrymore's wife in *Rasputin*, was showy but stilted and not successful. He won much more praise for his appearance as the French schoolteacher in RKO's *Topaze* (1933) and then as the alcoholic fading matinee idol in MGM's star-clustered *Dinner at Eight* (1933). The role was so biographical that many said John had to do little preparation for the assignment, which possibly was a large consideration, since he was already past the point where remembering lines was a simple matter.

The most remarkable quality of his performance in Elmer Rice's *Counsellor-at-Law* (1934) at Universal was his admirable restraint, a plus factor decidedly missing in the screwball romp, *Twentieth Century* (1934), which matched him with the energetic Carole Lombard. He was off the screen in 1935, during which time he and Dolores Costello were divorced. He began a distastefully flamboyant romance with an aspiring actress named Elaine Barrie, a nineteen-year-old former journalism student at Hunter College.

"Irving Thalberg saved me from the breadlines," said Barrymore when the MGM executive cast him as Mercutio in Metro's *Romeo and Juliet* (1936). Because of the actor's inability to remember his lines or to get away from the persistent Miss Barrie, Thalberg convinced John to enter a nearby sanitarium for the duration of the production. All this happened after Thalberg had almost decided to fire Barrymore and replace him with William Powell, but the latter refused to step into a part intended for an old friend. After completing *Romeo and Juliet*, Barrymore was physically unable to accept the role in Greta Garbo's *Camille* (1937) which was eventually played by Henry Daniell, and again he entered a sanitarium for treatment. Upon his release he played an aging impressario in *Maytime* (1937) but was a distinct second fiddle to stars Jeanette MacDonald and Nelson Eddy.

Between 1937 and 1942 Barrymore was demoted even further down the line of featured billing. He could no longer be counted on to carry his own, and he returned to MGM only once again, to play, in a magnificent manner, Louis XV in Norma Shearer's *Marie Antoinette* (1938). Paramount used his "presence" for several Bulldog Drummond programmers, and Carole Lombard graciously demanded that he be given a supporting assignment in her *True Confession* (1937). He sparkled once more on the screen in Billy Wilder's *Midnight* (1939), being cast as the aging Parisian aristocrat who hires Claudette Colbert to pretend to be his mistress in order to make his straying wife (Mary Astor) toe the line more closely. If it was sad to see him wearily parody himself in *The Great Profile* (1940), it was sadder still to think that he was Rudy Vallee's buffoon on the singer's radio show in 1941 and 1942.

Barrymore had married Elaine Barrie on November 8, 1936, after several "engagements," and they were divorced in 1940. On May 19, 1942, during a rehearsal for the Vallee radio show, he collapsed, saying, "This is one time I miss my cue." Ten days later, after being administered the last rites of the Catholic faith, and receiving a telephone call from a person from his past, Evelyn Nesbitt, which he was too weak to accept, the Great One died of pneumonia, complicated by chronic nephritis, cirrhosis of the liver, and gastric ulcers.

No Barrymore since has carried on with the tradition several generations of that family had established. For a time, John's daughter Diana tried, but she too could not cope, and her life was plagued by the same kind of notoriety and alcoholism as her father's had been. She died from an overdose of barbituates and alcohol in 1960, two years after the release of *Too Much, Too Soon*, a film based on her autobiography, in which Errol Flynn had given a sensible performance as her father. John's other daughter, Ethel, never pursued a theatrical career. His son, John Jr., likewise tried, and is still seen occasionally today in films and on television. Nevertheless, the Royal Family seems to be no more.

JOHN BARRYMORE

An American Citizen (Paramount, 1914)
The Man from Mexico (Paramount, 1914)
The Dictator (Paramount, 1915)
Are You a Mason? (Paramount, 1915)
The Incorrigible Dukane (Paramount, 1915)
Nearly a King (Paramount, 1916)
The Lost Bridegroom (Paramount, 1916)
The Red Widow (Paramount, 1916)
Raffles, the Amateur Cracksman (Hiller & Wilk, 1917)
On the Quiet (Paramount, 1918)
Here Comes the Bride (Paramount, 1919)

The Test of Honor (Paramount, 1919)
Dr. Jekyll and Mr. Hyde (Paramount, 1920)
The Lotus Eater (Associated First National, 1921)
Sherlock Holmes (Goldwyn, 1922)
Beau Brummell (WB, 1924)
The Sea Beast (WB, 1926)
Don Juan (WB, 1926)
When a Man Loves (WB, 1927)
The Beloved Rogue (UA, 1927)
Tempest (UA, 1928)
Eternal Love (UA, 1929)

With John Davidson and Edwin Maxwell in *Grand Hotel* (1932)

The Show of Shows (WB, 1929)
General Crack (WB, 1929)
The Man from Blankley's (WB, 1930)
Moby Dick (WB, 1930)
Svengali (WB, 1931)
The Mad Genius (WB, 1931)
Arsene Lupin (MGM, 1932)
Grand Hotel (MGM, 1932)
State's Attorney (RKO, 1932)
A Bill of Divorcement (RKO, 1932)
Rasputin and the Empress (MGM, 1932)
Topaze (RKO, 1933)
Reunion in Vienna (MGM, 1933)
Dinner at Eight (MGM, 1933)
Night Flight (MGM, 1933)
Counsellor-at-Law (Universal, 1934)
Long Lost Father (RKO, 1934)
Twentieth Century (Columbia, 1934)
Romeo and Juliet (MGM, 1936)
Maytime (MGM, 1937)
Bulldog Drummond Comes Back (Paramount, 1937)
Night Club Scandal (Paramount, 1937)
True Confession (Paramount, 1937)
Bulldog Drummond's Revenge (Paramount, 1937)
Bulldog Drummond's Peril (Paramount, 1938)
Romance in the Dark (Paramount, 1938)
Spawn of the North (Paramount, 1938)
Marie Antoinette (MGM, 1938)
Hold That Co-Ed (20th-Fox, 1938)
The Great Man Votes (RKO, 1939)
Midnight (Paramount, 1939)
The Great Profile (20th-Fox, 1940)

With Helen Hayes in *Night Flight* (1933)

The Invisible Woman (Universal, 1941)
World Premiere (Paramount, 1941)
Playmates (RKO, 1941)

With Basil Rathbone, Reginald Denny, and Leslie Howard in *Romeo and Juliet* (1936)

Lionel Barrymore

If John and Ethel were the royalty of the Barrymore acting family, brother Lionel was the journeyman actor of the clan. During his fifty-year film career, he avoided romantic leads, preferring to disguise his distinguished six-foot, 155-pound frame in unusual character assignments. Equally adept at sympathetic, heroic, villainous, comedic, avuncular, startling, or majestic roles, the excellence of his acting was overshadowed often in later years by his bulky wheelchaired presence. From the late 1930s onward he was forced to emote from a wheelchair as a result of a hip injury. His rasping voice and mobile bushy eyebrows forced critics to refer to him as the only living screen actor who consistently overacts and yet escapes being branded as a ham. During his movie decades he acted in front of the camera, and also directed and wrote scenarios. From 1926 until his death in 1954 he was under MGM contract. Not only did he hold together the lucrative Dr. Kildare series for fifteen episodes by his portrayal of the gruff but kindly Dr. Gillespie, but, more so than his fellow studio player Wallace Beery, he gave new meaning to the term of character star. When he performed a supporting or cameo assignment in a picture, it was not a case of a post–middle-aged actor reaching up for a moment of temporary glory, but that of a seasoned star graciously delving into his reservoir of experienced talent to bolster a production's impact on the public.

Lionel Blythe Barrymore was born on April 28, 1878 in the home of his grandmother, Mrs. John Drew, at 119 North Ninth Street in Philadelphia. Educated in private schools, Lionel's childhood, along with that of his sister Ethel and brother John, was a most transient one. In the summer of 1893, while on school vacation, he accompanied his grandmother on her tour as Mrs. Malaprop in *The Rivals*. Whenever the dynamic Mrs. Drew suggested that Lionel should become an actor, he would reply that he would much prefer to design scenery. Whereupon his forceful grandmother would exclaim, "First you will become an actor." And indeed his debut occurred when he took over the role of Thomas the coachman for one performance during that tour. Lionel hated this brief taste of acting and refused to appear on stage again. But the inevitability of an acting career was not to be denied. Although he enjoyed painting and etching—two avocations he pursued throughout his life—and for a time deserted the theatrical world to study art, family pressure and "obligation" to his determined grandmother and now to his stage actress sister, put him back on the road to acting. He made his Broadway debut on September 27, 1900 in *Sag Harbor*. Three years later, playing an Italian organ grinder, he appeared in *The Mummy and the Humming Bird* with his uncle John Drew, and literally stole the limelight from that famed matinee idol. Drew would later quip, when introducing Lionel to friends: "My nephew, in whose production I am playing quite a minor part."

Lionel got his first taste of the cinema by hanging around the Biograph Studio at 11 East 14th Street in Manhattan. Lionel would recall in his memoirs, *We Barrymores* (1951), how he had offered himself as a film actor to D. W. Griffith.

"He looked me up and down, peering over that fine, cantilevered nose of his, and he said:

'I'm not employing stage stars.'

'I'm not remotely any such creature,' I said, 'I will do anything. I mean absolutely anything. Believe me, I'm hungry. I want a job.'

'All right,' said Griffith, 'we'll put you on ... ' " Griffith hired him at $10 a day as an extra and paid him $25 for several scripts. He was the first of the Barrymore clan to turn to motion pictures, and he made his feature film debut in Griffith's biblical spectacle *Judith of Bethulia* (1914), playing several minor roles.

Barrymore became very active in motion pictures, playing opposite Lillian Russell in *Wildfire* (1915), and during the same year, first working for the Metro Company in *Dora Thorne* and *A Yellow Streak*. *Life's Whirlpool* (1917) for Metro-Rolfe found Lionel directing his sister Ethel in his own story–screenplay. Perhaps Lionel's most impressive performance in his early cinema years was in the lead role of Paramount's *The Copperhead* (1920), based on the famed Augustus Thomas drama in which he had starred on Broadway in 1918. Despite his busy film schedule, Lionel continued to ply his craft onstage. In 1917 he and brother John were in *Peter Ibbetson* and two years later costarred in *The Jest*. His *Macbeth* appeared on Broadway during the 1921 season.

Lionel's proclivity for meaty character parts led him to play a crook-turned-shoestring peddler in *Boomerang Bill* (1922), the secret head of the Italian Communist party in *The Eternal City* (1923), and the notorious Captain Walter Butler in D. W. Griffith's Revolutionary War epic *America* (1924). He was not above appearing in potboilers such as Chadwick's *The Iron Man* (1925) or B. P. Schulberg's *The Girl Who Wouldn't Work* (1925). Preferring the privacy of the film medium, Lionel moved permanently to California in 1925 and the following year signed a contract with the newly-merged MGM. His first effort for that studio was Rex Beach's *The Barrier* (1926) and later in the year played the cuckolded husband of Greta Garbo in *The Temptress*. When Gloria Swanson starred in United Artists' *Sadie Thompson* (1928), it was Lionel who played the fanatical reformer Alfred

Atkinson, the man who eventually seduces her and then commits suicide.

It was with the advent of sound that the fifty-year-old Lionel made his greatest screen impact, for his family-inherited stage-trained voice made him much in demand. He played a detective in MGM's first talkie, *Alias Jimmy Valentine* (1928) and won an Oscar as the alcoholic lawyer in *A Free Soul* (1931). In those early years at MGM he proved an industrious, if not particularly inventive, director, supervising Ruth Chatterton's *Madame X* (1929); John Gilbert's *His Glorious Night* (1929); Lawrence Tibbett's *Rogue Song* (1930); and, for Columbia, Barbara Stanwyck's *Ten Cents a Dance* (1931). One of Lionel's more restrained performances was playing the dying Kringelein, the meek clerk in *Grand Hotel* (1932), who finds a bit of happiness through the kindness of down-and-out aristocrat John Barrymore ("I may address the baron at any time?" queries the amazed Lionel) and the sympathetic attention of cynical stenographer Joan Crawford. Lionel was offered a wide selection of hardy screen roles due to a great extent to his rapport with Louis B. Mayer and his respect for Irving Thalberg. Lionel once said, "Irving was a motion picture man utterly. He was also extremely young. I used to go into his office with the feeling I was addressing a boy. In a moment I would be the one who felt young and inexperienced. I would feel he was not one but all the forty disciples." Lionel was offered a wide selection of hardy screen roles: the mad Russian monk in *Rasputin and the Empress* (1932), the sickly shipping magnate in *Dinner at Eight* (1933), Billy Bones in *Treasure Island* (1934), and Dan Peggotty in *David Copperfield* (1935). Foreshadowing his stereotyped screen image of the 1940s was his assignment as the gruff southern aristocrat who is melted by winsome Shirley Temple in Fox's *Little Colonel* (1935).

Two of MGM's rare excursions into the horrific featured Lionel in leading roles, *The Mark of the Vampire* (1935) and *The Devil-Doll* (1936). He was the scientist who hires hypnotist Bela Lugosi in the former, and in the latter he is an escaped convict masquerading as an old lady who has a collection of living miniature people. Having functioned as the father in *Ah, Wilderness!* (1935), Metro cast him as Judge Hardy in *A Family Affair* (1937), the first of the *Andy Hardy* series. Probably he would have continued in the part had not he tripped over a lighting cable while filming *Saratoga* (1937) and snapped his hip which he had injured the year before. The second accident to his hip confined him to a wheelchair, and for a time he thought his career was over. However, Louis B. Mayer assured him otherwise and loaned him to Columbia for Frank Capra's *You Can't Take It with You* (1938) to play the whacky Grandpa Vanderhof, a part which had been rewritten for him so he could play it from a wheelchair.

By the time Lionel returned to MGM, Lewis Stone was entrenched in the Judge Hardy assignment, and Reginald Owen had taken over the lead part of Scrooge in *A Christmas Carol* (1938). (Lionel had been playing Scrooge in an annual radio production of *A Christmas Carol* for some years. In the mid-1940s he would attain much popularity in that medium by starring in

With Frank Lawton and Maureen O'Sullivan in *The Devil-Doll* (1936)

With Chester Morris in *Public Hero Number One* (1935)

Mayor Of The Town.) Mayer came up with the Dr. Gillespie character for Barrymore and, beginning with *Young Dr. Kildare* (1938), he became everyone's favorite crochety but essentially kind medico. It was also the beginning of "Lionel the mugger" who, despite his confinement to a wheelchair, could rivet the audience's attention to his presence with a flick of his thick eyebrows. At Metro it became a standard gag that the L. B. in mogul Mayer's name stood for Lionel Barrymore, and the studio boss would admit on rare occasions to close associates, "I've got a lot of ham in me." If today's impersonators seem stuck on imitating Humphrey Bogart, Peter Lorre, and James Cagney, in the 1940s Lionel Barrymore headed the list of people most often mimicked, for his distinctive voice and flexible face mannerisms were easily identifiable by audiences of all sorts. Mickey Rooney became so adept in his impersonations of the elder star that on several radio broadcasts and in a few MGM pictures he would go into his "Lionel Barrymore bit."

When Metro bounced Lew Ayres from the Dr. Kildare series because of his pacifist stand in World War II, the studio spruced up Lionel's role, beginning with *Calling Dr. Gillespie* (1942) and continuing through *Dark Delusion* (1947), they used an assortment of Metro contractees to fill in as the younger doctor protégé, ranging from Van Johnson to James Craig. Besides this standard assignment, MGM found diversified use for Barrymore in the 1940s. He was a quizzical judge in *Lady Be Good* (1941), played the aging Thaddeus Stevens in *Tennessee Johnson* (1942), and narrated *Dragon Seed* (1944). On loanout to David O. Selznick he was used as the sermonizing clergyman in *Since You Went Away* (1944) and combated Margaret O'Brien for the limelight in *Three Wise Fools* (1946). It had been announced in 1944 that he would play President Roosevelt in *The Beginning of the End* (1945), but when another actor showed up in the role, it was presumed that the Roosevelts had protested, since Lionel had been an active supporter of Governor Thomas E. Dewey in the 1944 presidential race.

Lionel's last solid screen performance was as Lauren Bacall's father-in-law in Warner Brothers' *Key Largo* (1948). For this role the veteran player dropped all his Dr. Gillespie overtones and gave an energetic portrait of a proud and righteous man who fears neither gangster Edward G. Robinson nor death. Then Lionel played Andrew Jackson in *Lone Star* (1952), starring Clark Gable and Ava Gardner, a role he had essayed before in *The Gorgeous Hussy* (1936). His last screen appearance was as himself in *Main Street to Broadway* (1953) in which he shared scenes with sister Ethel, herself a studio contractee.

In the last years of his MGM tenure, it was a familiar sight to see Lionel's chauffeur-driven car arrive at the studio gate, with the actor thrusting out a box extended on a stick. The studio guard would drop the pay envelope into Barrymore's container, and then the star would drive off. Unfortunately, by this point, when Barrymore should have been able to enjoy the fruits of his long years of professional activities, he was in debt to the Internal Revenue Service, and much of his salary was immediately turned over to the tax bureau.

On November 15, 1954 he died at the age of 76, and with him an era died. He was the least flamboyant of the volatile Barrymores, his one vice being a gifted flair for profanity. He painted, etched, published a novel, *Mr. Cantonwine* (1951), and also composed music. His tone poem, *In Memoriam*, dedicated to his brother John, was performed by the Philadelphia Symphony Orchestra in 1942. He conducted his symphony, *Partita*, in New York City's Lewisohn Stadium in 1944 and, later, the San Francisco Symphony Orchestra performed his *Tableau Russe*. He married twice; first to Doris Rankin in 1904, by whom he had a daughter, Ethel Barrymore II. They divorced in 1923, and the same year he wed actress Irene Fenwick, the former Mrs. J. J. O'Brien. Irene died on Christmas eve, 1936, and the next day Lionel's brother John substituted for him in the annual performance of Scrooge in *The Christmas Carol* on radio.

LIONEL BARRYMORE

Judith of Bethulia (Biograph, 1914)
The Seats of the Mighty (World, 1914)
Under the Gaslight (Klaw & Erlanger, 1914)
Wildfire (World, 1915)
A Modern Magdalen (Life Photo, 1915)
The Curious Conduct of Judge Legarde (Life Photo, 1915)
The Flaming Sword (Metro, 1915)
Dora Thorne (Biograph, 1915)
A Yellow Streak (Metro, 1915)
Dorian's Divorce (Metro-Rolfe, 1916)
The Quitter (Metro-Rolfe, 1916)
The Upheaval (Metro-Rolfe, 1916)
The Brand of Cowardice (Metro-Rolfe, 1916)
The End of the Tour (Metro-Rolfe, 1917)
His Father's Son (Metro-Rolfe, 1917)
The Millionaire's Double (Metro-Rolfe, 1917)
Life's Whirlpool (Metro-Rolfe, 1917)
The Valley of Night (Monopol, 1919)
The Copperhead (Paramount, 1920)
The Master Mind (FN, 1920)
The Devil's Garden (FN, 1920)
The Great Adventure (Associated First National, 1921)
Jim the Penman (Associated First National, 1921)
Boomerang Bill (Paramount, 1922)
The Face in the Fog (Paramount, 1922)
The Enemies of Women (Goldwyn, 1923)
Unseeing Eyes (Goldwyn-Cosmopolitan, 1923)
The Eternal City (Associated First National, 1923)
America (UA, 1924)
Meddling Women (Chadwick, 1924)
I Am the Man (Chadwick, 1924)

The Iron Man (Chadwick, 1925)
Children of the Whirlwind (Arrow, 1925)
The Girl Who Wouldn't Work (B. P. Schulberg, 1925)
The Wrongdoer (Astor, 1925)
Fifty-Fifty (Associated Exhibitors, 1925)
The Splendid Road (FN, 1925)
The Barrier (MGM, 1926)
Brooding Eyes (Ginsberg Distributing, 1926)
The Lucky Lady (Paramount, 1926)
Paris at Midnight (Producers Distributing, 1926)
The Bells (Chadwick, 1926)
The Temptress (MGM, 1926)
The Show (MGM, 1927)
Women Love Diamonds (MGM, 1927)
Body and Soul (MGM, 1927)
The Thirteenth Hour (MGM, 1927)
Sadie Thompson (UA, 1928)
Drums of Love (UA, 1928)
The Lion and the Mouse (WB, 1928)
Road House (Fox, 1928)
West of Zanzibar (MGM, 1928)
The River Woman (Lumas, 1928)
Alias Jimmy Valentine (MGM, 1929)
The Hollywood Revue of 1929 (MGM, 1929)
The Mysterious Island (MGM, 1929)
Free and Easy (MGM, 1930)
A Free Soul (MGM, 1931)
Guilty Hands (MGM, 1931)
Yellow Ticket (Fox, 1931)
Mata Hari (MGM, 1931)
Broken Lullaby (Paramount, 1932)
Arsene Lupin (MGM, 1932)
Grand Hotel (MGM, 1932)

71

Washington Masquerade (MGM, 1932)
Rasputin and the Empress (MGM, 1932)
Sweepings (RKO, 1933)
Looking Forward (MGM, 1933)
Dinner at Eight (MGM, 1933)
Stranger's Return (MGM, 1933)
Night Flight (MGM, 1933)
One Man's Journey (RKO, 1933)
The Late Christopher Bean (MGM, 1933)
Should Ladies Behave? (MGM, 1933)
This Side of Heaven (MGM, 1934)
Carolina (Fox, 1934)

Cardboard City (Fox, 1934)*
Treasure Island (MGM, 1934)
Girl from Missouri (MGM, 1934)
David Copperfield (MGM, 1935)
Mark of the Vampire (MGM, 1935)
Little Colonel (Fox, 1935)
Public Hero Number One (MGM, 1935)
The Return of Peter Grimm (RKO, 1935)
Ah, Wilderness! (MGM, 1935)
The Voice of Bugle Ann (MGM, 1936)
The Road to Glory (20th-Fox, 1936)
The Devil-Doll (MGM, 1936)
The Gorgeous Hussy (MGM, 1936)
Camille (MGM, 1936)
Captains Courageous (MGM, 1937)
A Family Affair (MGM, 1937)
Saratoga (MGM, 1937)
Navy Blue and Gold (MGM, 1937)
Test Pilot (MGM, 1938)
A Yank at Oxford (MGM, 1938)
You Can't Take It with You (Columbia, 1938)
Young Dr. Kildare (MGM, 1938)
Let Freedom Ring (MGM, 1939)

Calling Dr. Kildare (MGM, 1939)
On Borrowed Time (MGM, 1939)
Secret of Dr. Kildare (MGM, 1939)
Dr. Kildare's Strange Case (MGM, 1940)
Dr. Kildare Goes Home (MGM, 1940)
Dr. Kildare's Crisis (MGM, 1940)
The Bad Man (MGM, 1941)
The Penalty (MGM, 1941)
The People vs. Dr. Kildare (MGM, 1941)
Lady Be Good (MGM, 1941)
Dr. Kildare's Wedding Day (MGM, 1941)
Dr. Kildare's Victory (MGM, 1942)
Calling Dr. Gillespie (MGM, 1942)
Dr. Gillespie's New Assistant (MGM, 1942)
Tennessee Johnson (MGM, 1942)
Thousands Cheer (MGM, 1943)
Dr. Gillespie's Criminal Case (MGM, 1943)
A Guy Named Joe (MGM, 1943)
Three Men in White (MGM, 1944)
Dragon Seed (Narrator: MGM, 1944)
Since You Went Away (UA, 1944)
Valley of Decision (MGM, 1945)
Between Two Women (MGM, 1945)
Three Wise Fools (MGM, 1946)
The Secret Heart (MGM, 1946)
It's a Wonderful Life (RKO, 1946)
Duel in the Sun (Selznick, 1946)
Dark Delusion (MGM, 1947)
Key Largo (WB, 1948)
Down to the Sea in Ships (20th-Fox, 1949)
Malaya (MGM, 1949)
Right Cross (MGM, 1950)
Bannerline (MGM, 1951)
Lone Star (MGM, 1952)
Main Street to Broadway (MGM, 1953)

*Unbilled Appearance

With Laraine Day in *Secret of Dr. Kildare* (1938)

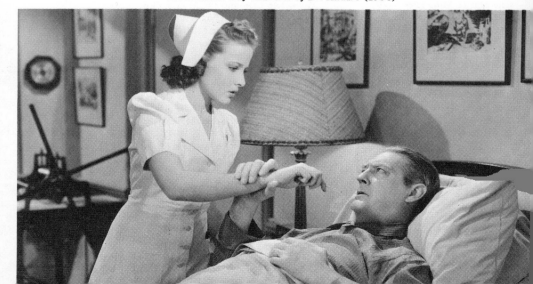

With Emma Dunn in *The Penalty* (1941)

With Clark Gable in *Lone Star* (1952)

Freddie Bartholomew

During the golden decades of Hollywood, MGM had the largest contingent of child actors in the industry, not only because they fit into Louis B. Mayer's idea of family entertainment, but also because the studio was willing to take the chance that a child actor may grow into further stardom as he or she gained adulthood. Thus all the MGM studio talent scouts were advised to keep an alert eye open for potential child players. Very often it was not a matter of them being discovered by talent scouts, but more a matter of mothers pushing their offspring into stardom despite their dubious credentials. During the 1930s, one of Metro's best known child stars was Freddie Bartholomew, a pretty, dimpled, curly-headed angelic English boy who found himself before the camera because his Aunt Cissie decided that he would become an actor. Bartholomew later admitted that he would never have known he could act, if indeed he could, had his Aunt not told him so. He made a name for himself in *David Copperfield, Anna Karenina, Little Lord Fauntleroy*, and *Captains Courageous*. At times he was quite effective, although some critics found Bartholomew's screen work shrill, stiff, and verging on the emetic. But any chance of maturing as an actor was thwarted by a combination of his pretty face, his English background, and the whole "Fauntleroy" business which so sissified his screen image that he was turned down as a possible costar with Mickey Rooney in *Boys Town* (1938). Studio executives considered him too much the gentleman to be believable as a tough orphan. However, such a role would have been the change of pace that Bartholomew needed to catapult him into a credible teenage performer.

He was born Frederick Llewellyn Bartholomew in a smoky factory section of London on March 28, 1924, where his father was a minor government employee who had had one leg shot off during World War I. At age three, Bartholomew's parents, who already had two daughters, farmed him out to his paternal grandparents and an aunt who lived in Westminister, some one hundred miles from London. Aunt Myllicent took charge of Freddie, tutored him in diction and the classics and determined that the youth should pursue an acting career. He began reciting poetry for local concerts and parties and did walkons in a few motion pictures that were being shot on location near his home. Aunt Cissie, as Bartholomew called her, arranged a

74

contractual agreement whereby any money he earned was divided between herself, his grandparents, and a trust fund for him. Bartholomew's parents were induced to sign the agreement.

When David O. Selznick, Mayer's son-in-law, was readying his production of *David Copperfield* (1935) for MGM, he turned down his father-in-law's persistent suggestion that he cast that "wonderful child" Jackie Cooper as Dickens' hero. Selznick sent director George Cukor to England in search for a child who would be more appropriate. Bartholomew was studying under Italia Conti in London at the time, who recommended the boy to Cukor. The director saw Bartholomew, approved him, and Aunt Cissie signed an agreement without telling her relatives. Together Cissie and Bartholomew set sail to visit "relatives" in the United States in 1934. His "relatives" turned out to be the Culver City studio where he was signed to a seven-year contract starting at $175 a week, with increases that would take him to $500 a week. *David Copperfield* had been the favorite book of Selznick's father, Lewis J. Selznick and, with Selznick's eye for detail, he turned out a screen classic that ran for two hours and thirteen minutes. Nicholas Schenck and Mayer urged Selznick to cut the picture but Selznick refused. Schenck said: "How long can it be?" Selznick replied: "How long is it good?!" The print remained intact and the resultant public screening made Bartholomew a box office favorite, with both the public and the critics generally agreeing that he brought life to Dickens' caricatured David.

Selznick used the youngster again in his MGM production of *Anna Karenina* (1935), and he was very good as Sergei, the son whom Greta Garbo relinquishes to his father, Basil Rathbone, when she falls in love with Fredric March. Bartholomew was now a property and MGM upped his salary to $1,000 a week. When Selznick left MGM to become an independent producer, his first project was a screen adaptation of another of his father's favorite books, *Little Lord Fauntleroy* (1936). He borrowed Bartholomew from Mayer for the starring role. *Fauntleroy* was the usual polished Selznick production but was not a hit like the prior Mary Pickford silent version. Essentially, Bartholomew was not the rambunctious type of child who appealed to the basic American audience, except perhaps to mothers, and a little performer named Mickey Rooney stole the picture in his role as a rugged young bootblack. *Little Lord Fauntleroy* typed Bartholomew as a dandy and made little boys across the country detest him when their mothers insisted they emulate him. He played another spoiled dandy opposite Mickey Rooney's tough New York street urchin in *The Devil Is a Sissy* (1936). In *Captains Courageous* (1937) he started out as the usual pampered brat, the son of business tycoon Melvyn Douglas, then fell overboard while sailing to Europe, was rescued by an illiterate Portuguese fisherman, played by Spencer Tracy, who teaches him the rudiments of manhood. It was his best role and the last good one he would have on the screen.

MGM continued to give Bartholomew such typed pretty-boy roles while offering more preferential treatment to the now virtuoso child actor,

Mickey Rooney, and refused to cast Bartholomew in *Boys' Town*. They loaned him out to other studios for several pictures, including Twentieth Century-Fox's *Kidnapped* (1938), but he came across more effete than youthfully adventurous in this adaptation of Stevenson's classic. The best of these loanouts was the pedestrian *Swiss Family Robinson* (1940). He finished his MGM tenure in *A Yank at Eton* (1942), in which the top-billed Rooney again walked away with the notices. Bartholomew was now eighteen, six-feet tall, had applied for American citizenship, and was nearly penniless. Ever since he had arrived in America, he had spent as much time in court as he had in making pictures. His major litigation involved a drawn-out battle between Aunt Cissie and his parents over his earnings, with his mother Lillian on one occasion coming to the United States and saying, "No one can love a child like his mother. I am anxious to see Freddie and take him in my arms again. I shall not be deprived of my own flesh. My husband and I believe we deserve a small share of his income, but we want him because we love him." A final settlement allocated Bartholomew's earnings as follows: ten percent to his parents, five percent to each of his two sisters, ten percent to Aunt Cissie, and the remainder set aside in a trust fund for the boy. There were further court actions to make Aunt Cissie his legal guardian and later she legally adopted him. By 1939, he had appeared in court on an average of twice a month since his arrival in America in 1934. During all these proceedings, Bartholomew sat in court, the perfect picture of dignified reserve.

On January 13, 1943, he was inducted into the U. S. Air Force. When he was discharged two years later, he formed a little theatre group on the West Coast and toured with it as an actor–director. In 1946, he married the publicity director of that group, Maely Daniele, and they had one daughter. They were divorced in 1953. He appeared in support of Billy Daniels in *Sepia Cinderella* (1947) and made his last picture in 1951, *St. Benny the Dip*, which was filmed on location in New York. Bartholomew took a fling in television in 1949, appearing in *Outward Bound*, and then hosted a video afternoon show. But a television performing career eluded him, and he next took a job as associate director of New York television station WPIX. In 1953 he married an employee of that station, Eileen Paul, and they now have two children, Kathleen and Frederick. In 1954 he joined the advertising firm of Benton and Bowles, where he is now a vice president and program manager. He and his family live on an estate in New Jersey.

Much of the $1 million he earned as an actor was dissipated in legal fees and taxes, but at age twenty-seven he was philosophical about his problems: "I'm not bitter. I'm healthy and young. I have a whole lifetime ahead of me." Aunt Cissie died in 1970. On one of the rare occasions when he talked publicly about his past film career, he remarked that his children associate him "in some vague way with stars like Clara Bow and others of a long-ago day," and added, "I have many happy memories of Hollywood, but I much prefer what I'm doing now." For him the pretty little Freddie is someone far in the past.

With Jean Cadell in *David Copperfield* (1935)

FREDDIE BARTHOLOMEW

Fascination (British, 1930)
Lily Christine (British, 1932)
David Copperfield (MGM, 1935)
Anna Karenina (MGM, 1935)
Professional Soldier (20th Fox, 1935)
Little Lord Fauntleroy (UA, 1936)
The Devil Is a Sissy (MGM, 1936)
Lloyds of London (20th-Fox, 1936)
Captains Courageous (MGM, 1937)
Kidnapped (20th-Fox, 1938)
Lord Jeff (MGM, 1938)

Listen, Darling (MGM, 1938)
Spirit of Culver (Universal, 1938)
Two Bright Boys (Universal, 1939)
Swiss Family Robinson (RKO, 1940)
Tom Brown's School Days (RKO, 1940)
Naval Academy (Columbia, 1941)
Cadets on Parade (Columbia, 1942)
A Yank at Eton (MGM, 1942)
The Town Went Wild (PRC, 1944)
Sepia Cinderella (Herald Pictures, 1947)
St. Benny the Dip (UA, 1951)

Wallace Beery

Wallace Beery was one of the screen's most lovable rogues as well as one of the top money-making stars for MGM in the 1930s and 1940s.* His film career had taken him from circus trainer to chorus boy to villain. He may have been nine parts personality and one part actor, yet on occasion he could, if he wanted, turn in a screen performance that earned sound critical praise, such as in *Viva Villa!* (1934). Coworkers frequently found Beery difficult to work with. He would not rehearse scenes and would often change his dialogue at whim. Besides, he upstaged all his coworkers and his manners at best were gauche. Although he was one of the biggest stars at MGM, where he worked full time from 1930 until his death in 1949, Louis B. Mayer disapproved so much of his working habits that he paid him $150,000 a year to work *only* twelve weeks a year. "Get Beery in and get him out" was his slogan.

The son of a policeman, Beery was born in Kansas City, Missouri on April 1, 1886. In addition, there were two brothers, William and Noah. The latter became an actor but always suffered under the shadow of his brother's acclaim. Beery's childhood name was Jumbo: He grew to be 6' 1" and weigh 250 pounds. He left school in the fourth grade and got a job working for the railroad. At sixteen he ran away from home and joined the Ringling Brothers circus as an elephant trainer at $3.50 a week. He stayed with the circus for two years but in 1904, he followed his older brother, Noah, to New York where Noah was pursuing a career as a chorus boy–actor. Beery worked in several shows, including *Babes in Toyland, The Prince of Pilsen, The Student Prince*, and *The Galloper*. He enjoyed a sizable role in *The Yankee Tourist*. Most of his work was in musicals as a chorus boy along with Noah: "But there was no lace on my cuffs." He further quipped: "Can you imagine two lummoxes like us prancing in a chorus?" He worked with the Woodward Stock Company and toured with several shows, taking whatever type of role he could wangle. His salary never reached more than $70 a week and 1912 found him flat broke. He joined Essanay Pictures in Chicago, where a tour of *The Balkan Princess* had ended and left him stranded.

At Essanay there were such stars as Francis X. Bushman, Beverly

*Beery was 7 at the boxoffice in 1932, 5 in 1933, 3 in 1934, 8 in 1935, and 8 in 1940.

Bayne, Charlie Chaplin, and a newcomer named Gloria Swanson. Beery said, "I liked the looks of this Swanson girl. She was a darned sweet kid, modest as could be and pretty." Definitely *early* Swanson! They married in 1916 and were divorced two years later in Hollywood, at which time Beery admitted, "She wanted the fancy life—to put on airs and all of that. Me, I like huntin' and fishin' and the simple life."

Beery worked at Essanay at $75 a week as a director and actor in short subjects. He played the Swedish housemaid, "Swedie," in a series of one-reeler comedies of which he made two a month. In 1915, G. M. "Broncho Billy" Anderson, co-owner of Essanay, hired Beery as the manager and director of his new studio in Niles, California. But that undertaking was a flop and a jobless Beery was forced to accept a bid to make some pictures in Japan. That venture never materialized, so he sought work as both director and actor at Universal. He then moved to Keystone, where he worked briefly with Swanson and more frequently with Ben Turpin. He attracted his first real attention as a screen actor by playing the Hun who attempts to rape Blanche Sweet in *The Unpardonable Sin* (1919). For the next five years he free-lanced in a string of pictures, playing mostly heavies, although occasionally he was the good guy, as with his Professor Challenger role in *The Lost World* (1925). That same year he signed a five-year pact with Paramount and gained a following with a series of comedies costarring Raymond Hatton: *Behind the Front* (1926), *We're in the Navy Now* (1926), and *Partners in Crime* (1928).

Paramount lost interest in the gruff-speaking Beery when talkies arrived, and he moved over to MGM in 1930 to play Butch, the murderous brute whose only redeeming quality was his childish naivete, in *The Big House*. This onscreen quality of childlike naivete was what made all of Beery's subsequent performances, whether in comedy or drama, acceptable to audiences who grew to love the big, loutish blunderer. Beery received an Academy Award nomination for playing Butch, but it was the uncanny pairing of Beery with Marie Dressler in *Min and Bill* (1930) which put him on top in Hollywood. He won the Oscar playing the washed-up prizefighter who is idolized by little Jackie Cooper in *The Champ* (1931). In two films about high society, he was the crude Prussian financier in *Grand Hotel* (1932) and the *nouveau riche* tycoon in *Dinner at Eight* (1933). In the latter, both he and Jean Harlow, who played his pampered, flirtatious wife, turned in charged performances. In one memorable moment Beery informs Harlow that he is going to Washington "because the President wants to consult me about the affairs of the nation." Harlow queries, "What's the matter with them?"

He and Dressler were reteamed in *Tugboat Annie* (1933) and the following year he played his favorite screen role, the Mexican bandit in *Viva Villa!* Dressler's death in 1934 left Beery without a topnotch screen *vis-à-vis*, but he continued to grind out formula pictures, in which he was the clumsy, overgrown bad boy who gets into all kinds of scrapes, more or less innocently. His typical reaction when caught in an onscreen predicament was his trademark reply, "Aw, shucks." By the 1940s, Metro relegated him to their lesser vehicles, knowing full well that the cheaply produced programmers starring Beery would clean up at the boxoffice, particularly with the rural trade. Marjorie Rambeau was a good foil for Beery in *Twenty Mule Team* (1940). Then MGM cast Marjorie Main opposite him in several pictures, including *Wyoming* (1940), *Barnacle Bill* (1941), *Jackass Mail* (1942), and *Bad Bascomb* (1946). Although the Beery–Main combination was a satisfying movie team, they never generated the same widespread approval as had Beery's pairing with Dressler. Main herself would find a more suitable screen partner in Percy Kilbride in Universal's *Ma and Pa Kettle* series. At one point when Berry was assigned to play in yet another picture with Main he said, "My idea of a good picture would be to team me with Billie Burke. I always go out with pretty ladies—in fact, beautiful girls. I can get inspired more if they'd give me a good pretty actress to work with." When filming *Big Jack* (1949) with Main he told one reporter: "If I have to make another picture with her, I'll have a heart attack." Beery, who had been suffering from a heart ailment, finally did just that, and died on April 15, 1949. *Big Jack* was released posthumously. The funeral services were held at Forest Lawn Memorial Park. Louis B. Mayer and MGM producer Edward J. Mannix were among the pallbearers.

Beery had married for a second time in 1924, to actress Rita Gilman, and in 1932, they adopted an eighteen-month-old girl, Carol Ann. He and Gilman divorced in 1939, with Beery stating "She fell in love with some gigolo, and so I'm letting her have him." Thereafter, Beery, who kept a table reserved at the Brown Derby in Hollywood three days a week, was seen dating a wide variety of Hollywood types, including ex-MGM star Mae Murray, and later socialite Cobina Wright, Sr. More often, Beery was seen escorting young girls, usually those not in the movie game. Shortly before his death, a small-time actress named Gloria Whitney, age thirty-two, involved Beery in a paternity suit. The sixtyish actor told the press, "I am flattered." A week before he died, she had rejected a $20,000 settlement, but later she and the Beery estate reached an undisclosed agreement.

On screen he was the perennial souse with the pot belly and outwardly seemed cavalier about his moviemaking. In his later years, he would frequently report to the sound stage for the day's shooting, crush his work hat in his hand, rub it in some dirt, smear a handful of dirt on his face, and announce to the director: "I'm ready. My makeup is on." But at heart he knew the vagaries of his craft: "This profession of mine has more ups and downs and swift reversals of fortune than any other profession on earth and I've always noticed that the people who go to the top and stay at the top are the people who were kicked around as kids. People who had too easy a time of it seldom last." Beery left an estate of nearly $2 million and he knew why he was able to earn that much money: "Like my dear old friend, Marie Dressler, my mug has been my fortune."

Beery acted the gruff gargantuan on the set and insisted on his rights as a star. When he took a daily nap in his trailer, he was not to be disturbed. He refused to give the usual rash of interviews, reasoning as follows: "Keep them guessing. As long as they spell the name right, that's okay by me. I'd rather go huntin' and fishin' and fly my big plane about the country than sit there balancin' a cup of tea, and have some sob sister simpering over me." On one occasion, when Beery had won a British film poll as the "No. 1 Favorite Star," a top film reporter was sent to Hollywood to present the actor with a trophy. The writer arrived at the Culver City lot just as Beery was beginning his daily snooze. Beery told a MGM publicity man: "Thank 'em again. Take 'em in the studio cafe and buy 'em some of that there good old Louis B. Mayer chicken soup, and put the check on me." Whenever Mayer presented Beery with his yearly contract, the star would tear up the lengthy typewritten document in front of the executive, and instead would jot down in longhand a simply worded agreement which always concluded with the term "quitting time is 5:30 P.M. punctually!"

During World War II Beery was a Commander in the U. S. Naval Reserve, a post in which he took enormous pride, almost as much as in his $30,000 cabin plane, or elaborate hunting shack, or his mansion on the corner of Sunset and Alpine in Beverly Hills. For a time he was quite proud to see his name listed in gold letters as a vice president of a Beverly Hills Bank. "But," Berry later recalled, "the bank went bust and I lost three and a half million dollars for that there prestige. After that I never let anyone sucker me, not even for a nickel."

WALLACE BEERY

The Slim Princess (Essanay, 1915)
Patria (Serial: International Film Service, 1917)
The Little American (Artcraft, 1917)
Johanna Enlists (Vitagraph, 1918)
The Love Burglar (Paramount, 1919)
The Unpardonable Sin (World, 1919)
Life Line (Paramount, 1919)
Soldier of Fortune (Realart, 1919)
Victory (Paramount, 1919)
Behind the Door (Paramount, 1919)
The Virgin of Stamboul (Universal, 1920)
The Mollycoddle (UA, 1920)
The Roundup (Paramount, 1920)
The Last of the Mohicans (Associated Producers, 1920)
The Rookies Return (Ince, 1920)
813 (Robertson-Cole, 1920)
The Four Horsemen of the Apocalypse (Metro, 1921)
Patsy (Truart, 1921)
A Tale of Two Worlds (Goldwyn, 1921)
The Golden Snare (FN, 1921)
The Last Trail (Fox, 1921)

The Rosary (Associated First National, 1922)
Wild Honey (Universal, 1922)
The Man from Hell's River (Western Pictures, 1922)
The Sagebrush Trail (Western Pictures, 1922)
Ridin' Wild (Universal, 1922)
I Am The Law (Affiliated, 1922)
Robin Hood (UA, 1922)
Trouble (Associated First National, 1922)
Hurricane's Gal (Associated First National, 1922)
Only a Shop Girl (C.B.C. Film, 1922)
The Flame of Life (Universal, 1923)
Stormswept (FBO, 1923)
Bavu (Universal, 1923)
Ashes of Vengeance (Associated First National, 1923)
Drifting (Universal, 1923)
The Eternal Struggle (Metro, 1923)
The Spanish Dancer (Paramount, 1923)
Three Ages (Metro, 1923)
Richard, the Lion Hearted (Allied Producers, 1923)
The Drums of Jeopardy (Truart, 1923)

With Paul Hurst, John Miljan, and Louis Natheaux in *The Secret Six* (1931)

With Joan Crawford in *Grand Hotel* (1932)

White Tiger (Universal, 1923)
Unseen Hands (Associated Exhibitors, 1924)
The Sea Hawk (Associated First National, 1924)
The Signal Tower (Universal, 1924)
The Red Lily (Metro-Goldwyn, 1924)
Another Man's Wife (Producers Distributors, 1924)
Dynamite Smith (Pathé, 1924)
Madonna of the Streets (FN, 1924)
So Big (FN, 1924)
Coming Through (Paramount, 1925)
The Devil's Cargo (Paramount, 1925)
Let Women Alone (Producers Distributing, 1925)
The Lost World (FN, 1925)
The Great Divide (Metro-Goldwyn, 1925)
Adventure (Paramount, 1925)
The Night Club (Paramount, 1925)
Rugged Water (Paramount, 1925)
In the Name of Love (Paramount, 1925)
The Pony Express (Paramount, 1925)
Behind the Front (Paramount, 1926)
The Wanderer (Paramount, 1926)
Volcano (Paramount, 1926)
We're in the Navy Now (Paramount, 1926)
Old Ironsides (Paramount, 1926)
Casey at the Bat (Paramount, 1927)
Fireman, Save My Child (Paramount, 1927)
Now We're in the Air (Paramount, 1927)
Wife Savers (Paramount, 1928)
Partners in Crime (Paramount, 1928)
The Big Killing (Paramount, 1928)
Beggars of Life (Paramount, 1928)
Chinatown Nights (Paramount, 1929)
River of Romance (Paramount, 1929)
Stairs of Sand (Paramount, 1929)
Big House (MGM, 1930)
Way for a Sailor (MGM, 1930)
Billy the Kid (MGM, 1930)
A Lady's Morals (MGM, 1930)
Min and Bill (MGM, 1930)
Secret Six (MGM, 1931)
Hell Divers (MGM, 1931)
The Champ (MGM, 1931)
Grand Hotel (MGM, 1932)
Flesh (MGM, 1932)
Dinner at Eight (MGM, 1933)
Tugboat Annie (MGM, 1933)
The Bowery (UA, 1933)
Viva, Villa! (MGM, 1934)
Treasure Island (MGM, 1934)
The Mighty Barnum (UA, 1934)
West Point of the Air (MGM, 1935)

With Stuart Erwin in *Viva, Villa!* (1934)

China Seas (MGM, 1935)
O'Shaughnessy's Boy (MGM, 1935)
Ah, Wilderness! (MGM, 1935)
A Message to Garcia (20th-Fox, 1936)
Old Hutch (MGM, 1936)
Good Old Soak (MGM, 1937)
Slave Ship (20th-Fox, 1937)
The Bad Man of Brimstone (MGM, 1938)
Port of Seven Seas (MGM, 1938)
Stablemates (MGM, 1938)
Stand Up and Fight (MGM, 1939)
Sergeant Madden (MGM, 1939)
Thunder Afloat (MGM, 1939)
The Man from Dakota (MGM, 1940)
20 Mule Team (MGM, 1940)
Wyoming (MGM, 1940)
The Bad Man (MGM, 1941)
Barnacle Bill (MGM, 1941)
The Bugle Sounds (MGM, 1941)
Jackass Mail (MGM, 1942)
Salute to the Marines (MGM, 1943)
Rationing (MGM, 1944)
Barbary Coast Gent (MGM, 1944)
This Man's Navy (MGM, 1945)
Bad Bascomb (MGM, 1946)
The Mighty McGurk (MGM, 1946)
Alias a Gentleman (MGM, 1948)
A Date with Judy (MGM, 1948)
Big Jack (MGM, 1949)

With Jackie Cooper and Nigel Bruce in *Treasure Island* (1934)

With Bob Watson and Marjorie Main in *Wyoming* (1940)

Marie Blake

One of the happier examples of nepotism in Hollywood of the 1930s was the case of Marie Blake. Few on the MGM lot, let alone the public, were aware that Marie, best known as Sally, the switchboard operator, in the *Dr. Kildare* series, was none other than the older sister of Metro's singing star, Jeanette MacDonald. In contrast to the glitter of Jeanette, Marie was a plain girl who, at best, resembled a pretty Alma Kruger. If Metro did a favor by hiring her, Marie returned it in kind by sprucing up the medical series with her comic abilities, a trait, by the way, which she and Jeanette shared. Marie was well experienced in the acting craft by the time she arrived at MGM in 1937, having had many years of versatile show business experience. She would remain with MGM five years after Jeanette had left the studio, and would later gain her greatest fan following as the kookie Granny on the bizarre *Addams Family* teleseries in the 1960s.

Marie was born Blossom MacDonald in 1896 in Philadelphia, the second of three daughters born to Daniel and Anne M. (Wright) MacDonald. Her father was a contractor and politician. Marie, Jeanette, and their older sister Elsie,* who would later run a dance school in Philadelphia, were all sent to local schools specializing in theatrical training. As youngsters, Marie and Jeanette played the vaudeville houses in Philadelphia on weekend nights, earning $10 an evening for their singing act. Marie was the first to move to New York to try for a professional show business career and landed a few musical comedy assignments. In 1926 she wed performer Clarence Rock, and together they toured the vaudeville circuit for three years. Marie first went to Hollywood in the early 1930s to visit Jeanette who had already become an established film personality. While there Marie had her first movie assignment in a bit part at Columbia Pictures. Returning to New York, Marie found vaudeville was dead, and wound up in a road tour of *Grand Hotel* with her husband. Other stage roles followed and, in 1936, she played a streetwalker in the Pulitzer Prizewinning play *Dead End*. A MGM talent agent saw her performance and she was signed to a studio contract, aided no doubt by being the sister of Metro operetta celebrity Jeanette.

For her movie career MGM gave her the new screen name of Marie Blake, and she "debuted" in Joan Crawford's *Mannequin* (1937), cast as a know-it-all domestic. It was the following year that she made her mark in the studio's *Dr. Kildare* series. Starting with *Young Dr. Kildare* (1938), she became a fixture of Blair General Hospital, playing as Sally, the loquacious and inquisitive switchboard operator.

*Elsie died in November 1971.

Like the other series regulars: hospital head Dr. Walter Carew (Walter Kingsford), floor nurse Parker (Nell Craig), ambulance driver Joe Wayman (Nat Pendleton), Marie supplied background flavor without distracting the audience from the major thrust of each episode which focused around crusty old Dr. Gillespie (Lionel Barrymore), Dr. Kildare (Lew Ayres), and for a time nurse Molly Lamont (Laraine Day). Marie remained with the series through the final entry, *Dark Delusion* (1947), which was long after Ayres had departed the series. Also, Van Johnson as Dr. Randall Stuart had come and gone, and James Craig coralled as Dr. Tommy Coalt in the last of the Kildare medical programmers. On rare occasions, Marie had an opportunity to do more than bits of comedy relief scenes in the series. In *Between Two Women* (1945) she becomes an emergency patient herself at Blair and undergoes a serious operation, from which she fully recovers and is able to step out on the town with the hospital staff.

As a general utility player, Marie was used on the home lot for minor assignments in Metro products, ranging from *The Women* (1939) to *Abbott and Costello in Hollywood* (1945). On loanout she often appeared in the lesser productions of other studios, such as the Andrew Sisters' *Give out Sisters* (1942) or Monogram's *Campus Rhythm* (1943). Occasionally she had minute assignments in grade A pictures such as the domestic servant in *The Major and the Minor* (1942), or as Bobby Blake's mother in Warner Brothers' *Pillow to Post* (1945).

With the conclusion of the Kildare series Marie left MGM and free-lanced in pictures for another five years. In *Mourning Becomes Electra* (1947) she was Walter Baldwin's cousin and part of the "Greek chorus." She played Mrs. Quigg, one of the boarders in June Haver's *Love Nest* (1951). Marie ended her theatrical film career with bits in Columbia's *The Brigand* (1952), whose cast included her old Blair General Hospital cohort, Walter Kingsford, at MGM in *Small Town Girl* (1953) and Fox's *From the Terrace* (1960).

Marie was a frequent television player in the 1950s, but it was in *The Addams Family* series (1964) that she gained her widest recognition, playing the white-wigged, rambunctious granny. She received much critical approval for her broad character interpretation in this long-running video show.

Today she lives in retirement at the Motion Picture Country Home in California. Her husband Clarence Rock, who was night manager at the Beverly Hilton Hotel for fifteen years, died in 1960. Regarding her famous sister, Marie says, "I had a wonderful relationship with my sister." (When Jeanette died in 1965, the star's husband, Gene Raymond, gave Marie much of Jeanette's jewelry.) One of Marie's fondest memories of her Hollywood years was in 1937: " . . . we gave a party called 'Come as You Think You'll Look in Fifty Years.' Jeannette and Gene came. MGM had made them up, and when they came to the door, I didn't recognize them. I thought they were just two old people who had stopped by.

"It was great fun. I went as the perennial ingenue with one foot in the grave. Attached to my ankle was a tombstone with an original poem which read:'As Blossom MacDonald she started life,

As Blossom Rock she became a wife.
For her movie career she was tagged Marie Blake.
The studio told her to jump in the lake.
P.S. She did!' "

MARIE BLAKE

Mannequin (MGM, 1937)
Love Finds Andy Hardy (MGM, 1938)
Man-Proof (MGM, 1938)
Woman Against Woman (MGM, 1938)
Love is a Headache (MGM, 1938)
Young Dr. Kildare (MGM, 1938)
Rich Man—Poor Girl (MGM, 1938)
Dramatic School (MGM, 1938)
Day-Time Wife (20th-Fox, 1939)
Calling Dr. Kildare (MGM, 1939)
I Take This Woman (MGM, 1939)*
The Women (MGM, 1939)
Blind Alibi (MGM, 1939)
Secret of Dr. Kildare (MGM, 1939)
Judge Hardy and Son (MGM, 1939)
They Knew What They Wanted (RKO, 1940)
They Drive By Night (WB, 1940)
Dr. Kildare's Strange Case (MGM, 1940)
A Child Is Born (WB, 1940)
Dr. Kildare's Crisis (MGM, 1940)
Jennie (20th-Fox, 1940)
Dr. Kildare Goes Home (MGM, 1940)
Sailor's Lady (20th-Fox, 1940)
The People vs. Dr. Kildare (MGM, 1941)
Caught in the Draft (Paramount, 1941)
Here Comes Happiness (WB, 1941)
Dr. Kildare's Wedding Day (MGM, 1941)
Small Town Deb (20th-Fox, 1941)
Dr. Kildare's Victory (MGM, 1941)
Blue, White and Perfect (20th-Fox, 1941)
Remember the Day (20th-Fox, 1941)
Give Out Sisters (Universal, 1942)
I Married a Witch (UA, 1942)
The Major and the Minor (Paramount, 1942)
Dr. Gillespie's New Assistant (MGM, 1942)
Good Morning Judge (Universal, 1943)
Dr. Gillespie's Criminal Case (MGM, 1943)
Campus Rhythm (Monogram, 1943)
Dubarry Was a Lady (MGM, 1943)
South of Dixie (Universal, 1944)
Sensations of 1945 (UA, 1944)

Gildersleeve's Ghost (RKO, 1944)
Between Two Women (MGM, 1945)
Abbott and Costello in Hollywood (MGM, 1945)
Pillow to Post (WB, 1945)
Christmas in Connecticut (WB, 1945)
Gentleman Joe Palooka (Monogram, 1946)
Dark Delusion (MGM, 1947)
Mourning Becomes Electra (RKO, 1947)
Christmas Eve (UA, 1947)
Don't Trust Your Husband (UA, 1948)
A Girl from Manhatten (UA, 1948)
The Snake Pit (20th-Fox, 1948)
Alimony (Eagle-Lion, 1949)
Angel in Disguise (Monogram, 1949)
Bad Boy (AA, 1949)
Paid in Full (Paramount, 1950)
A Woman of Distinction (Columbia, 1950)
Love Nest (20th-Fox, 1951)
FBI Girl (Lippert, 1951)
Gobs and Gals (Rep, 1952)
The Brigand (Columbia, 1952)
Small Town Girl (MGM, 1953)
Hilda Crane (20th-Fox, 1956)
She-Devil (20th-Fox, 1957)
From the Terrace (20th-Fox, 1960)
Human Jungle (AA, 1954)

In *Dr. Kildare's Crisis* (1940)

*Unreleased First Version

Ann Blyth

Even the most earnest of filmgoers is amazed to rediscover that the sweet lass who played Kathie in MGM's *The Student Prince* (1954) and Marsinah in MGM's *Kismet* (1955) is the same actress who, a decade before, emblazoned the screen as the vindictive bitch daughter of Joan Crawford in *Mildred Pierce* (1945). She received an Academy Award nomination for the latter picture and three years later was just as convincing playing Lillian Hellman's amoral Regina Hubbard in *Another Part of the Forest* (1948). But Ann was essentially a nice girl. She had a smile that was the envy of all toothpaste manufacturers, a lovely angular brunette beauty, and a pleasing singing voice. These latter attributes represented a personality which typed her in mostly good-girl roles. At MGM in the mid-1950s, she also starred in an occasional glossy musical.

She was born Ann Marie Blyth in Mt. Kisco, New York on August 16, 1928. Her parents separated when she was still a baby, and her Irish mother took her two daughters, Dorothy and Ann, to live on New York City's East 49th Street. While Dorothy went on to become a secretary, Ann set her sights on acting at a very early age. She made her professional debut as a radio actress on station WJZ. She was educated at St. Stephen's and St. Patrick's schools and then later at the New York Professional Children's School. During her grammar school years she was an established radio actress, and between the age of nine and twelve, she was a member of the San Carlo Opera Company. In 1941, she played the daughter of Paul Lukas in the Broadway production of Lillian Hellman's *Watch on the Rhine*, which ran for over eleven months. She then went on tour with the drama.

A talent scout for Universal Pictures spotted her in *Watch on the Rhine* and signed her to a seven-year contract with that studio. She debuted in *Chip off the Old Block* (1944) starring Donald O'Connor. A few more teenaged frivolities followed until Warner Brothers borrowed her to play Veda, the snobby daughter of struggling Joan Crawford in *Mildred Pierce*. As the girl who murders her mother's lover, Zachary Scott, in a fit of jealous rage, Ann acidly etched one of the most spoiled oncamera daughters the screen has seen. She was scheduled to be reteamed with Scott in Warner's *Her Kind of Man* (1946), but was involved in a tobogganing accident and was confined to a steel brace for over seven months. Janis Paige was given Ann's part in that film. After her recovery, Ann had one of the small women's roles in Universal's prison drama *Brute Force* (1947) and that same year was cast opposite Mickey Rooney in MGM's *Killer McCoy*, a boxing story. Ann's last gutsy part was playing the young Regina Hubbard in *Another Part of the Forest*, the drama which introduced the Hubbard dynasty which had already come full bloom in the earlier *The Little Foxes*. The character Ann portrayed was the younger version that Bette Davis had performed on the screen in 1941. As with *Mildred Pierce*, Ann received very respectable notices for her performance in *Another Part of the Forest* and might well have gone on to become a consistently strong, dramatic actress. However, she preferred to eschew any further demanding assignments such as this one, and, instead, slid into a comfortable rut of conventional screen ingenues.

MGM cast her as Mario Lanza's wife in *The Great Caruso* (1951) and then Universal had her and Claudette Colbert play nuns in *Thunder on the Hill* (1951). After that dim dramatic exercise, Ann's Universal contract expired and she signed with MGM. Even in the post–Golden Age of the early 1950s, Metro was still a sleek outfit. However, its roster of actors and technical talent were stagnating under the heavy-handed Dore Schary regime where uninspired, unentertaining "message" pictures were the order of the day. So it is no wonder that Ann languished at the Culver City studio, going from one colorless assignment to another. Under her MGM contract she first emoted in the nonmusical adventure yarn, *All the Brothers Were Valiant* (1953), playing opposite Robert Taylor and Stewart Granger. MGM cast her in two gaudily mounted but lethargic operetta remakes, *Rose Marie* (1954) and *The Student Prince*, the latter with Edmund Purdom. The next year she and Purdom adorned *The King's Thief* (1955), one of the more forgettable Cinemascope costume dramas churned out by the studio in the mid-1950s.

After a weak remake of *Kismet* with Howard Keel and an appearance in a small melodrama called *Slander* (1957), Ann left MGM. Her last two movie roles to date were in a duo of fatuous screen biographies. She played the wife of Donald O'Connor in what purported to be *The Buster Keaton Story* (1957) and then starred in *The Helen Morgan Story* (1957). Ann was rather effective as the mournful Helen, but the script was so dishonest that few people could recognize the real torch singer about whom the film had been made. Moreover, a short time before that picture went into general release, Polly Bergen had performed the same part in a much more exciting television version of that singer's troublesome life.

On June 27, 1953, Ann, a devout Catholic, married an Irish doctor, James McNulty, brother of radio–television singer–comedian Dennis Day. They have five children and Ann has lived in retirement these past years, save for periodic excursions into summer stock to star in such musicals as *The King and I* or *The Sound of Music*. Occasionally she can be seen in a television commercial.

Had Ann come to MGM in the early 1940s, there is little doubt but that she could have outdistanced such studio contractees as Kathryn Grayson or the later Jane Powell. Her singing was just as satisfying as anything those two performers could offer, and more importantly, Ann had a far greater dramatic range. However, she arrived at MGM when the musical film vogue was again on the wane, leaving her with little opportunity to become the screen's leading musical comedy lady. Then, too, by this time most of her high-powered career drive had been sublimated into a satisfying family life. Memories of her acting days are pleasant ones: "Hollywood has been very good to me. I was never hurt by the town or the profession. I had all the opportunities anyone could possibly ask for. I have only a deep love and respect for my profession and for all the joy it has brought me. I consider my husband, my children, my religion, my home, work when I want it, satisfaction enough to be truly fulfilled."

ANN BLYTH

With Brian Donlevy, Mickey Rooney, and Sam Levene in *Killer McCoy* (1947)

Chip off the Old Block (Universal, 1944)
The Merry Monahans (Universal, 1944)
Babes on Swing Street (Universal, 1944)
Bowery to Broadway (Universal, 1944)
Mildred Pierce (WB, 1945)
Swell Guy (Universal, 1946)
Brute Force (Universal, 1947)
Killer McCoy (MGM, 1947)
A Woman's Vengeance (Universal, 1947)
Another Part of the Forest (Universal, 1948)
Mr. Peabody and the Mermaid (Universal, 1948)
Red Canyon (Universal, 1949)
Once More, My Darling (Universal, 1949)
Top O' The Morning (Paramount, 1949)
Free for All (Universal, 1949)
Our Very Own (RKO, 1950)
The Great Caruso (MGM, 1951)
Katie Did It (Universal, 1951)
Thunder on the Hill (Universal, 1951)
I'll Never Forget You (20th-Fox, 1951)
The Golden Horde (Universal, 1951)
The World in His Arms (Universal, 1952)
One Minute to Zero (RKO, 1952)
Sally and Saint Anne (Universal, 1952)
All the Brothers Were Valiant (MGM, 1953)
Rose Marie (MGM, 1954)
The Student Prince (MGM, 1954)
The King's Thief (MGM, 1955)
Kismet (MGM, 1955)
Slander (MGM, 1957)
The Buster Keaton Story (Paramount, 1957)
The Helen Morgan Story (WB, 1957)

Lucille Bremer

One of the more spectacular cases of whatever-happened-to-what's-her-name is Lucille Bremer. In the mid-1940s she was groomed by MGM to replace the self-retired Eleanor Powell, and for a brief time seemed to be the loveliest dance discovery on the Hollywood scene. This red-haired Bette Davis look-alike was not only graceful in her onscreen terpsichore—particularly with slick partner Fred Astaire—but she radiated a pleasing patrician quality unspoiled by her dramatic inexpertise. However, she had both the misfortune of costarring in a musical flop, *Yolanda and the Thief* (1945), and becoming an unlucky pawn in studio politics. Three years after joining MGM, she was off the lot, a year hence she had retired from the screen, and by the 1960s she was just a vague memory of things past.

Lucille Bremer was born in Amsterdam, New York in 1923, but grew up in Philadelphia. At the age of seven she was taking dance lessons and five years later she was accepted as a ballet dancer in the Philadelphia Opera Company. In 1939 she became a Rockette at Radio City Music Hall and toured with that group in Europe. Later she had a chorus part in the Broadway cast of *Panama Hattie* (1940) and an ingenue role in Gertrude Lawrence's *Lady in the Dark* (1941). It was MGM producer Arthur Freed who later spotted Lucille in the dance line of the Versailles Restaurant floor show—she was the fastest kicker in the chorus. He had her screen-tested in a scene from *Dark Victory*, which seemed to prove Lucille's thesis: " . . . dancing was a lucky choice. It is an excellent showcase for a career. A small bit as a dancer seems to stand out above a straight stage role."

When Freed showed Lucille's test to Louis B. Mayer, the MGM mogul allegedly enthused: "Who is this girl? Don't let her do little things, Arthur. She's going to be big, very big." Signed to a MGM contract, Lucille was trained by studio drama coach Lillian Burns, and then assigned to Arthur Freed's *Meet Me in St. Louis* (1944). She was the eldest Smith daughter, Rose, a bit of a social snob whose long-distance romance causes the family much concern. The Technicolor musical clearly focused on the younger Smith girls, Judy Garland and Margaret O'Brien, leaving Lucille to pout prettily about being "left on the (matrimonial) shelf."

Having made a successful screen debut, Lucille was selected to be Fred

91

Astaire's dance partner for *Ziegfeld Follies*, but two later-made pictures were released before that extravaganza. *Yolanda and the Thief* (1945), directed by Freed's favorite director Vincente Minnelli, was considered daringly adult for its day, relying on Freudian fantasy and interpretive ballet to carry much of the story and provide the bulk of entertainment. Lucille was the naive South American heiress fresh from the convent who is almost conned out of her fortune by dapper Fred Astaire, whom she mistakes for her guardian angel. Instead, of course, they fall in love. In addition, there were Irene Shariff costumes, decors by Cedric Gibbons, and the antics of Mildred Natwick as the addled aunt, all filmed in glowing color. The picture's highlights, however, were two long ballet numbers, "Will You Dance With Me?" and the contrasting "Coffee Time" finale. Unfortunately audiences found the film tedious. By Hollywood standards, the failure was laid at Lucille's and Astaire's feet. He could survive the misfire; she could not.

In *Till the Clouds Roll By* (1946) she had a sequence as a dancer egged on by bandleader Van Johnson in the "I Won't Dance" number. She reached her cinema peak with the long-delayed release of *Ziegfeld Follies,* in which she shared two dance numbers with Astaire. In the film ballet number "This Heart of Mine" she gladly allows gentleman thief Astaire to steal her jewelry. In "Limehouse Blues," also choreographed by Robert Alton, Lucille and Astaire are two Orientals whose paths cross in Chinatown, only to have him killed in a robbery. "Limehouse Blues" is regarded as one of the best dance numbers in a

With Fred Astaire in *Yolanda and the Thief* (1945)

1940s film. Had *Ziegfeld Follies* been released before *Yolanda and the Thief*, Lucille's movie career might have lasted a lot longer.

By the end of 1946 MGM and Arthur Freed had lost interest in Lucille. Her final studio picture was the programmer *Dark Delusion* (1947), part of the Dr. Kildare series. As the wealthy psychopath suffering from a blood clot she gave a well-modulated performance, ironically disproving the "but she can't act" theory being touted as the cause of her MGM downfall.

Her remaining three pictures were would-be dramas done on loan to a low-budget facility, Eagle–Lion. In *Adventures of Casanova* (1948), set in eighteenth-century Sicily, she played the beauteous lady who draws Arturo de Cordoba's admiration. This silly swashbuckler was followed by the overly ambitious *Ruthless* (1948), in which she functioned as the bored wife of Sydney Greenstreet. She was involved with reporter Richard Carlson in *Behind Locked Doors* (1948), he having gotten himself committed to a mental institution to track down a runaway judge.

In July 1948 Lucille wed Abalardo Rodriguez, son of a former president of Mexico. She had met him while on location for the *Casanova* picture. She officially retired, although there were occasional announcements of a comeback, as when Lindsley Parsons wanted her to star in *A Moment of Fear* to be made for Allied Artists and to be filmed at La Paz, Mexico, where she was then living.

Currently, Lucille resides in La Jolla, California, and has five daughters. She owns a children's dress shop. For middleaged Lucille, Hollywood is just part of a long-ago past.

LUCILLE BREMER

Meet Me in St. Louis (MGM, 1944)
Yolanda and the Thief (MGM, 1945)
Till the Clouds Roll By (MGM, 1946)
Ziegfeld Follies (MGM, 1946)

Dark Delusion (MGM, 1947)
Adventures of Casanova (Eagle-Lion, 1948)
Ruthless (Eagle–Lion, 1948)
Behind Locked Doors (Eagle–Lion 1948)

Virginia Bruce

Outside of Nancy Carroll, who was a star, few nonlegendary screen actresses of the 1930s are as staunchly championed today by film enthusiasts as Virginia Bruce. There were several pictures which found her on the brink of establishing a marquee name—*The Mighty Barnum* (1934), *Society Doctor* (1935)—but each time she veered back into bland leading lady roles which fitfully capitalized on her cool blonde beauty. As was later demonstrated in *Wife, Doctor and Nurse* (1937) and *Careful, Soft Shoulders* (1942), her essential screen image was that of self-sufficient sophistication. She could deliver a song more than adequately, even if it were dubbed, and she had a sharp, tart way of handling dialogue, Nevertheless, MGM in the mid-1930s never wholeheartedly exploited these marketable qualities. Instead they wasted her prime years as a nondescript ingenue and she seemingly went along for the ride.

She was born Helen Virginia Briggs on September 29, 1910 in Minneapolis, Minnesota but grew up in Fargo, North Dakota. There was a younger brother, Stanley. While still in her late teens, Virginia gravitated to Los Angeles, planning to enter the University of California. But she happened to take a tour of the Fox studios and was spotted by director William Beaudine. He signed her to a $25 weekly contract, coaching her for a screen test as George O'Brien's female lead in a Fox western. She did not get the role but had a bit in Madge Bellamy's *Fugitives* (1929), directed by Beaudine, and in Helen Twelvetree's *Blue Skies* (1929). She next did a singing screen test at Paramount where she was hired at $75 weekly, and within the next two years appeared in thirteen features on the lot as well as being a Goldwyn girl in Eddie Cantor's *Whoopie* (1930) and having a bit in *Raffles* (1930). She often was little more than a glorified chorus girl at Paramount, as in *The Love Parade* (1929) where she was one of the Queen's Maids. Even in minor ingenue parts, such as in *Slightly Scarlet* (1930) with Clive Brook or in *Safety In Numbers* (1930) with Charles "Buddy" Rogers, she was no better or worse in vapid indistinctiveness than such other budding studio players as Jean Arthur or Carole Lombard.

Hoping to break out of her professional rut, she obtained through designer friend Jack Harkrider some small roles in Florenz Ziegfeld's Broadway production of *Smiles* (1930), starring Fred and Adele Astaire, and then was in the longer-lasting *America's Sweetheart* (1931) with Ann Sothern and Jack Whiting. She was a showgirl in this musical and understudied Jean Aubert. With a Ziegfeld girl tag, Virginia returned to Hollywood and maneuvered a screen test at MGM opposite Robert Young. The studio registered some interest, but she stated she had been signed for a New York play *East Wind* and was returning to Manhattan. On the way East, she changed her mind and, returning to Hollywood, became a MGM contractee. Her first appearance was a tiny role in *Hell Divers* (1931) with Wallace Beery and Clark Gable.

She had eight 1932 releases, but did better on loanout than at Metro, particularly in Warner's *Winner Take All* in which she was James Cagney's society doll. When MGM cast her opposite fading silent screen star John Gilbert in *Downstairs* (1932), a story he wrote himself, she fell in love with him and on August 1932, she became his fourth wife. The following year they had a daughter Susan, but were divorced in 1934. When he died in 1936, however, he left the bulk of his $250,000 estate to her and the child.

Having lost her screen momentum, Virginia was sent out to Monogram for *Jane Eyre* (1934) and then loaned to United Artists along with Wallace Beery for *The Mighty Barnum* (1934). Her playing of Jenny Lind caused a mild stir and established her as a "singing" lead. That her songs were dubbed was a fact left discreetly unstated. MGM gave her better parts, such as the sports promoter's daughter in *Times Square Lady* (1935). Most of the attention in this film, however went to newcomer Robert Taylor. She was featured in *Escapade* (1935), but again that film was more noteworthy as Luise Rainer's screen debut. Fox borrowed her to play the singing ingenue in *Metropolitan* (1935), which marked opera star Lawrence Tibbett's unsensational screen return. She was a bit stiff in the featured role of Audrey Lane, the show star who takes to drink and temperament in *The Great Ziegfeld* (1936). She introduced "I've Got You Under My Skin" in *Born to Dance* (1936) but the picture belonged to another new star, Eleanor Powell. At the time Virginia was causing more of a stir in fan magazines by being one of the last of the cinema's beauties to cut her long tresses for the new styles, and for such philosophizing as "Happiness is something you have to find within yourself ... "

She had the lead in Universal's minor *When Love Is Young* (1937) in which she sang two songs and played opposite Kent Taylor. *Bad Man of Brimstone* (1938) may have been a minor Wallace Beery–MGM folksy western, but the filming of it was noteworthy in that Virginia and its director J. Walter Ruben fell in love and were married in December 1937. (They had a son Christopher in 1941, and Ruben died of a blood clot in 1942). In *Let Freedom Ring* (1939) she was billed opposite Nelson Eddy and sang the "Star Spangled Banner," and in *Society Lawyer* (1939) with Walter Pidgeon she introduced "I'm In Love with the Honorable So And So." *Stronger Than Desire* (1939) also with Pidgeon concluded her MGM contract. She was now at the ripe age of thirty.

The 1940s found Virginia stuck in generally minor league screen products, cast in them to make use of her seminame and still unfaded looks. She supported George Brent in *The Man Who Talked Too Much* (1940) and played second fiddle to special effects and a dying John Barrymore in *The Invisible Woman* (1941). In *Careful, Soft Shoulders*, no more than a Twentieth Century-Fox programmer, she rose above the script and insipid leading man James Ellison with a wise, tongue-in-cheek performance, proving her much more versatile than her younger look-alike, Paramount contractee Hillary Brooke. She was George Sanders' mysterious *vis-à-vis* in *Action in Arabia* (1944), filmed on RKO's back lot and was a bolstering if wasted presence in Republic's *Brazil* (1944) with Tito Guizar.

In 1946, she wed Turkish writer–would-be producer Ali Ipar, who had just been drafted in the U. S. Army. He was twenty-three years old. They had a very checkered marital relationship. He returned to Turkey in 1947 to visit his enormously wealthy father and was refused reentry into the U. S. for over a year. In 1951, when he was conscripted into the Turkish army, Virginia divorced him because his country's law forbade a commission to any man wed to a foreigner. They remarried in 1952 and the following year she appeared in a film he produced, directed, and wrote. *Istanbul* (1953), shot in Turkey, cast Virginia as a Red Crescent nurse who helps save the populace during a plague. Later she and her husband returned to Hollywood to live and were in the news in 1960 when he reappeared in Turkey and was arrested during one of that country's government upheavals. He was jailed for over a year and a half, and during that time his American visa expired.

Virginia was occasionally seen on television in the 1950s, most notably in a *Lux Video Theatre* version of *Mildred Pierce* with Zachary Scott. In 1960 she made her final film to date, playing Kim Novak's mother in *Strangers When We Meet*. She seemed bewildered in her brief assignment.

Her last known residence was in Pacific Palisades, California, but by 1968 she had dropped completely out of sight, a victim of recurring illnesses.

VIRGINIA BRUCE

Fugitives (Fox, 1929)
Blue Skies (Fox, 1929)
Illusion (Paramount, 1929)
Woman Trap (Paramount, 1929)
Why Bring That Up? (Paramount, 1929)
The Love Parade (Paramount, 1929)
Lilies of the Field (Paramount, 1930)
Only the Brave (Paramount, 1930)
Slightly Scarlet (Paramount, 1930)
Paramount on Parade (Paramount, 1930)
Follow Thru (Paramount, 1930)
Raffles (UA, 1930)
Whoopee! (UA, 1930)
Young Eagles (Paramount, 1930)
Safety in Numbers (Paramount, 1930)

Social Lion (Paramount, 1930)
Hell Divers (MGM, 1931)
Are You Listening? (MGM, 1932)
The Wet Parade (MGM, 1932)
The Miracle Man (Paramount, 1932)
Sky Bride (Paramount, 1932)
Winner Take All (WB, 1932)
Downstairs (MGM, 1932)
Kongo (MGM, 1932)
A Scarlet Week-End (MGM, 1932)
Jane Eyre (Monogram, 1934)
The Mighty Barnum (UA, 1934)
Dangerous Corner (RKO, 1934)
Times Square Lady (MGM, 1935)
Society Doctor (MGM, 1935)

Shadow of Doubt (MGM, 1935)
Let 'Em Have It (UA, 1935)
Escapade (MGM, 1935)
Here Comes the Band (MGM, 1935)
The Murder Man (MGM, 1935)
Metropolitan (Fox, 1935)
The Garden Murder Case (MGM, 1936)
The Great Ziegfeld (MGM, 1936)
Born to Dance (MGM, 1936)
Woman of Glamour (Columbia, 1937)
When Love Is Young (Universal, 1937)
Between Two Women (MGM, 1937)
Wife, Doctor and Nurse (20th-Fox, 1937)
The First Hundred Years (MGM, 1938)
Arsene Lupin Returns (MGM, 1938)
Bad Man of Brimstone (MGM, 1938)
Yellow Jack (MGM, 1938)
Woman Against Woman (MGM, 1938)
There's That Woman Again (Columbia, 1938)
There Goes My Heart (UA, 1938)
Let Freedom Ring! (MGM, 1939)
Society Lawyer (MGM, 1939)
Stronger Than Desire (MGM, 1939)
Flight Angels (WB, 1940)
The Man Who Talked Too Much (WB, 1940)
Hired Wife (Universal, 1940)
The Invisible Woman (Universal, 1941)
Adventure in Washington (Columbia, 1941)
Pardon My Sarong (Universal, 1942)
Butch Minds the Baby (Universal, 1942)
Careful, Soft Shoulders (20th-Fox, 1942)
Brazil (Republic, 1944)
Action in Arabia (RKO, 1944)
Love, Honor and Goodbye (Republic, 1945)
The Night Has a Thousand Eyes (Paramount, 1948)
State Dept.—File 649 (Film Classics, 1949)
Istanbul (Turkish, 1953)
Two Grooms for a Bride (20th-Fox, 1957)
Strangers When We Meet (Columbia, 1960)

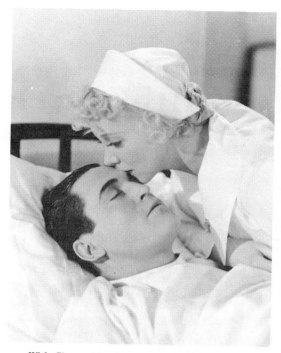

With Chester Morris in *Society Doctor* (1935)

Billie Burke

If a scenario called for an empty-headed society matron, everyone's first thought was "Get Billie Burke." Throughout the 1930s and 1940s, and especially at MGM from 1937–1941, she functioned as the aristocratic flibbertigibbet who invariably would end a piece of dialogue with her voice trailing off into a high squeak and her hands waving in the air, all the while fluttering her famed eyelashes. Her out-of-touch-with-reality gambit was not all one-keyed. In *Dinner at Eight* (1933) she exemplified the selfish, thoughtless society lady who *essentially* was incapable of caring one fig about anyone else's problems. Obviously, for her, such problems simply could not compare to the logistics of hostessing a dinner party. More tempered was her role in *Topper* (1937), also at MGM, which found her exasperating the life out of spouse Roland Young but still possessed of essential niceness. By the time of *Father of the Bride* (1950), she was essaying the affluent mother-in-law whose failure to grasp her own conventional and purposeless existence gave the viewer a twinge of sympathy for her plight. In short, with Metro geared to turning out gilt-edged society dramas and comedies, a Billie Burke was an invaluable piece of equipment.

She was born Ethelbert Burke August 7, 1885 in Washington, D. C., but soon adopted the nickname of her father William Burke, a clown with Barnum and Bailey Circus. Billie attended school in England and France, and made her stage debut at the age of fourteen in *The School Girl*. She had wanted to become a writer, but her dominating mother pushed her into acting. In 1907 producer Charles Frohman "imported" her to play opposite John Drew in *My Wife*, which established her Broadway reputation. This success was followed up by such ventures as *Mrs. Dot* (1909), *The Runaway* (1911), *The Amazons* (1913), and *Jerry* (1914). Of these efforts she once said: "I generally did light, gay things. I often had cute plays but never a fine one."

When she was offered $300,000 to star in the movie *Peggy* (1916) she could not resist the deal. Meanwhile, she had married flamboyant stage impresario Florenz Ziegfeld in 1914 and a daughter Patricia was born in 1916. Because Paramount then had a New York-based studio, Billie signed a five-year contract with them, making an assortment of popular but forgettable photoplays, which at least earned her number one rank in a motion picture popularity contest of 1922. But she preferred the stage and keeping a watchful eye on her errant husband.

By 1930 Ziegfeld was on the financial skids and Billie ventured back into the now-talking cinema, first in a few Pathé shorts and in 1932 director George Cukor asked her to essay the chic but irresponsible wife of John Barrymore in RKO's *A Bill of Divorcement*. That year Ziegfeld died, and she became a full-time film player with only occasional forays back to the stage. It was the all-star *Dinner at Eight* which established her mature screen image. She continued free-lancing as the flighty society matron until late 1936 when MGM offered her a featured player contract, reportedly because of her cooperation on their filming of *The Great Ziegfeld* (1936), in which Myrna Loy attempted to "be" Miss Burke to William Powell's Ziegfeld.

Once under MGM's aegis, Billie's career thrived on the home lot. For Hal Roach at Metro she was the skittish wife of Cosmo Topper (Roland Young) in *Topper* and he proved to be her most effective screen partner. Two years later came her role as Glinda, the Good Witch in the Technicolor fantasy *The Wizard of Oz* ("the role is as close as I have come in motion pictures to the kind of parts I did in the theatre"). *Wild Man of Borneo* (1941) concluded her MGM contract, During the remainder of the decade her screen highlights included *Topper Returns* (1941) and the addled mother of the household in *The Man Who Came to Dinner* (1941).

Success eluded her on Broadway in the mid-1940s and her biography *With a Feather on My Nose* (1949) was only moderately well received. MGM offered her a fine stereotyped Billie Burke role as Don Taylor's mother in *Father of the Bride* and its followup *Father's Little Dividend* (1951). There were stock tours in the mid-1950s, including *The Solid Gold Cadillac*, with Billie using painful skin clips to retain her smooth china doll face look. She had a solid cameo bit as a wise society matron in *The Young Philadelphians* (1959), published another book *With Powder on My Nose* (1959), then two more weak screen cameos, a bit on television's *77 Sunset Strip*, and then retirement. ("Television directors had no patience with little old ladies. It just wasn't fun anymore, and that's why I quit after 60 years in show business.")

For much of the last decade of her life, Billie resided at a home for the aged in the San Fernando Valley, forgotten by the many decades of filmgoers who had been amused by her flighty charm. When she was interviewed in 1965 she told the *National Enquirer* reporter: "I can't bear to watch most of my old movies. They depress me. Whenever I see one I turn it off. Mystery shows are my cup of tea these days." She remained beautifully vain until the end, refusing to allow even her relatives to refer to her matriarchal status of great-grandmother. She died May 14, 1970 at the age of eighty-four.

BILLIE BURKE

Peggy (Triangle, 1915)
Gloria's Romance (Serial: George Kleine, 1916)
The Mysterious Miss Terry (Paramount, 1917)
Arms and the Girl (Paramount, 1917)
The Land of Promise (Paramount, 1917)
Eve's Daughter (Paramount, 1918)
In Pursuit of Polly (Paramount, 1918)
Let's Get a Divorce (Paramount, 1918)
The Make-Believe Wife (Paramount, 1918)
Good Gracious, Annabelle! (Paramount, 1919)
The Misleading Widow (Paramount, 1919)
Sadie Love (Paramount, 1919)
Wanted, a Husband (Paramount, 1919)
Away Goes Prudence (Paramount, 1920)
The Frisky Mrs. Johnson (Paramount, 1921)
The Education of Elizabeth (Paramount, 1921)
Glorifying the American Girl (Paramount, 1929)*
A Bill of Divorcement (RKO, 1932)
Christopher Strong (RKO, 1933)
Dinner at Eight (MGM, 1933)
Only Yesterday (Universal, 1933)
Finishing School (RKO, 1934)

Where Sinners Meet (RKO, 1934)
We're Rich Again (RKO, 1934)
Forsaking All Others (MGM, 1934)
Society Doctor (MGM, 1935)
After Office Hours (MGM, 1935)
Doubting Thomas (Fox, 1935)
Becky Sharp (RKO, 1935)
She Couldn't Take It (Columbia, 1935)
Splendor (UA, 1935)
A Feather in Her Hat (Columbia, 1935)
Piccadilly Jim (MGM, 1936)
My American Wife (Paramount, 1936)
Craig's Wife (Columbia, 1936)
Parnell (MGM, 1937)
Topper (MGM, 1937)
The Bride Wore Red (MGM, 1937)
Navy Blue and Gold (MGM, 1937)
Everybody Sing (MGM, 1938)
Merrily We Live (MGM, 1938)
The Young in Heart (UA, 1938)
Topper Takes a Trip (UA, 1939)
Zenobia (UA, 1939)
Bridal Suite (MGM, 1939)
The Wizard of Oz (MGM, 1939)

*Unbilled Appearance

With Roland Young in *Topper* (1937)

With Judy Garland in *The Wizard of Oz* (1939)

Spring Byington

Spring Byington was once asked the secret of her success as a bubbling character star: "It's very simple. Lady Macbeth and I aren't friends." With a gay tilt of her head, a bit of her chic femininity, and some of her unpredictable comedy sense, she could turn the most pedestrian situation comedy scenes into a moment of joy. Unlike Billie Burke's flighty gallery of aunts, moms, grandmothers, Spring's characterizations always possessed that tomboy quality which made her asocial moments impish and beguiling. Although not officially a full-time member of the MGM stock company, she appeared in that studio's product so often during the years that she merits consideration.

Spring was born October 17, 1893 at Colorado Springs, Colorado. Her father was an educator and her mother a physician. At the age of fourteen she joined the Elitch Gardens Theatre in Denver at a weekly salary of $35. She later toured the United States and South America in shows before making her Broadway debut in *A Beggar on Horseback* (1924), followed by nineteen other shows, including *Once in a Lifetime* (1930) as the Hollywood columnist, and *When Ladies Meet* (1932). Meanwhile, she married Roy Carey Chandler. They had two daughters but were later divorced.

She made an impressive film debut as the brood mother in RKO's *Little Women* (1933) and then began a succession of free-lance assignments which usually cast her as a pixilated but conservative mother. Her first MGM film was as Franchot Tone's proper mater in *Mutiny on the Bounty* (1935). The next year she was Jed Prouty's homey small town wife in *Every Saturday Night* (1936) which launched Twentieth Century-Fox's popular programmer series, the Jones Family, which lasted through *On Their Own* (1940). Because she had done Mrs. Jones, Metro cast her as Lionel Barrymore's wife and Mickey Rooney's mother in *A Family Affair* (1937), the first of the Andy Hardy pictures. But the studio later decided that Fay Holden and Lewis Stone were more appropriate as the parents of a sensible, wholesome small town household. Her most impressive acting of the decade was as the eccentric mother who blithely went on writing her play amidst the confusion of *You Can't Take It with You* (1938), a role which won her an Oscar nomination.

Throughout the 1940s, Spring was frequently called upon to do "her thing" in several MGM entries, such as the high-toned *When Ladies Meet*

(1941) which had her re-creating her Broadway role as the heroine's fluttery confidant. She was the down-to-earth mom in *My Brother Talks to Horses* (1946). She was Judy Garland's coworker at the music shop in *In the Good Old Summertime* (1949), a general's wife in Mario Lanza's *Because You're Mine* (1952), and Doris Day's devilish mom in *Please Don't Eat the Daisies* (1960), her last film.

It was Universal's *Louisa* (1950), in which she was wooed by suitors Charles Coburn and Edmund Gwenn, that set the tone for her Lily Ruskin on *December Bride*, both on radio and then for five years on CBS-TV from 1954 onward. Along with coplayer Verna Felton, she capered about from episode to episode, proving to warm public response that mature women can still be schoolgirls at heart and in actions. Later, she was the cook on the *Laramie* teleseries and guested on *Batman* and other shows. Her reason for so much activity: "TV keeps me young because it keeps me busy, keeps my mind alert, my senses sharp and my interest up."

She died September 7, 1971, at the age of seventy-eight.

With Donna Corcoran and Harry Hayden in *Angels in the Outfield* (1951)

Little Women (RKO, 1933)
Werewolf of London (Universal, 1935)
Orchids to You (Fox, 1935)
Love Me Forever (Columbia, 1935)
Mutiny on the Bounty (MGM, 1935)
Way Down East (Fox, 1935)
Broadway Hostess (WB, 1935)
Ah! Wilderness (MGM, 1935)
The Great Impersonation (Universal, 1935)
The Voice of Bugle Ann (MGM, 1936)
Every Saturday Night (20th-Fox, 1936)
Palm Springs (Paramount, 1936)
Educating Father (20th-Fox, 1936)
Stage Struck (WB, 1936)
Back to Nature (20th-Fox, 1936)
Dodsworth (UA, 1936)
The Girl on the Front Page (Universal, 1936)
Charge of the Light Brigade (WB, 1936)
Theodora Goes Wild (Columbia, 1936)
Clarence (Paramount, 1937)
Green Light (WB, 1937)
Off to the Races (20th-Fox, 1937)
Penrod and Sam (WB, 1937)
Big Business (20th-Fox, 1937)
A Family Affair (MGM, 1937)
The Road Back (Universal, 1937)
Hotel Haywire (Paramount, 1937)
It's Love I'm After (WB, 1937)
Hot Water (20th-Fox, 1937)
Borrowing Trouble (20th-Fox, 1937)
Love on a Budget (20th-Fox, 1938)
The Adventures of Tom Sawyer (UA, 1938)
The Buccaneer (Paramount, 1938)
Jezebel (WB, 1938)
Penrod and His Twin Brother (WB, 1938)
A Trip to Paris (20th-Fox, 1938)
Safety in Numbers (20th-Fox, 1938)
You Can't Take It With You (Columbia, 1938)
The Jones Family in Hollywood (20th-Fox, 1939)
The Story of Alexander Graham Bell (20th-Fox, 1939)
Down on the Farm (20th-Fox, 1939)
Everybody's Baby (20th-Fox, 1939)
Chicken Wagon Family (20th-Fox, 1939)
Quick Millions (20th-Fox, 1939)
Too Busy to Work (20th-Fox, 1939)
Young as You Feel (20th-Fox, 1940)
The Blue Bird (20th-Fox, 1940)
The Ghost Comes Home (MGM, 1940)

A Child Is Born (WB, 1940)
My Love Came Back (WB, 1940)
On Their Own (20th-Fox, 1940)
Lucky Partners (RKO, 1940)
Laddie (RKO, 1940)
Arkansas Judge (Republic, 1941)
The Devil and Miss Jones (RKO, 1941)
Meet John Doe (WB, 1941)
Ellery Queen and the Perfect Crime (Columbia, 1941)
When Ladies Meet (MGM, 1941)
The Vanishing Virginian (MGM, 1941)
Roxie Hart (20th-Fox, 1942)
Rings on Her Fingers (20th-Fox, 1942)
The Affairs of Martha (MGM, 1942)
The War Against Mrs. Hadley (MGM, 1942)
Presenting Lily Mars (MGM, 1943)
Heaven Can Wait (20th-Fox, 1943)
The Heavenly Body (MGM, 1943)
I'll Be Seeing You (UA, 1944)
Salty O'Rourke (Paramount, 1945)
The Enchanted Cottage (RKO, 1945)
Thrill of a Romance (MGM, 1945)
Captain Eddie (20th-Fox, 1945)
A Letter for Evie (MGM, 1945)
Dragonwyck (20th-Fox, 1946)
Faithful in My Fashion (MGM, 1946)
My Brother Talks to Horses (MGM, 1946)
Cynthia (MGM, 1947)
Living in a Big Way (MGM, 1947)
Singapore (Universal, 1947)
It Had to Be You (Columbia, 1947)
B.F.'S Daughter (MGM, 1948)
In the Good Old Summertime (MGM, 1949)
The Big Wheel (UA, 1949)
Please Believe Me (MGM, 1950)
Devil's Doorway (MGM, 1950)
The Skipper Surprised His Wife (MGM, 1950)
Louisa (Universal, 1950)
Walk Softly, Stranger (RKO, 1950)
The Reformer and the Redhead (Voice Only: MGM, 1950)
According to Mrs. Hoyle (Monogram, 1951)
Angels in the Outfield (MGM, 1951)
Bannerline (MGM, 1951)
No Room for the Groom (Universal, 1952)
Because You're Mine (MGM, 1952)
The Rocket Man (20th-Fox, 1954)
Please Don't Eat the Daisies (MGM, 1960)

Louis Calhern

Most people recall the onscreen Louis Calhern only from his MGM period (1949–1956) when he was one of the busiest featured performers on the lot, appearing in as many as seven Metro releases in 1950. By that time, he was a well-seasoned stage veteran in his fifties. He had been in a few silent films and then did a long rash of generally villainous caricatures in 1930s features. At MGM he was utilized to add dignity and solidity to a variety of genres, usually emerging as the smooth Wall Street banker type. There was often a tinge of sneering venality or aristocratic ennui to his characterizations that prevented him from becoming a latter-day, mature William Powell type in his onscreen roles.

Louis Calhern was born Carl Henry Vogt in Brooklyn on February 19, 1895. At the age of nine he went to live with relatives in St. Louis and later, while playing on the high school football squad there, he was hired as an extra in a touring production of *Much Ado About Nothing*. Noting that actors only worked three hours an evening and had the days free, he decided upon a theatrical career. He quit school and returned to New York where at the age of fourteen he obtained a job with Cecil Spooner's stock company and soon adopted his professional name so he would not disgrace his family.

After serving in World War I with the field artillery in France, Calhern tried his luck in Los Angeles, performing in stock and as the nondescript male lead ingenue in a few feature films. But he wisely returned to Broadway and soon made his mark in a series of increasingly important roles: with George M. Cohan in *The Song and Dance Man* (1923), with Judith Anderson in *Cobra* (1924), with Laurette Taylor in *In a Garden* (1925), and with Ann Harding in *The Woman Disputed* (1926).

With the coming of sound silvery-voiced Calhern was brought back to Hollywood, but soon found himself typecast as a dark-haired heavy, as in James Cagney's *Blonde Crazy* (1931) in which he was counterfeiter Dapper Dan Barker, or as Irene Dunne's unwanted suitor in *Sweet Adeline* (1935). Tiring of his Hollywood roles, Calhern returned to the stage, spending three years in the road company production of and as an actual Broadway replacement in *Life with Father*, and then experiencing his greatest personal success in *The Magnificent Yankee* (1946). In the late 1940s, he gravitated back to Hollywood and signed a contract with MGM (he claimed he never read it).

He was British officer Walter Pidgeon's opposite number in the Russian army in *The Red Danube* (1949) and replaced the late Frank Morgan as Buffalo Bill in *Annie Get Your Gun* (1950). The best of his seven releases that year were as the corrupt lawyer whose mistress was Marilyn Monroe in *The Asphalt Jungle* and the picturization of *The Magnificent Yankee* in which he and Ann Harding were Judge and Mrs. Oliver Wendell Holmes. He functioned well in subsidiary parts in such costumers as *The Prisoner of Zenda* (1952) and *The Student Prince* (1954) but seemed overly arch in the title role of *Julius Caesar* (1954) and as Lana Turner's grasping high priest in *The Prodigal* (1955). His dapper quality uplifted such "comedies" and "romances" as *Latin Lovers,* (1953), *Athena* (1954), and *Forever Darling* (1956). His last screen role proved to be as Uncle Willie in *High Society* (1956), for he died of a heart attack on May 12, 1956 while on location in Tokyo for MGM's *The Teahouse of the August Moon* (1956). In this production he was replaced by Paul Ford.

Calhern was the first to admit that the MGM phase of his professional career was plush pickings, and when he returned to Broadway (having done *King Lear* in 1950) to direct–star in the short-lived *Wooden Dish* (1955), he stated that he: " ... wanted to get away from the easy life in Hollywood and get my blood in circulation with some kind of challenge." The bon vivant onscreen was equally so offscreen, having been four times married, each spouse an actress (Ilka Chase, Julia Hoyt, Natalie Schafer, and Marianne Stewart).

LOUIS CALHERN

What's Worth While? (Paramount, 1921)
The Blot (F. B. Warren Corp., 1921)
Too Wise Wives (Paramount, 1921)
Woman, Wake Up! (Associated Exhibitors, 1922)
The Last Moment (Goldwyn, 1923)
Stolen Heaven (Paramount, 1931)
Road to Singapore (WB, 1931)
Blonde Crazy (WB, 1931)
They Call It Sin (FN, 1932)
Night after Night (Paramount, 1932)
Okay America! (Universal, 1932)
Afraid to Talk (Universal, 1932)
The Woman Accused (Paramount, 1933)
20,000 Years in Sing Sing (WB, 1933)
Frisco Jenny (WB, 1933)
Strictly Personal (Paramount, 1933)
World Gone Mad (Majestic, 1933)
Diplomaniacs (RKO, 1933)
Duck Soup (Paramount, 1933)
Affairs of Cellini (UA, 1934)

Man with Two Faces (FN, 1934)
Count of Monte Cristo (UA,1934)
Sweet Adeline (WB, 1935)
The Arizonian (RKO, 1935)
Woman Wanted (MGM, 1935)
Last Days of Pompeii (RKO, 1935)
The Gorgeous Hussy (MGM, 1936)
Her Husband Lies (Paramount, 1937)
The Life of Emile Zola (WB, 1937)
Fast Company (MGM, 1938)
Juarez (WB, 1939)
Fifth Avenue Girl (RKO, 1939)
Charlie McCarthy, Detective (RKO, 1939)
I Take This Woman (MGM, 1940)
The Story of Dr. Ehrlich's Magic Bullet (WB, 1940)
Heaven Can Wait (20th-Fox, 1943)
Nobody's Darling (Republic, 1943)
Up in Arms (RKO, 1944)
The Bridge of San Luis Rey (UA, 1944)
Notorious (RKO, 1946)

Arch of Triumph (UA, 1948)
The Red Pony (Republic, 1949)
The Red Danube (MGM, 1949)
Annie Get Your Gun (MGM, 1950)
Nancy Goes to Rio (MGM, 1950)
The Asphalt Jungle (MGM, 1950)
Devil's Doorway (MGM, 1950)
A Life of Her Own (MGM, 1950)
The Magnificent Yankee (MGM, 1950)
Two Weeks with Love (MGM, 1950)
The Man with a Cloak (MGM, 1951)
It's a Big Country (Narrator: MGM, 1951)
Invitation (MGM, 1952)
We're Not Married (20th-Fox, 1952)
Washington Story (MGM, 1952)
The Prisoner of Zenda (MGM, 1952)

Confidentially Connie (MGM, 1953)
Remains to Be Seen (MGM, 1953)
Julius Caesar (MGM, 1953)
Latin Lovers (MGM, 1953)
Main Street to Broadway (MGM, 1953)
Rhapsody (MGM, 1954)
Executive Suite (MGM, 1954)
The Student Prince (MGM, 1954)
Men of the Fighting Lady (MGM, 1954)
Betrayed (MGM, 1954)
Athena (MGM, 1954)
The Blackboard Jungle (MGM, 1955)
The Prodigal (MGM, 1955)
Forever Darling (MGM, 1956)
High Society (MGM, 1956)

With Janet Leigh and Van Johnson in *Confidentially Connie* (1953)

Leslie Caron

Unlike most of her dancing predecessors in motion pictures—Lucille Bremer, Vera-Ellen, Cyd Charisse—winsome Leslie Caron made a major contribution to movie musicals with her ability to dance, sing, *and* act. She projected a piquant, elfin charm in some of the cinema's best musicals. Her smashing debut in *An American in Paris* (1951) made motion picture history, and she was Oscar-nominated for her portrayal of the ragamuffin in *Lili* (1953). She also provided much Gallic delight to the productions of *Gigi* (1958) and *Fanny* (1961). Above all, unlike her predecessors, she matured into a very good actress in nonmusical roles in both comedy and drama, and garnered a second Academy Award nomination in 1963, by playing the destitute pregnant young woman in *The L-Shaped Room*.

Leslie Claire Margaret Caron was born in Paris on July 1, 1931. Her father was a French chemist, and her American-born mother had been a ballet dancer of some success in America during the 1920s. Leslie began her ballet lessons at the age of eleven, but during the Nazi occupation she and her brother went to live in Cannes with her grandparents. When she returned to Paris after the war, Leslie attended the Convent of the Assumption and studied ballet at the National Conservatory. She became a member of Roland Petit's Ballet des Champs-Élysées at sixteen and attracted the attention of choreographer David Lichine who cast her as the Sphinx in his ballet, *La Recontre*. That production premiered in April 1948, and Leslie was an overnight sensation. American dancer Gene Kelly, and his wife, Betsy Blair, saw one of her performances, and two years later, when Kelly was back in Paris looking for a dancer to star with him in the musical ballet of George Gershwin's *An American in Paris*, he arranged for her to make a test on film. Then he had it sent to Culver City, where producer Arthur Freed and director Vincente Minnelli cabled Kelly their approval.

After the film test Leslie and her mother came to America where she was put under contract to MGM. While *An American in Paris* was being readied, Leslie did a small dramatic role as the young heroine in Barbara Stanwyck's *The Man with a Cloak* (1951), but wisely it was not released until after she had made her dancing debut with Kelly in *An American in Paris*. In this film she and Kelly did a song and dance to "Our Love Is Here to Stay" and danced in the finale, a seventeen-minute ballet to the title song, Gershwin's tone poem. The picture received six Academy Awards and critics found both Leslie's dancing and her fawn-faced, gaminlike innocence appealing. About adapting to the new medium, Leslie remarked: "But dancing before a camera instead of an audience was very confusing, until I learned to imagine an audience, and then it was all right."

While waiting for another suitable dancing role for her, MGM cast her in *Glory Alley* (1952), in which she played a New Orleans nightclub entertainer, and *The Story of Three Loves* (1953) where she had a thankless role as a priggish French governess. But in *Lili*, a whimsical story of a French waif, Leslie had the opportunity to dance two dream ballet numbers and to exude her infectious brand of childlike vulnerability. She won an Academy Award nomination for her performance.

Following *Lili*, she made her Broadway debut in Roland Petit's *Les Ballets de Paris*, dancing to *Deuil en 24 Heures*. Leslie received good notices but the program did not. Then Twentieth Century-Fox borrowed her to appear opposite Fred Astaire in *Daddy Long Legs* (1955). Astaire said it was one of his best scripts and recalls Leslie as "a fine artist; conscientious, rapt, and serious." While the Roland Petit choreography for the Cinemascope film was somewhat precious, she and Astaire delivered a simple but memorable rendition of "Something's Gotta Give" and performed a beautiful *pas de deux*. In MGM's *The Glass Slipper* (1955) Leslie was appropriately cast as the ugly duckling who falls for Prince Charming (Michael Wilding), but again, Petit's choreography inhibited her gracious dancing style. *The Glass Slipper* was not a moneymaker, unlike Jerry Lewis' later updated spoof of the fairy tale, *Cinderfella* (1960).

Because of her distinct Continental personality, it was difficult to cast Leslie in very American-oriented musicals, such as *It's Always Fair Weather* or *Meet Me in Las Vegas*. It was equally difficult to give a dancer of her magnitude a subordinate role in a multipersonality song-and-dance film, such as *Les Girls* (Leslie would have been perfect in the Taina Elg part). Thus the studio concocted a remake of *Waterloo Bridge* entitled *Gaby* (1956) whose final artistic outcome definitely rhymed with "flabby." With a weak script and an uneasy John Kerr as her World War II soldier lover, Leslie appeared very uncomfortable in her role as the ballerina. The movie was not well received.

When MGM could not get boxoffice magnet Audrey Hepburn for the title role of *Gigi* (1958), they entrusted it to Leslie. This now classic musical received nine Academy Awards and represented the peak of Vincente Minnelli's directing career. The movie grossed $7,740,000 with a good part of its success due to Leslie's performance as the bewildered young miss who rebels at being pushed into the mold of a polite mistress. Leslie's Metro contract ended with a nonmusical role in George Bernard Shaw's *The Doctor's Dilemma* (1958) filmed in England. It was a very dated tale in which a no longer petite but also not yet grown up Leslie played the wife of artist Dirk Bogarde.

Leslie then played in two boxoffice duds. Twentieth Century-Fox's *The Man Who Understood Women* (1959) with Henry Fonda had her eliciting sophistication to no avail, and in MGM's timid adaptation of Jack Kerouac's *The Subterraneans* (1960) Leslie found herself part of San Francisco's Bohemia, as bewildered as her costar George Peppard and the film audiences. By now she was definitely through with dancing: "Dancing is a wonderful way of expression until you reach twenty-five, but to have kept dancing would have left me stale as a human being and as a woman." Another reason for her abandonment of dance as a means of expression was her persistent anemia, which required her to spend much of her nonperforming time resting in bed. "Dancing is only fun when you can do it without pain."

Her career was rejuvenated with Warner Brothers' *Fanny* (1961), a nonmusical version of the sucessful stage musical. The film grossed $4.5 million. At age thirty, the onscreen Leslie seemed much younger, and more importantly made Joshua Logan's production of *Fanny* viable. After this Leslie moved abroad, where she found her acting services more in demand. She played with David Niven in the modest *Guns of Darkness* (1962) but regained stature with the well received *The L-Shaped Room*. As the pregnant French refugee in a sleazy London boarding house she displayed dramatic talent in full bloom and received a second Academy Award nomination, as well as her second British Oscar (the first had been for *Lili*). A trio of middling comedies followed which did not enhance her screen position. She was a mature gamine opposite Cary Grant in *Father Goose* (1964), which earned a tidy profit. However, the next film for Universal did not. *A Very Special Favor* (1965) cast her as Charles Boyer's daughter and Rock Hudson's *vis-à-vis*, but scripter Stanley Shapiro was running downhill in creativity since his prior Doris Day successes. *Promise Her Anything* (1966), set in Greenwich Village but shot in London, had an uptight Leslie cavorting with an overrelaxed Warren Beatty. That same year she had a cameo role in *Is Paris Burning?*

While in Hollywood Leslie married meat-packing plant heir George Hormel (September 23, 1951), but he divorced her three years later, charging that she preferred the artistic life to life with him. In 1956 she married the Royal Shakespeare's inventive director, Peter Hall, and they had two children: Christopher (born 1957), and Jennifer (born 1958). Under Hall's tutelage Leslie appeared in a West End production of *Ondine* in 1961 with Richard Johnson, but in 1964 Hall sued her for divorce, naming actor Warren Beatty as corespondent. Their divorce became final the next year, but Leslie and the elusive Beatty never married. Leslie adopted a somewhat Bohemian life style of semiretirement. She was hired to make the Israeli-filmed western *Madron* (1970) playing a "nun" very similar to Shirley MacLaine's role in *Two Mules for Sister Sara*. That project was as unfelicitous for Leslie's waning career as had been the Italian-made *Three Fables of Love* (1963).

On December 30, 1969 she wed producer Michael Laughlin. He is the producer of her recent programmer *Chandler* (1971), released through her old studio MGM. She and her husband sued MGM on several points: the financing of that film, the fact that Warren Oates was billed over her in the credits, and conflict about several other planned projects they were to do for Metro. Cast as the French moll of an American gangster, Leslie looked decidedly frazzled as the middle-aged waif in *Chandler*, and she had little to offer in this detective caper.

The mature Leslie, who was a presenter on the April 1972 Oscar telecast, now claims that she generally felt like a freak when she performed all those adolescent dancing screen roles. She has been quoted as saying: "I got what I have now through knowing the right time to tell terrible people when to go to hell."

With Jean Pierre Aumont in *Lili* (1953)

111

With Hermione Gingold and Louis Jourdan in *Gigi* (1958)

LESLIE CARON

With Mitchell Ryan in *Chandler* (1971)

John Carroll

Filmgoers generally recall John Carroll as merely the handsome, if stodgy, moustached screen baritone. But in 1939 he was considered by many, including Louis B. Mayer, to be the most likely rival to Clark Gable on the movie scene. His offscreen capering had fan magazines tagging him as "everything that Douglas Fairbanks, Sr. ever was in his prime, and then some." This epithet supposedly qualified the performer for oncamera charisma. He was duly hired by MGM as a threat to the cinema king but was never given the proper showcasing to live up to his promise. Hollywood decided that, after all, he was only a poor man's Rhett Butler. His economy-sized dapperness and perpetual swagger did not make for a resounding film image. So he left the studio to continue on for a decade more in motion pictures, mostly as a tongue-in-cheek leading man at Republic Pictures.

Carroll's background is filled with such a mixture of intriguing fact, deliberate fantasy, and resultant contradictions that the true story of his pre-Hollywood years has yet to be set straight. He was born Julian La Faye in New Orleans, Louisiana on July 17, 1913. At the age of twelve he ran away from home, heading for Houston, Texas. Along the way there and back to New Orleans, he worked as a newspaper seller, steel riveter, dock laborer, ranch hand, barnstorming pilot, merchant seaman, shop assistant, racing car driver in Chicago, and a steeple painter. He eventually returned home to complete his basic formal education and then decided to train his singing voice. He worked his way over to Europe and before long was studying in Italy with Victor Chesnais. He later performed in Paris, London, Berlin, Vienna, Rome, and Budapest, appearing as a concert performer with a salary of several thousand dollars per special performance. When he was not doing well financially, he supplemented his income by working as a taxi driver or café singer.

During his several global jaunts, Carroll stopped off in Hollywood on many occasions. In 1927 he had worked there as a laborer, building studio soundstages. Then he graduated to chorus work in several movie musicals, including Marion Davies' *Marianne* (1929) and Lawrence Tibbett's *New Moon* (1930), both at MGM. In 1935 he was back in America and in Hollywood, again performing in the chorus background of a film musical, this time Ruby Keeler's *Go into Your Dance*. RKO was then looking for an athletic singer type to star in *Hi, Gaucho* (1935). Carroll was tested and hired. His debonair Lucio earned him no critical praise, but he romanced the film's leading lady, Hungarian-born Steffi Duna, and they married. (They had a daughter, Juliana, born in 1936, and the couple were divorced in 1942.) RKO used Carroll in three more minor features, but in very subsidiary roles, and set him at liberty.

With his devil-may-care stunting prowess he convinced Republic to hire him for the lead in their twelve-chapter serial *Zorro Rides Again* (1937) and fought to save the California–Yucatan railroad from the nefarious gang headed by El Lobo. Twenty-two years later, this serial would be spliced into a sixty-eight-minute feature for theatrical and television release.

Puritan gave Carroll a spin in the lead in their aerial thriller *Death in the Air* (1937). Then he joined Monogram as an action lead player, finding time to take a small role in Columbia's *Only Angels Have Wings* (1939) and performing in Vitaphone short subjects.

With his Errol Flynnish offcamera life, it was only a matter of time before he came to the attention of Louis B. Mayer who took a liking to the performer. However, he was practical enough to hire Carroll on the proviso that he buy himself out of his previous studio commitments (it took him two years to do so). His starting salary at Metro was $150 a week, not much for the would-be successor to Gable. His first picture at that studio was *Congo Maisie* (1940), a twisted remake of *Red Dust*, and Carroll had the Clark Gable role. He was a jungle doctor who saves Dr. Shepperd Strudwick and flirts with the man's wife (Rita Johnson). The N.Y. *World-Telegram* was among those judging Carroll to " ... combine all the worst features of Cary Grant and Clark Gable." He next had the subordinate romantic lead in the Nick Carter entry, *Phantom Raiders* (1940) and then advanced to class productions for his other three 1940 Metro releases. In *Susan and God* he was an actor member of Joan Crawford's Long Island set, he played a gigolo in *Hired Wife*, and was Diana Lewis' *vis-à-vis* in the Marx Brothers' *Go West*. He and Lewis dueted "As If I Didn't Know."

Carroll was borrowed by RKO to support Anna Neagle and Ray Bolger in *Sunny* (1941) and then returned to MGM to bring up the rear in *Lady Be Good* (1941) as the crooner who really cares for Eleanor Powell, but who is thought by Robert Young to be romancing Ann Sothern. Following this, he played the singing straight man to Abbott and Costello in the updated remake of *Rio Rita* (1942), and then he had his first lead at MGM, in the B western adventure yarn *Pierre and the Plains* (1942). He was the French Canadian rogue who roams the north woods and flirts with saloon hostess Ruth Hussey. The picture was mild fun but certainly generated no sparks. It was the peak of Carroll's MGM stay.

Republic used Carroll again to be the mercenary, thoughtless army pilot in John Wayne's *Flying Tigers* (1942). The next year he capitalized on his roguish charms in Republic's "expensive" *Hit Parade of 1943*. He was the conscienceless Tin Pan Alley song publisher who steals any composer's work, including that of midwestern songwriter Susan Hayward (who was the actor's offscreen romance at the time). Back at MGM, he was Dr. Hercules, the professional strong man hired by Virginia Weidler to patch up a family marital problem in *The Youngest Profession* (1943). He then went into the Army Air Force, and, when he was discharged in 1945, he completed his MGM contract with the programmer *A Letter for Evie* (1945) and a supporting role as Esther Williams' fiancé in *Fiesta* (1947). Meanwhile, he had wed minor MGM film executive Lucille Ryman.

In the first of his pictures under a new Republic contract, he backed up William Elliott and Vera Hruba Ralston in *Wyoming* (1947). Studio head Herbert J. Yates then blessed Carroll with the honor of appearing in four additional pictures with his protégé and later wife, Ralston. These included *I, Jane Doe* (1948) in which Ralston is charged with killing playboy Carroll and the dead man's widow (Ruth Hussey) becomes her defense attorney; and *Surrender* (1950), a costumer with Ralston as a bitch and Carroll as a villainous gambler.

In 1951 Carroll came East to undertake a nightclub tour, returning to Hollywood a year later to play the Erie Canal barge boat owner in Betty Grable's *The Farmer Takes a Wife* (1953). At age forty, the 6' 4" actor looked well and seemed a better bet than the scripters' choice for Grable, Dale Robertson, in this musical. From this high-class production he went into Republic's very modest song-studded *Geraldine* (1953).

Carroll was off the screen for four years in the mid-1950s, but he had more than his share of headlines. A 1956 issue of *Confidential* magazine told "all" about a nude party he had tossed in 1947 in Hollywood. Then for several years he was in and out of court with a much-publicized law suit by a seventy-year-old widow who demanded the return of $228,000. She claimed to have loaned the sum to him. He insisted the amount was only half of that sum, and besides she had given it to him in the first place. The case was eventually settled on the quiet.

He and ex-Metro player Virginia Bruce were in a British-made budget entry made in 1952 but released in the U.S. as *Two Grooms for a Bride* in (1957). He next played a villain in Randolph Scott's *Decision at Sundown* (1957) and wrapped up his movie career with Republic's flabby *Plunderers of Painted Flats* (1959). One of his last acting appearances to date was in a two-part *Wonderful World of Walt Disney* television episode, *A Boy Called Nuthin'* (1967) in which he was teamed with Forrest Tucker.

Carroll was again in the news in 1968 when a honorary badge and personal letter from the late President John F. Kennedy was stolen from his New York City apartment.

JOHN CARROLL

Marianne (MGM, 1929)
Devil-May-Care (MGM, 1929)
Hearts in Exile (WB, 1929)
Rogue Song (MGM, 1930)
Dough Boys (MGM, 1930)
Monte Carlo (Paramount, 1930)
New Moon (MGM, 1930)
Reaching for the Moon (UA, 1930)
Go into Your Dance (FN, 1935)
Hi, Gaucho (RKO, 1935)
The Accusing Finger (Paramount, 1936)
Murder on the Bridle Path (RKO, 1936)
Muss 'Em Up (RKO, 1936)
We Who Are About to Die (RKO, 1937)
Zorro Rides Again (Serial: Republic, 1937)
Death in the Air (Puritan, 1937)
Rose of the Rio Grande (Monogram, 1938)
I Am a Criminal (Monogram, 1938)
Only Angels Have Wings (Columbia, 1939)
Wolf Call (Monogram, 1939)
Congo Maisie (MGM, 1940)
Phantom Raiders (MGM, 1940)
Susan and God (MGM, 1940)
Hired Wife (Universal, 1940)
Go West (MGM, 1940)
Sunny (RKO, 1941)

This Woman Is Mine (Universal, 1941)
Lady Be Good (MGM, 1941)
Rio Rita (MGM, 1942)
Pierre of the Plains (MGM, 1942)
Flying Tigers (Republic, 1942)
Hit Parade of 1943 (Republic, 1943)
The Youngest Profession (MGM, 1943)
Bedside Manner (UA, 1945)
A Letter for Evie (MGM, 1945)
Fiesta (MGM, 1947)
Wyoming (Republic, 1947)
The Fabulous Texan (Republic, 1947)
The Flame (Republic, 1947)
Old Los Angeles (Republic, 1948)
I, Jane Doe (Republic, 1948)
Angel in Exile (Republic, 1948)
The Avengers (Republic, 1950)
Surrender (Republic, 1950)
Hit Parade of 1951 (Republic, 1950)
Belle le Grande (Republic, 1951)
The Farmer Takes a Wife (20th-Fox, 1953)
Geraldine (Republic, 1953)
Two Grooms for a Bride (20th-Fox, 1957)
Decision at Sundown (Columbia, 1957)
Plunderers of Painted Flats (Republic, 1959)

With Raymond Hatton, Ruth Hussey, and Reginald Owen in *Pierre of the Plains* (1942)

Marge and Gower Champion

America's Dancing Sweethearts, Marge and Gower Champion, became so popular a husband–wife team for a short time in the 1950s, that they earned lofty comparison to Irene and Vernon Castle. Effusively described as "light as bubbles, wildly imaginative, infinitely meticulous and exuberantly young," this attractive pair of dancers made a name for themselves not just performing specialty numbers that were visually pretty, but by introducing to exhibition dancing the technique of making their routines of choreography tell a story of sorts. This technique was the result of Broadway's ballet influence, and it was crystallized in the MGM musicals of the Fifties, mainly via Gene Kelly. It replaced the old-style, Hollywood, show-stopping sequences that never quite fit into the movie plots. The Champions' few joint film appearances were made mostly during their brief MGM tenure, and, while they proved to be no cinematic Ginger Rogers and Fred Astaire, they were a more ingratiating pair than their television contemporaries Mata and Hari.

The distaff side of this team was born Marjorie Celeste Belcher in Los Angeles on September 2, 1923, the younger daughter of Ernest Belcher, ballet-master-to-the-stars. (He taught the rudiments of ballet to everyone from Vilma Banky to Betty Grable.) Marge learned dancing as a child at her father's side, and, by her teens, was teaching students her own age. She modeled for Walt Disney's *Snow White and the Seven Dwarfs* (1937), various dance roles in *Fantasia* (1940), and the Blue Fairy in *Pinocchio* (1940), being paid a fee of $10 a day. In between she obtained minuscule parts in three features, from playing a coed, along with the then equally unknown Veronica Lake, in *Sorority House* (1939), to background interest for Bob Baker and his horse in *Honor of the West* (1939). She had better success on the stage. She appeared in the Los Angeles production of *Tonight at 8:30* in 1937, after which she was in a short-lived Broadway musical, *The Little Dog Laughed*. She broke her toe doing that show and was unable to dance for two years. But in 1942 she played the ingenue in *Portrait of a Lady* with Ruth Gordon and was the blonde witch girl in *Dark of the Moon* in 1945. She was also in Duke Ellington's *Beggar's Holiday*, and was for a short time married to commercial artist Arthur Babbitt. Her biggest career disappointment at that time was not having become a Radio City Music Hall Rockette. She still nostalgically regrets it today. (Even when Gower Champion staged the television special *Mary Martin at Radio City Music Hall* in the early 1960s, Marge hoped to fulfill her ambition and be in the Rockette number, but Gower insisted she was the wrong type, and would not cast her for the bit.)

Gower Champion was born in Geneva, Illinois on June 22, 1921. When his parents divorced, he and his mother moved to Los Angeles where he attended Bancroft Junior High and later Fairfax High School. At the age of fifteen he won a dance contest at the Coconut Grove with high school partner Jeanne Tyler, and their prize was a thirteen-week engagement at that famous Hollywood club. Enthusiastic about their professional luck, the two quit school and were soon appearing in New York's Waldorf-Astoria and Radio City Music Hall, with Gower's mother traveling as chaperone. They did specialty numbers in Broadway's *Streets of Paris* in 1939, and the next year appeared in two shows, *The Lady Comes Across* and *Count Me In*. Gower entered the Coast Guard in 1942, where he toured in *Tars And Spars* before being transferred to troop transport. When he was discharged he found that Jeanne Tyler had retired, and Ernest Belcher suggested he contact Marge. He performed a solo dance in MGM's *Till the Clouds Roll By* (1946), then went to New York and talked Marge into becoming his partner.

In April 1947, billed as Gower and Bell (her professional name from her "movie" days), they played a Montreal club. They were married on October 5, 1947, a few days after they opened at the New York Plaza's Persian Room. Gower choreographed a Broadway revue called *Small Wonder* and did the choreography for a West Coast production of *Lend an Ear*. When that show was taken to Broadway in 1949, Gower received the Donaldson and Antoinette Perry awards for his creativity. That same year they received their first national attention as a dancing team on the *Admiral Broadway Revue*, a television show starring Mary McCarty, Sid Caesar, and Imogene Coca. They played a successful engagement at the Hollywood night spot, The Mocambo, and made their joint motion picture debut—as themselves—in Bing Crosby's *Mr. Music* (1950) at Paramount.

MGM offered the team a contract for two pictures a year for five years, and, while their acting drew no plaudits, their enthusiastic dancing did. They played the subsidiary roles of Ellie and Frank in *Show Boat* (1951), in which they glided through the routines of choreographer Robert Alton. They danced their way through *Lovely to Look At* (1952) in which Ann Miller was the brightest addition to this remake of *Roberta*. It was choreographed by Hermes Pan who had worked on the original. In the lower-case *Everything I Have Is Yours* (1952), Marge and Gower played characters based upon their own rise to fame, while Gower and Nick Castle choreographed the film. *Give a Girl a Break* (1953) also starred Marge and Gower in a backstage story, and proved to be the peak of their cinematic dancing, largely thanks to Stanley Donen's direction and his choreographing of the numbers with Gower. Two of the film's highlights were a rooftop dance sequence with the Champions, and a solo dance performed by Bob Fosse.

119

Although none of their "starring" film appearances had proven spectacular, MGM offered the Champions a new contract at higher salaries, stipulating no appearances on that rival medium, television. They refused and left the studio on March 3, 1953. In June of that year, Ed Sullivan's *Toast Of The Town* television variety show spotlighted them in a musical-dancing story of their lives. MGM finally had to recognize television as a reality, and they were invited back to the studio in 1955 to appear in Esther Williams' MGM swan song *Jupiter's Darling*. Marge and Gower were virtually reduced to a circus act, brought on for the Hermes Pan-inspired dancing interludes when the tongue-in-cheek widescreen version of *Road to Rome* was falling flatter than even director George Sidney could tolerate. That same year they joined with Betty Grable in her musical film finale at Columbia, *Three for the Show*, a listless remake of *Too Many Husbands*. The Champions took a very dim back row to both Jack Lemmon's clowning and to the occasional dancing interspots choreographed by Jack Cole. Gower later choreographed Jane Powell's *The Girl Most Likely* (1957), but the modest remake of *Tom, Dick and Harry* was quickly forgotten.

Nightclubs, a Broadway review, and more television work—they had their own CBS series for several months in 1957—kept them together as a dancing team, until Marge decided to retire in 1960 and raise their two sons, Gregg and Blake. Marge has said, "We took a lot of people by surprise when we quit. But Gower always wanted to direct and that was our real goal. The reason we called ourselves Marge and Gower Champion and now Gower and Marge Champion was to build his identity. ... I was happy to quit. We had danced together for thirteen years and I had had it. Trouble with me was I didn't mind the performance but dreaded the endless hours of rehearsal. It was wonderful to concentrate on being a wife and mother."

Gower went on to become one of Broadway's hottest choreographer–directors, once described as "Erich von Stroheim in an Ivy League suit." He was to participate in the staging of *My Fair Lady* but clashed with the producers over the show's concept. After directing several television commercials unbilled and often without salary in order to gain experience, he tackled *Bye Bye Birdie* (1960) and was credited with whipping that Broadway musical into a hit. Later there was *Carnival* (1961), *Hello, Dolly!* (1964), *I Do, I Do* (1966), and *The Happy Time* (1968). He received two more Tony awards, for *Dolly* and *The Happy Time*. The latter was a flop, but not as costly as Angela Lansbury's *Prettybelle* (1971), which Gower staged before it closed down in Boston, never reaching Broadway. By this point, he had been superseded in the name race as Broadway's best stager by Joe Layton, and by Bob Fosse, who went on to greater acclaim with his cinema staging of *Cabaret*. Even though he has slowed down his pace in recent years due to a severe ulcer condition. Gower returned to Broadway in 1972 as the stager of *Sugar*, and performed the same function in the spring of 1973 when he replaced John Gielgud as director of *Irene*, starring Debbie Reynolds, solidifying his reputation as one of the best show editors in the business. (He still considers

Jerome Robbins the best in the field and admits on occasion that he is not a particularly inventive choreographer but has the capacity for creating routines.) Gower made a faltering debut as film director of Debbie Reynolds' *My Six Loves* (1963). Differences of opinions with the producers of *Dr. Dolittle* and *Goodbye, Mr. Chips*, both in 1968, left him out of the final production. He has staged several television specials, including the 1968 Oscarcast.

In 1967, just for the fun of it, Marge accepted a small role in Burt Lancaster's bizarre *The Swimmer*, filmed on location in the East. She was plump and matronly, but not so out-of-tune as in the following year's *The Party*, a Peter Sellers' one-man misfire, directed by her friend Blake Edwards. She has spent a great deal of her time in recent years as an unpaid volunteer teacher of dance to black youths at the Mafundi Institute in Watts, California.

On Gower's fiftieth birthday, the couple announced a separation. No other parties were involved and no further explanation offered, although the couple still are often seen together. Several years before, while discussing their successful teamwork, where Gower was the choreographer and Marge the editor, Gower remarked, "We are almost repulsively in accord. We are a team in every way."

MARGE AND GOWER CHAMPION

Sorority House (RKO, 1939)*
The Story of Vernon and Irene Castle (RKO, 1939)*
Honor of the West (Universal, 1939)*
Till the Clouds Roll By (MGM, 1946)†
Mr. Music (Paramount, 1950)
Show Boat (MGM, 1951)

Lovely to Look At (MGM, 1952)
Everything I Have Is Yours (MGM, 1952)
Give a Girl a Break (MGM, 1953)
Jupiter's Darling (MGM, 1955)
Three for the Show (Columbia, 1955)
The Swimmer (Columbia, 1967)*
The Party (UA, 1968)*

*Marge Champion alone †Gower Champion alone

In *Give a Girl a Break* (1953)

Cyd Charisse

Cyd Charisse was Terpsichore incarnate to the MGM studio heads who needed a beautiful balletic dancing star to fill the bill that Broadway had opened in the 1940s with its musical dream ballets. MGM had endeavored to groom pretty Lucille Bremer along those lines, but she never had the proper opportunity to click with the public. So Cyd got her chance and for five years was the studio's dancing star. She was Fred Astaire's last major screen partner, and he called the leggy lass "beautiful dynamite." Onscreen, it did not matter that Cyd's lack of sustained energy concentration required her routines to be filmed in small fragments, and very carefully the studio avoided having her "sing" much before the camera, because she was nearly tone deaf. In the late 1950s her career veered to dramatic roles. Projecting a certain coolness and aloofness which enhanced her dancing image, she could never quite unbend in her nondancing screen moments, which suffered as a natural consequence. Nevertheless, when MGM was dropping most of its contract stars in the early 1950s, Cyd remained on their roster. Endowed with a great natural beauty and more than a slight resemblance to the studio's reigning goddess, Ava Gardner, she at least escaped playing the girl-next-door roles like her professional balletic rival Vera-Ellen.

She was born Tula Ellice Finklea in Amarillo, Texas on March 8, 1921 (or 1923) and acquired the nickname Sid, when her little brother could not pronounce Sis. She kept the nickname for professional use, giving it a more glamorous spelling. Her father, who owned a jewelry store, encouraged his daughter's ballet lessons which she had begun at the age of six. The family moved to Hollywood where Cyd was sent to study with ballet teacher Nico Charisse. Charisse was impressed with the dark-haired beauty and told her parents: "If your daughter will stay here and work, she will become a star."

Cyd was likewise impressed with her teacher to the point of falling in love with him. After one year of study, she auditioned for the Ballet Russe and was signed at $125 weekly as a member of that troupe's corps de ballet. Just as Cyd was to sail to London with the Ballet Russe, her father died. She cancelled her plans and returned home, but her mother sent her back to New York to join the troupe on its European tour. "We saw the great capitals of the world through hotel windows." Nico Charisse finally succumbed to his romantic feelings for the young dancer and followed her to Europe where they were married, in France, on August 12, 1939.

With the ensuing war in Europe, the troupe returned to the United States where, through choreographer David Lichine, Cyd met Russian actor–impresario–motion picture director Gregory Ratoff. He saw to it that she was used in Warner Brothers' *Mission to Moscow* (1943) and his own-directed *Something to Shout About* (1943). Cyd used the *nom de guerre* of Lily Norwood. With her husband's encouragement, Cyd decided to continue dancing in the movies, and the next year was signed to a MGM contract. After that studio's choreographer Robert Alton had introduced her to producer Arthur Freed, Metro used her unbilled in minor dancing roles in several motion pictures: *Ziegfeld Follies* (1946), where she danced a ballet "around" Fred Astaire but not with him; *The Harvey Girls* (1946); and *Three Wise Fools* (1946). Watching her on the set of *The Harvey Girls* was composer Harry Warren who turned to Freed and said: "Keep your eye on that girl." Both Freed and MGM did, and she got billing in such films as *Till the Clouds Roll By* (1946), *Fiesta* (1947), and *Words and Music* (1948). She was named one of the Stars of Tomorrow in the *Motion Picture Herald* Fame Poll in 1948, along with such already budding talent as Jane Powell, Ann Blyth, Angela Lansbury, Eleanor Parker, and Doris Day.

Just as she was offered the second lead plum with Fred Astaire and Judy Garland in *Easter Parade* (1948), she broke her leg and the role went to Ann Miller. MGM showcased Cyd to advantage with Ricardo Montalban and Miller in the "Dance Of Fury" sequence in *The Kissing Bandit* (1949) which starred Frank Sinatra and Kathryn Grayson, and gave her first straight dramatic portrayal as a chic, cool model in *East Side, West Side* (1949). One critic opined: "She's so lovely that you forget she is actually a dancer doing her first acting job." When the studio had no romantic dancing roles for her they assigned her to straight roles in small budget pictures. While she was a Greek Goddess when dancing, she was merely beautiful to look at when reciting lines.

Finally a choice part came along opposite Gene Kelly in *An American in Paris* (1951), but pregnancy prevented her from doing the picture. In 1947 Cyd had divorced Nico Charisse and the following year married Alice Faye's ex-husband, crooner–actor Tony Martin. On August 28, 1950 she gave birth to Tony, Jr. While Leslie Caron, the French gamin from Roland Petit's ballet, made her American film debut in *An American in Paris*.

Kelly did use Cyd in his next picture, however, and it was the turning-point of her dancing career. The film was *Singin' in the Rain* (1952), the polished musical satire about Hollywood's transition from silents to talkies. Cyd and Kelly performed the "Broadway Rhythm" ballet in that picture. After doing a tempestuous dance around an Aztec idol in the Mexican-localed *Sombrero* (1953), she was given the best film role of her MGM years, playing opposite Fred Astaire in *The Band Wagon* (1953). This film, by the long, contains Astaire's best cinema dancing. Cyd was "alive" when dancing with Astaire and they did a beautifully sensual routine to "Dancing in the Dark" which was matched by the later number "The Girl Hunt" ballet, a spoof on the Mickey Spillane detective novels. *The Band Wagon* is regarded as one of the best Hollywood musicals, but it received next to no public endorsement, heralding yet another decline of interest in movie song-and-dance films. Only in present-day reruns has this film gained the reputation it so richly deserves.

Cyd was at the peak of her form as a dancing star. But she was badly miscast in *Brigadoon* (1954), also directed by Vincente Minnelli. As the lassie Fiona Campbell she executed two dances, the opening fair piece "Waitin' for My Dearie," and with Gene Kelly, "Heather on the Hill." She was among those guests performing in the Sigmund Romberg story, *Deep in My Heart* (1954) and participated in the Gene Kelly–Stanley Donen musical *It's Always Fair Weather* (1955), a potentially excellent film marred by a soggy tale of the reunion of three World War II buddies and an overuse of gimmickery to fill out the Cinemascope screen. She was much better in *Meet Me in Las Vegas* (1956) as the haughty ballet star working a Las Vegas show, who encounters rancher-gambler Dan Dailey. The film was splashy, colorful, and joyfully reminiscent of the studio's product a decade back. Gene Kelly's three-part interpretative ballet work, *Invitation to the Dance* (1957), was artistically viable as a choreographed exercise, but it faltered even in art house release.

Cyd's last MGM musical was *Silk Stockings* (1957), the film tune version of Garbo's *Ninotchka* which had been a Broadway musical success with Hildegarde Neff. Cyd and Astaire were scintillating when dancing together, but the story line creaked and Cyd was no Garbo. Carole Richards dubbed Cyd's vocals for the film. After endeavoring to be the sultry murderess in Universal's *Twilight for the Gods* (1958) opposite Rock Hudson, Cyd ended her Metro tenure playing a showgirl in *Party Girl* (1958) with Robert Taylor. Her part in this Nicholas Ray antiquity looked like an Ava Gardner reject.

The forty-year-plus Cyd found the going increasingly difficult in the film world of the 1960s. She had a bit opposite Roland Petit in *Black Tights* (1962), a three-part story filmed in Paris, was the castrating actress Carlotta in Vincente Minnelli's *Two Weeks in Another Town* (1962), and had a guest spot as a nightclub dancer in the Dean Martin–Matt Helm entry *The Silencers* (1966). She followed the example of other one-time American stars and went to Europe to dabble in filmmaking. She was cast with Hugh O'Brian and Eleanor Rossi-Drago in *Assassination in Rome*, made in 1964 but not released in the U. S. until 1967. In *Maroc 7* (1967) she was the fashion magazine editor–jewel thief for the poorly conceived thriller which starred Gene Barry and Elsa Martinelli.

Since marrying Tony Martin, Cyd always has placed her home life before her career, and endeavored to travel whenever she could with Martin on his nightclub tours. In 1963 she made her club debut with her husband, billed as "Tony Martin and Cyd Charisse: A Two-Act Revue." She does an occasional summer theatre stint (e.g., *Illya, Darling*) and infrequently appears on television such as in a late 1960s dance special devoted to herself, or the 1972 *Fol-De-Rol* in which she was teamed with Yma Sumac in a dance–song sequence. When Betty Grable had to withdraw from the summer 1972 Australian production of *No, No Nanette*, Cyd was signed as her replacement. This strange casting substitution would indicate that the public, when in the mood for nostalgia entertainment, does not care from which decade representative talent is drawn.

CYD CHARISSE

Mission to Moscow (WB, 1943)
Something to Shout About (Columbia, 1943)
Ziegfeld Follies (MGM, 1946)
The Harvey Girls (MGM, 1946)
Three Wise Fools (MGM, 1946)
Till the Clouds Roll By (MGM, 1946)
Fiesta (MGM, 1947)
The Unfinished Dance (MGM, 1947)
On an Island with You (MGM, 1948)
Words and Music (MGM, 1948)
The Kissing Bandit (MGM, 1949)
East Side, West Side (MGM, 1949)
Tension (MGM, 1949)
Mark of the Renegade (Universal, 1951)
The Wild North (MGM, 1952)
Singin' in the Rain (MGM, 1952)

Sombrero (MGM, 1953)
The Band Wagon (MGM, 1953)
Easy to Love (MGM, 1953)
Brigadoon (MGM, 1954)
Deep in My Heart (MGM, 1954)
It's Always Fair Weather (MGM, 1955)
Meet Me in Las Vegas (MGM, 1956)
Invitation to the Dance (MGM, 1957)
Silk Stockings (MGM, 1957)
Twilight for the Gods (Universal, 1958)
Party Girl (MGM, 1958)
Five Golden Hours (Columbia, 1961)
Black Tights (Magna, 1962)
Two Weeks in Another Town (MGM, 1962)
The Silencers (Columbia, 1966)
Maroc 7 (Paramount, 1967)
Assassination in Rome (Walter Manley, 1967)

With Carl Milletaire (center) and Gene Kelly in *Singin' in the Rain* (1952)

1546-83

With Peter Lorre, Jules Munshin, and Joseph Buloff in *Silk Stockings* (1957)

Gladys Cooper

"I came to Hollywood for three weeks to do a movie, and I have stayed for twenty years." So spoke the doyenne of screen aristocrats, Gladys Cooper. She was fifty-one years old at the time, 1940, and the movie was *Rebecca*.

She was born Gladys Constance Cooper on December 18, 1888 in Lewisham, a less than fashionable suburb southeast of London. At the age of seventeen she defied the wishes of her father, journalist Charles Frederick Cooper, by going "onstage" in a provincial production of *Bluebelle in Fairyland*. For her inauspicious debut she played the lead role. Working her way up one more rung of the theatrical ladder, she made her London debut in the Gaiety Girls chorus line in 1906. A few years later, still struggling in the frivolity of the musical theatre, she became the British pinup girl of World War I. Unlike the more titilating pinups of World War II, hers was a picture postcard pose in a properly Edwardian Gibson Girl manner, and she was soon hailed as one of the great beauties of the century, indeed a veritable standard by which Britishers measured feminine beauty. Her stage credits included *The Kiss, The Diplomacy*, and *The Admirable Crichton*, and her costars numbered such luminaries as Ivor Novello, Charles Hawtrey, and Gerald du Maurier.

Gladys made her film debut in 1917 in *The Sorrows of Satan* and continued to make sporadic movie appearances throughout the 1920s, including two features opposite matinee idol Ivor Novello, *The Bohemian Girl* (1922—released in the U. S. in 1923) based on the Balfe opera, and *Bonnie Prince Charlie* (1923). However, Gladys' primary love was the stage, where in 1922 she established her reputation as a dramatic actress by starring in Pinero's *The Second Mrs. Tanqueray*. After another decade of English stage work, Gladys came to the United States to appear on Broadway in *The Shining Hour* (1934), and remained to play in *Othello, Macbeth, The Morning Star* (in which the juvenile lead was played by a pre–motion picture Gregory Peck), and *Call It a Day*.

When Alfred Hitchcock set out to direct his first Hollywood feature, *Rebecca*, and signed Gladys for a role, she had no pretensions to a new, sparkling screen career. She had performed in only two features in the 1930s, *Dandy Donovan* (1931) and *The Iron Duke* (1935) with George Arliss. Both were British-made and had an unspectacular boxoffice reception. She arrived in

127

Hollywood in early 1939 and guested with her old friend Nigel Bruce who would play her fat and genial husband in the Hitchcock adaptation of Du Maurier's popular novel. Her role as Beatrice Locy, the tweedy sister of Laurence Olivier, was not particularly demanding, but she made her blunt and chatty characterization vivid enough to be memorable. Gladys found the California climate congenial and decided to make her home there. After emoting as Dennis Morgan's screen mother in *Kitty Foyle* (1940), she settled down to a busy filmmaking schedule. Imperious on camera, she was not above appearing in such mock horror comedy as *The Black Cat* (1941) or the programmer whodunit, *The Gay Falcon* (1941) with George Sanders. Much more in keeping with her lofty theatre reputation was her assignment in Alexander Korda's *That Hamilton Woman* (1941) in which she was featured as the straitlaced Lady Hamilton. Her most famous screen part was the autocratic Back Bay Boston mother of repressed Bette Davis in *Now, Voyager* (1942), establishing a stereotype that Gladys would often re-create on the screen. She was nominated for a Best Supporting Actress Oscar award, but lost to Teresa Wright who won for *Mrs. Miniver*. The following year Gladys was again Oscar nominated for essaying the jealous and spiteful Sister Vauzous in *The Song of Bernadette*, but lost to Katina Paxinou of *For Whom the Bell Tolls*.

Having decided to remain in Hollywood, Gladys purchased a home in the Pacific Palisades where she maintained a small orchard of lemon and orange trees. The house became a refuge for the British colony, a gathering spot for English actors, writers, and directors who sought an intellectual camaraderie they found missing in Hollywood. Gladys was known as a gracious hostess and a witty woman with a keen sense of humor. She frankly admitted that she never watched the rushes of her films, for when she happened to see a day's shooting of *Rebecca* she could only exclaim, " 'That can't be me.' But it was and in horror I walked out." Whenever a friend would comment that he had liked her in this or that scene of a particular film, Gladys would reply in studied interest that she was glad to know finally what the film had been about and what her particular scenes meant to the story. She never went to see her own movies.

It was only a matter of time before Louis B. Mayer decided that he must align Gladys with his stable of British contractees. When he first met her he exclaimed: "I thought, Miss Cooper, you were much older." Evidently all he knew of her professional work stemmed from her performance as the unloving, elderly Mrs. Vale of *Now, Voyager*. She signed a five-year contract with the studio, and during that time was allowed to return to Broadway on several occasions to star in plays. On one occasion, MGM loaned her services to a British production company which permitted her to return to London in 1945 to make *Beware of Pity*, released in the U. S. in 1947.

At MGM Gladys was determined not to capture any awards, as she said, but simply to work. In *The White Cliffs of Dover* (1944) she was Peter Lawford's patrician grandmother, a decided contrast to her fellow English stage star Dame May Whitty, who played the effusive Nanny in this popular weeper film. Gladys functioned effectively as the Duchess of Brancourt in *Mrs. Parkington* (1944), played Gregory Peck's mother in *Valley of Decision* (1945), the Scottish grandmother in *The Green Years* (1946), and the mother of Lana Turner and Donna Reed in *Green Dolphin Street* (1947). She had one beautiful scene in RKO's *The Bishop's Wife* (1947) where, as the dowager patron of the church, she reveals to angel Cary Grant that her one true love had been a young poet, now dead, whom she refused to marry because she could not face the possibility of living in poverty. She played Judy Garland's patrician Aunt Inez in *The Pirate* (1948) and ended her MGM stay by playing Madame Dupuis in *Madame Bovary* (1949).

The remainder of her illustrious career was spent largely in the theatre and working on television. She is best known on the American stage for her portrayal of Mrs. St. Maugham in Enid Bagnold's *The Chalk Garden* (1955). Her greatest personal success in London was her portrayal of Felicity in Noel Coward's *Relative Values* (1957), and in 1967 she was made a Dame Commander of the Order of the British Empire for her distinguished stage work. On television she costarred with Charles Boyer, Gig Young, and Robert Coote in the NBC series *The Rogues* (1964), and was spry enough to do a bicycling sequence when the script demanded it. She was an occasional guest star on other video series, including a role as the Grand Duchess on an episode of the British-lensed *Persuaders* (1972). Her best film roles after leaving MGM were the overpowering mother of Deborah Kerr in *Separate Tables* (1958) and the mother of Henry Higgins in *My Fair Lady* (1964). For playing Rex Harrison's mater in this feature, she was again Oscar-nominated.

Gladys married English actor Philip Merivale in 1937. He died in 1946 while they were living in California. She had been married twice before in England: to Captain Herbert J. Buckmaster and Sir Neville Pearson. Her two daughters by her first marriage are wed to actors: Joan to Robert Morley and Sally to Robert Hardy. Her stepson, John Merivale, with whom she costarred on the London stage in Somerset Maugham's *The Sacred Flame* in 1960, was once married to actress Jan Sterling and was the frequent costar and companion of Vivien Leigh during the last years of that actress's life.

Gladys wrote her autobiography, *Gladys Cooper*, in 1931 and a followup biography was written by Sewell Stokes in 1953, entitled *Without Veils*. She continued to work up until almost the time of her death at the age of eighty-two (November 17, 1971). She never considered retiring because, as she said, "I am an old ham!" On celebrating her eightieth birthday the lively actress had exclaimed, "At my time in life I am pleased I can still remember my lines." Her good friend Sir Laurence Olivier regarded Gladys as a "brilliant hurdler of all epochs and fashions in the theatre."

With Paul Maxey and Judy Garland in *The Pirate* (1948)

GLADYS COOPER

The Sorrows of Satan (Samuelson, 1917)
Masks and Faces (Ideal, 1917)
My Lady's Dress (Samuelson, 1918)
Bonnie Prince Charles (Gaumont, 1923)
The Bohemian Girl (Selznick, 1923)
Dandy Donovan (British, 1931)
The Iron Duke (Gaumont–British, 1935)
Rebecca (UA, 1940)
Kitty Foyle (RKO, 1940)
That Hamilton Woman (UA, 1941)
The Black Cat (Universal, 1941)
The Gay Falcon (RKO, 1941)
This Above All (20th-Fox, 1942)
Eagle Squadron (Universal, 1942)
Now, Voyager (WB, 1942)
Forever and a Day (RKO, 1943)
Mr. Lucky (RKO, 1943)
Princess O'Rourke (WB, 1943)
The Song of Bernadette (20th-Fox, 1943)
The White Cliffs of Dover (MGM, 1944)
Mrs. Parkington (MGM, 1944)

Valley of Decision (MGM, 1945)
Love Letters (Paramount, 1945)
The Green Years (MGM, 1946)
The Cockeyed Miracle (MGM, 1946)
Green Dolphin Street (MGM, 1947)
The Bishop's Wife (RKO, 1947)
Beware of Pity (Two Cities, 1947)
Homecoming (MGM, 1948)
The Pirate (MGM, 1948)
The Secret Garden (MGM, 1949)
Madame Bovary (MGM, 1949)
Thunder on the Hill (Universal, 1951)
At Sword's Point (RKO, 1952)
The Man Who Loved Redheads (UA, 1955)
Separate Tables (UA, 1958)
The List of Adrian Messenger (Universal, 1963)
My Fair Lady (WB, 1964)
The Happiest Millionaire (BV, 1967)
A Nice Girl Like Me (Avco Embassy, 1969)

Jackie Cooper

Louis B. Mayer called Jackie Cooper a "wonderful kid," and Cooper remembers his star days: "At eleven, when most boys are delighted if they make twenty dollars a year, I was earning $2,000 a week as a child star with MGM, then the richest movie studio in Hollywood." By the time he was twenty-four years old, however, his professional career had nose-dived badly: "In 1946 I didn't earn a cent, but I spent $70,000." In a career that has seemingly had a larger number of ups than downs, Cooper progressed from stock member of the *Our Gang* short subject series to MGM junior screen luminary, where he was under contract from 1931–1936, to a twenty-five year old has-been who was rejected by New York's Actors' Studio. In the 1950s he became a successful television performer–producer–executive, and more recently, a motion picture director.

He was born John Cooper, Jr. in Los Angeles on September 15, 1922. His father operated a small music store but proved to be an inept businessman. When Cooper was two years old, his father skipped out of his life. Cooper's mother, Mabel Leonard Cooper, boarded her infant son with his grandmother and took a job playing the piano on the vaudeville circuit. Cooper's grandmother had worked as a movie extra on occasion and when he was three and a half years old, she got him jobs doing the same type of work. "My mother was on the road in vaudeville and my grandmother was baby-sitting. She took me to the studio and they dressed me up in a sailor suit and little wooden clogs and told me to dance." He began doing bit parts and, at six, became one of the stars of MGM's *Our Gang* series, along with Farina, Stymie Beard, Norman "Chubby" Chaney, and Bobby "Wheezer" Hutchins.

He sang for his feature film debut, *Fox Movietone Follies of 1929*. Two years later Paramount cast him as *Skippy*, and his pouting lower lip, blond locks, and button nose made him a star. *Motion Picture* magazine headlined, "Is Jackie Cooper a Midget? Skeptics Can't Believe The Boy Wonder Is Only Eight Years Old." He was nominated for an Academy Award but lost the Oscar to Lionel Barrymore who won for *A Free Soul*. MGM signed the 1930s answer to Jackie Coogan to a contract, and Cooper became the first child star at Metro. As Wallace Beery's son in *The Champ* (1931), Cooper proved his most winsome, and the youngster was utilized for similar sentimental effect in succeeding vehicles. His rather robust performance as Jim Hawkins in *Treasure Island* (1934) was a notable change of pace. But by 1936 MGM was more intrigued with the boxoffice potential of two other young contractees, Mickey Rooney and Freddie Bartholomew, both of whom appeared with Cooper in his last MGM contract assignment, *The Devil Is a Sissy* (1936).

Cooper found himself at liberty at age fourteen and it was difficult for the onetime star to obtain decent adolescent roles. He was the *Boy of the Streets* (1937) and *Gangster's Boy* (1938), both for Monogram. Paramount hired him to play Henry Aldrich in *What a Life!* (1939) and *Life with Henry* (1941). This series continued, however, with Jimmy Lydon replacing Cooper. Occasionally he was in a prime feature such as *The Return of Frank James* (1940), but more often he was cast in such indifferent double-bill items as *The Navy Comes Through* (1942) or *Where Are Your Children?* (1943).

Meanwhile he had enrolled at Beverly Hills High School but was snubbed by his classmates as "the kid" until he attended a prom with shapely Lana Turner as his date. He was seen around Hollywood with Judy Garland for a time, but his position was usurped by Mickey Rooney who got his driver's license first. Cooper's mother died in 1941, and he enlisted in the Navy, going off to the University of Notre Dame in a Naval Officers' training program. His academic background was so spotty that he flunked out. To add to his troubles, he was charged with contributing to the delinquency of a minor. "We were having a party at the La Salle Hotel and several girls and boys crashed the party. One guy and a girl went into the bedroom and stayed all night. The rest of us had to be on the base by midnight and we had all cleared out." Cooper was acquitted.

Since he had played drums in the movie *Syncopation* (1942), he was given a job of playing them again in the Navy band, and he spent several months touring the South Pacific in that capacity. Before his embarkment, he wed June Horne (1945), a girl he had known in Hollywood. They had a son, John Anthony, in 1946 and then were divorced in 1949. Cooper says, "I feel I might have married June just so someone would care that I was going overseas." When he was discharged in 1946, as a musician, second class, the only job he was offered was a television Western. But that was before the glamor days of television and Cooper turned it down. Each studio told him he was either too young or too old for any part he sought.

His savings were dwindling and his marriage was over, so he headed for New York. He obtained some television work but was refused membership in the Actors' Studio where he wanted to study drama. He married actress Hildy Parks (now the wife of Broadway producer Alexander Cohen) in 1950, but the union lasted only eight months. The following year, Cooper picked up a book entitled *The Will to Live*, by Dr. Arnold Hutschnecker, a noted authority on psychosomatic medicine. Cooper found Hutschnecker listed in the telephone directory and for the next two and a half years saw him regularly as a patient. His marriage failures, his inability to find a professional niche as a young adult, and his excessive drinking were left behind as Cooper endeavored to

132

replace his lost childhood with objective understanding via Hutschnecker's psychoanalytical assistance. Cooper recalls, "I lived in an all-adult world, studied at the studio, and seldom met kids my own age. I wasn't given an ounce of responsibility or taught the value of money. It makes you emotionally ill to be treated like an enlarged infant."

On April 29, 1954 he married for a third time, to Barbara Kraus, a New York advertising executive, whom he calls the "most understanding person I have ever known." After his move to Manhattan he did get some stage work. *Magnolia Alley* was a flop, but he did an eighteen-month stint as Ensign Pulver in *Mr. Roberts*, starred in *Remains to Be Seen* with Janis Paige, and later topcast *King of Hearts* (1954). But it was television that was to prove Cooper's professional salvation. He landed the lead in the teleseries, *The People's Choice*, which lasted three seasons. Then, as half-owner, he starred in a second teleseries, *Hennesey*. He played a Navy doctor and received two Emmy nominations during its three-year run. "I would lots rather work for a sponsor than a movie mogul. There is nothing now as dictatorial as they were. They controlled the scripts, the directors, and the actors' lives."

From 1964 to 1969, Cooper was vice president in charge of production of Screen Gems, the television arm of Columbia Pictures, where he displayed an astute capability of packaging successful video series. After leaving Screen Gems, the powerful executive formed his own television production company, but failed to sell a new series with himself as star, *Calhoun*. In 1971, after a ten-year absence he returned to screen acting, playing the television executive in Columbia's *The Love Machine*. His lacklustre performance in front of the camera underlined his previous wise choice of avoiding any performing chores in recent years. That same year he produced a telefilm, *Doctor Dan*, for NBC's *World Premiere* series. Columbia's Mike Frankovich allowed him to direct the feature *Stand Up and Be Counted* (1972).

Cooper resides in Beverly Hills and Palm Springs with his wife, Barbara, and their three children, none of whom he says will be a child performer.

JACKIE COOPER

Fox Movietone Follies of 1929 (Fox, 1929)
Sunny Side Up (Fox, 1929)
Skippy (Paramount, 1931)
Young Donovan's Kid (RKO, 1931)
The Champ (MGM, 1931)
Sooky (Paramount, 1931)
When a Feller Needs a Friend (MGM, 1932)
Divorce in the Family (MGM, 1932)
Broadway to Hollywood (MGM, 1933)
The Bowery (UA, 1933)
Lone Cowboy (Paramount, 1934)
Treasure Island (MGM, 1934)

Peck's Bad Boy (Fox, 1934)
Dinky (WB, 1935)
O'Shaughnessy's Boy (MGM, 1935)
Tough Guy (MGM, 1936)
The Devil Is a Sissy (MGM, 1936)
Boy of the Streets (Monogram, 1937)
White Banners (WB, 1938)
Gangster's Boy (Monogram, 1938)
That Certain Age (Universal, 1938)
Newsboys' Home (Universal, 1939)
Scouts to the Rescue (Serial: Universal, 1939)
Spirit of Culver (Universal, 1939)

Streets of New York (Monogram, 1939)
What a Life! (Paramount, 1939)
Two Bright Boys (Universal, 1939)
The Big Guy (Universal, 1940)
Seventeen (Paramount, 1940)
The Return of Frank James (20th-Fox, 1940)
Gallant Sons (MGM, 1940)
Life with Henry (Paramount, 1941)
Ziegfeld Girl (MGM, 1941)
Her First Beau (Columbia, 1941)
Glamour Boys (Paramount, 1941)

Syncopation (RKO, 1942)
Men of Texas (Universal, 1942)
The Navy Comes Thru (RKO, 1942)
Where Are Your Children? (Monogram, 1943)
Stork Bites Man (UA, 1947)
Kilroy Was Here (Monogram, 1947)
French Leave (Monogram, 1948)
Everything's Ducky (Columbia, 1961)
The Love Machine (Columbia, 1971)
Chosen Survivors (Metromedia, 1973)

With Wallace Beery and Roscoe Ates in *The Champ* (1931)

James Craig

James Craig was a tall, athletic bulk of a man, who, when sporting a moustache, bore a striking resemblance to Clark Gable. He was not a very good actor and he possessed none of the Gable celluloid charisma and power. During his MGM tenure in the 1940s he played mostly in B pictures and Westerns. Unlike the more jocular vocalizer John Carroll, Craig was not used as a second-string Gable, not only because such a role for him would have been improbable, but also because it simply was not necessary. Metro did feature him in two good bits of wartime Americana, *The Human Comedy* (1943) and *Our Vines Have Tender Grapes* (1945) in which he projected the honorable virtues of the rural American male. In addition, on loanout to RKO he was notable as the New Hampshire farmer in *The Devil and Daniel Webster* (1941). More often he was just the likeable but forgettable male lead of undistinguished movie entertainment.

He was born John Henry Meador on February 4, 1912, in Nashville, Tennessee, where his father was a building contractor. The family moved frequently during his childhood, to Kansas, New York, Virginia, and Florida, but he graduated from high school in Nashville in 1929. He then hitchhiked to Houston, Texas where the 6' 2" natural athlete enrolled in Rice Institute as a premedical student and placed as an All-Southern end on Rice's football team. He gave up the idea of becoming a doctor because the regimen was too rough and instead took a job at the General Motors factory in Houston. On a vacation from the factory he went to Hollywood where the idea of acting as a profession appealed to him. "I was out there on a vacation and lookin' around and I saw a lot of people makin' a lot of money. If they can do it, why couldn't I?"

Craig says he decided to take a tour of MGM where he talked with talent scout Oliver Hinsdell. Craig asked Hinsdell if he thought he would photograph well and how could a guy with no training learn to act? Once Hinsdell decided he was not a crackpot, he recommended that Craig hire a diction teacher and do some work with a little theatre group. Craig returned to Houston and took Hinsdell's advice, and appeared in local productions of *Holiday* and *The Last Mile*. He changed his name to Craig after *Craig's Wife* because he thought Meador sounded like a bad word in Spanish. On his next

135

vacation he returned to Hollywood and again looked up Hinsdell, who by now was working at Paramount. "I walked in on a Monday afternoon to face this talent-scout array. I had nothing to lose so I wasn't afraid of them. I showed them my one newspaper clipping and my photograph. They said they liked me, and if I would stay around for six weeks and take some lessons in screen acting, they would give me a test. I said, 'Oh, no. I'm here on a two weeks' vacation from a good job. I'm not going to give up that job on a gamble. If you don't want me, I'm going around to other studios.'"

Paramount put him under contract, and among his four pictures in 1937 were a supporting part in Gertrude Michael's *Sophie Lang Goes West* and the lead in a minor Western *Thunder Trail*. He did not like this studio treatment and asked for straight dramatic roles. Paramount skirted the issue and Craig recalls he left Hollywood one night about eleven o'clock and headed for New York where Guthrie McClintic gave him a part in *Mississippi Legend*, starring McClintic's wife Katharine Cornell. A Columbia Pictures talent scout saw the play and offered Craig a term contract, and it was back to the movies.

Craig left *Mississippi Legend* after only three weeks of work, but all he was given at Columbia was a rash of small parts in programmer features and a supporting part in two studio serials, *Flying G-Men*, and *Overland with Kit Carson*, both released in 1939. Disillusioned again, he went to Universal, where he was put into some quickies, including *Zanzibar* (1940), which he says "wasn't good but wasn't bad because it at least played in Hollywood." Craig has also said that during these early years he tested for the part of Rhett Butler in *Gone with the Wind*. Since there was very little question about who would play Butler, his statement sounds like very imaginative publicity on his part. At any rate Craig says he did make some tests with some of the actresses who were vying for the role of Scarlett O'Hara.

Despite all this professional work, it was not until director Sam Wood brought Craig to RKO to play Dr. Mark Eisen in *Kitty Foyle* (1940) that he attracted any attention. In that picture he and Dennis Morgan vied for Ginger Rogers and Craig walked away with good notices. Then, RKO used him as the flinty New Hampshire farmer in *The Devil and Daniel Webster* (a remake of *All That Money Can Buy*) and gave him the lead in *Valley of the Sun* (1942), a weakly scripted Western that Joel McCrea wisely turned down. His costar was Lucille Ball.

At long last, MGM took notice of the handsome actor and signed Craig to a seven-year contract, using him as a general utility minor leading man to fill in the gap left by those performers on leave from MGM to serve in World War II. Metro put him into two Westerns, and then gave him the role of the telegraph office manager in *The Human Comedy*. He played the flier whom Jean Rogers almost stole from Ann Sothern in *Swing Shift Maisie* (1943) and the reporter in *Lost Angel* (1943). He competed with William Powell for Hedy Lamarr in *The Heavenly Body* (1943); was a credible, if wooden, Caliph opposite Marlene Dietrich in one of the better versions of *Kismet* (1944); got a

Gablelike role opposite Lana Turner in *Marriage Is a Private Affair* (1944); and played the newspaper man who loves the schoolmarm, Frances Gifford, in *Our Vines Have Tender Grapes* (1945). His roles in 1946 and 1947 were insignificant since all the MGM males were back in the fold after military service. Craig was loaned to Eagle–Lion, a favorite pasture ground for soon-to-be-ousted Metro players, for two Westerns. After playing the movie star who is murdered in *Side Street* (1949) and the laconic immigration officer in *A Lady Without Passport* (1950), he concluded his MGM contract with Mickey Rooney's *The Strip* (1951).

Craig never made it to a "star" category at MGM, and throughout the subsequent two decades appeared in numerous programmers and economy Westerns, where his physique and not his acting abilities were required. In one of these Westerns, *Fort Utah* (1967), he was part of a "stellar" cast that included John Ireland, Virginia Mayo, Scott Brady, John Russell, Robert Strauss, and Richard Arlen. Craig did a teleseries entitled *Hannibal Cobb* for a short time and made his last film appearances to date in Cinerama's *If He Hollers, Let Him Go* (1969) and the science fiction entries *Bigfoot* (1971) and *The Doomsday Machine* (1973). In 1970 he appeared unbilled in a television commercial.

If Craig's film career seems lacklustre, his marital entanglements were quite the opposite. His first wife was a nonprofessional, Mary Ray, whom he married in 1939. They had three children: James, Jr., Robert, and Diane. On April 19, 1948 Robert, then three years old, died of a kidney ailment. On September 26, 1950, Mary was found on the highway near their home, clothed in a nightgown and suffering lacerations and bruises from a "beating." She was picked up by a passing driver and admitted to the San Fernando Valley hospital after which Jerry Geisler, the famed lawyer, was called, and no assault charges were invoked. Craig stated that possibly she had run into a tree after running from their home following an argument. They were divorced in 1954. In 1959 he married blonde starlet Jill Jarmyn, who had made headlines four years earlier when she walked into the bedroom of actor Don "Red" Barry, and found actress Susan Hayward in pajamas. There was an argument and Hayward assaulted the starlet. Craig's marriage to Jarmyn was a series of separations, and they finally divorced in 1962. He married divorcee Jane Valentine on March 17, 1964, but they separated and were divorced less than a year later. On May 30, 1967, Miss Valentine was staying in an Oceanside, California motel where she shot her small son (by a previous marriage) four times, then shot herself. She left an ambiguous note for her parents saying she didn't want her son "to grow up and suffer her mistakes." The note made no mention of Craig.

Like many another veteran performer, his career has been resurrected by the television grist mill, with a featured role as an attorney in ABC's ninety-minute daytime drama *Courtroom One* for the 1972–1973 video season.

Sophie Lang Goes West (Paramount, 1937)
Thunder Trail (Paramount, 1937)
Born to the West (Paramount, 1937)
Pride of the West (Paramount, 1938)
The Big Broadcast of 1938 (Paramount, 1938)
The Buccaneer (Paramount, 1938)
Blondie Meets the Boss (Columbia, 1939)
Cafe Hostess (Columbia, 1939)
Good Girls go to Paris (Columbia, 1939)
The Lone Wolf Spy Hunt (Columbia, 1939)
Missing Daughters (Columbia, 1939)
North of Shanghai (Columbia, 1939)
Romance of the Redwoods (Columbia, 1939)
A Woman Is the Judge (Columbia, 1939)
Behind Prison Gates (Columbia, 1939)
Taming of the West (Columbia, 1939)
The Man They Could Not Hang (Columbia, 1939)
Flying G-Men (Serial: Columbia, 1939)
Overland with Kit Carson (Serial: Columbia, 1939)
House Across the Bay (UA, 1940)
Winners of the West (Serial: Universal, 1940)
Konga, the Wild Stallion (Columbia, 1940)
Scandal Sheet (Columbia, 1940)
Zanzibar (Universal, 1940)
South to Karanga (Universal, 1940)
I'm Nobody's Sweetheart Now (Universal, 1940)
Seven Sinners (Universal, 1940)
Law and Order (Universal, 1940)
Kitty Foyle (RKO, 1940)
The Devil and Daniel Webster (RKO, 1941)
Unexpected Uncle (RKO, 1941)
Valley of the Sun (RKO, 1942)
Friendly Enemies (UA, 1942)
The Omaha Trail (MGM, 1942)
Northwest Rangers (MGM, 1942)
Seven Miles from Alcatraz (RKO, 1942)

The Human Comedy (MGM, 1943)
Swing Shift Maisie (MGM, 1943)
Lost Angel (MGM, 1943)
The Heavenly Body (MGM, 1943)
Kismet (MGM, 1944)
Marriage Is a Private Affair (MGM, 1944)
Gentle Annie (MGM, 1944)
Our Vines Have Tender Grapes (MGM, 1945)
Dangerous Partners (MGM, 1945)
She Went to the Races (MGM, 1945)
Boys' Ranch (MGM, 1946)
Little Mr. Jim (MGM, 1946)
Dark Delusion (MGM, 1947)
The Man from Texas (Eagle–Lion, 1948)
Northwest Stampede (Eagle–Lion, 1948)
Side Street (MGM, 1949)
A Lady without Passport (MGM, 1950)
The Strip (MGM, 1951)
Drums in the Deep South (RKO, 1951)
Hurricane Smith (Paramount, 1952)
Code Two (MGM, 1953)
Fort Vengeance (AA, 1953)
While the City Sleeps (RKO, 1956)
Massacre (20th-Fox, 1956)
The Women of Pitcairn Island (20th-Fox, 1956)
Shootout at Medicine Bend (WB, 1957)
The Persuaders (AA, 1957)
Cyclops (AA, 1957)
Ghost Diver (20th-Fox, 1957)
Naked in the Sun (AA, 1957)
Man or Gun (Republic, 1958)
Four Fast Guns (Universal, 1959)
Hostile Guns (Paramount, 1967)
Fort Utah (Paramount, 1967)
The Devil's Brigade (UA, 1968)
Arizona Bushwhackers (Paramount, 1968)
If He Hollers, Let Him Go! (Cinerama, 1969)
Bigfoot (Ellman, 1971)
The Doomsday Machine (Cine-find, 1973)

With Margaret O'Brien in *Our Vines Have Tender Grapes* (1945)

Joan Crawford

Joan Crawford—Superstar! That face, those arched eyebrows, that red slash for a mouth, those high cheekbones, those wide shoulders and wider shoulderpads, that stare, that walk: That is a *Movie Star*! No other cinema actress, before or since, has succeeded in establishing *and* maintaining so definite an impression as a glamorous star. Through her willful and highly concerted total efforts, with exhaustless energy and ambition, Joan set out to become the best of the movie stars, never entertaining thoughts of failure. Now in the forty-eighth year of one of the longest careers in cinema history, she continues unabated, seemingly never glancing back, except for a well-calculated nostalgic look.

She has never forgotten that she was the first unknown to be discovered and groomed into major stardom by the newly formed Metro-Goldwyn-Mayer in 1925, and placed in their newly created heaven of stars. She remained with that studio for eighteen years. While never the biggest star on the lot, since there was always a Norma Shearer, a Luise Rainer, or a Greer Garson, Joan Crawford nevertheless, is considered synonomous with the MGM of yester-year. Although she won her long-awaited Oscar in her post-Metro days, in Warner Brothers' *Mildred Pierce* (1945), she still had made what some consider her best picture, the tearjerker *A Woman's Face* (1941) at MGM, the studio to which her name is inextricably linked.

From ingenue to flaming flapper, to shop girl, to bitch goddess, and now cinema star emeritus, Joan Crawford is still the supreme luminary. It is no revelation to those in Hollywood who have known her over the course of her career that she has had no particular trouble in pursuing the real life job of career woman as a spokeswoman of the Pepsi Cola Company. Joan always has been able to recognize what is salable and has known full well how to market it.

Lucille LeSueur was born in San Antonio, Texas on March 23, 1908. Her parents separated before she was born. Her mother remarried a man named Cassin, and Lucille grew up as Billie Cassin. Her stepfather was a vaudeville theatre manager and the Cassins moved to Lawton, Oklahoma, where the youngster saw the backstage side of theatre life and became an avid dancer. By 1915 her mother had divorced Cassin. She and her daughter lived

140

in a cheap Kansas City hotel, and little Billie worked in a laundry. The girl performed menial tasks in exchange for tuition to two schools, while always setting her sights on something higher. She spent a very brief period at Stephens College in Columbia, Missouri. She quit, got a department store job, and, through the encouragement of a boyfriend, began appearing in amateur contests in hopes of a show business career.

Joan was hired for one week in the Katharine Emerine revue in Kansas City. In 1923 she won an amateur dance contest and set out for a job as a Chicago chorus girl. From Chicago she moved to Detroit where she performed eight routines a night at the Oriole Terrace. J. J. Shubert spotted her and hired Joan for the chorus of the New York production of *Innocent Eyes* (1924), starring Mistinguette. Harry Rapf of MGM caught the show, saw her "third from the left in the back row" and gave Joan a screen test. On New Year's Day, 1925, sixteen-year-old Joan was on her way to Hollywood and the movies.

From the beginning of her Hollywood years, the ambitious Miss Crawford was totally committed to her new career. Her first work before the camera was doubling for Norma Shearer in *Lady of the Night* (1925). Under the name of Lucille LeSueur, she debuted as a chorine in *Pretty Ladies* (1925), which starred Zasu Pitts. By the time her second picture, *Old Clothes* (1925), was released, the studio had renamed her Joan Crawford as a result of a *Photoplay* magazine contest. "I hated it at first," Joan recalls. "It sounded like Crawfish. Then I came to love it." MGM put her into anything that came along and Joan eagerly accepted. She wanted to learn. "No matter how lousy the dialogue, I believed every word of it." Certainly at the time of *Sally, Irene and Mary* (1925) Joan was the only one who had the true insight into her own nature to know she would outlast her two costars, Constance Bennett and Sally O'Neil, in the fickle world of the movies. On one of her rare loanouts, Joan played the ingenue who inspires the admiration of hobo Harry Langdon in First National's *Tramp, Tramp, Tramp* (1926). In the Tim McCoy historical melodrama *Winners of the Wilderness* (1927) Joan was the French commandant's daughter in love with the dashing officer McCoy. Later that same year, Joan turned up as the circus sideshow performer who earns Lon Chaney's warped devotion in *The Unknown*. But it was *Our Dancing Daughters* (1928) that made Joan a cinema star.

She had read the script and begged producer Hunt Stromberg for the Clara Bowlike flapper role. She was given the assignment, in which, as she described it, "I was the flapper, wild on the surface, a girl who shakes her windblown bob and dances herself into a frenzy while the saxes shriek and the trombones wail, a girl drunk on her youth and vitality." This picture caused F. Scott Fitzgerald to cite Joan as the "best example of the flapper."

Joan made her talkie debut in the all-star *Hollywood Revue of 1929*, singing "Gotta Feeling For You," did the first tap dance audible in a feature film, and joined the other principals in the concluding number, "Singin' in the Rain." There was a followup to *Our Dancing Daughters* entitled *Our Modern*

Maidens (1930) which proved that Joan could be as contemporary 1930s style as she had been during the past decade. When Norma Shearer became pregnant, Joan fought to replace her as the shopgirl in *Paid* (1930). *Variety* reported "Histrionically she impresses us as about ready to stand up under any directorial assignment." The statement was somewhat of an exaggeration; she nonetheless gave her all to each role. She and Clark Gable sparkled as a team in *Dance, Fools, Dance* (1931). The following year she proved to be much more than a popular movie chorine, playing Flammchen the stenographer in *Grand Hotel*. Her role in this memorable production bore a striking resemblance to one facet of Joan's own personality: a perpetual awe of life's fineries. But unlike Joan, the Flammchen of *Grand Hotel* had second thoughts about the price one must pay for living the high life. By the time of this film, Joan was an established member of the studio hierarchy, although far behind the lot's prime stars, Norma Shearer and Greta Garbo.

Joan's two other 1932 releases did not prove as felicitous as *Grand Hotel*. No sooner had *Letty Lynton* been released than it was withdrawn due to a high-pressure copyright infringement suit, and even today it remains one of the few major Crawford vehicles unavailable for general screening. Joan had long been agog at the special status of Hollywood's reigning 1920s queen Gloria Swanson, and naturally jumped at the opportunity to re-create one of that star's most notable successes, Sadie Thompson in *Rain*, made on loanout to United Artists. Joan's performance pleased neither the critics nor her legions of fans. So Metro quickly thrust her back into her established mold: either as the glamorous socialite in *Today We Live* (1933), or as the hard-working shopgirl who rises to riches, but not always for love, as in *Sadie McKee* (1934). The Joseph L. Mankiewicz production of *The Gorgeous Hussy* (1936) gave her a bevy of male admirers (Robert Taylor, Franchot Tone, Melvyn Douglas, James Stewart) and period costumes by Adrian, but Joan as Peggy O'Neal, an innkeeper's daughter in the Washington, D. C. of the 1830s was no more convincing than the flabby script. *The Bride Wore Red* (1937) asked the audience once again to empathize with a beautiful cabaret dancer who must choose between romance with the well-to-do Robert Young or marriage to a Swiss postman, Franchot Tone. The formula had run its course and Joan was labeled boxoffice poison by some exhibitors.

MGM ignored the "poison" label and renewed her contract for five years at $1,500,000 for three pictures a year. *Mannequin* (1938) with Spencer Tracy was Joan's penultimate shopgirl role. Whether pushing her way through the morning subway crowd or peeling potatoes in her parents' tenement flat, no one before or since, including Gloria Swanson, has ever worked harder at being the glamorous, martyred proletarian. Equally specious but more outside the established Crawford genre was *The Shining Hour* (1938) in which Fay Bainter was a most effective villainess while Joan, Melvyn Douglas, Margaret Sullavan, and Robert Young pondered who belonged to whom and with whom. Then Metro carelessly tossed Joan into a piece of "trash," *The Ice Follies of 1939*. At this point Joan put her ankle-strapped shoes firmly on the

With Zasu Pitts in *Pretty Ladies* (1925)

With Lon Chaney in *The Unknown* (1927)

ground and demanded better scripts. Surprisingly, she got them! She was Crystal Allen, the predatory salesgirl, in *The Women* (1939) and willingly played second fiddle to Norma Shearer. (Joan once said she would play Wallace Beery's mother if it were a good part.) Joan later recalled that during the filming of *The Women*, "Norma Shearer made me change my costume sixteen times because every one was prettier than hers. I love to play bitches and she *helped* me in this part." *Strange Cargo* (1940) was her eighth and final costarring picture with Clark Gable. *A Woman's Face* (1941) under George Cukor's direction, had Joan as a horribly scarred criminal who seeks a better life after plastic surgery. Many consider this the best screen performance she ever gave.

By 1942 Norma Shearer and Greta Garbo had retired. It seemed natural for Joan, then age thirty-eight, to inherit the title of Queen of the Lot. But she was a demanding actress and Louis B. Mayer turned his attentions to a more pliable contestant, in the person of Greer Garson. After three more mediocre features on the home lot and a loanout to Columbia in 1942 (when Carole Lombard was killed in a plane crash, the ever-practical Joan was quick to put in her bid to replace the late star in *They All Kissed the Bride*), Joan asked out of her MGM contract and was released. At one time Mayer liked to brag that the millions of dollars earned from Joan's pictures had made it possible to build the Writers' Building on the Culver City Lot. But now, after eighteen years, the lady was leaving.

The day she left, she signed with Warner Brothers for two pictures at one-third her MGM salary. But Warners could not come up with suitable scripts for Joan, particularly when the prime properties automatically were offered to their own reigning dignitary, Bette Davis. After a brief cameo in *Hollywood Canteen* (1944) Joan was floundering at Warners. Producer Jerry Wald stepped into the breach and decided that she would be right for *Mildred Pierce*. Some studio powers thought the film was a perfect vehicle for contract star Ann Sheridan, and director Michael Curtiz wanted Barbara Stanwyck, fresh from her triumph in *Double Indemnity*. Curtiz allegedly screamed about Joan, "Her and her damned shoulder pads!" "But," Joan remembers, "when he broke down and cried watching my test scene, I knew he'd support me, and he did."

Mildred Pierce was the quintessence of what Joan Crawford wanted to be all about: the crafty businesswoman who retains her feminine frailties. The polished soap opera, along with its campaign of "Please don't tell what *Mildred Pierce* did," netted Joan her Oscar. Having emerged successfully into a new genre, Warner next cast her as the society patroness of violinist John Garfield in *Humoresque* (1946). This feature contains her most beautifully photographed poses, and her suicidal walk into the sea is one of filmdom's most memorable endings. She enjoyed playing opposite rebel John Garfield as much as she had with Gable and Spencer Tracy, but says, "unlike them, he was mixed up." The following year she had another good meaty role as the schizophrenic dame in *Possessed*. She received another Oscar nomination but lost out to another cinema tyro, Loretta Young, who won for *The Farmer's Daughter*.

It was yet again a new Joan who greeted moviegoers in *Flamingo Road* (1949), playing the tough carnival broad who marries politician David Brian for convenience and yet comes to love him, having undergone the salubrious pleasure of killing grafter Sydney Greenstreet in self-defense. This successful picture was followed with a string of new breed Crawford soap operas which asked, "not whether she will cross from the wrong side of the tracks to the right side, but *how* she will do it." Interspersed between her Warners' trilogy of castrating dames, was a remake of *Craig's Wife* gussied out in pseudo-1950s style as *Harriet Craig* (1950). One of Joan's most underrated performances was in Warners' *Goodbye, My Fancy* (1951). Not since her post-flapper period had Joan appeared so emotionally liberated onscreen, despite the watered-down script, but also greatly aided by her *Mildred Pierce* straight gal, Eve Arden.

After the carbon-copy *This Woman Is Dangerous* (1952), Joan left Warners and agreed to star in RKO's thriller, *Sudden Fear* (1952), in which she had a sizzling onscreen adversary in Jack Palance. She performed without salary, accepting a percentage of the profits, which turned out to be an advantageous deal for all concerned. When Joan heard that Metro was preparing *Torch Song* (1953), she set her sights on the role and refused to take no for an answer. If anyone had loved the notion that Joan had passed her prime in her ability to essay a dancing stage star, the veteran star proved them wrong. In her first on-camera dancing role since the 1930s, she kicked her taut limbs higher and harder than anyone her age had a right to do. *Torch Song* did not emerge the hit it could have been, but it assured audiences that Joan's glamor was still very much intact.

Joan's remaining 1950s vehicles were a series of bizarre encounters. The Western *Johnny Guitar* (1954), filmed in garish Republic Trucolor, offered saloon owner Joan pitted against crazed Mercedes McCambridge in one of the decade's strangest screen battles for supremacy. It made one wonder how Joan would have interpreted her *From Here to Eternity* assignment had she not walked off the project and been replaced by Deborah Kerr. *Autumn Leaves* (1956) was devoted to the dubious question of whether a woman past forty can find happiness with a younger man (Cliff Robertson) who just happens to be suffering from mental ills. Perhaps the peak moment of the disappointing *The Story of Esther Costello* (1957) occurs early in the feature when Joan makes her entrance stalking down a flight of stairs, revealing to the audience her still shapely gams encased in her trademark ankle strap shoes. Her final 1950s role was an "also-starring" job for Twentieth Century-Fox in *The Best of Everything* (1959), a Cinemascope confection which focused more on the younger cast members than on such veterans as Joan, Brian Aherne, and Martha Hyer. The picture revealed Joan with carrot-colored hair as Amanda Farrow, who relinquishes her executive post at a big Manhattan publishing outfit, only to learn that it is too late for her to find domestic bliss.

But most of Joan's energies from the mid-1950s onward were devoted to her role as the wife to Alfred N. Steele, Chairman of the Board of the Pepsi Cola Company, whom she had married in 1955. He was her fourth husband. She had married Douglas Fairbanks, Jr. in 1929, but they were divorced in 1933. That marriage brought the ex-chorus girl social acceptability from everyone except Fairbanks' stepmother, Mary Pickford. She next married Franchot Tone in 1935, but they divorced in 1939. This union introduced her to the world of books, artists, and music. Her third marriage was to a minor actor named Phillip Terry (1942–1946). Of this marriage Joan says, "I married because I was unutterably lonely. Don't ever marry because of loneliness. I've owed him an apology from the first." During her marriage to Steele, Joan traveled with him on his promotional tours for Pepsi Cola. He was quoted as saying, "I hate to use my wife to help me sell, but let's face it—she does. On these trips most of our business is done through top officials of governments. At those levels, Crawford is fabulous."

When Steele died of a heart attack in April 1959, Pepsi Cola named Joan their ambassadress, a position to which she brought all the business acumen of her Hollywood years. Since then she has become one of the most respected businesswomen in America.

In 1962 Joan and Bette Davis showed what two old-timers could do with a bit of Grand Guignol in *Whatever Happened to Baby Jane?* This boxoffice bonanza led each lady on to new careers in the 1960s. The next year Joan was in the horrific *Strait-Jacket* in which the script allowed her to emote as a maturely attractive if cheaply adorned mother of ax murderess Diane Baker. She and Davis were reunited in *Hush, Hush, Sweet Charlotte* (1964) but during production, Joan was hospitalized three times for pneumonia. When production could be held up no longer, she was replaced by Olivia de Havilland. Joan has said of her onscreen rival Davis, "I'm the quiet one and Bette's explosive. I have discipline. She doesn't. I don't know who suffers the most. Holding it in is an awful thing. Believe me, I know." Miss Davis would hardly agree that she is without discipline.

Since the mid-1960s, Joan's screen and television work has been in second-rate programs, but she rationalizes, "Inactivity is one of the great indignities of life. The need to work is always there, bugging me." No one can make a greater show or fanfare for doing what other performers take in their stride than Joan.

Joan has four adopted children: Christina, Christopher, and twins, Cathy and Cynthia. All are grown and married. She no longer speaks to her son, who has left his movie star family life far behind. Her relationship with her oldest daughter, actress Christina, was strained for years, but recently has been reconciled. Now a grandmother, Joan frankly declares, "I absolutely will not allow anybody to call me grandmother. They can call me Aunt Joan, Dee-Dee, Cho-Cho, or anything they want, but I hate the word grandmother. It pushes a woman almost into the grave."

Joan misses the glamorous days of MGM and says, "I think stars being glamorous ended, as an industry policy, when Louis B. Mayer was ousted from MGM. He has been much maligned. No matter how busy he was I could go to him if I had a problem. He was the kindest and gentlest person I have ever known." With equal emphasis, she says, "If you have an ounce of common sense and one good friend you don't need an analyst." And, "If you're going to be a star, you have to look like a star, and I never go out unless I look like Joan Crawford the movie star. If you want to see the girl next door, go next door."

Regarding her old movies being shown on television: "If you start watching the oldies, you're in trouble. I feel ancient if *Grand Hotel* or *The Bride Wore Red* comes on. I have a sneaking regard for *Mildred Pierce*, but the others do nothing for me." In the Spring of 1973, she was the guest of John Springer in his Legendary Ladies of the Movies series at Town Hall in New York City, and proved again her inimitable ability to be outspoken about her Hollywood. She was critical of the Academy Awards, saying everyone on the 1973 awards show seemed to have a case of the *cutes*. "The dignity and the beauty of the Academy Awards has been lost. I was appalled at the presenters' behavior and with Marlon Brando." She is saddened by the demise of Hollywood and the lack of roles for stars her age. "Today there are no jobs. I wish I were Duke Wayne. Everything that I have was all given to me by the motion picture industry. I was born in front of a camera. I don't know anything else."

Of her chosen life style, Joan says, "I don't know anyone who isn't lonely. You just learn to live with it. You don't dwell on it. That's the only way to handle it. I never look on the past. I live today to prepare for tomorrow."

JOAN CRAWFORD

Lady of the Night (MGM, 1925)	The Boob (MGM, 1926)
Proud Flesh (MGM, 1925)	Tramp, Tramp, Tramp (FN, 1926)
Pretty Ladies (MGM, 1925)	Paris (MGM, 1926)
Old Clothes (MGM, 1925)	The Taxi Dancer (MGM, 1927)
The Only Thing (MGM, 1925)	Winners of the Wilderness (MGM, 1927)
Sally, Irene and Mary (MGM, 1925)	The Understanding Heart (MGM, 1927)

In *I Live My Life* (1935)

With Orville Caldwell in *Mannequin* (1938)

With Margaret Sullavan in *The Shining Hour* (1938)

With Clark Gable in *Strange Cargo* (1940)

The Unknown (MGM, 1927)
Twelve Miles Out (MGM, 1927)
Spring Fever (MGM, 1927)
West Point (MGM, 1928)
Rose Marie (MGM, 1928)
Across to Singapore (MGM, 1928)
The Law of the Range (MGM, 1928)
Four Walls (MGM, 1928)
Our Dancing Daughters (MGM, 1928)
Dream of Love (MGM, 1928)
The Duke Steps Out (MGM, 1929)
Hollywood Revue of 1929 (MGM, 1929)
Our Modern Maidens (MGM, 1929)
Untamed (MGM, 1929)
Montana Moon (MGM, 1930)
Our Blushing Brides (MGM, 1930)
Paid (MGM, 1930)
Dance, Fools, Dance (MGM, 1931)

Laughing Sinners (MGM, 1931)
This Modern Age (MGM, 1931)
Possessed (MGM, 1931)
Grand Hotel (MGM, 1932)
Letty Lynton (MGM, 1932)
Rain (UA, 1932)
Today We Live (MGM, 1933)
Dancing Lady (MGM, 1933)
Sadie McKee (MGM, 1934)
Chained (MGM, 1934)
Forsaking All Others (MGM, 1934)
No More Ladies (MGM, 1935)
I Live My Life (MGM, 1935)
The Gorgeous Hussy (MGM, 1936)
Love on the Run (MGM, 1936)
The Last of Mrs. Cheyney (MGM, 1937)
The Bride Wore Red (MGM, 1937)
Mannequin (MGM, 1938)

With Ludwig Stossel, Fred MacMurray, and Lisa Golm in *Above Suspicion* (1943)

With Harry Morgan in *Torch Song* (1953)

Hume Cronyn

"To act, you must have a sense of truth and some degree of dedication," says character actor Hume Cronyn. Being rather short (5' 6") and plain-looking, Cronyn never had illusions of being a cinema leading man but hoped to follow in the path of the more star-conscious and showier Paul Muni. When Cronyn joined the MGM roster in the early 1940s he expected to exercise his penchant for portraying crotchety old men on one day's shooting and then handling light comedy assignments on the next. Such imaginative casting was antithetical to the studio's pigeonhole typing system and therefore he was rarely allowed to push his acting resources to their obvious potential. Most of his best screen work in the 1940s was done away from his contract employer, MGM.

Cronyn was born in London, Ontario on July 18, 1911, the youngest of his parents' five children. His great-grandfather was the first Bishop of Huron. As a youth he was sent to board at a Ottawa day school and then went to Bishop Ridley College, a Canadian preparatory school. By the age of ten he was already drawn to acting, putting on his own production of *The Green Goddess* for an audience composed of himself. ("It was pure living in a dream world, which was much richer, much gayer, and much more delightful than the world I really lived in.") Cronyn was in a prelaw course at McGill University when he became very ill, and, while recuperating, was introduced to the director of the National Theatre Stock Company in Washington. He joined this company at a salary of $15 weekly, and debuted as a newspaper boy in *Up Pops the Devil*. In 1932–1933 he studied at the American Academy of Dramatic Arts in New York, and made his Broadway bow in *Hipper's Holiday* (1934) as a janitor. For two seasons he toured in the lead role of Erwin in *Three Men on a Horse*, did a road company of *Boy Meets Girl*, and finally returned to Broadway in *Room Service* (1937), *High Tor* (1937), and *Three Sisters* (1939). From 1942–1943 he directed and appeared in U.S.O. camp shows, and then went to Hollywood with his English-born actress wife, Jessica Tandy, whom he married in 1942. Each had been previously married and together they had two children, Christopher and Tandy.

Cronyn made his film debut at Universal in Alfred Hitchcock's *Shadow of a Doubt* (1943) as the bespectacled Herbie Hawkins, the literal-minded

153

friend of Patricia Collinge's household. He is the armchair detective who thrives on pulp fiction and on his own snoops into everyone else's business. His comic touches were a great asset to the film. But then in the same studio's remake of *Phantom of the Opera* (1943) he was reduced to playing Gerard, assistant to police inspector Edgar Barrier of the Paris Sûreté. In his flunky's role Cronyn had fewer scenes and even fewer lines of dialogue.

Cronyn next joined MGM's stable, where he remained through 1947. In *The Cross of Lorraine* (1943) he breathed some life into this mawkish venture as the appeasing French soldier who collaborates with the Nazis. As Paul Roder, the German factory worker who finally realizes what the Third Reich is all about, in *The Seventh Cross* (1944), he won an Oscar nomination for best supporting player against stiff competition. He lost out to Barry Fitzgerald who won for *Going My Way*. Jessica Tandy played his onscreen wife in *The Seventh Cross*. His friend Hitchcock borrowed him to work in Twentieth Century-Fox's *Lifeboat* (1944) as the ship's radio operator who proposes to Mary Anderson.

He had been set by MGM for a role in Judy Garland's *The Clock* (1945), but the studio suddenly decided he would be more useful portraying Gregory Peck's brother in *Valley of Decision* (1945). Cronyn showed up on the Peck set, where director Tay Garnett speedily observed what the casting office had overlooked. Peck towered over Cronyn. So he was yanked from that film and Marshall Thompson substituted. Meanwhile, Keenan Wynn had been given his role in *The Clock*. But that year was not a loss as Cronyn did play in *A Letter for Evie* (1945), his first MGM comedy role. He was the timid soldier who sends Marsha Hunt the picture of his handsome buddy (John Carroll). *The Green Years* (1946) found him playing Jessica Tandy's father, Papa Leckie, and in *The Postman Always Rings Twice* (1946) he was the defense attorney. For *The Ziegfeld Follies* (1946), Fannie Brice repeated her popular vaudeville routine "The Sweepstakes Ticket" and Cronyn was effectively used as her henpecked husband.

His most memorable 1940s film role was done away from MGM at Universal, where he created the sadistic, high-voiced Captain Munsey in *Brute Force* (1947), a landmark of perversion and cruelty on the screen. If MGM had indulged in more realistic film fare in those days, Cronyn might have developed into a strong movie heavy. Instead, he ended his MGM contract with the featherweight *The Bride Goes Wild* (1948) as a frustrated publisher, but it was just a variation of his boss characterization in the earlier *The Sailor Takes a Wife* (1945), also with June Allyson. During his free time, Cronyn adapted both *Rope* (1948) and *Under Capricorn* (1949) for Hitchcock. The director later admitted: "I wanted him [Cronyn] because he's a very articulate man who knows how to voice his ideas. But as a scriptwriter he hadn't really sufficient experience."

Cronyn returned to Broadway to direct his wife in *Now I Lay Me Down to Sleep* (1949) but had better luck supervising *Hilda Crane* (1950), which also starred his wife. They appeared together on Broadway in *The Four Poster*

(1951), *A Day by the Sea* (1955), *The Man in the Dog Suit* (1958), and *Triple Play* (1958), gaining the reputation as the junior league Alfred Lunt–Lynn Fontanne acting duo.

He had first appeared on television in 1939 in *Her Master's Voice.* He and Tandy re-created their *The Four Poster* roles on a video special, in 1954 costarred in the comedy series *The Marriage,* and later were in Laurence Olivier's television production of *The Moon and Sixpence* (1959).

Cronyn has been an infrequent film performer in the past two decades. He played the small-minded physician whose jealousy starts the investigation in *People Will Talk* (1951), joined with Nancy Kelly in the New York-lensed *Crowded Paradise* (1956), and portrayed Franklin Delano Roosevelt's gruff friend and counselor, Louis Howe, in *Sunrise at Campobello* (1960). He was Sosigenes in *Cleopatra* (1963), and Polonius in the filmed version of Richard Burton's stage production *Hamlet* (1964), in which he had won a Tony Award for his stage role. In the mid-1960s he was active with Tyrone Guthrie's Minneapolis Theatre Company, but late in the decade returned to the screen for a trio of films, none of them, unfortunately, commercial successes. *Gaily, Gaily* (1969) found him as politican, "Honest" Tim Grogan. He was the attorney friend of Deborah Kerr in *The Arrangement* (1969) and offered a full-scale performance as the domesticated homosexual in the Western *There Was a Crooked Man* (1970).

Due to a recurring eye ailment, Cronyn underwent surgery for the removal of his left eye in 1970. He recovered sufficiently to tour later that year as Fr. William Rolfe in *Hadrian VII,* and more recently costarred with John Forsythe in the tour of *The Caine Mutiny Court-Martial,* with Henry Fonda directing. With the husband and wife team of Anne Jackson and Eli Wallach he starred briefly on Broadway in the multi-episode chronicle comedy, *Promenade, All!* (1972) with *The New York Times* approving his "wry charm." That fall he and his wife Jessica Tandy performed a month of repertory of Samuel Beckett plays at Lincoln Center. One of his rare recent television appearances was in a guest shot on *Hawaii Five-O* (1971) as an arch-criminal.

Once, when asked for the requirement most necessary for an active performer, he answered: "To go on being an actor, you need sheer animal energy. If you can't restock your energy, you have to hide your lack of it."

Shadow of a Doubt (Universal, 1943)
Phantom of the Opera (Universal, 1943)
The Cross of Lorraine (MGM, 1943)
The Seventh Cross (MGM, 1944)
Main Street after Dark (MGM, 1944)
Lifeboat (20th-Fox, 1944)
A Letter for Evie (MGM, 1945)
The Sailor Takes a Wife (MGM, 1945)
The Green Years (MGM, 1946)
The Postman Always Rings Twice (MGM, 1946)
The Ziegfeld Follies (MGM, 1946)
The Secret Heart (Voice only MGM, 1946)

The Beginning or The End (MGM, 1947)
Brute Force (Universal, 1947)
The Bride Goes Wild (MGM, 1948)
Top O' the Morning (Paramount, 1949)
People Will Talk (20th-Fox, 1951)
Crowded Paradise (Tudor, 1956)
Sunrise at Campobello (WB, 1960)
Cleopatra (20th-Fox, 1963)
Hamlet (WB, 1964)
Gaily, Gaily (UA, 1969)
The Arrangement (WB-7 Arts, 1969)
There Was a Crooked Man (WB, 1970)

With John Carroll in *A Letter for Evie* (1945)

Arlene Dahl

"With enthusiasm, anything is possible," claims Arlene Dahl, a pink and white screen beauty who has made a successful post-film career as a popular columnist on the art of beauty. She arrived at MGM in the retrenchment days of 1947 and from the start was utilized as pure adornment for middling studio products, including three lesser Red Skelton films. Dore Schary's Metro regime had only a skin-deep professional interest in Arlene: would her green eyes, red hair, and supple figure photograph well? (Louella Parsons wrote at the time: "The only two totally natural beauties in Hollywood who could step in front of the camera without one spot of makeup are Liz Taylor and Arlene Dahl.") No real attempt was made to sell Arlene to the public as a new this or a fresh that. She was just there. By the end of 1951 the last of her nine studio pictures had been released and she was "the" star of none of them. She had been a commodity used and then discarded.

Arlene Carol Dahl, of Norwegian heritage, was born in Minneapolis, Minnesota on August 11, 1924. She studied art in high school and had a part-time job as a junior copywriter at the local Dayton's Department Store. Occasionally she had a small role on a Minneapolis radio program. She briefly attended the University of Minnesota, dabbled in local drama groups, worked as an assistant to the loungewear buyer at Marshall Field and Company, and then as a model came to New York City where she eventually worked for the Walter Thornton agency. She had a part on Broadway in the quick-closing *Mr. Strauss Goes to Boston* (1945) and was in the pre-Broadway casualty *Questionable Ladies* (1946). Then there was a road tour and work in the chorus line of the Latin Quarter. ("I wore more on my head than they wear all over now.") A talent scout saw one of her magazine photos, brought her to the attention of Warner Brothers' director Curtis Bernhardt and she was brought to Hollywood. At Warners' she made a screen test in studio star Alexis Smith's *San Antonio* outfit and was signed to a $500 weekly contract. Studio mogul Jack Warner proclaimed: "You could be another Ann Sheridan." But Arlene was not that thrilled by her sudden brush with potential fame. As she later recalled: "I ended up in Hollywood where I never wanted to be in the first place, but I never considered those Hollywood years as anything but marking time. In my mind, it was an interim. In my heart I have always wanted nothing else but to be a musical comedy star."

In Warners' *Life with Father* (1947) she had a walkon as a girl at Delmonico's, but in the same studio's *My Wild Irish Rose* (1947), a sham-shamrock tale filmed in color, she was the title figure and the inspiration of ballad writer Chauncey Olcott (Dennis Morgan).

While Jack Warner was away in Europe on a business trip, Arlene's Warners' option came due. Meanwhile, Metro's Louis B. Mayer had seen *My Wild Irish Rose* and had his studio offer Arlene a contract. She quickly accepted. She was sixth-billed in *The Bride Goes Wild* (1948) as illustrator June Allyson's comely rival for the affection of children's book writer Van Johnson. Arlene proved one of Red Skelton's most attractive, if unsubtle, leading ladies as the Dixie girl who is attracted to bumbling Northern spy Skelton in *A Southern Yankee* (1948). She was loaned to Eagle–Lion to prettify a French Revolution costumer, *Reign of Terror* (1949), and then back at Metro as the wife of police detective Van Johnson in *Scene of the Crime* (1949). She continued being a mobile mannequin as the army general's blonde daughter in Robert Taylor's Western, *Ambush* (1949).

Arlene was Red Skelton's *vis-à-vis* in two 1950 releases. In *Three Little Words*, the musical biography of composers Bert Kalmar (Fred Astaire) and Harry Ruby (Skelton), Arlene was the girl who sings (including "I Love You So Much") her way into Skelton's heart. However, most of the film was centered on Astaire's dancing and his relationship with his screen wife (Vera-Ellen). In *Watch the Birdie*, a reworking of Buster Keaton's silent comedy *The Cameraman*, Skelton was a trouble-prone photographer and Arlene the wealthy lady who is involved with the dunce. *Watch the Birdie* proved to be one of the most abysmal of Skelton's comedies, with the comedian playing not only the lead but the character's onscreen father and grandfather. Near the end of the tale, while Skelton, Dahl, and the other principals were still conversing on important plot matter, the end title was suddenly flashed on the screen. Seemingly even MGM decided the picture was a lost cause and posthaste had dropped the curtain on the film.

Arlene was the dance hall hostess who matches schemes with card sharp David Brian in *Inside Straight* (1951), and her final Metro picture, *No Questions Asked* (1951), was ironically the only picture at that studio which gave any indication of what Arlene might have became on the screen. She was the calculating doll who walks out on her insurance attorney husband (Barry Sullivan), weds another, and then renegotiates love and plots a fraud scheme with Sullivan.

For a spell in the mid-1950s, in between hostessing television's *Pepsi Cola Playhouse*, Arlene was used as a substitute for such performers as Rhonda Fleming, Patricia Medina, or Yvonne De Carlo in such empty low-priced adventure pictures as John Payne's *Caribbean* (1952), Alan Ladd's *Desert Legion* (1953), Fernando Lamas' *Sangaree* and *The Diamond Queen* (both 1953), and Rock Hudson's *Bengal Brigade* (1954). She posed as the vain beauty who disgusts her husband Van Heflin in *Woman's World* (1954), and was a stately fixture in the Jules Verne entry *Journey to the Center of the Earth* (1959). But sandwiched in between these vapid assignments were a trio of bad girl parts that contained her best screen work. In RKO's *Slightly Scarlet* (1956) she revealed unusual dimension as the mentally unbalanced sister of Rhonda Fleming. In *Wicked as They Come* (1957) she played the scheming vixen who craves an unobtainable Philip Carey. Finally, in another British-made film, *She Played with Fire* (1958), she was an arsonist who leads insurance investigator Jack Hawkins down the wrong path.

In 1951 Arlene wed Tarzan actor Lex Barker, but they were divorced in 1952. She married Fernando Lamas in 1954, had a son Lorenzo in 1958 and was again divorced in 1960. She married Texas oil tycoon Christian R. Holmes III in 1960, had a daughter Carol in 1961 and, repeating a pattern already set, divorced him in 1964. The next year she married business executive Alexis Lichine but they also were divorced in 1969. That same year she wed industrialist Rounsevelle W. Schaum, who later became a television executive. A son was born in December 1970.

It was in 1952 that Arlene launched Arlene Dahl Enterprises in order to distribute her own line of lingerie and nightwear. In addition, she frequently modeled the merchandise at trade shows. A few years later she commenced writing a syndicated beauty column, which is still active. And in 1963 her first book, *Always Ask a Man*, appeared, followed shortly by a series of twelve Beautyscope-Zodiac paperback beauty care books. In 1967 she became a vice president of Kenyon and Eckhardt, heading the agency's Woman's World division which advised companies marketing female products.

Arlene sporadically returned to show business in the 1960s. She made her Las Vegas club debut in 1962 and in 1964 worked for director Curtis Bernhardt again, appropriately cast as the glamorous head of a cosmetic company in the movie *Kisses for my President*. Arlene frequently appears on television talk shows to discuss feminine beauty care, a subject still popular despite the onslaught of woman's liberation.

In May 1972 Arlene returned to Broadway to replace Anne Baxter in *Applause!*, her first main stem assignment since playing Roxanne to José Ferrer's *Cyrano De Bergerac* in 1952. In the intervening years she has also starred in such summer stock musicals as *I Married an Angel, One Touch of Venus*, and *The King and I. Applause!* lasted only a few weeks once Arlene assumed the part of Margo Channing, but she seemingly enjoyed the brief Broadway fling. Thereafter, Arlene began preparations for good will trips to Moscow to teach Russian women how to use makeup, with a packaged demonstration show titled *Beauty Happening*. President Nixon's State Department is planning to send Arlene to other Communist countries, including Yugoslavia, Albania and Rumania.

Arlene once told Louella Parsons about her complicated workday schedule: "It's like walking a tightrope carrying a heavy load. You have to find out how much weight you can carry without falling."

With Red Skelton in *Watch the Birdie* (1950)

ARLENE DAHL

Life with Father (WB, 1947)
My Wild Irish Rose (WB, 1947)
The Bride Goes Wild (MGM, 1948)
A Southern Yankee (MGM, 1948)
Reign of Terror (Eagle–Lion, 1949)
Scene of the Crime (MGM, 1949)
Ambush (MGM, 1949)
The Outriders (MGM, 1950)
Three Little Words (MGM, 1950)
Watch the Birdie (MGM, 1950)
Inside Straight (MGM, 1951)
No Questions Asked (MGM, 1951)
Caribbean (Paramount, 1952)
Jamaica Run (Paramount, 1953)

Desert Legion (Universal, 1953)
Sangaree (Paramount, 1953)
The Diamond Queen (WB, 1953)
Here Come the Girls (Paramount, 1953)
Woman's World (20th-Fox, 1954)
Bengal Brigade (Universal, 1954)
Slightly Scarlet (RKO, 1956)
Wicked as They Come (Columbia, 1957)
She Played with Fire (Columbia, 1958)
Journey to the Center of the Earth (20th-Fox, 1959)
Kisses for My President (WB, 1964)
The Land Raiders (Columbia, 1969)

Marion Davies

From the deluge of screen star biographies and memoirs that have poured out of Hollywood in the last two decades, it is sometimes difficult to separate fact from fiction. But one fact that all of these biographies substantiate is that Marion Davies was one of the most beloved of stars. This charming little blonde evoked a whole thesaurus of admiring adjectives: warm, witty, generous, fun-loving, beautiful, spunky, personable, giddy, saucy, vivacious, joyous, and sentimental. Even the egomanical Charles Chaplin, in his fatuous autobiography, said "To my surprise, she was quite a comedienne, with charm and appeal and would have been a star in her own right without the cyclonic Hearst publicity."

Countervailing this verisimilitude is the fact that, as the mistress of the elephantine William Randolph Hearst for some thirty-odd years, Marion was the butt of multitudinous Hollywood jokes resulting from the preposterous amount of publicity about her carried in the Hearst newspapers. Hearst had decreed that a day should not pass without some mention of the actress in his chain of newspapers and much of that prose came from the pen of Louella O. Parsons, Hearst's powerful and loyal movie columnist. Recently in a biting satire of Parsons, female impersonator T. C. Jones has built a sequence describing Hollywood's social milieu around the phrase, "And Marion never looked lovelier!" Ironically, that phrase, a perennial Hollywood joke, was *actually* created by Louella herself in her October 10, 1924 column when, in reviewing one of Marion's many costume potboilers, *Yolande*, she said, "Marion Davies, in costumes of the English period, has never looked lovelier." That joke was amusing as most of them were, and Marion herself could have enjoyed laughing over it, but other "jokes" were not as harmless. One of the most malicious was a poem, usually attributed to Dorothy Parker: "Upon my honor,/ I saw a Madonna,/ Standing in a niche,/Above the door,/Of a prominent whore,/Of a prominent son of a bitch." This doggerel was composed in reference to a Madonna over the front door of Irish Marion's fourteen-room "bungalow" on the MGM lot in Culver City.

The most notorious of the Marion Davies "jokes" was of course, the character of Susan Alexander in Orson Welles' *Citizen Kane* (1941), as the no-talent mistress of newspaper baron Charles Foster Kane, Susan is pushed into an operatic career which is unequivocably beyond her abilities. The similarities between her and Marion are obvious as they are, in part, to the career of Hope "Hopeless" Hampton, first mistress to, and later wife of, Eastman Kodak executive Jules Brulator. The fact is that Marion was *not* a no-talent actress. She was indeed a delightful mimic and vivacious comedienne, and if her singing and dancing were not topnotch, she was far better than many another cinema favorite who deemed it necessary to become part of the musical talking film craze of the late 1920s. But Hearst saw her only in a fantasy of romanticism and female dignity, and he built her career around a series of ridiculous costume dramas, thwarting her talents as a comedienne. Marion, who loved "Pops" and did not give a damn about her career most of the time, usually acquiesced.

Half of Marion's twenty years in motion pictures were spent under the aegis of MGM (1925–1934), but she was never really a part of that studio. She was just part of a business arrangement between Hearst and Louis B. Mayer. A list of Marion's screen credits places her in a very small niche in film history, but her life style and the manner in which her career was conducted makes her an important part of Hollywood folklore and the MGM story.

Marion Cecilie Douras was born in Brooklyn on January 3, 1897, the youngest of four daughters born to Bernard and Rose Douras. Mr. Douras, an attorney, was a small-time politician. Marion was educated in local parochial schools and later at the Convent of the Sacred Heart in Hastings, New York, where she participated in a production of *Twelfth Night*. Marion's sister Reine had wed producer George W. Lederer, and he was the influential show business figure who got Marion a chorus girl post in *The Sunshine Girl* (1913), followed by a similar job in *The Queen of the Movies* and *Chin-Chin*, both produced in 1914. Years later Marion would recall of the latter musical: "I was one of 500 chorus girls, more or less. We had to stick our heads through holes in the backdrop; we were supposed to be flowers. I was on the top tier. All went well until the framework I was standing on crashed down on the girl below; she had to go to the hospital. It left me chinning myself on the backdrop. I hung there until rescued, a most unhappy-looking blossom."

In Jerome Kern's *Nobody's Home* (1915) Marion first received billing as "Marion Davis," the progenitor of her final professional name. Then came *Miss Information* and *Stop, Look and Listen*, and Florenz Ziegfeld put her in his *Ziegfeld Follies of 1916*. At this time she also returned to her career as a fashion model, posing for such well-known commercial artists as James Montgomery Flagg and Howard Chandler Christy.

William Randolph Hearst, thirty-four years Marion's senior, supposedly first saw the young blonde hoofer in the *Follies* (1916), although Hedda Hopper maintains it was in the chorus of *Queen of the Movies* at the Globe Theatre in 1914. He was so stricken with her bouncyness that he attended every evening performance for eight weeks, purchasing two tickets, one for himself and one for his hat.

Hearst, the perennial collectomaniac with a high-pitched voice, made his intentions known from the beginning, and Marion with her catchy stutter soon became his *objet d'art supreme.* Marion had made her debut for her brother-in-law George Lederer in *Runaway Romany* (1917), filmed on location in Florida. But it was Hearst who decided that she would become a bigger star than even Mary Pickford. She moved into an apartment at the Beaux Arts Building on Sixth Avenue and Hearst purchased Sulzer's Harlem River Park Casino on Second Avenue and 127th Street. He turned it into a movie studio. Their first joint venture was *Cecilia of the Pink Roses* (1918), a title which aptly describes Heart's idolization. The picture premiered in New York in June 1918 and the Hearst press heralded Marion Davies as a "triumph" saying, "Only a marble heart could have withstood the charming Marion Davies." Hearst arranged with Adolph Zukor to release Marion's Cosmopolitan pictures through Paramount. Pickford had already left that studio to form United Artists. He made a string of dull epics enlivened only by Marion's personal charm, and they were all so lavishly produced they could not earn back their investments. (Everyone but the motion picture exhibitors loved Marion. They had to show her pictures.)

In 1922, one of her films, *When Knighthood Was in Flower*, did make money despite the $1.5 million production cost. Marion was Mary Tudor, wife of Louis XII of France, and Victor Herbert composed "The Marion Davies March" to be played in theatres showing the picture. The Hearst press proclaimed her trumph in such phrases as, "Marion Davies in Greatest Role of Career" and "Marion Davies Soars to New Heights." Even New York mayor John F. Hylan, a Hearst political puppet, got into the act by stating, "No person can afford to miss this great screen masterpiece." Louella Parsons, the motion picture editor of the N. Y. *Morning Telegraph* (not a Hearst paper) had already interviewed Marion three years earlier and found her to be "naive and unspoiled." In reviewing *Knighthood,* she complimented Marion but took Hearst to task for his lavish expenditure. Hearst found this amusing and asked Marion to introduce him to the woman, and on November 19, 1923, Parsons went to work for Hearst at $250 weekly as motion picture editor of his N. Y. *American.*

The following year, Hearst had the Cosmopolitan Theatre in New York refurbished at the cost of $225,000 for the premiere of Marion's *Little Old New York* (1923), hired Victor Herbert's orchestra to provide the music and handed out programs with gilt covers to his first-night audience. According to W. A. Swanberg, Hearst's biographer, when the gilt came off on the gowns of the ladies, the theatre management made an announcement that it would pay for the dry cleaning bills. That evening Hearst's newspaper screamed: "Marion Davies' Greatest Film Opens Tonight," and Mayor Hylan, in the act again, said, "Marion Davies is the most versatile screen star ever cast in any part."

Little Old New York was released through Samuel Goldwyn's distributing facilities, and the next year when Metro-Goldwyn was formed, Hearst began releasing Marion's pictures through the new outfit, while his press kept her name constantly in front of the public. When *Janice Meredith* opened in

1924, Louella Parsons regretted that the author, Paul Leicester Ford, "could not have lived to see Marion Davies play his character."

Late in 1924, Hearst, wanting to move his movie interests to the West Coast became involved in one of Hollywood's most talked about scandals: the mysterious death of Thomas H. Ince, a prominent independent producer. Hearst and Ince were about to culminate a deal whereby Ince would produce Marion's pictures. A weekend party was held aboard Hearst's 280-foot yacht, the *Oneida*. The party included Hearst, Marion, Charles Chaplin, and Elinor Glyn. On Sunday evening, November 16th, at a celebration honoring Ince's 43rd birthday, Ince was stricken with "acute indigestion." The next morning he was removed from the yacht, put under the care of two physicians, and on Tuesday, November 19th, died. The cause of death was listed as "angina pectoris" and Ince was cremated after a private funeral on November 21st. Supposedly the mystery over *how* Ince died was created by rival Los Angeles newspapers and the versions of what happened are varied: (1) that Hearst discovered Ince and Marion in *flagrante delicto* and shot Ince: (2) that Hearst discovered Charles Chaplin and Marion in *flagrante delicto*, and while a group of guests gathered, Hearst shot, missing Chaplin and hitting Ince. In both instances, Louella Parsons was allegedly a witness to the shooting and thus her job with Hearst was insured. The fact is, Parsons was writing her column from New York and did not arrive in Hollywood until the following May.

Following the Ince episode Hearst contracted with Louis B. Mayer to have the new MGM produce Marion's pictures, pay her a $10,000 weekly salary, and share in the profits of her films with him. Mayer, of course, knew that Marion's films rarely made money, but one unwritten dividend of the agreement was that Hearst's powerful press would be aligned with the studio, and Mayer jumped at the chance. Indeed, Marion's pictures at MGM were not moneymakers, but her regal bungalow became the center of the studio's social life, with a parade of notable visitors including Winston Churchill and George Bernard Shaw. The bungalow was only a prelude to the "social" life Hearst and Marion would bring to Hollywood. An invitation to Hearst's fabled San Simeon in San Luis Obispo County was already coveted, while Marion's presence made it more fun. (Everything was more staid when Hearst's wife was in residence. Millicent Willson, a former showgirl, wed Hearst in 1903 and bore him five sons. She refused to grant him a divorce no matter what offer he made. Marion's one regret in life was never having been able to marry Hearst.)

In addition to her bungalow, Hearst built Marion a beach house at Santa Monica at a cost of $7 million. The house consisted of 118 rooms and 55 baths. The furnishings included twelve full-length oil portraits showing Marion in various cinema roles. Ordinary film folk referred to the beach house as the Versailles of Hollywood. Marion's parties at the beach house were livelier than usual when Hearst wasn't around. After one such evening, attended by Louella Parsons, Marion stuttered: "If W. R. hears about this, one of us is going to lose his job, an-an-and it won't be me."

164

Marion's film career was a secondary factor in her busy life. Had she been able to marry Hearst, she would probably have retired from the cinema. But Hearst took her career very seriously and the "romantic" films rolled out of MGM. Of her silent films there were two good comedies. *The Patsy* (1928) had her play a flapper and mimic Lillian Gish, Pola Negri, and Mae Murray; and *Show People* (1928), loosely based on Gloria Swanson's film career, told the story of the rise of an actress from slapstick queen to femme fatale. Both were very ably directed by King Vidor. In the latter entry, Hearst refused to have Marion hit in the face with a custard pie. He thought it undignified and had a stream of seltzer water substituted. He wanted Marion to play nothing "sordid" in her pictures and refused to allow her to play Sadie Thompson. Gloria Swanson did so and received an Academy Award nomination.

It had originally been decided to have Marion make her starring sound film debut in a screen version of the Broadway musical, *The Five O'Clock Girl*. After a few weeks of production in January 1929, the project directed by Alfred E. Green and featuring Marion, Charles King, Aileen Pringle, Polly Moran, and Joel McCrea was abandoned. Instead, Marion appeared as a World War I French farm girl in *Marianne* (1929), singing, dancing, mimicking Maurice Chevalier and Sarah Bernhardt and falling for the rough charms of doughboy Lawrence Gray. Marion had already appeared in the studio's allstar talkie pastiche, *The Hollywood Revue of 1929*, singing and dancing to the song "Oh What a Man, What a Man." Hearst had had her coached carefully to keep her from stuttering and Marion recalled: "Somebody told me I should put a pebble in my mouth to cure my stuttering. Well, I tried it, and during a scene I swallowed the pebble. That was the end of that."

Marion completed a musical version of *Rosalie* in mid-1930, but it was shelved by MGM. Instead the public was "treated" to a new rendition of *Dulcy*, now entitled *Not So Dumb* (1930), and *The Floradora Girl* (1930), which reteamed her with Lawrence Gray. Marion would have much preferred doing broad comedy, but Hearst insisted that she should play romantic, dramatic heroines. Even Irving Thalberg's urging that she be allowed to do what she did best—(comedy)—was ignored by Hearst. Finally in 1934, after the stagnant Civil War spy yarn *Operator 13* which matched her with Gary Cooper, the break with MGM came. Hearst had set his sights on *The Barretts of Wimpole Street* as a perfect vehicle for Marion. However, Thalberg had that dramatic plum reserved for his own consort, Norma Shearer, and Mayer sided with him. Undaunted, Hearst then chose *Marie Antoinette* as a showcase for Marion. This time Marion was convinced she wanted the assignment. But Thalberg also had that part in his plans for Norma, Another impasse. Finally, Mayer told Hearst he could have *Marie Antoinette* if he would pay the entire production cost. Hearst declined and moved Marion and the bungalow to Warner Brothers.

Marion and Shearer had always been good friends. She was one of Shearer's bridesmaids at the 1927 wedding to Thalberg. But after her MGM departure, Hearst forbade the name of Shearer to appear in his newspapers.

Marion did four pictures at Warner Brothers and Jack Warner says they made money, Years later, Dick Powell, who played Napoleon Bonaparte's younger brother who woos Dixie American Marion in the costume musical *Hearts Divided* (1936), would recount his experiences on the set of a Marion Davies picture. He recalled that Hearst would not allow Marion to perform unless he was on the set. Usually the great man would be accompanied by three bulky associates, who said nothing but looked about with great intentness. "The love scenes," Powell remembered, "were sheer torture. If I didn't make them look real, the director would never use me again. If I made them too real, I was sure I was going to get a bullet in the back. Marion was doing her part in the long kissing closeups, but I was damn near choking to death. That picture lasted ten weeks, and I thought I'd die before I got out. I was still shaking months afterwards."

By 1937 Hearst's empire was beginning to crumble and Marion at age forty retired from the cinema. Her last performance was in a dramatization of *The Brat* on *Lux Radio Theatre* in July 1936. Over the years there would be rumors of "comebacks," such as the mother's role in *Claudia*, but nothing transpired. In 1945 Marion sold her beach house for $600,000 and purchased a home on North Beverly Drive for $200,000. One Hollywood wag at the time suggested an appropriate newspaper headline for the event would be: "Marion Davies closes Beach House. Thousands homeless!" Marion and Hearst moved into the Beverly Hills mansion with the twelve portraits. At one point, when Hearst was in financial difficulties, she loaned him $1 million. On August 14, 1951 Hearst died at the age of eighty-eight. Marion, who had drowned her sorrow in alcohol, was sleeping under sedation when the family had his body removed from the house. When she awakened, she said, "I asked where he was and the nurse said he was dead. His body was gone, whoosh, like that. Old W. R. was gone, the boys [Hearst's sons] were gone. I was alone. Do you realize what they did? They stole a possession of mine. He belonged to me. I loved him for thirty-two years and now he was gone. I couldn't even say goodbye." She was not invited to the funeral nor was she mentioned in the will, since she had been provided for separately, but his death did leave her in voting control of the Hearst organization. After lengthy meetings with the family and the lawyers, Marion agreed to relinquish her voting rights and serve as an advisor only at the salary of $1 per year. Thus Hearst finally disappeared from her life.

The same year, on October 31st, Marion eloped to Las Vegas with a former naval officer and ex-stuntman, Captain Horace Brown. As Hearst-owned L. A. *Examiner* noted, "It was Miss Davies' first marriage." Marion's name was now out of the papers, she lived her last years in solitude, and the public simply forgot her. On January 9, 1960, Hedda Hopper presented a one-hour television special *Hedda Hopper's Hollywood*, and one of the guests was Marion Davies. (After her film retirement, Marion saw little of Louella Parsons. At one social gathering in 1948, a drunken Marion greeted the "revered" columnist with: "Hello, Louella, you old shit.")

On September 22, 1961, Marion died at age sixty-four, leaving an estate of eight million dollars. Perhaps Mary Astor, who worked with Marion in Warner Brothers' *Page Miss Glory* (1935), summed up the off-screen Marion best: "She was not sharp and inquisitive, nor was she a dumb blonde. She was bright and funny. Her warmth and kindness could have taught many of us a great deal about the art of loving."

MARION DAVIES

In *Little Old New York* (1923)

Runaway Romany (Pathé, 1917)
Cecilia of the Pink Roses (Select, 1918)
The Burden of Proof (Select, 1918)
The Belle of New York (Select, 1919)
Getting Mary Married (Select, 1919)
The Dark Star (Paramount, 1919)
Cinema Murder (Paramount, 1920)
April Folly (Paramount, 1920)
Restless Sex (Paramount, 1920)
Buried Treasure (Paramount, 1921)
Enchantment (Paramount, 1921)
The Bride's Play (Paramount, 1921)
Beauty's Worth (Paramount, 1922)
The Young Diana (Paramount, 1922)
When Knighthood Was in Flower (Paramount, 1922)
Adam and Eva (Paramount, 1923)
Little Old New York (Goldwyn, 1923)
Yolande (Metro-Goldwyn, 1924)

Janice Meredith (Metro-Goldwyn, 1924)
Zander the Great (Metro-Goldwyn, 1925)
Lights of Old Broadway (Metro-Goldwyn, 1925)
Beverly of Graustark (MGM, 1926)
The Red Mill (MGM, 1927)
Tillie the Toiler (MGM, 1927)
The Fair Co-ed (MGM, 1927)
Quality Street (MGM, 1927)
The Patsy (MGM, 1928)
The Cardboard Lover (MGM, 1928)
Show People (MGM, 1928)
The Hollywood Revue of 1929 (MGM, 1929)
Marianne (MGM, 1929)
Not So Dumb (MGM, 1930)
Floradora Girl (MGM, 1930)
Bachelor Father (MGM, 1931)
It's a Wise Child (MGM, 1931)
Five and Ten (MGM, 1931)
Polly of the Circus (MGM, 1932)
Blondie of the Follies (MGM, 1932)
Peg O'My Heart (MGM, 1933)
Going Hollywood (MGM, 1933)

Operator 13 (MGM, 1934)
Page Miss Glory (WB, 1935)
Hearts Divided (WB, 1936)

Cain and Mabel (WB, 1936)
Ever Since Eve (WB, 1937)

In *The Red Mill* (1927)

With Lester Vail in *It's a Wise Child* (1931)

With Onslow Stevens in *Peg O' My Heart* (1933)

Laraine Day

Laraine Day is best known to movie audiences for her sympathetic portrayal of dedicated nurse Mary Lamont, the fiancée of Lew Ayres in the *Dr. Kildare* series. Laraine played the Blair General Hospital nurse in seven episodes of the series. When her part was finally written out of the series, the script writers did so by having her fatally hit by a truck. The picture was melodramatically entitled *Dr. Kildare's Wedding Day* (1941), and MGM was inundated with letters from a grieving public. Laraine's second claim to fame was for having been the "First Lady of Baseball," a title she earned by her marriage to Leo Durocher, the manager of the New York Giants, and her resultant interest in America's national sport.

She was born LaRaine Johnson in Roosevelt, Utah on October 13, 1919, of a family of Mormons. Her grandfather had been a Brigham Young elder and the father of fifty-two children. LaRaine was one of eight children, twin to a brother, Lamar. The Johnsons moved to Long Beach, California in 1931, where Laraine attended George Washington Junior High and Poly-technic High Schools. Laraine had been star-struck ever since seeing her first movie at age six, and she eagerly joined the Long Beach Players among whose members was a yet undiscovered Robert Mitchum. Laraine appeared in several plays there and adopted "Day" as her professional name in honor of the playhouse manager, Elias Day.

Talent scout Marty Martyn took Laraine to the Goldwyn Studios where she was cast as the girl on a stool at a soda fountain in *Stella Dallas* (1937). She had all of four lines to say. Her option was dropped six months later because she "lacked talent." Nevertheless, RKO used her in several Westerns. Then MGM's assistant casting director, Billy Gordon, who had seen her at the Long Beach Players, had her audition at Metro for the role of Wallace Beery's "daughter" in *Sergeant Madden* (1939). In that programmer she projected a warm personality as the Irish lass who is adopted by policeman Beery. She had a small role in a picture called *I Take This Woman*, but because of script and cast changes, it was not released until 1940. Laraine and Richard Denning were briefly seen as a British couple who are killed in a plane crash in Africa, with their young son (Johnny Sheffield) being adopted by Johnny Weissmuller and Maureen O'Sullivan in *Tarzan Finds A Son!* (1939). Then

171

came her casting as Mary Lamont in *Calling Dr. Kildare* (1939). The public liked her well enough for MGM to keep her in the series for six more pictures.

Laraine's work in the Kildare series so typed her that MGM failed to consider her for anything else, much to her chagrin. "They never really wanted me for anything. I was always the one who happened to be free when their first choice was not." MGM did loan her to United Artists for the role of the tragic Maeve, the girl suicide, in *My Son, My Son* (1940) when Frances Dee collapsed on the set during the first week's shooting. One fan magazine at the time touted Laraine as an "Oscar Menace" for her sensitive performance as the actress in *My Son, My Son,* but no Academy Award nomination was forthcoming. Back at MGM she had the lead in the remake of *The Trial of Mary Dugan* (1941), playing an innocent girl accused of murder and saved from false prosecution by clever lawyer Robert Young. That same year she was written out of the Kildare series so newer MGM contractees such as Ann Ayars and Donna Reed could be showcased opposite Ayres. Nevertheless, Laraine and Ayres were reunited for the mild whodunit, *Fingers at the Window* (1942). She gave a moving performance as the young matron suffering from emotional shock in *Journey for Margaret* (1942), but moppet Margaret O'Brien was the real focal point of that weeper. On loan to RKO Laraine played her favorite role, the sophisticated Park Avenue socialite opposite Cary Grant in *Mr. Lucky* (1943). Cecil B. De Mille and Paramount borrowed her to portray a nurse in *The Story of Dr. Wassell* (1944), which, if not viable drama, at least provided Laraine with the most prestigious assignment of her movie career.

RKO borrowed Laraine again to star with Robert Young in a mild sudser called *Those Endearing Young Charms* (1945). MGM brought her back home to play a WAC in *Keep Your Powder Dry* (1945). After making this meandering Lana Turner vehicle, Laraine requested her contract release, and economy-bent MGM obliged in May 1946. Returning to RKO, Laraine was not very effective as the jewel-snatching psychopath who drives artist Robert Mitchum to suicide in *The Locket* (1946), but the fault was more the script writers' than her emoting. She was better as the wealthy, half-Spanish daughter of Sir Cedric Hardwicke who falls in love with engineer John Wayne in *Tycoon* (1947).

Good roles or bad, it was suddenly no longer important, for Laraine, through her marriage to Leo Durocher, the gregarious manager of the New York Giants, had found a new interest, baseball. Laraine had been married before to former dance band singer James Ray Hendricks. She and Hendricks had married on May 16, 1942, and they adopted three children: Angela, Michele, and Christopher. They were divorced in 1947, and she flew to El Paso to marry Durocher on January 21, 1947. Durocher, or Leo the Lip as he often was called, was one of the most colorful personalities of baseball and was fifteen years older than Laraine, now his third wife. Laraine said: "I had to learn about baseball." She learned so much about the sport and took so much interest in it that she was able to conduct knowledgeably a radio show on which she talked with famous baseball players. This show led to a half-hour variety show on ABC television in 1957, *The Laraine Day Show*, and a fifteen-minute evening television spot which evolved around sports figures and was called *Daydreaming with Laraine*. In 1952 she wrote a book called *Day with the Giants*, and in 1953 she and her husband appeared in a television sports series, *Double Play with Durocher and Day*. She said at the time with all the dedication she had earned as nurse Mary Lamont of the Dr. Kildare series: "My life is Mrs. Leo Durocher and baseball comes first."

Laraine did appear in a few motion pictures right after she and Durocher were married, including the offbeat red-baiting RKO production *I Married a Communist* (a.k.a. *Woman on Pier 13*). She and Gregory Peck starred in a version of *Angel Street* at the La Jolla Playhouse, and the duo took the play on a brief tour. In 1954 she was very convincing as Sidney Blackmer's wife who is paid court by David Brian in *The High and the Mighty*. In 1956 she starred in two lightweight features, but seemed to mean it when she said, "Let someone else be the world's greatest actress; I'll be the world's greatest baseball fan." She remained the First Lady of Baseball until she divorced Durocher in 1960. That same year she made a murder mystery called *The Third Voice*, her last film appearance for twelve years. Laraine had been an occasional television guest star on drama anthologies, including a most effective performance as a persecuted office worker in the "Pattern of Deceit" (1955) episode of the *Loretta Young Show*. One of her rare recent appearances in the video medium was in a segment of *Sixth Sense* (1972), playing opposite Leif Erickson. Eventually she accepted a role in First Leisure's *House of Dracula's Daughter* (1972).

In 1960 Laraine wed television producer Michael Grilkhas. They have two children, Gigi and Dana, and live in the fashionable Trusdale Estates in Beverly Hills. She says she was always more popular with the public than with the studios because she never played politics and never would submit to trumped-up "dates" for publicity purposes. She very much wanted to play the part Maureen Stapleton got in *Airport* (1970), but the producer turned her down. "People think it is easy if you have a name to get a job. It isn't. Believe me, for every part that comes up for a woman my age there are at least two dozen former stars who are up for it and really want it."

Today, in her mid-fifties, Laraine is the grandmother of four. In recent years she was the spokeswoman for the "Make America Better Program" of the National Association of Real Estate Boards and wrote the brochure, "The America We Love." She now runs a small boutique in her home for her friends, with the aid of her former movie stand-in. Laraine says, "I keep young by keeping busy. I am deeply involved with the Mormon church and that takes a lot of time and thought. It gives me strength in a confusing world."

With Billie Burke, Frank Milan, and Jean Muir in *And One Was Beautiful* (1940)

With Alma Kruger in *The People vs. Dr. Kildare* (1941)

Stella Dallas (UA, 1937)
Border G-Men (RKO, 1938)
Scandal Street (Paramount, 1938)
Painted Desert (RKO, 1938)
The Arizona Legion (RKO, 1939)
Sergeant Madden (MGM, 1939)
Calling Dr. Kildare (MGM, 1939)
Tarzan Finds a Son! (MGM, 1939)
Secret of Dr. Kildare (MGM, 1939)
My Son, My Son (UA, 1940)
I Take This Woman (MGM, 1940)
And One Was Beautiful (MGM, 1940)
Dr. Kildare's Strange Case (MGM, 1940)
Foreign Correspondent (UA, 1940)
Dr. Kildare Goes Home (MGM, 1940)
Dr. Kildare's Crisis (MGM, 1940)
The Bad Man (MGM, 1941)
The Trial of Mary Dugan (MGM, 1941)
The People vs. Dr. Kildare (MGM, 1941)
Dr. Kildare's Wedding Day (MGM, 1941)
Unholy Partners (MGM, 1941)

Kathleen (MGM, 1941)
Journey for Margaret (MGM, 1942)
Fingers at the Window (MGM, 1942)
A Yank on the Burma Road (MGM, 1942)
Mr. Lucky (RKO, 1943)
The Story of Dr. Wassell (Paramount, 1944)
Bride by Mistake (RKO, 1944)
Those Endearing Young Charms (RKO, 1945)
Keep Your Powder Dry (MGM, 1945)
The Locket (RKO, 1946)
Tycoon (RKO, 1947)
My Dear Secretary (UA, 1948)
I Married a Communist (RKO, 1949)
Without Honor (UA, 1949)
The High and the Mighty (WB, 1954)
Toy Tiger (Universal, 1956)
Three for Jamie Dawn (AA, 1956)
The Third Voice (20th-Fox, 1960)
House of Dracula's Daughter (First Leisure, 1972)

Gloria DeHaven

When MGM's musical *Two Girls and a Sailor* went into production in 1943, it was a toss-up which of the picture's two singing-and-dancing "sisters," Gloria DeHaven or June Allyson would emerge as the studio's new musical soubrette. Allyson, in that Joe Pasternak production, won gob Van Johnson and became Metro's popular girl next door. Gloria was relegated, as she says, to: "the immature, snooty, glamour-girl type." But the honey blonde Gloria had tremendous verve then, as now, and might well have been .... .

Gloria Mildred DeHaven was born in Los Angeles, California on July 23, 1924, and says: "I'm the product of divorce, show business, very little stability, and no roots. We were always traveling." The "we" included father, Carter DeHaven; mother, Flora Parker; a brother, Carter, Jr.; and a sister, Marjorie. The traveling was through the vaudeville circuit where her parents were popular performers. (They also appeared in some silent films, notably *Twin Beds*.) When Gloria was eleven years old, her father was an assistant director on Charles Chaplin's *Modern Times* (1936), and Gloria and a girlhood chum, Gloria Delson, played Paulette Goddard's two ragamuffin sisters, with two brief scenes and no dialogue.

Gloria attended the Ken-Mar Professional School in Hollywood, during which time she spent: "Making the rounds and taking lessons from Mother. That's all I knew." She had bit parts in Chaplin's *The Great Dictator* (1940) and in four MGM films: *Susan and God* (1940), *Keeping Company* (1941), *Two-Faced Woman* (1941), and *The Penalty* (1941). Louis B. Mayer was all set to give Gloria a term contract, but he discovered that she had an iron-clad agreement with an agent whom he had barred from the lot, so the teenager was unable to accept the Metro offer. She then sang with the Bob Crosby and the Jan Savitt orchestras. It was while appearing with the latter in New Orleans that an MGM talent scout spotted Gloria and offered her a screen test. She informed him she was a Hollywood native and had already been in three Metro pictures, but she accepted the screen test and, now being free from her previous agent, was able to sign a seven-year contract beginning at $50 weekly.

From the start, she and June Allyson found themselves groomed along the same lines: They both were school girls involved in an athletic dance in

Best Foot Forward (1943) and together with Virginia O'Brien did a rendering of "In a Little Spanish Town" in *Thousands Cheer* (1943). Gloria and Kenny Bowers were the juvenile team in *Broadway Rhythm* (1944), a mild rendering of Jerome Kern's unsuccessful musical *Very Warm for May*.

Then came the watershed mark, the film *Two Girls and a Sailor*, in which she and Allyson played sisters with contrasting personalities who work in a serviceman's canteen and fall in love with the same sailor (Van Johnson). In *Step Lively* (1944), a musical remake of the Marx Brothers' *Room Service*, tailor-fitted to Frank Sinatra, showgirl Gloria gave the crooner his first real screen kiss. She followed this stint with two nonshowy "dramatic" roles. In *The Thin Man Goes Home* (1944) she functioned as the spoiled rotten society girl, and the next year was seen in *Between Two Women* (1945), a Van Johnson–Lionel Barrymore Dr. Gillespie entry, as a show business type suffering from a rare disease (one of its symptoms gave her a fixation about not eating). At least she sang "I'm in the Mood for Love."

If it were not bad enough that the June Allyson faction at MGM was burying Gloria's film career, she up and retired for two years when she wed actor John Payne, ex-husband of actress Anne Shirley. Gloria had had more than enough of being tied to Mama and wanted out. Marriage to thirty-two year-old Payne seemed the ideal solution. Mrs. DeHaven remained true to form. When told that Gloria had married, she yelled at her daughter: "You can't do this to *me!* Not to *me!*" Mostly all Gloria did was harm her own professional career.

After giving birth to daughter Kathleen in 1945, she returned to MGM the following year to appear as Mickey Rooney's high school sweetheart in *Summer Holiday*, the Rouben Mamoulian musical remake of *Ah, Wilderness*! Marilyn Maxwell, the social worker in *Between Two Women*, who won out over Gloria in that film, played the corrupting chanteuse in *Summer Holiday* who nearly lures naive Rooney into a night of sin. Maxwell received the most attention when this picture was finally released by MGM in 1948 to generally unpopular results.

In 1947, Gloria's son Thomas was born, and then she returned to the studio again. She played a torch singer who falls in love with married detective Van Johnson in *Scene of the Crime* (1949) and the sister of Glenn Ford in *The Doctor and the Girl* (1949). Janet Leigh was the sweet young thing of the title in this picture and Gloria the Park Avenue socialite, unmarried and with child. MGM loaned her to Universal for *Yes Sir, That's My Baby* (1949) in which she and Donald O'Connor played a college married couple, and then brought her back to the home lot to play straight gal to Red Skelton's antics in *The Yellow Cab Man* (1950).

In 1950, the year she divorced Payne, she had two of her best screen roles. In *Three Little Words* she appeared in a cameo as her real-life mother Flora Parker DeHaven, and sang "Who's Sorry Now?". That picture was a musical biography of songwriters Bert Kalmar and Harry Ruby, who had written that song for Gloria's mother years before. In *Summer Stock*, she was

Judy Garland's stagestruck but temperamental sister, who ends up out of the big show and stuck with Garland's castoff, Eddie Bracken. MGM loaned Gloria to Twentieth Century-Fox to play June Haver's sister in *I'll Get By* (1951) where, in a tuxedo and top hat, she sang "Fifth Avenue" with Haver. Gloria was also loaned to RKO, along with Ann Miller and Janet Leigh, for *Two Tickets to Broadway* (1951) where she sang "Baby, You'll Never Be Sorry" with Eddie Bracken, and joined Miller, Leigh, and Barbara Lawrence in "The Wrong Bird" number.

Two Tickets to Broadway ended her MGM contract and she left because she claimed she wanted to get away from the glamor girl image. However, she looks back on the studio system with fondness: "You lived there, you worked there, you grew up there. You knew everyone around you. We were groomed, step by step, for stardom. Nobody was thrown into something before they were ready for it. And I miss the movies that were made for the sheer entertainment of the audience."

Gloria did three more pictures, had a short-lasting marriage in 1953 to older real estate man Martin Kimmel and then moved to New York with her two children. She made her stage debut as the streetwalker in the Victor Young musical, *Seventh Heaven* (1955). Another stage play, *Have I Got One for You*, was a flop. She since has appeared in stock productions of *The Unsinkable Molly Brown, Oliver*, and *The Sound of Music*, and the London company of *Golden Boy* with Sammy Davis, Jr. She has played supper clubs throughout the U. S. and done both musical and dramatic roles on television on *The Bob Hope Show, The Red Skelton Show, Wagon Train, The Defenders, The Dick Powell Show*, and *Burke's Law*. In 1966–1967 she played Sara Fuller, the menacing femme fatale on CBS's afternoon soap opera, *As the World Turns* and, as a result, has become a popular guest on television talk shows. In 1969 she began hostessing the ABC *Prize Movie* for several seasons, chatting with telephone guests in breaks between the old movies. In the telefeature *Call Her Mom* (1972), Gloria had a zappy cameo as the ex–chorus girl wife of college president Van Johnson.

In 1957, Gloria had married Miami Beach auto dealer Richard W. Fincher. They had two children—Harry (1958) and Faith (1962) and were divorced in 1963; they remarried in 1964 and were divorced for a second time in 1968. Fincher later became a Florida state senator. In 1971, at the persuasion of her good friend June Allyson, the now vibrant red-headed Gloria moved back to California. She still sports the beauty mark on her left cheek (actually a mole highlighted by makeup) and remains a conscious glamor gal throwback to her MGM days. She says, "I didn't begin to grow up until I was forty; and now I can face reality anytime, but escaping from it via 'sheer entertainment' can be fun now and then."

With Van Johnson in *Scene of the Crime* (1949)

With Judy Garland, Phil Silvers, and Hans Conried in *Summer Stock* (1950)

GLORIA DEHAVEN

Modern Times (UA, 1936)
The Great Dictator (UA, 1940)
Susan and God (MGM, 1940)
Keeping Company (MGM, 1941)
Two-Faced Woman (MGM, 1941)
The Penalty (MGM, 1941)
Best Foot Forward (MGM, 1943)
Thousands Cheer (MGM, 1943)
Broadway Rhythm (MGM, 1944)
Two Girls and a Sailor (MGM, 1944)
Step Lively (RKO, 1944)
The Thin Man Goes Home (MGM, 1944)
Between Two Women (MGM, 1945)

Summer Holiday (MGM, 1948)
Scene of the Crime (MGM, 1949)
The Doctor and the Girl (MGM, 1949)
Yes Sir, That's My Baby (Universal, 1949)
The Yellow Cab Man (MGM, 1950)
Three Little Words (MGM, 1950)
Summer Stock (MGM, 1950)
I'll Get By (20th-Fox, 1950)
Two Tickets to Broadway (RKO, 1951)
Down Among the Sheltering Palms (20th-Fox, 1953)
So This is Paris (Universal, 1955)
The Girl Rush (Paramount, 1955)

Melvyn Douglas

He was 6' 2", handsome, with a twinkling mischievousness in his eyes; had a pencil-thin moustache, elegant manners, an aristocratic bearing, and a way of performing little tricks with the pitch of his voice that made him one of the screen's most accomplished farceurs. He was at once suave and debonair, frivolous and quizzical, always self-confident but rarely sarcastic. By his own definition he was "a commodity," the necessary sophisticated leading man for the greatest of the Hollywood ladies, including Gloria Swanson, Greta Garbo, Joan Crawford, Irene Dunne, Marlene Dietrich, Myrna Loy, and Ava Gardner. He rode a motor bike with Irene Dunne in *Theodora Goes Wild* (1936) and was "the man who makes Garbo laugh" in *Ninotchka* (1939). Not all of the romantic comedies he did in the 1930s and 1940s were as good as those two: "The roles were boring and I was soon fed up with them. It's true they gave me a worldwide reputation I could trade on, but they also typed me as a one-dimensional, nonserious actor."

Douglas was born Melvyn Edouard Hesselberg on April 5, 1901 in Macon, Georgia. His father, a Russian Sephardic Jew, came to the United States as a young concert piano prodigy and stayed to teach music in Colorado. There he met his wife-to-be, Lena Shackleford, a Kentuckian of Scottish descent. There was a second child, George, two and one half years younger than Melvyn. The Hesselbergs moved several times during Douglas' childhood and he attended high school in Lincoln, Nebraska. Halfway through his junior year he was expelled from school for smoking, beer-drinking, and being a member of a secret fraternity. His time being his own he hung around the community theatrical stock company performing a few walkons which earned him a few dollars. At seventeen he ran away to Omaha where he enlisted in the Army, serving at camps in Wyoming and Washington as a medical orderly. It was in the Army that he met a well-read friend who introduced him to the works of Isaac Newton, Spinoza, and Schopenhauer. For the first time, Douglas seriously began to learn about the arts.

Douglas' family had moved to Chicago by the time he was discharged from the Army, and he joined them there. He recalls the Chicago of 1919 with Maxwell Bodenheim, Floyd Dell, Ben Hecht, and Charles MacArthur as a "yeasty" atmosphere. He met actor William Owen, who had organized a

Shakespearean repertory company, and Douglas joined the group. Stints with several other stock companies followed, and he began to realize that acting was a creative experience. Up until that time, "I thought acting meant sleeping late and being rich enough to buy silk shirts." During this period he married a girl he had first met in Madison, Wisconsin. They had a son named Gregory, but the marriage soon broke up. He sailed to Europe for five months with money he had saved. The trip was ostensibly to go to Berlin to work with Max Reinhardt's theatre group, but when he got as far as Paris he found another "yeasty" atmosphere to distract him. He remained in Paris for several months, and when he returned to the States he found employment with Jessie Bonstelle's Detroit stock company. In 1926, the career-climbing Douglas signed a three-year stage contract with Broadway producer William A. Brady and made his New York debut on January 12, 1928, playing the gangster in *A Free Soul*. Several more plays and tours followed when David Belasco hired him at $500 weekly to essay the Unknown Gentleman in *Tonight We Sing*. That play opened in November 1930 and his costar was reputed to be one of the ten most beautiful women in the world, Helen Gahagan. They fell in love and were married on Douglas' birthday in 1931.

Gloria Swanson had asked Samuel Goldwyn, then production head of United Artists, to purchase a stage vehicle for her. Goldwyn bought the rights to *Tonight We Sing* (1931) and signed Douglas to a personal contract at $900 a week. Swanson, who was then under a $250,000-per-picture agreement with United Artists, "would arrive late, serve tea from a silver service at 4:30, and go home." "With that kind of a beginning," Douglas says, "I got an erroneous impression of how movies were made." Goldwyn loaned him to MGM as Greta Garbo's leading man in *As You Desire Me* (1932), and their love scenes proved at least civilized if not passionate. That picture was released after he had appeared in three more Goldwyn loanouts. None of these, or for that matter *As You Desire Me*, made him a hot cinema property. Goldwyn continued to loan out the actor for increasingly bad scripts. Douglas asked out of his contract and Goldwyn complied. Despite this less than rewarding film beginning, Douglas recalls Goldwyn as a "marvelous, untypical mogul."

Douglas and his wife took a trip around the world which cost them $750 each at the time and returned to California where their son Peter was born. Free-lancing, Douglas played the impoverished grafter in *Counsellor-at-Law* (1933), which starred John Barrymore, and then returned to New York to stage and star in a production of *No More Ladies*. He directed his wife in a production of *Moor Born* which opened in April 1934, in which she played Emily Brontë. He staged the New York production of Sean O'Casey's *Within These Gates* starring Lillian Gish, and thereafter he and his wife starred in *Mother Lode*, which he also directed. When his wife went to Hollywood to appear in the only picture she would ever make, *She* (1935), Douglas joined her. He made three quickies for RKO and then was signed to a Columbia contract which was the start of his boost to stardom.

In his first film for Columbia, a cheery comedy called *She Married Her*

Boss (1935), he played a department store czar who romances his executive secretary, Claudette Colbert. He says, "My comedy role in that one successful movie was a salable commodity. They began exploiting what was supposed to be the comic Melvyn Douglas. I earned what became an international reputation for being one of the most debonair and witty farceurs in Hollywood." MGM borrowed him to play Senator John Randolph in Joan Crawford's costume drama, *The Gorgeous Hussy* (1936). After noting the excellent reviews for Douglas' performance in *Theodora Goes Wild*, MGM negotiated with Columbia to share his contract. Since MGM already had their own proficient farceur, William Powell, they used Douglas for whatever sophisticated roles were left over. He was the tycoon father of Freddie Bartholomew in *Captains Courageous* (1937), a French jewel thief in *Arsene Lupin Returns* (1938), Luise Rainer's cuckolded husband in *Toy Wife* (1938), a suave detective in *Fast Company* (1938), and a gentleman farmer in *The Shining Hour* (1938).

Back at Columbia Douglas fared a little better. They loaned him to Paramount for two comedies. One was *I Met Him in Paris* (1937) which teamed him again with Colbert and did well at the boxoffice; the other was the too-precious *Angel* (1937), with Marlene Dietrich, which was not well received. Then there were three outings with that bit of "fizz on the soda," Joan Blondell: *There's Always a Woman* (1937), *Good Girls Go to Paris* (1939), and *The Amazing Mr. Williams* (1939). When William Powell took ill and was unable to star with Garbo in *Ninotchka*, Douglas was cast as the flippant Parisian who romances the grim Russian commissar, Garbo. He enjoyed working with Garbo again and called her the first hippie, "a very easy person to be with."

That Certain Woman (1941) was a less successful Ernst Lubitsch picture, and *A Woman's Face* (1941), while popular, was little more than the typical Joan Crawford woman's picture. Douglas had the dubious distinction of playing with Garbo and Norma Shearer in their last pictures, *Two-Faced Woman* (1941) and *We Were Dancing* (1942), respectively. After starring with Ann Sothern in *Three Hearts for Julia* (1943), Douglas enlisted in the Army as a private. In 1942 he had spent time in Washington as director of the Arts Council of the Office of Civilian Defense and had become involved in the Fight For Freedom Committee headed by Wendell Willkie and Herbert Agar. He felt strongly about taking part in the war, but says: "MGM thought I was a traitor; that I was deserting them." He was serving in the Chinese–Burma–India theatre of operations when he learned that his wife had been elected as a Democratic Congresswoman from California. She served from 1945 to 1949.

Douglas was discharged from the service in November, 1945, with the rank of major. He was still under contract to both Columbia and MGM. He made one picture for MGM, *The Sea of Grass* (1947) and a clinker for Columbia, *The Guilt of Janet Ames* (1947). His lawyer found a loophole in his studio contracts and he was a free agent again. After a few more free-lance assignments, he returned to the New York stage for the most fruitful and rewarding years of his career. He starred in Samuel Spewack's *Three Blind Mice* (1949), and then played in *The Little Blue Light* (1951) and *Glad Tidings* (1951). After performing in *Time Out for Ginger* (1952) on Broadway, he went on tour in the U. S. and Australia for two years. When Paul Muni fell ill during the run of *Inherit the Wind* (1955), Douglas replaced him and also took that show on tour, playing Harry Drummond, the Clarence Darrowlike character. He said it was not until this role that he was considered as a serious actor. He repeated his performance in a television version aired on November 18, 1965. This assignment was followed by a tour of *The Waltz of the Toreadors* (1957), with Paulette Goddard, and a Broadway musical version of Sean O'Casey's *Juno and the Paycock* entitled *Juno* (1959), with Shirley Booth. This production was short-lived, as was *The Gang's All Here*, done later that year. In 1960 he received a Tony award for portraying the presidential aspirant in Gore Vidal's *The Best Man*.

After an eleven-year absence, a much aged Douglas returned to the screen in *Billy Budd* (1962), and the following year he received an Academy Award as best supporting actor of the year for playing the honorable rancher–father of Paul Newman in *Hud* (1963). For his television performance as the elderly carpenter who must create a new life for himself in a rest home in *Do Not Go Gentle into That Good Night* (1967), he won an Emmy, making him the fifth actor or actress in history to have won all three of the major acting awards, the Oscar, the Tony, and the Emmy. Ingrid Bergman, Shirley Booth, Helen Hayes, and Thomas Mitchell are the other four.

While many critics thought Douglas' performance as the old man of eighty in the movie *I Never Sang for My Father* (1970) was the best performance of his career, some others view this characterization as more a modification of Douglas' past acting assignments than any new height of achievement. He was nominated for an Oscar again, but George C. Scott won for *Patton*. Douglas was at the Award ceremony to make the touching presentation of a Special Oscar to "Miss Lillian" (Lillian Gish).

Douglas has starred in several telefeatures in recent years, and one, *Death Takes A Holiday* (1971), costarred him with one of his MGM leading ladies, Myrna Loy, of whom he says: " ... [she] is the only one from that period I'd really still enjoy seeing as a friend." For theatrical release, Douglas was in the San Francisco-lensed *The Candidate* (1972), starring Robert Redford. In MGM's *One Is a Lonely Number* (1972), a drama about the problems of divorce, Douglas essayed an old storekeeper, a widower who helps, somewhat, the heroine, Trish Van Devere, to find her own way.

Douglas and his wife now live in an apartment on Manhattan's Riverside Drive. They have two children, Peter and Mary, and nine grandchildren. Douglas has been politically oriented ever since he made a trip to Europe in the pre-Nazi days. He was the first actor to be a delegate to a National convention, the 1940 Democratic one, and he was an anti-Fascist supporter of Loyalist Spain. He has stated, "I've always been a strongly anti-Communist liberal. I've never vacillated." In 1950 his wife ran as the Democratic candidate for U. S. Senator from California against Republican Richard M. Nixon. The campaign was an acrimonious and dirty fight in which she finally was defeated. Douglas is a frank observer of the political scene and says, about present U. S. foreign policy, "I'm angry over the administration's handling of the war in Vietnam. It is a tragic, horrendous mistake."

MELVYN DOUGLAS

Tonight or Never (UA, 1931)
Prestige (RKO, 1932)
The Wiser Sex (Paramount, 1932)
Broken Wing (Paramount, 1932)
As You Desire Me (MGM, 1932)
The Old Dark House (Universal, 1932)
Nagana (Universal, 1933)
The Vampire Bat (Majestic, 1933)
Counsellor-at-Law (Universal, 1933)
Woman in the Dark (RKO, 1934)
Dangerous Corner (RKO, 1934)
People's Enemy (RKO, 1935)
She Married Her Boss (Columbia, 1935)
Mary Burns — Fugitive (Paramount, 1935)
Annie Oakley (RKO, 1935)
The Lone Wolf Returns (Columbia, 1936)
And So They Were Married (Columbia, 1936)
The Gorgeous Hussy (MGM, 1936)
Theodora Goes Wild (Columbia, 1936)
Women of Glamour (Columbia, 1937)
Captains Courageous (MGM, 1937)
I Met Him in Paris (Paramount, 1937)
Angel (Paramount, 1937)
I'll Take Romance (Columbia, 1937)
There's Always a Woman (Columbia, 1937)
Arsene Lupin Returns (MGM, 1938)
The Toy Wife (MGM, 1938)
Fast Company (MGM, 1938)
That Certain Age (Universal, 1938)
The Shining Hour (MGM, 1938)
There's That Woman Again (Columbia, 1938)
Good Girls Go to Paris (Columbia, 1939)

Tell No Tales (MGM, 1939)
The Amazing Mr. Williams (Columbia, 1939)
Ninotchka (MGM, 1939)
Too Many Husbands (Columbia, 1940)
He Stayed for Breakfast (Columbia, 1940)
Third Finger Left Hand (MGM, 1940)
This Thing Called Love (Columbia, 1941)
That Uncertain Feeling (UA, 1941)
A Woman's Face (MGM, 1941)
Our Wife (Columbia, 1941)
Two-Faced Woman (MGM, 1941)
They All Kissed the Bride (Columbia, 1942)
We Were Dancing (MGM, 1942)
Three Hearts for Julia (MGM, 1943)
The Sea of Grass (MGM, 1947)
The Guilt of Janet Ames (Columbia, 1947)
Mr. Blanding Builds His Dream House (RKO, 1948)
My Own True Love (Paramount, 1948)
A Woman's Secret (RKO, 1949)
The Great Sinner (MGM, 1949)
My Forbidden Past (RKO, 1951)
On the Loose (RKO, 1951)
Billy Budd (AA, 1962)
Hud (Paramount, 1963)
Advance to the Rear (MGM, 1964)
The Americanization of Emily (MGM, 1964)
Rapture (International Classics, 1965)
Hotel (WB, 1967)
I Never Sang for My Father (Columbia, 1970)
One Is a Lonely Number (MGM, 1972)
The Candidate (WB, 1972)

185

With Charles D. Brown and Louise Platt in *Tell No Tales* (1939)

With Greta Garbo in *Ninotchka* (1939)

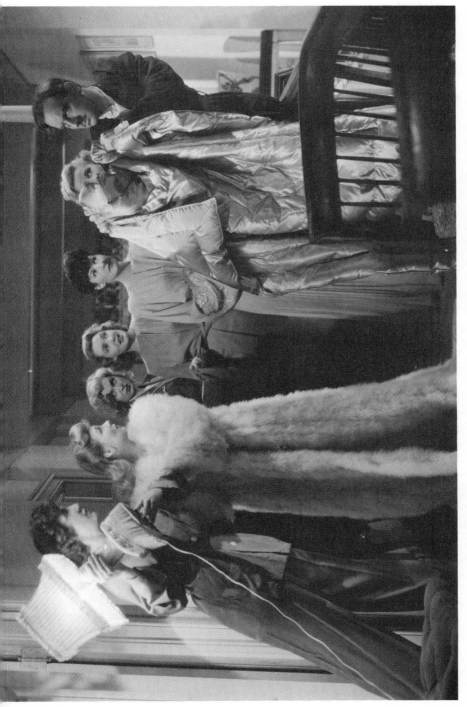

With Elvia Allman, Ann Sothern, Kay Medford, Ann Richards, Marta Linden, and Jacqueline White in *Three Hearts for Julia* (1943)

Tom Drake

Each decade has its personification of wholesomeness, and in the 1940s, MGM's Van Johnson led the pack with this all-American screen image. But not too far behind for a spell in the mid-1940s was the same studio's Tom Drake. Once Judy Garland sang of her love for "The Boy Next Door" in *Meet Me in St. Louis* (1944), he was stuck with that career tag for life. Not that Drake has ever demonstrated on screen any desire to shake such a casting rut. The years have weather-beaten his looks very little. He still projects that languid smile, staring for reassurance with those moist eyes that seem incapable of conveying any semblance of gutsiness.

Drake was born Alfred Alderice in Flatbush, Brooklyn, on August 5, 1918, and was educated at the Iona School and then at Mercersberg Academy in Virginia. After acting in stock from the age of eighteen, he graduated to Broadway in *June Night* (1938), followed by roles in *Central Casting, Dance Nights, Run, Sheep, Run*, and *Clean Bed*. He went to California to try his luck in movies and was cast for a small part in Columbia's *The Howards Of Virginia* (1940), billed as Richard Alden. But when there were no further film offers, he returned to New York and eventually obtained the juvenile lead in *Janie* (1942) with Gwen Anderson, Linda Watkins, and Herbert Evers. It was his role in this highly popular comedy which brought him to the attention of MGM, then more eager than Buddy De Sylva's regime at Paramount in garnering the corner on performers who could essay small town Americana on the World War II screens.

Drake's Metro debut was in *Two Girls and a Sailor* (1944), a loose reworking of *Broadway Melody*, in which he was a soldier friend of army man Van Johnson, the latter involved in a romantic triangle with June Allyson and Gloria DeHaven. Despite Jimmy Durante's scene-stealing presence, the musical interludes of Lena Horne and the orchestras of Xavier Cugat and Harry James, Drake was noticed for his clean-cut, unaffected performance. In *Maisie Goes to Reno* (1940) he was again a G. I., but this time a penniless one wed to heiress Ava Gardner, who is herself being hoodwinked by her crooked business manager, Paul Cavanagh. Drake was a soldier in the classy *The White Cliffs of Dover* (1944), and in *Marriage Is a Private Affair* (1944) he was one of the fellows involved in Lana Turner's reckless life. He played Ned Talbot, the nice young gentleman intertwined in the dynasty of Major Walter Pidgeon and Greer Garson, in *Mrs. Parkington* (1944). But it was as John Truett, the Kensington Avenue neighbor of maturing Judy Garland in *Meet Me in St. Louis* (1944), that insured his cinema mark. He portrayed the basketball-playing youth with whom Garland falls in love, shares a trolley ride, and who is lured by her into helping to turn off the gas lights after the house party. It is he who suffers her pummeling when she mistakenly believes he was responsible for sister Tootie's (Margaret O'Brien's) accident. As a result of these six pictures, Drake was named a "Star of Tomorrow" in 1945, along with such others as Metro's Keenan Wynn and Twentieth Century-Fox's William Eythe.

Drake was a younger member of *This Man's Army* (1945) with Wallace Beery and James Gleason. In the highly touted *The Green Years* (1946) Drake was trusted by the studio with the prettified John Dall-type lead as the adult Robert Shannon (played by Dean Stockwell as a child) who matures in Ireland, loved only by his old grandfather Charles Coburn. He was the soldier on leave in *Faithful in My Fashion* (1946) who discovers his best girl (Donna Reed) is now engaged to another. The other professional high point of 1946 for Drake and his last well-remembered cinema role was in *Courage of Lassie*. He was the army sergeant stationed in the Aleutians who gains possession of the dog and turns the gentle collie into a war killer animal, with it remaining for the animal to be recivilized by his past owner, Elizabeth Taylor. This feature is still revived for children matinees at movie theatres.

By 1947 all the actors who had gone into World War II service had been demobilized, which made the competition for screen roles tougher, a problem compounded for Drake by the country's changing tastes which no longer held vapid, nice young men in such high repute. On loanout to Universal for *I'll Be Yours* (1947), he was caught on the outskirts as Deanna Durbin pursued baron Adolphe Menjou. At Metro he was just a good guy in *Cass Timberlane* (1947) and Beverly Tyler's husband in *The Beginning or the End* (1947). It was also in 1947 that Drake divorced actress Christopher Curtis, whom he had wed in the early 1940s.

Drake was a good influence on Dorothy Patrick, the daughter of weary jailbird Wallace Beery in *Alias a Gentleman* (1948). In the lesser Lassie vehicle *Hills of Home* (1948) he was being persuaded to become a physician. Since it was strictly a cardboard biography, it seems plausible in retrospect that MGM cast mild Drake to play composer Richard Rodgers in *Words and Music* (1948). A very freshlooking Janet Leigh was Drake's girl and later wife.

After supporting police lieutenant Van Johnson in the mild whodunit *Scene of the Crime* (1949), Drake's Metro contract expired. With his limited acting range it is amazing he got even the few screen breaks he did on the lot. Thereafter his movie career took a decided nosedive. He was Jessie Royce Landis' son in *Mr. Belvedere Goes to College* (1949), was second string to Dane Clark in *Never Trust a Gambler* (1951), and was baffled by the inhumane treatment to Peggy Knudsen and Beverly Michaels in the women's prison yarn, *Betrayed Women* (1955). He was one of the trio of human actors playing foil to the *Cyclops* (1957). It was Elizabeth Taylor, his studio friend from the days of Lassie, who obtained for him the featured role of her brother in MGM's roadshow costumer, *Raintree County* (1957).

During the 1950s, Drake performed on Broadway in *Hook and Ladder* (1952) with Vicki Cummings and played *Stalag 17* (1953) at the Arena Stage in Washington, D. C. He was a frequent if nondescript television performer, such as on *Studio One's The Brotherhood of the Bell* (1958).

The 1960s were even leaner for Drake in the entertainment industry. He was Barbara Rush's dying husband in *The Bramble Bush* (1960) and five years later played in Elizabeth Taylor's *The Sandpiper* as an understanding friend of Eva Marie Saint. The following year—also at MGM—he was in the old contract player's reunion picture *The Singing Nun* (1966). He made two A. C. Lyles budget westerns, *Johnny Reno* (1966) and *Red Tomahawk* (1967) which qualified him for has-been status, and the following year teamed with George Montgomery in the Philippines-lensed action picture *Warkill*. His latest theatre movie to date is *The Spectre of Edgar Allan Poe* (1973), a low-budget horror exploitation feature starring Robert Walker, Jr.

In the 1970s, Drake guested on episodes of *Mannix, Marcus Welby, M.D.*, and *Owen Marshall*. Recently he was the subject of a small trade paper advertisement which announced he had joined the sales and leasing division of a car company located in Culver City, near his old MGM stamping grounds.

With Frank Sully and Van Johnson in *Two Girls and a Sailor* (1944)

TOM DRAKE

The Howards of Virginia (Columbia, 1940)
Two Girls and a Sailor (MGM, 1944)
Maisie Goes to Reno (MGM, 1944)
The White Cliffs of Dover (MGM, 1944)
Marriage Is a Private Affair (MGM, 1944)
Mrs. Parkington (MGM, 1944)
Meet Me in St. Louis (MGM, 1944)
This Man's Navy (MGM, 1945)
The Green Years (MGM, 1946)
Courage of Lassie (MGM, 1946)
Faithful in My Fashion (MGM, 1946)
I'll Be Yours (Universal, 1947)
Cass Timberlane (MGM, 1947)
The Beginning or the End (MGM, 1947)
Alias a Gentleman (MGM, 1948)
Hills of Home (MGM, 1948)
Words and Music (MGM, 1948)
Mr. Belvedere Goes to College (20th-Fox, 1949)

Scene of the Crime (MGM, 1949)
The Great Rupert (Eagle–Lion, 1950)
Never Trust a Gambler (Columbia, 1951)
Disc Jockey (AA, 1951)
FBI Girl (Lippert, 1951)
Sangaree (Paramount, 1953)
Sudden Danger (AA, 1955)
Betrayed Women (AA, 1955)
Cyclops (AA, 1957)
Raintree County (MGM, 1957)
Warlock (20th-Fox, 1959)
The Bramble Bush (WB, 1960)
The Sandpiper (MGM, 1965)
The Singing Nun (MGM, 1966)
Johnny Reno (Paramount, 1966)
Red Tomahawk (Paramount, 1967)
Warkill (Universal, 1968)
The Spectre of Edgar Allan Poe (First Leisure, 1973)

Marie Dressler

Marie Dressler may not have been "just another pretty face," but she was a *Star*. With an ample figure like a rain barrel and a face that fell into folds like those of a St. Bernard, the lovable if unlovely Miss Dressler was paid tribute just before her death in 1934 by Will Rogers: "Marie Dressler is the real queen of our movies," and she was indeed that for several years. In 1930, after a long career in vaudeville, theatre, and films, her career was all but forgotten. Then, at the age of 61, she was cast as Greta Garbo's drinking buddy in *Anna Christie* and the public almost forgot to notice that this was the picture in which Garbo "talked." For the next four years, Marie was Number One at the boxoffice, earned an Oscar for *Min and Bill* (1930) and was the highest paid star on the MGM lot, $5,000 weekly. She was equally adept at comedy and drama. Her harridans were proud, her grand dames were down to earth, and her appeal was universal. She was proud of her long career and reveled in her belated social acclaim. Having suffered a series of ups and downs in her career and having been bankrupt on several occasions, she never forgot the importance of steady work and maintaining the facade of stardom. She is credited with having uttered one of the more viable quips about Hollywood: "You're only as good as your last picture."

"I was born homely," she said in her autobiography, *My Own Story*, published posthumously in 1934, and told readers the name of the place, Coburg, Canada, and her real name, Leila von Koerber. But with true femininity she failed to mention the date—November 9, 1869. She also failed to mention her two broken romances (they may have been marriages) to actors George Hoppeit and James Dalton, but she did reveal the amount of hard work it took to achieve stardom. Her father, whom she disliked, was a frustrated organist and music teacher and the von Koerbers moved from town to town during her childhood. By the time she was fourteen, she was determined not to quietly resign herself to struggling with poverty like her hard-working mother. So she joined a "cheap dramatic stock company" managed by the brother of opera diva Emma Nevada. Her sister, Bonita, five years her senior, joined the company with her, but left after a few months to marry a playwright. When her father objected to Leila's being an actress and said she would not drag the family name "through the mud," she adopted her professional name after an old aunt in Germany whom she had never seen.

Her first role was as Cigarette in *Under Two Flags*, and she said she never did overcome the stage fright she had before that first performance. Her salary was $6 a week. After nearly a year she joined the Maurice Grau Grand Opera Company where she displayed a strong, natural operatic singing voice but left when she was not paid her weekly salary of $8. She had enough money to get to Philadelphia but not enough for a hotel room and said she persuaded the desk clerk to give her a room (would that that persuasion scene were on film). The next day she got a job with the Deshon Company playing one of her favorite roles, Katisha, in Gilbert and Sullivan's *The Mikado*. After that, she joined the George Baker Opera Company and was so good at spoofing opera that she stayed for several years. In Chicago she supported Eddie Foy and Adele Harrington in a musical comedy, *Little Robinson Crusoe*, and made her New York bow on May 28, 1892, playing a brigand in *The Robber of the Rhine*, a romantic comedy written by Maurice Barrymore, father of Lionel, Ethel, and John. The show was a flop but Barrymore told the young actress: "You were born to make people laugh, Marie."

To pay her rent, Marie sang in New York City beer halls, finally landing a job supporting Lillian Russell in *The Princess Nicotine*, playing a duchess. She and Russell hit it off as friends and the Broadway set referred to them as Beauty and the Beastie. She finally got a starring role in *The Lady Slavey* in 1896, playing a music hall queen opposite Dan Daly, the popular eccentric dancer of the day. At first, Daly did not want to dance with an "elephant," but before rehearsals were over, he asked Marie to work up some dances they could use as encores. Joe Weber used her in two productions at his Music Hall, *Higgledy-Piggledy* which featured Anna Held, and *Twiddle Twaddle*. After these productions she scored her greatest stage success in *Tillie's Nightmare*. Billed as a "melange of mirth and melody in three acts," it opened in 1910. As the boarding house drudge, Marie immortalized the song "Heaven Will Protect the Working Girl." Two other plays, *Marie Dressler's All-Star Gambol* (1913) and *A Mix Up* (1914) took her on tour to the West Coast where Mack Sennett talked her into doing a silent picture based on her Tillie.

Tillie's Punctured Romance (1914) was the first American feature-length film farce, six reels in length rather than the usual two, and *Variety* noted that the unique Marie was ably supported by Charles Chaplin and Mabel Normand. The film has become a classic, but subsequent silent movie ventures (including two shorts—*Tillie's Tomato Surprise* (1915) and *Tillie Wakes Up* (1917) were disappointments. Her vaudeville career also suffered a setback. She championed the labor grievances of the chorus girls' strike in 1917, which resulted in the formation of Actors' Equity, and became an enemy to management. By the 1920s she was down and out.

There was a Broadway show called *The Dancing Girl* (1923), some one-reel comedies made in France, and a small role in Fox's *The Joy Girl* (1926), but at age 57, it looked like her long professional career had fizzled out, and it was rumored she had applied for a housekeeper's position on a Long Island estate. But a young MGM screenwriter named Frances Marion came to the rescue. She had met Marie more than a decade before in San Francisco when, as a news reporter, she requested an interview with the vaudeville queen. When Elisabeth Mayberry, a top New York literary agent, wrote Frances at MGM to inform her of "poor" Marie's financial plight, Frances energetically readied a script entitled *The Callahans and the Murphys* (1927). When Frances presented the project to her friend and studio executive Irving Thalberg, she advised him it would be a great role for studio contractee Polly Moran as Mrs. Murphy, and that the role of Mrs. Callahan would be perfect for "one of the greatest comediennes on Broadway." Thalberg knew little about Marie but recalled her Broadway career had been somewhere in the past. He agreed to cast her and Marion said they could get her for $2,000 weekly. Louis B. Mayer objected, and the figure was changed to $1,500. The picture made a popular team out of Marie and Moran as two slatterns guzzling gin and swapping lines such as, "This stuff makes me see double and feel single," but the studio had to withdraw it from release when it aroused the ire of Hibernian societies.

Once again it seemed Marie's career was over, but Frances Marion advised her to stay in Hollywood and accept supporting roles. A few such roles came along such as *Bringing up Father* (1928) with Moran and *The Patsy* (1928) with Marion Davies. She quickly adapted to talkies, albeit unimportant ones: Corinne Griffith's *The Divine Lady* (1929) at First National; *Dangerous Females* (1929), again with Miss Moran; and a comic role as Venus rising from the sea in MGM's all-star *The Hollywood Revue of 1929*. Finally Frances pulled the magic rabbit out of MGM's hat, when she convinced Thalberg that Marie would be right as Marthy in Eugene O'Neill's *Anna Christie* with Greta Garbo. A test convinced not only Thalberg, but Mayer and director Clarence Brown as well, that Marie could handle this dramatic assignment. That film was ballyhooed for being Garbo's talkie debut and prerelease publicity all but overlooked Marie. But her performance was so beautiful, so effortlessly human and tragic, that critics praised her far more than Garbo. In fact, Garbo herself visited Marie's home with a bouquet of chrysanthemums. Marie had landed back on top.

MGM now realized they had a star in the person of the fat old comedienne and she agreed to stay with the studio. In her autobiography she stated: "Our contract is a gentlemen's agreement. I have no written contract. I don't want one. My word is my bond. And so is Metro's." Marie was given a few more supporting roles after which the prolific Frances Marion came up with another project especially for her friend. This time it was a starring role opposite Wallace Beery (whose career was presently at a low ebb) in *Min and Bill*. They played two down-and-out residents of dockside slums, at once irascibly comic and human. The public adored the two ugly stars who radiated warm love, and Marie was voted the Academy Award as the best actress of the year. As her award was presented to her by Norma Shearer, Marie paid tribute to her screenwriting friend: "You can be the best actress in the world and have the best producer, director, and cameraman, but it won't matter a bit if you don't have the story."

She was now not only the favorite person on the MGM lot, but the studio returned the affection and billed her as "The World's Greatest Actress." More importantly, she was tremendous at the boxoffice. She and Polly Moran did two more pictures as bickering bosom buddies, *Reducing* (1931) and *Politics* (1931). Frances Marion wrote another starring vehicle for her in *Emma* (1932) as Jean Hersholt's beloved maidservant, for which she again was nominated for an Academy Award. She and Beery were teamed in the popular *Tugboat Annie* (1933) where she was the salty captain and Beery her ne'er-do-well husband, "who never struck me except in self defense." She was especially poignant as Carlotta Vance, the decaying theatrical grand dame in David O. Selznick's all-star *Dinner at Eight* (1933), stealing scenes from the satin-ensconced braless blondeness of Jean Harlow. Her best role, as Abby, the housekeeper in *The Late Christopher Bean* (1933), was also her last.

Success had come late, and it was to be short-lived, for on July 28, 1934, Marie died of cancer. During her last months, when she knew she was dying, Louis B. Mayer, who adored her, took to personally looking after her every need, so much so that she fended him off gallantly with, "You are trying to run my life." She was proud of her comeback and the important friends she had made during her long career, including Presidents Theodore Roosevelt, Harding, and Wilson, and she visited with the Franklin D. Roosevelts for weekends at the White House. Marie was the first to admit to friends: "I have been known to grand dame it, at times." She did and the world loved it.

MARIE DRESSLER

Tillie's Punctured Romance (Keystone, 1914)
The Joy Girl (Fox, 1926)
The Callahans and the Murphys (MGM, 1927)
Breakfast at Sunrise (FN, 1927)
Bringing up Father (MGM, 1928)
The Patsy (MGM, 1928)
The Divine Lady (FN, 1929)
The Vagabond Lover (RKO, 1929)
Hollywood Revue of 1929 (MGM, 1929)
Chasing Rainbows (MGM, 1930)
The Girl Said No (MGM, 1930)
Anna Christie (MGM, 1930)

One Romantic Night (UA, 1930)
Caught Short (MGM, 1930)
Let Us Be Gay (MGM, 1930)
Min and Bill (MGM, 1930)
Reducing (MGM, 1931)
Politics (MGM, 1931)
Emma (MGM, 1932)
Prosperity (MGM, 1932)
Tugboat Annie (MGM, 1933)
Dinner at Eight (MGM, 1933)
The Late Christopher Bean (MGM, 1933)

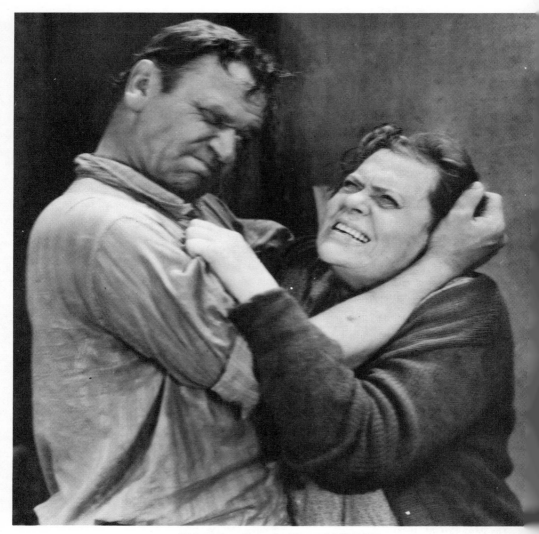

With Wallace Beery in *Min and Bill* (1930)

With Polly Moran in *Reducing* (1931)

With Madge Evans in *Dinner at Eight* (1933)

Jimmy Durante

Referring to his joke repertory, Jimmy Durante is wont to say, "I've got a million of 'em." In 1930 Irving Thalberg played a hunch that the popular Schnozzola could become a money-making member of the MGM family. The razzmatazz Brooklynese garbler was slated to fill the gap somewhere between the spot held by declining star Buster Keaton and the pinnacle occupied by the boisterous Wallace Beery and Marie Dressler. But Thalberg aside, MGM was pretentiously high-toned in those days, seemingly incapable of concealing its embarrassment at presenting film buffoonery to the public. So, instead of giving Durante a proper showcase buildup as a comedy star, he was wrongfully passed off as foolish comic relief and soon wore out his screen welcome. It was not until the more middlebrow atmosphere of the 1940s at Metro that the great comedian returned to the home lot as an appealing featured performer.

James Francis Durante was born February 10, 1893 in New York City, the son of a sideshow barker. The actor recalls that his oversized nose always bothered him, even as a small child. "Everytime I went down the street, I'd hear, 'Look, it's the big-nosed kid!' Even if they said nothin', nothin' at all, I'd shrivel up and think they was sayin', 'What an ugly kid! What a monster!' And then I'd go home and cry. All through life, even when I am makin' a fortune on account of the big beak, and while I am out there on stage laughin' and kiddin' about the nose, at no time was I ever happy about it." By the time he was sixteen, he was playing ragtime piano in Bowery nightclubs and by 1923 he joined with vaudeville partners Lou Clayton and Eddie Jackson and opened the impressive Club Durant in midtown Manhattan. The team made their Broadway debut in Ziegfeld's *Show Girl* (1929), and the next year jaunted out to Paramount's Astoria studio to participate in *Roadhouse Nights*, a picture written especially for them by Ben Hecht and Charles MacArthur.

The team disbanded in 1930 when Thalberg hired Durante for a five-year MGM contract at a hefty salary. As costar of William Haines in *New Adventures of Get-Rich-Quick Wallingford* (1931) he was cast as a con artist, but really just played himself, the Schnozz, quipping as of old: "I'm mortified." He was one of Lawrence Tibbett's prankster buddies in the dismal *Cuban Love Song* (1931), and then was teamed with Buster Keaton in a farce version of *Her Cardboard Lover* entitled *Passionate Plumber* (1932). It was not well received, but the studio paired them again in *Speak Easily* (1932) and *What! No Beer?* (1933), with Durante getting most of the screen time. On loan to Paramount, he outdistanced two George M. Cohans (in a dual role) in *Phantom President* (1932), and in the *Wet Parade* (1932) he managed a sympathetic straight role as a government agent killed by bootleggers. Louis B. Mayer was extremely fond of Durante. He would often visit the comic's dressing room accompanied by A. P. Giannini of the Bank of America, and the two executives would rub the star's famed proboscis for good luck. But Mayer could not find decent roles for Durante.

The comedian returned to New York to do *Strike Me Pink* (1933) on the stage, and then finished out his MGM contract with the revue-style *Hollywood Party* (1934), a spot in *Student Tour* (1934), and on loanout as a frantic Knobby Walsh to Stu Erwin's *Joe Palooka* (1934). He wrote and sang "Inka Dinka Do" for this picture.

Durante was on Broadway throughout the 1930s in *Jumbo* (1935), *Red, Hot And Blue* (1936), *Stars in Your Eyes* (1939), and *Keep off the Grass* (1940), returning to Hollywood for occasional featured comedy relief roles. His sharp spot in *The Man Who Came to Dinner* (1941) awoke new screen interest in him, but Durante was undergoing a career lull largely due to domestic problems. He had married Jeanne Olsen in 1921 and over the years she had become a depressive alcoholic, claiming her husband spent more time with his stage partners than with her. In the last years before she died in 1943, she became an invalid whose nervousness would cause her to cry at the slightest provocation.

It was MGM producer Joe Pasternak who convinced Durante to take another crack at the silver screen, offering the performer a five-year contract at $75,000 per film for two films per year. In *Two Girls and a Sailor* (1944) he was the old vaudeville headliner attempting a comeback, making the role really too close to home for comfort. Audiences and critics alike noted that, refreshingly, he had tightened his performance routine and there was an immediate clamor for more Durante screen ventures. Metro rewrote the five-year agreement at $150,000 per one picture a year. His remaining five Metro assignments, however, mostly wasted his talents with uninspired lowjinks. The best of these was *It Happened in Brooklyn* (1947) in which he was the Mr. Chips-aspiring school janitor who performed "The Song Gotta Come From The Heart" with star Frank Sinatra.

Away from Metro, Durante surprised many by his sensitive performance in *The Great Rupert* (1950) and then launched into a multimillion dollar television career which has spanned more than two decades. In 1960 he married ex-Copacabana hat-check girl Marge Little, thirty-three years his junior, and the couple adopted a daughter. It was again Joe Pasternak who lured Durante back to the movies. He was hired to play Martha Raye's *vis-à-vis* in the Doris Day musical *Billy Rose's Jumbo* (1962), filmed at MGM. As Day's circus owner dad, he livened up a pretty deadly affair. Next, in the comic marathon *It's a Mad, Mad, Mad, Mad World* (1963), he had one of the few genuinely funny bits as he literally kicked the bucket.

Since then he has returned to nightclub work, showing no signs of retiring. There have been two fair biographies about the hot-cha-cha man who once insured his nose with Lloyds of London for $1 million: *Schnozzola* (1951) by Gene Fowler, and *Good Night, Mrs. Calabash* (1963) by William Cahn. Wherever he goes, Durante is still surrounded by an entourage of friends and flunkies ("Everybody wants tuh get inta da act") and claims that his success is due to, "Dere's a million good lookin' guys, but I'm a novelty."

JIMMY DURANTE

Roadhouse Nights (Paramount, 1930)
New Adventures of Get-Rich-Quick Walling-
　ford (MGM, 1931)
Cuban Love Song (MGM, 1931)
Passionate Plumber (MGM, 1932)
The Wet Parade (MGM, 1932)
Speak Easily (MGM, 1932)
Phantom President (Paramount, 1932)
Blondie of the Follies (MGM, 1932)
Meet the Baron (MGM, 1933)
What! No Beer? (MGM, 1933)
Hell Below (MGM, 1933)
Broadway to Hollywood (MGM, 1933)
George White's Scandal (Fox, 1934)
Hollywood Party (MGM, 1934)
Joe Palooka (UA, 1934)
She Learned about Sailors (Fox, 1934)
Strictly Dynamite (RKO, 1934)
Student Tour (MGM, 1934)
Carnival (Columbia, 1935)
Forbidden Music (World, 1938)

Sally, Irene and Mary (20th-Fox, 1938)
Start Cheering (Columbia, 1938)
Little Miss Broadway (20th-Fox, 1938)
Melody Ranch (Republic, 1940)
You're in the Army Now (WB, 1941)
The Man Who Came to Dinner (WB, 1941)
Two Girls and a Sailor (MGM, 1944)
Music for Millions (MGM, 1945)
Two Sisters from Boston (MGM, 1946)
It Happened in Brooklyn (MGM, 1947)
This Time for Keeps (MGM, 1947)
On an Island with You (MGM, 1948)
The Great Rupert (Eagle-Lion, 1950)
The Milkman (Universal, 1950)
Beau James (Paramount, 1957)*
Pepe (Columbia, 1960)
The Last Judgment (Astor, 1961)
Jumbo (MGM, 1962)
It's a Mad, Mad, Mad, Mad World (UA, 1963)

*Unbilled Appearance

With Buster Keaton, Ruth Selwyn, Hedda Hopper, and Ed Brophy in *Speak Easily* (1932)

Nelson Eddy

Nelson Eddy and Jeanette MacDonald were dubbed "America's Sweethearts," and, between 1935 and 1942, they were one of the cinema's most popular romantic teams and certainly the best-liked singing duo ever on the screen. Their eight costarring film vehicles were fluffy, glossy operettas, pure romantic escapism produced with the very best of MGM's excellent polish. Audiences overlooked the inane plots, the often inanimate acting, and the vocal imperfections. They lined up for tickets and added many millions of dollars to the MGM bank balance. MacDonald was the better-liked of the two, more relaxed and more personable. But Eddy, with his manly baritone, appealed to a large portion of the audience, to wit, the women. When either of the singing twosome appeared in a picture with some other costar, the public disapproved. Their fans liked them as a singing team. Little did filmgoers know that the smiling singers held a special animosity toward one another.

Eddy was born in Providence, Rhode Island on June 29, 1901, of a musical family who traced their ancestry back to President Martin Van Buren. "My ancestors did not come over on the Mayflower. They missed by ten years," Eddy once stated. His mother, father, and grandmother had each been a singer, and his grandfather had been a bass drummer for fifty-five years with the Reeves American Band. Eddy began his singing as a boy soprano in the church choir, and the only career he ever considered was one of singing. His family's musical heritage did not provide him any professional entrees, however, and for a number of years he could not afford a professional teacher. He first learned singing by listening to opera recordings of famous singers and then imitating their voices. In 1915 his mother took him to Philadelphia where he studied his school lessons via correspondence course and worked as a telephone operator in an iron foundry. He sold classified ads for the Philadelphia *Press, Evening Public Ledger*, and *Bulletin*, and for a short time was a copywriter for an advertising firm. He got a part in a musical play, *The Marriage Tax*, at the Philadelphia Academy of Music and later joined the Savoy Opera Company where he appeared in several Gilbert and Sullivan operettas.

He met veteran opera singer Dr. Edouard Lippe, who coached him and believed in him enough to lend him the money to travel to Dresden and Paris in order to study with a noted teacher, William V. Vilmont. Just when he was offered a regular position with the Dresden Opera Company, Eddy opted to return to Philadelphia where he won a singing competition and sang the role of Amonasro in *Aida*. He made his professional operatic debut with the Philadelphia Civic Opera Company in an appearance at the New York Metropolitan, singing Tonio in *Pagliacci*. Years later his press agents exploited that Metropolitan appearance, intimating that he had been a member of that renowned company. Eddy gave his first concert recital in Philadelphia in 1928, and for the next five years earned a reputation as a concert baritone and also sang on radio.

At a concert in Los Angeles in 1933, he sang eighteen encores for an enthusiastic audience, and among that audience was Louis B. Mayer's first-class helper Ida Koverman. Koverman took the 6-foot blond singer to Mayer who signed him to a seven-year contract with the studio. The studio tested his boxoffice appeal with rather brief singing spots in three pictures —*Broadway to Hollywood* (1933), *Dancing Lady* (1933), and *Student Tour* (1934). However, musicals suited to his formal screen image were not the thing of the day, so while he waited for his career to get off the ground, he began studying drama with the MGM coaches and appeared in several more concerts.

MGM producer Hunt Stromberg had held up the production of Victor Herbert's *Naughty Marietta* (1935) while he searched for an appropriate lead to appear opposite Jeanette MacDonald, a singer whose screen career was faltering since her earlier Paramount success in several good Maurice Chevalier musicals. Mayer urged Stromberg to take on Eddy, but Stromberg was hesitant and warned Mayer that the picture's main song, "Ah, Sweet Mystery of Life," was the Forest Lawn Cemetery's theme song and could make or break the film. Finally Eddy was given the role, playing the Yankee scout to MacDonald's French princess, and audiences were spellbound as they delivered the Forest Lawn theme. It was a great boxoffice success and, since it had come in on a small budget, it made the profits all the sweeter.

Eager to use Eddy again, Mayer readied Rudolph Friml's *Rose Marie* (1936), planning to cast Metropolitan Opera star Grace Moore opposite Eddy. But Moore had concert commitments and MacDonald replaced her. Eddy played the Canadian Mountie and she the opera star, and after singing "Indian Love Call," they became the patron saints of operetta. After Grace Moore again proved unavailable for *Maytime* (1937) and Eddy and MacDonald were teamed again to even more successful results, there was no question as who should costar with whom. Everyone was happy except the two singing leads. They simply did not like each other.

The studio kept the duo busy in *The Girl of the Golden West* (1938), *Sweethearts* (1938), *New Moon* (1940), and the color film *Bitter Sweet* (1940), with each plot becoming sillier. None of these pictures gave MacDonald much opportunity to display her charming sense of comedy. While most of them cast Eddy in impossible roles, his acting still took a beating from critics who

With Jeanette MacDonald in *Maytime* (1937)

With Ilona Massey and Roland Varno in *Balalakia* (1939)

mentioned his "painful pomposity," "embarrassing lack of ease," and dubbed him "personality minus." Their movies together could hardly be evaluated on realistic terms (one critic said he could not talk about them without lapsing into impudence) and both stars were cognizant of this fact. Both of them aspired to more serious singing. When *I Married an Angel* (1942) was completed, they called it quits as a screen team, never filming *Show Boat* which MGM had purchased as a vehicle for them. Eddy called *I Married an Angel* a mess, his contract expired, and he left. MacDonald did one more picture, *Cairo* (1942), and then also left.

MGM had used Eddy in several pictures without MacDonald—*Rosalie* (1937) and *Balalaika* (1939), both with Ilona Massey, *Let Freedom Ring* (1939) with Virginia Bruce, and *The Chocolate Soldier* (1941) with Risé Stevens. These films, and with his costarring vehicles with MacDonald, made him the highest-paid baritone in the movies. While he refused to see his own films, "simply because I was too ashamed of them," he was a profit-making star. As one studio executive explained; "Nelson always has a profitable following. If he makes an extraordinary picture, if we happen to find an unusual story for him, the returns on it of course, are unusual. But no matter what he makes, there seems to be a basic return we can always count on."

After leaving MGM, Eddy made four more pictures. *The Phantom of the Opera* (1943) was a huge success, but his acting was unanimously panned. Sporting a dark wig he looked decidedly middle aged in this remake which found Claude Rains in the title role. Nevertheless, Universal thought of pairing him and MacDonald in a musical rehash of the operetta *East Wind*, but the project fell through. Eddy did loosen up a bit in *Knickerbocker Holiday* (1944), but the plodding fantasy was not popular with World War II audiences. He did the voice of Willie the Whale in Walt Disney's *Make Mine Music* (1946) and ended his motion picture career in Republic's Western *Northwest Outpost* (1947), reunited with another faded screen figure, Ilona Massey.

Eddy had a large radio following throughout the years he was in pictures. The schmaltzy "Short'nin' Bread" was his theme song. He also appeared in concert and sang at Carnegie Hall in 1944. After a number of years of retirement, he and MacDonald were persuaded in 1959 to record some of their movie hits for RCA. The LP album sold well. When MacDonald died in 1965, she willed a print of *Rose Marie* to Eddy, who had said he never saved any momentos from his career.

In the 1960s Eddy made a comeback via the nightclub circuit with singer Gale Sherwood. This proved to be a popular and lucrative undertaking, consisting of some nostalgia and satire based on his old pictures. As he told reporters; "I want to keep going till I drop." On March 6, 1967, just a few hours after performing at the Hotel San Souci in Miami Beach, he was with friends in his hotel suite when he suddenly exclaimed: "Oh, I can't talk. Something's wrong. I can't see," and he collapsed and died of a stroke. He was survived by his wife, Anne Denitz. She was three years his senior and had been formerly married to director Sidney Franklin. She and Eddy were married in 1939 but they had no children. At his funeral Eddy was eulogized as a "simple, straightforward man."

NELSON EDDY

Broadway to Hollywood (MGM, 1933)
Dancing Lady (MGM, 1933)
Student Tour (MGM, 1934)
Naughty Marietta (MGM, 1935)
Rose Marie (MGM, 1936)
Maytime (MGM, 1937)
Rosalie (MGM, 1937)
Girl of the Golden West (MGM, 1938)
Sweethearts (MGM, 1938)
Let Freedom Ring (MGM, 1939)

Balalaika (MGM, 1939)
New Moon (MGM, 1940)
Bitter Sweet (MGM, 1940)
The Chocolate Soldier (MGM, 1941)
I Married an Angel (MGM, 1942)
The Phantom of the Opera (Universal, 1943)
Knickerbocker Holiday (UA, 1944)
Make Mine Music (Voice Only: RKO, 1946)
Northwest Outpost (Republic, 1947)

With Jeanette MacDonald in *I Married an Angel* (1942)

John Ericson

If an actor is fortunate, he has one lucky break in his career. John Ericson had two in the early 1950s. Each led to MGM screen commitments, but neither opportunity pushed him into the realm of a cinema leading man.

Ericson was born Joseph Meibes in Dusseldorf, Germany on September 25, 1927, where his father headed a food-flavoring concern. His mother was Ellen Wilson, a former Shakespearian actress and operatic singer. Ericson was still an infant when the family moved to Antwerp, Belgium to avoid the growing political unrest in Germany. He was only three years old when the family relocated to New York. Because the Meibes continued to move around the United States, Ericson had quite a wide-ranging education: at the Jackson Heights, N. Y. public school, then at the Faulkner School in Chicago, and finally at Newton High School in Elmhurst, N. Y.

After attending the American Academy of Dramatics Arts, Ericson spent three years working in stock, first at the Barter Theatre in Arlington, Virginia in 1949 and then at the Gateway Theatre in Gatlenburg, Tennessee. When director Fred Zinnemann was auditioning actors in New York for MGM's *Teresa* (1951), to be shot largely on location in Italy, Ericson tried out and was eventually hired. He was cast as the World War II G.I. who weds an Italian girl (Pier Angeli) and encounters tremendous prejudice when he brings his bride back to his small hometown, particularly from his unrelenting mother (Patricia Collinge). The film was typical of MGM product at the time, laced full with "messages," but uncourageous enough to be realistic in the face of boxoffice disdain. The resulting film satisfied few. Had Ericson risen above the sticky script, MGM or other producing companies might have taken more interest in his showcasing screen debut.

Instead, by the time *Teresa* was released, Ericson was already performing on Broadway as Sefton in José Ferrer's production of *Stalag 17*. (William Holden won an Oscar for starring as the collaborating G.I. in the film version.) Ericson received good notices for his top featured assignment and won the N. Y. Critics Award as the most promising newcomer of the season. But there was a strong critical reserve about Ericson's too slavish following of the Marlon Brando school of acting. He remained with *Stalag 17* throughout its Broadway run, and when the show closed June 21, 1952, he went on tour with the production for six months. During this period he performed on radio's *Voice of the Army* and was on television with *Studio One, Philco Playhouse*, and *Hawkins Falls*. Also in 1953 Ericson wed songstress Milly Cory, and they later had a son and a daughter.

In early 1953 Ericson accepted MGM's contract offer and went to the Coast. It was a period when boxoffice favorites were of the healthy, clean-cut type, such as Tab Hunter, Robert Wagner, Jeffrey Hunter and the soon-to-emerge Paul Newman. Ericson certainly qualified in the looks department (6' 2", blonde, blue eyes), having a far stronger potential screen appeal than such MGM contractees as Dewey Martin, Jeff Richards, or Richard Anderson. But, like Warner Brothers, which did not know how to handle the build-up of Richard Davalos, Ericson was dropped into four Metro A features. His roles were always subordinate to the main thrust of the film, and he languished on the sidelines, where his untapped middle-European charm went unutilized.

In Charles Vidor's *Rhapsody* (1954) Elizabeth Taylor was a wealthy, culture-craving girl entranced with fledgling violinist Vittorio Gassman, but loved by student pianist Ericson. MGM, still in its Latin Lovers phase, gave Gassman the flashier scenes, allowing Ericson to capture Taylor on the rebound by saving her from a suicide attempt. Several sequences required Ericson to simulate piano playing. In the Cinemascope remake of *The Student Prince* (1954), Ericson was the moustachioed Count Von Asterburg, the ill-tempered nobleman who conflicts with Prince Karl (Edmund Purdom on screen—but the singing voice of Mario Lanza) over the affections of Heidelberg barmaid Ann Blyth. Ericson and Purdom have a duel, and Purdom is forced to wed stodgy princess Betta St. John. Ericson emerged a distinct "also" in this soggy picture. *Green Fire* (1954) confronted a patrician coffee plantation owner with tough emerald mining engineer Stewart Granger. Also in the cast was Paul Douglas as Granger's wise-cracking partner. Ericson? . . . well, he was Grace Kelly's wastrel brother, clearly lost in the wide-screen, color shuffle, in which the Colombian scenery was most memorable.

Ericson's last MGM assignment was in John Sturges' *Bad Day at Black Rock* (1955). Spencer Tracy arrives in the shambling southwestern town of Black Rock in 1945 to deliver a posthumous war medal to the Japanese father of an American soldier. Only the farmer has "disappeared." Sixth-featured Ericson, husband of fourth-billed Anne Francis, is among those responsible for the Oriental's death. However, Ernest Borgnine, Robert Ryan, and Lee Marvin were more vicious and more likely villains than Ericson.

Written off by MGM, Ericson became an independent screen player. His film career, however, dissipated slower than many former studio contractees. He was the son of the notorious criminal in *The Return of Jack Slade* (1955). But in his other two Allied Artists pictures, he was far less in control of his performance: *The Cruel Tower* (1956) as the man afraid of heights bullied by his brutish boss, Steve Brodie, and *Oregon Passage* (1957) as the cavalry lieutenant in love with an Indian maid. He was just one of the brothers of a gunslinger up against Barbara Stanwyck's gang in *Forty Guns* (1957), and in *Day of The Bad Man* (1959) he was the sheriff trying to cope with the rigid honesty of Judge Fred MacMurray.

In the European-produced *Under Ten Flags* (1960), Ericson played his first onscreen German since *The Student Prince* days. He was Kruger, an officer on Van Heflin's Nazi sea raider who got to romance Mylene Demongeot. *Pretty Boy Floyd* (1960) offered Ericson his last real starring film role to date, playing the Prohibition days gangster. The movie had no subtlety of style, but, in its sleazy way, it recaptured the flavor of those cheap gangster melodramas of the 1930s. At least Ericson was somewhat convincing when he mouthed such lines as, "I don't know whether to clout you or kiss you." He does the former to one moll in the film. (Ten years later American International released *A Bullet for Pretty Boy*, a considerably less successful rendering of the same material, with former singer Fabian in the lead role.)

Ericson joined the legion of once-Hollywood performers making cloak and sandal pictures in Italy (*I Semiramis* (1963), the first of many he would make on the continent. But he returned to California and to MGM to play a staunch citizen of the dim-witted Western town visited by Tony Randall's oriental carnival in the bizarre *Seven Faces of Dr. Lao* (1964).

In the late 1950s, Ericson returned to television (he was twice on *Shirley Temple's Storybook* in 1958) and did some additional stage work, notably *Mister Roberts* in 1959. He traveled the video series route, costarring with Anne Francis in *Honey West,* a 1965–1966 entry that lasted only thirty episodes. She had the lead as a private detective, and he was her partner Sam Bolt.

In the late 1960s Ericson was in three economy features that soon were relegated to television, putting him in the same used-out anonymous category as Richard Egan, David Brian, Lois Nettleton, and Patricia Owen—his costars in these pictures. Two other quickie films he made, Universal's *Heads or Tails* and Allied Artists' *Treasure of Pancho Villa* (1967) have been shelved and may eventually be debuted on television in America. In Walt Disney's *Bedknobs and Broomsticks* (1971), Ericson had a featured role as the Nazi colonel leading a landing party on Peppering Eye, England. He seemed ill at ease in this cardboard characterization.

Approaching the age of fifty, Ericson still has the babyface look of a Richard Jaeckel, but he has yet to create a suitable screen identity for his personality.

JOHN ERICSON

Teresa (MGM, 1951)

Rhapsody (MGM, 1954)

The Student Prince (MGM, 1954)

Green Fire (MGM, 1954)

Bad Day at Black Rock (MGM, 1955)

The Return of Jack Slade (AA, 1955)

With Edmund Purdom, James Dobson, and Charles Victor in *The Student Prince* (1954)

Madge Evans

Decorous and capable Madge Evans had already amassed sixteen years of screen and stage experience before she arrived at MGM in 1931 at the age of twenty-two. During the 1910s she achieved the same degree of screen popularity that decades later would come to Shirley Temple and Margaret O'Brien. In the late 1920s Madge was a frequent Broadway stage ingenue, although not in the same league with Claudette Colbert, Miriam Hopkins, or Sylvia Sidney. If MGM can be blamed for not promoting Madge beyond her minor but steady leading lady roles, part of the responsibility for her cinema casting rut must be thrust at the actress herself. She was civilized and charming in her modest way but never generated any sparks of onscreen distinctiveness that would have made her more a public favorite due to the *quality* rather than the *quantity* of her film acting.

Madge was born in New York City on July 1, 1909, the daughter of Arthur John and Maude Mary Evans. Her father was a native of Liverpool, England, and her mother was a Manhattan magazine model. Madge's brother Tom would later become a Hollywood still photographer. Madge began her professional career before she was a year old, posing for painter George DeForest Brush. Like her mother, Madge frequently modeled for magazine illustrators, appearing in the *Saturday Evening Post*, and posed for consumer product advertisements. She was the Fairy Soap girl. Madge was educated by private tutors and at the age of five struck out into new fields. Baby Madge, as she was known professionally, made her Broadway stage debut in *The Highway of Life* (1914), and later that year appeared in Paramount's film, *Sign of the Cross*. She was in three more Paramount films before being signed to a contract by William A. Brady. For her films Madge was usually cast as the orphaned waif or as the daughter of a trouble-ridden widow as in *The Corner Grocer* (1917). That same year Madge appeared on screen with Brady's famous daughter Alice in *Maternity* and also returned to the stage to play Mimsey Seraskier in the Shuberts' prestige production of *Peter Ibbetson*, starring John and Lionel Barrymore and Constance Collier. Madge continued in films until 1919, playing in such tearjerkers as *The Love Nest* and *Home Wanted*. At the age of ten, however, she obviously had outgrown her very popular toddler roles and had to wait four years before she was mature enough physically to

210

portray virginal ingenues. Vitagraph cast her as the sweetheart of inventor James Morrison in *On the Banks of the Wabash* (1923), the title suggested by Paul Dresser's song. The next year she was the aristocratic girl friend of West Point cadet Richard Barthelmess in the romantic drama *Classmates*, released by First National.

Madge was making very little impression as a cinema leading lady and wisely decided to return to the stage. She shed her Mary Pickford blonde curls and became a pert flapper type, appearing to good advantage in *Daisy Mayne* (1926), *The Marquise* (1927), *Our Betters* (1928), and *Philip Goes Forth* (1931). Madge's performance in the last play was sufficiently impressive to bring her to the attention of a MGM executive and she was signed to a term contract.

MGM cast the former child star opposite Ramon Novarro in her first studio effort, *Son of India* (1931). He was the wise native of India who rejects Boston Back Bay girl Madge. The N.Y. *Times* noted she "played very well in view of everything." She and Lew Cody were dealers at Clark Gable's racetrack gambling joint in *Sporting Blood* (1931). In *Guilty Hands* (1931) Madge was the daughter of attorney Lionel Barrymore. The film had her fiance Alan Mowbray killed by her father. She was rather unconvincing as an Austrian countess in love with American flyer Charles Farrell in *Heartbreak* (1931). These four features established Madge as a popular modern ingenue, a fine type casting for a screen beginner, but a professional category not likely to keep an actress on top of the status heap unless she delves into meatier roles. Madge never took the necessary step. For instance on loan to United Artists, she was only one of the three gold diggers in *The Greeks Had a Word for Them* (1932), and for the same studio she was mayor Frank Morgan's blah girl friend in the offbeat recitative musical *Hallelujah, I'm a Bum* (1933), starring Al Jolson. The best of her nine releases in 1933 was the important all-star *Dinner at Eight*. Madge was the maturing daughter of Billie Burke and Lionel Barrymore. She is having an ill-fated affair with fading screen star John Barrymore throughout the film. At best, in such illustrious company, Madge was crisp and competent, but hardly memorable. The hodgepodge variety show *Broadway to Hollywood* (1933) reunited her with Alice Brady, who again played her mother. Madge was scheduled to star in MGM's *Louisiana Lou*, a project to be directed by Tod Browning, and based on a William Faulkner script. But the novelist clashed with MGM authorities, and the film was eventually abandoned. The next year she was with Robert Montgomery in *Fugitive Lovers*, a project which suffered by comparison with the very similar *It Happened One Night*.

Irving Thalberg, who is said to have lost interest in promoting Madge's screen career once he put Myrna Loy under MGM contract, gave Madge one more "break" when he cast her in Helen Hayes' *What Every Woman Knows* (1934). She was the flirtatious Lady Sybil who temporarily snatches away Hayes' husband (Brian Aherne). The assignment failed to breathe any new life into Madge's stagnating career, and for the next three years she continued on at MGM with bland ingenue roles. Playing the role of Agnes in *David*

Copperfield (1935), she was billed below Maureen O'Sullivan, and in Paramount's *Men Without Names* (1935) she was a stereotyped dashing lady reporter. Ironically, the British-made *Transatlantic Tunnel* (1935) showcased her to good advantage as the blinded wife of engineer Richard Dix, and she demonstrated a forcefulness noticeably absent in her Hollywood films. But thereafter it was back to stock assignments such as the persistent social worker in Bing Crosby's *Pennies from Heaven* (1936). She finished her MGM contract with the old-hat *The Thirteenth Chair* (1937), a thriller in which she had the lead. Madge slipped downhill rapidly on the Hollywood screen scene thereafter, first as John Boles' island romance in *Sinners in Paradise* (1938) and later that year as the daughter of Colonel H. B. Warner in Republic's *Army Girl*.

Unable to resurrect her screen standing, Madge went back to Broadway, appearing in Philip Barry's *Here Come the Clowns* (1938). The next year she wed playwright Sidney Kingsley, then age thirty-six, whom she had met while doing stock in Suffern, New York. Since that time the couple has resided in New York City, where Madge was a frequent straw hat performer in the late 1930s and early 1940s, appearing in such plays as *Biography, Brief Moment, The Greeks Had a Word for It, Mr. and Mrs. North*, and *Private Lives*. She was announced for the pre-Broadway tour of *Two-Story House* in 1941, but at the last minute Karen Morley took over the assignment. Madge was back on Broadway in Kingsley's *The Patriots* in 1943, and the next year played Jo in *Little Women* at Bucks County Playhouse.

Madge remained in semiretirement from acting and her name popped up only in the social columns as the wife of playwright Kingsley, who in the 1950s became a CBS television network executive. Madge made a few guest-starring appearances on early 1950s video anthology shows. As a lark, she had a brief spot on *The Verdict Is Yours* and appeared with Lonny Chapman in an episode of *The Investigators*, both produced for CBS in 1958. But since then the Shirley Temple of the 1910s has been content just to be Mrs. Kingsley, devoting her nonsocial hours to charitable causes.

MADGE EVANS

Sign of the Cross (Paramount, 1914)
Zaza (Paramount, 1915)
The Garden of Lies (Universal-Broadway, 1915)
Seven Sisters (Paramount, 1915)
The Revolt (World, 1916)
Seventeen (Paramount, 1916)
Husband and Wife (Brady-World, 1916)
Sudden Riches (World, 1916)
The Hidden Scar (World, 1916)
Broken Chairs (World, 1916)
Beloved Adventuress (Peerless-World, 1917)

The Little Duchess (Peerless-World, 1917)
The Burglar (Peerless-World, 1917)
The Volunteer (World, 1917)
Web of Desire (Peerless-Brady-World, 1917)
The Corner Grocer (Paramount, 1917)
The Adventures of Carol (World, 1917)
Maternity (Peerless-Brady-World, 1917)
Gates of Gladness (World, 1918)
Woman and Wife (World, 1918)
The Golden Wall (World, 1918)
The Power and the Glory (World, 1918)
Stolen Orders (Brady-World, 1918)

Neighbors (World, 1918)
Wanted–a Mother (Peerless-World, 1918)
Seventeen (Frohman-Paramount, 1919)
The Love Nest (World, 1919)
Home Wanted (World, 1919)
The Love Defender (World, 1919)
Heidi (Prizma, 1921)
On the Banks of the Wabash (Vitagraph, 1923)
Classmates (FN, 1924)
Son of India (MGM, 1931)
Sporting Blood (MGM, 1931)
Guilty Hands (MGM, 1931)
Heartbreak (Fox, 1931)
West of Broadway (MGM, 1932)
Are You Listening? (MGM, 1932)
Lovers Courageous (MGM, 1932)
The Greeks Had a Word for Them (UA, 1932)
Huddle (MGM, 1932)
Fast Life (MGM, 1932)
Hell Below (MGM, 1933)
Hallelujah, I'm a Bum (UA, 1933)
Made on Broadway (MGM, 1933)
Dinner at Eight (MGM, 1933)
The Nuisance (MGM, 1933)
The Mayor of Hell (WB, 1933)

Broadway to Hollywood (MGM, 1933)
Beauty for Sale (MGM, 1933)
Day of Reckoning (MGM, 1933)
Fugitive Lovers (MGM, 1934)
The Show-Off (MGM, 1934)
Stand up and Cheer (Fox, 1934)
Death on the Diamond (MGM, 1934)
Grand Canary (Fox, 1934)
Paris Interlude (MGM, 1934)
What Every Woman Knows (MGM, 1934)
Helldorado (Fox, 1935)
David Copperfield (MGM, 1935)
Age of Indiscretion (MGM, 1935)
Transatlantic Tunnel (Gaumont-British, 1935)
Calm Yourself (MGM, 1935)
Men Without Names (Paramount, 1935)
Moonlight Murder (MGM, 1936)
Exclusive Story (MGM, 1936)
Piccadilly Jim (MGM, 1936)
Pennies from Heaven (Columbia, 1936)
Espionage (MGM, 1937)
The Thirteenth Chair (MGM, 1937)
Sinners in Paradise (Universal, 1938)
Army Girl (Republic, 1938)

With Robert Young in *Paris Interlude* (1934)

Mel Ferrer

The enigmatic Mel Ferrer has often been classed as a pint-sized *wunderkind*, whose multifaceted entertainment career dissipated itself into nonsuperiority in all areas. He had already functioned in directing–production capacities at Columbia and RKO before he came to MGM in the early 1950s. At MGM he was generally limited to being a performer. He had the same elegant remote air as the earlier Joseph Schildkraut, but Ferrer was far more wooden. In the "new" Hollywood suave aesthetes were not much in demand, onscreen or off, particularly at MGM which was struggling for its survival. Once he met and married actress Audrey Hepburn, his interest in acting, which he always insisted was just a means to become a director, lessened even further. He was more concerned with being a Svengali to her Trilby.

Melchior Gaston Ferrer was born in Elberon, New Jersey on August 25, 1917, the son of Dr. José Ferrer, a Cuban who became a New York City surgeon, and Irene O'Donohue, a Manhattan socialite. He attended the Canterbury Preparatory School and then went to Princeton University where he quit in his sophomore year to work in the theatre. He acted at the Cape Playhouse in Dennis, Massachusetts, was an editor for a time for the Stephen Day Press in Brattleboro, Vermont, and wrote a children's book, *Tito's Hat*. He entereed the Broadway scene as a chorus dancer in two musicals, *You Never Know* and *Everywhere I Roam*, both in 1938. In *Cue for Passion* (1940), directed by Otto Preminger, he played a reporter. His stage career was interrupted when he contracted polio and was forced to spend a year recuperating. In the interim he developed a facility for radio commentary and, once recovered, found employment as a disc jockey–commentator in network stations at Little Rock, Arkansas, and at Long View, Texas. Then in 1943, NBC hired him as a producer–director for many of its top radio shows such as *The Hit Parade, The Hildegarde Show*, and *Mr. District Attorney*. He left this post in 1945 when Columbia Pictures offered him a wide-range contract to function in whatever capacity the studio required, actor, director, or story consultant. He directed a low-budget remake of *The Girl of the Limberlost* (1945), but the picture went over schedule and the studio promptly dropped his option.

Ferrer returned to Broadway to act in Lillian Smith's short-lasting

Strange Fruit (1945) directed by José Ferrer—no relation—and the following year starred in a revival of *Cyrano de Bergerac*, directed by José Ferrer and later restaged by Guthrie McClintic. His performance in this play led to David O. Selznick and RKO hiring Ferrer on much the same terms that he had had at Columbia. He worked in Mexico with John Ford on *The Fugitive* (1947) and returned to Hollywood to help salvage the multimillion-dollar fiasco, *Vendetta*, finally released in 1950.

Meanwhile, Ferrer made his film acting debut in Louis de Rochemont's *Lost Boundaries* (1949), playing the New Hampshire black physician who passed for white. He was an onlooker to Joan Fontaine's bitchery in *Born to Be Bad* (1950), directed Claudette Colbert in *The Secret Fury* (1950), was borrowed by Columbia to play the fear-wracked matador in *The Brave Bulls* (1951), and ended his RKO stay by playing Frenchy Fairmont in Marlene Dietrich's *Rancho Notorious* (1952).

Then MGM head Dore Schary, who had known Ferrer when they both were at RKO, hired him on an acting capacity. In the swashbuckler *Scaramouche* (1952) he was fourth-billed as the imperious Marquis de Maynes, the thoroughbred who first duels with star Stewart Granger and then loses Janet Leigh to him. The rather wooden Ferrer was ideally cast by Metro in *Lili* (1953) as Paul Berthalet, the lame puppeteer who eventually expresses his abiding affection for French carnival waif Leslie Caron. In the European-lensed mishmash *Saadia* (1953), Ferrer was the doctor competing with French-educated sheik Cornel Wilde for native Rita Gam. He played King Arthur in *Knights of the Round Table* (1953), where his queen, Ava Gardner, preferred top-billed Lancelot (Robert Taylor) to him.

It was at this juncture that Ferrer met and fell in love with Audrey Hepburn. He convinced her to star in a Broadway production of *Ondine* with him, directed by Alfred Lunt. The show opened in February 1954, to great acclaim, and that September they were married. (He had been previously wed to sculptress Frances Pilchard. They had had a son and a daughter, and then the couple were divorced. He next wed and divorced Barbara C. Tripps, by whom he had a son and daughter, and remarried and again divorced Pilchard.)

Based in Europe, Ferrer was in the British *Oh Rosalinda* (1955), the Italian *Probito* (released in 1961 in the U. S. as *Forbidden*), and then costarred with Hepburn in the Italian-lensed *War and Peace* (1956). His portrayal of Prince Andrey was most ineffectual and cold. Metro then used him as John Kerr's brother in the French-made *The Vintage* (1957) which ended up on double-bill programs. That same year he was among a group of actors miscast in *The Sun Also Rises*, and joined with Hepburn in an elaborate but sterile video production of *Mayerling*, directed by Anatole Litvak.

MGM had begun filming W. H. Hudson's *Green Mansions* in 1954 with Vincente Minnelli directing and Edmund Purdom and Pier Angeli slated as stars. The project was abandoned, only to be picked up again in July 1958, with Ferrer directing and Hepburn and Anthony Perkins in the leads. It was

216

not at all well received. Ferrer completed his Metro contract by appearing with Harry Belafonte and Inger Stevens in *The World, the Flesh and the Devil* (1959).

In the 1960s Ferrer jumped about the Continent, starring as a sensitive type in such horror tales as *The Hands of Orlac* (1960) and *Blood and Roses* (1961), doing a cameo as Major General Robert Haines in *The Longest Day* (1962), projecting a most baffled Cleander in the laughable *The Fall of the Roman Empire* (1964), squirming with embarrassment as the psychiatrist in *Sex and the Single Girl* (1964), and floundering as the painter *El Greco* (1966). Having coscripted and directed *Cabriola* (1965) and produced *Every Day Is a Holiday* (1966), both filmed in Spain, Ferrer returned to Hollywood to produce the screen version of *Wait until Dark* (1967), starring his wife. Later that year she filed for divorce in France, and it became final in 1968.

Since then, Ferrer has remarried—Elizabeth Soukutine, a Belgian who edits children's books and is twenty years his junior. He remains based on the Continent. His most recent film appearance was in *Time for Loving* with Joanna Shimkus and Britt Eklund, made a few years ago, but just released in 1972.

MEL FERRER

Lost Boundaries (Film Classics, 1949)
Born to Be Bad (RKO, 1950)
The Brave Bulls (Columbia, 1951)
Rancho Notorious (RKO, 1952)
Scaramouche (MGM, 1952)
Lili (MGM, 1953)
Saadia (MGM, 1953)
Knights of the Round Table (MGM, 1953)
Oh Rosalinda (British, 1955)
War and Peace (Paramount, 1956)
The Vintage (MGM, 1957)
Paris Does Strange Things (WB, 1957)
The Sun Also Rises (20th-Fox, 1957)
Fraulein (20th-Fox, 1958)
The World, the Flesh and the Devil (MGM, 1959)
The Hands of Orlac (French–English, 1960)
L'Homme a Femmes (French, 1960)

Blood and Roses (Paramount, 1961)
Legge Di Guerra (Italian–French–German, 1961)
Forbidden (Casolaro-Giglio Film Distributing, 1961)
Le Diable et les 10 Commandements (Italian–French, 1962)
The Longest Day (20th-Fox, 1962)
I Lancieri Neri (Italian–French, 1963)
The Fall of the Roman Empire (Paramount, 1964)
Paris When It Sizzles (Paramount, 1964)*
Sex and the Single Girl (WB, 1964)
El Señor de la Salle (Spanish, 1964)
El Greco (20th-Fox, 1966)
Time for Loving (Hemdale, 1972)

*Unbilled Appearance

Anne Francis

At the tail end of MGM's golden age, shapely Anne Francis (36–24–35 1/2) was signed as a general utility leading lady. Metro saw her as another glamor doll, but failed to promote her beyond a hackneyed sexy-gal type of campaign. None of her string of MGM pictures required any great acting ability from Anne; she was just a living prop. In any case, given the lackluster production values of 1950s MGM films, there were no longer any lush backdrops to showcase even an animated puppet. Anne, who says, "I've been fighting my face all my life," perhaps best analyzed her MGM failure, as a lack of "A. I." (audience identification), which held her back from gaining any momentum of cinema success.

Anne was born September 16, 1930, in Ossining, New York, not too far from Sing Sing Prison. She was the only child of Philip Francis, a sales manager for a New York City concern, and Edith Abbertson Francis. Because of Anne's unusually good looks, her mother quickly decided the girl was just right for a modeling career. By the age of five Anne was an established magazine cover model for such prestigious publications as *Ladies' Home Journal*. Anne's trademark then, and throughout her professional career, was the large mole located to the right of her lower lip. The family moved to Manhattan when Anne was seven, and thereafter she was made to pursue a professional career on a full-time basis. She became a John Powers model and was taken by her mother from audition to audition, eventually being heard on scores of radio shows, including such programs as *When a Girl Marries, Big Town*, and *Aunt Jenny*. She soon become known as the "Little Queen Of Soap Opera."

When Anne was eleven she made it to Broadway, playing Gertrude Lawrence as a child in the musical *Lady in the Dark*, and was the star of her own daily CBS-TV show, which was taken off the air after seven months only because of the outbreak of World War II and the shutdown of commercial TV. For a while Anne was being considered for a part in MGM's *Mrs. Miniver* (1942). However, the studio decided she was too old for the role of the Miniver girl, and the part was given to Clare Sanders. In 1946, however, MGM did bring Anne to Hollywood under a term contract where she was promptly rechristened "The Fragile Blonde with the Mona Lisa Smile." After playing the small role of high school Elsie Rand in the Mickey Rooney musical *Summer Holiday*, not released until 1948, she had a bit in Esther Williams' *This Time for Keeps* (1947), and was loaned to David Selznick for a minute assignment in *Portrait of Jenny* (1948). For the most part Anne languished in the MGM School, waiting for a decent role. In the end all she did receive was a pink slip. Her option had been dropped during the television scare economy wave of 1947.

Back in New York Anne found a new career for herself as one of the Bonny Maid Versatile Varieties girls on the weekly NBC television show. She and two other blondes, Carol Ohmart and Jean Eyres, became well known figures as video pitch girls for the linoleum company, dressed in kilts. Along the way there was a stock engagement of *My Sister Eileen*, and finally she was cast in *So Young, So Bad* (1950) an United Artists budget picture shot on location in New York. She, Anne Jackson, Enid Pulver, and Rita Moreno were four of the teenaged inmates at a reform school for girls, while Paul Henreid played the understanding psychiatrist at the school. It was a low-grade *Caged* all the way. Next Anne was seen as Lloyd Bridges' girl friend in the drama *The Whistle at Eaton Falls* (1951), a labor union story shot in Portsmouth, New Hampshire.

After this varied apprenticeship, Anne was finally spotted and tested by Twentieth Century-Fox, which signed her to a contract. She arrived in Hollywood in December 1950. Her new studio labeled her "The Palomino Blonde" and she was featured in color photographs posed next to a Palomino. "The one without the mole," Ann says, "was the horse." Her first Fox film was *Elopement* (1951), in which she and William Lundigan were the central figures of the plot, but the focal point was on their in-laws, played by Clifton Webb and Charles Bickford respectively. The N. Y. *Times* made this observation about Anne: " . . . [she is] both easy to watch and hear." *Dreamboat* (1952) cast her again as Clifton Webb's daughter; this time he was a professor trying to live down his past as a silent screen romantic hero. Her big "break" at Fox was in the title role of *Lydia Bailey* (1952), based on Kenneth Roberts' novel of early nineteenth-century Haiti. Dale Robertson played the swashbuckling lawyer, and Charles Korvin as her guardian was the villain. Anne was the expatriot American, who one reviewer carped was, "as out of place as an iceberg in this setting." Fox loaned her to Warner Brothers to play a tart in James Cagney's *A Lion Is in the Streets* (1953). She had a caustic role as Dick Powell's ex-fiancée in RKO's *Susan Slept Here* (1954) and wound up her Fox contract by playing in *The Rocket Man* (1954), a budget vehicle for child performer George "Foghorn" Winslow.

Meanwhile in 1952 Anne had wed Bamlet Laurence Price, Jr. a small-time producer. Three years later they were divorced. She claimed that he expected her to clean the house when she returned home after a twelve-hour workday.

MGM was her next home base. That studio took full advantage of the Marilyn Monroe craze and promoted Anne as a sexpot in the Lana Turner tradition. No one took the campaign too seriously except members of the production line at MGM. Anne was seen as George Raft's castoff mistress in *Rogue Cop* (1954), loaned to Warner Brothers to play Rae, the San Diego V-girl, in *Battle Cry* (1955), and then had a change of pace as the sympathetic pregnant wife of teacher Glenn Ford in *The Blackboard Jungle* (1955). Her best-remembered role at Metro was in their elaborate science fiction entry, *Forbidden Planet* (1956), in which she played Walter Pidgeon's scantily clad daughter. However, Robby the Robot got the best notices in that Cinemascope color entry. *The Great American Pastime* (1956) was ostensibly about baseball but more concerned with the bedroom habits of suburban couples. One of the performers in this comedy, besides Anne, Tom Ewell, and Ann Miller, was Anne's toy poodle, whom she had named Walter Smidgeon. (The year before there had been a mild rhubarb when hard-of-hearing gossip columnists had mistaken her dog for actor Walter Pidgeon and had had the two MGM players vacationing together in Palm Springs.) Anne's last MGM assignment was as the curvaceous nurse with the upsweep hairdo in the comedy *Don't Go Near the Water* (1957), but most of the camera time was spent on Glenn Ford's romance with South Seas island teacher Gia Scala.

Anne emerged from 5 1/2 years of psychoanalysis around 1960. She recalls, "When I went into analysis I didn't know whether I'd come out of it quitting the business or what. I came out of it ... knowing that I love it. It was the greatest investment I ever made." That same year she eloped to Las Vegas to wed dentist Dr. Robert Abeloff. They had a daughter Elizabeth Jane in 1963, but were divorced the next year. She received child support in the decree but no alimony since her average income of $200,000 yearly was more than he earned in his profession.

Anne's 1960s films have been a rather dismal lot. She was a call girl in the sugar-coated *Girl of the Night* (1960) in which John Kerr was her gentle pimp. That same year she was an unnerved airline stewardess in *The Crowded Sky* (1960) with a distraught John Kerr as her boyfriend. Five years later she returned to the screen as Dana Andrews' daughter in the adventure tale, *The Satan Bug* (1965), and the same year showed up in *Brainstorm* as Andrews' wife. When Anne signed for the movie musical *Funny Girl* (1968) she thought she had a costarring role as a chorus girl friend of Barbra Streisand. But she and Streisand feuded, resulting in most of Anne's scenes being eliminated from the final print. She sued to have her name removed from the credits, but it remained. She performed as a painter from the East in the B Western *More Dead than Alive* (1968) and was relegated to performing two secondary roles as a straight lady to Don Knotts in *The Love God?* (1969) and then to Jerry Lewis in *Hook, Line and Sinker* (1969). These two comedies flopped badly on the theatrical market. Her last features to date were *Lost Flight* (1970), a telefeature released to theatres instead, and the Spanish-lensed *Pancho Villa* (1972).

Anne has not fared much better on television in the last decade. After guest starring in such series as *Ben Casey, Arrest and Trial*, and *Twilight Zone*, she was given her own video series, *Honey West* (1965), in which she played a female James Bond. Despite her looks, a knack for karate, and some wild plots, the series did not spark audience interest and died after only one season. In the 1970s she became one of the busiest guest actresses on television, making an average of two appearances a month on various network series and features. While she has proven to be always more than competent and usually very splashy in appearance, none of her assignments have been memorable roles.

Although Anne has had no intention of remarrying, she adopted six-month-old Margaret West Francis in early 1971. As she says, "You have to be independent, both financially and spiritually, to make a decision like I did. But I don't think either of the girls will suffer because they haven't got a father around all the time." About men: "Having a man doesn't work unless the strength and will to survive are there within you first. The mistake people make about love is trying to find it in others without finding it in themselves first."

ANNE FRANCIS

This Time for Keeps (MGM, 1947)
Summer Holiday (MGM, 1948)
Portrait of Jennie (Selznick, 1948)
So Young, So Bad (UA, 1950)
The Whistle at Eaton Falls (Columbia, 1951)
Elopement (20th-Fox, 1951)
Lydia Bailey (20th-Fox, 1952)
Dreamboat (20th-Fox, 1952)
A Lion Is in the Streets (WB, 1953)
The Rocket Man (20th-Fox, 1954)
Susan Slept Here (RKO, 1954)
Rogue Cop (MGM, 1954)
Bad Day at Black Rock (MGM, 1954)
Battle Cry (WB, 1955)
The Blackboard Jungle (MGM, 1955)
The Scarlet Coat (MGM, 1955)

Forbidden Planet (MGM, 1956)
The Rack (MGM, 1956)
The Great American Pastime (MGM, 1956)
The Hired Gun (MGM, 1957)
Don't Go Near the Water (MGM, 1957)
Girl of the Night (WB, 1960)
The Crowded Sky (WB, 1960)
The Satan Bug (UA, 1965)
Brainstorm (WB, 1965)
Funny Girl (Columbia, 1968)
More Dead than Alive (UA, 1968)
Impasse (UA, 1969)
The Love God? (Universal, 1969)
Hook, Line and Sinker (Columbia, 1969)
Lost Flight (Universal, 1970)
Pancho Villa (Scotia International, 1972)

With Glenn Ford in *Don't Go Near the Water* (1957)

Clark Gable

Clark Gable was the KING of Hollywood and even now, more than a decade after his death, there is no contender for the lofty throne that was his. Projecting intelligent masculinity beyond that of a mere brute, his appeal was universal. He was the hero of MGM. To be cast opposite him meant the achievement of stardom to many an actress, even the aloof Grace Kelly. During his reign he was the most important male star of the American screen.

William Clark Gable was born in Cadiz, Ohio on February 1, 1901, of German ancestry. His mother died when he was seven months old and his stepmother, a kind and gentle woman, became the first of many women to influence his life. He quit school at sixteen to work in a tire factory in Akron, where, after seeing a play called *The Bird of Paradise*, he decided to become an actor. For the next seven years he knocked around with various stock companies, working in oil fields and selling neckties whenever unemployed. He arrived in Los Angeles in 1924 as the result of meeting the manager of a Portland, Oregon, theatre group. This was Josephine Dillon, an ex-actress, who became the foremost influence in Gable's career. She patiently and expertly taught him the rudiments of acting and, although seventeen years his senior, married him that same year.

It was through her influence that Gable got jobs as an extra in films such as the John Gilbert–Mae Murray *The Merry Widow* (1925) and Clara Bow's *The Plastic Age* (1926). But when film success continued to elude him—his rugged presence was incompatible with the wan sensitivity of 1920s leading men—he returned to the theatre. He struck up a lifelong friendship with Lionel Barrymore who gave him a part in the West Coast production of *The Copperhead*. Gable finally reached Broadway and created a bit of a stir in *Machinal*, a drama of the inhumanity of city life. While in New York, he started keeping company with a wealthy, thrice-married Texas socialite, Rhea Lucas Langham, also several years his senior, and it was supposedly through her influence that Gable starred in the West Coast production of *The Last Mile* (Spencer Tracy's Broadway success) at $300 weekly.

Lionel Barrymore saw Gable's performance and screen-tested him at MGM, but the test was a failure, as was his next one at Warners, where Darryl F. Zanuck turned him down as the lead in *Little Caesar* (1931) by saying: "His

223

With Greta Garbo in *Susan Lennox—Her Fall and Rise* (1931)

ears are too big. He looks like an ape." However, Hal Wallis' sister, agent Minna Wallis, saw Gable's MGM test and got him a part in a Pathé Western, *The Painted Desert* (1931), a talkie starring William Boyd. Gable's perform-ance as the leering villain displayed the qualities that would later make him famous. Meanwhile, Barrymore instituted another screen test of Gable which pleased MGM's Irving Thalberg. Thus in December 1930 he was signed to a two-year contract at Metro at $350 a week. He was put to work in the small role as the husband of Anita Page in Constance Bennett's *The Easiest Way* (1931), and, after viewing his performance in that film, Joan Crawford requested him to play opposite her in *Dance, Fools, Dance* (1931).

After a few weak starts, director Clarence Brown urged Thalberg to allow him to use Gable's cynical magnetism against Norma Shearer in *A Free Soul* (1931) in which he played the villain who manhandles MGM's "first lady." Although Lionel Barrymore walked off with an Oscar for that picture, it was Gable the public loved, and MGM took to promoting him as a new kind of hero. Shearer would later recall: "It was Clark who made villains popular." Thalberg then cast his new star opposite the majestic Greta Garbo in *Susan Lenox—Her Fall and Rise* (1931), one of his eleven releases that year. Even the elusive Swede showed moments of response to the rough-edged Gable. Joan Crawford performed one of her remarkable metamorphoses from factory worker to sophisticate for him in *Possessed* (1931) and, back with Shearer, he was a believable Eugene O'Neill hero in *Strange Interlude* (1932).

But it was *Red Dust* (1932) which sent Gable to the boxoffice top and set the pace for years to come. An earthly, braless Jean Harlow and an earthier, unshaven Gable had audiences blinking at their smoldering love-making, which left little to the viewers' imagination. This picture entrenched Gable as the *most* important MGM star. Gable was not unaware of his studio importance and when he refused to do another rags-to-riches Crawford entry, Mayer punished Gable by farming him out to Harry Cohn's Columbia. The script Cohn had in mind was a "bus picture" to be directed by Frank Capra, a project which had already been rejected by the likes of Robert Montgomery, Myrna Loy, Miriam Hopkins, and Constance Bennett. Claudette Colbert reluctantly agreed to appear in it only when she was paid $50,000, twice her per-picture take at Paramount. The script in question was released as *It Happened One Night* (1934), and Colbert got to show legs while hitchhiking and the King displayed his no-undershirt look. For some excellent comedic acting the two of them surprised the industry by winning Oscars.

Back at his home studio, Gable was now given preferential treatment with scripts, and his salary was climbing to $4,000 weekly with pictures such as *Call of the Wild* (1935), *China Seas* (1935), *Mutiny on the Bounty* (1935), *San Francisco* (1936), *Test Pilot* (1938), and *Idiot's Delight* (1939). The oft-repeated story behind the production of David O. Selznick's masterpiece *Gone with the Wind* (1939) has become an indelible Hollywood legend. Suffice it to say that Gable was indeed the public's choice for the role of Rhett Butler which, it is said, Margaret Mitchell wrote with him in mind. With his splendid portrayal

With Mary Astor in *Red Dust* (1932)

With Jack Holt, Harold Huber, and Edgar Kennedy in *San Francisco* (1936)

in this road show production Gable reached the apogee of his career. Each time the lengthy film is rereleased by MGM, it attracts a new legion of Gable admirers.

Gable's popularity continued undimimshed with films such as *Boom Town* (1940) and *Honky Tonk* (1941) in which he and Lana Turner sparked onscreen. By this time he had divorced Josephine Dillon and married and divorced Mrs. Langham to marry one of filmdom's most beautiful and beloved actresses, Carole Lombard. The public adored them and she is considered to be the most important woman in Gable's personal life. The marriage ended tragically less than twenty-two months after it began when Lombard and her mother died in a plane crash in Nevada on January 16, 1942 while returning home from a War Bond selling tour. Gable was grief-stricken and, immediately upon finishing *Somewhere I'll Find You* (1942), he joined the Army Air Corps and was off the screen for three years.

He returned to films opposite Greer Garson in *Adventure*, a commercially successful but mediocre film. *The Hucksters* (1947), *Homecoming* (1948), and *Command Decision* (1948) put him back on top, but conditions in the film industry and at MGM were changing. As the number of pictures produced in the 1950s decreased, Dore Schary, Mayer's successor as head of the studio, began cutting costs by releasing from contract many of the studio's over-4,000 employees. Gable's salary was a prohibitive $520,000 a year and when his contract expired in 1954, it was not renewed. The parting was acrimonious for the fifty-three-year-old star felt he was being put out to pasture before his time, even granting that his 1950s releases, save for the African-filmed *Mogambo* (1953), had faltering gross receipts. Gable now turned to free-lancing with largely programmer-level pictures at tremendous profit-making percentages. Gable was clearly showing his age, and the scripters had some fancy maneuvering to explain his onscreen lovemaking to Doris Day (*Teacher's Pet*) (1959), to Carrol Baker (*But Not for Me*) (1959), and to Sophia Loren (*It Started in Naples*) (1960).

In 1949 Gable had briefly married international butterfly Lady Sylvia Ashley (formerly married to Douglas Fairbanks, Sr.) and six years later wed Kay Williams Spreckels, a union which has often been compared to his happy, short-lived marriage to Carole Lombard.

In 1960 Gable embarked upon the fateful production of *The Misfits* (1961), from a screenplay written by playwright Arthur Miller for his wife Marilyn Monroe. In the midst of production Gable proudly announced his wife was pregnant and that at age fifty-nine he was about to become a father for the first time. Two months later he was dead of a heart attack. His widow blamed his insistence on performing his own strenuous stunts for the film as part of the cause of his death. As he was laid to rest in Forest Lawn Cemetery beside Lombard, the world mourned their King. A son, John Clark, was born posthumously.

Several years later, Joan Crawford, his costar in eight MGM films, succinctly stated what all the biographies of Gable wanted to convey: "Clark

With Joan Crawford in *Love on the Run* (1936)

Gable was the King of an empire called Hollywood. The empire is not what it once was—but the King has not been dethroned, even after death."

CLARK GABLE

Forbidden Paradise (Paramount, 1924)
The Merry Widow (MGM, 1925)
The Plastic Age (FBO, 1925)
North Star (Associated Exhibitors, 1926)
The Painted Desert (Pathé, 1931)
The Easiest Way (MGM, 1931)
Dance, Fools, Dance (MGM, 1931)
The Secret Six (MGM, 1931)
The Finger Points (FN, 1931)
Laughing Sinners (MGM, 1931)
A Free Soul (MGM, 1931)
Night Nurse (WB, 1931)
Sporting Blood (MGM, 1931)
Susan Lennox—Her Fall and Rise (MGM, 1931)
Possessed (MGM, 1931)
Hell Divers (MGM, 1931)
Polly of the Circus (MGM, 1932)
Strange Inerlude (MGM, 1932)
Red Dust (MGM, 1932)

No Man of Her Own (Paramount, 1932)
The White Sister (MGM, 1933)
Hold Your Man (MGM, 1933)
Night Flight (MGM, 1933)
Dancing Lady (MGM, 1933)
It Happened One Night (Columbia, 1934)
Men in White (MGM, 1934)
Manhattan Melodrama (MGM, 1934)
Chained (MGM, 1934)
Forsaking All Others (MGM, 1934)
After Office Hours (MGM, 1935)
Call of the Wild (UA, 1935)
China Seas (MGM, 1935)
Mutiny on the Bounty (MGM, 1935)
Wife vs. Secretary (MGM, 1936)
San Francisco (MGM, 1936)
Cain and Mabel (WB, 1936)
Love on the Run (MGM, 1936)
Parnell (MGM, 1937)
Saratoga (MGM, 1937)

With Myrna Loy in *Parnell* (1937)

With Lorraine Kreuger, Virginia Grey, Paula Stone, Joan Marsh, Bernadette Hayes, and Virginia Dale in *Idiot's Delight* (1939)

With Vivien Leigh in *Gone with the Wind* (1939)

Test Pilot (MGM, 1938)
Too Hot to Handle (MGM, 1938)
Idiot's Delight (MGM, 1939)
Gone with the Wind (MGM, 1939)
Strange Cargo (MGM, 1940)
Boom Town (MGM, 1940)
Comrade X (MGM, 1940)
They Met in Bombay (MGM, 1941)
Honky Tonk (MGM, 1941)
Somewhere I'll Find You (MGM, 1942)
Adventure (MGM, 1945)
The Hucksters (MGM, 1947)
Homecoming (MGM, 1948)
Command Decision (MGM, 1948)
Any Number Can Play (MGM, 1949)
Key to the City (MGM, 1950)

To Please a Lady (MGM, 1950)
Across the Wide Missouri (MGM, 1951)
Callaway Went Thataway (MGM, 1951)
Lone Star (MGM, 1952)
Never Let Me Go (MGM, 1953)
Mogambo (MGM, 1953)
Betrayed (MGM, 1954)
Soldier of Fortune (20th-Fox, 1955)
The Tall Men (20th-Fox, 1955)
The King and Four Queens (UA, 1956)
Band of Angels (WB, 1957)
Run Silent, Run Deep (UA, 1958)
Teacher's Pet (Paramount, 1958)
But Not for Me (Paramount, 1959)
It Started in Naples (Paramount, 1960)
The Misfits (UA, 1961)

With Grace Kelly in *Mogambo* (1953)

Greta Garbo

It seems properly fitting that the screen's greatest actress should be mysterious and elusive—an enigma. And whether out of shyness or design Greta Garbo is the most enigmatic of cinema actresses, both onscreen and in her much-documented private life. Film historian Gary Carey maintains that "Garbo's Marguerite Gautier [*in Camille* (1937)] is the single most beautiful performance in the American sound film. The force of its intelligence and delicacy fills us with the awe and admiration awarded the legendary actresses of the past. We respond not merely to great acting, though assuredly this *is* great acting, but rather to some supreme intensity of personality, so pure that we are mystified and exalted." The scope of Garbo's acting technique has been argued endlessly and inconclusively for decades. No one critic seems to be able to pinpoint what it was about Garbo's acting style that was so naturally suited to the screen. While she never appeared in any really great motion pictures, there was a touch of genius in her performances which derived from her own intelligence and her instinctual ability to *respond* to all that was around her, always with the utmost restraint and always eliciting a carnal spirituality from her audiences. Long before the word charisma became a cliché, Garbo was its quintessence. When Garbo arrived in the United States in 1925, she had appeared in three feature films in Europe. She arrived under contract to MGM and remained with the studio to make twenty-four feature films.

Greta Lovisa Gustafsson was born on September 18, 1905 at 32 Blekingegatan Street in Stockholm. Her parents were of peasant stock and she has said that as a child she always "preferred being alone. I could give my imagination free rein and live in my world of lovely dreams." Her brother once recalled, "She always wanted to act. It was just in her, I guess." Greta's father died when she was fourteen, and she went to work first in a barbershop as an apprentice and then in the millinery department of a local department store. She appeared as a mannequin in some newspaper advertisements and made two short commercial films. When film director Erik Petschler happened to visit the store in which she was working, she asked him for a job. He cast her as the ingenue in *Peter the Tramp* (1922), after which he suggested she enroll in the Royal Academy of Dramatic Art. Through the Academy she was

233

recommended for a role in *The Saga of Gösta Berling* (1924) directed by Mauritz Stiller. Stiller had a reputation for being the D. W. Griffith of the Swedish film industry. Garbo was seventeen, he was forty. In his diary he wrote, "I immediately saw how easily one could dominate her by looking straight into her eyes." He soon became her Svengali, changed her name first to Mona Gabor, finally settling for Greta Garbo. This now classic film revealed a plump Garbo, but it launched her career.

Under Stiller's tutelage she soon was glamorized, and her next picture, G. W. Pabst's *The Street of Sorrow* (1925), revealed a sleeker, more sophisticated Garbo. In 1924, Louis B. Mayer traveled to Rome to investigate the troubled set of *Ben Hur* and went on to Berlin where he asked to meet Stiller and to see *The Saga of Gösta Berling*. Before leaving Berlin, Mayer settled a contractual agreement that brought both Stiller and Garbo to work for MGM. One story states that Mayer wanted Stiller and that Garbo was an afterthought. Another version has it that it was Garbo that Mayer was after and in order to get her, he had to sign Stiller. Whichever is true, before leaving Berlin, Mayer said, "Tell her that in America men don't like fat women."

Garbo and Stiller arrived in the U. S. in the summer of 1925. The studio had no idea what to do with either of them. Many critics maintain that MGM *never* knew what to do with Garbo. From the beginning Garbo eschewed the usual starlet publicity, although Metro did persuade, the aloof Swede into posing for a few silly press shots, including one with an MGM lion. At first Greta attended a few social functions–(Beatrice Lillie remembers a Garbo who used to laugh and enjoy herself at parties). After experiencing the bizarreness of her initial press interviews and publicity chores, Greta announced, "I've never been so afraid in my life. If I ever become as great as Lillian Gish, I shall have it in my contract that I'm to be spared such idiocies. And no shaking hands with professional boxers." Her shyness became an accepted fact, as did the closed sets on her pictures.

Metro debuted her in *The Torrent* (1926) starring Ricardo Cortez. When Monta Bell and not Stiller was chosen to direct the vehicle, it was a blow for both Greta and her mentor. Cortez was in a huff that he had been forced to emote with an "unknown," but when that romantic melodrama was released there was no doubt whom the star of the picture had been. Garbo was overjoyed that Stiller was to be the director on *The Temptress* (1926), but when he and her costar, Antonio Moreno, failed to get along, Stiller was replaced by Fred Niblo. The disillusioned Stiller went over to the more Continental-oriented Paramount where he directed three films and then returned to his native Sweden in 1927. Greta wanted to leave with him, but MGM refused permission. A year later he died, a crushed man. Greta wailed, "Since Mauritz went, there's no one to look after me. I feel lonely and abandoned." Garbo's third film was one she did not wish to make, as she thought it was too romantic. But *The Flesh and the Devil* (1927) managed to establish her and John Gilbert as one of the screen's greatest romantic teams.

When that picture was released to enthusiastic boxoffice results, Greta

With Antonio Moreno in *The Temptress* (1926)

With John Gilbert in *A Woman of Affairs* (1929)

With Nils Asther in *Wild Orchids* (1929)

With Richard Tucker, Paul McAllister, Arthur Hoyt, John Miljan, Lewis Stone, Judith Vosselli, Karen Morley, and Gwen Lee in *Inspiration* (1931)

demanded her $600 a week salary be increased to $5,000, and it was. She also stipulated that her salary be paid over a 52-week year, rather than the usual contractual forty weeks. She and Gilbert became close friends and Hollywood's most talked-about romance. The duo starred again in *Love* (1927), based on Tolstoy's *Anna Karenina*. (At one point the project had been titled *Heat* until the publicity department suddenly realized what that title would look like on marquees, i.e., "Greta Garbo in *Heat*.") Garbo was by now the ultimate screen love goddess, and graced such ultimately specious products as *The Divine Woman* (1928), *The Mysterious Woman* (1929), and *A Woman of Affairs* (1929). The latter was with Gilbert, who that year surprised the movie colony by marrying stage actress Ina Claire.

Greta's last silent picture was *The Kiss* (1929) with Lew Ayres. Her talking film debut was delayed so much that, next to Chaplin, who was the longest holdout against talkies, Greta's belated sound movie debut was the most auspicious of Hollywood. The picture was *Anna Christie*, and when it premiered on March 14, 1930, critics not only raved about her dramatic abilities, but applauded her husky, sensuous voice as well. Greta's luminescence was a perfect counterpart to Clark Gable's brashness in the confessional *Susan Lenox—Her Fall and Rise* (1931) and she was sleekly treacherous in *Mata Hari* (1932). In MGM's all-star *Grand Hotel* (1932) she played the fading ballerina who informs baron John Barrymore, "I want to be alone." It became her tag line. Of her performance in that often-revived picture, Kenneth Tynan has evaluated, "Her technical skill is unsleeping; note how she keeps her passionate lips an inch or two higher than Barrymore's, thereby upscreening an actor too wily to be upstaged. In the poetic intensity with which she gives voice to banalities, Garbo has no modern rivals, except possibly Callas."

One of her more popular sound film roles was in *Queen Christina* (1933) in which she romped in men's attire. For her costar, she refused to accept Laurence Olivier, demanding John Gilbert, who was then struggling with a failing career in sound pictures. The famous final shot in this picture shows Garbo's face, beginning with a long view on board ship and ending with an enormous closeup that runs approximately 85 feet. Garbo's enigmatic expression during this telling sequence has produced paragraphs of explanation by critics as to its meaning. Director Rouben Mamoulian delights in explaining that for this shot he told Garbo to think of "nothing, absolutely nothing. You must make your mind and your heart a complete blank. Make your face into a mask; do not even blink your eyes while the camera is on you."

In *Anna Karenina* (1935) Greta made literature's most famous average woman more interesting than thought possible, and she was never more felicitously cast than in *Camille* (1937). But by this time, Greta, like her rival Paramount star, Marlene Dietrich, was no longer popular with mass audiences. Their vehicles had become top-laden with esoteric frills. Searching for a property to make the elusive Greta more compatible to contemporary tastes, Metro cast her as the proleterian Russian in *Ninotchka* (1939). The film revealed comic nuances in Greta that surprised critics and audiences alike. Still not yet satisfied with the remolded image of the distinctive Swede, Metro pushed her into yet a new guise as the capricious, sexy sweater girl in *Two-Faced Woman* (1941). The general public was indifferent to the "new" Garbo, while the more sophisticated were astounded at the tampering done to the cinema queen. Greta left the movies after *Two-Faced Woman*, planning an extended rest, which turned into permanent exile.

During her Hollywood years Greta was nominated three times for Academy Awards: in 1930 for *Anna Christie* and *Romance*, in 1937 for *Camille*, and in 1939 for *Ninotchka*. In 1954 she was presented with a Special Oscar "for her unforgettable screen performances." Nancy Kelly accepted the award for the absent Greta. At first it had not been Greta's intention to retire permanently, but as film projects were announced, each time she hesitated, "I'm sorry, I can't go through with it. I don't have the courage to make another picture." She refused to play the mother of Rosalind Russell in O'Neill's *Mourning Becomes Electra* (Greta was 42, Russell 40); and a film based on the life of George Sand with Laurence Olivier as costar fell through the same year. In 1949 she was actually signed by Walter Wanger to star in Balzac's *La Duchesse de Langeais*, but lack of proper financing caused the project to be dropped. In 1952 she refused a comeback opportunity in *My Cousin Rachel*, which was made with Olivia de Havilland and Richard Burton. Several years later Burton met Garbo at a party and recalls, "I asked her to do me a favor. I asked Garbo if I could kiss her knee." She replied, 'certainly.' And I leaned over and did. It was an experience I'll never forget."

Greta's life since her retirement has been completely private. She supposedly has no money worries. It is said that she invested in Beverly Hills real estate soon after she arrived in this country, and at the time of the stock market crash, she sent home to Sweden $1 million in gold coin. She lives in New York City and makes frequent visits to Europe. Her home in recent years has been a seven-room sparsely furnished cooperative apartment at 450 East 52nd Street in Manhattan, the same building in which her good friend, the late George Schlee, resided.

Garbo's male friends have been a series of celebrities. After her "affair" with Gilbert she said, "You are aware I was in love with John Gilbert; he was a fine man. I can never answer the question, 'Why weren't you two married then?' " Later on she said, "God, I wonder what I ever saw in him. Oh well, I guess he *was* pretty." Since then her male companions have included dietician Gaylord Hauser, conductor Leopold Stokowski, designer Cecil Beaton, and millionaire Aristotle Onassis. The one person who had the greatest influence on Greta since Stiller was financier George Schlee, whose wife is Valentina, the couturière. For many years, until his death in 1964, he was Greta's constant companion. They had met when Hauser had taken Greta to be fitted for some clothes by Valentina. Soon Greta moved into an apartment in the same building as the Schlees. One evening would find Schlee escorting Greta, the next his wife, and the next accompanying both of the ladies, dressed in

With Helen Jerome Eddy, Blanche Frederici, Edmund Breese, Ramon Novarro, and Alec B. Francis in *Mata Hari* (1932)

With Herbert Marshall in *The Painted Veil* (1934)

With Henry Daniell in *Camille* (1937)

With Leif Erikson and Henry Stevenson in *Conquest* (1937)

identical Valentina dresses, wearing identical coiffures. In the summer of 1964 Greta and Schlee checked into adjoining suites in Paris' Hotel Crillon and the next day, Schlee died of a heart attack. His widow barred Greta from the plane carrying his body back to the United States. Today, while both women continue to live in the same building, the elevator man has been instructed by Greta that under no circumstances are the ladies to meet.

Other publicized friends of Greta include director George Cukor, screenwriter Salka Viertel (mother of Peter who is married to Deborah Kerr), and Greta's closest confidante, Cecile de Rothschild, daughter of French banker Robert de Rothschild. Greta often visits Cecile in Paris, and in turn Cecile visits her in New York.

In 1970 Greta was photographed sporting a chic coiffure while attending the wedding of one of the young Rothschilds in Paris. In 1971 Italian motion picture director Luchino Visconti said he had been informed by Rothschild sources that Greta was interested in playing the small part of Maria Sophia, Queen of Naples, in Visconti's forthcoming screen version of Marcel Proust's *Remembrance of Things Past*. Visconti exclaimed, "I am very pleased at the idea that this woman, with her severe and authoritarian presence, should figure in the decadent and rarefied climate of the world described by Proust." Garbo has reportedly turned down offers extending to $1 million for her memoirs. Early in her career she had said, "Being in the newspapers is awfully silly to me. It's all right for important people who have something to contribute, to talk. I have nothing to contribute."

Upon her exodus from the movies, Greta was asked about her future plans. She stated most prophetically, "I don't know. I suppose I'm just drifting."

GRETA GARBO

Peter the Tramp (Erik A. Petschler, 1922)
The Story of Gosta Berling (Svensk Filmindustri, 1924)
The Street of Sorrow (Sofar-Film, 1925)
The Torrent (MGM, 1926)
The Temptress (MGM, 1926)
Flesh and the Devil (MGM, 1927)
Love (MGM, 1927)
The Divine Woman (MGM, 1928)
The Mysterious Lady (MGM, 1928)
A Woman of Affairs (MGM, 1929)
Wild Orchids (MGM, 1929)
The Single Standard (MGM, 1929)
The Kiss (MGM, 1929)
A Man's Man (MGM, 1929)*
Anna Christie (MGM, 1930)

Romance (MGM, 1930)
Inspiration (MGM, 1931)
Susan Lenox—Her Fall and Rise (MGM, 1931)
Mata Hari (MGM, 1932)
Grand Hotel (MGM, 1932)
As You Desire Me (MGM, 1932)
Queen Christina (MGM, 1933)
The Painted Veil (MGM, 1934)
Anna Karenina (MGM, 1935)
Camille (MGM, 1937)
Conquest (MGM, 1937)
Ninotchka (MGM, 1939)
Two-Faced Woman (MGM, 1941)

*Guest appearance

Ava Gardner

Ava Gardner bears the distinction of being MGM's final cinema Aphrodite. The mold never quite made a perfect fit and was broken by the actress' own volatile will and the beginning of the decline of MGM and the star system. After Louis B. Mayer was ousted from power, the outspoken Ava was quoted as saying, "MGM's no great shakes now, but it was a damned sight better when the old man was around. I never liked him very much, but at least you knew where you stood. This joint's come down a lot in the world."

It was a tremendous transformation for the backwoods Southern girl to become onscreen the full-blown, full-grown woman who brought life and a healthy lustfulness to Lady Brett in *The Sun Also Rises* (1957), Eloise Kelly in *Mogambo* (1953), Jean Ogilvie in *The Hucksters* (1947), *The Barefoot Contessa* (1954), *Pandora and the Flying Dutchman* (1951), and *One Touch of Venus* (1948). With her earthy eroticism and unique voice, Ava is comparable to France's Jeanne Moreau, but her excellent photogenic face prevented her from developing into the tart comedienne for which she showed such potential. Nevertheless, those occasional roles in which she was allowed to exhibit her lusty, cynical wit, e.g., *Mogambo*, proved her to be the most real of Hollywood's latter-day femme fatales.

Ava Lavinia Gardner was born December 24, 1922, the youngest of the six children of a tenant farmer in Grabtown, North Carolina. Of her strict, poverty-filled childhood, Ava recalls, "I never had any ambitions to be anything but dead in those days." After finishing high school in nearby Smithfield and taking some secretarial courses at Atlantic Christian College in Wilson, North Carolina, eighteen-year-old Ava saved enough money for a trip to New York City to visit her sister Beatrice and to find work as a secretary.

Ava arrived in Manhattan in the summer of 1940, and when Beatrice's husband, Larry Tarr, saw her, he was immediately struck by her green-eyed beauty. Tarr's father owned several photography studios in New York and he proceeded to take numerous photographs of the young girl, displaying some of them in the Fifth Avenue window of one of his father's shops. Barney Duhan, then a clerk in MGM's legal department and later a New York policeman, saw the display and was so affected by the "vibrant face," that he distributed some sixty copies of the photographs throughout the MGM offices. The result was fairly predictable—a \$50-a-week contract and Ava's move to the West Coast.

Despite this sudden rash of interest, it was six years before Ava attracted any attention on the screen. She was groomed, coached, and taught how to walk, how to dress, and how to use her instinctively sultry voice more effectively. One of Ava's earliest MGM credits was in the Pete Smith specialty short subject, *Fancy Answers* (1941), in which Ava can be spotted sitting in the studio audience of a quiz show and applauding a concert singer's question-and-answer prowess. Her first feature picture was a walkon in one of Norma Shearer's worst pictures, *We Were Dancing* (1942).

In the interim she had married one of MGM's top boxoffice draws, child prodigy Mickey Rooney. About the studio press agent who accompanied the youngsters on their honeymoon, Ava once stated: "When you came down to breakfast, he was there. When you had dinner, he was there. When you went to bed, he was damn near." Sixteen months later they were divorced: "We were babies, just children. Our lives were run by a lot of other people. We didn't have a chance."*

Meanwhile, Ava continued with her bit assignments in studio productions. In *Kid Glove Killer* (1942) she was a carhop, and *Hitler's Madman* (1943) found her as one of the Czech villagers threatened by the Nazis. On loanout to poverty row Monogram Pictures, she was little more than set dressing in the East Side Kids' *Ghosts on the Loose* (1943). Finally, in *Three Men in White* (1944) she received a billing. She played a girl whose mother is suffering from advanced arthritis and comes to Blair General Hospital for expert treatment from Dr. Gillespie (Lionel Barrymore) and staff.

By the time of *She Went to the Races* (1945) Ava had risen to third billing, even if this slight comedy was built about Edmund Gwenn's quiet charm rather than her personality. On loanout to United Artists, she was George Raft's girl friend in *Whistle Stop* (1946), and for Universal she was the siren in the excellent cinematization of Hemingway's *The Killers* (1946). All of a sudden MGM woke up to Ava's potential and gave her the part of the smart-mouthed other girl in its quality production, *The Hucksters* (1947). She was expert enough in her nightclub singer role to steal scenes from stars Clark Gable and Deborah Kerr.

By now (October 17, 1945), Ava had wed bandleader Artie Shaw. It was his fifth marriage. Shaw, a self-brewed culture fiend, induced Ava to take courses at UCLA in economics and English literature. She proved adept in her studies, but thereafter still maintained the facade of being "just a dumb broad." The marriage lasted less than a year. Shaw later said he attributed MGM's interference as one of the causes. Ava's public statement on the

---

*Shortly after her divorce from Rooney, Howard Hughes installed Ava in a lush abode. Soon after, it became apparent that the peripatetic Hughes was not devoting sufficient attention to her, and Rooney began stopping by. Reportedly, Hughes confronted Ava and slapped her. She retaliated by hitting him over the head with a copper-based ashtray, knocking him out cold. He was taken to a hospital where his ever-busy press agents managed to have the injuries officially listed as stomach trouble.

matter was less complex: "He told me to leave, so I left."

At Universal Ava costarred with Fred MacMurray in an inept melodrama *Singapore* (1947) and, although she had the focal role in *One Touch of Venus* (1948), Universal had managed to extract most of the joy from the Broadway play that originally had starred Mary Martin. There were three MGM releases in 1949; she was the enticing wife of smuggler John Hodiak in the Caribbean-set *The Bribe*, a world-weary daughter of a Russian general in the adaptation of Dostoievski's *The Gambler*, retitled *The Great Sinner*, and the other woman out to grab James Mason away from his wife (Barbara Stanwyck) in *East Side, West Side*. The latter film found Ava at her most vampish, breathing sensuality into her every scene.

About this time, Ava informed the press: "Apparently, I am what is known as a 'glamor girl.' Now that is a phrase which means luxury, leisure, excitement, and all things lush. No one associates a six A.M. alarm, a 13-hour workday, several more hours of study, housework, and business appointments, with glamor. That, however, is what glamor means in Hollywood. At least, it does to me."

My Forbidden Past (1951) found Ava at RKO essaying a Southern belle in a disappointing costume melodrama. Back on the home lot, she made her first color feature, *Pandora and the Flying Dutchman* (1951) the film was filled with all the cultural symbolism of which director Albert Lewin was so fond, but it lacked any significant boxoffice appeal. Ava portrayed the oft-loved playgirl who yearns for the ability to love in return. After Judy Garland and MGM parted ways, Ava was given the plum role of the mulatto Julie in *Show Boat* (1951) and was impressive in the part of the alcoholic singer. She fought to be allowed to do her own singing, but MGM officials would have none of it. Onnette Warren dubbed her songs. They did allow her voice to be used on the original cast album. Ava always relishes the fact that she still collects royalties for that album.

On November 7, 1951, Ava married Frank Sinatra, whom she had been dating since February 1950. The union proved extremely stormy and provided the press with a barrage of stories that made Ava look anything but sweet. Ava and Sinatra were separated in 1954 and thereafter divorced. As Ave described it: "When he was down he was sweet but when he got back up he was hell."

If *Lone Star* (1952) opposite Clark Gable was an undistinguished Western, Twentieth Century-Fox's *The Snows of Kilimanjaro* (1952) more than made up for it. She was extremely well cast as one of Hemingway's "lost generation." Then it was back to the range—this time on the Mexican border—for *Ride Vaquero!* (1953) in a Katy Juradolike role as the wife of Howard Keel while letching for free-wheeling Clark Gable. In *Band Wagon* (1953) Ava did an unbilled guest bit as a Hollywood star arriving in New York on a train.

It was in *Mogambo* that Ava gave what most regard as her best performance. In this remake of Clark Gable's *Red Dust* (1932) which had starred Jean Harlow, Ava vied with Grace Kelly for the affections of Gable.

With Ann Sothern, Tom Drake, Marta Linden, and Paul Cavanagh in *Maisie Goes to Reno* (1944)

With (front row): Charles Halton, James Craig, Frances Gifford; (second row): Sig Rumann, Reginald Owen, Edmund Gwenn, and Clyde Fillmore in *She Went to the Races* (1945)

With Agnes Moorehead and Kathryn Grayson in *Show Boat* (1951)

With Anthony Quinn, Howard Keel, and Robert Taylor in *Ride Vaquero!* (1953)

Critics likened Ava to Carole Lombard and she received her only nomination for an Academy Award. Her sister Inez says this is the role most like the "real" Ava.

In a particularly static historical yarn, *Knights of the Round Table* (1953), filmed in England, Ava was excessively wooden as Queen Guinevere. On the other hand, as the barefoot dancer who becomes a famed movie star, Ava came to grips with the title role of *The Barefoot Contessa* (1954) and worked well opposite Humphrey Bogart. Nevertheless, by the end of that year, Ava had left Hollywood for good and moved to Madrid. Her explanation: "Being a movie star in America is the loneliest life in the world. In Europe they respect your privacy. No one believes me when I say I'm going to Europe to live, but I am, and I won't be back." She has not returned, save for a rare movie role.

It was two years before Ava had another release, *Bhowani Junction* (1956). She acquitted herself well under George Cukor's direction and made her role as the Indian half-caste creditable. Just to wrap up her MGM contract, Ava played in the tasteless sex comedy, *The Little Hut* (1957), and the vulgar but dull *The Naked Maja* (1959), the latter released by UA. Ava's embarrassing portrayal of the Duchess of Alba was matched by Anthony Franciosa's method interpretation of painter Goya. Despite extensive publicity suggesting the film was highly salacious, audiences stayed away in droves. In *Ava: Portrait of a Star* (1960), author David Hanna quotes Ava as saying: "In a few days I'll be through with Metro. I wouldn't admit this to anyone else but I'm afraid. I never worked for any other company. I never had another job. I hate their guts but for 17 years they've been there and I just did what they told me to, going from one lousy picture to the other."

Sandwiched between these last two cinematic fiascos was her appearance in *The Sun Also Rises* (1957) made on loan to Twentieth Century-Fox. This film did not do justice to Hemingway and Ava, a friend of the author, sensed the incredulity from the beginning. But she still managed to make her portrayal of Lady Brett effective. However, like her costars, she was too old for her role, and telltale signs of her high-stepping personal life were beginning to catch up with her. And yet, these same haggard qualities were particularly effective in Stanley Kramer's underrated *On the Beach* (1959) in which she is the former Australian playgirl waiting for the end to come and regretful that married submarine skipper Gregory Peck will not share the final hours with her.

The 1960s found Ava professionally adrift in much the same manner as one-time movie queen Rita Hayworth was experiencing. She was unconvincing as the alluring Spanish prostitute in *The Angel Wore Red* (1960) and was seen to minimal advantage in the weak spectacle *55 Days at Peking* (1963) in which she was a titled Russian who does not survive the Boxer Rebellion. Ava was used for boxoffice lure in John Frankenheimer's *Seven Days in May* (1964). She was so adept in her brief role as a former mistress of general Burt Lancaster that audiences for the first time in a long while found themselves wishing there was more scenes of Ava in this overthrow-the-government drama. That same year, Ava was the third-billed star in Tennessee Williams' *The Night of the Iguana*, playing the Bette Davis stage role of the resort hotel owner who yearns for defrocked clergyman Richard Burton. When the picture was made on location in Mexico, the press expected fireworks between Ava and Burton's wife Elizabeth Taylor who was along for the ride. Despite the extensive coverage, there was little interesting gossip to report, except for allusions to the fact that Ava's role of a middle-aged woman who dallies with her native houseboys might be taken from her own private life.

Also for John Huston who had directed her in *The Night of the Iguana*, Ava appeared as Sarah in *The Bible* (1966), aging from a young girl to a very old woman. In MGM's European-filmed remake of *Mayerling* (1968) Ava had an also-starring role as the Austrian queen mother of Omar Sharif. She was well gowned in this costumer, but had little to do beyond registering basic reactions to the goings-on.

In 1968 Ava made *The Devil's Widow* under Roddy McDowall's direction, playing a tremendously wealthy widow who tries to retain her youth by paying for the company of a group of young decadents who cater to her whims. This Scottish-set color feature was caught in the middle of a production company liquidation and subsequently was purchased by American International Pictures who had director McDowall complete the editing for a much-delayed opening in 1972. The film has already been sold to TV. Ava had the opportunity to act her age and, although the drama is no great shakes, she turned in a competent characterization.

In late 1971 John Huston lured Ava back to the States to appear in the Paul Newman–Jacqueline Bisset Western, *The Life and Times of Judge Roy Bean*. Her "also-starring" status in this production does not phase her, because being a movie star and making pictures has always been pretty much of a drag for Ava. She would much have prefered being a contented housewife. "I was much better equipped for having babies."

She still leads a hearty Continental life, but disclaims that she is lonely. "The lonely, lovely Ava bit is just the crazy idea everybody has about me. My God! If I were really as sad and lonely as some of the stories say, I'd blow my brains out." Unlike others in her age group who have drifted into television and stage work or business of some kind to avoid stagnation and maintain an image, Ava remains her own woman, keeping whatever ghost-chasing she may do a strictly private matter. She once proudly admitted: "I'm one Hollywood star who hasn't tried to slash her wrists, take sleeping pills or kick a cop in the shins."

248

AVA GARDNER

We Were Dancing (MGM, 1942)
Joe Smith, American (MGM, 1942)
Sunday Punch (MGM, 1942)
This Time for Keeps (MGM, 1942)
Calling Dr. Gillespie (MGM, 1942)
Kid Glove Killer (MGM, 1942)
Pilot No. 5 (MGM, 1943)
Hitler's Madman (MGM, 1943)
Ghosts on the Loose (Monogram, 1943)
Reunion in France (MGM, 1943)
Du Barry Was a Lady (MGM, 1943)
Young Ideas (MGM, 1943)
Lost Angel (MGM, 1943)
Swing Fever (MGM, 1944)
Music for Millions (MGM, 1944)
Three Men in White (MGM, 1944)
Blonde Fever (MGM, 1944)
Maisie Goes to Reno (MGM, 1944)
Two Girls and a Sailor (MGM, 1944)
She Went to the Races (MGM, 1945)
Whistle Stop (UA, 1946)
The Killers (Universal, 1946)
The Hucksters (MGM, 1947)
Singapore (Universal, 1947)
One Touch of Venus (Universal, 1948)
The Great Sinner (MGM, 1949)
East Side, West Side (MGM, 1949)
The Bribe (MGM, 1949)

My Forbidden Past (RKO, 1951)
Pandora and the Flying Dutchman (MGM, 1951)
Show Boat (MGM, 1951)
Lone Star (MGM, 1952)
The Snows of Kilimanjaro (20th-Fox, 1952)
Ride, Vaquero! (MGM, 1953)
Band Wagon (MGM, 1953)*
Mogambo (MGM, 1953)
Knights of the Round Table (MGM, 1953)
The Barefoot Contessa (UA, 1954)
Bhowani Junction (MGM, 1956)
The Little Hut (MGM, 1957)
The Sun Also Rises (20th-Fox, 1957)
The Naked Maja (UA, 1959)
On the Beach (UA, 1959)
The Angel Wore Red (MGM, 1960)
55 Days at Peking (AA, 1963)
Seven Days in May (Paramount, 1964)
The Night of the Iguana (MGM, 1964)
The Bible (20th-Fox, 1966)
Mayerling (MGM, 1968)
The Devil's Widow (AIP, 1972)
The Life and Times of Judge Roy Bean (National General, 1972)

*Unbilled Appearance

With Bill Travers in *Bhowani Junction* (1956)

With James Mason in *Mayerling* (1968)

Judy Garland

"There is a haste and a lack of dignity to film stardom," said Marlene Dietrich, who certainly had gained her place in that realm. No longer is there a member of the film cognoscenti who does not know about Louis B. Mayer's haste in the transformation of Judy Garland into a star. Too few know about her own haste. While in all of the latter years of her wavering career Judy trounced on Mayer's commercialization of her, she herself was a prepubescent climber. Mayer did not have too high an opinion of her until he had lost Deanna Durbin to Universal and then later needed a replacement for Shirley Temple in *The Wizard of Oz* (1939). But by that time Judy had been climbing for over a decade.

Judy was not Mayer's personal discovery. Rather his secretary-gal Friday-major domo, Ida Koverman, found her via the girl's ambitious mother, Ethel Gumm. It was Ida who foisted Judy on Mayer. Using his auditor's brain, he found a beautiful vein of gold in a little vaudevillian girl and turned her into what street people term a "junkie" and social workers tag an addict. As a plump teenager-pup, with her sparkling eyes, retroussé nose and ability to belt a song, Judy was pushed by both her mother and Mayer into a continuous disciplined work pattern which resulted in constant dieting, pep pills, sleeping tablets, and "medical" treatment when needed. The child–woman who was the singing "girl next door" had the emotional and psychological problem of being a star without dignity on her own lot until she demanded it, at which point she was termed a "prima donna."

Mayer gave appropriate treatment to his Greer Garsons who could not compete with Judy at the boxoffice, but Judy was not his sexually fantasized "great lady." She was only a little broad from the sticks. It can't be disputed that the "factory" system was at once at its most creative and its most baleful where Judy was concerned. Harry J. Anslinger, former head of the U. S. Bureau of Narcotics, said that in 1949 he concerned himself with Judy's addiction to morphine and succeeded in removing her from the "care" of a physician who was a drug addict himself. However, when he requested Mayer to give her a year off for sanatorium treatment, Mayer replied, "I couldn't afford your plan. We've got 14 million dollars invested in her and she's at the top of her box office right this minute." Judy was quite right. Mayer helped kill her. Her death was not quite as tragic to the public as that of Marilyn Monroe, but it was certainly a Hollywood-inspired death.

When she later sang "Born in a Trunk," Judy was drawing from personal experience. She was born on June 10, 1922 in Grand Rapids, Minnesota, the third daughter of Frank Gumm, a crooner in vaudeville who had married the house pianist, Ethel Milne. Billed as "Jack and Virginia Lee, the Sweet Southern Singers," the couple toured the lesser vaudeville circuits and finally settled in Grand Rapids where Gumm leased the New Grand Theatre and took over the managerial duties. Ethel Gumm continued to be house pianist and occasionally she and her husband would revive their act, sometimes incorporating their two daughters, Mary Jane (later called Suzanne) and Virginia into the show. Their third child, to their disappointment, turned out to be another daughter, and they named her Frances Ethel.

At the age of three, little Frances decided she too would get into the act and ran onto the stage, did seven choruses of "Jingle Bells," and had to be carried off by her father. Naturally, after that, she was included in the act. By 1927 the family had moved to Lancaster, California, due to Frank Gumm's frail health. Gumm took to managing a silent movie house, and while the two older girls were sent to public school, Mrs. Gumm believed enough in the talents of her youngest daughter to enroll her in Lawler's Professional School. There her work in school plays and revues led to a professional part with the Meglin Kiddies, a troupe of tots who toured California. Little Frances' solo was "I Can't Give You Anything But Love, Baby." One night vaudevillian impresario Gus Edwards went backstage to congratulate the charming youngster and talked her mother into working all three of her daughters into a vaudeville act. With home-sewn costumes, they debuted at the Biltmore Hotel in Los Angeles for the salary of $1.50. Mrs. Gumm then toured with the girls who were billed as the Gumm Sisters. No matter what they did, their act was always second rate.

Arriving at the Oriental Theatre in Detroit in 1931 ("as close to New York as we ever got," recalled Judy) they found themselves billed as The Glum Sisters. Headliner George Jessel not only persuaded the management to correct the error, but gave the act an entirely new last name, Garland, after his good friend, New York drama critic Robert Garland. Following this engagement, the trio did a gig at the Chicago World's Fair in which Frances perched on a piano in the style of Helen Morgan, and sang "My Bill." About this time, and against her mother's objections, Frances took the name of Judy because of Hoagy Carmichael's popular song of that title and because she thought it "peppy." She *was* beginning to climb. None of this action, however, led to instantaneous success, and the family eventually returned to California in 1934, with the girls going back to school.

At school Judy excelled in sports. On a vacation Judy and her mother went to Lake Tahoe where Judy sang for a campfire group. Songwriter Lew Brown heard her there and provided an entrée to the Hollywood studios. Mother and daughter made the rounds, but while Columbia and a few other

252

With Gwen Lee and Richard Powell in *Every Sunday* (1936)

companies said they "liked" Judy, they did not have a suitable role for her.

In the meantime, Judy became one of the regulars on the weekly vaudeville shows presented at the Wilshire-Ebell Theatre and finally got a chance for a MGM audition when that studio's musical arranger Roger Edens caught her act. He arranged for her to sing "Dinah" for Ida Koverman and she was so impressed that she called in her boss, Mayer himself. Mayer agreed with Koverman and took little Judy on a tour of the studio, had her sing for his employees all along the way and, before the day ended, signed her to a contract. The first time in the studio's history a contract had been given without a screen test. The year was 1935, and Mayer proclaimed: "We have just signed a baby Nora Bayes." In 1964 Judy recalled: "I was very thrilled by it, though I actually didn't sign the contract. Nobody asked me. That should be the title of my life: *Nobody Asked Me*."

Shortly after joining MGM's roster Judy's father, whom she adored, died of meningitis. At first MGM had no projects in mind for Judy. They used her to sing at countless studio functions and put her into a two-reeler entitled *Every Sunday* (1936)* along with another fourteen-year-old, for whom they had likewise not found a niche, Deanna Durbin. Judy sang "hot" and Deanna vocalized "sweet." As a result of that short, Universal snapped up Durbin, and Mayer roared about his assistants' incompetence. Judy did some radio broadcasts, made several recordings for Decca, and was loaned to Twentieth Century-Fox for her first feature, *Pigskin Parade*, in which she sang "Balboa."

Then Roger Edens, Judy's early and lifelong booster, arranged a special lyric to the old standard "You Made Me Love You," which he called "Dear Mr. Gable." On Clark Gable's 36th birthday, February 1, 1937, he had Judy sing the song at the studio-hosted party. Mayer liked the song so much he had it and Judy written into the pending *Broadway Melody of 1938* (1937). Billed seventh as "That New Hot Little Singing Sensation," she played the child star of stage mother Sophie Tucker and sang her song as she wrote Gable a fan letter. The New York *Times* declared her solo "probably the greatest tour de force in recent screen history."

MGM quickly sandwiched Judy into four more films, none of which used her full potential, but each spotlighting her in song. One of them, *Love Finds Andy Hardy* (1938), paired her ever so platonically with that studio's precocious virtuoso Mickey Rooney, and Judy demonstrated an undeveloped flair for handling wry lines in a tart manner. The project that catapulted her into stardom was one that had not been planned for her. This, of course, was, *The Wizard of Oz*. Producer Mervyn LeRoy had wished to borrow Twentieth Century-Fox's Shirley Temple. When the loan could not be conveniently worked out, Judy was substituted. She was a bit mature at seventeen and was corseted and carefully made up to play the innocent, young

---

*Prior to this short subject released in December 1936, Judy had appeared in as many as six Vitaphone short subjects with the Meglin Kiddies, and at MGM was in the short *La Fiesta of Santa Barbara* with Steffi Duna and others, released in April 1936.

With Fanny Brice in *Everybody Sing* (1938)

Dorothy. The picture made her a full-fledged star and earned her a special little Oscar. The song "Over The Rainbow," (which was nearly cut out of the overlong picture) became her trademark. As a result of *Oz*, Judy showed up as Number Ten in the top moneymaking stars of 1940. The only other female in the group was Bette Davis in Number Nine spot, while Mickey Rooney was at the head of the list.

MGM continued using the seventeen-year-old in childlike roles, and in the next two years she appeared in seven features, five of them with Master Rooney. In July 1941, over stern objections from her mother and the studio, she married composer–musician David Rose, twelve years her senior and recently divorced from Martha Raye. It was during these first years of stardom that the regimented dieting began and the resultant fatigue led to the pep and sleeping pills. Years later, Judy recalled: "When we [she and Rooney] were in production, they had us working days and nights on end. They'd give us pep-up pills to keep us up after we were exhausted. Then they'd take us to the studio hospital and knock us cold with sleeping pills—Mickey sprawled out on one bed, and me on another."

Judy received singular billing above the title for the first time in 1942 with *For Me and My Gal*, a homey show biz yarn about a struggling song and dance team—Judy and Gene Kelly (in his screen debut). Judy had some good songs, the best of which was her memorable "After You've Gone."

That same year, Joseph L. Mankiewicz, then a scripter under MGM contract, noticed the beginnings of Judy's emotional problems. He wanted her to see psychologist Karl Menninger but could not arrange it secretly. So he talked her into seeing another noted psychologist, Dr. Ernst Simmel. Judy's mother discovered her clandestine visits and reported them to Mayer. Mankiewicz recalled that Mayer was in a rage to think that professional help was better than the attention he and Judy's mother were capable of giving. As a result of this confrontation, Mankiewicz left MGM and Judy stopped psychiatric visits. This event was also a turning point in her relationship with her mother, which had always been a strained one. Judy said: "Mother was the real-life Wicked Witch of the West. ... Mother ... was no good for anything except to create chaos and fear. She didn't like me because of my talent .... She had a crude voice and my sisters had lousy voices too. ... When I review my financial problems, I have to admit they began with mother." Estranged off and on over the years, Judy and her mother were not speaking when Mrs. Gumm died in 1953.

In 1943, Judy appeared in three films, the best of which was *Presenting Lily Mars*, in which she, as the young performer, and Connie Gilchrist, as the scrubwoman, sang the memorable "Every Little Movement." She played her first concert on July 1 that year in Philadelphia and was a smash hit, singing Gershwin songs and numbers from her films. She also did an extensive USO tour that year as well as seeing her marriage to Rose end. ("The studio never gave our marriage a chance.").

Her best MGM role was as Esther Smith in *Meet Me in St. Louis* (1944).

With Ray Bolger, Bert Lahr, and Jack Haley in *The Wizard of Oz* (1939)

The film was a beautiful bit of Americana which epitomized the family-brand sentiment that Mayer loved so dearly. The picture was directed by sophisticated Vincente Minnelli and when Judy began work on her next film, *The Clock* (1945), she took a disliking to Fred Zinnemann and asked that he be replaced by Minnelli. Her wish was granted and she and Minnelli were married on June 15. Their daughter Liza May was born on May 12, 1946.

The Clock was Judy's only nonsinging role at MGM, something Judy had wanted to do, and critics credited Minnelli with bringing her talent into "unmistakable bloom." While Judy enjoyed and was excellent in her dramatic debut, the public wanted to hear her sing, and sing she did in *The Harvey Girls* (1946), particularly wowing her audience in the rousing number "On the Atchison, Topeka and the Santa Fe." A brilliant piece of musical satire of a Greer Garsonlike movie queen entitled "The Interview" in *Ziegfeld Follies* (1946) had the N.Y. *Times* exclaiming: "Miss Garland gives promise of a talent approaching that of Beatrice Lillie and Gertrude Lawrence." The plaudits also rolled in with *Till the Clouds Roll By* (1946), in which she played Marilyn Miller and sang "Who?" and "Look for the Silver Lining."

Her personal life seemed ostensibly happy and Judy kept working. *The Pirate* (1948), directed by Minnelli, was not her biggest boxoffice success, but *Easter Parade* (1948), turn-of-the-century vaudeville fluff, was both tuneful and popular and she and costar Fred Astaire did the now famous tramp routine, "A Couple of Swells." Astaire had been persuaded to come out of "retirement" for *Easter Parade* when Gene Kelly broke his ankle during rehearsals. The team of Garland and Astaire was so well received that MGM planned a second project for them, *The Barkleys of Broadway* (1949), but Judy's emotional problems and exhaustions forced them to call in Ginger Rogers instead. After a rest Judy returned to work in the all-star biopic of Rodgers and Hart, *Words And Music* (1948), doing a ten-minute appearance as herself singing "Johnny One Note" and a duet with Mickey Rooney "I Wish I Were in Love Again." She looked thin and drawn.

When called upon in 1949 to replace a pregnant June Allyson in *In the Good Old Summertime*, there were many delays. Producer Joseph Pasternak said: "There was never a word uttered in recrimination when she was late, didn't show up, or couldn't go on. Those of us who worked with her knew her magical genius and respected it." Meanwhile, MGM purchased, for more money than they had paid for any project up to that time, the screen rights to Irving Berlin's *Annie Get Your Gun*. At first the project was delayed because they could not find a leading man. Finally Howard Keel was signed and shooting began with Busby Berkeley as director. Judy and Berkeley failed to get along and he was replaced by George Sidney. In May 1949 Judy had recorded the score to the film and over $1 million had been spent on the production when it was agreed she was unable to continue. An irate MGM suspended her and sent her to a Boston sanatorium for a "checkup" and a rest. Betty Hutton was called in as her replacement.

Three months later, Judy returned to MGM and began work on

Summer Stock (1950). She was not well and there were more delays, and MGM called the psychiatrist who had treated her in Boston to come to Culver City and help her get through the filming. The production took six months to complete and her fluctuating weight was evident on the screen. She asked for a vacation when the film was completed but June Allyson was pregnant again, and the studio cajoled Judy into taking over *Royal Wedding* (1951) opposite Fred Astaire. She could not go on. Jane Powell was given the assignment and Judy collapsed at home.

On June 20, 1950, with her marriage to Minnelli faltering and her career on the rocks, she attempted suicide by slashing her throat with a piece of glass. The wound was superficial but the cry for help was real. The projects that MGM had lined up for her, such as the Helen Morgan role of Julie in *Show Boat* (1951), were reshuffled and Judy's $5,000 weekly studio contract cancelled. Propitiously, Judy met Michael Sidney Luft, a onetime test pilot and former secretary to Eleanor Powell, as well as producer of B pictures and ex-husband of Lynn Bari. Luft became her impresario and began planning a new career for Judy: concertizing. Judy was scared, but Luft convinced her it was a step she had to take and could do it. Oddly she relaxed for the first time in her career. "I stuffed myself with food, went window-shopping and got up and went to bed when I liked. It was my first real fling."

Luft's plans worked well. She was a sensation at the London Palladium in 1951, and in October that year, she revived the two-a-day vaudeville policy at New York's Palace Theatre. Her four-week engagement extended into nineteen frames and grossed $750,000. She married Luft in June 1952 and on November 21 gave birth to a daughter, Lorna. Their second child, Joseph Wiley, was born March 29, 1955. Riding the wave of a new-found success, the Lufts formed Transcona Productions and contracted with Warner Brothers for three motion pictures. The first was *A Star Is Born* (1954), a musical remake of Janet Gaynor's 1937 dramatic hit. (Judy had appeared in the *Lux Radio Theatre* version of the film in 1942.) The film ran into interminable delays, the major cause of which was Judy's faltering health. The film was finally released in October 1954. Judy turned in the best screen work of her career and earned an Academy Award nomination.

The last fifteen years of Judy's life were an unending series of emotional and professional highs and lows. There was a successful television debut in 1955 on the *Ford Star Jubilee*, and she was one of the most enthusiastic campaigners for John F. Kennedy: "One of the best friends I ever had." She reached the zenith of her concertizing with her appearances at Carnegie Hall on April 23, 1961, and the two-record live recording of that performance has sold over two million copies. That same year she accepted a small dramatic role in Stanley Kramer's *Judgment at Nuremberg* and earned another Oscar nomination, this time as best actress in a supporting role.

In 1963 she embarked upon her own weekly television series, *The Judy Garland Show*. It ran for twenty-six shows but there were too many problems, mostly on the executive level. Besides, CBS foolishly allowed the variety

With Diana Lewis in *Andy Hardy Meets Debutante* (1940)

With Lucille Bremer in *Meet Me in St. Louis* (1944)

With Edward Earle, Ben Carter, and William Hall in *The Harvey Girls* (1946)

With Robert Walker and Paul Langdon in *Till the Clouds Roll By* (1946)

program to compete with *Bonanza*, the most popular video series on the air. Mel Tormé, who functioned as musical writer and advisor for Judy's series, published an account of his experiences in *The Other Side of the Rainbow with Judy Garland on the Dawn Patrol* (1971), a lucid but fatuous recollection of what working with the tormented and tormenting Judy Garland was like.

Her last two feature films were released in 1963. *A Child is Waiting* interestingly channeled her nervous presence as a novice music teacher in an institution for mentally retarded children. The British-lensed *I Could Go on Singing* presented her as a singer, a role similar to her own life, and she was good in several highly-charged onstage vocalizing scenes. Throughout these years there were more collapses, hospitalizations, and comebacks. There were headlines about pills, booze, romances, and cancelled performances. Having divorced Luft in 1965, she briefly married a young actor named Mark Herron, and dropped out of the quickie Electronovision rendition of *Harlow* (1965), being replaced by Ginger Rogers. She likewise signed for an appearance in the filming of Jacqueline Susann's *Valley of the Dolls* (1967). But after recording two song numbers for the film, she found she just could not go on, and Susan Hayward was rushed in to replace her as the aging Broadway star.

In 1969 she married discotheque manager Mickey Deans, who was twelve years younger than she, and Judy made another comeback at the Talk of the Town Club in London. Again there were headlines about late appearances and irate audiences. On June 22, 1969 Judy was found dead in her London flat by her husband from an "accidental" overdose of barbituates. The funeral service was held in New York, and a crowd of some 20,000 mobbed the funeral home to pay their last respects or just to gawk. Deans would later write in a national magazine that Judy had been happy during their marriage but that she was plagued by the fear she could no longer hold an audience. According to many of her co-workers, that lack of confidence began in the 1940s and reached disastrous proportions in the last years at MGM.

In Judy's last years, an increasingly large percentage of her audience was homosexual. Fully cognizant of this, and grateful for their unswerving adulation through thick and thin, Judy nonetheless could appraise the scene in her inimitable bitter humor: "When I die, I have visions of fags singing 'Somewhere over the Rainbow' and the flag at Fire Island being flown at half-mast." Curiously, her cult has helped make female impressionist Jim Bailey famous because of his uncanny recreation of Judy in concert via costumes and his own voice. His appearance at Carnegie Hall in 1972 brought out that homosexual cult in large numbers, and when Bailey left the stage, they stood, applauded, and cried, "We want Judy!"

Pigskin Parade (20th-Fox, 1936)
Broadway Melody of 1938 (MGM, 1937)
Thoroughbreds Don't Cry (MGM, 1937)
Everybody Sing (MGM, 1938)
Listen Darling (MGM, 1938)
Love Finds Andy Hardy (MGM, 1938)
The Wizard of Oz (MGM, 1939)
Babes in Arms (MGM, 1939)
Strike up the Band (MGM, 1940)
Little Nellie Kelly (MGM, 1940)
Andy Hardy Meets Debutante (MGM, 1940)
Ziegfeld Girl (MGM, 1941)
Life Begins for Andy Hardy (MGM, 1941)
Babes on Broadway (MGM, 1941)
For Me and My Gal (MGM, 1942)
Presenting Lily Mars (MGM, 1943)
Girl Crazy (MGM, 1943)

Thousands Cheer (MGM, 1943)
Meet Me in St. Louis (MGM, 1944)
The Clock (MGM, 1945)
The Harvey Girls (MGM, 1946)
Ziegfeld Follies (MGM, 1946)
Till the Clouds Roll By (MGM, 1946)
The Pirate (MGM, 1948)
Easter Parade (MGM, 1948)
Words and Music (MGM, 1948)
In the Good Old Summertime (MGM, 1949)
Summer Stock (MGM, 1950)
A Star Is Born (WB, 1954)
Pepe (Voice only: Columbia, 1960)
Judgment at Nuremberg (UA, 1961)
Gay Purr-ee (Voice only: WB, 1962)
A Child Is Waiting (UA, 1963)
I Could Go on Singing (UA, 1963)

With Fred Astaire and Peter Lawford in *Easter Parade* (1948)

Betty Garrett

One of the bigger talent wastes engineered by MGM was Betty Garrett. After gaining a sizable musical comedy reputation on Broadway in the mid-1940s as a new Charlotte Greenwood who might well equal or outdo Ethel Merman, she was hired by Metro and enlivened five of their major productions with her singing, dancing, and especially comic presence. Then in the McCarthy Red scare of the early 1950s, she chose to stick by her husband, actor Larry Parks, and, as a result, saw her screen career fizzle out completely.

Betty was born on May 23, 1919 in St. Joseph, Missouri, but grew up in Seattle, Washington, where her traveling salesman father had reestablished his home base. Her father died when Betty was still a teenager, which meant in those Depression days that she and her mother were on the move constantly, always one step ahead of unpaid rooming house bills. Betty did find time to participate in sports in high school, winning the northwestern women's javelin championship as well as later winning a poetry scholarship to the Annie Wright Seminary. She graduated from there with honors and, following her ambitions, auditioned for and won a scholarship to the Neighborhood Playhouse in New York City. To support herself while studying acting, she had jobs as a saleswoman and an elevator operator. It was at this time she met Larry Parks, then part of the Group Theatre. They married in September 1944 in Hollywood, where he was under contract to Columbia Pictures.

After being heard as an offstage baby crying in the Orson Welles Mercury Theatre production of *Danton's Death* (1938), Betty danced with Martha Graham's troupe, played the Catskill resort hotel circuit, and sang at various night spots, such as the Village Vanguard and La Martininque in New York City, the Drake Hotel in Chicago, and the Clover Club in Hollywood. Meanwhile, Betty had been working with a revue group in Brooklyn and Manhattan, and they worked up a World War II topical satire, *Of V We Sing*, which they produced. In 1942 they presented Harold Rome's *Let Freedom Ring* on Broadway. The sketch show was not very enduring, but Cole Porter, among others, saw Betty's energetic performance, and hired her as an understudy to Ethel Merman in *Something for the Boys* (1943). This was followed by *Jackpot* with Allan Jones and the frenetic *Laffing Room Only*

(1944) with Olsen and Johnson. Harold Rome used her again in *Call Me Mister* (1946), with Betty's show-stopping number being "South America, Take It Away!" She won the Donaldson Award for best musical comedy performance of the year.

MGM was impressed with Betty and signed her to a contract. She debuted in *Big City* (1948). Betty was the saloon singing sweetheart of Irish cop George Murphy, and sang "I'm Goona See a Lot of You." "Don't Blame Me," and the novelty number "Ok'l Baby Dok'l," reprised by the picture's star, Margaret O'Brien. That same year she was among the MGM musical stable used in *Words and Music*. It was certainly not the real Rodgers and Hart story, but Betty, as the apple of Lorenz Hart's (Mickey Rooney) eye, sang "There's a Small Hotel" in a winning manner.

Take Me out to the Ball Game (1949) topcast a mostly nonswimming Esther Williams as the manager of the Wolves baseball team, whose star members are vaudevillians Gene Kelly and Frank Sinatra. Sinatra has his heart set on Williams, but she prefers Kelly, leaving the sly crooner to accept the advances of a pursuing Shirley Delwyn (Betty) in the comic duet, "It's Fate, Baby, It's Fate." This Arthur Freed-produced Technicolor period musical was popular, but not as successful as the next Freed tune venture, the screen version of *On the Town* (1949). Jules Munshin, who had been on Broadway with Betty in *Call Me Mister* was again, as in *Ball Game*, the third wheel to sailors Sinatra and Kelly. The trio have a twenty-four-hour shore leave in New York and each is searching for a doll to make the day perfect. Kelly falls for Miss Turnstiles (Vera-Ellen), Munshin is overjoyed with anthropologist Ann Miller, and Sinatra is reluctantly agreeable to the dynamic advances of taxi driver Brunhilde Esterhazy (Betty). In the is comic role played on Broadway by Nancy Walker, Betty has a difficult time urging Sinatra to "Come up to My Place" and is the first to agree in a most congenial way that "You're Awful." The labored ballet dancing of Kelly and Vera-Ellen in this Leonard Bernstein musical is less impressive with passing years, but Betty's man-hungry performance, along with the performance of her cold-sneezing wallflower roommate Lucy Schmeeler (Alice Pearce) is as endearing now as ever.

Betty's third release of the year was MGM's *Neptune's Daughter* (1949) with Esther Williams a bathing suit designer and Betty her male-chasing sister who mistakes polo club masseur Red Skelton for a South American polo star. Esther wins Fernando Lamas, and Betty has Skelton firmly entrapped, having proven in her Latin number "I Love Those Men," and that romancing is much more appropriate because "Baby, It's Cold Outside." This latter Frank Loesser tune won an Oscar that year.

During 1949 Betty and Parks had performed a club act and were on tour in Scotland and at London's Palladium. When Garland went out of *Annie Get Your Gun* (1950), Betty was touted as a stronger contender for the role, but eventually it went to Paramount's Betty Hutton. Due to the birth of sons Garrett in 1950 and Andrew in 1951, Betty was generally unavailable for screen assignments. It was at this time that Parks testified at the House UnAmerican Activities Committee that he had been a card-carrying Communist from 1941 to 1945 but left the party when he realized he was misguided. Columbia dumped their *Jolson Story* star and Dore Schary's all-American MGM gave Betty the polite gate. The jobless Parkses finally went overseas to play their club act and then returned to the U. S. to tour with the play *Anonymous Lover*.

Ironically, it was Columbia who next hired the new Betty—she had had plastic surgery on her nose—to play Ruth Sherwood in their musical version of *My Sister Eileen* (1955). The role had been played onstage by Shirley Booth, and then in films by Rosalind Russell who also did a different musical version of the play, called *Wonderful Town*. Later, Elaine Stritch would be Ruth Sherwood in a television series version. Bringing her own brand of wisecracking good humor to the assignment, Betty played the older, literary-bent "ugly" sister of attractive Eileen (Janet Leigh). The Jule Styne–Leo Robin tunes were eminently forgettable and the script overly farcical, but Betty got to perform "As Soon as They See Eileen," "Give Me a Band and My Baby," "I'm Great" (with Leigh, Dick York, and Kurt Kasznar) and "There's Nothing Like Love" (with Leigh). Jack Lemmon also starred as the magazine editor who sings "It's Bigger than You or Me," as he goes on the prowl for cigarette-dangling, would-be-writer Betty.

It was two years before she did another film, *The Shadow on the Window* (1957), a mild melodrama for Universal in which she was the mother of trauma-muted Jerry Mathers and was held hostage by homicidal robbers.

Since then she has done occasional television work, such as a few thirty-minute comedies with Parks (*The Penlands and the Poodle, A Smattering Of Bliss*), an appearance with Art Carney in a TV special, (1959), and as a guest on *The Fugitive* and other similar programs. Mostly she and Parks have worked on stage, replacing Judy Holliday and Sydney Chaplin in 1957 in *Bells Are Ringing*, and then starring in the flop musical *Beg, Borrow or Steal* (1960). In addition, Betty has been in Theater West's (California) production of Edgar Lee Masters' free verse collection *Spoon River Anthology* and appeared in the short-lived Broadway edition in 1963, receiving excellent notices. In 1964, she played with Pat Hingle in a quick-closing two-character comedy, *A Girl Could Get Lucky*.

In recent years the Parkses have continued to perform together in stock shows, while most of the family's income has been derived from a construction business the actor had formed years before with his movie revenues. On her own, Betty has become quite a favorite with Chicago audiences. She was very popular with her version of *Plaza Suite* and recently starred with Sandy Dennis in a well-received edition of *And Miss Reardon Drinks a Little*.

BETTY GARRETT

The Big City (MGM, 1948)
Words and Music (MGM, 1948)
Take Me Out to The Ball Game (MGM, 1949)
Neptune's Daughter (MGM, 1949)

On the Town (MGM, 1949)
My Sister Eileen (Columbia, 1955)
The Shadow on the Window (Columbia, 1957)

With Mickey Rooney in *Words and Music* (1948)

Greer Garson

" ... I guess if you're going to be typed, there are worse molds in which you can be cast." So spoke Greer Garson who became the 1940s personification of the genteel, unneurotic woman who deemphasized her sexuality in order to *be* the self-sacrificing, noble heroine of good causes in such films as *Mrs. Miniver* (1942), *Random Harvest* (1942), and *Madame Curie* (1943). For five years, covering the equally self-sacrificing World War II span, she reigned supreme as the epitome of Louis B. Mayer's fantasized womanhood and hence the star of MGM's most lavishly expansive women's pictures. The mixture of her Irish charm, natural red-haired beauty, and her uncanny capacity to project the shopgirl's vision of the great lady made her an incontestable star to a decade that required a staunch, wholesome ideal.

Many critics insist Mayer's influence on Greer's artistic growth was deplorable, considering that her apprenticeship on the English stage had made her a popular and well-thought-of young actress in roles of a classical nature, such as Shaw, Sheridan, and Shakespeare. James Agee maintained that if she had not been "suffocated and immobilized by Metro's image," she could have made an interesting Lady Macbeth. Many of her detractors claim she even began to believe Mayer's image of herself. But even she had the foresight to call herself "Metro's Glorified Mother" in the late 1940s when she was trying to break the Mrs. Miniver "curse." Mayer's reaction to her "ingratitude" was to label her "rebellious" and import another English lass, Deborah Kerr, as a threat. However, by the time Kerr had been promoted as a proper American star, Mayer was out of MGM and Greer soon took leave of the studio voluntarily. Her rationale was, "We were not making the big romantic type picture that is my forte." To this day, she is one of the most stalwart supporters of the Louis B. Mayer legend.

Greer Garson was born in County Down, Ireland (the Presbyterian part of Northern Ireland) on September 29, 1908 (some say 1914). While still in her teens, she moved to London with her mother. She graduated with honors from the University of London. Having been stagestruck since she had recited poems in the town hall at the age of four, she joined the Birmingham Repertory Theatre and made her stage debut in Elmer Rice's *Street Scene.* She toured in Shaw's *Too True to Be Good* and played an American girl opposite

Laurence Olivier in a short-lived item called *Golden Arrow* (1935). She was soon a popular young star of London's West End, being directed by Noel Coward in *Mademoiselle*, and broadening her acting experience in *Twelfth Night* and *School for Scandal*.

It was in the West End's St. James Theatre that Louis B. Mayer saw her in a little melodrama, *Old Music*. He attended the performance believing the show's title implied a musical and sat throughout the play fidgeting every time the lovely red-haired actress was not on stage. He was enchanted with her innocent beauty and invited her to have supper with him at the Savoy Grill after the performance. The always ladylike Greer (known as the "Duchess of Garson" to the London gallery girls) rushed home, put on her best gown, and brought her mother along. The next day she was carefully screen-tested, given a $500-a-week contract, and told to report to Culver City as soon as she could gain release from the play.

She did just that but found that Mayer was not in any rush to find a film project for her—there were still Greta Garbo and Norma Shearer on the home lot—and Greer was about to disenchantedly return to London. But she was suggested for the small role of Kathy, the young wife who dies early in *Goodbye, Mr. Chips* (1939). Thus Greer did go home, but only to make that film in London. When she returned to Hollywood, she was hailed as an international star and nominated for an Oscar.

Just to keep her on the screen, she was assigned to a mediocre comedy *Remember?* (1939) with Lew Ayres and Robert Taylor. However, she was perspicaciously cast as Elizabeth Bennett in the film version of Jane Austen's *Pride and Prejudice* (1940), in which her costar was her old friend Laurence Olivier. (Vivien Leigh, fresh from her Scarlett O'Hara success, wanted the role desperately, and it even had originally been planned as a Norma Shearer–Clark Gable vehicle.) The results were feliticious and middle America found itself sitting through a classic without an intolerable case of the squirms.

It was in Mervyn LeRoy's Technicolor *Blossoms in the Dust* (1941) that Greer was initially teamed with Walter Pidgeon, the first of their eight films together. This film set the self-sacrificing image which became her cinematic stock in trade. Greer paraded through the maudlin piece with saintly self-confidence and convinced moviegoers that, contrary to the global war then in progress, there were still wondrous examples of human courage and fortitude to be found, even if the scripters had to turn the clock back several decades to do so. The real-life Mrs. Edna Gladney, a crusader for the humane treatment of illegitimate children, might well have blushed at the contrived schmaltz added to her life story. Next, Greer confronted Joan Crawford in the remake of Rachel Crothers' play *When Ladies Meet* (1941). It was a draw match with the audience being the main loser in this over-talky debate on women's rights.

Greer was finally cajoled by Mayer into starring in her most famous screen role, *Mrs. Miniver*. Norma Shearer had refused the part because she did not wish to play the mother of a grown son, and Greer initially refused on the same pretext. After much pleading by Mayer, whose performance everyone says could have won him an Oscar, she accepted the role. With Walter Pidgeon as her husband she was splendid as the gallant wartime English wife. Franklin D. Roosevelt was so impressed with the film that he requested its hasty release and had the vicar's lofty speech at the end of the film printed in leaflet form and dropped by airplanes over Nazi-occupied Europe. Greer received the Academy Award for her performance and, at the awards dinner in 1943, gave a thank-you speech that lasted nearly forty-five minutes. Thereafter, recipients were requested to make their acceptance speeches "brief." There was a romantic footnote to *Mrs. Miniver*: Greer fell in love with the actor who played her son in the film, Richard Ney, age twenty-six. MGM persuaded her to delay her marriage for several months during the film's initial release to avoid any distasteful publicity. (She had been married to Edwin A. Snelson from 1932 to 1937.)

The die had been cast, and the films which followed rarely allowed Greer to assert her vivacious Irish charm, let alone expand her acting abilities. In *Random Harvest* she gallantly nursed amnesiac Ronald Colman. She also had a bit as a be-kilted music hall entertainer, and sang while she jigged, revealing a trim figure. In *Madame Curie*, again with Pidgeon, she portrayed fifty years of the scientist's heroic quest, and lost her Oscar bid to the more noble performance of Jennifer Jones in *The Song of Bernadette* (1943). *Mrs. Parkington* (1944) cast her as the glamorous matriarch of a fortune earned by scoundrel Walter Pidgeon. Again she was Oscar nominated and, though she lost the award to Ingrid Bergman in MGM's *Gaslight* (1944), she had won a new seven-year contract with very prestigious terms.

It was now that Greer Garson jokes were becoming part of Hollywood folklore, proving she was an established institution. (One quipster noted: Lassie is Greer Garson with fur.) But Mayer did little to appease her in her effort to burst the clinical cocoon of her stereotyped roles. *Valley of Decision* (1945) had her as a Pittsburgh servant girl in love with mining scion Gregory Peck. This family saga was her last big hit. She was a librarian picked up by sailor Clark Gable in *Adventure* (1946), but second lead Joan Blondell received what little critical approval this out-of-key film merited. *Desire Me* (1947) with Robert Mitchum was so bad that director George Cukor refused to put his name in the credits.

A teen-aged Elizabeth Taylor attracted more attention than either Greer or Walter Pidgeon in *Julia Misbehaves* (1948), confirming that Greer had past her top-ten-at-the-boxoffice peak. *That Forsyte Woman* (1949), based on the Galsworthy epic, pitted her against Errol Flynn, Pidgeon, and Robert Young, and found her acting on a suitable level again. In retrospect, it is easy to say that MGM was foolish in casting her in a sequel to *Mrs. Miniver* entitled *The Miniver Story* (1950). Ultimately the film made filmgoers uncomfortably leery of their positive judgment eight years before when witnessing the charming if equally phony original. A black-wigged Greer was no asset to the spiritless *The Law and the Lady* (1951), yet another remake of *The Last of Mrs.*

Cheyney.

Greer requested the almost cameo role of Calpurnia in *Julius Caesar* (1953). She did a last film with Pidgeon, *Scandal at Scourie* (1953), about religious tolerance in a small Canadian town, and ended her MGM association in March, 1954 with *Her Twelve Men* (1954). (Eleanor Parker inherited *Interrupted Melody* [1955] which had been slated for Greer.) When she left the lot Greer told reporters: "For the first time in my life, I'm not planning or worrying . . . . I want to do a picture now and then but I won't do any more potboilers."

After making a Western at Warners, *Strange Lady in Town* (1955), which did not click, Greer found herself at a professional impasse. Now well into her forties, she was being passed over in favor of the younger Deborah Kerr or the even younger Jean Simmons. Unlike determined Metro stablemate Joan Crawford, she refused to besmirch her once lofty screen image by working in modestly budgeted products.

On a turnabout, Greer then replaced Rosalind Russell in *Auntie Mame* on Broadway and might have reestablished herself as a popular stage performer. However, she had wed oil magnate Elijah E. "Buddy" Folgelson in 1949, and he did not like his wife away from the home fires for too long a stretch. She did return to films in 1960 with a cleverly etched portrayal of the young Eleanor Roosevelt in *Sunrise at Campobello* (a part Loretta Young is said to have badly wanted to play) but the road show production failed at the boxoffice. Greer received her seventh Oscar nomination for her performance. Her remaining 1960s films are negligible: a gratuitous cameo in *Pepe* (1960), an overly grand mother superior in *The Singing Nun* (1966) back at MGM, and a forgettable assignment opposite Fred MacMurray in Walt Disney's *The Happiest Millionaire* (1967).

She has been an occasional television performer without notable success, ranging from *Reunion in Vienna* (1955) and *The Little Foxes* (1956), to Trevor Howard's wife in *The Remarkable Mr. Disraeli* (1963), and condescending guest appearances as herself on the *Father Knows Best* series and *Laugh-In*. Finally, in 1971, she essayed a woman lawyer on the *Men from Shiloh* Western teleseries.

With homes in Dallas, Texas and Pecos, New Mexico, Greer remains an avid champion of her late MGM mentor and actively supports the Louis B. Mayer Foundation.

GREER GARSON

Goodbye, Mr. Chips (MGM, 1939)
Remember? (MGM, 1939)
Pride and Prejudice (MGM, 1940)
Blossoms in the Dust (MGM, 1941)
When Ladies Meet (MGM, 1941)
Mrs. Miniver (MGM, 1942)

Random Harvest (MGM, 1942)
The Youngest Profession (MGM, 1943)
Madame Curie (MGM, 1943)
Mrs. Parkington (MGM, 1944)
Valley of Decision (MGM, 1945)
Adventure (MGM, 1945)

271

Desire Me (MGM, 1947)
Julia Misbehaves (MGM, 1948)
That Forsyte Woman (MGM, 1949)
The Miniver Story (MGM, 1950)
The Law and the Lady (MGM, 1951)
Julius Caesar (MGM, 1953)
Scandal at Scourie (MGM, 1953)

Her Twelve Men (MGM, 1954)
Strange Lady in Town (WB, 1955)
Sunrise at Campobello (WB, 1960)
Pepe (Columbia, 1960)
The Singing Nun (MGM, 1966)
The Happiest Millionaire (BV, 1967)

With Robert Taylor in *Remember?* (1939)

With Claire Sanders, Christopher Severn, Richard Ney, and Teresa Wright in *Mrs. Miniver* (1942)

With Ronald Colman in *Random Harvest* (1942)

With Walter Pidgeon in *Madame Curie* (1943)

With Selena Royle and Walter Pidgeon (photograph) in *Mrs. Parkington* (1944)

With Walter Pidgeon in *Julia Misbehaves* (1948)

With Tom Drake, Ed Sullivan, and Ricardo Montalban in *The Singing Nun* (1966)

Frances Gifford

For those who wonder whatever happened to Frances Gifford, the star of Republic's action serial *Jungle Girl* (1941), she did not swing off into obscurity. After playing Nyoka in that chapter play and a pagan princess in *Tarzan's Triumph* (1943), the auburn-haired beauty went contemporary and joined MGM, where for five years she played pert "other women." Had not an automobile accident caused emotional damage, she undoubtedly would have gone on to better roles in films and on television. She was a beautiful girl and among the many who deserved a better chance from Hollywood during the industry's Golden Age.

Mary Frances Gifford was born in Long Beach, California on December 7, 1922. She was an only child. She attended Woodrow Wilson High School, where in her senior year she took commercial law as a major subject. During summer vacation she had been employed as a fashion model. She intended to enter the University of California at Los Angeles as a prelaw student, but shortly before she was to start there, she accompanied some friends on a visit to the Samuel Goldwyn studios to watch a film being made. While on the set, Frances was "spotted" and offered a screen test. According to the official story, during her oncamera audition she was posed before a mirror and as she turned to face the lens she suddenly made a face at herself in the mirror. This flash of innate humor so appealed to the Goldwyn executives that she was signed to a contract. That was in 1936, and in the same year she was among the ten promising newcomers chosen by the Hollywood Press Photographers Association as "Flash-Lighters' Starlets." The other girls were: Helen Burgess, Kay Hughes, Janice Jarrett, Rosina Lawrence, Cecilia Parker, Barbara Pepper, Joan Perry, and June Travis.

During Frances' stay at the Goldwyn studio, all she did was pose for publicity spreads, mostly of the bathing suit variety. She was seen very briefly onscreen in Miriam Hopkins' *Woman Chases Man* (1937). Leaving that studio, Frances signed with RKO in 1937, only to receive at first more of the nonexposure syndrome. That studio eventually did utilize her as animated background for such studio releases of the year as *New Faces of 1937, Stage Door*, and *Living on Love*. By 1938 Frances had departed from RKO and married actor James Dunn. He had starred with Whitney Bourne in *Living on*

Love but found time to make Frances' acquaintance during the shooting of that picture. Dunn was then thirty-two and past his cinema prime. For two years Frances was just a housewife and did nothing to advance whatever career she had. But in 1939 she had a walkon in Columbia's *Mr. Smith Goes to Washington*, and the next year she and Dunn were teamed in two quickie films for Producers Releasing Corporation. Neither *Mercy Plane* nor *Hold That Woman* broke the professional jinx for Dunn or improved Frances' fledgling screen status. She was used by Walt Disney in 1941 for his animated–live action feature *The Reluctant Dragon*. More important, Republic selected her to play the lead in its fifteen-chapter serial, *Jungle Girl* (1941), based on Edgar Rice Burrough's novel of the same title. In the part of Nyoka, the girl of the title, Frances was becomingly garbed in abbreviated jungle wear, "swung" through the trees and niftily revived the tradition of such past great serial queens as Pearl White and Ruth Roland. Republic was so pleased with audience reaction to Frances' starring vehicle that they announced her to star in a followup chapter play, *Perils of Nyoka* (1942). But by that time she was under contract to Paramount and had divorced Dunn (she never remarried). Instead, Kay Aldridge became the new Nyoka.

At Paramount, Frances initially graced the background of Bob Hope's *Louisiana Purchase* (1941) but then was given the female lead in *Border Vigilantes* (1941), the thirty-fourth of the William Boyd Hopalong Cassidy films. She even got to sing a song in that Western. On the whole, Frances was not well used by the Paramount casting department: She supported Anne Shirley in *West Point Widow* (1941), was outdone by burlesque stripper Martha O'Driscoll in *My Heart Belongs to Daddy* (1942), and played a conventional role as Preston Foster's wife in *American Empire* (1942), which was released by United Artists. She was just in the finale production number of *Star Spangled Rhythm* (1942). In the remake of *The Glass Key* (1942) she had the small part of the nurse, played by Ann Sheridan in the original. Dorothy Lamour's *Beyond the Blue Horizon* (1942) found Frances cast as one of the civilized society set who scoff at former jungle girl Lamour. However, Frances did have a sizable role in *Henry Aldrich Gets Glamour* (1943) in which she was the femme fatale movie sarong queen who immobilizes, at least temporarily, hyperactive Jimmy Lydon. Her role was similar to Lucille Ball's part in Metro's *Best Foot Forward*, released that same year. Next to *Jungle Girl*, Frances' most remembered assignment was in RKO's *Tarzan's Triumph* (1943), the first of the Johnny Weissmuller series to be made away from MGM. Since Maureen O'Sullivan was no longer available to play Jane (the script had her away in England), Frances appeared as Zandra, the pagan princess from the hidden city. Years later, in a fantasy sequence within the British-produced *Morgan!* (1966), clips from *Tarzan's Triumph* were used, showing Weissmuller and Frances swimming.

Frances next moved over to MGM. She was first utilized there in *Cry Havoc* (1943), a more entertaining production about World War II nurses than was Paramount's similar *So Proudly We Hail*, released the same year. Frances was not quite lost in the large cast of women in *Cry Havoc*. She played Helen, the nurse who cannot stop talking about men. MGM then cast her in *Marriage Is a Private Affair* (1944) as the girl romanced by Hugh Marlowe. She had little screen time in that Lana Turner vehicle, but the next year was more in evidence in *Thrill Of a Romance* as the "other woman" standing in the way of Esther Williams' romance with soldier Van Johnson. Next came a trio of film assignments opposite MGM's budget leading man James Craig. Frances was the citified country school teacher in love with local newspaper publisher Craig in *Our Vines Have Tender Grapes* (1945), and horse trainer Craig's love interest in *She Went to the Races* (1945) in which she has developed a scientific system for winning at the horse races. Finally, she is the mother of Jackie "Butch" Jenkins in *Little Mr. Jim* (1946). When she dies partway through the story, her army husband, Craig, takes to drink, ignoring his son.

Although Arch Oboler's *The Arnelo Affair* (1947) was an economy picture, it offered Frances a real lead role and a chance to "suffer" in the best cinema tradition of Joan Crawford and Ann Sheridan. She played the wife of Chicago attorney George Murphy who nearly comes to grief due to her attraction to disreputable nightclub owner John Hodiak. Then it was back to a supporting assignment in the musical *Luxury Liner* (1948), as the shipboard passenger whom star Jane Powell attempts to match up with her ship's captain father (George Brent). Frances looked lovely but had little to do in this Technicolor nonsense.

After completing *Luxury Liner*, Frances was supposedly set for bigger and better things at MGM. There was even mention of her starring in several remakes of Norma Shearer pictures. Suddenly however, she was in a serious automobile accident, suffering severe head injuries. The accident required a long recuperatory period and her MGM contract was terminated. It was two years before she returned to the screen in Paramount's *Riding High* (1950), Frank Capra's remake of *Broadway Bill*. Frances was relegated to the supporting role of a pretty rich girl who is jilted by horse lover Bing Crosby. After that it was three years before Frances made what proved to be her final film. It was Columbia's programmer *Sky Commando* (1953), set in World War II. As the female war correspondent she had a relatively unimportant role.

In the early 1950s Frances was a frequent television performer, appearing on such series as *Fireside Theatre*. She and Allyn Joslyn costarred in a domestic comedy series pilot, *My Wife, Poor Wretch*, but it never sold.

Evidently Frances continued to suffer repercussions from the accident, for by the late 1950s she had retired from the acting scene and in 1958 was admitted to the Camarillo (California) State Hospital. This has been the last her public has heard of her.

Woman Chases Man (UA, 1937)
New Faces of 1937 (RKO, 1937)
Living on Love (RKO, 1937)
Stage Door (RKO, 1937)
Mr. Smith Goes to Washington (Columbia, 1939)
A Fugitive from Justice (WB, 1940)
Mercy Plane (PRC, 1940)
Hold That Woman (PRC, 1940)
The Reluctant Dragon (RKO, 1941)
Jungle Girl (Serial: Republic, 1941)
Louisiana Purchase (Paramount, 1941)
Border Vigilantes (Paramount, 1941)
West Point Widow (Paramount, 1941)
The Remarkable Andrew (Paramount, 1942)
Tombstone, the Town Too Tough to Die (Paramount, 1942)

Beyond the Blue Horizon (Paramount, 1942)
The Glass Key (Paramount, 1942)
My Heart Belongs to Daddy (Paramount, 1942)
American Empire (UA, 1942)
Star Spangled Rhythm (Paramount, 1942)
Tarzan Triumphs (RKO, 1943)
Cry Havoc (MGM, 1943)
Marriage Is a Private Affair (MGM, 1944)
Thrill of a Romance (MGM, 1945)
Our Vines Have Tender Grapes (MGM, 1945)
She Went to the Races (MGM, 1945)
Little Mr. Jim (MGM, 1946)
The Arnelo Affair (MGM, 1947)
Luxury Liner (MGM, 1948)
Riding High (Paramount, 1950)
Sky Commando (Columbia, 1953)

With John Hodiak and George Murphy in *The Arnelo Affair* (1947)

Connie Gilchrist

If ever MGM got its money's worth from a contract character player it was with Connie Gilchrist. She was salty in the tradition of Marjorie Rambeau and Marjorie Main but more restrained than either of those two grand dames. Her gallery of domestics and Gallic mothers rivals those created by free-lancer Mary Gordon, but Connie was outspoken and wisecracking in her characterizations in comparison to Gordon's persistent gentleness. Best of all for Metro's purposes, her solid build and openness of look made her suitable for almost any genre of screenfare. Therefore, between 1940 and 1948, she popped up in MGM's Westerns, musicals, war tales, and costumes pieces, as well as the contemporary-set films.

She was born Rose Gilchrist in Brooklyn Heights, N. Y. on February 2, 1906, the daughter of actress Martha Daniels. After being educated at a convent and then Assumption Academy, she decided to pursue a stage career. She made her debut in London at the age of sixteen, playing a Cockney in *The Enchanting Mistress*. Thereafter she toured in repertory in France for three years and later returned to the U. S. to manage a small theatre company in Connecticut. In 1922 she wed actor Edwin O'Hanlon and their daughter Dorothy was born in 1930. She was on Broadway in Langston Hughes' *Mulatto* (1935), played a tough, slangy salesgirl in *Excursion* (1937), and then was in *Work Is for Horses* (1937). Her radio debut was on the soap opera *John's Other Wife*. It was playing Mrs. Rudd in Helen Hayes' *Ladies and Gentlemen* (1939) which led to a screen career. She was spotted in the West Coast pre-Broadway tour of the show and signed by MGM.

After a bit in *Hullabaloo* (1940), Connie quickly hit her stride with eleven Metro releases in 1941. She was Bonita Granville's mother in *The Wild Man of Borneo* and had a secretarial bit in Greta Garbo's *Two-Faced Woman*. In *Barnacle Bill* she was Marjorie Main's energetic rival for Wallace Beery's affection, a screen assignment she would repeat with that comedy duo in *Rationing* (1944) and *Bad Bascomb* (1946). She had her meatiest role that year in *A Woman's Face* (1941), as one of Joan Crawford's disrespectful, outspoken criminal underlings.

Connie was equally at ease adding local color as the Mexican dancing partner of Spencer Tracy in *Tortilla Flat* (1942), as a squaw in *Apache Trail*

(1942), or as a combat nurse in *Cry Havoc* (1943). She is perhaps best remembered as the scrubwoman who sings "Every Little Movement" with Judy Garland in *Presenting Lily Mars* (1943).

Throughout the 1940s she continued as the perennial cinema domestic, whether on loan to Twentieth Century-Fox for *Junior Miss* (1945) or as the maid in *Valley of Decision* (1945) and the middle-aged cook in *Good News* (1947). She was merely a lady with a baby in *Song of the Thin Man* (1947) and she finished off her MGM contract as yet another servant in *Little Women* (1949). The previous year she had had an excellent role as Linda Darnell's wrong-side-of-the-tracks mother who spends her time boozing with pal Thelma Ritter in *A Letter to Three Wives*.

Throughout the 1950s she was again busy in films, playing a nun in *Thunder on the Hill* (1952), Purity Pinker in *Long John Silver* (1955), and exuding one of the few touches of sincerity as the former candy store owner turned barfly in Frank Sinatra's *Some Came Running* (1958). She was a housekeeper again in *Auntie Mame* (1958) and cleaner-upper of Bing Crosby's rectory in *Say One for Me* (1959). The latter film allowed her to be gussied up for the Debbie Reynolds–Robert Wagner wedding scene. Then it was more domestics in the 1960s: a day cleaning lady in *Two on a Guillotine* (1965), a hotel maid in *Fluffy* (1965), and Hilda the handy woman in Elvis Presley's *Tickle Me* (1965). A small part in Dick Van Dyke's *Some Kind of a Nut* (1969) is her last picture to date.

Connie has been equally active on television, particularly in the 1950s and 1960s, appearing in episodes of most of the major series ranging from *Wagon Train* to *Alfred Hitchcock* to *Hawaiian Eye* to *Bachelor Father*.

She and her husband are semiretired and live in a rustic house high in the hills of Los Angeles. Her husband still calls her "Gertie," a nickname she picked up years ago from an artist who painted her portrait (which now hangs in the Whitney Museum). At MGM she was the studio cutup and was affectionately called "The Countess."

CONNIE GILCHRIST

Hullabaloo (MGM, 1940)
Down in San Diego (MGM, 1941)
Billy the Kid (MGM, 1941)
Dr. Kildare's Wedding Day (MGM, 1941)
The Wild Man of Borneo (MGM, 1941)
A Woman's Face (MGM, 1941)
H. M. Pulham, Esq. (MGM, 1941)
Barnacle Bill (MGM, 1941)
Johnny Eager (MGM, 1941)
Two-Faced Woman (MGM, 1941)
Married Bachelor (MGM, 1941)
We Were Dancing (MGM, 1942)
This Time for Keeps (MGM, 1942)

Sunday Punch (MGM, 1942)
Tortilla Flat (MGM, 1942)
Grand Central Murder (MGM, 1942)
Apache Trail (MGM, 1942)
The War Against Mrs. Hadley (MGM, 1942)
Thousands Cheer (MGM, 1943)
Presenting Lily Mars (MGM, 1943)
Swing Shift Maisie (MGM, 1943)
Cry Havoc (MGM, 1943)
The Heavenly Body (MGM, 1943)
Rationing (MGM, 1944)
Nothing But Trouble (MGM, 1944)
Music for Millions (MGM, 1944)

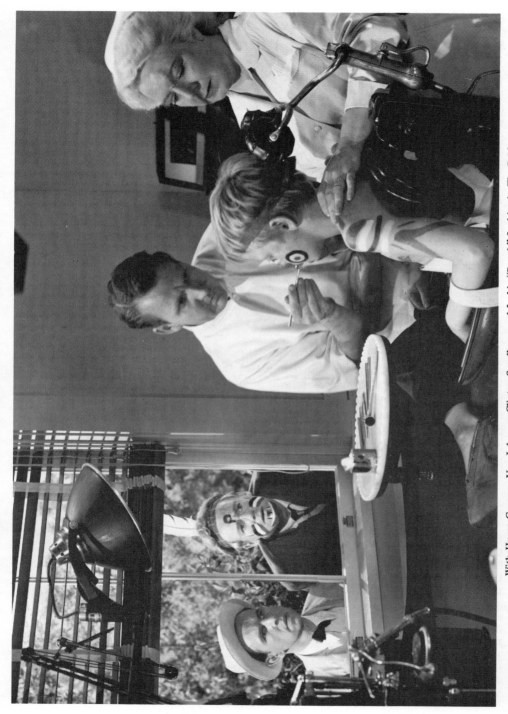

With Hume Cronyn, Van Johnson, Clinton Sundberg, and Jackie "Butch" Jenkins in *The Bride Goes Wild* (1948)

The Seventh Cross (MGM, 1944)
Valley of Decision (MGM, 1945)
Junior Miss (20th-Fox, 1945)
Young Widow (UA, 1946)
Bad Bascomb (MGM, 1946)
Faithful in My Fashion (MGM, 1946)
The Hucksters (MGM, 1947)
Song of the Thin Man (MGM, 1947)
Good News (MGM, 1947)
Tenth Avenue Angel (MGM, 1948)
The Bride Goes Wild (MGM, 1948)
The Big City (MGM, 1948)
Luxury Liner (MGM, 1948)
Act of Violence (MGM, 1948)
A Letter to Three Wives (20th-Fox, 1948)
Chicken Every Sunday (20th-Fox, 1948)
Little Women (MGM, 1949)
The Story of Molly X (Universal, 1949)
Stars in My Crown (MGM, 1950)
Buccaneer's Girl (Universal, 1950)
A Ticket to Tomahawk (20th-Fox, 1950)
Louisa (Universal, 1950)
Peggy (Universal, 1950)
Undercover Girl (Universal, 1950)
Tripoli (Paramount, 1950)
The Killer That Stalked New York (Columbia, 1950)
Here Comes the Groom (Paramount, 1951)

Thunder on the Hill (Universal, 1951)
Chain of Circumstances (Columbia, 1951)
One Big Affair (UA, 1952)
The Half-Breed (RKO, 1952)
Flesh and Fury (Universal, 1952)
Houdini (Paramount, 1953)
The Great Diamond Robbery (MGM, 1953)
It Should Happen to You (Columbia, 1954)
The Far Country (Universal, 1955)
Long John Silver (DCA, 1955)
The Man in the Gray Flannel Suit (20th-Fox, 1956)
Machine Gun Kelly (AIP, 1958)
Auntie Mame (WB, 1958)
Some Came Running (MGM, 1958)
Say One for Me (20th-Fox, 1959)
The Interns (Columbia, 1962)
Swingin' Along (20th-Fox, 1962)
A Tiger Walks (BV, 1964)
The Misadventures of Merlin Jones (BV, 1964)
A House is Not a Home (Embassy, 1964)
Two on a Guillotine (WB, 1965)
Sylvia (Paramount, 1965)
Fluffy (Universal, 1965)
Tickle Me (AA, 1965)
The Monkey's Uncle (BV, 1965)
Some Kind of a Nut (UA, 1969)

Gloria Grahame

If, as legend has it, the Oscar can be a jinx, then Gloria Grahame's screen career is an excellent example. At the top of her public and critical acclaim in 1952, she received the best supporting actress Academy Award for her performance as the Southern tramp in MGM's *The Bad and the Beautiful*, and the remainder of her career went downhill. However, legends aside, a quick perusal of the biographical facts of Gloria's career reveal it was not so much Oscar as Gloria who ruined her career. She spent her film apprenticeship at MGM in the mid 1940s, but the studio was even less interested in molding a commercial cinema image for her than with flashy MGM contemporary Audrey Meadows. Gloria left the lot after three uneventful years to make a name for herself as a sexually alluring cinema siren. Her sensuous pout (did she stuff Kleenex under the upper lip of her already flamboyantly puckered mouth?) became a lucrative stock in trade on the screen. Whether her pictures were first- or second-rate, and they were usually the latter, her convincing performances made her the typical girl that screen skunks loved to smash about and kill. MGM even found itself borrowing Gloria's professional service for *The Bad and the Beautiful* and *The Cobweb* (1955). But everything turned sour for the thirty-year-old Gloria. Her rude and arrogant attitude to the press caught up with her, several stormy marriages diverted her from retaining her movie status, and then it was all over, except for a reflex-action "comeback" syndrome in the 1970s.

She was born Gloria Grahame Hallward in Los Angeles on November 28, 1925. Her mother, Jean Grahame, had been an actress of minor note in London, and Gloria decided at an early age that she also wanted to be a performer. Her father was a commercial and industrial designer and, during her childhood, the family moved several times. While living in Pasadena Gloria made her stage debut at the age of nine at the Pasadena Community Playhouse, and when the Hallwards moved to Hollywood she attended Hollywood High School where she had a featured role in the senior class play of 1942. Producer Howard Lang saw her in that performance and gave her a job as understudy in his San Francisco production of *Good Night Ladies*. After six weeks of understudying, Gloria got to go on stage when one of the actresses took ill. Gloria traveled with the play to Chicago, and when it closed in 1943 she headed for the Broadway stage.

Her first New York job was again as an understudy, but this time to much older Miriam Hopkins, who had replaced Tallulah Bankhead in Thornton Wilder's *The Skin of Our Teeth*. That play's producer, Michael Meyerberg, took a liking to Gloria and gave her a part in his new production, *Star Dust*. But the show closed out of town, and she finally made her Broadway debut in the Jed Harris production of Nunnally Johnson's *The World's Full of Girls*. The play opened on December 6, 1943, and was a flop, but at least she attracted some attention from the critics. One writer called her a "flamboyant and amusing floozy." George Abbott hired her for the role of the barmaid in his *A Highland Fling*. Gloria spoke with a Scottish burr and the N.Y. *Herald-Tribune*, among others, thought her excellent. However, the play was not, and it closed in less than a month, but luckily not before an MGM talent scout saw her performance.

She was signed to a MGM contract in July 1944 at $250 a week. Louis B. Mayer had her name shortened to Gloria Grahame because he thought Gloria Hallward was far "too theatrical." Gloria did not have the beautiful face that typified the MGM femmes—she would have been much better off at Warners playing in tandem with their lineup of tough screen mugs—and the studio made no effort to promote her toward stardom, particularly when it had Audrey Totter on hand to essay in a more conventional manner the quasi tough broads that even Metro found itself forced to depict on the screen. Gloria's screen debut was as a waitress in *Blonde Fever* (1944) followed by a bit as a flower girl in *Without Love* (1945).

Gloria filled her spare time with a USO tour and a marriage to actor Stanley Clements (August 29, 1945). After numerous, noisy separations, they were divorced in 1948. Her career finally got off the the ground when producer–director Frank Capra telephoned MGM's casting head Billy Grady and told him he needed a "young blonde sexpot" for the small role of the village flirt in *It's a Wonderful Life* (1946). In Capra's autobiography, *The Name Above the Title,* he says Grady's response went like this: "For crissake, I'm up to here in blonde pussies that've never been to the post. Let me show you some tests." During the tests Capra saw Gloria on the screen and said "Hey, Bill! Who's that dame?"

"Who is she, for crissake?," said Grady. "She's a star. But do you think I can get any of our jerks to listen? Two years she's been around here snapping her garters. You can have her for a cuppa coffee. Her name's Gloria Grahame."

Her success in that small role prompted MGM to cast Gloria as the frizzy blonde Brooklyn nurse who gets Frank Sinatra in *It Happened in Brooklyn* (1947). Following this, she was cast as a silent screen vamp in *Merton of the Movies* (1947), and suffered her first onscreen death scene as the nightclub singer in *Song of the Thin Man* (1947). MGM was still uninterested and allowed RKO production head Dore Schary to buy up her contract and sign her with RKO at $750 a week. In *Crossfire* (1947), her first RKO film, Gloria was Oscar-nominated for her role as a kind-hearted tart. However, the best supporting actress award went to Celeste Holm for her work in another anti-Semitism study, *Gentleman's Agreement*. But Schary was soon to move to MGM as vice president in charge of production, and Gloria's career still floundered in such roles as the pouty blonde manbait in Humphrey Bogart's *In a Lonely Place* (1950) or as the croupier girl friend of Brad Dexter in Jane Russell's *Macao* (1952). When Cecil B. De Mille had to replace a pregnant Lucille Ball in the role of Angel, the elephant girl of *The Greatest Show on Earth* (1952), he borrowed Gloria from RKO, and she received considerable prerelease publicity when she refused to have a stand-in perform in the scene where the elephant holds his foot just inches over her face as she is lying on the ground.

It was the best year of her film career, not only because of her appearance in that Academy Award-winning circus picture. Her own studio gave her the good role as the lover of Joan Crawford's husband (Jack Palance) in *Sudden Fear* which contained another of her death scenes. This time she was run down by an automobile. To top the year off, MGM borrowed her *back* from RKO to play Rosemary Bartlow, the Dixie trollop wed to screen writer Dick Powell, in *The Bad and the Beautiful*. Cy Howard, who had created Marie Wilson's *My Friend Irma*, was even planning a video series, *Miss Ruby Stevens*, to star Gloria, but it never developed. One vixen role followed another mostly in bad films such as *Prisoners of the Casbah* (1953). One of her best portrayals was Lee Marvin's moll in *The Big Heat* (1953), a quintessential 1950s picture, a particularly grotesque, but memorable scene had Marvin throwing scalding coffee in her face. To even the score, the now-scarred Gloria attempts to return the favor to Marvin just before he shoots her to death.

She received unanimous critical boos for her performance as the wealthy small-town widow who seduces Dr. Robert Mitchum in *Not as a Stranger*, more likely due to her unbecoming appearance than for her cardboard acting. She bounced back as the delightfully naughty Ado Annie in *Oklahoma!* (1955), in the role Celeste Holm had created on Broadway. A musical seemed an unlikely place setting for her feline petulance, but critics adored her sexually inviting delivery of "I Cain't Say No" and "All 'er Nothin'." The sympathetic role of the American librarian in *The Man Who Never Was* (1956) confirmed her versatility as an actress but it was her last good part.

The Man Who Never Was was filmed in London and at the time she was married to her third husband, writer–producer–director, Cy Howard, whom she had wed in 1954. (Her second marriage had been to director Nicholas Ray whom she had met at RKO. They married on June 2, 1948 and in November of that year she gave birth to Timothy Nicholas. They divorced in 1952.) The Howards moved to France, where in 1956 Gloria gave birth to a daughter, Marianne Paulette. They returned to the United States where she sued for divorce in 1957, saying the marriage was "over and done with" and that she planned to resume her career. There were rumors that while in Europe she had

had operations on her chin and lips. Whether this was a rumor or not, photographs revealed a Gloria with a different, although not particularly more attractive face.

There were two bad movies, a few television appearances, including a role on Edmond O'Brien's *Sam Benedict* (1962) series, plus summer stock in *The Country Girl* and *A Shot in the Dark*. In 1962 it was revealed that she had secretly married her former stepson, Tony Ray, and one film historian, Ray Hagen, went to the trouble to unravel the resultant relationships: "This means her former husband is her current father-in-law, and that her son Timothy has become his half-brother's stepson and, to add to the tangle, Gloria bore her new husband a daughter in October 1963, and is now her own sister-in-law."

Gloria had a small assignment in Columbia's *Ride Beyond Vengeance* (1966) a Western one step above A. C. Lyles' budget efforts at Paramount, and filled with once-famous performers. A more matronly-looking Gloria, still sporting that pouty, quiver-lip look, has wandered in and out of several recent economy features, including the detective entry *Chandler* (1971) released by MGM, in which she had one brief scene as the bedraggled owner of a run-down health club frequented by Warren Oates. On television she was in the telefeature *Black Noon* (1971) starring Ray Milland and Roy Thinnes, and had a tiny part in a Los Angeles stage production of *The Time of Your Life* (1972), after which she took a bus tour of the States with Henry Fonda in *The Time of Your Life*. It was a popular success and Fonda came away exclaiming, "She's a riveting actress!" Along with ex-MGM child star Dean Stockwell she appeared in the motorcycle feature *The Loners*, released in 1972, and co-starred with Sue Lyon in the Spanish-lensed *Tarot* (1973).

Regarding her show business return, Gloria recently mused, "I don't know how I feel about it. It's hard to get a good script. Maybe I should just keep doing housework and not try to come back at all, you know what I mean?"

GLORIA GRAHAME

Blonde Fever (MGM, 1944)
Without Love (MGM, 1945)
It's a Wonderful Life (RKO, 1946)
It Happened in Brooklyn (MGM, 1947)
Merton of the Movies (MGM, 1947)
Crossfire (RKO, 1947)
Song of the Thin Man (MGM, 1947)
A Woman's Secret (RKO, 1949)
Roughshod (RKO, 1949)
In a Lonely Place (Columbia, 1950)
Macao (RKO, 1952)
The Greatest Show on Earth (Paramount, 1952)
Sudden Fear (RKO, 1952)
The Bad and the Beautiful (MGM, 1952)
The Glass Wall (Columbia, 1953)
Man on a Tightrope (20th-Fox, 1953)

The Big Heat (Columbia, 1953)
Prisoners of the Casbah (Columbia, 1953)
Human Desire (Columbia, 1954)
Naked Alibi (Universal, 1954)
The Good Die Young (UA, 1955)
Not as a Stranger (UA, 1955)
The Cobweb (MGM, 1955)
Oklahoma! (Magna, 1955)
The Man Who Never Was (20th-Fox, 1956)
Ride Out for Revenge (UA, 1958)
Odds Against Tomorrow (UA, 1959)
Ride Beyond Vengeance (Columbia, 1966)
Blood And Lace (AIP, 1971)
The Todd Killincs (National General, 1971)
Chandler (MGM, 1971)
The Loners (Fanfare, 1972)
Tarot (Vagar, 1973)

With Mary Astor and Philip Dorn in *Blonde Fever* (1944)

Stewart Granger

Stewart Granger frankly admits this of his more than seventy motion picture roles, "I am not proud of one." In fact, the Britisher once complained, "to me acting is torture ... a man who works with his hands for a living knows he's doing a man's work in a man's world. But not actors." Granger was one of England's top film stars in the post–World War II years, playing romantic leads in several popular melodramas. He then came to the United States to star in MGM's *King Solomon's Mines* (1950), and during his seven-year stay with Metro was showcased in nearly twenty historical–adventure–swashbuckling roles. He was a distinct throwback to the dashing screen heroics made famous by Errol Flynn in the 1930s. None of Granger's MGM assignments required much emoting. All they demanded was the actor's 6' 3" physique and his darkly handsome profile, aided not a little by his stage-trained resonant voice. After his MGM contract expired, Granger continued to play in the same type of potboiler films. At age fifty-seven he was hired as the leading man type for the teleseries *The Virginian* (1970) and two years later emerged as the video's newest Sherlock Holmes.

He was born James Lablanche Stewart in London on May 6, 1913. During his twenties, while pursuing an acting career, he changed his professional name for obvious reasons. His first choice of careers had been medicine and for two years he attended Epson College as a premed student. However, he left Epson when his friend Michael Wilding, then beginning his own acting career, suggested that he should work as a film extra. Granger later studied at the Webber-Douglas School of Dramatic Arts and obtained acting parts with the Hull Repertory Company, the Birmingham Repertory, the Malvery Festival, and the Old Vic where he became a matinee idol playing opposite Vivien Leigh in *Serena Blandish* in 1939. He made his full-fledged film debut in *So This Is London* (1940), a lowbrow farce starring George Sanders. World War II interrupted his new movie career and he joined the Black Watch Regiment. When a stomach ulcer forced him out of the regiment he returned to film work, signing a seven-year contract with British impresario J. Arthur Rank. His forte was romantic leads, particularly opposite star Phyllis Calvert, and soon he was one of England's top boxoffice draws. He played a dashing Cavalier in *The Man in Grey* (1945), a villain who menaces schizophrenic Phyllis Calvert in *Madonna of the Seven Moons* (1946), and Mark Anthony to Vivien Leigh's Cleopatra in *Caesar and Cleopatra* (1946).

While making the epic *Cleopatra* Granger met the beautiful sixteen-year-old Vivien Leigh look-alike, Jean Simmons. In the film, Jean played the harp in Cleopatra's palace. At the time, Granger was married to actress Elspeth March by whom he had two children, Jaimie and Lindsay. Miss March had introduced Granger to the right people in the right places, pushing forward his career to a great extent. By 1948 Granger had become Jean's professional advisor, had instigated divorce proceedings against March, which became final in 1949, and promised Jean's family that they would not marry for at least two years. It was Granger who advised Jean not to accept Laurence Olivier's offer to play Ophelia in his film production of *Hamlet* (1948) because of her ignorance of Shakespeare. Olivier won out over Granger's objections, and Jean won international stardom for that picture.

After appearing opposite Phyllis Calvert again in *Fanny by Gaslight* (a.k.a. *Man of Evil*) (1948), he played one of his better roles, that of the draft-dodging black marketeer in *Waterloo Road* (1949). In *Adam and Evelyne* (1949) he had Jean as his leading lady. His contract with Rank expired with this picture and he signed with MGM to play Alan Quartermain in the remake of *King Solomon's Mines*. Shortly afterward, Jean followed him to Hollywood and they were married on December 20, 1950, with Granger's friend Michael Wilding as best man and the only guest. When Jean came to Hollywood, Howard Hughes, then head of RKO, bought up the remaining six months of her Rank contract. In addition, Hughes made an alleged oral agreement with her for services at RKO beyond those six months. The oral contract became a point of contention between Granger as Jean's advisor and husband, and Hughes as her employer. A lawsuit followed, with Hughes' attorney claiming that Granger had demanded that RKO pay $500,000 to Jean, $100,000 to him for their new Beverly Hills home, and to purchase an option on a story property he owned. Granger accused Hughes of slander and libel and the case was finally settled by RKO paying the Grangers $250,000, plus $35,000 in lawyers' fees. Jean agreed to be loaned to other studios at $200,000 per picture. That legal victory over Hughes is the proudest achievement of his life, according to Granger. The second item in which he takes enormous pride is having brought to the U. S. the Charolais, a snow-white breed of French beef cattle, which he had imported to the Arizona ranch which he bought in the early 1950s.

Granger's Technicolor fare at MGM now makes up the bulk of features on television's late, late show. *Scaramouche* (1952), *The Prisoner of Zenda* (1952), *Young Bess* (1953), *Beau Brummell* (1954), *Bhowani Junction* (1956), and *The Little Hut* (1957). All these roles are similar to ones that Robert Taylor might have done in an earlier decade.

Jean's film career was much the same: *The Robe* (1953), *The Egyptian* (1954), *Desiree* (1954), and a few filmed soap operas added. But the husband–wife performers enjoyed life in America and were an oft-photographed part of the Hollywood social scene. They had a daughter born in 1956 and named her Tracy after Jean's costar in *The Actress* (1953), Spencer Tracy. Their closest friends in Hollywood were Michael Wilding and Elizabeth Taylor. Of his marriage at the time, Granger said: "I have the perfect wife. She cannot cook. She does Gene Kelly routines around the pool while I prepare supper. She cannot make a bed. She will not pick up things. She simply lives in her work. She dotes on fan magazines, fish-and-chips, and she'd die for winkles [a shellfish sold in paper bags on London's seedier streets]."

Granger's MGM tenure expired in 1957 with a second-rate Western, *Gun Glory*, in which his British accent was all too obvious. Thereafter he appeared in a rash of European-lensed adventure yarns, more imaginative in their titles than in their story lines. If he was no longer big boxoffice, his name on the marquee still had some money value. More important for his faltering film career, he had not gone to seed like so many of his on-screen contemporaries. Even today he still retains a virile screen image.

In 1960 Jean Simmons divorced Granger when she fell in love with director Richard Brooks while starring in *Elmer Gantry*. Granger commented on the change in his life: "I don't mind Jean leaving me. It's like a child breaking away from an overprotective parent. But it's the guy she chose —that's what got me. Can you imagine anyone wanting to marry Richard Brooks? The trouble with me is that I did everything for Jean in our marriage. I taught her how to read, how to walk, how to carry herself. I taught her art, literature, current events. She was such a child. Our entire relationship was like Pygmalion. She would hear my conversation at the dinner table, my point of view on various subjects, and then when we had guests, she would spout my point of view as her own—I must say she had the decency to leave the Mercedes 190 I had given her when she and Brooks decided to elope."

Granger sold his Arizona ranch for over $2 million at an enormous capital gain, and continued to earn his paycheck in standard programmers without any apparent ambition for better roles. In the mid-1960s it was reported he planned to remarry his first wife. While he did refurnish her apartment at his expense, he put an end to rumors by saying, "She is my very best friend." In 1964, with David Niven as best man, Granger wed twenty-two-year-old blonde Miss Belgium of 1962, Caroline Lecerf. They have a daughter, Samantha, and were divorced in 1969. The next year Granger decided to become a working actor and took over the lead role in the long-running teleseries *The Virginian*. Already worn out, the series died at the end of Granger's year with the show. In February 1972 Granger appeared as Sherlock Holmes, with Bernard Fox as Dr. Watson in the Universal teleseries pilot, *The Hound of the Baskervilles*.

During a recent interview with *TV Guide*, Granger recalled that once Hedda Hopper alleged that he had had an homosexual affair with another actor. Granger laughed and said: "My God, I have been married three times and have four children." The actor in question was his old friend Michael

With Richard Carlson and Deborah Kerr in *King Solomon's Mines* (1950)

With John Dehner and Mel Ferrer in *Scaramouche* (1952)

Wilding, who had at one time been wed to Margaret Leighton and later to Elizabeth Taylor. When Hedda Hopper published her second book of memoirs in 1963, *The Whole Truth and Nothing But*, her first chapter covered the life of Elizabeth Taylor. Hedda related how she had called the young actress and her fiancé Michael Wilding to her home in an effort to dissuade them from marriage, saying, "In the first place, he's too old for you. And the rumor around town is that Michael Wilding and Stewart Granger are very, very close." Wilding supposedly sat there and listened to Hopper, but when that book was published he filed a libel suit for $3 million on April 4, 1963. The case was settled out of court with Hopper and her publisher Doubleday sharing in the $100,000 payment to Wilding.

Granger claims he is retired from pictures after too many years of less than great roles. "I'm just an old leading man. And every time I get dignified, someone calls me Farley Granger." He has occasionally produced films but finds the new product not to his liking. Of his past career he says: "You know, if I'd done just one film like *Inherit the Wind*, I could have retired and said I did that. I would have been proud."

STEWART GRANGER

Give Her a Ring (Alliance, 1935)
A Southern Maid (Alliance, 1936)
So This Is London (20th-Fox, 1940)
Convoy (RKO, 1941)
Thursday's Child (British, 1943)
The Lamp Still Burns (Two Cities-General, 1943)
Secret Mission (English Films, 1944)
The Man in Grey (Universal-Gainsborough, 1945)
Madonna of the Seven Moons (Universal-Gainsborough, 1946)
Caesar and Cleopatra (UA, 1946)
The Magic Bow (Universal, 1947)
Caravan (Eagle–Lion, 1947)
A Lady Surrenders (Universal, 1947)
Captain Boycott (Universal, 1947)
Man of Evil (Universal, 1948)
Blanche Fury (Eagle–Lion, 1948)
Saraband (Eagle–Lion, 1949)
Woman Hater (Universal, 1949)
Waterloo Road (Eagle–Lion, 1949)
Adam and Evelyne (Universal, 1949)
King Solomon's Mines (MGM, 1950)
Soldiers Three (MGM, 1951)
The Light Touch (MGM, 1951)
Scaramouche (MGM, 1952)
The Wild North (MGM, 1952)

The Prisoner of Zenda (MGM, 1952)
Salome (Columbia, 1953)
Young Bess (MGM, 1953)
All the Brothers Were Valiant (MGM, 1953)
Beau Brummell (MGM, 1954)
Green Fire (MGM, 1954)
Moonfleet (MGM, 1955)
Footsteps in the Fog (Columbia, 1955)
The Last Hunt (MGM, 1956)
Bhowani Junction (MGM, 1956)
The Little Hut (MGM, 1957)
Gun Glory (MGM, 1957)
The Whole Truth (Columbia, 1958)
Harry Black and the Tiger (20th-Fox, 1958)
North to Alaska (20th-Fox, 1960)
The Secret Partner (MGM, 1961)
Swordsman of Siena (MGM, 1962)
Sodom and Gomorrah (20th-Fox, 1963)
The Secret Invasion (UA, 1964)
Commando (AIP, 1964)
The Crooked Road (7 arts, 1965)
Frontier Hellcat (Columbia, 1966)
Rampage at Apache Wells (Columbia, 1966)
Consigna: Tanger 67 (Spanish–German–Italian, 1966)
The Last Safari (Paramount, 1967)
Flaming Frontier (WB-7 Arts, 1968)
The Trygon Factor (WB-7 Arts, 1970)

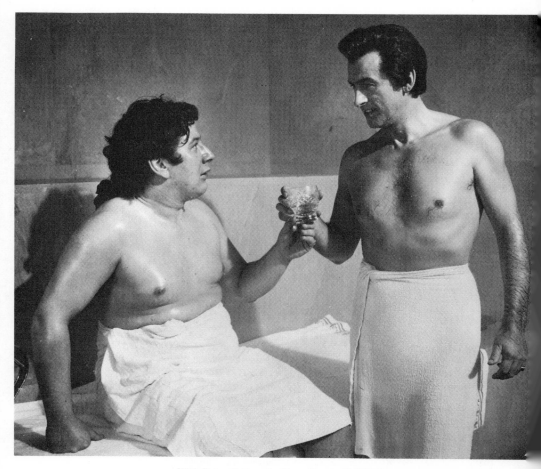

With Peter Ustinov in *Beau Brummel* (1954)

Kathryn Grayson

Pert little Kathryn Grayson, with her heart-shaped face and dimpled cheeks, once remarked: "I must be the oldest living child soprano." She had indeed worked diligently toward a career as a singing star, hopefully as a luminary of the opera, and particularly the Metropolitan Opera. That girlhood dream never came true, but during the 1940s and early 1950s this voluptuous young woman, who eschewed cheesecake poses because with her 39 1/2" bust she did not want to be known as an operatic Jane Russell, delighted movie audiences, if not music critics, with her pretty, florid coloratura vocalizing in twenty cream-puff musicals. Because MGM deemed it commercially expedient to showcase her mainly in lightweight, lower case musicals, she was never presented to the public as "the" singing star of the lot. There was still the refined presence of vibrant Jeanette MacDonald on tap and later in the 1940s more snooty Jane Powell would alternate with Kathryn in a series of pleasant but generally unmemorable tune films. Thus Kathryn's achievements never quite matched her professional aspirations and by the time she made her two favorite pictures, *Show Boat* (1951) and *Kiss Me, Kate!* (1953), her career, like the cycle of movie musicals, was nearing its end. Even after "retiring" from the screen she exclaimed "I want to do something intelligent, and movie musicals don't classify."

She was born Zelma Kathryn Hedrick in Winston Salem, North Carolina on February 9, 1922. Her father was a contractor–realtor and the Hedricks lived in St. Louis during most of her childhood. It was there at the Municipal Opera that she met Frances Marshall, a singer with the Chicago Civic Opera. He encouraged Kathryn to work hard at her vocal lessons. When the Hedricks moved to Hollywood Kathryn attended the Manual Arts High School there and began taking voice lessons from Minnaletha White. After hearing Kathryn sing at a Hollywood music festival, Louis B. Mayer offered her a movie contract, and Kathryn accepted against the wishes of Miss White, who wanted the teenager to continue her studies in preparation for an opera career. This was something Kathryn also wanted, but the movies were enticing and she signed with the studio in 1940.

At first an ordeal of lessons in drama, elocution and music for several months had to be endured. Interspersed with these drudging chores were appearances on Eddie Cantor's radio show and other radio programs. During this time she met and married MGM contract actor John Shelton, but after six separations, reconciliations, and a miscarriage, that marriage ended in divorce in 1946. (He died in May 1972.)

MGM debuted her in *Andy Hardy's Private Secretary* (1941), one of the Andy Hardy series, which had become the training ground for many studio ingenues such as Lana Turner, Judy Garland, Donna Reed, Ruth Hussey, and Esther Williams. She was the girl of the title, poor in finances but not in musical talent, who is hired to help Mickey Rooney sort out his mounting extracurricular activities at Carvel High. The script was maneuvered to give graduating senior Rooney a big dose of humility and allowed Kathryn to perform the mad scene from *Lucia di Lammermoor* and Strauss' "Voci de Primavera." After supporting Frank Morgan in *The Vanishing Virginian* (1941), which dealt with the suffragette movement down South, and playing the romantic lead opposite John Carroll in the Abbott and Costello remake of *Rio Rita* (1942), she had the first of her major film assignments, *Seven Sweethearts* (1942), in which S. Z. Sakall's brood of daughters couldn't wed until the eldest (Kathryn) did. Van Heflin was the spouse-to-be and the song was Paul Francis Webster-Walter Jurmann's "You and the Waltz and I."

In Metro's all-star *Thousands Cheer* (1943) Kathryn was the romantic lead as Colonel John Boles' daughter who is beguiled by disgruntled army private Gene Kelly. She sang such operatic songs as "Sempra Libre" and the more proletarian "I Dug a Ditch in Wichita." The memorable moments in the picture were contributed by the rash of guest stars who performed at the finale big camp show, leaving Kathryn a distinct "also" in the film. *Anchors Aweigh* (1945) again teamed her with Gene Kelly and fiesty Frank Sinatra as his gob cohort. The thin film plot had her as a Hollywood extra out to win an audition with José Iturbi. Kelly and Sinatra copped most of the attention with their dancing and dueting, and young Dean Stockwell as Kathryn's nephew was more winning. She delivered "My Heart Sings," which assured audiences that she and Kelly would have a happy future together (Sinatra is paired off with Pamela Britton).

Two Sisters from Boston (1946) was a turn-of-the-century musical with Kathryn and June Allyson, who was fast becoming more popular but was still second-billed, going to work in Jimmy Durante's Bowery saloon and Kathryn becoming the establishment's singing sensation, "High C Susie." Peter Lawford supplied the romantic interest in this money-making Joe Pasternak production. In *Ziegfeld Follies* (1946), Kathryn imperiously rendered "There's Beauty Everywhere," by far the least effective of that film's musical interludes, and at revivals today it is one of the few segments to be booed by cinema buffs. In *Till the Clouds Roll By* (1946) she was Magnolia in the *Show Boat* sequence, doing a public screen test for the studio's forthcoming edition of that musical.

Trying to find a proper niche for her, MGM put Kathryn into two pictures opposite the singer that had made all America swoon, Frank Sinatra.

It Happened in Brooklyn (1947) was okay for Sinatra, but Kathryn was simply not capable at opera in her full-dress excerpt from Delibes' *Lakmé* and a Mozart duet with the crooner. The second picture, *The Kissing Bandit* (1948), was a commercial disaster, but she did introduce "Love Is Where You Find It."

Oddly enough, despite Kathryn's lengthy and lackluster screen apprenticeship, filmgoing audiences liked her. She finally got an "operatic" costar in Mario Lanza in *That Midnight Kiss* (1949) (he was a truck driver with operatic aspirations) and the more popular *The Toast of New Orleans* (1950). The audience thought them a sensation, and she got to sing excerpts from her favorite role, Cho-Cho-San, in Puccini's opera, *Madame Butterfly*. In *Grounds for Marriage* (1950), Kathryn was an onscreen opera singer, who spends most of the film's 91 minutes rejecting and rewooing ex-husband, physician Van Johnson.

It was Metro's new singing find, Howard Keel, who proved to be Kathryn's best screen teammate and they were acceptably cast as Gaylord and Magnolia in the still-melodious *Show Boat*. Though the Arthur Freed production was a substantial grosser ($5.2 million) it can hardly be said that Kathryn was the star, and had Judy Garland not been replaced by Ava Gardner, Garland would have been the picture's focal point. As it was, people recall the 1936 version of *Show Boat* for Irene Dunne's Magnolia and vice versa, but no such strong impression remains of the 1950s Magnolia.

Kathryn ended her MGM contract playing with Keel in a film they both detested, *Lovely to Look At* (1952). She left MGM in August of that year and the next month signed with Warner Brothers for four musicals. The agreement stated that one of the projects would be a biographical picture about the beloved opera diva Grace Moore. Kathryn and Warners' top male singing star, Gordon MacRae, looked rather silly in the studio's latest version of *The Desert Song* (1953), but she did get to do the Grace Moore story, *So This Is Love* (1953), which did very modestly in theatrical release.

Her Warners' contract ended up being for only two pictures, and MGM called her back for one of their best 1950s musicals, *Kiss Me, Kate!*. Nevertheless, the picture was memorable more for Ann Miller's vivaciousness, and for being Keel's best role, than for Kathryn's singing or petulant emoting. She says that singer Marjorie Lawrence vetoed her for *Interrupted Melody* (1955), the dramatic story of that singer's life, because she was "too pretty." Eleanor Parker played the part first offered to Greer Garson, and she earned an Oscar nomination for doing the role. Kathryn's last screen appearance was in Paramount's *The Vagabond King* (1956) where her costar was Oreste, the "new" Lanza, but it was simply too late for screen operetta to grab hold of public appeal.

By now Kathryn was tired of her cinema career and decided to be a full-time mother to daughter Patricia Kathryn, born October 7, 1948, during her marriage to singer and MGM contractee Johnny Johnston. She and Johnston had wed in 1947 but were divorced in 1951, when Kathryn accused him of being a golf fiend and a party man. She has never remarried, though often is seen on the arm of attractive men. In 1958 her frequent escort was young Robert Evans, now head of Paramount Pictures and once spouse of Ali McGraw. Kathryn's comment on Hollywood's romantic life is this: "You can never tell what a man has in mind when he asks you for a date in this town. He may be thinking of romance or he may just want his name in the papers." And she further added that a career woman should not marry a man who does not have his own successful career.

She made some concert appearances in Hollywood and London (at the Palladium) in the early 1950s and nightclub stints in Las Vegas and New York a few years later. Her first stage appearances were in operetta in 1961, in *The Merry Widow* and *Naughty Marietta*. In 1963 she briefly toured in *Camelot* but collapsed from "nervous exhaustion" and could not appear as a Broadway replacement for Julie Andrews as announced. In March 1965 she was hospitalized for what was described as an accidental overdose of barbituates, and three years later, she and her former film costar Howard Keel, were reunited successfuly for several nightclub appearances. She has appeared on a number of television shows but in 1958 turned down a five-year contract for $1 million from Revlon Cosmetics to appear as their video salesgirl.

Kathryn says that the only typically Hollywood part of her behavior is that she remains friendly with her two former husbands. She recently told film historian John Kobel about her MGM years: "Louis B. Mayer really did go on. I told him after I had been with the studio about a year that I didn't want a film career. I didn't feel I was very good in films, and that the films I was in weren't any good for me. Besides, I wanted very much to leave so I could go back and train for the operatic stage. Well, when he saw that I was determined, I guess it really took him by surprise. He said, 'Here we are making you a big star and you tell me you don't want to be one. You ungrateful little bitch!' Well, I was only sixteen (she was really nineteen) and at home we never even said Damn! So I said, 'It's you who's the son of a bitch and a pants-presser too!' I think I had heard that he started off in the clothing business and that seemed to me the worst thing I could call him. Then he had one of his famous attacks. This upset me! Later on, I found out that he had them with everybody when he couldn't get his own way."

Kathryn was really MGM's answer to the more popular Deanna Durbin, whom they had had under contract but lost to Universal before she became a star. As for lost illusions, Kathryn's voice, despite its vocal range of G below middle C to C above high C, was not properly suited or trained for the operatic career to which she always had aspired.

Andy Hardy's Private Secretary (MGM, 1941)
The Vanishing Virginian (MGM, 1941)
Rio Rita (MGM, 1942)
Seven Sweethearts (MGM, 1942)
Thousands Cheer (MGM, 1943)
Anchors Aweigh (MGM, 1945)
Two Sisters from Boston (MGM, 1946)
Ziegfeld Follies (MGM, 1946)
Till the Clouds Roll By (MGM, 1946)
It Happened in Brooklyn (MGM, 1947)

The Kissing Bandit (MGM, 1948)
That Midnight Kiss (MGM, 1949)
The Toast of New Orleans (MGM, 1950)
Grounds for Marriage (MGM, 1950)
Show Boat (MGM, 1951)
Lovely to Look At (MGM, 1952)
The Desert Song (WB, 1953)
So This Is Love (WB, 1953)
Kiss Me, Kate! (MGM, 1953)
The Vagabond King (Paramount, 1956)

With Natalie Thompson and Frank Morgan in *The Vanishing Virginian* (1941)

With Frank Jenks, Frank Sully, Wally Cassell (top), and Ben Blue in *Thousands Cheer* (1943)

With Van Johnson, Barry Sullivan, and Paula Raymond in *Grounds for Marriage* (1951)

Virginia Grey

If endurance medals were awarded on Oscar night, sweet-faced Virginia Grey would certainly rate one. She made her screen debut in 1927 at the age of ten and five decades later is still hoping for that featured role just over the next casting call. At best, she played second league ingenues at MGM in such pictures as *Thunder Afloat* (1939) and *Blonde Inspiration* (1941), but she lacked that visible personality spark that helped the more snappy Ruth Hussey, Laraine Day, and Marsha Hunt up the ladder. Because she radiated such concentrated sweetness and earnestness, she ran amok in the 1950s and thereafter when age prevented her from essaying the sweet young thing any longer. If only her real-life gutsiness could have been intelligently captured onscreen, she might well have become an established "other woman" type.

Virginia was born in Los Angeles, March 22, 1917, the daughter of comedy film director Ray Grey. When he died in the mid-1920s, Virginia's mother went to work at Universal as a film cutter to support her three daughters. Hearing that the studio was casting *Uncle Tom's Cabin* (1927), she had Virginia audition and the ten-year-old was given the role of Little Eva. The following year Virginia had a small part in Mary Astor's *Heart to Heart*, Jean Hersholt's *Jazz Mad* (1928), and in Universal's Western, *The Michigan Kid* (1928), she was Rene Adoree as a child.

Virginia was then off the screen for three years, first to complete her schooling and then to study nursing. For a time in the mid-1930s she was a doctor's assistant. Nevertheless she occasionally appeared—virtually an extra —in a number of pictures, such as Mary Pickford's *Secrets* (1933) and the Busby Berkeley staged musicals *Dames* (1934) and *Gold Diggers of 1935*. At other times she worked as a stand-in for actresses Madge Evans and Florence Rice, often at MGM. MGM's talent scout Billy Grady then hired her as a chorus worker-bit player at $50 weekly.

In Wallace Beery's *Old Hutch* (1936) she was seen briefly as a "girl" and she was just one of the Glorified Girls in *The Great Ziegfeld* (1936). That same year she also appeared in Metro's short, *Violets in Spring*. In Metro's B Picture, *Bad Guy* (1937), she was elevated to female lead opposite power lineman Bruce Cabot. But she registered as just another pretty face in this assignment and it was back to minuscule film parts. Meanwhile, she had been

301

dating the kingpin of the Metro lot, Clark Gable. He eventually divorced Rhea Langham and wed star Carole Lombard instead, leaving Virginia well out into the cold. Nevertheless, the same year (1939) she was one of the six-chorine troupe traveling in war-torn Europe with hoofer Gable in *Idiot's Delight*, and in the *Hardys Ride High* (1939) she was passable as the hard-boiled chorus girl. Her next "big" chance came when Metro gave her a sizable buildup in *Thunder Afloat* (1939) in which she was Wallace Beery's daughter. But the necessary screen charisma was still missing—at Warners she might have done nicely in Joan Leslie-type roles—and it was back to such minor assignments as the sales girl in *The Women* (1939) and as C. Aubrey Smith's relative in *Another Thin Man* (1939). After the nominal lead opposite John Shelton in *Blonde Inspiration*, she reached her last studio peak as Tony Martin's kidnapped girlfriend in the Marx Brothers' *The Big Store* (1941). The studio admitted she was showing new potential and renegotiated her contract. But she was only to remain another year on the lot, competing with Ann Rutherford for Red Skelton in *Whistling in the Dark* (1941), and concluding her MGM tenure as Lee Bowman's love interest in the Marjorie Main misfire *Tish* (1942).

Throughout the 1940s, Virginia free-lanced, functioning as second female leads in a few major pictures such as *Sweet Rosie O'Grady* (1943) with Betty Grable, and in several programmers such as *The Men in Her Diary* (1945) with Louise Allbritton and *Wyoming* (1947) with Vera Hruba Ralston. She had a small featured role in Cecil B. De Mille's *Unconquered* (1947). Having played opposite Johnny Weissmuller in his first non-Tarzan role since 1929, *Swamp Fire* (1946), she was used as the female lead in the kickoff entry for his new series *Jungle Jim* (1949). Her *Unknown Island* (1948), dealing with scientists who encounter prehistoric life, was standard fare on television.

In the early 1950s, Virginia became quite active in television, giving her career another boost of continuance. At the same time, onscreen, she played undemanding minor roles in several Westerns, *The Fighting Lawman* (1952), *The Last Command* (1955). One of her few meaty assignments in years was *Jeanne Eagels* (1957) in which she was fading actress Elsie Desmond who sees Kim Novak winning "her" part in the stage production of *Rain*.

Most important for Virginia's film career in the last twenty years has been her friendship with producer Ross Hunter. He first utilized her in his plush soap opera, *All That Heaven Allows* (1955), as the wife of Charles Drake. Her other roles in Hunter films have been the well-dressed but lonesome Miss Robson in the Sandra Dee–John Saxon *The Restless Years* (1958); a loyal spinster secretary in *Portrait in Black* (1960); the headmistress in *Tammy, Tell Me True* (1961), an actress in a film within a film in *Flower Drum Song* (1961); Susan Hayward's hard-working sister in *Back Street* (1961); and as society set dressing in *Madame X* (1966) and *Rosie!* (1968). In Hunter's *Airport* (1970) she had a tiny part as a plane passenger with an overprecocious brat of a child.

Perhaps her most telling role in the 1960s was as one of the two middle-aged Americans (Ruth Roman was the other) seeking gigolo love south of the border in Lana Turner's *Love Has Many Faces* (1965). Decked out to look as youthful as possible, Virginia had that desperate, pathetic look which, combined with her latter-day emaciated presence, made her characterization a telling commentary on her own life.

Virginia has never married.

VIRGINIA GREY

Uncle Tom's Cabin (Universal, 1927)
Heart to Heart (FN, 1928)
The Michigan Kid (Universal, 1928)
Jazz Mad (Universal, 1928)
Misbehaving Ladies (WB, 1931)
Secrets (UA, 1933)
The St. Louis Kid (WB, 1934)
Dames (WB, 1934)
The Firebird (WB, 1934)
She Gets Her Man (Universal, 1935)
Gold Diggers of 1935 (WB, 1935)
Old Hutch (MGM, 1936)
Secret Alley (20th-Fox, 1936)
The Great Ziegfeld (MGM, 1936)
Bad Guy (MGM, 1937)
Rosalie (MGM, 1937)
Test Pilot (MGM, 1938)
Rich Man, Poor Girl (MGM, 1938)
Ladies in Distress (Republic, 1938)
Youth Takes a Fling (Universal, 1938)
Dramatic School (MGM, 1938)
Shopworn Angel (MGM, 1938)
Idiot's Delight (MGM, 1939)
Broadway Serenade (MGM, 1939)
The Hardys Ride High (MGM, 1939)
Thunder Afloat (MGM, 1939)
Another Thin Man (MGM, 1939)
The Women (MGM, 1939)
Three Cheers for the Irish (WB, 1940)
The Captain Is a Lady (MGM, 1940)
Hullabaloo (MGM, 1940)
The Golden Fleecing (MGM, 1940)
Keeping Company (MGM, 1941)
Blonde Inspiration (MGM, 1941)
Washington Melodrama (MGM, 1941)
The Big Store (MGM, 1941)
Whistling in the Dark (MGM, 1941)
Mr. and Mrs. North (MGM, 1941)
Tarzan's New York Adventure (MGM, 1942)
Grand Central Murder (MGM, 1942)
Tish (MGM, 1942)
Bells of Capistrano (Republic, 1942)
Secrets of the Underground (Republic, 1943)

Idaho (Republic, 1943)
Stage Door Canteen (UA, 1943)
Sweet Rosie O'Grady (20th-Fox, 1943)
Strangers in the Night (Republic, 1944)
Grissly's Millions (Republic, 1945)
Flame of Barbary Coast (Republic, 1945)
Blonde Ransom (Universal, 1945)
The Men in Her Diary (Universal, 1945)
Smooth as Silk (Universal, 1946)
Swamp Fire (Paramount, 1946)
House of Horrors (Universal, 1946)
Wyoming (Republic, 1947)
Unconquered (Paramount, 1947)
Who Killed "Doc" Robbin? (UA, 1948)
Glamour Girl (Columbia, 1948)
So This Is New York (UA, 1948)
Unknown Island (Film Classics, 1948)
Miraculous Journey (Film Classics, 1948)
Mexican Hayride (Universal, 1948)
When My Baby Smiles at Me (20th-Fox, 1948)
Leather Gloves (Columbia, 1948)
Jungle Jim (Columbia, 1949)
The Threat (RKO, 1949)
Highway 301 (WB, 1950)
The Bullfighter and the Lady (Republic, 1951)
Three Desperate Men (Lippert, 1951)
Slaughter Trail (RKO, 1951)
Desert Pursuit (Monogram, 1952)
The Fighting Lawman (AA, 1952)
A Perilous Journey (Republic, 1953)
Captain Scarface (Astor, 1953)
Hurricane at Pilgrim Hill (Howco, 1953)
The Forty-Niners (AA, 1954)
Target Earth (AA, 1954)
The Eternal Sea (Republic, 1955)
The Last Command (Republic, 1955)
All That Heaven Allows (Universal, 1955)
The Rose Tattoo (Paramount, 1955)
Accused of Murder (Republic, 1956)
Crime of Passion (UA, 1957)
Jeanne Eagels (Columbia, 1957)
The Restless Years (Universal, 1958)
No Name on the Bullet (Universal, 1959)

Portrait in Black (Universal, 1960)
Tammy, Tell Me True (Universal, 1961)
Flower Drum Song (Universal, 1961)
Back Street (Universal, 1961)
Bachelor in Paradise (MGM, 1961)
Black Zoo (AA, 1963)

The Naked Kiss (AA, 1964)
Love Has Many Faces (Columbia, 1965)
Madame X (Universal, 1966)
Rosie! (Universal, 1968)
Airport (Universal, 1970)

With Clem Bevans, Beulah Bondi, Charles Coburn, Dan Dailey, and Francis Pierlot in *The Captain Is a Lady* (1940)

Sara Haden

As Sara Haden saw her movie image: "I'm just an old frozenface. Nobody loves me." Onscreen she invariably played women much older and plainer than she was, often cast as a hard-boiled confidential secretary or a spinster school teacher. She rarely had any sizable cinema roles, certainly no such opportunity as those tossed at Agnes Moorehead. Rarely did Sara have the chance to be contracast in lighthearted parts, such as those given to equally stern-looking Margaret Hamilton or Doro Merande. Then Sara joined the Andy Hardy stock company as poor Aunt Milly. She was considered the least essential of the Carvel family regulars—her billing and screen time was proof of that—but the series kept her occupied at MGM for a decade.

Sara was born in Galveston, Texas, in 1897, the daughter of Dr. John B. Haden and Charlotte Walker, a stage actress. At age eight Sara was traveling with her mother who was playing in Washington, D. C. with a stock show. When the cast's juvenile performer was taken ill, Sara was substituted and thus began her professional career. A decade later she would again perform with her mother in *Nancy Lee*. Later she moved to New York and appeared with Walter Hampden's Shakespearian Repertory Company in such plays as his *Hamlet* (1921). Sara was seen in New York productions of *The Last of Mrs. Cheyney* (1925) and *Trigger* (1927), and at the end of the decade was in London with a show entitled *Sun Up*. During this period she wed actor Dick Vanderberg.

When RKO decided to film *Trigger* as a vehicle for Katharine Hepburn, Sara was brought to Hollywood to re-create her stage assignment. The story was retitled *Spitfire* (1934) and proved to be the best part Sara would have in the movies. She was Etta Dawson, the not-so-bright Ozark neighbor of tomboy faith healer Hepburn. Five of Sara's nine releases that year were for RKO, but it was Fox's *Music in the Air* (1934) which set the pattern for her screen roles to come. As the private secretary to Reginald Owen, a Munich music publisher, she had little to do but look shocked as musical comedy star Gloria Swanson flirted with Douglass Montgomery. But Sara looked real! She and Jane Darwell were senior nurses in *The White Parade* (1934) and Sara was the prim nurse–companion to Irene Dunne in *Magnificent Obsession* (1935).

During her Fox period, Sara was often utilized as rural local color such

305

as in *Way Down East* (1935). Her best-remembered Fox appearance was as the relentless truant officer Agatha Morgan who chased after Shirley Temple in *Captain January* (1936).

At MGM, her next contract employer, Sara quickly settled into form. She was briefly seen in *Under Cover of Night* (1937) as the genius physicist murdered by her jealous husband (Henry Daniell). Later in the year, she was used in the first Andy Hardy picture, *A Family Affair* as the resigned spinster sister of Ma Hardy (Spring Byington). From the start, Sara's character faded into the background. Most of her screen activities were devoted to helping in the Hardy kitchen, or sitting stiff-backed at the dinner table anxious to add a bit of advice to the words of wisdom being passed on to Andy (Mickey Rooney) and Marian (Cecilia Parker). For two of the 1938 Hardy entries *Judge Hardy's Children*, and *Love Finds Andy Hardy*, she was replaced by character actress Betsy Ross Clarke, but by *Out West with the Hardys* (1938) she was back in place, and in *The Hardys Ride High* (1939), she had her finest screen moments in the series. When a sudden legacy throws the Hardys into a state of emotional jubilation, Sara gets carried away and thinks a gentleman paying a good deal of attention to her wants to wed her, but really, as she learns to her humiliation and ultimate betterment, he just wants her money.

When not engaged in the Hardy series, Sara had brief character roles in an assortment of Metro releases: as a nurse in both *Four Girls in White* (1939) and *The Secret of Dr. Kildare* (1939), or as Miss Barnes in *Boom Town* (1940). Her best variety of movie assignments came in 1943: She was Sister Lassie in *The Youngest Profession*, the stern companion of Ann Shoemaker in *Above Suspicion*, and in the Frank Morgan medical examination skit of *Thousands Cheer*, she was the new nurse.

When Sara left MGM in 1946, she was still playing the perennial secretary, as in Sylvia Sidney's *Mr. Ace* (1946). By then she had developed a philosophy about her career "rut": " ... by the end of a day's work before the cameras I sometimes get quite sick of it all. Those are the nights I go home and sit down in front of a mirror and just laugh my head off for about an hour and a half."

Once she started free-lancing, her film roles became fewer. She was the disdaining Mildred Cassawy in *The Bishop's Wife* (1947) and the wife of Parson Tom Tully in *Rachel and the Stranger* (1948). She played James Bell's wife in the Western *Roughshod* (1949), Margaret Phillips' nurse Smitty in *A Life of Her Own* (1950) back at Metro, and added local color as Lulu May in James Cagney's *A Lion Is in the Street* (1955).

Sara has been an occasional performer on such television shows as the NBC special *Of Time and the River* (1953) opposite Thomas Mitchell. After a three-year absence from the screen, she returned to MGM to play Aunt Milly again in *Andy Hardy Comes Home* (1958), her last movie to date. She now lives quietly in retirement in California.

SARA HADEN

Spitfire (RKO, 1934)
Finishing School (RKO, 1934)
Hat, Coat, and Gloves (RKO, 1934)
Life of Vergie Winters (RKO, 1934)
The White Parade (Fox, 1934)
Anne of Green Gables (RKO, 1934)
Music in the Air (Fox, 1934)
The Fountain (RKO, 1934)
Affairs of a Gentleman (Universal, 1934)
Mad Love (MGM, 1935)
O'Shaughnessy's Boy (MGM, 1935)
Way Down East (Fox, 1935)
Black Fury (FN, 1935)
Magnificent Obsession (Universal, 1935)
Everybody's Old Man (20th-Fox, 1936)
Little Miss Nobody (20th-Fox, 1936)
Captain January (20th-Fox, 1936)
Half Angel (20th-Fox, 1936)
Poor Little Rich Girl (20th-Fox, 1936)
The Crime of Dr. Forbes (20th-Fox, 1936)
Can This Be Dixie? (20th-Fox, 1936)
Reunion (20th-Fox, 1936)
Under Cover of Night (MGM, 1937)
The Last of Mrs. Cheyney (MGM, 1937)
Laughing at Trouble (20th-Fox, 1937)
A Family Affair (MGM, 1937)
First Lady (WB, 1937)
The Barrier (Paramount, 1937)
You're Only Young Once (MGM, 1938)
Out West with the Hardys (MGM, 1938)
Four Girls in White (MGM, 1939)
The Hardys Ride High (MGM, 1939)
Tell No Tales (MGM, 1939)
Andy Hardy Gets Spring Fever (MGM, 1939)
Judge Hardy and Son (MGM, 1939)
The Secret of Dr. Kildare (MGM, 1939)
Remember? (MGM, 1939)
The Shop Around the Corner (MGM, 1940)
Andy Hardy Meets Debutante (MGM, 1940)

Boom Town (MGM, 1940)
Hullabaloo (MGM, 1941)
The Trial of Mary Dugan (MGM, 1941)
Andy Hardy's Private Secretary (MGM, 1941)
Washington Melodrama (MGM, 1941)
Love Crazy (MGM, 1941)
Keeping Company (MGM, 1941)
Barnacle Bill (MGM, 1941)
Life Begins for Andy Hardy (MGM, 1941)
H. M. Pulham, Esq. (MGM, 1941)
The Courtship of Andy Hardy (MGM, 1942)
The Affairs of Martha (MGM, 1942)
Andy Hardy's Double Life (MGM, 1943)
The Youngest Profession (MGM, 1943)
Above Suspicion (MGM, 1943)
Best Foot Forward (MGM, 1943)
Thousands Cheer (MGM, 1943)
Lost Angel (MGM, 1943)
Andy Hardy's Blonde Trouble (MGM, 1944)
Bathing Beauty (MGM, 1944)
Our Vines Have Tender Grapes (MGM, 1945)
Bad Bascomb (MGM, 1946)
So Goes My Love (Universal, 1946)
She Wouldn't Say Yes (Columbia, 1946)
Our Hearts Were Growing Up (Paramount, 1946)
She Wolf of London (Universal, 1946)
Mr. Ace (UA, 1946)
Love Laughs at Andy Hardy (MGM, 1946)
The Bishop's Wife (RKO, 1947)
Rachel and the Stranger (RKO, 1948)
The Big Cat (Eagle–Lion, 1949)
Roughshod (RKO, 1949)
A Life of Her Own (MGM, 1950)
A Lion Is in the Street (WB, 1953)
The Outlaw's Daughter (20th-Fox, 1954)
Betrayed Women (AA, 1955)
Andy Hardy Comes Homes (MGM, 1958)

With Esther Williams in *Bathing Beauty* (1944)

Jean Hagen

In reviewing MGM's *The Asphalt Jungle* (1950), the N.Y. *Herald-Tribune's* Howard Barnes observed; "Incidentally, Jean Hagen is very good as the Doll who gets mixed up in a major robbery." That "incidentally" seems to be the best description for this versatile actress' unfulfilled screen career. During her Metro contract years (1949–1953) she was good despite the studio's offhanded policy of casting her as a knowing dame or insipid best friend in a run of B pictures. Occasionally, even MGM had to sit up and take notice, as the time she was Oscar-nominated for her Lina Lamont in *Singin' in the Rain* (1952). But Metro had even fewer ideas of how to present Jean to the public than did Columbia with the similar Judy Holliday, and in Jean's case she was never considered a prize studio commodity. Instead, she became just a useful gap filler in MGM pictures.

She was born Jean Shirley Ver Hagen in Chicago, Illinois on August 3, 1924 (or 1925), one of five children of C. M. Ver Hagen, who had immigrated to the U. S. when he was twenty-five, planning to study voice. His opera career never materialized. Her family moved to Elkhart, Indiana when Jean was twelve, and by the time she attended Lake Forest College and Northwestern University, where she was a drama major, she was set on being an actress. Her Northwestern roommate was Patricia Neal. When Jean was graduated in December 1945 she headed for New York and the stage. The theatre offered no jobs at first so she sought radio work, since she had performed on radio to help finance her education. She got recurring parts on *Grand Central Station, Hollywood Story*, and *Light of the World*, and when radio work was not to be had she worked as a cigarette girl in a nightclub or ushered in theatres. *Swan Song* was playing at the Booth Theatre when she was ushering there, and one night the authors of that play, Ben Hecht and Charles MacArthur, overheard the opinionated Jean making some tart remarks on the quality of the show. Rather than ignore her, the playwrights, known for their own outspokenness, offered her a role in the play, replacing an ailing member of the cast.

Jean took the part, and when the play closed in September, 1946, she was cast two months later in the role of Laurette Sincee in Lillian Hellman's *Another Part of the Forest*. Her former roommate Patricia Neal was Regina in that play and, when it opened, Jean earned praise from the critics for her telling portrayal of the brazen trollop. It was Neal who introduced her to actors' agent (later building contractor) Tom Seidel, whom Jean married on July 3, 1947,

After *Another Part of the Forest*, Jean did a summer stock stint of *Dear Ruth*, and played Regina in Eva Le Gallienne's translation of Ibsen's *Ghosts*, which lasted five nights on Broadway. She had better luck in Herman Wouk's *The Traitor*, which opened on March 31, 1949. MGM producer producer Sam Zimbalist and director Anthony Mann saw her in this drama and thought she would be right as the alcoholic nightclub singer in *Side Street* (1949) starring Farley Granger. Jean was tested and then was given a MGM contract. When she left *The Traitor* in May 1949, she was replaced by Eileen Heckart.

Before *Side Street* was released Jean made her motion picture debut as the agreeable homewrecker who dallies with Judy Holliday's husband (Tom Ewell) in *Adam's Rib* (1949). Jean's Beryl Caighn, "that tall job," was effective, but it was Judy Holliday as the dumb blonde who shoots her erring spouse, who garnered most attention away from stars Katharine Hepburn and Spencer Tracy, and who won an Oscar as well. Jean was married to drunk Bruce Cowling in *Ambush* (1950) and then had one of her two memorable screen assignments as the sympathetic girl friend of jewel thief Sterling Hayden in *The Asphalt Jungle* (1950). Hayden was the crook who wanted to go home to Kentucky and buy back the farm he had left and, in the end, he and Jean escape by car to Kentucky. Hayden, however, suffering from bullet wounds, dies as they reach his home. Critics and the public overlooked Jean because of the electric presence of a luscious newcomer named Marilyn Monroe. Jean says of this picture: "There were only two girl roles, and I obviously wasn't Marilyn Monroe."

In 1952 Jean essayed the screen role which has made her an original camp heroine, the egomanical blonde, silent screen star in *Singin' in the Rain*. Her portrayal of Lina Lamont, who talks "with a microphone in her bosom and a parakeet in her throat" is an excellent satire of an actress making the transition from silents to talkies. Having admirably suffered a cake in the face from Debbie Reynolds, the loss of Gene Kelly, as romantic attachment, and being made a professional fool, all within the screen musical, she was a loser on Oscar night when MGM contractee Gloria Grahame won over Jean in the best supporting actress category for her role in *The Bad and the Beautiful* (1952).

Jean's remaining MGM pictures were all downhill for her: she was the girl friend of psychotic war veteran Ralph Meeker in *Shadow in the Sky* (1952), and James Stewart's understanding wife in *Carbine Williams* (1952). Pregnancy prevented her from playing the sour farm wife in *My Man and I* (1952) and Claire Trevor replaced her. Jean's son, Aric Philip was born on August 19, 1952. A daughter, Christina Patricia (named after Patricia Neal) had been born two years earlier on August 26th. Then Jean was Lana Turner's secretary in *Latin Lovers* (1953), the wife of clown Harry Morgan in *Arena* (1953), and ended her contract as the wife of Red Skelton in the suburbia comedy *Half a Hero* (1953).

Leaving MGM, Jean joined Danny Thomas in *Make Room for Daddy* (premiere: ABC-TV, September 29, 1953), playing Thomas' forceful, pleasantly caustic wife. She did the role for three seasons, earned two Emmy nominations and became recognizable to a larger audience than any of her films had afforded her. Jean became tired of the one-dimensional role she played on the teleseries and made a big interview hoopla that she was ready for meatier challenges. She was replaced on *The Danny Thomas Show* by a subdued Marjorie Lord and returned to films playing the slightly blowsy nymphomaniac in Clifford Odets' *The Big Knife* (1955). Her cameo as the pathetic two-timer was well etched. Two years later, when Betty Hutton, in her own movie comeback attempt, had Florence Halop removed from the cast of *Spring Reunion* (1957), Jean was substituted as the high school classmate, now a mother of four.

Jean's career momentum was all gone, and when she appeared in a major picture, *Sunrise at Campobello* (1960), it was in the unrewarding role as Franklin Delano Roosevelt's secretary, Missy LeHand. Then in 1964 she showed every bit of her age as one of the overripe participants in Bette Davis' *Dead Ringer* (1964), in which Jean was the social butterfly who flirts with Davis' lover, Peter Lawford.

After *Dead Ringer* Jean retired. But each revival of *Singin' in the Rain* causes at least one new devotee of the picture to ponder aloud: "Geez, whatever happened to that Hagen girl?"

JEAN HAGEN

Adam's Rib (MGM, 1949)
Side Street (MGM, 1949)
Ambush (MGM, 1950)
The Asphalt Jungle (MGM, 1950)
A Life of Her Own (MGM, 1950)
Night into Morning (MGM, 1951)
No Questions Asked (MGM, 1951)
Singin' in the Rain (MGM, 1952)
Shadow in the Sky (MGM, 1952)
Carbine Williams (MGM, 1952)

Latin Lovers (MGM, 1953)
Arena (MGM, 1953)
Half a Hero (MGM, 1953)
The Big Knife (UA, 1955)
Spring Reunion (UA, 1957)
The Shaggy Dog (BV, 1959)
Sunrise at Campobello (WB, 1960)
Panic in Year Zero (AIP, 1962)
Dead Ringer (WB, 1964)

With Gene Kelly in *Singin' in the Rain* (1952)

Jean Harlow

Jean Harlow was unique. She was the female equivalent of the bad guys of the 1930s (James Cagney, Edward G. Robinson, Humphrey Bogart) a nonstop, rat-a-tat-tat moll for tough guys. She was a hard-as-nails, phosphorescent tart who thought like a man and, just like a man, took what she wanted when she wanted it. If fate was not always on her side, her sense of humor was. There had been vamps before (Theda Bara, Pola Negri, and Clara Bow) but when Harlow hit the scene in a big way in 1930 with *Hell's Angels*, she was something totally different. Her darkly lipsticked, pouting lips, white, white skin, that platinum blonde hair, and her onscreen narcissism meant enticement and destruction for any male in sight. Jean was probably the first of the mammary-oriented sex symbols, and her braless, nubile body was erotically swathed in white satin for the duration of her career. She was not simply the other woman, nor the typical whore with a heart of gold. She was a proficient, self-sufficient sex machine who used and disposed of men with a gleeful insouciance.

MGM acquired her early in her career and she remained at that studio until her premature death at the age of twenty-six. She was an oddity among that studio's female contingent, where actresses represented Louis B. Mayer's stereotyped reverence towards womanhood. Her tough girl image was gradually softened over the years at MGM (more in publicity stills than in actuality on the screen) and she developed from an atrociously bad actress into an adept instinctual comedienne. It is astonishing to realize that her peak career lasted for little more than seven years and equally astonishing that her colleagues recall her offscreen character as a childlike, amiable, not dumb, but not too bright, likable gal.

Harlean Carpentier, as she was christened, was born in Kansas City, Missouri on March 3, 1911. Her father was a dentist and, when she was seven, her parents were divorced. She went to live with her domineering, fanatically Christian Scientist mother and her stepfather Marino Bello. She was educated in private schools and at sixteen eloped with a wealthy young Chicagoan, Charles F. McGrew. That marriage was dissolved and Jean moved to Los Angeles with her mother, where, taking her mother's maiden name of Jean Harlow, she halfheartedly sought a career as an extra in motion pictures. She

In *The Beast of the City* (1932)

worked at Paramount in Richard Dix's *Moran of the Marines* (1928), did two Hal Roach comedies with Laurel and Hardy, and was an extra in Chaplin's *City Lights* (1931) at United Artists. She received eleventh billing in Clara Bow's *The Saturday Night Kid* (1929).

All hell broke loose when Howard Hughes selected her for the lead in *Hell's Angels* in 1930. Hughes had fired Swedish actress Greta Nissen because of her accent and cast Harlow as the British girl who seduces both Ben Lyon and James Hall. The three-million-dollar film about the British Royal Flying Corps was technically superior, but the acting was poor, and no one for a minute believed Jean as a Britisher. But her screen magnetism was overpowering, and audiences were aghast at her blatant sexuality as she purred to Lyon, "Pardon me while I slip into something more comfortable." Hughes signed her to a contract with his Caddo Company at $250 a week, and loaned her out for seven films in rapid succession. Two were noteworthy: *Public Enemy* (1931), because it cast her opposite her perfect male counterpart James Cagney; and *Platinum Blonde* (1931), while miscasting her as a socialite, tagged her with its title.

Her last loanout was to MGM for *The Beast of the City* (1932), opposite Walter Huston, after which Jean asked out of her Hughes contract. Louis B. Mayer fortuitously bought up her contract for $60,000 and signed her at $1,250 per week. MGM's Irving Thalberg gave little thought to her until his intellectual right arm, Paul Bern, took her under his wing. Bern persuaded Thalberg to feminize Jean's image via comedy and he was responsible for her being cast in *Red-Headed Woman* (1932), in which she played the bad girl with a sense of humor. MGM had tested so many actresses for the part before they could make a decision that jovial Marie Dressler put on a blonde wig and did a test also. Bern's persistence proved the turning point for Jean and MGM began to exploit their blonde sex symbol with all its technical finesse.

Before *Red-Headed Woman* was released, Bern, an effete forty-two-year-old bachelor, shocked the film colony by marrying the twenty-one-year-old Jean. During their courtship the unprepossessing blonde had been quoted as exclaiming, "My God, he wants to take me to an opera." That marriage was short-lived and tragic, and produced the first public scandal in MGM's history. On Labor Day 1932 (they had wed in July) Bern's nude body was found dead of a pistol wound in his bedroom. Presumably a suicide, he left the following note:

> Dearest dear,
> Unfortunately this is the only way to make good
> the frightful wrong I have done you and to wipe
> out my abject humiliation. You understand that
> last night was only a comedy.
>
> > Paul

MGM was shaken, and in an effort to decide how to handle the ensuing publicity, heeded William Randolph Hearst's suggestion to simply "shut up" about it. Hearst's tactic worked and, two months later, with the

With Clark Gable in *Hold Your Man* (1933)

release of *Red Dust* (1932) opposite Clark Gable, Jean was a STAR. The Gable-Harlow chemistry in *Red Dust* proved one of the most memorable of Hollywood screen loves, and audiences howled when a nude Jean in a rain barrel commands Gable to "Scrub my back." Thereafter, Jean quickly married a third husband, cinematographer Harold G. Rosson, seventeen years her senior, but was divorced a year later, complaining that "he read in bed."

While her personal life was chaos, her motion picture career flourished. *Hold Your Man* (1933) was another good one with Gable, and the unforgettable *Dinner at Eight* (1933) earned her a *Time* magazine cover story as the vixenish, scheming wife of Wallace Beery. Marie Dressler, as the *grand dame* actress, sizes Jean up perfectly when, in response to the blonde's, "Do you know machinery is going to take the place of every profession?" Dressler bitchily replies, "Oh, my dear, that is something *you* need never worry about."

Boxoffice successes followed with *The Girl from Missouri* (1934) with Franchot Tone, *Reckless* (1935) with William Powell, *China Seas* (1935) with Wallace Beery, *Wife vs. Secretary* (1936) with Gable, *Suzy* (1936) with Cary Grant, *Libeled Lady* (1936) with Spencer Tracy, and *Personal Property* (1937) with Robert Taylor.

On June 7, 1937, while making *Saratoga* (1937) with Gable, Jean died after a ten-day illness diagnosed as uremic poisoning.* Her mother's religious beliefs prevented her from receiving the medical treatment which might have saved her life. Hollywood was shocked and truly mourned their amiable blonde. At the time of her death it was assumed she would shortly marry William Powell who was recently divorced from Carole Lombard. At her funeral at Forest Lawn, where Jeanette MacDonald sang "Indian Love Call" and Nelson Eddy sang "Ah, Sweet Mystery of Life," Powell was a grief-stricken mourner. For many months following, he provided fresh flowers daily for her grave.

It is almost impossible to speculate what turn Jean's career may have taken had she lived. Many think she would have married Powell and retired. Nonetheless, there has been a procession of Harlow imitators, none of whom have captured the magnetism of the original. Only one blonde ever surpassed her as a sex symbol, but Marilyn Monroe is another story entirely.

When Irving Schulman published a titillating but suspect biography of Jean in 1964, two film companies jumped on the bandwagon to profit from the renewed interested in the blonde bombshell. Neither Joseph E. Levine's *Harlow* (1965), starring Carrol Baker, nor the Electronovision quickie, with Carol Lynley, came close to depicting the raw sensuality that was Jean's trademark, and their haphazard attempts to re-create the Hollywood of the 1920s and the 1930s were pathetic.

---

*Some sources state that Jean's condition was caused by an induced abortion, with William Powell cited as the father of the unborn child.

JEAN HARLOW

Moran of the Marines (Paramount, 1928)
Fugitives (Fox, 1929)
Close Harmony (Paramount, 1929)
Love Parade (Paramount, 1929)
The Saturday Night Kid (Paramount, 1929)
New York Nights (UA, 1929)
Hell's Angels (UA, 1930)
City Lights (UA, 1931)
Secret Six (MGM, 1931)
Iron Man (Universal, 1931)
Public Enemy (WB, 1931)
Goldie (Fox, 1931)
Platinum Blonde (Columbia, 1931)
Three Wise Girls (Columbia, 1932)
The Beast of the City (MGM, 1932)

Red-Headed Woman (MGM, 1932)
Red Dust (MGM, 1932)
Dinner at Eight (MGM, 1933)
Hold Your Man (MGM, 1933)
Bombshell (MGM, 1933)
The Girl from Missouri (MGM, 1934)
Reckless (MGM, 1935)
China Seas (MGM, 1935)
Riffraff (MGM, 1935)
Wife vs. Secretary (MGM, 1936)
Suzy (MGM, 1936)
Libeled Lady (MGM, 1936)
Personal Property (MGM, 1937)
Saratoga (MGM, 1937)

With Lee Tracy in *Bombshell* (1933)

With Franchot Tone in *The Girl from Missouri* (1934)

With Cary Grant in *Suzy* (1936)

In *Personal Property* (1937)

With Lionel Barrymore and Clark Gable in *Saratoga* (1937)

Richard Hart

Among the many actors who have burst upon the Hollywood scene with great fanfare and then burnt out their welcome before they had developed a screen image is Richard Hart. Unlike the more conventional William Eythe or the more rebellious Robert Walker and James Dean, both of whom also died young, Hart never achieved film stardom and is little remembered today. Within a year of his arrival at MGM he was rushed into the second male lead roles of three studio films. Each was a stinker for different reasons, but the critics complained that Hart was nothing more than an imitation Laurence Olivier. Shelved by Metro, he made one more independent film and then returned to the New York stage whence he had come.

Hart was born in Providence, Rhode Island on April 14, 1915 where he grew up and attended Brown University as a psychology and English major. During his junior year at college he was an all-American center halfback in soccer. When he graduated he thought he would become a newspaper reporter, but instead worked at a silverware plant for three years. One summer he played juvenile leads in the stock theatre at Twerton, Rhode Island. His appetite for theatre work whetted by this experience, he moved to New York and was hired for the stock company at the Ridgeway Theatre in White Plains. For the O. P. A. he was in *It's up to You*, directed by Elia Kazan, and performed in the New York City area at movie theatres. In 1943–1944 he did juveniles and then leads at the Cambridge Summer Theatre. In between, there was a road tour of *Without Love* with Constance Bennett.

Hart made his Broadway debut in a bit role in *Pillar to Post* (1944) and the following season starred with Carol Stone in *Dark of the Moon*, roles they each had played at Cambridge. This fantasy play was based on the Barbara Allen legend, dealing with the witch boy (Hart) who wants to wed a mortal, only to later wonder why he ever wanted to be human. The offbeat subject matter caused a critical stir, and in the showy lead Hart received much publicity, the N.Y. *Sun* stating that the main role was " ... played with excitement and vigor by the lithe Richard Hart."

MGM was sufficiently impressed by Hart's Broadway success to sign him to a contract without a screen test. As a "hot" young property, he was rushed into Greer Garson's *Desire Me* (1947) when Robert Montgomery departed the much-plagued film. Hart was the Frenchman who, upon hearing about Garson from her husband (Robert Mitchum), a fellow p. o. w., falls in love with her sight unseen. He later appears at Garson's home, tells the loyal wife all about her husband's supposed death while escaping, and proceeds to make love to her. She becomes enamored of him, but then Mitchum comes home. The public did not buy this hogwash—director George Cukor had had his name removed from the credits—and third-billed Hart did not fare well either. As the deceiving army buddy he was labeled "more promising than expert" by Howard Barnes of the N.Y. *Herald-Tribune*.

Less than a month after *Desire Me* premiered came the expensively mounted ($4 million plus) *Green Dolphin Street* (1947), based on the Elizabeth Goudge novel. Hart was fourth-featured as the son of Frank Morgan who deserts from British military service and escapes to 1840s New Zealand. While there and in a drunken stupor, he writes to Lana Turner to wed him, when he really meant to request the hand of her sister (Donna Reed) in marriage. The film proved viable boxoffice, largely because of Turner's name, plus the special effects of an earthquake and a tidal wave, as well as a native uprising tossed into the plot for good measure. As the weakling husband, the moustached Hart was soundly rapped for being too preoccupied with aping the mannerisms of a swashbuckling Laurence Olivier.

MGM gave Hart half a chance more. This chance was the disastrous *B. F.'s Daughter* (1948), purportedly based on John P. Marquand's novel. Industrialist Charles Coburn's daughter (Barbara Stanwyck) attempts to dominate the career of her husband (Van Heflin). This domestic squabble chronicle ranged from the 1930s to the middle of World War II. Hart was given a subsidiary role as the stuffed shirt who becomes a war hero. His *vis-à-vis* was Margaret Lindsay.

With no additional projects lined up for Hart, the studio was agreeable to loaning him out to Eagle–Lion for *Reign of Terror* (1949) (a. k. a. *The Black Book*) along with MGM coworker Arlene Dahl. Robert Cummings was the swashbuckling "hero" of this revolution-torn France entry, but it was Richard Basehart as Robespierre and Arnold Moss as Fouche who stole the limelight. Once again Hart was lost in the shuffle, his Francois Barras a forgettable characterization.

Since his Hollywood career had fizzled, Hart requested and received permission from MGM to return to Broadway. After appearing in the short-lived *Leaf and Bough* (1948), he replaced Sam Wanamaker as the *Life* magazine photographer Matt Cole in *Goodbye, My Fancy*. In the days of live television drama in New York City, there was plenty of work for experienced actors, and he starred on such anthology series as *Studio One* in *The Passionate Pilgrim*. He also was the first actor to play Ellery Queen on television when he debuted on *The Adventures of Ellery Queen* (October 19, 1950).

In 1950 Hart was costarred with Claude Dauphin in *The Happy Time*. He was young Uncle Desmonde, the *bon vivant* traveling salesman. The warmhearted stage comedy was doing commercially well when Hart, on January 2, 1951, died of a heart attack at the age of thirty-five. He was survived by his actress wife Louise Valery (they wed in 1945) and their daughter Hillary. For those who had seen the vitality of Hart's stage work, his early death was a sad loss to the theatre.

RICHARD HART

Desire Me (MGM, 1947)
Green Dolphin Street (MGM, 1947)

B.F.'s Daughter (MGM, 1948)
Reign of Terror (Eagle–Lion, 1949)

With Lana Turner, Linda Christian, and Van Heflin in *Green Dolphin Street* (1947)

Helen Hayes

When Helen Hayes celebrated her Golden Jubilee in 1955, one of the more pungent tributes came via tape from Mae West: "I knew she was the most when she starred in a piece called *What Every Woman Knows!*" For years Helen has been known as the First Lady of the Theatre, a tag that has been bestowed upon several actresses over the decades by energetic press agents. This title has remained most closely associated with Miss Hayes not necessarily because she was the *best* stage actress, but mainly for the longevity of her career. She began acting when five years old, and is still active today in her seventies. Her less than two dozen motion picture performances are really a footnote to her theatrical career, and the only reason she originally traveled to Hollywood was to be with her husband, playwright–screen writer Charles MacArthur. Once there at MGM, she found herself a square peg in a round hole without the sex appeal and physical beauty of a "movie star." as a result, the roles offered her failed to establish her as a First Lady of the American Screen.

Helen Hayes Brown was born in Washington, D. C. on October 10, 1900, of Irish Catholic ancestry. Her mother, an independent-thinking young actress, sent her daughter to Catholic schools and the Minnie Hawkes School of Dance ("because I was pigeon-toed"). She allowed Helen to make her stage debut at the age of five, playing Prince Charles in the Columbia Players production of *The Royal Family*. That was the beginning of a prolific career as a child actress, and she made her Broadway debut in 1909, in *Old Dutch*. During that play she had her first "crush," she says, for dancer Vernon Castle and jealously resented, in her own nine-year-old way, Castle's interest in an unknown named Irene Foote. Helen made a Vitagraph two-reeler entitled *Jean and the Calico Doll* with Maurice Costello; played in *The Prodigal Husband* (1914) with Broadway's greatest star of the day, John Drew; toured for several seasons in *Pollyanna*; and two days before Christmas in 1918, she began her Broadway star years when she opened in Sir James M. Barrie's *Dear Brutus*, playing Margaret. The next day she was hailed as one of the greatest young actresses of her time.

From then on she became one of the more pleasant permanent fixtures on Broadway in such plays as Booth Tarkington's *Clarence* (1919) and *Babs*

(1920); the George S. Kaufman–Marc Connolly *To the Ladies* (1922); *Caesar and Cleopatra* (1925); and the play that saw her come of age, Barrie's *What Every Woman Knows* (1926). While doing a two year stint in *Coquette*, Helen married Charles MacArthur (August 17, 1928) and later left the play to have a baby daughter, Mary, born in 1930. The management of the play sued her, and during the publicity and litigation that followed, Helen had what was known as an Act of God baby.

MacArthur had accepted a lucrative contract from MGM to write screen scenarios and quickly established himself as one of their best script doctors and writers of dialogue. When MacArthur became restless because of the separation from his wife, Irving G. Thalberg wired Helen, proposing a motion picture contract with Metro. Helen accepted reluctantly only after MacArthur implored her to accept and after the studio agreed to double their first salary bid. Unlike Paramount, which had successfully raided Broadway of its finer young players, Claudette Colbert, Miriam Hopkins, Sylvia Sidney, Fredric March, and Phillips Holmes, MGM had been particularly leery of importing Broadway figures to handle talking film assignments, with Alfred Lunt and Lynn Fontanne, who quickly left after one disappointing feature, *The Guardsman*, and Robert Montgomery, who succeeded in Hollywood, being the notable MGM exceptions. When Helen arrived at the Culver City lot she was, to say the least, put off by such standard queries as, "What's your specialty?" Wisely, she allowed such questions to remain rhetorical.

Wishing to retain MacArthur's valuable services, Thalberg tried to assuage Helen of her fears of the big screen, and Thalberg and his wife Norma Shearer and the MacArthurs became good friends, even traveling to Europe together in 1933. But the scripts the studio offered Helen were far from satisfactory. The first was *Lullabye*, which borrowed heavily from the old *Madame X* mother-love plot, and had Helen age from girlhood innocence in to an old whore and then a decrepit charwoman. When MacArthur saw the first version of the script, he exclaimed: "My God, this thing would sink Garbo!" After considerable reworking by both MacArthur and Thalberg, the entire film was virtually remade and the picture was released as *The Sin of Madelon Claudet* (1931). Helen hated it, but at the preview, Louis B. Mayer wept openly and proclaimed it the greatest thing he had even seen. The public agreed with him and a few months later Mayer proudly presented Helen with an Academy Award for her "human portrayal." The picture's success still did not establish a niche for Helen in the MGM roster, largely because Mayer doubted her sex appeal with audiences. As Mayer put it, he did not know if she had sex appeal or not. Helen modestly replied, "Mr. Mayer, I don't know either."

So with her uneasy status as Great-Actress-come-to-the movies, MGM loaned her to United Artists to play the wife of idealistic doctor Ronald Colman in Sinclair Lewis' *Arrowsmith* (1931), and to Paramount for the best film version of Hemingway's *A Farewell to Arms* (1932) in which she played Catherine opposite Gary Cooper. These two assignments proved to be her least mannered screen portrayals. Her next four assignments from MGM, *The Son–Daughter* (1933), *The White Sister* (1933), *Another Language* (1933), and *Night Flight* (1933), demonstrated that the studio still did not know how to promote the actress who had a strong penchant for screen posturing. She returned briefly to Broadway to star in Maxwell Anderson's *Mary Of Scotland*. MGM enticed her to return with a script of the Barrie play she had done so successfully onstage, *What Every Woman Knows* (1934), but the picture was not up to her expectations. Costar Brian Aherne recalls her as difficult, touchy, and remote in her uneasiness over her cinema career. She refused to do the next assignment they chose for her, a dated Hugh Walpole novel, *Vanessa, Her Love Story* (1935), but Mayer reminded her she was under contract and that she would be sued for $90,000 if she did not comply. Helen acquiesced but, before the picture was released, it being the last commitment on her contract, she announced succinctly, "I am leaving the screen because I don't think I am very good in the pictures, and I have a beautiful dream that I'm elegant on stage." She turned down an offer to star in *Pride and Prejudice*.

Returning to Broadway, she experienced the personal triumph of her career, *Victoria Regina*, which she played from 1935 to 1938. After this there was *The Merchant of Venice* (1938), *Twelfth Night* (1940), *Harriet* (1943–1945), and a London production of *The Glass Menagerie* (1948). The following year her nineteen-year-old daughter Mary died of infantile paralysis. Their second child, James, who is now an actor, was adopted in 1937.

After two more Broadway appearances, Helen briefly resumed her motion picture career. She was the mother of Communist Robert Walker in *My Son John* (1952) and played herself in *Main Street to Broadway* (1953), as she had done in *Stage Door Canteen* (1943). In one of her best film roles she played the Grand Duchess in *Anastasia* (1956), the film which brought Ingrid Bergman back to American audiences. In 1947 it had been Helen who presented Bergman with the Tony Award for her stage performance in *Joan of Lorraine*, saying: "We thank you, Miss Bergman, for bringing the theatre back to Broadway." Later in 1956 Charles MacArthur died of a heart attack.

She returned to the stage in *Time Remembered* in 1958. The next year she opened at the Helen Hayes Theatre in O'Neill's *A Touch of the Poet*, exclaiming, "An actress's life is so transitory! Suddenly you're a building!" In the early 1960s she toured Europe in *The Skin of Our Teeth* and *The Glass Menagerie*, appeared with Maurice Evans in a Shakespeare recital, and joined the APA–Phoenix Repertory Company. After performing in *The Show-Off* with that company in her home town in 1968, she announced in a moment of fatigue that she was retiring. But she gave second thoughts to these plans, "I must refrain from making any more statements about my dream of retirement. It's beginning to sound absurd." She accepted the opportunity to appear with James Stewart on Broadway in a limited engagement of *Harvey* (1970). Producer Ross Hunter lured her back to the movies to play the cute little old stowaway in the motion picture *Airport* (1970), in which she was billed as "Miss Helen Hayes." She received the Academy Award as best actress in a

327

supporting role in that year. Her theatrical performance may have added a broad comic touch to the melodrama, but it did not endear her to more discriminating audiences.

Helen has done much television work from the 1950s to the present, winning an Emmy in 1952 as best actress. She is still plying her craft in the 1970s: a cute little old lady in the telefeature *Do Not Fold, Spindle or Mutilate* with veterans Myrna Loy, Sylvia Sidney, and Mildred Natwick; a video rendition of *Harvey* (1972) with James Stewart; a polite but nervous hostess on the April 1972 Oscarcast; and a costarring role with Mildred Natwick in the telefeature *The Snoop Sisters* (1972). Also in 1972 she was awarded Rome's Santa Susanna Guild's St. Genesius Gold Medal for "outstanding dedication to the promotion of Christian principles in the acting profession."

Once asked to explicate her professional success, Helen analyzed, "I am the triumph of the familiar over the exotic." She freely admits that, "Durability is the thing. They're loving me more than they ever loved me twenty years ago when I was much better than I am now."

HELEN HAYES

The Sin of Madelon Claudet (MGM, 1931)
Arrowsmith (UA, 1931)
A Farewell to Arms (Paramount, 1932)
The Son–Daughter (MGM, 1933)
The White Sister (MGM, 1933)
Another Language (MGM, 1933)
Night Flight (MGM, 1933)
What Every Woman Knows (MGM, 1934)
Crime without Passion (Paramount, 1934)*

Vanessa, Her Love Story (MGM, 1935)
Stage Door Canteen (UA, 1943)
My Son John (Paramount, 1952)
Main Street to Broadway (MGM, 1953)
Anastasia (20th-Fox, 1956)
Third Man on the Mountain (BV, 1959)*
Airport (Universal, 1970)
The Further Adventures of the Love Bug (BV, 1973)

*Unbilled appearance.

With Robert Montgomery and Louise Closser Hale in *Another Language* (1933)

With Brian Aherne in *What Every Woman Knows* (1934)

With Robert Montgomery in *Vanessa, Her Love Story* (1935)

Van Heflin

Early on in his acting career, Van Heflin realized: "I just don't have the looks and if I don't do a good acting job I look terrible." Despite his sturdy talents he had to push hard to gain and maintain professional recognition. His screen reputation rests largely on three roles: the drunken scholar in *Johnny Eager* (1942), for which he received an Oscar; the stalwart homesteader in *Shane* (1953); and the mad bomber in *Airport* (1970).

He was a stage-trained actor who did not take to the motion picture medium at first. Even after he was firmly entrenched at MGM in the 1940s, his personal restlessness and rebellious nature drew him back to the stage. His cragged looks did not qualify him for romantic leads, but he never regretted playing the heavy, because he knew the audience would remember him. He was frequently likened to Spencer Tracy and was often thought of as one of the screen's best male performers, but stardom in the pre–Dustin Hoffman days eluded him. Heflin spent eight years at MGM (1941–1949), after which he free-lanced in motion pictures, theatre, and television. During the early 1960s he gained a respectable European following as the result of making several pictures in Italy and Spain, but he never used the foreign-made pictures as a tax break. His home and bank account were in the United States. He was a private man and rarely took part in the Hollywood social life and, while he plied his trade in all media, he always came back to motion pictures. "They're good because they keep your name before the audience, and they're good financially. Success or not, you always get paid."

Emmett Evan Heflin, Jr. was born on December 13, 1910 in Walters, Oklahoma, where his French–Irish father was a dentist. He spent his early years vacillating between academic studies and the sea. At the early age of fourteen he drifted to Long Beach, California, where he shipped out to sea. He arrived in New York after one voyage, and there at a cocktail party, a relative goaded him into reading for a play entitled *Mr. Moneypenny* where his "strange mixture of college-bred gentleman and two-fisted sailor" won him the part. The play by Channing Pollock opened in October 1928 and was a flop. Cast adrift again, the eighteen-year-old actor earned a diploma from the University of Oklahoma in 1931, joined the Hedgerow Theatre in Philadelphia, and spent a year with the Yale School of Drama.

With this formal theatre training and work in summer stock behind him, Heflin returned to New York and was soon actively involved in a Broadway career. In 1934 he and Jean Arthur appeared in *The Bride of Torotzko*. Not only was the play bad, but Heflin took a beating from the critic Percy Hammond who stated that Heflin was "an unreasonably bad actor." (Heflin would save this notice the remainder of his life.) Next he understudied the lead in a musical entitled *Sailor Beware*, and appeared with Ina Claire in *End of Summer* (1936), which was his first Broadway success. Of these early theatre years, Heflin once said, "In those days, Burgess Meredith was the brilliant one, Tom Ewell the man not to be underestimated, Hank Fonda and Jim Stewart were the ones who sold themselves for movie gold."

But Heflin was human also, and when Katharine Hepburn, who had seen his *End of Summer* performance, asked RKO to sign the actor for her new picture *A Woman Rebels* (1936), he followed the footsteps of Fonda and Stewart to Hollywood. The film was a Victorian costume drama in which an emancipated Hepburn defies her faithful suitor (Herbert Marshall) to have a child out of wedlock by her young, virile lover (Heflin). This static picture was creaky, but RKO gave Heflin several more assignments in B pictures. He did not cotton to the bad scripts or the medium, and asked out. "What I thought of them is exactly what they thought of me. I felt like a failure and, come to think of it, I was."

He went back to New York and, after some radio work, was cast in Philip Barry's play *The Philadelphia Story* (1939) in the role of the sardonic journalist which Barry supposedly had written for him. The star of that play was Katharine Hepburn, but Heflin earned his share of good reviews. N.Y. *Times'* Brooks Atkinson opined, "It would be hard to improve upon Van Heflin's honest and solid description of a tough-minded writer." Hollywood, however, did. Hepburn owned one-fourth of the theatre production of *The Philadelphia Story* and when the hit play ended its run, she sold her previously purchased screen rights to MGM. But to guarantee its commercial success, she insisted Cary Grant and James Stewart be cast in the film version, Stewart in the role that Heflin had done onstage. Stewart won an Oscar for same.

Heflin drifted back to Hollywood and did two films, one a big Errol Flynn Western at Warner Brothers, *Santa Fe Trail* (1940), in which he was the villain. Then he telephoned MGM talent scout Billy Grady and requested a screen test. Heflin did a test opposite studio contractee Donna Reed and recalled, "It came out remarkable for her and good for me." MGM signed him on and cast him in Rosalind Russell's *The Feminine Touch* (1941). He played the cynical adman in *H. M. Pulham, Esq.* (1941), after which he was the alcoholic, Shakespeare-quoting conscience of gangster Robert Taylor in *Johnny Eager*, for which he won a best supporting actor Oscar. MGM gave him the lead as the likable scientist in *Kid Glove Killer* (1942) and a romantic lead opposite Kathryn Grayson in *Seven Sweethearts* (1942).

If anything sealed Heflin's fate at MGM, it was the rather costly *Tennessee Johnson* (1943), an idealistic but plodding chronicle of the ill-fated

With Robert Taylor in *Johnny Eager* (1941)

With Ruth Hussey in *Tennessee Johnson* (1942)

1257-

Andrew Johnson. Heflin was intense and robust in the role, but he could not drag life into the historical film, and, more importantly, his solid masculinity did not incite strong interest from the female filmgoers. He was properly sincere as the playwright in *Presenting Lily Mars* (1943), but the tale was simply a Judy Garland showcase.

Heflin spent three years as a combat cameraman with the Ninth Air Force during World War II and returned to finish out his MGM contract. He was loaned to Paramount as the righteous ex-lover of a nasty Barbara Stanwyck in *The Strange Love of Martha Ivers* (1946), and as the scoundrel who arouses Joan Crawford's unstable love in Warners' *Possessed* (1947). That same year he played a man of honest intentions in the costumer *Green Dolphin Street* but, like the film's audience, both female leads Lana Turner and Donna Reed had their twisted hearts set on Richard Hart, a new MGM leading man. Heflin had already asked to be released from his contract, but Metro called him ungrateful, stating that now he wanted to sell his talents to competitor studios after they had groomed his screen image. A compromise was reached, and he finished off his studio commitments with such unsatisfactory assignments as Athos in *The Three Musketeers* (1948) and Charles Bovary in *Madame Bovary* (1949).

As a free-lancing film player in the 1950s, Heflin had a very shaky time. He turned in his best work as the homesteader opposite Alan Ladd's gunfighter in George Stevens' *Shane*. Two years later he gave a notable Broadway performance as Eddie, the self-destructive longshoreman in Arthur Miller's *A View from the Bridge* (1955). One controversial scene in that play called for Heflin to kiss another actor (Richard Davalos) on the lips, and Heflin wryly explained: "The kiss always got gasps from the audiences. But we got away with it, I suppose, because neither of us looks effeminate. We haven't even had any passionate letters from *the boys*."

He continued to turn in craftsmanlike performances on the screen: as the major who is killed in *Battle Cry* (1955), the ambitious executive in *Patterns* (1956), the impoverished rancher in *3:10 to Yuma* (1957), and one of the five riffraffs turned into an instant hero in *They Came to Cordura* (1959). On Broadway in 1964 he created a thoughtful performance of trial lawyer Louis Nizer in *A Case of Libel* and received an Emmy nomination three years later after re-creating the role on television. Of all the tough, weather-beaten screen roles he undertook in the 1960s, his last two were the most intriguing. He was the emotionally burned-out motel owner who befriends Ryan O'Neal in *The Big Bounce* (1969), which a major studio film which had the distinction of setting new frontiers in blatant obscenity. In *Airport* he was the down-at-the-heels husband of waitress Maureen Stapleton. His crazed mind devises a plot to blow up a jet passenger plane so his wife can collect insurance on him. He lent much-needed believability to both pictures.

Heflin married actress Frances Neal in 1942, and she retired from acting to become wife and mother. They had two daughters, Vana and Cathleen. Cathleen is now Mrs. Robert Westbrook, daughter-in-law of

With Jennifer Jones and Louis Jourdan in *Madame Bovary* (1949) columnist Sheilah Graham. Heflin and his wife divorced in 1967. (An earlier, unrecorded marriage ended after six months.) Heflin's sister Frances is an actress and is currently appearing on the television soaper *All My Children*.

On June 6, 1971 Heflin was found clinging to the ladder of the swimming pool at his apartment house in Hollywood. He had suffered a heart attack while taking his daily swim. He never regained consciousness and died the following July 23 at the age of sixty. He had recently completed work on *The Last Child*, an ABC telefeature aired in October 1971, for which the late actor received fine notices.

A modest, self-effacing man, he took his degree of success in stride: "The great danger an actor faces is that he may take himself more seriously than he does his work. There are a few who read their own publicity and begin to believe it. But if you don't let it go to your head, you can go on and live a normal life."

VAN HEFLIN

A Woman Rebels (RKO, 1936)
Outcasts of Poker Flat (RKO, 1937)
Flight from Glory (RKO, 1937)
Saturday's Heroes (RKO, 1937)
Annapolis Salute (RKO, 1937)
Back Door to Heaven (Paramount, 1939)
Santa Fe Trail (WB, 1940)
The Feminine Touch (MGM, 1941)
Johnny Eager (MGM, 1941)
H. M. Pulham, Esq. (MGM, 1941)
Kid Glove Killer (MGM, 1942)
Seven Sweethearts (MGM, 1942)
Grand Central Murder (MGM, 1942)
Tennessee Johnson (MGM, 1942)
Presenting Lily Mars (MGM, 1943)
The Strange Love of Martha Ivers (Paramount, 1946)
Till the Clouds Roll By (MGM, 1946)
Possessed (WB, 1947)
Green Dolphin Street (MGM, 1947)
Tap Root (Universal, 1948)
B.F.'s Daughter (MGM, 1948)
The Three Musketeers (MGM, 1948)
Act of Violence (MGM, 1948)
The Secret Land (Narrator: MGM, 1948)
Madame Bovary (MGM, 1949)
East Side, West Side (MGM, 1949)
Tomahawk (Universal, 1951)
The Prowler (UA, 1951)

Weekend with Father (Universal, 1951)
My Son, John (Paramount, 1952)
Wings of the Hawk (Universal, 1953)
Shane (Paramount, 1953)
Tanganyika (Universal, 1954)
The Golden Mask (UA, 1954)
The Raid (20th-Fox, 1954)
A Woman's World (20th-Fox, 1954)
Black Widow (20th-Fox, 1954)
Count Three and Pray (Columbia, 1955)
Battle Cry (WB, 1955)
Patterns (UA, 1956)
3:10 to Yuma (Columbia, 1957)
Gunman's Walk (Columbia, 1958)
They Came to Cordura (Columbia, 1959)
Tempest (Paramount, 1959)
Five Branded Women (Paramount, 1960)
Under Ten Flags (Paramount, 1960)
Cry of Battle (AA, 1963)
The Wastrel (Medallion, 1963)
To Be a Man (Medallion, 1964)
The Greatest Story Ever Told (UA, 1965)
Once a Thief (MGM, 1965)
Stagecoach (20th-Fox, 1966)
The Man Outside (AA, 1967)
The Ruthless Four (Golden Eagle, 1969)
The Big Bounce (WB-7 Arts, 1969)
Airport (Universal, 1970)
The World of Sport Fishing (AA, 1972)

Katharine Hepburn

Of Hollywood's indomitable triumvirate of wilful, emancipated women—Bette Davis, Katharine Hepburn, Joan Crawford—each is unequivocally a *star*. Each has her assorted moments of brilliant emoting and public adulation. Katharine Hepburn's career, however, is unique in Hollywood history. Except for one brief stretch at the end of her RKO tenure in 1937–1938, she has been *on top* all the time. There have been the unavoidable flops and the inactive years that occur in all such long show business careers. Yet Hepburn is the only actress who has been able to maintain her stellar position in today's realistic market. She is the sole actress to receive three Academy Awards, two of which were awarded in the last decade, thirty-one years after her motion picture debut. The appreciation of Katharine's work has been generally deserved and the admiration bestowed on her fitting. But ironically, when she commenced her multimedia career, she was little more than an expert showoff with a magnetic spark. "When I started out, I didn't have any great desire to be an actress or to learn how to act. I just wanted to be famous." Today that spark is in no way diminished. In her own eccentric fashion, she is still the obstreperous showoff, but she has also become one of our finer actresses.

She has said, "I'm a personality as well as an actress. Show me an actress who isn't a personality and I'll show you a woman who isn't a star." Rebellious by nature, her impulsiveness has been part of her admittedly selfish desire to maintain and exert her independence. Joan Blondell recently observed, "I really don't have envy in my gut, but I admire Hepburn a hellava lot. I have great respect for the way she maps things out. She'll lay into you if she thinks you're not doing the right thing." Katharine's resilient independent nature has earned her the admiration of today's young filmgoing generation and has caused her to be championed by the Women's Libbers. She eschews any association with such groups, continuing to go about her business as she always has.

Katharine Houghton Hepburn was born on November 18, 1907 in Hartford, Connecticut. She was a tomboy during her childhood and adored her brother Thomas. When she was twelve, she and Thomas had gone to New York to see a play, *A Connecticut Yankee in King Arthur's Court*. Both were intrigued with the scene in which a man does a trick with a noose around his neck. In their Hartford home the next day, Kate found her brother's body hanging in the attic. It was never determined whether the boy took his life deliberately, but Kate grieved for months. Her father was head urologist of the Hartford Hospital and her mother a noted suffragette and crusader for birth control. Kate was educated largely by private tutors and in 1924 enrolled in her mother's alma mater, Bryn Mawr.

She found that in order to pursue her childhood affinity for theatricals, she had to maintain her grades at Bryn Mawr. She managed to do so and participated in several drama productions at college. She was expelled on one occasion for smoking a cigarette. She was graduated in 1928 and joined a Baltimore stock company managed by Edwin H. Knopf (brother of the publisher and later a MGM producer). She studied drama with Frances Robinson-Duff, who had coached Cornelia Otis Skinner, Helen Hayes, and Ruth Chatterton, and studied dancing with Mordkin. Kate debuted with the Knopf company in 1928 in *The Czarina*, playing a lady-in-waiting. In the course of her theatrical apprenticeship on tour, she was fired from a production for blowing her lines, and finally made a Broadway name with *The Warrior's Husband*. That play opened on March 11, 1932. Kate played an athletic Amazon queen to sufficient critical and public interest that Hollywood offered her movie contracts. But snobbish Kate, now a stage veteran of four years, chastised Hollywood for taking notice of her only after she had appeared in a "leg show."

When RKO approached her, she asked what she considered a ridiculous salary, $1,500 weekly (she was currently earning $100 per week). To her surprise the studio agreed to the salary demands. On July 4, 1932, a skinny, freckled, snooty typhoon Kate hit Hollywood. For eight years it kept hitting her back and almost knocked her out of the business. To quote film historian Romano Tozzi, "Hepburn arrived in Hollywood determined to put the movie industry in its place. She immediately set out to break all the rules and was as unpleasant and uncooperative as possible. She fought senselessly with practically everyone, from top producer to lowest technician. She was insulting and abusive to the press and gave out ridiculous, inane interviews in which she deliberately distorted the facts of her personal life. She allowed herself to be photographed without makeup, in all her freckles, and, even worse, dressed hideously in mannish garb—sloppy slacks, sweaters, and men's trousers and suits. She hired a Rolls-Royce to take her to and from the studio. She read her mail sitting on the curb outside the RKO lot."

Hollywood had not seen her likes. Fortunately, director George Cukor, viewing her screen test in which she performed a scene from the play *Holiday*, saw in one tragic moment how she set a glass of water down, and detected a nobility he had been searching for in the actress to play Sydney, the daughter of John Barrymore in *A Bill of Divorcement* (1932). It was a much-coveted role and Norma Shearer had already put her bid in for the part. It proved to be an auspicious screen debut for Kate, and a star was born. Her early screen work was either very good or very bad. She overplayed in *Christopher Strong* (1933) but received an Oscar as the struggling young actress in *Morning Glory* (1933). Then she offered one of her best performances as Jo in *Little Women* (1933), which earned her the Cannes Film Festival Award.

Kate talked RKO into allowing her to return to Broadway for *The Lake* (1933). The show was a big flop and provided Dorothy Parker with the opportunity to make one of her best barbs. Of Kate's emoting she quipped, "She ran the gamut of emotions from A to B." Back at RKO Kate renegotiated for six pictures to be made within a two-year period at a salary of $300,000. Kate had now replaced Ann Harding as RKO's most prestigious property. The remaining RKO films, however, were not her best. Only *Alice Adams* (1935) and the John Ford–directed *Mary of Scotland* (1936) advanced her career. Again Kate renegotiated with the studio, this time for four pictures at an undisclosed amount. She proved a first-rate comedienne in *Stage Door* (1937), in which she spoke the much-imitated line, "The calla lilies are in bloom again." Her next picture, *Bringing Up Baby* (1938), was her first screwball comedy and also presented a much sexier and sleeker Kate than ever before on the screen. It was a zany costarrer with Cary Grant and a great boxoffice success. However, the exhibitors had become disillusioned by her recent string of films and chose this year to label her boxoffice poison.

When RKO offered her a B picture as her next assignment, she bought out her contract for $200,000. She went over to Columbia, the temporary home of many dethroned cinema queens, and made one picture, *Holiday* (1938), with Cukor as director and Grant again as her costar. It was one of the best performances of her career. Years later, critic Pauline Kael analyzed, "Her wit and nonconformity made ordinary heroines seem mushy, and her angular beauty made the round-faced ingenues look piggy and stupid. She was hard when they were soft in both head and body." After *Holiday*, Kate begged David O. Selznick for the role of Scarlett O'Hara in *Gone with the Wind*, exclaiming, "The part was practically written for me. I *am* Scarlett O'Hara." Selznick replied, "I just can't imagine Clark Gable chasing you for ten years." Kate walked out of Hollywood in the summer of 1938, returned to Hartford, and sat it out for a few months.

Then she returned to Broadway, with a share in the profits, as the star of Philip Barry's *The Philadelphia Story*. It opened on March 28, 1939, with Van Heflin, Joseph Cotten, and Shirley Booth in the cast, and emerged as a great success. In June 1940 Kate arrived back in Hollywood and sold the picture rights to Louis B. Mayer for $250,000, insisting that Cary Grant and James Stewart be her leading men. She even conceded star billing to Grant. The picture was directed by George Cukor with supposedly no retakes on scenes. Upon release it proved to be one of the all-time great sophisticated comedies. Kate received her third Academy Award nomination, but Hollywood was not about to forget her early misbehavior, and gave the Oscar she so richly deserved to another RKO star, Ginger Rogers, for her performance in *Kitty Foyle*.

339

With James Stewart in *The Philadelphia Story* (1940)

With Spencer Tracy in *Woman of the Year* (1942)

With Spencer Tracy in *Without Love* (1945)

With Edmund Gwenn in *Undercurrent* (1946)

Kate signed with MGM and became a prize contractee for Hollywood's largest studio. There was mutual respect between Kate and Louis B. Mayer. Her ten years at Metro were important both professionally and personally because of her association with Spencer Tracy. For the first time on the screen, while acting with Tracy, Hepburn became almost conventionally feminine. Seemingly disparate in personality and acting style, the two stars worked amazingly well and natural in tandem. Besides their professional rapport, they became fast and lasting friends. Their relationship was one of the oddest in film history, and not at all what the public has been indulgently led to believe. Their first joint vehicle was their best, *Woman of the Year* (1942), for which Kate garnered another Academy Award nomination. Occasionally during the decade, Kate would emote on camera without Tracy, such as playing the Chinese farmer's wife in *Dragon Seed* (1944), or the wife of psychotic Robert Taylor in *Undercurrent* (1946), or the pianist Clara Schuman in *Song of Love* (1947). If the soap opera prairie Western *The Sea of Grass* (1947) was minor Hepburn–Tracy, *Adam's Rib* (1949) found the duo in stellar comedy form.

In 1951 Metro loaned Kate to United Artists for one of her greatest roles, the spinster in *The African Queen*. She received her fifth Oscar nomination. Her costar, Humphrey Bogart, was a great friend and admirer of Kate and said, "She talks like a blue streak. We listened for the first couple of days when she hit Africa and then began asking ourselves, 'How affected can you be in the middle of Africa?' She used to say that everything was 'divine.' The God damn stinking natives were 'divine.' 'Oh, what a *divine* native!' she'd say. 'Oh, what a divine pile of manure!' You had to ask yourself, 'Is this really the dame or is this something left over from *Woman of the Year*?' She does pretty much as she God damn pleases. She came in lugging a full-length mirror and a flock of tooth brushes. She brushed her teeth all the time and habitually takes four or five baths a day. She talks at you as though you were a microphone. I guess she was nervous, though, and scared of John [Huston] and me. She lectured the hell out of us on temperance and the evils of drinking. She's actually kind of sweet and lovable, though, and she's absolutely honest and absolutely fair about her work. None of this late on the set or demanding closeups or any of that kind of thing. She doesn't give a damn how she looks. She doesn't have to be waited on either. I don't think she tries to be a character. I think she is one!"

After the effulgent comedy *Pat and Mike* (1952), made with Tracy, Kate finished her MGM contract and was off the screen for three years. She returned playing spinsters in both *Summertime* (1955) and *The Rainmaker* (1956), and also receiving Oscar nominations for both pictures. In 1957 she and Tracy costarred in *The Desk Set* at Twentieth Century-Fox. Working in the picture with them was Joan Blondell who later recalled, "It was a pleasure to watch her work with Spencer Tracy. They never kissed on the screen yet did some of the tenderest love scenes there have ever been. And they'd tease each other. He'd always call for another actress when they had finished a scene together, and she'd call him a 'dirty old man.' They had a lovely, divine relationship."

After receiving her eighth Academy Award nomination for playing the twisted mother figure in *Suddenly, Last Summer* (1959), Kate moved into semiretirement from the screen. The primary reason was to nurse Tracy who was in increasingly poor health. She did return to the movies in 1962 to give a marathon performance as the dope-addicted, flight-of-fantasy mother in *Long Day's Journey into Night*, proving she could be one of the best screen tragediennes when so inclined. Five more years of inactivity followed, until she and Tracy signed to star in Stanley Kramer's *Guess Who's Coming to Dinner* (1967), their ninth and final picture together. In the last moving sequence of the picture, Tracy talks about the upcoming marriage of his daughter to a black man, and turns to his screen wife (Hepburn), saying, "If what they feel for each other is even half what *we* felt, then that is everything." The tears in Hepburn's eyes were very real. Two weeks later Tracy was dead. The Academy voted Kate her second Academy Award, which was accepted by her good friend, George Cukor. Later she told the press, "I am enormously touched. It was delightful, a total surprise. I feel I have received a big, affectionate hug from my fellow workers. They don't usually give these things to old girls, you know."

The next year the Academy further surprised her, when she and Barbra Streisand tied for Best Actress, Kate for *The Lion in Winter* and the songstress-cum-cinema player for *Funny Girl*. After Tracy's death, Kate threw herself into her work with ferocity and undertook one of her most ambitious projects, the musical stage production, *Coco*, which cost $900,000 to mount. This musical biography of French dress designer Coco Chanel opened December 18, 1969. The show was big and splashy, but it was Kate's radiance, if not her talk–singing, which kept the play from being a bore. She will presumably star in the film version, when and if it is done. Thereafter, she was miscast in *The Madwoman of Chaillot* (1968) but proved again she was an adept dramatic player as Hecuba in *The Trojan Women* (1971). Both were arty productions that kept customers away from the boxoffice in droves. In 1972 she walked out of plans to film Graham Greene's *Travels with My Aunt* and a much younger Maggie Smith was substituted after which she signed to star in a cinemazation of Edward Albee's *A Delicate Balance*, to be made in London, and co-starring Paul Scofield, Kate Reid, Joseph Cotten and Lee Remick.

Kate has been married once, in 1928, to Philadelphia socialite, Ludlow Ogden Smith. Although they did not divorce until 1934, they lived together but a very short time, time enough for Kate to insist he legally change his name to Ogden. She did not wish to be the second Kate Smith.

Kate has warred with the press most of her life, saying, "My privacy is my own and I am the one to decide when it shall be invaded." Shortly before Tracy's death, she said, "Spencer Tracy is one of the few actors capable of total concentration. All based on truth. He and Laurette Taylor are the two best actors I've ever seen." About herself, she remains ambivalent, and when

With Spencer Tracy in *State of the Union* (1948)

With Spencer Tracy, William "Bill" Phillips, and Edgar Buchanan in *The Sea of Grass* (1947)

her longtime acquaintance, Garson Kanin, husband of Ruth Gordon, published a fatuous "intimate memoir" titled *Tracy and Hepburn* (1971), Kate, with good reason, took offense. Since 1934 she has lived in a town house on East 49th Street in Manhattan.

Her occasional statements to the press, while usually not very revealing, are colorful. "In the film business I was considered a freak. It's becoming stylish now to look upon me as though I had been lovely. We all say now I have a classic beauty with a delicately proportioned face. But at the beginning I was always caricatured as a horse. But artists—sculptors and painters—they thought me very good looking.

"If you survive in the film business you become a legend. I'm a legend because I've survived over a long period of time. I'm revered rather like an old building. Yet I still seem to be the master of my fate. I'm still paddling the boat myself, not sitting, being paddled by anybody. It may just be a canoe, but I'm paddling it.

"There comes a time in your life when people get very sweet to you. I don't mind people being sweet to me. In fact, I'm getting rather sweet back to them. But I'm a madly irritating person, and I irritated people for years. Anything definite is irritating—and stimulating. I think people are beginning to think I'm not going to be around much longer. And what do you know: They'll miss me like an old monument—like the Flatiron Building."

KATHARINE HEPBURN

A Bill of Divorcement (RKO, 1932)
Christopher Strong (RKO, 1933)
Morning Glory (RKO, 1933)
Little Women (RKO, 1933)
Spitfire (RKO, 1934)
The Little Minister (RKO, 1934)
Break of Hearts (RKO, 1935)
Alice Adams (RKO, 1935)
Sylvia Scarlett (RKO, 1935)
Mary of Scotland (RKO, 1936)
A Woman Rebels (RKO, 1936)
Quality Street (RKO, 1937)
Stage Door (RKO, 1937)
Bringing Up Baby (RKO, 1938)
Holiday (Columbia, 1938)
The Philadelphia Story (MGM, 1940)
Woman of the Year (MGM, 1942)
Keeper of the Flame (MGM, 1942)
Stage Door Canteen (UA, 1943)
Dragon Seed (MGM, 1944)
Without Love (MGM, 1945)

Undercurrent (MGM, 1946)
The Sea of Grass (MGM, 1947)
Song of Love (MGM, 1947)
State of the Union (MGM, 1948)
Adam's Rib (MGM, 1949)
The African Queen (UA, 1951)
Pat and Mike (MGM, 1952)
Summertime (UA, 1955)
The Rainmaker (Paramount, 1956)
The Iron Petticoat (MGM, 1956)
Desk Set (20th-Fox, 1957)
Suddenly, Last Summer (Columbia, 1959)
Long Day's Journey into Night (Embassy, 1962)
Guess Who's Coming to Dinner (Columbia, 1967)
The Lion in Winter (Embassy, 1968)
The Madwoman of Chaillot (WB-7 Arts, 1968)
The Trojan Women (Cinerama, 1971)
A Delicate Balance (American Film Theatre, 1973)

With Spencer Tracy and William Ching in *Pat and Mike* (1952)

With Alan Gifford, Bob Hope, and Paul Carpenter in *The Iron Petticoat* (1956)

Jean Hersholt

Even before Jean Hersholt became indelibly associated with the kindly Dr. Christian of radio and motion picture fame, he had become typed as the screen's leading physician. Few may recall that in the 1920s he had been one of Hollywood's leading versatile character stars until the coming of sound made this Scandinavian-accented actor much less in demand. It was at this point that MGM signed him to a featured player's contract, utilizing him like Lewis Stone, C. Aubrey Smith, C. Henry Gordon, and others of like ilk to add instant professionalism to a variety of 1930s pictures. That Hersholt's demeanor and build fit the then current stereotype of the physician proved yet another turning point in his career. He exemplified the good old-fashioned country doctor so perfectly that, even three decades after his last appearance as RKO's *Dr. Christian*, he is still remembered for this characterization.

Hersholt was born in Copenhagen, Denmark on July 12, 1886, the son of Henry and Claire Hersholt, both leading artists at the Royal Theatre. After high school Hersholt attended the Copenhagen Art School but at the same time developed an interest in the stage and took acting lessons. He became a student actor at the Dagmar Theatre where he served a two-and-a-half-year apprenticeship. He made his film debut in a short film for Louis Hellerstade at the Great Northern Studios. In 1914 he came to America and made his professional bow at the Pan American Pacific Exposition of San Francisco in 1914, where he not only acted but assisted in staging the shows. By this time he had wed Via Anderson, and a son Allan was born in December 1914.

The Hersholts moved to Los Angeles and the actor determined to break into film. He went to Thomas Ince's studio and was hired, not initially because of his stage experience, but because he had had the foresight to borrow a cutaway from a friend to bring to the "audition." Among his features at that studio were *The Disciple* (1915), *The Deserter* (1916), and *Bullets and Brown Eyes* (1916) with a young John Gilbert. When it was discovered that Hersholt was mortally afraid of horses he was dismissed from the studio's payroll, since cowboy-and-Indian pictures were one of the studio's principal outputs. After a few months of no work, he was signed by Universal and remained there through 1917. He undertook a variety of roles including Christ in *The Saintly*

Sinner (1917). For a time he shared a dressing room at Universal with fellow contract player Lon Chaney.

In 1919 Hersholt went to Portland, Oregon to join the new American Lifegraph Company as a film director–actor. His big acting break came when Mary Pickford selected him to play the murderer Ben Letts in her *Tess of the Storm Country* (1922) which in turn, led to such strong roles as Marcus Schouler, Zasu Pitts' frustrated suitor, in Erich von Stroheim's *Greed* (1925) at Metro-Goldwyn. That same year he played Belle Bennett's salesman friend in *Stella Dallas* at United Artists, although he was working mostly at Universal where he had signed a five-year contract at $2,000 weekly. Nevertheless, he returned to MGM to play Dr. Juttner the tutor of prince Ramon Novarro in Ernst Lubitsch's *The Student Prince of Heidelberg* (1927).

With the coming of sound Universal lost interest in Hersholt. After his contract expired he free-lanced, until his agent Jerry Mayer got him an MGM featured player contract at $500 weekly, $3,000 less than he had received at his Universal peak. After appearing in Ramon Novarro's *Daybreak* (1931), he was the farmer Ohlin who attempts to marry off his illegitimate daughter (Greta Garbo) to brutish Alan Hale in *Susan Lennox—Her Fall and Rise* (1931). *The Sin of Madelon Claudet* (1931) started him on his bespectacled physician image, as he was the doctor who knows, and eventually tells all the facts of Helen Hayes' indiscretion. He was in eleven 1932 releases, including *Grand Hotel* as the desk clerk overanxious about the condition of his expectant wife, and in *The Mask of Fu Manchu* in which he found himself being impaled between two spikestudded walls. He was Broadway producer Jo Stengel who is persuaded to offer drunken actor John Barrymore a stage job in *Dinner at Eight* (1933). Having worked well with Marie Dressler in *Emma* (1932), Hersholt was used as her employer in *The Late Christopher Bean* (1934). After the dedicated doctor's part in *Men in White*, (1934), he was seen as Professor Talma in Katharine Hepburn's *Break of Hearts* (1935) at RKO. Because of his craftsmanlike work and his genial nature, Hersholt had won the unswerving devotion of Louis B. Mayer who told him, "You and Lew Stone can stay here for the rest of your lives. If there's a part you don't like, tell me and you won't have to do it." Mayer remained true to his word.

Darryl F. Zanuck was preparing a film at Twentieth Century-Fox to feature the headline-grabbing Dionne quintuplets, with studio star Will Rogers cast in the lead as *The Country Doctor* (1936). But Rogers was killed in a plane crash and Hersholt, with his reputation as the screen's best physician, was requested for the assignment. Mayer reluctantly sold Hersholt's contract to Fox. Hersholt made two more films with the Dionne babies, *Reunion* (1936) and *Five of a Kind* (1938). He was cast as Sonja Henie's pop in *One in a Million* (1936) and also in *Happy Landing* (1938), joined with Shirley Temple in *Heidi* (1937), was a professor in Alice Faye's *Alexander's Ragtime Band* (1938), and even got involved with Peter Lorre's Puerto Rican escapades in *Mr. Moto in Danger Island* (1939). None of these Fox films taxed his acting abilities one iota.

Meanwhile, Hersholt had already begun playing Dr. Paul Christian on CBS radio (the weekly show lasted fourteen years), and in 1939 the first of the six RKO pictures, *Meet Dr. Christian*, about the kindly small town physician appeared. The programmer series concluded with *They Meet Again* in 1941. After a cameo in *Stage Door Canteen* (1943), Hersholt retired from the screen until he performed a role in *Dancing in the Dark* (1949) His part, however, was cut from the release print. In 1955 he played Viveca Lindfors' Swedish immigrant father in James Cagney's Western *Run for Cover*.

The following year, although he was already dying from cancer, he appeared in the opening installment of the *Dr. Christian* teleseries, starring MacDonald Carey as the big city doctor nephew of the original Dr. Christian.

Hersholt died on June 2, 1956. At the Forest Lawn funeral service, both James Stewart and Walter Pidgeon spoke eulogies. During his decades in Hollywood, Hersholt had founded the Motion Picture Relief Fund and served as its head for many years, as well as being a president of the Academy of Motion Pictures Arts And Sciences. He won three Oscars over the years, not for acting but for his general benevolence. One of the annual awards since has borne his name—the Jean Hersholt Humanitarian Award.

JEAN HERSHOLT

The Disciple (Triangle, 1915)
The Aryan (Triangle, 1916)
Hell's Hinges (Triangle, 1916)
The Deserter (Triangle, 1916)
Kinkaid—Gambler (Universal, 1916)
Bullets and Brown Eyes (Triangle, 1916)
Fighting for Love (Universal, 1917)
Love Aflame (Universal, 1917)
The Terror (Universal, 1917)
The Saintly Sinner (Universal, 1917)
The Show-Down (Universal, 1917)
Southern Justice (Universal, 1917)
The Greater Law (Universal, 1917)
Stormy Knights (Universal, 1917)
49-17 (Universal, 1917)
Princess Virtue (Universal, 1918)
Madame Spy (Universal, 1918)
In the Land of the Setting Sun (Multnomah Film, 1919)
The Servant in the House (FBO, 1920)
The Red Lane (Universal, 1920)
Merely Mary Ann (Fox, 1920)
The Four Horsemen of the Apocalypse (Metro, 1921)
A Certain Rich Man (Goldwyn, 1921)
The Deceiver (Arrow, 1921)
Golden Trail (Arrow, 1921)

With Madge Evans in *Are You Listening?* (1932)

Man of the Forest (W. W. Hodkinson, 1921)
The Servant in the House (FBO, 1921)
Golden Dreams (Goldwyn, 1922)
The Gray Dawn (W. W. Hodkinson, 1922)
Tess of the Storm Country (UA, 1922)
When Romance Rides (Goldwyn, 1922)
Heart's Haven (W. W. Hodkinson, 1922)
The Stranger's Banquet (Goldwyn, 1922)
Jazzmania (Tiffany, 1923)
Quicksand (Selznick, 1923)
Red Lights (Goldwyn, 1923)
Torment (FN, 1924)
The Woman on the Jury (Associated First National, 1924)
Sinners in Silk (Metro-Goldwyn, 1924)
Her Night of Romance (FN, 1924)
Cheap Kisses (FBO, 1924)
So Big (FN, 1924)
Greed (Metro-Goldwyn, 1925)
Fifth Avenue Models (Universal, 1925)
Dangerous Innocence (Universal, 1925)
A Woman's Faith (Universal, 1925)
If Marriage Fails (FBO, 1925)
Don Q, Son of Zorro (UA, 1925)
Stella Dallas (UA, 1925)
My Old Dutch (Universal, 1926)
Greater Glory (FN, 1926)
It Must Be Love (FN, 1926)
Flames (Associated Exchange, 1926)
The Old Soak (Universal, 1926)
The Wrong Mr. Wright (Universal, 1927)
The Student Prince in Old Heidelberg (MGM, 1927)
Alias the Deacon (Universal, 1928)
13 Washington Square (Universal, 1928)
The Secret Hour (Paramount, 1928)
The Battle of the Sexes (UA, 1928)
Jazz Mad (Universal, 1928)
Give and Take (Universal, 1928)
Abie's Irish Rose (Paramount, 1929)
The Younger Generation (Columbia, 1929)
Modern Love (Universal, 1929)
The Girl on the Barge (Universal, 1929)
Hell Harbor (UA, 1930)
Climax (Universal, 1930)
The Case of Sergeant Grischa (RKO, 1930)
Mamba (Tiffany, 1930)
Viennese Nights (WB, 1930)
The Cat Creeps (Universal, 1930)
East Is West (Universal, 1930)
Third Alarm (Tiffany, 1930)
Daybreak (MGM, 1931)
A Soldier's Plaything (WB, 1931)

Susan Lennox—Her Fall and Rise (MGM, 1931)
Phantom of Paris (MGM, 1931)
Transatlantic (Fox, 1931)
The Sin of Madelon Claudet (MGM, 1931)
Private Lives (MGM, 1931)
Beast of the City (MGM, 1932)
Emma (MGM, 1932)
Are You Listening? (MGM, 1932)
Grand Hotel (MGM, 1932)
Night Court (MGM, 1932)
New Morals for Old (MGM, 1932)
Skyscraper Souls (MGM, 1932)
Unashamed (MGM, 1932)
Hearts of Humanity (Majestic, 1932)
Flesh (MGM, 1932)
The Mask of Fu Manchu (MGM, 1932)
Crime of the Century (Paramount, 1933)
Dinner at Eight (MGM, 1933)
Song of the Eagle (Paramount, 1933)
The Late Christopher Bean (MGM, 1933)
Cat and the Fiddle (MGM, 1934)
Men in White (MGM, 1934)
The Fountain (RKO, 1934)
The Painted Veil (MGM, 1934)
Mark of the Vampire (MGM, 1935)
Murder in the Fleet (MGM, 1935)
Break of Hearts (RKO, 1935)
Tough Guy (MGM, 1936)
The Country Doctor (20th-Fox, 1936)
Sins of Man (20th-Fox, 1936)
His Brother's Wife (MGM, 1936)
Reunion (20th-Fox, 1936)
One in a Million (20th-Fox, 1936)
Seventh Heaven (20th-Fox, 1937)
Heidi (20th-Fox, 1937)
Happy Landing (20th-Fox, 1938)
Alexander's Ragtime Band (20th-Fox, 1938)
I'll Give a Million (20th-Fox, 1938)
Five of a Kind (20th-Fox, 1938)
Mr. Moto in Danger Island (20th-Fox, 1939)
Meet Dr. Christian (RKO, 1939)
Courageous Dr. Christian (RKO, 1940)
Dr. Christian Meets the Women (RKO, 1940)
Remedy for Riches (RKO, 1940)
Melody for Three (RKO, 1941)
They Meet Again (RKO, 1941)
Stage Door Canteen (UA, 1943)
Dancing in the Dark (20th-Fox, 1949)*
Run for Cover (Paramount, 1955)

*Scenes deleted from release print

John Hodiak

"I was an awfully homely kid, but even then I wanted to be an actor," John Hodiak once reflected. He was a toothy, square-jawed masculine man who diligently pursued his acting career. Unlike his three screen idols, Clark Gable, Robert Montgomery, and Gary Cooper, Hodiak lacked that one undefinable but salient requirement for film immortality—star quality. His solid physical stature made him perfect for several roles as a military man during the 1940s, most notably *A Bell for Adano* (1945), but he was equally effective as the worldly saloonkeeper who falls under the spell of a little waitress, Judy Garland, in *The Harvey Girls* (1946). For nine of his twelve years on the screen he was under contract to MGM, and three years after he left that studio, he was dead from a heart attack at the age of forty-one.

Hodiak was his real name and he was born on April 16, 1914 in Pittsburgh, Pennsylvania where his Ukrainian father and Polish mother had settled after emigrating to the United States. A few years later, they moved to Hamtramck, Michigan, the largest Polish settlement in the United States, where Hodiak's childhood ventures into church plays made him decide to be an actor. While his family used to laugh at him when he told them he would have his name in lights one day, they did encourage his interest. He also took music lessons, studying the clarinet, and was an excellent baseball player. He turned down an offer to sign with a minor league, as he was determined to pursue his dramatics.

He took a job as a stock clerk in the Chevrolet factory in Detroit and in the evenings did part-time work on WXYZ radio at no salary, playing in such series as *The Green Hornet*. Finally, he was made a regular member of that station's stock company at $35 a week, ten dollars less than he was making in the factory. With a little experience under his belt, he moved to Chicago where he was soon earning $110 a week on radio. In 1939 he auditioned for the radio part of *Li'l Abner:* "I spent hours trying to create a voice—a sort of portrait of that naive, gangling hunk of hillbilly muscle." His efforts paid off and he got the part, and for the next three years he worked steadily in such audio series as *The Story of Mary Marlin, Ma Perkins,* and *Wings of Destiny*.

Marvin Schenck, an MGM talent scout, heard Hodiak, sent him to New York for a screen test, and signed him to a long term contract with that studio. Louis B. Mayer suggested they change his surname, but Hodiak refused, saying: "I look like a guy named Hodiak." At one point he or Peter Lawford were considered to replace the injured Van Johnson in *A Guy Named Joe* (1943), but that film's star Spencer Tracy insisted that the director shoot around Johnson's part until that actor recovered. Hodiak did have a walkon in Frank Morgan's *A Stranger in Town* (1943), a factory clerk in *Swing Shift Maisie* (1943), and after a small role in *Song of Russia* (1943), he was loaned to Twentieth Century-Fox to play the seaman Communist in Alfred Hitchcock's wartime allegory, *Lifeboat* (1944). That picture starred the indomitable Talullah Bankhead, and Hodiak called her a "trouper" and said working with her was an "education."

MGM brought him back to Culver City to play Lana Turner's wartime husband in *Marriage is a Private Affair* (1944), and he was one of the few males who did not succumb offscreen to the charms of that busy blonde. He was loaned out to Fox again, this time for two pictures. One was *Sunday Dinner for a Soldier* (1944), World War II rural Americana at its stickiest, with Charles Winninger as "Grandfeathers" and Anne Baxter as the real head of the houseboat home near Tarpon Springs, Florida. One overenthusiastic advertisement for Lloyd Bacon's film read: "Their eyes met! Their lips questioned! Their arms answered!" That pap was more true of the soon-budding offscreen romance of Hodiak and Baxter, who married two years later.

The other Fox picture was one of his most popular roles, that of the American Major Joppolo, who falls for a blonde Italian girl named Tina, unconvincingly played by Gene Tierney, in the cinema realization of John Hersey's Pulitzer Prize-winning novel, *A Bell for Adano*. The N.Y. *Times* called Hodiak: "firm and unquestionably sincere, with just the right shade of emotion in his response to human problems."

For Hodiak 1946 and 1947 were not good years professionally. Many of MGM's stellar male stars—Clark Gable, Robert Taylor, *et al.*—had returned from the war, and the better scripts were handed to them instead. (Hodiak had not been accepted for military service due to hypertension.) Nevertheless he was right in the part of the New Mexico saloonkeeper whom Judy Garland chases out of Angela Lansbury's arms in *The Harvey Girls,* but the musical was all Garland and little else, particularly for a straight man.

Hodiak and Baxter were wed on July 7, 1946 and MGM borrowed her from Twentieth Century-Fox to play with Hodiak, in support of Clark Gable and Lana Turner in *Homecoming* (1948). He was in support of Gable again in *Command Decision* (1949), the story of Allied bomber efforts to destroy German production of a new, superior jet fighter. Hodiak was the colonel who is killed in the successful raid. The remaining three years of his MGM contract found him largely in supporting roles in pictures that were vehicles for the studio's big boxoffice males. He was an FBI agent in Spencer Tracy's *Malaya* (1950), was the treasury agent in a dubious Hedy Lamarr film, *A Lady Without Passport* (1950), was a law enforcer in *People Against O'Hara* (1951) with Tracy again, and played an Indian in *Across the Wide Missouri* (1951), starring his idol, Gable. His last studio assignment for the studio was in *The Sellout* (1951), a newspaper yarn starring Walter Pidgeon.

Upon free-lancing, Hodiak's screen success further declined. Among other nonfulfilling roles, he was the Indian rebel in *Conquest of Cochise* (1953). His marriage to Anne Baxter ended in divorce on January 27, 1953. Their daughter, Katrina Baxter Hodiak, was born on July 7, 1951. Baxter said: "I loved him very deeply, but two careers are murder, and two in the same profession is double murder." Hodiak appeared in the New York theatre production of *The Chase* (1952) as the sheriff, and later received excellent notices as Lt. Maryk in *The Caine Mutiny Court Martial* on Broadway. His last good film role was as the district attorney in Glenn Ford's *Trial* (1955) at MGM. On October 16, 1955, *The Loretta Young Show* telecast a half-hour sequence he had made for that series, and three days later, he died of a coronary thrombosis while shaving in his home in Tarzana, California, where he was living with his parents. His ex-wife said it was "very, very sad." She added: "He suffered from a lack of confidence and never realized how damned good an actor he really was."

JOHN HODIAK

A Stranger in Town (MGM, 1943)
Swing Shift Maisie (MGM, 1943)
I Dood It (MGM, 1943)
Song of Russia (MGM, 1943)
Maisie Goes to Reno (MGM, 1944)
Marriage Is a Private Affair (MGM, 1944)
Lifeboat (20th-Fox, 1944)
Sunday Dinner for a Soldier (20th-Fox, 1944)
A Bell for Adano (20th-Fox, 1945)
The Harvey Girls (MGM, 1946)
Somewhere in the Night (20th-Fox, 1946)
Two Smart People (MGM, 1946)
The Arnelo Affair (MGM, 1947)
Desert Fury (Paramount, 1947)
Love from a Stranger (Eagle–Lion, 1947)
Homecoming (MGM, 1948)
Command Decision (MGM, 1948)

The Bribe (MGM, 1949)
Battleground (MGM, 1949)
Malaya (MGM, 1949)
Ambush (MGM, 1949)
A Lady without Passport (MGM, 1950)
The Miniver Story (MGM, 1950)
Night unto Morning (MGM, 1951)
The People against O'Hara (MGM, 1951)
Across the Wide Missouri (MGM, 1951)
The Sellout (MGM, 1951)
Battle Zone (AA, 1952)
Mission over Korea (Columbia, 1953)
Conquest of Cochise (Columbia, 1953)
Ambush at Tomahawk Gap (Columbia, 1953)
Dragonfly Squadron (AA, 1954)
Trial (MGM, 1955)
On the Threshold of Space (20th-Fox, 1956)

With Spencer Tracy and James Stewart in *Malaya* (1949)

With Carl Milletaire in *A Lady Without Passport* (1950)

Fay Holden

One of Louis B. Mayer's favorite fantasized images was of the middle-class WASP household and its apple-pie American mother. He saw to it that MGM churned out an appropriate number of films built around this human fortress of the homefront and to do so, he needed an assortment of varied actresses to fill the bill. Fay Bainter, Mary Astor, and Spring Byington generally graced the class productions as the "mom," but their personalities were too strong to handle the warm, solid mother to be featured in the studio's programmer crop of Americana, which turned out to be the *Andy Hardy* series. Fay Holden came along at the right moment and for over eight years filled the niche as the nation's Number One matronly screen mom. She became Mrs. Judge Hardy of Carvel, America, the mother of Mickey "Andy Hardy" Rooney.

She was born Fay Hammerton in Birmingham, England, August 20, 1895, and began her stage career at the age of nine by joining a dance troupe. The following year she won her first dramatic part and adopted the professional name of Gaby Fay. In her adult years, she gravitated to sophisticated society roles and in 1927 came to America with Mrs. Pat Campbell for a tour of *The Adventurous Age*, which flopped. She stayed in New York to join Leslie Howard in *Elizabeth Steps Out*, and then returned to England. It was at the persuasion of her actor brother-in-law Andy Clyde (she had married actor–producer–manager David Clyde in 1914) that they came to Hollywood in 1934.

Fay accepted character roles at the Pasadena Playhouse and the part of an English governess in *Hollywood Holiday* landed her a movie part in *I Married a Doctor* (1936). In a later film that year, Joe E. Brown's *Polo Joe* (1936), in which she played Aunt Minnie, she was typecast on screen as the warm-hearted relative. It was Paramount's *Double or Nothing* (1937) which proved the turning point in her career. Although the role of Mary Carlisle's mother called for her to be disdainful and skeptical, it convinced MGM that she was a good choice to play "Ma" Hardy to Lewis Stone's Judge Hardy in the Andy Hardy series, now that Spring Byington and Lionel Barrymore had been removed from the lineup after *A Family Affair* (1937).

Beginning with *You're Only Young Once* (1938) through *Love Laughs at*

Andy Hardy (1946), Fay functioned in fourteen of the series entries. She never really came out of the detailed background, since her function was to exemplify the concept that the ideal American mother is a well-adjusted part of the woodwork, content just to keep the household running smoothly. Occasionally she would hypothesize on the solution of family problems with spinster Aunt Milly (Sara Haden), but it was always Judge Hardy (Lewis Stone) who did the actual decision making. Every problem for her would vanish at the dining table just watching Rooney gobble up his dinner. And should he ask for a second wedge of her home-baked pie, she was in seventh heaven.

Fay was one actress who claimed she thoroughly enjoyed the rut of typecasting and happily acknowledged: "It's odd how a role can actually become a part of one's life." There were assorted other mother roles at MGM along the way, but the Mickey Rooney pictures became her *raison d'être* at the studio, and when the series folded in 1946 she left the lot. But she still continued to essay the same stock in trade, as in Universal's color Western *Canyon Passage* (1946), in which she was fiery Susan Hayward's mom. She returned to MGM in 1950 to be Elizabeth Taylor's mother in *The Big Hangover*. Throughout the 1950s she was an infrequent performer on television, appearing in such dramatic anthology shows as *Ford Theatre's Mr. Kagle and the Baby Sitter* (1956) with Charles Coburn. She went into retirement until 1958 when Rooney joined with MGM in an over-the-hill attempt to resurrect the *Hardy* series in *Andy Hardy Comes Home* (1958). Looking remarkably much as she did twenty years before, she was again Mrs. Hardy, but this time a widow, since Lewis Stone had passed away.

Now in her late seventies, Fay lives alone in her San Fernando Valley home, her husband having died in 1945. She spends most of her time puttering about the garden and doing charity work.

FAY HOLDEN

I Married a Doctor (FN, 1936)
The White Angel (FN, 1936)
Wives Never Know (Paramount, 1936)
Polo Joe (WB, 1936)
Bulldog Drummond Escapes (Paramount, 1937)
Internes Can't Take Money (Paramount, 1937)
King of Gamblers (Paramount, 1937)
Double or Nothing (Paramount, 1937)
Exclusive (Paramount, 1937)
You're Only Young Once (MGM, 1938)
Judge Hardy's Children (MGM, 1938)
Love Is a Headache (MGM, 1938)
Battle of Broadway (20th-Fox, 1938)
Hold That Kiss (MGM, 1938)

Test Pilot (MGM, 1938)
Love Finds Andy Hardy (MGM, 1938)
Out West with the Hardys (MGM, 1938)
Sweethearts (MGM, 1938)
Sergeant Madden (MGM, 1939)
The Hardys Ride High (MGM, 1939)
Andy Hardy Gets Spring Fever (MGM, 1939)
Judge Hardy and Son (MGM, 1939)
Andy Hardy Meets Debutante (MGM, 1940)
Bitter Sweet (MGM, 1940)
Ziegfeld Girl (MGM, 1941)
Andy Hardy's Private Secretary (MGM, 1941)
Washington Melodrama (MGM, 1941)
I'll Wait for You (MGM, 1941)
Blossoms in the Dust (MGM, 1941)

With Lewis Stone, Cecilia Parker, and Mickey Rooney in *The Hardys Ride High* (1939)

Lena Horne

Lena Horne, a woman of rare exotic beauty and finely honed vocalizing talent, has long been held up as an example of how 1940s Hollywood, and MGM in particular, could stifle a potential screen star. She was the first black performer to sign a long-term screen contract with a major studio, but in 1941 the movie industry was still afraid to buck the racial issue for fear of commercial recriminations in the South. Thus Lena, who refused to essay onscreen domestics, was caught in a professional vacuum that found her guest appearing in assorted Metro musicals, usually in solo spots which could be easily excised when shown in areas where her presence might offend. Her only solid characterizations were in two all-black musical films.

Lena Calhoun Horne was born in Brooklyn, N. Y. on June 30, 1917. When she was four her father left home, which made money in her household even less plentiful. Her mother returned to a stage career, and Lena was shipped around the Eastern seaboard and the Midwest, boarding with one family after another. She recalls the mood of those days: "It was a mood of loneliness and self-protectiveness, broken occasionally by the hope that somehow I might finally be allowed to settle down in one place permanently —and occasionally, by some act of kindness or cruelty that stands out from the gray tones of the background."

Through her mother, Lena developed an interest in a show business career. She made her professional debut as a chorus girl at the Cotton Club in Harlem, a joint then run by hoods. ("My mother didn't want me in that atmosphere, and she'd come with me every night—or my stepfather. One night they pushed his head in the toilet because they didn't want him coming around.") Next she was a dancer with Noble Sissle's orchestra and then had a short run in the Broadway revue, *Blackbirds of 1939*, followed by a vocalist's stint with Charlie Barnett's band. By this time she had appeared in an all-black feature, *The Duke Is Tops* (1938), filmed in New York, and had married Lewis Jones. They had two children, Gail and Terry, and the couple later were divorced.

After performing at Cafe Society Downtown in Greenwich Village, Lena went to Hollywood where she appeared at the Little Troc Club. MGM musical supervisor Roger Edens heard her and asked her to audition for

Arthur Freed at Metro. Freed was impressed and agreed to sign Lena to a contract. A few days later Lena returned to Freed's office with her father, who had come back into her life, and the agents. Says Lena: "I know those MGM executives had had to deal with the parents of child stars at the start of their careers, but I'm sure this was the first time a grown Negro woman ever arrived with a handsome, articulate, and unimpressed father who proceeded to show them the many disadvantages, spiritually and emotionally, that his daughter might suffer should she be foolish enough to sign with them. It was marvelous for me to watch them listening to him. Since neither one of us believed in the damn thing, we must have been infuriating."

Metro planned to feature Lena in *Cabin in the Sky*, an all-black Broadway musical they had just acquired. Since that film was not yet set for production, Lena was tested for the role of Jeanette MacDonald's flippant maid in *Cairo* (1941), but the part was given to Ethel Waters who seemed much more the dark-skinned domestic type.

Panama Hattie (1942) established the mold for Lena at MGM. She was briefly featured in a specialty number—billed as herself—singing the rhumba rhythm song, "The Spring." By now the studio had devised a special pancake makeup to even further lighten her skin tones. Her next film, *Cabin in the Sky* (1943), was her best screen assignment. She was the chanteuse sent by the devil to woo Eddie "Rochester" Anderson away from his homey wife, Ethel Waters. Lena vibrated as the shameless seductress and gave a strong interpretation to "Honey in the Honeycomb." Despite her heady performance, MGM did not see fit to give Lena further stellar assignments. She was loaned to Twentieth Century-Fox for their all-black *Stormy Weather* (1943), a musical revue loosely built around the career of Bill "Bojangles" Robinson. In *Thousands Cheer* (1943) Lena was sandwiched into the big army camp show, singing "Honeysuckle Rose." She teamed with pianist–singer Hazel Scott in a guest spot in Red Skelton's *I Dood It* (1943), offering a hot rendition of "Jericho." In *Swing Fever* (1943) Lena sang "You're So Indifferent." MGM was gracious enough to give her an onscreen character name, Fernway De La Fer, in *Broadway Rhythm* (1944), and she did "Brazilian Boogie" and "Somebody Loves Me."

Two Girls and a Sailor (1944) found Lena "by herself" (as the casting list read) to do "Paper Doll." In *Ziegfeld Follies* (1946) she performed "Love" in a West Indies joint setting. It was in the *Show Boat* sequence of *Till the Clouds Roll By* (1946) that she essayed Julie, singing "Why Was I Born?" and proving she should have had the Ava Gardner part in the studio's 1951 picturization of that musical. After a spot in *Words and Music* (1948), performing "Where or When" and "The Lady Is a Tramp," she wrapped up her MGM contract with a brief appearance in *Duchess Of Idaho* (1950), singing "Baby, Come out of the Clouds."

Of her relatively unproductive MGM days, Lena has said, "I was always told to remember I was the first of my race to be given a chance in the movies, and I had to be careful not to step out of line, not to make a fuss. It was all a lie. The only thing that wasn't a lie was that I did make money; if I didn't, they wouldn't have kept me."

In 1948 Lena wed Caucasian Lennie Hayton, MGM's chief music director from the 1940s on. ("It wasn't easy to make the decision to marry. My father wouldn't speak to me for three years because I had married a white man.") As a favor to Hayton, Lena performed the specialty number "If You Can Dream" in Metro's *Meet Me in Las Vegas* (1956).

During the early 1950s Lena found herself blacklisted in the entertainment field because of her long-standing friendship with Communist sympathizer Paul Robeson. But she persevered and retained her status as a chic chanteuse of the nightclub circuit. Her LP albums all contained the distinctive Lena sound. In 1957 she made an impressive Broadway splash in the musical *Jamaica* with Ricardo Montalban as her costar. She had her *Nine O'Clock Revue* on Broadway in the early 1960s and made occasional guest appearances on television, capped by a video special with Harry Belafonte in the late 1960s. There was much publicity when she returned to Hollywood to essay a dramatic role in the Richard Widmark Western, *Death of a Gunfighter* (1969). She played his black companion, although race was tactfully left untouched in the screenplay.

Since her biography *Lena* appeared in 1965, the public has become conscious of her difficult role in attempting to maintain her integrity as a performer while trying to advance the cause of her race, and still having to accept the criticisms of many black groups who call her an Uncle Tom. In the early 1970s Lena lost her father, her husband, and her son Terry—all within the course of a year.

Although the Lena of today is devoting herself primarily to racial causes, she was among the celebrities who appeared at the "Fabulous Forties" night at Manhattan's Roseland in June 1972. Looking twenty years younger than her real age, she mingled with such fellow ex-MGM-ites as Lana Turner, and sang a few tunes. As she recently stated, "In my early days I was a sepia Hedy Lamarr. Now I'm black and a woman, singing my own way."

LENA HORNE

The Duke Is Tops (Popkin, 1938)
Panama Hattie (MGM, 1942)
Cabin in the Sky (MGM, 1943)
Stormy Weather (20th-Fox, 1943)
I Dood It (MGM, 1943)
Thousands Cheer (MGM, 1943)
Swing Fever (MGM, 1943)
Broadway Rhythm (MGM, 1944)

Two Girls and a Sailor (MGM, 1944)
Ziegfeld Follies (MGM, 1946)
Till the Clouds Roll By (MGM, 1946)
Words and Music (MGM, 1948)
Duchess of Idaho (MGM, 1950)
Meet Me in Las Vegas (MGM, 1956)
Death of a Gunfighter (Universal, 1969)

In *Broadway Rhythm* (1944)

Marsha Hunt

When Marsha Hunt made her Broadway debut in *Joy to the World* in 1948, one theatre critic said her intelligent beauty possessed a charm that had been intangible in her screen work. At that point Marsha was midway in her prodigious screen career (over sixty films) in which stardom had somehow illuded her. For seven of those Hollywood years, 1939–1945, she was under MGM contract. That studio cast her either as leads in B pictures or in supporting roles in top budget productions. While her versatility caused her to be labeled Hollywood's "youngest character actress," the camera never made tangible that mysterious characteristic called star quality.

Marsha was born Marcia Virginia Hunt in Chicago on October 17, 1917. Her father was an attorney and her mother was a vocal coach with a modest reputation in concert and opera circles. When the Hunts moved to New York City, Marsha attended Horace Mann High School and studied at the Theodore Irving School of Dramatics. Later she became a John Robert Powers model. When she was seventeen she visited friends in California and her reputation as a model earned her a screen test and a motion picture contract with Paramount Pictures.

She made her debut at that studio in a small assignment in *The Virginia Judge* (1935). She learned the rudiments of facile screen acting while working with the Paramount Actors Training School, but all her pictures, from a loanout to Twentieth Century-Fox for Jane Withers' *Gentle Julia* (1936) to RKO's *Annapolis Salute* (1937) in which she was the gal pursued by two midshipmen, James Ellison and Van Heflin, were strictly second-rate.

In 1939 she signed with MGM where she was notably one of the studios best supporting actresses. She was the perennial bridesmaid in the amusing *These Glamour Girls* (1939) starring Lana Turner, the young widow in Ann Sothern's *Joe and Ethel Turp Call on the President* (1939), and Mary Boland's bespectacled daughter in *Pride and Prejudice*. Perhaps her finest MGM work was in the lushly mounted woman's picture *Blossoms in the Dust* (1941), in which she played a foundling who commits suicide. In *The Penalty* (1941) she was Lionel Barrymore's granddaughter who falls in love with farmer Robert Sterling. Among her few starring parts was her role as a lab assistant to scientist Van Heflin in *Kid Glove Killer* (1942) and as the wife of superpatriot Robert Young in *Joe Smith, American* (1942). MGM kept her busy in their chin-up wartime efforts, the best of which was as the fiancée of James Craig in *The Human Comedy* (1943). She played one of the nurses on wartorn Bataan in *Cry Havoc* (1943), and was opposite Craig again in the Margaret O'Brien vehicle *Lost Angel* (1943). Her last MGM assignment had her as the girl who carries on a romance via correspondence with soldier Hume Cronyn in *A Letter for Evie* (1945), but that programmer was just a pale imitation of the Broadway hit *Dear Ruth*. Stuck in a professional wasteland like other ex-MGM contractees Ruth Hussey, Rita Johnson, and Ann Richards, Marsha had no choice but to leave MGM. For whatever consolation it provided, Marsha had amassed a thin but steady following among the filmgoing public, which placed her a cut above other contemporary MGM players such as Diana Lewis, Helen Gilbert, or Pamela Blake.

Marsha had married Jerry Hopper, a Paramount film editor and cousin of actress Glenda Farrell, on November 23, 1938. They divorced in 1943, and on February 10, 1946, she married screen writer Robert Presnell, Jr. Presnell was the son of Robert Presnell, Sr., who had written the scripts for such features as *Bureau of Missing Persons, My Man Godfrey*, and *Meet John Doe*. Following in his father's footsteps, Presnell has written the scripts for many television shows and such films as *Legend of the Lost* and *Let No Man Write My Epitaph*. Marsha was off the screen for a year after her marriage, during which time she gave birth to a daughter who died on July 2, 1947, only one day old.

Marsha returned to films playing the slinky vamp in *Smash-Up* (1947) and gave a beautiful performance as the mother of the musical prodigy in *Carnegie Hall* (1947). Her stage debut was opposite Alfred Drake in *Joy to the World* (1948), directed by Jules Dassin, and while in New York played a cameo in the Manhattan-lensed *Jigsaw* (1949). Her stage work includes Shaw's *The Devil's Disciple* (1950) with Maurice Evans, Christopher Fry's *The Lady's Not for Burning* (1952) with Vincent Price, *Affairs of State, The Cocktail Party, Tunnel of Love* with Johnny Carson, *The King and I*, and *Major Barbara*. After debuting on television as Viola in *Twelfth Night*, she played the mother of Patty McCormack in the mid-1950s video series, *Peck's Bad Girl*, and has made numerous guest appearances on *Gunsmoke, The Breaking Point* (particularly fine as the mother in the 1963 episode, *And James Was a Very Small Snail*), *The Defenders, Laramie*, and *My Three Sons*. In 1970 she played a trial judge on an *Ironside* segment and appeared as a psychiatrist on the telefeature *Jigsaw* (1972).

Marsha was among those exiled from Hollywood film making during the Red scare of the early 1950s and seldom was able to obtain film work. She was Natalie Wood's mother in *Bombers B-52* (1957) and the mother in *Blue Denim* (1959). After appearing in Jeff Chandler's Western *The Plunderers* (1960) it was eleven years before she made another picture. Former blacklisted Hollywood scenarist Dalton Trumbo hired Marsha to play Timothy Bottoms' small town mother in *Johnny Got His Gun* (1971). Her screen time was minimal.

The Marsha of today says her recreations are people and peace. She has been actively involved in civil rights, the United Nations, the March of Dimes, the Red Cross, Cerebral Palsy, and Freedom from Hunger, and she has a wall in her home devoted to scrolls and awards for her efforts. Her political views are "liberal," and in 1962, while taking part in a symposium, The Extreme Right Threat to Democracy, in Los Angeles, the homes of two ministers who participated in the program were bombed. Marsha's home was put under guard as a result. The organization criticized extreme right wing politics and when questioned by reporters about the bombing, Marsha said, "it was probably some poor soul who imagines he loves America."

MARSHA HUNT

The Virginia Judge (Paramount, 1935)
The Accusing Finger (Paramount, 1936)
Gentle Julia (20th-Fox, 1936)
Desert Gold (Paramount, 1936)
Arizona Raiders (Paramount, 1936)
Hollywood Boulevard (Paramount, 1936)
Easy to Take (Paramount, 1936)
College Holiday (Paramount, 1936)
Murder Goes to College (Paramount, 1937)
Easy Living (Paramount, 1937)
Thunder Trail (Paramount, 1937)
Born to the West (Paramount, 1937)
Annapolis Salute (RKO, 1937)
The Long Shot (Grand National, 1938)
Come on, Leathernecks (Republic, 1938)
The Hardys Ride High (MGM, 1939)
The Star Reporter (Monogram, 1939)
These Glamour Girls (MGM, 1939)
Joe and Ethel Turp Call on the President (MGM, 1939)
Winter Carnival (UA, 1939)
Pride and Prejudice (MGM, 1940)
Flight Command (MGM, 1940)
Irene (RKO, 1940)
Woman in Hiding (Universal, 1940)
Ellery Queen, Master Detective (Columbia, 1940)
Blossoms in the Dust (MGM, 1941)
I'll Wait for You (MGM, 1941)
The Trial of Mary Dugan (MGM, 1941)
The Penalty (MGM, 1941)
Cheers for Miss Bishop (UA, 1941)

Unholy Partners (MGM, 1941)
Kid Glove Killer (MGM, 1942)
Joe Smith, American (MGM, 1942)
The Affairs of Martha (MGM, 1942)
Panama Hattie (MGM, 1942)
Seven Sweethearts (MGM, 1942)
Thousands Cheer (MGM, 1943)
Pilot No. 5 (MGM, 1943)
The Human Comedy (MGM, 1943)
Cry Havoc (MGM, 1943)
Lost Angel (MGM, 1943)
Bride by Mistake (RKO, 1944)
None Shall Escape (Columbia, 1944)
Music for Millions (MGM, 1944)
Valley of Decision (MGM, 1945)
A Letter for Evie (MGM, 1945)
Smash-Up (Universal, 1947)
Carnegie Hall (UA, 1947)
The Inside Story (Republic, 1948)
Raw Deal (Eagle–Lion, 1948)
Jigsaw (UA, 1949)
Take One False Step (Universal, 1949)
Mary Ryan, Detective (Columbia, 1950)
Actors and Sin (UA, 1952)
The Happy Time (Columbia, 1952)
Diplomatic Passport (Eros, 1954)
No Place to Hide (AA, 1956)
Bombers B-52 (WB, 1957)
Back from the Dead (20th-Fox, 1957)
Blue Denim (20th-Fox, 1959)
The Plunderers (AA, 1960)
Johnny Got His Gun (Cinemation, 1971)

With Edward G. Robinson and Laraine Day in *Unholy Partners* (1941)

Ruth Hussey

After viewing Ruth Hussey as Robert Taylor's wife in *Flight Command* (1940), the N. Y. *Times* complimented the lovely actress' portrayal but took MGM to task for making her look too much like studio star Myrna Loy. This observation has been voiced by others and it seems a fact that MGM failed to individualize this intelligent player's screen image, because she *did* resemble Loy at times. A quick look at the kind of roles they assigned her reveals a succession of ladylike, nice roles, and wife roles. They were not as good as the ones Loy played, neither as sophisticated nor as witty but simply respectable, enduring, supportive portrayals. True, she was humorous as the photographer in *The Philadelphia Story* (1940) and earned a best supporting actress Oscar nomination, but that was an exception. It was largely in her stage work after she left MGM that Ruth's talents as an actress were realized. By that time she was more interested in being a wife and a mother, and her stage career was only an afterthought.

Ruth Carol O'Rourke was born in Providence, Rhode Island on October 30, 1914 (or 1915), the daughter of a jewelry firm owner. She received her degree in philosophy from Pembroke Women's College at Brown University. Following her graduation, she attended the University of Michigan, studying at the School of Drama to perfect her diction in preparation for a theatre career. Her first job was as a radio fashion commentator on Providence's KPRO station at $13.50 a week. She then got work in New York as a Powers model and landed a part in the touring production of *The Old Maid*. A few minor stage roles followed, after which she auditioned for and was accepted as Kay, the heroine, in a touring company of Sidney Kingsley's *Dead End*.

That tour took her to Los Angeles where MGM's ubiquitous talent scout Billy Grady got her a screen test and a five-year contract. The studio objected to her professional name of Hussey (her mother's maiden name). The executives thought it did not sound ladylike, but she assured them that it was a perfectly acceptable name back East. She made her screen debut in a walkon appearance in *The Big City* (1937) which starred Spencer Tracy and Luise Rainer. In *Judge Hardy's Children* (1938) she was Margaret Bee, one of that series' perennial youths, and in *Marie Antoinette* (1938) she functioned briefly

366

as Mme. LePolignac. She was loaned to Twentieth Century-Fox for a ninth-billed role in the Michael Whalen–Gloria Stuart programmer *Time Out for Murder* (1938), and in *Spring Madness* (1938) was elevated to a top supporting role, but the fluff was focused on the collegiate romance of Lew Ayres and Maureen O'Sullivan. In *Honolulu* (1939) she was buried at the bottom of the cast list with a three-minute bit as Robert Young's forgiving lady in the film-within-the-film entitled *Women Who Say No*.

After this rash of small roles, Ruth was ready to leave the studio. "I was the five-minute star because of the size of my roles." Finally after going through a second test, this time with emphasis on her sex appeal, she began to receive larger screen assignments. In *Within the Law* (1939), one of the several versions of Bayard Veiller's play, she was the shop girl wrongly imprisoned who later studies law and weds the son of the man who sent her to jail. In *Maisie* (1939) she lived up to her professional surname, being the erring wife of Westerner Ian Hunter who would not mind seeing ranch foreman Robert Young blamed for Hunter's suicide. She was Miss Watts in *The Women* (1939) and dropped down to ninth billing in *Another Thin Man* (1939). She was Edward G. Robinson's woman in *Blackmail* (1939), Robert Young's fianceé in *Northwest Passage* (1940), and a Long Island socialite in *Susan and God* (1940) with Joan Crawford.

After this siege of professional seesawing, she was handed the role of the magazine photographer and sidekick of James Stewart in *The Philadelphia Story* (a role played on the stage by Shirley Booth and in the later musical film remake *High Society* [1956] by Celeste Holm.) Having earned an Academy Award nomination, MGM's reward to her was a starring role, albeit a minor one, opposite Robert Taylor in *Flight Command*. After this status elevation, Ruth was still level-headed enough to realize: "I'll probably never be a star, but it's an interesting way to earn a living and I like it." She was loaned to Columbia for *Our Wife* (1941), a marital comedy with Melvyn Douglas, and then was Robert Young's consoling wife in *H. M. Pulham, Esq.* (1941). In the latter picture some critics thought her so beautiful that they felt Young's yearning for Hedy Lamarr was unjustified.

After playing Mrs. Andrew Johnson in *Tennessee Johnson* (1942) with Van Heflin, Ruth's MGM contract expired and she departed from the Culver City lot. She would later say: "Hollywood treated me well. I learned a lot about acting and I even got a mink coat." On August 2nd of that year she married C. Robert Longenecker, then a radio executive and now one of Hollywood's most successful artists, managers, and her career soon began to take second place to her marriage. She played a momentarily erring wife in RKO's *Tender Comrade* (1943), starring Ginger Rogers; was the victim's wife in Republic's *I, Jane Doe* (1948); and played F. Scott Fitzgerald's Jordan Baker in Paramount's rendition of *The Great Gatsby* (1949) with Alan Ladd.

By this time she was also appearing in the theatre. In 1945 she had starred with Ralph Bellamy in *State of the Union* to excellent reviews and in June 1949, she took over Madeleine Carroll's role of the romantic congresswoman in Broadway's *Goodbye, My Fancy*. Then there was a tour of *The Royal Family* in 1951. She earned an Emmy nomination for her television portrayal of *Craig's Wife* (1955) and that same year played the Norma Shearer role in the video version of *The Women*. Her last feature film part to date was as Bob Hope's wife in *The Facts of Life* (1960), a sensible and warmhearted comedy of middle-aged adulterers who decide that playing around is not worth the trouble. In the mid-1960s she was Jack Benny's wife in a televersion of *Time Out for Ginger* and in 1972, she made guest appearances on two television series: in *The Jimmy Stewart Show*, and on *Marcus Welby, M. D.* which stars Robert Young; both Stewart and Young were costars in her MGM days.

Ruth devotes most of her time to her family and occasionally appears with actor Allan Gruener in a two-hour dramatic program called *Great Moments in Theatre*, which they tour on the luncheon circuit before Women's Clubs in California. The Longeneckers live in Brentwood and have a mountain retreat at Lake Arrowhead. They have three children, George Robert, John William, and Mary Elizabeth. John, who studied cinema at the University of Southern California, received an Academy Award in 1970 for the best short subject, *The Resurrection of Broncho Billy*, and on his arm at the Awards ceremony was his mother.

Of her former film career, Ruth says: "I just faded out of sight, I guess. I probably didn't seek work, but producers didn't seek me.

"You come into an age bracket where you don't play leads any more—I think the men fare better in this respect.

"So you play the mother, the aunt, the woman next door. Merle Oberon, Joan Crawford, Bette Davis ... I don't think they've had parts they'd ... well, you can finish that sentence."

With Rita Johnson in *Within the Law* (1939)

RUTH HUSSEY

The Big City (MGM, 1937)
Madame X (MGM, 1937)
Judge Hardy's Children (MGM, 1938)
Man-Proof (MGM, 1938)
Marie Antoinette (MGM, 1938)
Hold That Kiss (MGM, 1938)
Rich Man—Poor Girl (MGM, 1938)
Time Out For Murder (20th-Fox, 1938)
Spring Madness (MGM, 1938)
Honolulu (MGM, 1939)
Within the Law (MGM, 1939)
Maisie (MGM, 1939)
The Women (MGM, 1939)
Another Thin Man (MGM, 1939)
Blackmail (MGM, 1939)
Fast and Furious (MGM, 1939)
Northwest Passage (MGM, 1940)
Susan and God (MGM, 1940)
The Philadelphia Story (MGM, 1940)
Flight Command (MGM, 1940)

Free and Easy (MGM, 1941)
Our Wife (Columbia, 1941)
Married Bachelor (MGM, 1941)
H. M. Pulham, Esq. (MGM, 1941)
Pierre of the Plains (MGM, 1942)
Tennessee Johnson (MGM, 1942)
Tender Comrade (RKO, 1943)
The Uninvited (Paramount, 1944)
Marine Raiders (RKO, 1944)
Bedside Manner (UA, 1945)
I, Jane Doe (Republic, 1948)
The Great Gatsby (Paramount, 1949)
Louisa (Universal, 1950)
Mr. Music (Paramount, 1950)
That's My Boy (Paramount, 1951)
Woman of the North Country (Republic, 1952)
Stars and Stripes Forever (20th-Fox, 1952)
The Lady Wants Mink (Republic, 1953)
The Facts of Life (UA, 1960)

José Iturbi

Today he is considered 1940s kitsch, but at the time José Iturbi was hot stuff with more mass appeal and seemingly more musical talent than today's Leonard Bernstein. He had the uncanny knack of being able to spoon-feed classical music to lower-brow audiences and make them accept it as entertainment. This ability made him an ideal asset to MGM which reveled in having the prestigious orchestra conductor–pianist–composer in its fold to add painless longhair class to their rash of proleterian musicals.

Iturbi was born November 28, 1895 in Valencia, Spain of Basque ancestry. The family was poor, with his father Ricardo working for the local gas company and tuning pianos on the side. By the age of eight, Iturbi was supporting himself; his first steady job was playing the piano in a local movie theatre on the 2 P.M. to the 2 A.M. shift. His talents were so appreciated by the townspeople of Valencia that they collected a purse to send him to study music, first with Joaquin Malata of Barcelona, and then at the Conservatoire de Musique in Paris. He played in Parisian cafés to earn money for food and lodging while studying, and finally he was graduated from the Conservatory with first honors at the age of seventeen. His big break came in 1919 when the President of the Conservatory of Geneva heard him in a Zurich café and offered him the post of head of the piano faculty, a position Franz Liszt had once held. Meanwhile Iturbi had wed Maria Giner, who died in 1929, the year of his first American success, and they had a daughter Maria, who died in 1944. In 1923 he went out on his own and in 1929 made his piano debut in the U. S., playing with the Philadelphia Orchestra under Leopold Stokowski. In 1933 he started a parallel career as a conductor in an orchestral concert in Mexico City. After this engagement he was a guest conductor with several orchestras in the United States and was appointed permanent conductor of the Rochester Philharmonic Orchestra, a post he held until 1944.

From the start, Iturbi's flair for bravura publicity became evident, typified by his later stunt of flying his own plane from concert to concert. His lightning temperament was renowned, particularly when he felt mismatched on rare radio guest stints—i.e, he once refused to be on the same show with Benny Goodman when the latter announced he was going to play jazz: "You can arrange for a picnic with hamburger, but when you have a stiff shirt and white tie dinner, you serve caviar." In another instance of his artistic temperament, he once interrupted in mid-performance a national radio broadcast of Philadelphia's Robin Hood Dell Orchestra, for which he was guest conductor, when he felt that the light semi-classical music scheduled was beneath the dignity of the orchestra and the occasion. While the network filled in with an emergency organ recital, the program was hastily revised to include music of more intellectual substance, and then Iturbi and the orchestra returned to the air to finish the concert.

Iturbi had long been sought for films. In fact, he had been signed to portray himself in MGM's *Sweethearts* (1938), but his part was written out of the musical. Joe Pasternak, who had done well by Leopold Stokowski in *One Hundred Men and a Girl* (1937), persuaded Iturbi to join his musical film unit at MGM. (Iturbi had meanwhile performed in a straight concert-style art house picture, *Adventure in Music* [1944].) Iturbi grasped the concept of cinema showmanship from the start with his specialty number in *Thousands Cheer* (1943). He banged out boogie-woogie rhythms on the keyboard while Judy Garland sang "Jumpin' Down at Carnegie Hall." Producer Joe Pasternak said enthusiastically of Iturbi: "He has the hottest left hand you ever heard." In *Two Girls and a Sailor* (1944) he was joined by his musically accomplished sister Amparo in a piano duet. In *Music for Millions* (1944) June Allyson was a bass fiddle player in his orchestra, and he rendered a piano solo of "Claire de Lune," among other pieces. *Anchors Aweigh* (1945) found gobs Frank Sinatra and Gene Kelly out to win movie extra Kathryn Grayson an audition with Iturbi, with the latter offering a boogie-woogie rendition of "Donkey Serenade." Everyone in the cast of *Holiday in Mexico* (1946) seemed to have a chance to vocalize, from Jane Powell to Walter Pidgeon as her ambassador-to-Mexico father. Second-billed Iturbi performed duets with sister Amparo and kidded with his two real-life grandchildren, and was around to play a swing Polonaise and an abridged Rachmaninoff Concerto—all in tandem with the Latin rhythms of MGM contractee Xavier Cugat and orchestra. Along the way, Iturbi was not seen in Columbia's *A Song to Remember* (1945), but he was heard playing, while Cornel Wilde as Chopin fingered the keyboard, the famous Polonaise in A Flat, the single disc of which became a million-seller record.

The high point of Iturbi's MGM tenure, and by now critics were bemoaning the screen presence of his corny clowning and blushless pseudo-charm, was *Three Daring Daughters* (1948) in which onscreen he weds grass widow Jeanette MacDonald. When not emoting, he played "Route 66," "The Dicky Bird Song," and "Ritual Fire Dance." *That Midnight Kiss* (1949) cast him as a stern opera impresario who is not initially impressed with Mario Lanza. With Amparo, he played Chopin's Revolutionary Etude and soloed at the piano in Liszt's E-Flat Piano Concerto.

Iturbi did not renew his MGM contract. As he said, "The critics and the professional music lovers say I have prostituted myself. It is tough on me." Instead, as permanent conductor of the Valencia Orchestra, he went on tour of

371

Britain and France in 1950. He and Amparo, who had jointly given a Carnegie Hall concert in 1937, did a return engagement there in 1951. He made his opera conducting debut in 1957 at New York's City Center with *La Vida Breva* and in 1961 gave a Lewisohn Stadium concert. He appeared very occasionally on television: He quit a $7,500 guest spot on a variety show because he would not be on the same program with Rosemary Clooney whom he termed "cheesecake," but he did perform Liszt's Hungarian Fantasy on the *Bell Telephone Hour* in 1959.

His sister Amparo died in 1969 of a heart condition, an ailment which has plagued him as well over recent decades. After her death Iturbi withdrew from public performances, remaining secluded in his home in Beverly Hills or visiting his estate in Valencia, Spain. He came out of retirement in October of 1970 to perform with his beloved Rochester Philharmonic Orchestra and was well received by the city at the scene of former triumphs. Nevertheless, now in his late seventies, Iturbi is seldom seen as a performer in public anymore.

JOSE ITURBI

Thousands Cheer (MGM, 1943)
Adventure in Music (A.F.E., 1944)
Two Girls and a Sailor (MGM, 1944)
Music for Millions (MGM, 1944)
Anchors Aweigh (MGM, 1945)

A Song to Remember (Soundtrack playing only: Columbia, 1945)
Holiday in Mexico (MGM, 1946)
Three Daring Daughters (MGM, 1948)
That Midnight Kiss (MGM, 1949).

With Mary Eleanor Donahue, Ann E. Todd, and Jane Powell in *Three Daring Daughters* (1948)

Claude Jarman, Jr.

One of the few child performers to win a special Academy Award, Claude Jarman, Jr. nurtured no intentions of becoming a screen actor until he was discovered in a MGM nationwide talent search for *The Yearling* (1946). By the time of its release and his acclaim he was already an awkward twelve years old, and, although it kept him under contract through 1950, MGM made no real effort to promote him as a major find. He was particularly excellent for *The Yearling* but lacked conventional good looks or childish appeal to be promotable boxoffice. (Compare him to Ted Donaldson of Columbia's *Rusty* series, or television series stars Lee Aaker in *The Adventures of Rin Tin Tin* or Tommy Rettig and Jon Provost in *Lassie*.)

Jarman was born in Nashville, Tennessee on September 27, 1934, the son of a railroad accountant. There was an older sister, Mildred Ann. When Claude was in the fifth grade, he noticed a man surveying the various classrooms of his school. He was told the stranger was a building inspector. It turned out to be MGM director Clarence Brown on the prowl for a youth to play the role of Jody Baxter in Marjorie Kinnan Rawlings' *The Yearling*. This was to be the second try on this long-planned project. In 1941 MGM had sent Spencer Tracy on location to Florida for *The Yearling*, but the filming was abandoned after a few weeks. The original cast included Anne Revere as his wife and young Gene Eckman as Jody.

Jarman was signed by MGM for *The Yearling*, to portray the tow-headed Florida farm boy who has a mischievous pet fawn Flag. Gregory Peck and Jane Wyman played his hickish parents. Having succeeded with such other animal pictures as *National Velvet* and *Lassie Come Home*, MGM knew its market well, and the Technicolor feature grossed $5.25 million over the years. The N.Y. *Times'* Bosley Crowther raved over Jarman's performance: " . . . [he] achieves a child characterization as haunting and appealing as any we've seen." At the 1946 Academy Awards presentation, Jarman was awarded a miniature Oscar.

With the success of *The Yearling*, the Jarman family moved to California permanently, and Claude continued in the MGM studio school, while future screen plans for him were being formulated. MGM came up with only one 1947 assignment for Jarman, *High Barbaree*, in which he played Van

Johnson as a child. The film had Johnson and Cameron Mitchell as two Navy pilots stranded in the Pacific, with Johnson recalling his flavorful childhood. *High Barbaree* was not well received.

Then Jarman was in three 1949 releases. In Jeanette MacDonald's last movie and the fifth in the studio's series of *Lassie* pictures, *The Sun Comes Up*, she was a widowed concert singer who has lost her own son. The combination of orphan lad Jarman and Lassie rekindle her human warmth. In the RKO Western *Roughshod,* Jarman was seen as a tough range kid, and in the adaptation of William Faulkner's *Intruder in the Dust*, Jarman was Chick Mallison, the youth who inspires attorney David Brian to defend condemned black man Juano Hernandez. It was the last important role of Jarman's acting career.

MGM used Jarman as Arlene Dahl's brother in *The Outriders*, but most of the action focused on three Confederate soldiers (Joel McCrea, Barry Sullivan, James Whitmore) who escape Yankee confinement to join up with Quantrill's Raiders. On loan to Republic, Jarman played the teenaged son of John Wayne and Maureen O'Hara in *Rio Grande* (1950). As Jeff Yorke, who has flunked out of West Point and has enlisted in the army, he finds himself assigned to the Western fort commanded by his lieutenant colonel father.

In his final MGM movie, *Inside Straight* (1951), Jarman played San Francisco gambler David Brian at the age of sixteen and was seen in gold mining scenes with sourdough Lon Chaney, Jr. The following year he was the callous member of Randolph Scott's Confederate band in *Hangman's Knot* (1952), and then returned to Republic to be one of Fred MacMurray's crew in *Fair Wind to Java* (1953). He had minimal screen time in both pictures. Three years later he had a very subsidiary role in Walt Disney's Civil War–localed actioner *The Great Locomotive Chase* (1956).

During these awkward years, Jarman had returned to Nashville to complete high school, and then attended Vanderbilt University where he took a prelaw course. He spent three years in the Navy, assigned to a public relations post.

When he returned to Hollywood in 1959 he was married and had a son, Claude Jarman III. When asked about his acting comeback, he reasoned, "If it works out, fine. If not, I won't settle for becoming a second-rate performer in inferior pictures." He was in a *Wagon Train* video episode and a few other television guest shots in 1959, and then disappeared from the public scene.

In the later 1960s, he emerged as executive director of the San Francisco Film Festival, a post he still holds. He recently acquired the screen rights to the novel *The Bushwhacked Piano* but was quick to explain that he only intended to produce the venture: " . . . you can bet I won't be in front of the camera. That's all behind me."

He has since produced the rock concert feature *Fillmore* (1972).

CLAUDE JARMAN ,JR.

The Yearling (MGM, 1946)
High Barbaree (MGM, 1947)
The Sun Comes Up (MGM, 1949)
Roughshod (RKO, 1949)
Intruder in the Dust (MGM, 1949)
The Outriders (MGM, 1950)

Rio Grande (Republic, 1950)
Inside Straight (MGM, 1951)
Hangman's Knot (Columbia, 1952)
Fair Wind to Java (Republic, 1953)
The Great Locomotive Chase (BV, 1956)

With Lon Chaney, Jr. in *Inside Straight* (1951)

Jackie "Butch" Jenkins

There have always been a plethora of cutesy child actors on the Hollywood scene, but rarely has the cinema had such a find as Jackie "Butch" Jenkins. He was not handsome in the typical sense—with his big front teeth, freckles, and uncombed mop of hair. But unlike the physically similar Kevin Corcoran of more recent times, he projected the image of a real child. Best of all, he lacked the telltale theatrical mannerisms of those goody-goody stage children who have peppered films with their synthetic all endearing young charms. Jenkins made only eleven films in a five-year span (1943–1948), all at MGM, but he is one of the better remembered former child stars of the cinema. He certainly outranks the studio's earlier Bobs Watson or Jenkins' Metro contemporary Claude Jarman, Jr. Had not dewy-eyed Margaret O'Brien been the queen of Metro's juvenile division, it is likely Jenkins would have been promoted much faster and to a greater degree than he was.

Jenkins was born in Los Angeles on August 19, 1937 (or 1938), the son of Captain Jack Jenkins of the U. S. Ferry Command and of stage–screen performer Doris Dudley. Her father was Bide Dudley, an actor and New York drama critic.

Even as a youngster Jenkins was affectionately known as a holy terror, a free-wheeling child more interested in self-expression than being a plain brat. One day a Metro scout noted Jenkins cutting up on his favorite haunt, Santa Monica beach, and had him screen-tested for the role of Mickey Rooney's younger brother in Clarence Brown's *The Human Comedy* (1943). As Ulysses he functioned well in this William Saroyan piece of Americana and was actually memorable in such scenes as waving to a black soldier passing by on a train and trying to comprehend the meaning of his older brother's (Van Johnson) death, killed in action. Interacting with Rooney and his onscreen parents (Fay Bainter and Ray Collins), he displayed a novel, natural rambunctiousness that insured his utilization in further MGM films.

He was next seen as the son of Anne Revere and Donald Crisp in *National Velvet* (1944). Bewildered by his older, boy-chasing sister, Angela Lansbury, he was more intrigued by sister Elizabeth Taylor's total concentration on training her lottery-won horse. In *An American Romance* (1944), he was one of Brian Donleyy and Ann Richards' children. Jenkins was next

376

teamed with Margaret O'Brien as her fun-loving younger cousin in *Our Vines Have Tender Grapes* (1945) and seen briefly in *Bud Abbott and Lou Costello in Hollywood* (1945). Along with Skip Homeier, he was raised on James Craig's Texas spread in *Boys' Ranch* (1946). And he again had the lead part in *Little Mr. Jim* (1946) in which he is forced to regenerate his ex-Army officer father (James Craig) who has become a tippler since his wife died.

The high point of Jenkins' relatively brief screen career was *My Brother Talks to Horses* (1946). He played Lewis Penrose, a young Baltimore boy who confines most of his communication to an "understanding" horse, who just happens to give him, so to speak, the latest racetrack dope. All of which delights his brother Peter Lawford and confounds his mother Spring Byington. The latter part of Fred Zinnemann's film bogs down as the muted child grows into a new emotional maturity, but just from the camp value of the title alone, the film has stuck in people's mind. In *The Bride Goes Wild* (1948) he was the nice hellion "adopted" by child-hating Van Johnson who is out to woo June Allyson. Jenkins again played support to star Margaret O'Brien in *The Big City* (1948) as her feuding sidekick. His final picture was the musical version of *Ah, Wilderness!*, entitled *Summer Holiday* (1948). Filmed in lush Technicolor in the summer of 1946, the studio did not drop it onto the market until two years hence, after being unconvinced of its potential. Jenkins inherited the role Mickey Rooney had played in the studio's 1935 straight film version, with Rooney now the older brother.

In 1947, after he completed his releases for 1948, Jenkins' mother decided that the emotional pressures of a film career were too great on her son, especially when the youth began stuttering (which he still does). So she took him and his brother Ted to Dallas to be schooled. He later attended the State University of Iowa. In 1957 he married and, before the couple were divorced in 1964, they had three daughters. He remarried in 1966, and the 6' 4" 200-pound ex–child star now lives in Quinlan, Texas, close by Dallas, where his mother owns a real estate subdivision. Jenkins owns several car wash establishments and the East Texas Water System.

Recently Jenkins stated: "I have never regretted leaving the picture business and am very grateful to my mother for taking me away from it. I enjoyed the first few years of acting in movies but I certainly don't miss it. In fact, when I've had offers to return a few times, I wasn't even tempted. There may be a better way to live than on a lake with a couple of cows, a wife, and children but being a movie star is not one."

JACKIE "BUTCH" JENKINS

The Human Comedy (MGM, 1943)
National Velvet (MGM, 1944)
An American Romance (MGM, 1944)
Our Vines Have Tender Grapes (MGM, 1945)
Bud Abbott and Lou Costello in Hollywood
   (MGM, 1945)

Boys' Ranch (MGM, 1946)
Little Mr. Jim (MGM, 1946)
My Brother Talks to Horses (MGM, 1946)
The Bride Goes Wild (MGM, 1948)
The Big City (MGM, 1948)
Summer Holiday (MGM, 1948)

With Spring Byington in *My Brother Talks to Horses* (1946)

Rita Johnson

Some young screen actresses fit so snugly into caustic and or sympathetic "other woman" film roles that they are considered too good to waste in insipid second-string leading lady assignments. Yet they still do not possess enough charisma to qualify for cinema stardom. Such was the tragedy-struck Rita Johnson. Physically she was more robust than Martha Scott and certainly less mechanical than the pre-"star" Jane Wyman, and for four years (1937–1940) she was employed by MGM to bolster a string of mostly B pictures as the snappy but wholesome miss who knew all about her worldly rights long before woman's lib had become fashionable.

She was born August 13, 1912 in Worcester, Massachusetts as Rita McSean. (For professional allure, she changed the Gaelic surname to its Anglo-Saxon equivalent, Johnson.) She had always been intrigued by a stage career and upon graduation from high school worked in summer stock. She made her Broadway debut in the short-lasting *If This Be Treason* (1935) and then turned to radio playing such leads as *Joyce Jordan, Girl Interne*. She then returned to the stage in George M. Cohan's *Fulton of Oak Falls* (1937), and her attention-getting part in that play brought her a MGM contract.

Since Jean Harlow had just died during the filming of *Saratoga* (1937), it was initially thought to have Rita redo the star's scenes. However, the studio decided to save costs by using a double to complete that picture, and stated they did not want to type the young actress into a screen image. So Rita made her cinema bow in the murder mystery *London by Night* (1937), playing the coquettish heroine to George Murphy's newspaper reporter lead. She was then a pal to crusading women's rights heiress Maureen O'Sullivan in *My Dear Miss Aldrich* (1937), a bridesmaid to Rosalind Russell in *Man-Proof* (1938), and the sister of Robert Young in *Rich Man—Poor Girl* (1938). These assignments were enough to type Rita as a well-bred other woman in the screen manner of Gail Patrick and Lynn Bari, and she was loaned to RKO for *Smashing the Rackets* (1938). In Universal's show business tale, *Letter of Introduction* (1938), she was fortuitously allowed a change of professional pace in being cast as George Murphy's dancing partner, although Andrea Leeds had the lead. This role was one of Rita's favorites.

MGM got good value from Rita in 1939 by sandwiching her into eight of their releases. As a made-over blonde, refined Marian Martin-type, she got to wed the right Robert Young (he had dual roles) in Eleanor Powell's *Honolulu*, and in *Broadway Serenade* she gave good backup to Jeanette MacDonald as the chorine "protégé" of theatrical producer Frank Morgan. She gets to wed him in that picture, once she pushes chorus line competitor Virginia Grey well out of the way. Two of the year's efforts were prison melodramas in parts Gertrude Michael would have played at Paramount a few years back: *6,000 Enemies* (as a wrongly convicted girl) and *They All Come Out* (as a gun moll). Her emoting in the latter led the N.Y. *World-Telegram* to label her "Leo's new White Hope." Such praise, as usual, went unheeded by the front office. She was in the remake of *Evelyn Prentice*, titled *Stronger Than Desire*, and her fifth film, with Walter Pidgeon, was *Nick Carter, Master Detective*. She played an airline stewardess in this caper.

Her last year at MGM had her in the Mary Astor role in their remake of *Red Dust*, now labeled *Congo Maisie* (1940), and she was Lew Ayres' girl friend in *The Golden Fleecing* (1940). While playing the waitress whose abandoned baby is mothered by girls' school professor Eddie Cantor in *Forty Little Mothers* (1940), she worked on a nearby soundstage as Spencer Tracy's understanding wife in *Edison, the Man* (1940). This was the one film role she fought to get at Metro and it proved the most prestigious of her career, leading many critics to comment she outshone Tracy in this followup production to the more entertaining *Young Tom Edison* (1940). Metro executives still could not see Rita as a potential leading lady and slated her for supporting wisecracking roles in *Ziegfeld Girl* (1941) and *Maisie Was a Lady* (1941). She was staunch enough in her self-esteem to refuse and asked to be released from her studio contract which had four years to go. Meanwhile she had wed stockbroker L. Stanley Kahn in 1940. They divorced in 1943 and then she married Captain Edwin Hutzler, whom she also divorced later.

As a free-lancer Rita found herself stuck with the "other woman" tag. She was the murdering lover of John Emery in Columbia's *Here Comes Mr. Jordan* (1941) and the actress ex-love of playwright Charles Boyer in *Appointment for Love* (1941). Billy Wilder used her as Diana Lynn's short-tongued older sister and as Ray Milland's jealous fiancée in *The Major and the Minor* (1942). In a contrasting, sympathetic role, she was the Wyoming ranch mother of Roddy McDowall in the Technicolor *My Friend Flicka* (1943) and its sequel *Thunderhead, Son of Flicka* (1945). Back in her usual form, she was volatile Mona Kent, the bitchy actress in Joan Fontaine's *The Affairs of Susan* (1945). Following this, she was wasted as a show boat con artist in Abbott and Costello's *The Naughty Nineties* (1945) and was second lead to Marguerite Chapman and Fred MacMurray in *Pardon My Past* (1946).

It was a mature (thirty-five-year-old) Rita who played Robert Young's infinitely possessive wife in *They Won't Believe Me* (1947), meeting a grisly end. But in *Sleep, My Love* (1948) she was Claudette Colbert's effusive Boston chum. In *The Big Clock* (1948) she reached villainess status as the homicidal mistress of bulbous publishing tycoon Charles Laughton.

In September 1948 Rita was operated on for a brain concussion that nearly cost her her life. It seems that, sometime before, she had been struck on the head by a hair dryer in her home. Although the police surgeon noted several old, minor bruises on her body, the investigation disclosed nothing to substantiate that the wounds were not accidental. After a slow recovery Rita showed up in *The Second Face* (1950), a budget melodrama with her onscreen friend Ella Raines being transformed into a beauty by plastic surgery. For whatever reasons, it was four years later before she appeared in a minuscule assignment as Dick Powell's psychiatrist in the pseudo-titillating *Susan Slept Here* (1954). Her role as warden Chester Morris' wife in *Unchained* (1955) was chopped out of the release print. She was just a nurse in *Emergency Hospital* (1956) and the pioneer woman who adopts orphaned Patty McCormack in *All Mine to Give* (1957).

Rita was not heard of again until October 31, 1965, when she died of a brain hemorrhage in County General Hospital in Hollywood. So ended the life of an accomplished actress who never quite made the grade to which she aspired.

RITA JOHNSON

London by Night (MGM, 1937)
My Dear Miss Aldrich (MGM, 1937)
Man-Proof (MGM, 1938)
Rich Man—Poor Girl (MGM, 1938)
Smashing the Rackets (RKO, 1938)
Letter of Introduction (Universal, 1938)
Honolulu (MGM, 1939)
The Girl Downstairs (MGM, 1939)
Broadway Serenade (MGM, 1939)
Within the Law (MGM, 1939)
6,000 Enemies (MGM, 1939)
Stronger Than Desire (MGM, 1939)
They All Come Out (MGM, 1939)
Nick Carter, Master Detective (MGM, 1939)
Congo Maisie (MGM, 1940)
The Golden Fleecing (MGM, 1940)
Forty Little Mothers (MGM, 1940)
Edison, the Man (MGM, 1940)
Here Comes Mr. Jordan (Columbia, 1941)
Appointment for Love (Universal, 1941)

The Major and the Minor (Paramount, 1942)
My Friend Flicka (20th-Fox, 1943)
Thunderhead, Son of Flicka (20th-Fox, 1945)
The Affairs of Susan (Paramount, 1945)
The Naughty Nineties (Universal, 1945)
Pardon My Past (Columbia, 1946)
The Perfect Marriage (Paramount, 1946)
The Michigan Kid (Universal, 1947)
They Won't Believe Me (RKO, 1947)
Sleep My Love (UA, 1948)
The Big Clock (Paramount, 1948)
Don't Trust Your Husband (UA, 1948)
Family Honeymoon (Universal, 1948)
The Second Face (Eagle–Lion, 1950)
Susan Slept Here (RKO, 1954)
Unchained (WB, 1955)*
Emergency Hospital (UA, 1956)
All Mine to Give (Universal, 1957)

*Scenes deleted from release print

With John Carroll in *Congo Maisie* (1940)

Van Johnson

During the mid-1940s Van Johnson was the cause of what Hedda Hopper termed the Bobby-Soxer Blitz. As the blue-eyed, red-haired, freckle-faced boy-next-door, he set the hearts of all the maternal females in the audience, young and old, pounding. No other young movie idol except MGM cohort Frank Sinatra sent as many screaming fans running to the boxoffice during the World War II years. In 1945 Johnson was the Number Two cinema moneymaker and Number Three in 1946. He could act a little, sing and dance a smidgeon, and had such a perpetual air of naive helplessness that ladies wanted to mother him. Despite some male critics who wished he were less Baby LeRoy and more Richard Dix, those ladies sent him 8,000 letters a week begging him not to get married, but to wait for them. Van Johnson was as awe-stricken a movie fan himself as was his audience. He loved the glamor of MGM where he was under contract for fourteen years (1942–1956). He never asked for a new contract or a raise, just having his studio agreement renewed, until, at the time of his departure, he was earning $8,000 weekly.

He was born Charles Van Johnson on August 25, 1916 in Newport, Rhode Island, of Swedish, *not* Irish ancestry, as some sources would have it. His parents divorced when he was three and he was raised by his father, a real estate agent. He was an only child, a star-struck loner who worked at various odd jobs including selling magazines, delivering groceries, and playing beach boy. He took lessons in singing, dancing, and the violin. At Rogers High School he failed to make the drama club but did play the violin in the orchestra, and with a top hat and cane, performed musical entertainment for the local Kiwanis and Lions, clubs. When he graduated from high school in June 1935, his father urged him to enroll in prelaw studies at Brown University, but he opted for a theatrical career.

When he got to New York that fall, Johnson obtained a four-week stint in a musical revue, *Entre Nous*, at the Cherry Lane Theatre in Greenwich Village and toured as a substitute dancer with a musical show playing the New England circuit. Next he played for forty weeks in *New Faces of 1936*, which included Imogene Coca in the cast. He did a tour, emceeing the vaudeville act of Buster West and Lucille Page, and performed in a club act in 1939 called "Eight Young Men of Manhattan." His show business break occurred when

383

he was hired by George Abbott as understudy to the three male leads in Rodgers and Hart's *Too Many Girls*, which opened on Broadway on October 18, 1939. The three leads were Desi Arnaz, Eddie Bracken, and Richard Kollmar. When Kollmar left the show to wed reporter Dorothy Kilgallen, Johnson took over his part. When RKO filmed *Too Many Girls* (1940) starring Lucille Ball, Desi Arnaz, Eddie Bracken, and Ann Miller, Johnson was used in the film, but only in a small chorus boy role. He returned to Broadway to appear in George Abbott's next show, *Pal Joey*, also by Rodgers and Hart, which opened Christmas Day, 1940. Johnson had only ten lines of dialogue in the play, and he danced with June Havoc.

Johnson had come to the attention of Warner Brothers and that studio gave him a six-month contract at $300 a week. He was cast opposite Faye Emerson in a 59-minute programmer *Murder in the Big House*. Warners decided Johnson was no John Garfield or Jeffrey Lynn and dropped his option. He was about to leave Hollywood and return to New York when he dropped by the home of Desi Arnaz and Lucille Ball to say goodbye. When Ball heard of his decision she telephoned MGM casting head Billy Grady, who, in turn, arranged a screen test for Johnson opposite Donna Reed, which was successful.

MGM signed him to a seven-year contract and immediately put him to work. He was the Irish-faced soldier in *Somewhere I'll Find You* (1942) with Clark Gable and Lana Turner, and had another soldier bit in *The War Against Mrs. Hadley* (1942). When MGM ignominiously dropped pacifist Lew Ayres from their roster, Mayer thought enough of Johnson's screen potential to cast him as *Dr. Gillespie's New Assistant* (1942). He would play Dr. Red Adams in three other entries in the medico series but never with the same degree of success as Ayres had done with his parallel Dr. Kildare role. Johnson played Marcus, the older son of Fay Bainter in *The Human Comedy* (1943), and during the course of the film he is the soldier finally killed in action. Then he was just a reporter in *Madame Curie* (1943).

It was Victor Fleming's *A Guy Named Joe* (1943) which boosted Johnson to stardom. That picture starred Irene Dunne and Spencer Tracy, who was Johnson's idol. During the shooting, Johnson was driving his closest friends, Keenan Wynn and his wife Eve, to a special screening of Tracy's *Keeper of the Flame* (1942). Johnson's automobile, a convertible, was hit broadside by another car which ran through a stop light. Johnson's passengers were not hurt, but Johnson's head was smashed against the top lock of his convertible in the middle of the windshield. His injury was serious enough to require a metal plate to be inserted in his forehead and incidentally disqualified him for World War II military service. When Tracy learned that MGM was considering replacing the ailing Johnson with either John Hodiak or Peter Lawford, Tracy insisted that if Johnson were dropped from the film, he would not film another scene. Louis B. Mayer finally relented and agreed to shoot around Johnson's scenes until he recovered, *if* Tracy would start behaving more gentlemanly toward Irene Dunne. That gesture on Tracy's part created the basis for a lifelong friendship between the two actors. When *A Guy Named Joe* was released on December 24, 1943, it made Johnson a star.

Johnson's ascendancy at MGM was faster than normal due to the shortage of actors during the War years. The studio featured his boyish charm in *Two Sailors and a Girl* (1944), the first of his five films opposite June Allyson, *Thrill of a Romance* (1945) the first of five costarring vehicles with Esther Williams, *The Romance of Rosie Ridge* (1947), and *State of the Union* (1948). Soon he became a boxoffice star, a top moneymaker, and had as many fans as Clark Gable.

On January 25, 1947, Johnson married Eve Abbott Wynn, the wife of his very best friend Keenan Wynn. Wynn had wed Eve in 1938 and they had two children. The Wynns had "adopted" their bachelor friend when he arrived in Hollywood and the trio were a frequent sight on the Hollywood social scene. It was Eve who nursed Johnson through his convalescence after his accident. The wedding disappointed many of Johnson's female fans, but both Johnson and MGM were a little tired of his baggy-pants-and-romantic image and took the opportunity to cast him in two good military pictures, *Command Decision* (1948) and *Battleground* (1949). These two films revealed the spark of serious actor potential that Johnson had earlier displayed when he essayed the disillusioned but loyal aide of Spencer Tracy in *State of the Union*. But it was much easier for MGM to cast Johnson in lightweight fluff, and he continued playing the juvenile leads with remarkable aplomb and lack of concern for his own advancing age or expanding waistline. MGM loaned him to Columbia to play Lt. Maryk in *The Caine Mutiny* (1954) which contains Johnson's most solid emoting. Again on loan to Columbia, he and Deborah Kerr waddled through a distortion of Grahame Greene's *The End of the Affair* (1955). The next year he ended his fourteen-year tenure with MGM by playing the television personality with a prison record in *Slander* (1956), a well-made little topical programmer.

Like June Allyson, Johnson had matured way beyond his accepted screen image but appeared unable to find a suitable substitute guise to make himself viable to the new generations. In 1959 Johnson, his wife, and their daughter Schuyler moved to Switzerland. When Eve tired of Europe and also of Johnson, she took their daughter and returned to the U. S., announcing an official separation. Johnson remained in Europe continuing to appear in above-par feature programmers. Then he signed for the London production of *The Music Man* (1961), which proved to be a personal triumph for him. He had slowly overcome his fear of live audiences after being talked into performing in nightclubs by Rosalind Russell in 1953. When he had made his Las Vegas debut in the 1950s, his wife and her ex-husband Keenan Wynn sat at the same ringside table. During one performance of *The Music Man* in 1963, Johnson lost the tip of his finger in an onstage accident. He was rushed to the hospital where the top piece of his finger was stitched back on. He returned to the U. S. to star in a Broadway vehicle called *Come on Strong* (1962) with Carol Baker.

Johnson worked up a nightclub act and played several dates before his tour was interrupted by an operation for skin cancer on his left thigh in 1963. The following year a second operation was performed to remove a lymph gland as preventive treatment against the cancer. Both operations seemed to be successful in arresting his disease. Hal Wallis used Johnson to backstop an outmoded marital comedy *Wives and Lovers* (1963), and the actor did more of the same in *Divorce American Style* (1967). Lucille Ball was thoughtful enough to use him as second male lead in *Yours, Mine and Ours* (1968). His last theatrical feature to date has been *Company of Killers* (1970), a telefeature thought too brutal for television airing and shoved into theatres on a double bill. Johnson was actually effective as the tough cop coping with a Murder, Inc. gang.

He has not fared well in the television game. Johnson was talked out of starring in *The Untouchables* series, and since then has made several series which never sold, including *Take Her, She's Mine* and *Man in the Middle*. He continues to guest star in the medium, but usually in the added-attraction category, as in Jack Warden's pilot *Wheeler and Murdoch* (1972) and Connie Stevens' telefeature *Call Her Mom* (1972). Likewise Johnson continues to dabble in summer stock. Having done *A Thousand Clowns* in the mid-1960s, Johnson turned to *Help Stamp out Marriage* for his 1972 outing on the straw hat circuit.

Since his separation from his wife, Johnson has lived in a Manhattan penthouse apartment. For a time it was necessary for him to live in the East because Eve instituted such financially involved divorce proceedings in California that he could not enter that state without fear of court battles. They were finally divorced in 1968. Johnson says, "I'll never get married again, and if I do, throw something at me."

Johnson recalls that the MGM days were exciting and that it was a big kick to be around the studio's top stars. Spencer Tracy used to tell him to stop running around with his autograph book, and once Ingrid Bergman said, "If that boy annoys me once more, I'm going to scream." Today he is friends with many of those stars: Greta Garbo, Rosalind Russell, Lucille Ball, and Ingrid Bergman too. He acknowledges that he was never a fighter for better pictures at MGM and that there are only a few of his assignments of which he is proud: *A Guy Named Joe, Thirty Seconds over Tokyo, Command Decision, Battleground,* and *The Caine Mutiny.*

VAN JOHNSON

Too Many Girls (RKO, 1940)	Dr. Gillespie's Criminal Case (MGM, 1943)
Somewhere I'll Find You (MGM, 1942)	The Human Comedy (MGM, 1943)
Murder in the Big House (WB, 1942)	Pilot No. 5 (MGM, 1943)
The War Against Mrs. Hadley (MGM, 1942)	Madame Curie (MGM, 1943)
Dr. Gillespie's New Assistant (MGM, 1942)	White Cliffs of Dover (MGM, 1944)
A Guy Named Joe (MGM, 1943)	Two Girls and a Sailor (MGM, 1944)

Thirty Seconds over Tokyo (MGM, 1944)
Three Men in White (MGM, 1944)
Between Two Women (MGM, 1944)
Weekend at the Waldorf (MGM, 1945)
Thrill of a Romance (MGM, 1945)
Ziegfeld Follies (MGM, 1946)
Till the Clouds Roll By (MGM, 1946)
No Leave, No Love (MGM, 1946)
Easy to Wed (MGM, 1946)
High Barbaree (MGM, 1947)
The Romance of Rosy Ridge (MGM, 1947)
State of the Union (MGM, 1948)
The Bride Goes Wild (MGM, 1948)
Command Decision (MGM, 1948)
Mother Is a Freshman (20th-Fox, 1949)
Scene of the Crime (MGM, 1949)
In the Good Old Summertime (MGM, 1949)
Battleground (MGM, 1949)
Grounds for Marriage (MGM, 1950)
The Big Hangover (MGM, 1950)
Duchess of Idaho (MGM, 1950)
Too Young to Kiss (MGM, 1951)
Go for Broke (MGM, 1951)
It's a Big Country (MGM, 1951)
Three Guys Named Mike (MGM, 1951)
Invitation (MGM, 1952)
When in Rome (MGM, 1952)

With Barry Nelson, Don DeFore, and Spencer Tracy in *A Guy Named Joe* (1943)

th Alma Kruger and Walter Kingsford in
ween Two Women (1944)

Washington Story (MGM, 1952)
Plymouth Adventure (MGM, 1952)
Confidentially Connie (MGM, 1953)
Remains to Be Seen (MGM, 1953)
Easy to Love (MGM, 1953)
The Caine Mutiny (Columbia, 1954)
The Siege at Red River (20th-Fox, 1954)
Men of the Fighting Lady (MGM, 1954)
The Last Time I Saw Paris (MGM, 1954)
Brigadoon (MGM, 1954)
The End of the Affair (Columbia, 1955)
Slander (MGM, 1956)
Miracle in the Rain (WB, 1956)
The Bottom of the Bottle (20th-Fox, 1956)
23 Paces to Baker Street (20th-Fox, 1956)
Kelly and Me (Universal, 1957)
Action of the Tiger (MGM, 1957)
The Last Blitzkrieg (Columbia, 1958)
Web of Evidence (AA, 1959)
Subway in the Sky (UA, 1959)
The Enemy General (Columbia, 1960)
Wives and Lovers (Paramount, 1963)
Divorce American Style (Columbia, 1967)
Yours, Mine and Ours (UA, 1968)
Where Angels Go ... Trouble Follows (Columbia, 1968)
El Largo Dia Del (Spanish–French, 1969)
Company of Killers (Universal, 1970)

With Esther Williams in *Duchess of Idaho* (1950)

With Patricia Collinge and Patricia Neal in *Washington Story* (1953)

With June Allyson in *Remains to Be See* (1953)

Howard Keel

Howard Keel, a natural, untrained singing actor, was one of the best of the screen's romantic, musical leading men, combining the sophistication of a Douglas Fairbanks, Jr. and the masculinity of a Clark Gable. However, he arrived on the Hollywood scene at an inopportune time. While MGM was still turning out big-budget musicals which provided a showcase for his talents, such as *Annie Get Your Gun* (1950) and *Show Boat* (1951), the many executive changes at the studio did not allow for his sustained grooming. One good picture would be followed by two bad ones and at such times, the public went to see his competitors, Gordon MacRae, Mario Lanza, or Tony Martin. Keel was better than his wooden predecessor at MGM, Nelson Eddy, but musicals were in the process of one of their periodic dips in popularity, so his stardom was short-lived.

Keel was born in Gillespie, Illinois on April 13, 1919 (or 1917). His name was originally Harry Leek. His father died when Keel was eleven years old and he and a younger brother moved with their mother to Fallbrook, California, where he attended high scool. He was known as a kid who liked to sing, but he showed no serious aspirations for a career as a singer until a friend introduced him to "Mom" Rider, a widow who ran a Los Angeles boarding house and played the piano. She taught Keel a few vocal tricks and induced him to accept a job as a singing waiter in a Los Angeles café at $15 weekly. Keel had a lot of fun at the job, but he had to earn more money to help support his mother and brother. So he went to work for Douglas Aircraft. When word got around the plant that he could sing, he was soon promoted as a "traveling manufacturer's representative," performing at various entertainments for the company and its clients. He began to realize that singing might very well provide him with a respectable living and started to appear with the American Music Theatre in Pasadena. There he was coached by that organization's founder, George Huston, who had helped such singers as George London, Brian Sullivan, and John Raitt. Keel won a few prizes at music festivals and hired an agent to obtain concert bookings. The agent also got him an audition with Oscar Hammerstein II, who put him in as a Broadway replacement for the second male lead in *Oklahoma!* He then did the London production of *Oklahoma!*, playing the more substantial lead role of Curly.

389

About this time Warner Brothers screen-tested him but offered him nothing since they already had Gordon MacRae under contract. He did, however, make his motion picture debut while in London in a small, nonsinging role in *The Small Voice* (1948) (released in the U. S. as *Hideout*). He played the escaped convict. His name was spelled "Harold" in the credits, so when he returned to the U. S., he kept the new first name. His return to the States was propitiously timed, because MGM was polishing up Irving Berlin's *Annie Get Your Gun* (1950) for Judy Garland and was looking for a Frank Butler, the male lead. Producer Arthur Freed happened to see Keel's Warners' test and hired him at $850 weekly, changing his name to Howard. The problems that beset *Annie* are legend, the most regretable of which was that Garland had to be replaced by Betty Hutton. During his first eight months under contract to the studio, Keel was idle while *Annie* was being readied, and studio producers suggested him for the Robert Young role in *That Forsyte Woman* (1949) and the David Brian role in *Intruder in the Dust* (1949). But Louis B. Mayer desisted, since he wanted Keel to "debut" in a first-rate musical. As production on the film began, Garland insisted that Busby Berkeley be replaced as director, and he was, by George Sidney. Then Keel broke his leg when his horse fell on him and for six weeks they shot around him. Frank Morgan, who was to play Buffalo Bill, died and had to be replaced by Louis Calhern. And finally, Garland suffered from "nervous exhaustion" and in stepped Hutton. Keel recalls that the blonde bombshell was self-centered (an out-of-touch perfectionist is more appropriate) and he did not enjoy working with her. However, the resultant film was a lively and quite-popular ($4.6 million gross to date) musical romp, and Keel was impressive as the masculine, singing cowboy.

While Mayer showed concern about Keel's initial MGM outing, he apparently turned his head the other way when Keel was allowed to be cast in the foolish *Pagan Love Song* (1950) with Esther Williams. Likewise, when he played the nonsinging pilot in *Three Guys Named Mike* (1951), a pleasant enough comedy with Jane Wyman, Van Johnson, and Barry Sullivan, Keel came off well in his role, but the audience wanted to hear him sing, which they did, splendidly, in *Show Boat* (1951) with its still beautiful Jerome Kern score. Keel was effectively cast as Gaylord Ravenal, a singing Rhett Butler, and he and Kathryn Grayson proved as likable a singing team as Jeanette MacDonald and Nelson Eddy. But up popped Esther Williams again in his next film, *Texas Carnival* (1951), and this time Red Skelton was on the scene too. Keel looked as though he would have given up his waistcoat and walking stick to be back on a Mississippi riverboat.

An amusing but at the time unpopular satire of television Westerns followed, *Callaway Went Thataway* (1951). Then he was reteamed with Grayson in *Lovely to Look At* (1952), distinctly a B musical. MGM seemed to have forgotten him momentarily. After having him sing to Polly Bergen and a race horse in *Fast Company* (1953) and having him play Ava Gardner's husband in a Mexican-set Western, *Ride, Vaquero* (1953), they loaned him to Warners for *Calamity Jane* (1953) with Doris Day. This last picture was a flop when released because, Keel says, studio head Jack Warner did not get behind it and push it. The song "Secret Love," however, won the Academy Award and the film is now a popular entry on television late shows.

By this time Keel was despairing over his restrictive MGM contract and fought to be cast in *Kiss Me, Kate!* (1953). Producer Jack Cummings had already signed Kathryn Grayson as the feminine lead but wanted Laurence Olivier as the male star and planned to dub his voice. Director George Sidney, however, promoted Keel sufficiently for him to be given the part in this 3-D color production. It is by far his best role.

Keel did not want to do the wide-screen remake of the Jeanette MacDonald–Nelson Eddy *Rose Marie* (1954) opposite Ann Blyth, because he thought the Mountie a "blithering idiot." MGM insisted, nevertheless and then rewarded him with *Seven Brides for Seven Brothers* (1954), which is regarded as a high point for both director Stanley Donen and the latter-day MGM musicals. Keel introduced the song "Bless Yore Beautiful Hide" and gave the production a creditable ruggedness. He also worked well with leading lady Jane Powell.

MGM renewed his contract at $3,000 weekly, but did not see fit to give him any decent assignment. So while he was taking home his weekly paycheck—splash—there was Esther Williams again in *Jupiter's Darling* (1955), followed by the tepid remake of *Kismet* (1955) with Ann Blyth. Keel's discomfort in this endeavor showed all too clearly on the screen. It was his last MGM picture. "I was typed as a singer and they weren't making musicals then. No studio was willing to take a chance on an actor in a dramatic role. Furthermore, actors were not as marketable as 'personalities.'"

In the years since his release from MGM, Keel has appeared in several nonsinging movie roles, such as Simon-Peter in *The Big Fisherman* (1959), and a succession of Westerns of diminishing importance. He played a character role as a friendly Indian in *The War Wagon* (1967) and had the male lead in three of A. C. Lyles' budget Westerns geared to draw a fast buck by utilizing once-popular boxoffice names. *Red Tomahawk* (1967) was slated to reteam him with Betty Hutton, but she withdrew and Joan Caulfield was substituted.

He has kept his voice active by summer theatre tours. A case of pneumonia prevented him from starring on Broadway in Dore Schary's *Sunrise at Campobello*, and Ralph Bellamy played FDR both onstage and in the screen version. In 1959 a Broadway presentation of *Saratoga*, a musical based on Edna Ferber's *Saratoga Trunk*, pairing him with Carol Lawrence, was a flop, but he did have moderate success with stock editions of Richard Rodgers' *No Strings* and Neil Simon's *Plaza Suite*. He recently worked up a nightclub act with his often film costar Kathryn Grayson. The act has been well received in Las Vegas and abroad. He and Danielle Darrieux starred in a lavish but impressive musical version of Henry James' *The Ambassador* in London in early 1972, which was remounted later in the year for a Broadway

With Louis Calhern, Betty Hutton, and Keenan Wynn in *Annie Get Your Gun* (1950)

With Chief Yowlachie (on bier) and Abel Fernandez in *Rose Marie* (1954)

airing. In the summer of 1972 he toured the straw hat circuit in *Man of La Mancha.*

Married in 1943 to actress Rosemary Cooper, they divorced after five years. In 1949, he married former dancer Helen Anderson, by whom he had three children, one of whom is now married and a parent himself. This second marriage ended in divorce in 1970, and on December 21 of that year Keel married Judy Magamoll. When Keel announced not long ago that he was moving his residence to a houseboat, he claimed it was to offer him a new sense of freedom. Other more cynical souls sighed that things are not what they used to be for the one-time cinema celebrity.

HOWARD KEEL

The Small Voice (British Lion, 1948)
Annie Get Your Gun (MGM, 1950)
Pagan Love Song (MGM, 1950)
Three Guys Named Mike (MGM, 1951)
Show Boat (MGM, 1951)
Texas Carnival (MGM, 1951)
Callaway Went Thataway (MGM, 1951)
Across the Wide Missouri (Narrator: MGM, 1951)
Lovely to Look At (MGM, 1952)
Desperate Search (MGM, 1952)
I Love Melvin (MGM, 1953)
Fast Company (MGM, 1953)
Ride, Vaquero (MGM, 1953)
Calamity Jane (WB, 1953)
Kiss Me, Kate! (MGM, 1953)

Rose Marie (MGM, 1954)
Seven Brides for Seven Brothers (MGM, 1954)
Deep in My Heart (MGM, 1954)
Jupiter's Darling (MGM, 1955)
Kismet (MGM, 1955)
Floods of Fear (Universal, 1959)
The Big Fisherman (BV, 1959)
Armored Command (AA, 1961)
The Day of the Triffids (AA, 1963)
The Man from Button Willow (United Screen Arts, 1965)
Waco (Paramount, 1966)
Red Tomahawk (Paramount, 1967)
The War Wagon (Universal, 1967)
Arizona Bushwhackers (Paramount, 1968)

With Dolores Gray in *Kismet* (1955)

Gene Kelly

Bob Hope once quipped that, "Every time Gene Kelly starts dancing, Fred Astaire starts counting his money." Comparisons of these two men are inevitable in any discussion of dance on film. But the careers of these two gentlemen are as different as their styles: Astaire with his sophisticated, romantic élan and Kelly with his ingratiating, all-American athletic Irish appeal. While Kelly was at first regarded as only another hoofer, he soon became recognized as a singing–acting dancer with a cinematic instinct as to how dance could be effectively presented on celluloid. His contribution to the art of dance on film was pioneering and unique. Busby Berkeley had expanded the screen dance by utilizing kaleidoscopically photographed chorines. Astaire went a step further and moved his film dancing away from the stage proscenium and into the reality of skating rinks, stairways, and parks. But it was Kelly who expanded upon both these improvements to devise a cinemantic language of dance in which the Terpsichorean activity, be it tap, soft shoe, or ballet, replaced dialogue and became an integral part of the scenario's framework.

Eugene Curran Kelly was born in Pittsburgh, Pennsylvania on August 23, 1912, the third of five children. His mother encouraged all her children to take lessons in dance, music, and French. Kelly and his brother Fred excelled at dance, but Kelly preferred playing sports, such as basketball, football, and hockey. In fact, he later recalled: "I hated dancing . . . . I thought it was sissy. I bless her now for making me go . . . ." Kelly attended Pennsylvania State College where he studied journalism. But when the Depression came, he was forced to quit school and take a job teaching gymnastics at Camp Porter, a YMCA camp near Pittsburgh. He and his brother worked up a hoofing act, tap dancing on roller skates, for local amateur nights. When he could afford it he returned to college, this time to the University of Pittsburgh where he first studied economics, then switched to law, and earned his bachelor of arts degree in 1933. During this time he worked at numerous odd jobs, while he and Fred continued their dancing duo. Simultaneously he took over teaching in the dancing school where he had studied as a youngster. He proved so popular in this capacity that he developed it into The Gene Kelly Studio of the Dance, and opened a second branch in Johnstown, Pennsylvania.

Kelly and his brother performed in local clubs and in a children's theatre show at the Chicago World's Fair in 1933–1934. In 1937 Kelly went to New York for a job as a dance teacher. He got no offers, so he returned home where his dance schools were earning $8,000 a year. He tried New York again the next year and landed in the chorus of *Leave It to Me!* (1938). In this Cole Porter musical, he and three other boys backed up Mary Martin as she sang "My Heart Belongs to Daddy." He danced and spoke some lines in *One for the Money* (1939) and did the choreography for three shows at the Theatre Guild's summer theatre in Westport, Connecticut. In the fall of 1939 for twenty-two weeks he played the role of the comedian in William Saroyan's *The Time of Your Life*, and then spent the next summer as the dance director for Billy Rose's *Diamond Horseshoe Revue*. While there, he met a sixteen-year-old dancer named Betty Blair, and they were married September 22, 1941.

Word soon got around that Kelly was a professional dancing actor on the rise. He was selected as the heel–hero in the Broadway production of John O'Hara's *Pal Joey* (1940). It was this role that really made him a star. Producer David O. Selznick put him under a personal contract and planned to use him as a dramatic screen actor. Kelly recalls that Selznick said, "You're a great actor. This nonsense about your doing musicals, that's fine. You can do them for a hobby. I have a property for you. You are going to play the priest in *The Keys of the Kingdom.* Kelly said they finally agreed he was not right for the part, which was given to another Broadway actor, Gregory Peck. It was then decided Kelly would play the Scottish doctor in the same picture. He studied with a speech teacher and made a test. In the end, Selznick cast Thomas Mitchell in the role and sold one-half of Kelly's screen contract to MGM, loaning him to that studio to play Judy Garland's leading man in *For Me and My Gal* (1942). Later Selznick would sell the second half of his contract to MGM.

In *For Me and My Gal*, Kelly played an opportunistic vaudevillian, a character very similar to his role in *Pal Joey*. MGM next put him in two small musical roles and two dramatic ones, then loaned him to Columbia as Rita Hayworth's costar in *Cover Girl* (1944). Although the choreography was credited to Seymour Felix, Kelly, with the assistance of a young friend, Stanley Donen, whom he had met while starring in *Pal Joey*, actually devised the dance steps for the successful "Alter Ego" number where Kelly danced with and around his conscience. The popularity of this film induced the studio to let Kelly choreograph his next film, *Anchors Aweigh* (1945), one of the most popular of MGM's musicals, where he and Frank Sinatra played two sailors after the same girl, Kathryn Grayson. Kelly had two excellent numbers: one in which he danced with the cartoon characters, Tom and Jerry, and the other, the famous "Mexican Hat Dance." After doing "The Babbitt and The Bromide" routine with Fred Astaire in MGM's colorful grab bag, *Ziegfeld Follies* (filmed in 1944 and 1945 but not released until 1946), Kelly joined the Navy.

Upon his discharge, Louis B. Mayer induced Kelly and Stanley Donen to devise some dance routines for *Living in a Big Way* (1947), in order to help promote Marie "The Body" McDonald, whom Mayer prophesied would be a great star. Next Kelly was cast in the lavish Vincente Minnelli production *The Pirate* (1948) with Judy Garland. Kelly's acrobatic "Be a Clown" number, which he choreographed with Robert Alton, was lively enough, but Kelly's strolling actor characterization was criticized by James Agee as, "a misguided conception by John Barrymore by way of the elder Douglas Fairbanks." Foolish is the best that can be said of Kelly's portrayal of D'Artagnan in *The Three Musketeers* (1948). For the meandering *Words and Music* (1948), Kelly choreographed Richard Rodgers "Slaughter on Tenth Avenue," which he danced with Vera-Ellen.

Producer Arthur Freed gave Kelly and Donen the go-ahead with *Take Me out to the Ball Game* (1949) which they wrote and choreographed. It led to their sharing the choreography and direction of *On the Town* (1949) based on the Broadway show by Betty Comden, Adolphe Green, and Leonard Bernstein. The latter film is frequently regarded as an example of the motion picture musical comedy in its purest form and remains Kelly's favorite picture. Kelly and Vincente Minnelli collaborated on *An American in Paris* (1951), a synthesis of what Kelly had long been endeavoring to do with dance in the film medium. The seventeen-minute ballet sequence to Gershwin's tone poem was the high point of that Technicolor picture, and it cost $450,000 to produce. Kelly was awarded a special Oscar "in appreciation of his versatility as an actor, singer, director, and dancer, and especially for his brilliant achievements in the art of choreography on film."

Singin' in the Rain (1952) teamed Kelly and Donen again as choreographer and director and is a mother classic of the musical film genre. After *Singin' in the Rain*, MGM assigned him to three pictures to be made abroad, whereby he was the first U. S. actor to benefit from the 1951 income tax law which exempted an American from federal income taxation if he worked abroad for eighteen months or more. One of the pictures Kelly made on the Continent was *Invitation to the Dance*, not released until 1956. It was an experimental attempt to present a dance film without dialogue but was not a success. He returned to the United States just as the musical was declining in popularity. *Brigadoon* (1954), in which he starred and choreographed while Minnelli directed, was a failure. The last-minute decision to film this musical entirely on soundstages was a major factor in the picture's synthetic flavor. *It's Always Fair Weather* (1955), which he did with Donen, had little of the sparkle of their earlier successes, despite its Cinemascope and color expensiveness. George Cukor directed Kelly's next film, the stylish but ignored *Les Girls* (1957), in which Kelly was surrounded by a trio of musical comedy performers, Kay Kendall, Mitzi Gaynor, and Taina Elg.

Throughout his film career, Kelly had mingled musical comedy roles with straight dramatic assignments. He was only mildly ludicrous as the opportunist husband in Deanna Durbin's *Christmas Holiday* (1944). In *The Black Hand* (1950) he was among those battling the Mafia in turn-of-the-century New York. *The Devil Makes Three* (1952) found him at his pretentious worst as the American G.I. returning to Munich to thank a family who had helped him during World War II. *Crest of the Wave* (1954) was a little picture in which Kelly appeared as a Navy officer who joins a British research team on a demolition assignment. When Warner Brothers announced that Kelly would play the Jewish heel, Noel Airman, in *Marjorie Morningstar* (1958), there was mild dismay from all quarters. However, this type of role was in keeping with Kelly's brand of screen dramatics, and the only substantial complaint about his performance was that he was a shade too old for the role. In *Inherit the Wind* (1960) Kelly was singularly inoffensive as the cynical reporter covering the controversial trial.

Kelly's last assignment for MGM was directing *Tunnel of Love* (1958), a one-joke sex comedy with Doris Day. Upon leaving MGM, Kelly choreographed the Broadway production of Rodgers and Hammerstein's *Flower Drum Song* (1959) and then tried his hand at presenting dance on television. Two of his video efforts were well received: an *Omnibus* production called *Dancing is a Man's Game*, and a special in which he danced to a poem read by Carl Sandburg, which the poet had written expressly for a dance sequence. But Kelly found the small-screen medium very limiting and preferred to do film and stage work. In 1960 he wrote and choreographed a ballet, *Pas de Deux*, to Gershwin's Piano Concerto in F. When it was presented by the Paris National Opera Ballet, he received twenty-three curtain calls.

Kelly directed the Parisian-filmed *Gigot* (1962) with Jackie Gleason. However, he had so many conflicts with that star and with the producing company, Seven Arts, that he got out of doing two more commitments for them. He starred in an unsuccessful television series, *Going My Way* (1963), which was based on the old Bing Crosby movie. Then he choreographed and starred in a segment of Shirley MacLaine's *What a Way to Go!* (1964), and had the lead in Jacques Demy's *The Young Girls of Rochefort* (1968) in which he played a dancing American concert pianist. *A Guide for the Married Man* (1967), which Kelly directed, was relatively successful, due more to the plethora of guest comedians than to the lackadaisical presentation. Twentieth Century-Fox planned to have Kelly direct a musical feature based on the *Tom Swift* novels but abandoned that project and put him in charge of their colossally expensive musical, *Hello, Dolly!* (1969). Barbra Streisand was not liked in the title role and Kelly's direction was euphemistically termed old-fashioned.

He ventured into yet another new entertainment medium when *Clown Around* premiered at the Coliseum in Oakland, California in April 1972. Kelly directed the elaborately mounted traveling kiddie's show, which headlined Ruth Buzzi and Dennis Allen of TV's *Laugh-In*. After two weeks of bad business in San Francisco in early May, the $650,000-plus arena show closed, sustaining a terrific loss.

Kelly divorced his first wife in 1957. They have a daughter Kerry. On August 6, 1960 he married Jeanne Coyne, a dancer who had studied at the

Gene Kelly Studio in Pittsburgh. Since 1949 she had been assistant choreographer on all his films and television specials. They have a son Timothy, born March 3, 1962.

The old days at MGM were ones of hard work, camaraderie and excitement for Kelly. He recalls, "Marvelous! What a group! Minnelli and Donen and Walters and Freed and Edens and Sol Chaplin. These are guys. And the musicans around them! Like Connie Sallinger and Lennie Hayton and Johnnie Green. Everyone was sympatico, one with another. Everyone was pitching in. It was like a repertory company, except very few of us were players. The players were Judy, Astaire, Cyd Charisse, and myself. But the guys around us were the reasons we had such good musicals. We had real collaboration. It was fun. We didn't think it was work."

GENE KELLY

For Me and My Gal (MGM, 1942)
Pilot No. 5 (MGM, 1943)
Dubarry Was a Lady (MGM, 1943)
Thousands Cheer (MGM, 1943)
The Cross of Lorraine (MGM, 1943)
Cover Girl (Columbia, 1944)
Christmas Holiday (Universal, 1944)
Anchors Aweigh (MGM, 1945)
Ziegfeld Follies (MGM, 1946)
Living in a Big Way (MGM, 1947)
The Pirate (MGM, 1948)
The Three Musketeers (MGM, 1948)

Words and Music (MGM, 1948)
Take Me out to the Ball Game (MGM, 1949)
On the Town (MGM, 1949)
The Black Hand (MGM, 1950)
Summer Stock (MGM, 1950)
An American in Paris (MGM, 1951)
It's a Big Country (MGM, 1951)
Singin' in the Rain (MGM, 1952)
The Devil Makes Three (MGM, 1952)
Love Is Better Than Ever (MGM, 1952)
Brigadoon (MGM, 1954)
Crest of the Wave (MGM, 1954)
Deep in My Heart (MGM, 1954)
It's Always Fair Weather (MGM, 1955)
Invitation to the Dance (MGM, 1956)
The Happy Road (MGM, 1957)
Les Girls (MGM, 1957)
Marjorie Morningstar (WB, 1958)
Inherit the Wind (UA, 1960)
Let's Make Love (20th-Fox, 1960)
What a Way to Go! (20th-Fox, 1964)
The Young Girls of Rochefort (WB-7 Arts, 1968)
Forty Carats (Columbia, 1973)

With Marie McDonald, William "Bill" Phillips, and Paul Godkin in *Living in a Big Way* (1947)

With Leslie Caron in *An American in Paris* (1951)

With Donald O'Connor, Douglas Fowley, and Bill Lewin in *Singin' in the Rain* (1952)

With Cyd Charisse in *It's Always Fair Weather* (1955)

With Diana Adams in *Invitation to the Dance* (1956)

Deborah Kerr

"Her name will rhyme with star and not with cur," was Louis B. Mayer's dictate when he imported British Deborah Kerr to Hollywood in 1946. She was to be a lever against another red-headed English star, Greer Garson, who was proving too headstrong for her adoring but practical MGM studio boss. Deborah came to California full of professional enthusiasm but soon discovered " ... all I had to do was to be high-minded, long-suffering, white-gloved and decorative." Her studio employers were convinced that once installed in her screen image as a British gentlewoman, Deborah should not stray afield in her pictures. There was an occasional offbeat assignment doled out to her such as the dipsomaniac in *Edward, My Son* (1949), but, despite public approval of this contracasting, Mayer continued thrusting her into films as the dignifed, and reserved upper-crust lady. Departing MGM in 1953, she surprised everyone concerned by her sensuous American dame characterization in *From Here to Eternity* (1953) and gained a long-overdue reputation as an actress of authoritative versatility on Broadway in *Tea and Sympathy*. Then, taking up the reins of her own film career, she became the internationally respected star she is today.

Deborah Kerr-Trimmer was born in Helensburgh, Scotland on September 30, 1921 and recalls the first fourteen years of her life as a lonely childhood and an unbearable tenure at boarding school. At fifteen she went to Bristol to attend the School of Dramatic Art, an establishment run by her aunt. While there she studied dancing briefly, and then went on to study ballet with the Sadler's Wells. She soon realized her height (5' 7") relegated her to the ballet chorus line only. She decided to try her hand at acting, setting out for London alone. She performed small roles in London repertory and made her West End theatrical debut in *Heartbreak House* (1940), starring Dame Edith Evans and Robert Donat. "Dame Edith taught me so much. She was very strict with me. She taught me timing and economy of gestures. Once she made me do a whole scene sitting on my hands because she said I used them too much."

One day Deborah was lunching in a fashionable restaurant with her agent, when she caught the eye of Hungarian director Gabriel Pascal. She says he approached her, asking her agent: "Who is this sweet virgin?" Then, turning to her, he declared, "You should wear your hair down around your shoulders. Pinned up that way, you look like a tart." With that off his chest, the flamboyant Pascal offered her an audition at which he had her recite the Lord's Prayer. Immediately he cast her as the Salvation Army girl, Jenny Hill, in his movie version of Shaw's *Major Barbara* (1941). She was quite effective in this excellent film and Pascal put her under contract.

Pascal did not use her again in any of his own films but kept her busy for other producers. He allowed her to be cast as a wench in *Love on the Dole* (1941) which proved to be successful for her. She then had a good part as the father-dominated girl in *Hatter's Castle* (1941) with James Mason. Her acting facility became clearly evident in 1943 when she played three different characters in *The Life and Death of Colonel Blimp*. She was acclaimed for her performances in two films released by the J. Arthur Rank Organisation. In *The Adventuress* (1946) she was very touching as the Irish colleen who is the foil of Nazi agents in a not entirely successful comedy–melodrama and, as the overconfident mother superior who finally achieves spiritual humility in the Technicolor *Black Narcissus* (1947), she was superb. These two films brought her the New York Film Critics Award—she had been named a star of tomorrow in 1942 by the *Motion Picture Herald*—and a contract from Louis B. Mayer.

The financial arrangements of Deborah's contract with MGM suggest that Mayer was greatly impressed by the British actress. He supposedly paid Pascal $200,000 to release her from his contract and offered her a seven-year contract which started at $3,000 weekly and which was to escalate to $7,000 during the last two years. This placed her immediately in the top ranks of the Metro stable, a fact that did not sit too well with many of the studio's domestic players. Before the end of 1947 she and her husband (Anthony Bartley whom she wed November 28, 1945) were settled in California, and she had given birth to daughter Melanie Jane. Said Deborah: " ... I am a part of the movies, and I like the fact that life in Hollywood revolves around the movies."

Her domestic bliss was not matched on the professional front. Her first MGM assignment was as the docile war widow in *The Hucksters* (1947), an expensively mounted film largely memorable for the blossoming of Ava Gardner as a love goddess and Sydney Greenstreet's characterization of the crude soap company executive. Her second role was more of the same as Walter Pidgeon's inamorata in *If Winter Comes* (1947). She returned to England with Spencer Tracy and director George Cukor to film *Edward, My Son*, the story of a businessman who corrupts and destroys in order to give his son everything. While Tracy was miscast, Deborah turned in one of the best performances of her career to date as his long-suffering wife who, unable to combat Tracy's egomaniacal whims, resorts to alcoholism.

But these types of roles were not to be her reward from MGM and the studio bullishly reserved their less gutsy parts for her. She was stuck with the "Lady" tag and in the next four years was continuously cool and classy in Africa, *King Solomon's Mines* (1950); in ancient Rome, *Quo Vadis* (1951); in

Graustark, *The Prisoner Of Zenda* (1952); and in King Henry the Eighth's England, *Young Bess* (1953). She was bored with this glib filmmaking and requested a supporting role as Portia in *Julius Caesar* (1953) which also featured her friendly rival Greer Garson as Calpurnia.

MGM was now under the aegis of Dore Schary and Deborah saw even less reason to stick around, "I suffered from too much respect for the boss. I took for granted that the heads of studios, with all their experience, knew instinctively what was best for me. It took me six years to learn that perhaps they didn't."

When Joan Crawford departed from the cast lineup of Columbia's *From Here to Eternity*, zealous agent Bert Allenberg fought for Deborah being given the plum of Karen Holmes, the promiscuous army wife. When Allenberg approached Columbia head Harry Cohn, the mogul reportedly screamed: "Why, you stupid son of a bitch!" Nevertheless, he finally agreed when producer Buddy Adler, director Fred Zinnemann, and screenwriter Daniel Taradash convinced him the surprise casting would be unique. The rest is film history, with the Deborah Kerr–Burt Lancaster surfside love scene becoming a classic. She was Oscar-nominated, but lost out to Audrey Hepburn who won for *Roman Holiday*.

Deborah next went to New York to appear in Robert Anderson's *Tea and Sympathy* (1953) and confounded Broadway and the public by her sensitive, dazzling performance. She remained a full season with the hit drama and later went on a national tour with it.

Tea and Sympathy marked the beginning of Deborah's career prime as a free-lance star. She was Anna in *The King and I* (1956), splitting her vocal duties with Marni Nixon, and earning the second of her five Academy Award nominations to date. *Tea and Sympathy* (1956) rejoined Deborah with MGM, but the picturization was too hedgy to be viable drama. Her second costarring vehicle with David Niven, *Separate Tables* (1958), earned them both Oscar nominations. Niven won his Oscar, but her seaside resort spinster lost out. She was a wavering Sheilah Graham to Gregory Peck's miscast F. Scott Fitzgerald in Twentieth Century-Fox's *Beloved Infidel* (1959) but regained stature the following year with her fifth Oscar bid, in the Australian-filmed *The Sundowners* (1960).

It was on July 23, 1960 that Deborah wed writer Peter Viertel (she and Bartley had a second child in 1950) and they were divorced amid some nasty publicity in 1968. Fortuitously, Deborah's public image remained intact during these domestic hassles, most likely due to the fact that her well-bred lady image stood her in very good stead. Hedda Hopper concluded the speculation on Deborah's moral status by kindly chiding, "Deborah always made the mistake of boasting about her 'perfect marriage' when we all knew it wasn't true."

Throughout the 1960s, Swiss-based Deborah was very much a part of the international social set, while retaining her film celebrity membership with more than competent performances in a variety of inartistic cinema productions. She was the tormented governess in an adaptation of Henry James' *Turn of the Screw*, titled *The Innocents* (1961), and a very much different sort of nursemaid in the glossy but empty edition of *The Chalk Garden* (1964). In that same year she was the frustrated spinster awakened to life by Richard Burton in *The Night of the Iguana*. The production publicity for the film so far exceeded what emerged on the screen that everything about the film, including Deborah's controlled neurotic performance, was a disappointing anticlimax. Some of her artistic lapses were such roles as the bored wife in the Frank Sinatra–Dean Martin sex comedy *Marriage on the Rocks* (1965), the untamed clan head capering about the Scottish countryside in *Casino Royale* (1967), as Kim Novak's replacement in *Eye of the Devil* (1967). She reteamed with Niven in the alleged birth control comedy *Prudence and the Pill* (1968) which sat badly with the public.

Deborah's last two films to date, both released in 1969, were small, top female lead assignments, each requiring the forty-seven-year-old actress to tackle nude love scenes. She was attracted to professional parachutist Burt Lancaster in *The Gypsy Moths*, and was Kirk Douglas' nonunderstanding wife in the unentertaining *The Arrangement*. She was drawn to the latter film, not only because of its prestigious nature and the fact that it offered her "a" role in the diminishing market for mature female stars, but because "I play a very human wife—that is, I'm part wonderful and part bitch."

She has only made an occasional television appearance, gracing a few Oscarcasts, hostessing the Tony Awards in April 1972, narrating a documentary here and there, and performing in a European-lensed video trilogy, *Three Roads to Rome*.

Although Deborah is terrified by public appearances, she returned to the London stage in the fall of 1972 in Frank Harvey's new play, *The Day After the Fair*. Explaining this career decision she says: "It's nerve-wracking but it's an extension of life . . . . I like it because I can hide myself in so many different parts." Regarding her fears of public scrutiny: "When you're young, you just go barging along, but you're more sensitive as you grow older. Your ego becomes less. You have higher standards of what's really good and you're fearful that you won't live up to what's expected of you."

Perhaps the key to Deborah's *only* near-legendary career status was best summed up by the actress herself a few years ago: "All the most successful people seem to be neurotic these days. Perhaps we should stop being sorry for them and start being sorry for me—for being so confounded normal."

DEBORAH KERR

Major Barbara (UA, 1941)
Love on the Dole (British National, 1941)
The Courageous Mr. Penn (British National, 1941)
Hatter's Castle (British National, 1941)
The Avengers (General Film Distributors-Paramount, 1942)
The Life and Death of Colonel Blimp (Archer Films-UA, 1943)
Vacation from Marriage (MGM-London, 1945)
The Adventuress (Rank-Eagle–Lion, 1946)
Black Narcissus (Rank-Universal, 1947)
The Hucksters (MGM, 1947)
If Winter Comes (MGM, 1947)
Edward, My Son (MGM, 1949)
King Solomon's Mines (MGM, 1950)
Please Believe Me (MGM, 1950)
Quo Vadis (MGM, 1951)
Prisoner of Zenda (MGM, 1952)
Thunder in the East (Paramount, 1953)
Young Bess (MGM, 1953)
Dream Wife (MGM, 1953)
Julius Caesar (MGM, 1953)

From Here to Eternity (Columbia, 1953)
The End of the Affair (Columbia, 1955)
The Proud and Profane (Paramount, 1956)
The King and I (20th-Fox, 1956)
Tea and Sympathy (MGM, 1956)
Heaven Knows, Mr. Allison (20th-Fox, 1957)
An Affair to Remember (20th-Fox, 1957)
Bonjour Tristesse (Columbia, 1958)
Separate Tables (UA, 1958)
The Journey (MGM, 1959)
Count Your Blessings (MGM, 1959)
Beloved Infidel (20th-Fox, 1959)
The Sundowners (WB, 1960)
The Grass Is Greener (Universal, 1960)
The Naked Edge (UA, 1961)
The Innocents (20th-Fox, 1961)
The Chalk Garden (Universal, 1964)
The Night of the Iguana (MGM, 1964)
Marriage on the Rocks (WB, 1965)
Casino Royale (Columbia, 1967)
Eye of the Devil (MGM, 1967)
Prudence and the Pill (20th-Fox, 1968)
The Gypsy Moths (MGM, 1969)
The Arrangement (WB-7 Arts, 1969)

With Ian Hunter and Spencer Tracy in *Edward, My Son* (1949)

With James Whitmore in *Please Believe Me* (1950)

With James Mason in *Julius Caesar* (1953)

With John Kerr in *Tea and Sympathy* (1956)

With Maurice Chevalier, Martin Stephens, and Rossano Brazzi in *Count Your Blessings* (1959)

With Donald Pleasance in *Eye of the Devil* (1967)

Hedy Lamarr

Venus, as envisioned by Botticelli, came from the sea and so Hedwig Kiesler was reborn Hedy Lamarr, with the blessings of Louis B. Mayer, on the ocean voyage taking her to Hollywood. Internationally famous as a teenager because of her nude aquatic scene in *Ecstasy* (1933) produced in Prague, Czechoslovakia, Hedy was utilized by Mayer in one undistinguished picture after another. Undeniably the most beautiful screen actress of the late 1930s and early war years, the bulk of her career was spent as merely a marble mannequin. After a sensational American film debut in *Algiers* (1938) on loanout from MGM, Mayer put her in two pictures which flopped and then lost interest in her. With no Svengali to replace Mayer, Hedy singlehandedly tried to fathom what was right for herself as an actress, but her decisions frequently proved disastrous. Despite this mismanagement the public was enchanted by this ethereal beauty and, since it is the public which makes cinema stars, her dubious reign in Hollywood lasted a full decade.

Hedy was born Hedwig Eva Maria Kiesler in Vienna (November 9, 1915). Her father was a director of the Bank of Vienna and she was raised in a luxurious household surrounded by servants and private tutors. At a private academy in Switzerland she spent her allowance on movie magazines and, while attending a finishing school later in Vienna, she skipped classes and got a two-day job at the Sascha Film Studio. After the part of an ingenue in another film, she persuaded her parents to allow her to go to Berlin to study with Max Reinhardt. Reinhardt, whom she recalls as a kind and gentle man, gave her small roles in several theatrical productions. She did a comedy film for German director Carl Boese, then attracted international notoriety by playing in a film called *Symphonie der Liebe* (1933), directed by Gustav de Machatz, and widely released under the exotic title *Ecstasy*. The plot was little more than ordinary soap opera, but two revealing sequences made it famous: one had Hedy swimming nude in a lake and then running likewise nude through a forest, and the second showed her face in a closeup during orgasm. The film won the Grand Prix at the Vienna Film Festival in 1934 and set a precedent for nudity in the commercial film.

By this time, Hedy had returned to her native Vienna. While appearing in a play called *Cissy*, based on the life of Queen Elizabeth of Austria, she was

407

introduced to, courted by, and married to Fritz Mandl, owner of the Hirstenberger-Patronen-Fabrik Industries, one of the world's four largest manufacturers of munitions. Mandl, then in his fifties, seemed to collect actresses as a hobby. He had married and divorced one, and another had committed suicide when he refused to marry her. As the teenaged Madame Mandl Hedy found herself presiding over a ten-room apartment in Vienna, a castle in Salzburg, and entertaining such dinner guests as Gustav Mahler and Franz Werfel on a solid gold dinner service, while on another occasion, her hand was being kissed by Adolf Hitler, and her chair was being held by Benito Mussolini.

Despite the extravagance of her life style, Hedy sought to escape Mandl and his obsession with her as just another *objet d'art*. She finally did just this, by disguising herself as one of her servants and fleeing to Paris by train with only a few jewels. She obtained a divorce in the French courts, and sold some of her jewelry to pay for her passage to England. Her arrival there did not go unnoticed and an American agent named Bob Ritchie took her to Mayer's hotel suite. Mayer agreed she was beautiful but was skeptical as to how this star of "nude" films could fit into the proper MGM family. Offhandedly, he offered her a six month contract at $125 weekly with no traveling expenses. Hedy refused, whereupon Ritchie devised a scheme to have her book passage on the *Normandie*, the ship on which Mayer was returning to America. She was to be the "governess" of another of Ritchie's clients, a fourteen-year-old violin prodigy named Grisha Goluboff. Before they docked, Hedy had in hand a seven-year contract starting at $500 weekly and a new name. Mayer named her after silent film actress Barbara LaMarr whom he considered the most beautiful of all Hollywood stars.

When they finally docked, Hedy was greeted by a swarm of newsmen who all clamored to look at the star of *Ecstasy*, much to Mayer's dismay. Once in Hollywood, Mayer had no immediate plans for her and advised her to learn English. While she was waiting for the studio to decide her professional fate, she was escorted through Hollywood's social whirl by debonair Reginald Gardiner, and on one such occasion, Charles Boyer introduced her to Walter Wanger, suggesting her for the part of the society girl in *Algiers*. Wanger had wanted Sylvia Sidney, but that star had temporarily deserted Hollywood for Broadway. So Mayer loaned Hedy to Wanger at $1,500 weekly. This exotically set film had Boyer as a criminal seeking refuge in a North African *casbah*, and when he sang "C'est la Vie" to the exquisite Hedy, the public swooned. "Come wiz me to the Casbah," a line *never* in the film, became the catch phrase of the day and American males soon were fantasizing over the Lamarr allure.

Mayer was unprepared for this enthusiasm but, with his usual bravura touch, set out to make her his "most important star." Would that he had! His tactic was to capitalize on her continental background and for this purpose he hired Josef von Sternberg (the alleged Svengali to Marlene Dietrich) to direct *I Take This Woman* (1940). The film costarred Spencer Tracy, and was one of Charles MacArthur's worst scripts. The dictatorial von Sternberg proceeded to rewrite and after two weeks he was replaced by Frank Borzage, who had to stop shooting when production overlapped with the starting date of Tracy's next commitment, *Stanley and Livingstone* (1939). By the time *Woman* resumed, cast members had been changed and a new director, W. S. Van Dyke, was assigned because he worked fast. By this time Hollywood was referring to it as "I Re-Take This Woman," but Mayer was not laughing as this was probably the only feature film he actually personally produced. When finally released, it was a flop and Mayer was heard exclaiming: "I told them they were making a lousy picture, but they wouldn't listen to me."

In the interim, Hedy completed *Lady of the Tropics* (1939), a little melodrama set in Saigon which was hardly more than a series of breathtaking black and white stills of Hedy and Robert Taylor. Another flop! At this point, Hedy wisely requested the supporting role with star billing in *Boom Town* (1940) whose featured stars were Clark Gable, Spencer Tracy, and Claudette Colbert. It was a boxoffice smash and Gable and Hedy were so effective onscreen together that they were subsequently cast in *Comrade X* (1940), a quite charming imitation of Ernst Lubitsch's *Ninotchka*, with Hedy as a Russian streetcar conductor. Hedy says she found Gable a warm and friendly man but never quite understood his sex appeal.

By now Mayer curiously, and unfortunately, had lost interest in Hedy's career and she became the foil of the studio's scriptwriters whenever they needed an actress with ultra exotic appeal. Her effort to manage her own career, which at the time earned her the reputation of being difficult, resulted in some grave miscalculations. She turned down Otto Preminger's *Laura* (1944), as well as two of Ingrid Bergman's biggies, *Gaslight* (1944) and *Saratoga Trunk* (1945). MGM refused to loan her to Warners for *Casablanca* (1942) (Bergman did that one, too) and Warners did not bother to borrow her for *Mr. Skeffington* (1944), the role many thought she should have played instead of Bette Davis. The films in which she did star were mostly second-rate. She was only decorative in *Ziegfeld Girl* (1941), but quite good with Robert Young in *H. M. Pulham, Esq.* (1941). While everyone, including Spencer Tracy and John Garfield, was miscast in John Steinbeck's *Tortilla Flat* (1942), Hedy regards her performance as the Mexican beauty her best and she may very well be right. *White Cargo* (1942) had her as a half-caste who utters "I am Tondelayo" and Hedy in one of her less enlightened moments said of the picture, "I thought with some interesting makeup, a sarong, and some hip-swinging, I would be a memorable nymphomaniac."

Her role as the intimidated wife of maniacal Paul Lukas in RKO's *Experiment Perilous* (1944) is the one critics regard as her best. With *Her Highness and the Bellboy* (1945) she ended her MGM contract. She formed her own company, but her poor judgment of scripts—*The Strange Woman* (1946), *Dishonored Lady* (1947), *Let's Live a Little* (1948)—capsized her enterprise. Furthermore, she was not the brightest star in heaven when in 1949 Cecil B. De Mille cast her in *Samson and Delilah*. De Mille had wanted an unknown for the part but had second thoughts and cast Hedy because he knew she could fill the audience's conception of the Biblical seductress. The film was a top moneymaker but Hedy found working with the autocratic De Mille so taxing that she foolishly refused to star in his next picture, *The Greatest Show on Earth* (1952). Hedy's career was virtually over.

She continued to appear in an occasional film through 1957, but her name was kept alive more by the foibles of her personal life. She had married and divorced five husbands since Mandl: writer Gene Markey, actor John J. Loder, restaurateur Ernest Stauffer, Texas oilman W. Howard Lee, and lawyer Lewis W. Boles, Jr. She also raised three children. In 1966 two events resulted in unpleasant headlines. In January she was arrested for supposedly shoplifting a pair of $85 gold slippers in Los Angeles' May Company. At the time she was reportedly carrying $14,000 in uncashed checks, and when the case came to trial she was found not guilty. The publicity, however, ruined her chance at a comeback in the Joseph E. Levine minor thriller *Picture Mommy Dead*. Later the same year a book purporting to be an an authorized autobiography called *Ecstasy and Me* was published, and its scurrilous sexposelike content made it a best seller. Hedy maintained the book was full of falsities and that she never saw the final galleys, and she instituted a multimillion-dollar lawsuit. That lawsuit, plus two others—one against ex-husband Lee and one against a film company over an unreleased picture made in Italy—have occupied her for the past seven years, and she steadfastly says she will win.*

Now living in New York, her courage and perseverence are indeed admirable if, indeed, somewhat sad. Film historian Richard Griffith once wrote: "The emotional binge of stardom leaves its victims in a state of perpetural hangover." This would seem to apply aptly to the current-day Hedy, who has been wont to state, "Would you believe I was once a famous star. It's the truth!"

*In May 1972 Hedy lost another round in her multimillion-dollar lawsuit against the publisher, writer and collaborator of her supposed autobiography. The Court of Appeals of the State of New York ruled it lacked jurisdiction to hear the cause of action.

The prior November, Hedy had failed to show up in court in a false arrest suit brought against her by a machine repairman. The workman had gone to her home to adjust her air-conditioner, and Hedy brought suit charging attempted rape. The repairman counter-charged that the actress had willingly accepted his advances. When Hedy did not appear at the court hearing, she was ordered to pay $15,000.

HEDY LAMARR

Sturme Ein Vaser Glase (Sascha, 1929)
Mein Braucht Kein Geld (Sascha, 1930)
Das Geld Liegt auf der Strasse (Sascha, 1930)
Die Blumenfrau Von Lindenau (Sascha, 1931)
Die Koffer der Herr I. F. Herne (Allianz Film, 1931)

Symphonie Der Liebe (Ecstasy) (Elecktra, 1933)
Algiers (UA, 1938)
Lady of the Tropics (MGM, 1939)
I Take This Woman (MGM, 1940)
Boom Town (MGM, 1940)

With Joseph Schildkraut in *Lady of the Tropics* (1939)

With Kent Taylor and Verree Teasdale in *I Take This Woman* (1940)

Comrade X (MGM, 1940)
Come Live with Me (MGM, 1941)
Ziegfeld Girl (MGM, 1941)
H. M. Pulham, Esq. (MGM, 1941)
Tortilla Flat (MGM, 1942)
Crossroads (MGM, 1942)
White Cargo (MGM, 1942)
The Heavenly Body (MGM, 1943)
The Conspirators (WB, 1944)
Experiment Perilous (RKO, 1944)

With Donald Meek in *Come Live With Me* (1941)

With Clark Gable in *Comrade X* (1940)

Her Highness and the Bellboy (MGM, 1945)
The Strange Woman (UA, 1946)
Dishonored Lady (UA, 1947)
Let's Live a Little (Eagle–Lion, 1948)
Samson and Delilah (Paramount, 1949)
A Lady Without Passport (MGM, 1950)
Copper Canyon (Paramount, 1950)

411

In *White Cargo* (1942)

With William Powell in *The Heavenly Body* (1943)

With Ferdinand Munier, Ludwig Stossel, Agnes Moorehead, Marie Melish, Bertha Feducha, and Symona Boniface in *Her Highness and the Bellboy* (1945)

My Favorite Spy (Paramount, 1951)
The Loves of Three Women (Italian, 1954)
Femmina (Italian, 1954)
The Story of Mankind (WB, 1957)
The Female Animal (Universal, 1957)

412

Fernando Lamas

By the 1950s the Latin Lover screen image was an anachronism in Hollywood folklore, a fact recognized all too well by the two major stars who were being promoted as Lovers—Fernando Lamas and Ricardo Montalban. MGM, however, took a while before they admitted such roles were a commodity no longer salable on the Hollywood market. Both Lamas and Montalban were handsome and Lamas sang well while Montalban was the better dancer. Lamas possessed more of the charisma for romantic leads than did his competitor, and for a time MGM utilized him as a tuxedoed puppet who sang an occasional song in musical or adventure films which required that romantic touch. Inanely, his publicity labeled him "The First of the Red-Hot Lamas," and MGM tried to use him as a threat to the self-indulgent, overweight Mario Lanza. Lamas' stardom was short-lived and the Latin Lover publicity and his romances with Lana Turner and Arlene Dahl overshadowed anything he did professionally. Finally he decided all the hoopla was just simply not worth it.

Fernando Alvaro Lamas was born in Buenos Aires, Argentina, on January 9, 1915. He was orphaned at the age of four and raised by his grandparents with whom he did much global traveling. By the age of seventeen he was a handsome, well-developed, athletic youngster who had firmly decided to become an actor. His career began with small roles on stage, in radio, and in motion pictures. In 1940 he wed Argentinian actress Pearla Mux. They were both ambitious, career-minded individuals, and their marriage did not last. During the 1940s he moved to Mexico where he acquired better roles in Spanish-speaking films and was married for a second time, in 1946, to Lydia Babachi, the daughter of a socially prominent Uruguayan family. Two years later he gained stardom appearing opposite Dolores Del Rio in a handsome cinemazation of Oscar Wilde's *Lady Windemere's Fan* (*Historia de una Mala Mujer*). When Republic made *The Avengers* (1950) on location in South America, Lamas had a small role in the John Carroll feature, and in the Spanish version of the picture he dubbed Carroll's voice. Carroll's wife, Lucille Ryman, a drama coach and talent scout for MGM, arranged for the virile actor to be screen-tested at that studio.

During the first seven months at Culver City, MGM tutored Lamas in

English, making it the fifth language he speaks fluently. He also speaks Portuguese, Spanish, Italian, and French. But they had no role for him. Lamas' wife, Lydia, followed him to the United States in an effort to reconcile their marital problems. They had a daughter, Alejandre, but Lydia's family felt she had married below her station and the marriage was never very peaceful. Supposedly, pianist and MGM artist Jose Iturbi saw the tall Lamas at a party at the home of producer Joe Pasternak and said; "Joe, Joe! Here's a prize; a gaucho for the girls!" With that, Pasternak cast him in a small role in a Jane Powell musical, *Rich, Young and Pretty* (1951), which was followed by his portrayal of a South American cowboy in Greer Garson's *The Law and the Lady* (1951).

Then the studio promoted him to full-fledged stardom as a Latin Lover opposite Lana Turner in the remake of *The Merry Widow* (1952). As Prince Danilo Lamas displayed a very attractive baritone singing voice, and he and Turner were well costumed and photographed. The public responded to the two obvious sex symbols on the screen. Turner virtually glowed in that picture, and it was not just because of the costumes and the lighting. MGM cohorts recall that when the two performers met, it was spontaneous combustion, and the romance was a lead item in all the columns. Lamas resented the publicity attending their romance, although he could not deny it made him a much hotter screen commodity. As the gossip hens began predicting a marriage, Lamas firmly denied any intention of divorcing Lydia, despite their unsuccessful reconciliation attempts. He said "I have no intention of starting divorce proceedings against my wife. It is not up to a man to ask for a divorce, anyway." His attitude did not sit well with the possessive Turner, and one evening, at a $25,000 bash that Marion Davies threw in honor of singer Johnny Ray, the big romance ended. Turner flirted with handsome muscleman Lex Barker, and Lamas and she exchanged bitter words in front of the guests. Even Louella Parsons admitted she was "shocked" at their behavior. The ending of their courtship received greater coverage than their romance, particularly when Turner not only dated but married Barker. Furthermore, Lamas, whose wife by now had gotten a divorce, took to courting and then marrying Barker's ex-wife, Arlene Dahl. It was almost too much for even an astute columnist to keep straight, but they all got properly switched and legally hitched in the end. And if it did not last a lifetime, at least some of the foursome must have been happy some of the time.

As soon as *The Merry Widow* was wrapped up, MGM had announced that Lamas and Turner would be reteamed in *Latin Lovers* (1953), but wisely decided to replace Lamas with Ricardo Montalban and put Lamas into *Dangerous When Wet* (1953) instead, opposite Esther Williams, who was by now used to having Montalban as her costar. Lamas' manly physique was splashed by mermaid Williams in that aquatic spectacular. Then MGM capitalized on his romance with Arlene Dahl and loaned him out to Paramount for *Sangaree* and then to Warner Brothers for *Diamond Queen*, both released in 1953. Metro used his singing ability in a remake of the

Jeanette MacDonald–Nelson Eddy musical, *Rose Marie* (1954), with toothy Ann Blyth. His MGM contract expired with that picture and he said: "I left MGM because everything I had done—6 or 7 expensive pictures—I always played the same roles and I realized I was not going anyplace with all the *Merry Widows* and *Rose Maries*. It got so I didn't need a new set of tails."

Lamas wed Arlene Dahl in 1954, made two more Hollywood pictures, and signed for the singing lead in the Broadway musical, *Happy Hunting* at $2,000 weekly. Ethel Merman was the star of that show and, when it opened on December 6, 1956, Lamas' reviews were good, but he and Merman ended up hating each other and refused to speak to one another offstage. Each accused the other of upstaging. When the play closed Lamas made several nightclub appearances as a singer and appeared in a stock version of *The King and I* with Dahl. Arlene bore him a son, Lorenzo Fernando, in 1958, and two years later their marriage ended in divorce.

He taped a television special with Esther Williams in Cypress Gardens, Florida in 1959, and when she flew to Europe to make a film, Lamas followed. They became steady companions. Lamas directed a motion picture in Spain entitled *The Magic Fountain* (1961) in which he and Williams costarred, but it never was released in the States. When Williams appeared in Ft. Lauderdale, Florida in 1967 to be named a member of the Swimming Pool Hall of Fame, Lamas was her escort, and it was announced that they had been married that year in Europe. On December 31, 1969 they were wed a second time at the Founders Church of Religious Science. Lamas had become associated with that metaphysical school of thought while still married to Arlene Dahl. Lamas and Williams live in Santa Monica, California, with her three children by a previous marriage.

Lamas made two minor motion picture appearances in 1969: *100 Rifles*, starring Raquel Welch, and *Backtrack* for Universal. He has also directed a number of television episodes, including *The Bold Ones* series. In 1972 he and Williams began working up a nightclub routine. Lamas once said that, for his string of Latin Lover and swashbuckling roles, all he needed for props were "a sword in one hand, a blonde in the other, and a horse outside." He seems to enjoy the current lack of headlines about his private life. Occasionally he appears on television talk shows and impresses his audiences as a charming and level-headed man. Of his Latin Lover image, he says, "The difference between Latin and American men is that the Latins give you a little more of everything, I think. More headaches, more temper, more tenderness."

FERNANDO LAMAS

En el Ultimo Piso (Argentinian, 1942)
Frontera Sur (Argentinian, 1942)
Villa Rica del Espiritu Santo (Argentinian, 1945)
Navidad de los Pobres (Argentinian, 1947)
Evasion (Argentinian, 1947)
El Tango Vuelve a Paris (Argentinian, 1947)
Historia de una Mala Mujer (Argentinian, 1948)
La Rubia Mireya (Argentinian, 1948)

With Lana Turner in *The Merry Widow* (1952)

La Otra y Yo (Argentinian, 1948)
De Padre Desconocido (Argentinian, 1949)
Vidalita (Argentinian, 1949)
La Historia del Tango (Argentinian, 1949)
The Avengers (Republic, 1950)
Rich, Young and Pretty (MGM, 1951)
The Law and the Lady (MGM, 1951)
The Merry Widow (MGM, 1952)
The Girl Who Had Everything (MGM, 1953)
Dangerous When Wet (MGM, 1953)
Sangaree (Paramount, 1953)
Diamond Queen (WB, 1953)
Rose Marie (MGM, 1954)
Jivaro (Paramount, 1954)
The Girl Rush (Paramount, 1955)
The Lost World (20th-Fox, 1960)
The Magic Fountain (Spanish, 1961)
Valley of Mystery (Universal, 1967)
Kill a Dragon (UA, 1967)
100 Rifles (20th-Fox, 1969)
Backtrack (Universal, 1969)

With Jack Carson and Esther Williams in *Dangerous When Wet* (1953)

416

Angela Lansbury

Angela Lansbury was a late-blooming cereus who, like Lauren Bacall (in *Applause*!), did not come into her own as an actress or a woman until twenty-three years after making her motion picture debut. With her acidly comic portrayal of the sophisticated earth mother in *Mame*, Angela became the toast of Broadway, received international press coverage as well as a cover story in *Life* magazine, was voted a Tony Award, and accolade of accolades, her framed caricature was moved from the back wall of Sardi's Restaurant to a more prominent location by the entranceway to that Broadway eatery. Her husband, MGM executive Peter Shaw, exclaimed, "Suddenly, after beating her brains out, Angie's really a star."

Angela Brigid Lansbury was born in London on October 16, 1925. Her father died when she was nine, leaving her mother and Angela's twin brothers, Bruce and Edgar. (Her mother, an actress named Moyna MacGill, had earlier been wed to actor–manager Reginald Denham, and she still pursues an acting career, while both Bruce and Edgar have become entertainment producers.) Angela recalls that she never shared her mother's strong acting ambitions but, willingly enough, began to study drama to avoid being shipped off to boarding school. After a brief tenure at the Webber-Douglas School of Singing and Dramatic Art, Miss MacGill decided wartime England was not the place to raise her brood, and they emigrated to the United States. In September 1940 Angela enrolled in the Feagin School of Drama and Radio in Rockefeller Center and immediately became aware that she was essentially a character actress and not a typical ingenue.

A fellow student at Feagin worked up an arrangement of Noel Coward's "I Went to a Marvelous Party," having Angela imitate Beatrice Lillie's style, and soon Angela found herself booked into a Montreal nightclub at $65 weekly. By the time the stint had ended, her mother had moved to Los Angeles and Angela followed. Both mother and daughter found acting jobs elusive at first and hired themselves out as salesladies in Bullock's Department Store on Wilshire Boulevard, mother in the toy department and Angela in cosmetics.

Soon after she arrived in Los Angeles, Angela met aspiring young actor Michael Dyne, who was being considered for the lead in MGM's *The Picture of Dorian Gray* (1945). He suggested she go to MGM's Culver City lot and test for the role of the Cockney maid in *Gaslight* (1944). She performed her test for director George Cukor, playing opposite Hugh Marlowe (Charles Boyer played the role in the picture). Louis B. Mayer liked her and signed her to a seven-year contract at $500 weekly. She resigned from Bullock's over the telephone. When *Gaslight* was released, critics noted that, even though she was but eighteen years old and this was her motion picture debut, she was mature in both presence and technique, and she was nominated for an Academy Award as best supporting actress. After playing Elizabeth Taylor's older sister in *National Velvet* (1944), she earned a second Oscar nomination for *The Picture of Dorian Gray*, playing the virginal Sibyl Vane. The lead was essayed by Hurd Hatfield. Her portrayal of the fragile music hall singer who warbles "Little Yellow Bird" prompted critic James Agee to opine, "She is touching and exact in her defenseless romanticism and ... evocative of milkmaids in eighteenth-century pornographic prints."

Despite the fact that Mayer liked her, and she says she could always talk to him ("he did not chase me around the desk"), he did not give her the kind of roles she wanted to play ("I always wanted to be Jean Arthur"). Most of her parts required her to display the more venal aspects of the feminine psyche and not the comedic. She was so good at being a bad girl that after playing the honky-tonk singer in *The Harvey Girls* (1946), she was actually hissed in public for being mean to Judy Garland.

Angela's ability to play callous women had her briefly considered for the title role in Twentieth Century-Fox's *Forever Amber* (1947), for unlike many fellow character players who specialized in bitchery, (such as Agnes Moorehead), Angela combined a man-eating sexual allure with her grasping ways. Whether or not Angela was seriously considered as the replacement for star Peggy Cummins, who was withdrawn from the part, Angela was quoted as saying "Whatever would I have used for bosoms?" When Fox resumed production on that ballyhooed flop, Linda Darnell had the title role. A part Angela did fight for was as Milady De Winter in *The Three Musketeers* (1948). Mayer did not agree with her and she was relegated to playing Queen Anne in support to MGM's hot sex symbol Lana Turner. It was no contest.

Meanwhile, MGM had loaned her to United Artists for *The Private Affairs of Bel Ami* (1947). For a change she was the one stepped upon by a worse onscreen skunk, George Sanders. Then she was cast on the home lot as Walter Pidgeon's middle-aged spiteful wife in *If Winter Comes* (1947). She cynically used her sexual allure to gain political power in *State of the Union* (1948), with Spencer Tracy and Katharine Hepburn, and was speared to the wall while playing Hedy Lamarr's sister Semadar in Cecil B. De Mille's *Samson and Delilah* (1949) at Paramount. She ended her MGM association in 1951 by terrorizing Ethel Barrymore in *Kind Lady*. She says that being under contract was "terribly confining" and, after Dore Schary became MGM's vice president in charge of production and studio operations in 1948, she got lost in the shuffle.

After leaving the studio, she sought theatre work in summer stock because it paid well, and played character roles in films and television when they were available. She says her professional low was playing the seamstress in *The Purple Mask* (1955), a swashbuckler starring Tony Curtis. She made her Broadway debut in 1957 with Bert Lahr in the Georges Feydeau farce, *Hotel Paradiso*. While the play was not a success, she credits Lahr with teaching her the art of stage craft. In 1960 theatrical producer David Merrick cast her as the floozy mother in *A Taste of Honey* which gave her a longer run and much critical acclaim. She gave two striking film performances in 1962: the tragic–comic prototype mother of Warren Beatty in *All Fall Down* (released by MGM) and the monstrously malevolent mother of Laurence Harvey in *The Manchurian Candidate*. Those two portrayals earned her the best supporting actress award from the National Board of Review, and the latter one earned her a third Academy Award nomination.

Angela is philosophical about her typecasting problem. "I've played so many old hags, most people think I'm sixty-five years old. I didn't want to play all those nasty ladies, but in Hollywood, you're either a member of the working group or not, and if not, you're easily forgotten. I've had high spots, medium spots, and a couple of low spots, but I've always been in there pitching." She never pitched harder then when she was approached to star in the Broadway production of *Mame*, the Jerry Herman–Jerome Lawrence–Robert E. Lee musical version of Patrick Dennis' *Auntie Mame*, which was performed originally on the stage by Rosalind Russell. Literally every top stage and film actress from Russell to Simone Signoret was mentioned as a candidate for the part, and Angela was not anyone's first choice. Finally, after two auditions and no affirmative answer, Angela exasperatedly exclaimed, "I'm going back to California and, unless you tell me now, yes or no—let's face it—I have prostrated myself—that's the end of it." She got the part! The musical opened May 24, 1966 and was a sensation. Said *Time* magazine: "The woman all moviegoers remember as a worn, plump old harridan with a snake pit for a mouth, is the liveliest dame to kick up her heels since Carol Channing opened in *Hello, Dolly!*" Angela had finally come into her own, and for months she was the Queen of the Great White Way.

It was also during the run of this triumph that Angela faced the biggest test in her personal life. She had been married in 1945 for nine months to actor Richard Cromwell. Four years later she wed agent Peter Shaw by whom she had two children—Anthony (born 1952) and Diedre (born 1953). During the run of *Mame*, Angela did not question her son's repeated requests for his allowance in advance at first, but in time she discovered that Anthony had become addicted to heroin. The battle to face the problem and learn how to handle it led to several years of hospitals, withdrawal clinics, and psychiatrists. During this time Angela appeared in the expensive Broadway flop, *Dear World*, a musical version of Jean Giraudoux's charming *The Madwoman of Chaillot*. Another even more costly stage flop was *Prettybelle* (1970) which the producer closed in Boston. Meanwhile, when all efforts to completely cure her son failed, Angela and her husband opted to find a retreat, taking their son away from the frustrations and temptations of metropolitan life. They purchased a home in Ballycotton, Ireland, a small town near Cork, where they lived in exile for a year. Now cured, Anthony lives in London in his own apartment and is studying drama.

On the crest of her *Mame* popularity, Angela had starred in Harold Prince's black comedy film *Something for Everyone* (1970) which failed to generate the popularity it so wickedly deserved. A year later Angela followed in the footsteps of Julie Andrews and starred in a Walt Disney supermusical, *Bedknobs and Broomsticks* (1971). Despite her very animated Mary Poppinslike amateur witch portrayal, the movie was no successor either in quality or boxoffice receipts to the predecessor, (*Mary Poppins* [1964]), it so strove to imitate.

Since the much-delayed film version of *Mame* was cast with Lucille Ball and not Angela, she chose to stay near her son in London and starred in the English version of Edward Albee's *All Over* in 1972. In the Spring of 1973 she was showcased in the opening musical number on the televised Academy Awards presentations, reminding Hollywood again that she is a superior musical-comedy stylist. Returning to London, she starred in a stage revival of one of the best American musicals, *Gypsy* (1973).

ANGELA LANSBURY

Gaslight (MGM, 1944)
National Velvet (MGM, 1944)
The Picture of Dorian Gray (MGM, 1945)
The Harvey Girls (MGM, 1946)
The Hoodlum Saint (MGM, 1946)
Till the Clouds Roll By (MGM, 1946)
Private Affairs of Bel Ami (UA, 1947)
If Winter Comes (MGM, 1947)
Tenth Avenue Angel (MGM, 1948)
The Three Musketeers (MGM, 1948)
State of the Union (MGM, 1948)
The Red Danube (MGM, 1949)
Samson and Delilah (Paramount, 1949)
Kind Lady (MGM, 1951)
Mutiny (UA, 1952)
Remains to Be Seen (MGM, 1953)
A Life at Stake (Filmakers, 1955)
A Lawless Street (Columbia, 1955)
The Purple Mask (Universal, 1955)
Please Murder Me (DCA, 1956)
The Court Jester (Paramount, 1956)

The Reluctant Debutante (MGM, 1958)
The Long Hot Summer (20th-Fox, 1958)
The Dark at the Top of the Stairs (WB, 1960)
A Breath of Scandal (Paramount, 1960)
Blue Hawaii (Paramount, 1961)
Season of Passion (UA, 1961)
All Fall Down (MGM, 1962)
The Manchurian Candidate (UA, 1962)
The Four Horsemen of the Apocalypse (Voice Only: MGM, 1962)
In the Cool of the Day (MGM, 1963)
The World of Henry Orient (UA, 1964)
Dear Heart (WB, 1964)
The Greatest Story Ever Told (UA, 1965)
Harlow (Paramount, 1965)
The Amorous Adventures of Moll Flanders (Paramount, 1965)
Mister Buddwing (MGM, 1966)
Something for Everyone (National General, 1970)
Bedknobs and Broomsticks (BV, 1971)

With Peter Lawford in *The Red Danube* (1949)

With James Garner in *Mister Buddwing* (1966)

Mario Lanza

Mario Lanza possessed a powerful tenor voice with a tonal richness and a considerable range that made concert and movie audiences proclaim him as a possible successor to Enrico Caruso. His singing had a definite emotional appeal but his voice was largely untrained, certainly undisciplined without the subtlety or musicality that might have made him a great singer. Lanza could belt an operatic song so that indiscriminate audiences sat up and listened, and he was masculine enough so that the men in the audience would not be put off. But he was *not* a great singer, and it was his personal lack of discipline, a schizophrenic combination of ego and insecurity, which resulted in his premature death at age thirty-eight. His career was a constant battle with his weight—it varied from 169 pounds to 300 pounds—and the overeating, overdrinking, crash dieting, and barbiturates took their toll in every aspect of his life. There were legal battles, temper tantrums, cancelled performances, and shortly after his own tragic death, his emotionally distraught wife died of asphyxiation, an apparent suicide. Lanza emerged from a South Philadelphia Italian background and was already a top recording star when Louis B. Mayer signed him to an MGM contract after hearing him sing at the Hollywood Bowl. Never a convincing actor, it was his singing that drew his audiences, and his eight starring motion pictures grossed millions of dollars.

He was born Alfred Arnold Coccozza on January 31, 1921 in Philadelphia. His father Antonio was a disabled veteran who had been gassed during World War I and his mother Maria worked as a seamstress in an Army quartermaster depot. The child's music interest evolved from hearing the recordings of Caruso at a neighbor's house, and to be an opera singer became his one ambition. His mother sacrificed everything to pay for his vocal lessons. At school he was a lazy student, hating to study, but excelling in sports. In fact, he was expelled two months before his graduation from high school and went to work in his grandfather's wholesale grocery. In 1942 his music teacher Irene Williams arranged for him to meet William K. Huff, concert manager of the Philadelphia Academy of Music, who subsequentally arranged an audition for Lanza with Dr. Serge Koussevitzky, then in charge of the Berkshire Music Center in Tanglewood at Lenox, Massachusetts. Koussevitzky recognized the young tenor's natural abilities after hearing him sing "Vesti la Guibba" from *I Pagliacci,* and offered him a scholarship at Tanglewood.

Lanza changed his name, using his mother's maiden name, and, after serious preparation, sang in Nicolai's *The Merry Wives of Windsor* at the Berkshire Summer Festival on August 7, 1942. He earned praise for his promising voice. Columbia Concerts signed him to a tour, albeit prematurely, for he should have considered only further studies at the time. His induction into the army on January 5, 1943 precluded any concert work and he was assigned to the Military Police. It was discovered he was a singer when he attempted to pass off a recording by Ezio Pinza as being his own, and he was transferred to Special Services. He joined the fifty-man choral cast of *On the Beam* and later was a member of the *Winged Victory* chorus. *Winged Victory* was a play produced by Moss Hart and, when it traveled to the West Coast where it was filmed by George Cukor for Twentieth Century-Fox, there were a round of parties to which the servicemen were invited. At the home of Warner Brothers' musical comedy performer Irene Manning, Lanza's singing prompted Manning to take him to see Jack Warner. Warner agreed his voice was intriguing but stated he did not need a 270-pound tenor. At a later party at the home of Frank Sinatra, Lanza met agent Art Rush who obtained a recording contract with RCA Victor for him.

Lanza was discharged from the Army early in 1945 for a catarrhal condition and, on April 13, 1945, married Betty Hicks, the sister of an Irish army buddy. Between his Columbia Concerts and RCA recording sessions, Lanza was kept so busy that he put aside his dreams of performing in grand opera. When he was scheduled to sing at the Hollywood Bowl on August 28, 1947, Mannie Sachs, an RCA executive, mailed a test recording and a photograph of Lanza to Louis B. Mayer's personal assistant, Ida Koverman. She and Mayer attended the concert, after which Lanza was signed to a seven-year contract, which left him free six months each year to make recordings and go on concert tours.

MGM debuted him in the Joe Pasternak production, *That Midnight Kiss* (1949), and, to assure that he got the proper cinema start, the picture had everything for everyone: Lanza played a singing ex-G.I. truck driver, Kathryn Grayson was the heiress who aspires to be an opera singer, Jose Iturbi appeared as the opera impresario, Ethel Barrymore was the imperious music patron, and Keenan Wynn played the general fourflusher. *That Midnight Kiss* was "class" all the way. Lanza sang "Celeste Aida" from Verdi's *Aida*; Donizetti's "Una Furtiva Lagrima" from the opera *L'Elsis d'Amore*; "Mama Mia Che Vo Sape" from Mascagni's *Cavalleria Rusticana*; and "They Won't Believe Me." The picture was a blockbuster success, outdistancing Mayer's expectation that here was an "opera" singer with more screen popularity than either Lawrence Tibbet or Nelson Eddy. Mayer gave Lanza a $10,000 bonus.

Lanza and Grayson were put into *The Toast of New Orleans* (1950), with the tenor receiving costarring billing this time. He sang "M'appari" from von Flotow's *Martha*; "Brindisi" from Verdi's *La Traviata;* "The Flower

Song" from Bizet's *Carmen*; "O Paradiso" from Ponchielli's *La Gioconda*; "Tina Lina"; and "Be My Love." The latter song, which had been written for Lanza by Nicholas Brodsky, became the singer's theme song and one of RCA Victor's big single song hits. He and Grayson were sent on a cross-country concert tour to promote the picture, and Lanza became a household word.

Having long worshiped the late Caruso, Lanza was eager to star in a film biography of the famed personality. Louis B. Mayer agreed that such a film would be a very marketable item, but by the late 1940s Mayer was on the way out. Lanza was unaware of the intercorporate hassling, and he sizzled; "Those bastards in New York with all the dough don't think I'm good enough to star in Caruso's life story. Who the hell do they think can play Caruso! Nelson Eddy? There is nobody but me who can play that role. I am Caruso!" The film was finally made with Lanza and released in 1951. Lanza had his chance to sing fifteen solos of his idol's favorite arias, and the picture grossed a hefty $4.5 million. Despite the popularity of *The Great Caruso* and the adulation of the critics, who said Lanza was on a par with Caruso, the new screen tenor was incensed. He was convinced he was better than Caruso!

Lanza's MGM mentor Joe Pasternak scheduled *Because You're Mine* (1952) as the star's next venture, reasoning that the inexpensive-to-mount story would bring in huge returns. Lanza's reaction to the script was immediate: "This stinks so much, it would louse me up with my fans." He refused to make the picture and turned on his former friend Pasternak: "If it weren't for people like me, he'd be back washing dishes. I make the pictures—I sing—and that bastard thinks it's him." Mario boasted to the other MGM stars that for once there was a person of virility on the lot who would not put up with front-office dictates. However, the studio had an ironclad contract, and Lanza had no legal option but to make the film. He had his revenge, though. He showed up on the set drunk, overate extravagantly and taunted costar Doretta Morrow mercilessly with lewd behavior and vile language. *Because You're Mine* was pushed into release and did good business. Lanza later said: "I personally got 'The Lord's Prayer' number into the film. And that, I think, gave it some dignity and helped save it."

After only four pictures Lanza had earned the reputation of being one of the most temperamental actors on the MGM lot. He called himself "tiger boy" and there were rumors of various romances. He proclaimed that he was a genius and was named the most uncooperative actor by the Hollywood press. MGM's next assignment was to be *The Student Prince* (1954), a vehicle Lanza requested, but in a moment of pique he walked out of the picture. MGM sued him for $5 million. Dore Schary, who had by now taken over operation of the studio after Mayer's ousting, managed to settle the dispute by using Lanza's already recorded songs for the film to be mouthed by actor Edmund Purdom. However, Schary considered Lanza paranoiac and refused to take him back at MGM, and his contract was cancelled. At one point Lanza summed up his studio problems by telling columnist Hedda Hopper: "My biggest beef with Metro was that the studio wanted to be commercial and I wanted artistic betterment. Put them together—they don't mix. I rebelled because of sincerity to the public and my career."

Part of the dual nature of Lanza was his conviction that, on one hand, he had a God-given voice which he must share with the world and that, on the other, the world at large did not appreciate him. He would fly into rages when he read a critical report that questioned the artistry of his singing: "Does *Time* magazine think a Dead End Kid from North Philadelphia, not yet 33, could have grossed more than $5,250,000 in five years and paid Uncle Sam more than $4,000,000 in taxes—clean up to date—if he didn't sing? What do they think, that I'm a ventriloquist?"

In 1954 Lanza made his television debut on *Showers of Stars* and, weakened from dieting, he had to lip-synch the words to his own recordings. The next day the headlines screamed that he had lost his voice. The publicity forced Paramount to cancel him as the lead in *The Vagabond King* (1956), and he was replaced by Oreste. However, Jack Warner was always willing to take a gamble on proven talent, and he agreed to pay Lanza $150,000 to star in *Serenade* (1956). To help promote that unlikely film, Warner booked Lanza into the New Frontier Hotel in Las Vegas for a one-week engagement. The boxoffice was completely sold out way in advance. On opening night Lanza was unable to appear, because he had taken an overdose of seconal with champagne, and more bad publicity ensued when the week's engagement had to be cancelled.

Lanza's career was at a low ebb and he decided to accept a two-picture deal from Titanus Films in Italy which would have MGM as the releasing company in the U. S. He and his family moved to Rome where they rented the expensive villa once presented by Mussolini to Marshal Badoglio, reasoning, "I'm a movie star, and I think I should live like one." Lanza starred in *The Seven Hills of Rome* (1958) with Peggie Castle and *For the First Time* (1959) with Zsa Zsa Gabor. They did only average business.

On October 7, 1959, after struggling through several months with pneumonia, phlebitis, and more dieting, Lanza died in the Villa Guilia Clinic when a blood clot in his leg moved to his heart. He left his wife Betty and their four children: Colleen, Elisa, Damon, and Mark. Betty Lanza went into a deep depression after her husband's death. On one occasion, when her sister took the four children to Chicago with her, Betty accused her of kidnaping them. Betty's mother stepped in and had a lawyer draw up affidavits to have her committed to a sanitarium. All during her tempestuous marriage to Lanza she had used barbiturates. In an effort to regain her equilibrium she moved in with her friend Kathryn Grayson and later rented the home of actor Fred Clark and moved in to that home with her four children. On March 11, 1960, she died of asphyxiation. The coroner's report listed a high alcoholic content in her blood. Lanza's parents, Antonio and Maria Cocozza, became guardians of the four children and moved them to their Pacific Palisades home. Much of Lanza's reported income had been devoured by taxes and numerous litigations, but the royalties from his recordings bring in an estimated $100,000 each year. In 1968, Lanza's oldest daughter Colleen signed a recording contract and later became engaged to musician Bobby Bregman. Lanza's mother died on July 6, 1970.

The Lanza legend lives on via his recordings and a legion of fans. Philadelphia has proclaimed October 7 Mario Lanza Day, and even named a park after him.

With J. Carrol Naish in *The Toast of New Orleans* (1950)

With Eula Guy and Ann Blyth in *The Great Caruso* (1951)

With James Whitmore, Jeff Donnell, Doretta Morrow, and Celia Lovsky in *Because You're Mine* (1952)

MARIO LANZA

That Midnight Kiss (MGM, 1949)
The Toast of New Orleans (MGM, 1950)
The Great Caruso (MGM, 1951)
Because You're Mine (MGM, 1952)

The Student Prince (Voice only: MGM, 1954)
Serenade (WB, 1956)
The Seven Hills of Rome (MGM, 1958)
For the First Time (MGM, 1959)

With Johanna Von Kocsian in *For the First Time* (1959)

Laurel and Hardy

As a comedy team Laurel and Hardy occupy their own well-deserved niche in cinema history. Their in-tandem screen antics are as rewarding an entertainment experience to watch today as when first viewed decades ago. However, their status in the MGM constellation of stars is a purely technical one, deriving largely from the association between their employer Hal Roach and the MGM distribution facilities. Occasionally, between churning out their two-reelers, Metro would utilize their services in a studio-produced revue, such as *Hollywood Revue of 1929* or *Hollywood Party* (1934), or very occasionally to bolster a potentially dubious straight vehicle, such as Lawrence Tibbett's *Rogue Song* (1930). In their declining professional days, they returned to MGM to crank out two minor comedy features, both unworthy reminders of their past triumphs. However, in the main, Laurel and Hardy under Roach's aegis, were a separate unit, uninvolved with the mainline of MGM production, politics, and social activities. Unlike the Marx Brothers, who were brought into the Metro fold by Irving Thalberg, there was scant linkage between Laurel and Hardy and the Culver City hierarchy.

Stan Laurel was born Arthur Stanley Jefferson on June 16, 1890, in Ulverston, Lancashire, England. Laurel was the son of an actor and theatre manager. He made his stage debut in Glasgow at Pickard's Museum in 1906. He was part of the Juvenile Pantomine Company for a time and then later joined Fred Karno's Company, with whom he traveled to the U. S. in 1910 and 1913. Charlie Chaplin was also with Karno, and Laurel was frequently his understudy and also did imitations of Chaplin. On a later trip, Laurel, as he now called himself, remained in America after being cast in a two-reeler, *Nuts in May* (1918). After this outing, he signed with Metro for a series of shorts, moved on to the Hal Roach Studios for more of the same, when Universal signed him up for the Stan Laurel series. He rejoined Roach in 1926, and gradually began to become well known to film audiences.

Oliver Norvell Hardy was born in Atlanta, Georgia on January 18, 1892. His parents were of Scottish–English descent and had never been in show business. At the age of eight Hardy was so adept a singer in community sessions that he took to performing with minstrel shows and, although he did not continue with a professional singing career, he continued to take music

428

lessons. Studying law did not prove as much fun as running a movie house, which he did for a time in 1910. Then he joined the Lubin Company in Florida in 1913 as a comedy player. For several years he moved around the movie business, and was a bit player in *Lucky Dog* (1917), a short starring Laurel. It was when Hardy went to work for Larry Semon as actor and codirector of comedy shorts in the 1920s that he gained prominence.

Historian William K. Everson lists *Forty-Five Minutes from Hollywood* (1926), released through Pathé, as probably being the first Hal Roach two-reeler in which both comedians appeared together. By the time of *Slipping Wives* (1927) and *Sailors Beware* (1927), the two baby-faced comics were permanently teamed and turning out two-reelers on the average of one a month. *Sugar Daddies* (1927), with the ever-present James Finlayson, was the first of the Roach–Laurel and Hardy two-reelers to be released through MGM. *From Soup to Nuts* (1928), directed by funnyman Edgar Kennedy, is the first of the comedies in which the team received star billing. *Liberty* (1929), directed by Leo McCarey and with Jean Harlow in the cast, was the first of the boys' vehicles to be released in both silent and limited sound versions.

Not to be left off the Hollywood bandwagon, MGM produced its own musical variety picture, *Hollywood Revue of 1929*, to exploit its versatile roster of players, sound, and Technicolor. In one of the more entertaining episodes of this otherwise rather dreary picture, Hardy plays a magician with Laurel his fumbling assistant, and with master of ceremonies Jack Benny involved in their act. Lionel Barrymore had already completed his direction of *Rogue Song* which introduced Metropolitan Opera star Lawrence Tibbett to the screen, when front office officials decided comedy relief was needed to give the production some extra boxoffice luster. Thus additional scenes of the operetta were shot, featuring Laurel and Hardy in tandem with the Russian bandit king (Tibbett) who is busy courting a wary princess (Catherine Dale Owen). Laurel and Hardy received no featured billing in the film, nor did contemporary reviewers consider their presence much of an aid to the picture. But then the highbrow critics were too intent on extolling the virtues of this prestigious movie, to acclaim the antics of proletarian favorites Laurel and Hardy. At the moment, this is the only major film work of Laurel and Hardy unavailable for present-day reassessment. Apparently both the release prints and negative of this Technicolor feature have long since decomposed.

Pardon Us (1931), directed by James Parrott, was the team's first feature-length starring vehicle. As with the later Laurel and Hardy features, reviewers and audiences alike much preferred their more compressed two-reelers. Roach took advantage of the standing sets from Metro's prison melodrama, *The Big House*, and used them for this comic caper of two cards jailed for brewing illegal beer during Prohibition. It was their three-reeler, *The Music Box* (1932), which won the team an Oscar in the new category of short subjects. An enduring favorite among Laurel and Hardy followers, the basic one-gag premise has the boys carting a piano up an interminable flight of hillside steps, with the expected misadventures along the way up and down.

Twice Two (1933) presented Laurel and Hardy in dual roles, playing themselves and each other's wives, while the feature *Fra Diavolo* (1933) (a. k. a. *The Devil's Brother*) offered the comedians in a burlesque of the well-known operetta, aided and abetted by Dennis King, Thelma Todd, and James Finlayson. *Hollywood Party* was intended to be a potpourri all-star production, but it resulted in a dismal offering that mixed the disparate comedic talents of Laurel and Hardy, Jimmy Durante, Lupe Velez, and Charles Butterworth to the disadvantage of all concerned. In Roach's feature, *Pick a Star* (1937), a slight musical tale with a Hollywood background, Laurel and Hardy appeared as themselves. The following year's *Blockheads* was the last Laurel and Hardy feature released by MGM in this period. Thereafter, Roach negotiated an agreement with United Artists to handle his product.

The 1940s saw the comedy team on a decline. After they ended their tenure with Roach they signed on with Twentieth Century-Fox where they appeared in six modest programmers which lacked the zest of their earlier work. The boys were just not capable of turning out inspired work when shoved into production-line low-budget comedy in which they were allowed no freedom to plan their extemporaneous shenanigans. In between their Fox years (1941–1945) the duo returned to MGM to appear in *Air Raid Wardens* (1943) and *Nothing but Trouble* (1944), the latter featuring Mary Boland, Henry O'Neill, and Connie Gilchrist. As William K. Everson summed up the 1944 entry: "[it] was another weak entry in Laurel and Hardy's tragically fading career."

Hardy appeared without Laurel in *The Fighting Kentuckian* (1949) and *Riding High* (1950), and after several European stage tours, the team made a final picture in France, the abortive *Atoll K* (1951). In 1960 a special Oscar was awarded Laurel "for his creative pioneering in the field of cinema comedy." Hardy, his partner, had died three years earlier in poverty, and in 1965, Laurel would also die broke.

Ironically, from the mid-1950s onward, the Laurel and Hardy short subjects and features became a staple of television and earned the team new generations of fans, but no income. The profits went to seemingly everyone else but the two performers who deserved them the most. Many of the duo's better works have been reedited into several compilation features, and even their Twentieth Century Fox output was utilized as filler to bolster the story line of *Myra Breckingridge* (1970).

Today a New York-based fan club, "The Sons of the Desert," persists in promulgating the artistry of the two clowns. But the team needs no such well-meant boosting, for via television showings and home movie purchases, their prolific work is readily available for all to enjoy.

LAUREL AND HARDY

Fortune's Mask (Vitagraph, 1922)*
Little Wildcat (Vitagraph, 1922)*
One Stolen Night (Vitagraph, 1923)*
Three Ages (Metro, 1923)*
The Girl in the Limousine (FN, 1924)*
The Wizard of Oz (Chadwick, 1925)*
The Gentle Cyclone (Fox, 1926)*
Stop, Look, and Listen (Pathé, 1926)*
No Man's Law (Pathé, 1927)*
Hollywood Revue of 1929 (MGM, 1929)
Rogue Song (MGM, 1930)
Pardon Us (MGM, 1931)
Pack up Your Troubles (MGM, 1932)
Devil's Brother (MGM, 1933)
Sons of the Desert (MGM, 1933)
Hollywood Party (MGM, 1934)
Babes in Toyland (MGM, 1934)
Bonnie Scotland (MGM, 1935)
The Bohemian Girl (MGM, 1936)
Our Relations (MGM, 1936)
Way Out West (MGM, 1936)

Pick a Star (MGM, 1937)
Swiss Miss (MGM, 1938)
Blockheads (MGM, 1938)
Zenobia (UA, 1939)*
The Flying Deuces (RKO, 1939)
A Chump at Oxford (UA, 1940)
Saps at Sea (UA, 1940)
Great Guns (20th-Fox, 1941)
A-Haunting We Will Go (20th-Fox, 1942)
Air Raid Wardens (MGM, 1943)
Jitterbugs (20th-Fox, 1943)
The Dancing Masters (20th-Fox, 1943)
The Big Noise (20th-Fox, 1944)
Nothing but Trouble (MGM, 1944)
The Bull Fighters (20th-Fox, 1945)
The Fighting Kentuckian (Republic, 1949)*
Riding High (Paramount, 1950)*
Atoll K (Utopia-Fortezza Films, 1951)

*Hardy appeared without Laurel

In *Babes in Toyland* (1934)

In *Bonnie Scotland* (1935)

With David Leland in *Nothing But Trouble* (1944)

Peter Lawford

Although he has never won any acting awards and most likely never will, Peter Lawford has spent well over thirty semisuccessful years in the entertainment business projecting his rather elegant personality. Initially he played the very proper, gentlemanly glamor boy with a clipped British accent, qualities which endeared him professionally to Louis B. Mayer at MGM and made him a semihit with the bobby-soxer filmgoers of the 1940s. After a brief television apprenticeship which utilized to an extent his modest talents for sophisticated comedy, the Lawford oncamera personality was transformed into that of the perennial swinger via his association with the Hollywood Rat Pack and Frank Sinatra. His image was further enhanced by marrying into America's political kingpin family, the Kennedys, and then again by his close friendship with his brother-in-law, Robert F. Kennedy.

Peter Aylen Lawford was born in London on September 7, 1923. His father, Sir Peter Sydney Ernest Lawford, was a military man decorated in World War I who later turned to character acting in motion pictures. His mother, Lady May, was something of an indomitable grand dame who loved having an actor in the family. Lawford was educated in private schools and at age seven his mother allowed him to appear in a British film called *Old Bill* (1930), in which he was billed as the English Jackie Cooper. When the Lawfords visited California in 1938, he played the Cockney boy in *Lord Jeff* (1938), an MGM picture starring Freddie Bartholomew and Mickey Rooney. However, Lawford's mother preferred her son completing a proper education rather than becoming a teenaged actor. So it was not until four years later that he turning to acting on a full-time basis.

In 1942, after working at several odd jobs including ushering in a Westwood, California movie house, Lawford was signed with MGM, and played a pilot in Greer Garson's *Mrs. Miniver* (1942). Thereafter, whenever MGM or another studio required the services of a well-bred British young man, Lawford was summoned. In his first two years under MGM contract he appeared briefly in twenty-two pictures, fourteen on loan to other companies. He had a moving death scene in *The White Cliffs of Dover* (1944), played the RAF flyer in *Son of Lassie* (1945), performed as Jackie "Butch" Jenkins' older brother in *My Brother Talks to Horses* (1946), made an attempt at being a song-and-dance man opposite sprightly June Allyson in *Good News* (1947), was led around by the nose by voluptuous Ann Miller in *Easter Parade* (1948), and played Laurie, the nice young man in the anemic remake of *Little Women* (1949). He was so persistently tongue-in-cheek elegant in his roles that the whole scene was a bit nauseating, but the teenagers adored him. In the "new" Hollywood and Dore Schary MGM regime of the 1950s Lawford was an outmoded commodity, and he left the studio to free-lance.

He went to Columbia to play Judy Holliday's wealthy beau in *It Should Happen to You* (1954), his last feature for five years. In 1954 he also starred in the teleseries *Dear Phoebe*, playing the advice-to-the-lovelorn editor of a city newspaper. Regardless of what the part actually demanded, Lawford was still just the British glamor boy going through listless high-jinks in a domestic comedy. *Dear Phoebe* lasted two seasons. He and Phyllis Kirk in 1959 starred in a video series based on MGM's feature series, *The Thin Man*. Lawford owned twenty-five percent of that show. It ran for two seasons and contains his best acting work. He carefully avoided imitating William Powell and made quite an agreeable comedian–playboy–wolf–sleuth.

Lawford's playboy–swinger reputation in his personal life came forth in the 1950s with his membership in Hollywood's famed Rat Pack, a fraternity of outspoken actors who eschewed social functions and gossip colums. The group had centered around Humphrey Bogart and Lauren Bacall. After Bogart's death, Frank Sinatra became Rat Pack leader and the clan grew to include Dean Martin and Sammy Davis, Jr., and Lawford, whose friendship with Sinatra stemmed from their costarring MGM film *It Happened in Brooklyn* (1947).

On April 24, 1954 Lawford married Patricia Kennedy, daughter of the patriarch of America's foremost political dynasty. Joseph P. Kennedy was outraged over the match and Lawford never became an intimate member of the Kennedy "family circle." He did, however, become a confidant of Patricia's brother Robert, and was on the fringe of Washington's political life as long as Robert was alive. The Lawfords purchased Louis B. Mayer's Santa Monica beach house and an apartment at 990 Fifth Avenue in Manhattan. Their first attempt to purchase a cooperative apartment in Manhattan was thwarted when the landlord refused their application because he was an actor and she was a Democrat. The Lawfords had four children: Christopher, Sydney, Victoria Frances (named after Sinatra), and Robin. Contrary to the Rat Pack association, Lawford once said, "Really, I'm not sophisticated. Actually Pat and I lead a simple life. We have a house on the beach, and Sunday night we play poker with the gang, and Pete Rugulo comes over and makes spaghetti."

On August 5, 1962 Marilyn Monroe died tragically from an overdose of barbiturates. In the frenetic publicity that ensued, Lawford told police that he was probably one of the last people to talk with her before she died, as he had telephoned to ask her to come to dinner with friends. Monroe declined, saying she was sleepy. Later publicity alleged there had been a romance between

Monroe and Robert Kennedy, with Lawford as the go-between. Lawford spoke to reporters again when he said how "shocked" he and Pat were because they had not been invited to the actress's private funeral, the arrangements having been made by Marilyn's ex-husband, Joe DiMaggio.

On January 1, 1966 Lawford and Patricia were divorced, the first divorce to take place in the ultra-Catholic Kennedy family. Five years later (October 30, 1971) he and Mary Rowan, daughter of television star Dan Rowan, had a much-publicized wedding in Puerto Vallarta, Mexico. Asked about the twenty-seven-year difference between himself and the bride, Lawford replied: "I'm just trying to do my small bit for the generation gap."

Lawford's post-MGM features have been more a series of social outings than serious acting. As a subsidiary member of the Rat Pack he had subservient assignments in three Frank Sinatra films: *Never So Few* (1959), *Ocean's Eleven* (1960), and *Sergeants Three* (1962). He played the anti-Semitic British officer in *Exodus* (1960) and was the overfed lover of Bette Davis in *Dead Ringer* (1964). He was in much better form as the cynical agent of Sammy Davis, Jr. in *A Man Called Adam* (1966). He and Davis made a pseudo–James Bondish entry in Britain called *Salt and Pepper* (1968), with Lawford as the hip Soho club owner, Pepper. The followup to this picture, *One More Time* (1970), was badly directed by Jerry Lewis and fizzled on the release market. Like many former "leading" men type, Lawford continues to make movie appearances whenever the cash offer is right. In the low budget *Clay Pigeon* (1971), an independently-produced anti-Establishment thriller released by MGM, Lawford had an unbilled role as a government agent.

When not playing the cool playboy onscreen or off, Lawford has presided over his own production company, Chrislaw, which produced several feature films, including *Johnny Cool* (1963), with Elizabeth Montgomery, and *Billie* (1965), with Patty Duke. Lawford is likely to turn up in any number of guises on television. He was among those in a video version of *The Farmer's Daughter* (1962) and a decade later was a most unconvincing Ellery Queen in *Don't Look Behind You*, a telefeature pilot for a projected series. In between he has graced numerous quiz shows, talk shows, and television commercials, one of the more recent ones presenting him as the spokesman for Western Union Candygrams. Neither the circumstances nor his stockier appearance and gray temples have changed Peter Lawford from his congenial playboy image, which made him a perfect choice for the semi-regular role of Doris Day's doctor boyfriend on her recent teleseries.

PETER LAWFORD

Old Bill (British, 1930)
Lord Jeff (MGM, 1938)
Mrs. Miniver (MGM, 1942)
Eagle Squadron (Universal, 1942)
Thunder Birds (20th-Fox, 1942)

Junior Army (Columbia, 1942)
A Yank at Eton (MGM, 1942)
London Blackout Murders (Republic, 1942)
Random Harvest (MGM, 1942)
Girl Crazy (MGM, 1943)

435

The Purple V (Republic, 1943)
The Immortal Sergeant (20th-Fox, 1943)
Pilot No. 5 (MGM, 1943)
Above Suspicion (MGM, 1943)
Someone to Remember (Republic, 1943)
The Man from Down Under (MGM, 1943)
Sherlock Holmes Faces Death (Universal, 1943)
The Sky's the Limit (RKO, 1943)
Paris After Dark (20th-Fox, 1943)
Flesh and Fantasy (Universal, 1943)
Assignment in Brittany (MGM, 1943)
Sahara (Columbia, 1943)
West Side Kid (Republic, 1943)
Corvette K-225 (Universal, 1943)
The White Cliffs of Dover (MGM, 1944)
The Canterville Ghost (MGM, 1944)
Mrs. Parkington (MGM, 1944)
Son of Lassie (MGM, 1945)
The Picture of Dorian Gray (MGM, 1945)
Two Sisters from Boston (MGM, 1946)
Cluny Brown (20th-Fox, 1946)
My Brother Talks to Horses (MGM, 1946)
It Happened in Brooklyn (MGM, 1947)
Good News (MGM, 1947)
On an Island with You (MGM, 1948)
Easter Parade (MGM, 1948)
Julia Misbehaves (MGM, 1948)
Little Women (MGM, 1949)
The Red Danube (MGM, 1949)
Please Believe Me (MGM, 1950)

Royal Wedding (MGM, 1951)
Just This Once (MGM, 1952)
Kangaroo (20th-Fox, 1952)
You for Me (MGM, 1952)
The Hour of 13 (MGM, 1952)
Rogues' March (MGM, 1952)
It Should Happen to You (Columbia, 1954)
Never So Few (MGM, 1959)
Ocean's Eleven (WB, 1960)
Exodus (UA, 1960)
Pepe (Columbia, 1960)
Sergeants Three (UA, 1962)
Advise and Consent (Columbia, 1962)
The Longest Day (20th-Fox, 1962)
Dead Ringer (WB, 1964)
Sylvia (Paramount, 1965)
Harlow (Paramount, 1965)
The Oscar (Paramount, 1966)
A Man Called Adam (Embassy, 1966)
Salt and Pepper (UA, 1968)
Buona Sera, Mrs. Campbell (UA, 1968)
The April Fools (National General, 1969)
Hook, Line and Sinker (Columbia, 1969)
One More Time (UA, 1970)
Clay Pigeon (MGM, 1971)*
Return to the Land of Oz (Voice only: WB, 1972)
They Only Kill Their Masters (MGM, 1972)

*Unbilled appearance

With Esther Williams in *On an Island with You* (1948)

With Telly Savalas in *Clay Pigeon* (1971)

Janet Leigh

Janet Leigh was one of the screen's loveliest ingenues. With her fresh-faced, all-American beauty, she was the perfect candidate for that screen cliché, the girl next door. However, no sooner had she mastered the rudiments of screen acting and made a pleasing impression as the hopeful young actress in *Two Tickets to Broadway* (1951) than her "perfect" real life marriage to Tony Curtis catapulted her into a new screen image. She became a sexy chick in half a dozen ghastly costume romancers which were enough to sink even an Eleanora Duse. All this took place during the seven years Janet was under contract to MGM (1947–1954). It was not until she was stabbed to death by a deranged Anthony Perkins in the shower scene of *Psycho* (1960) that audiences considered her an actress of some substance.

Jeanette Helen Morrison was born on July 26, 1927 in Merced, California. Janet's father was in the insurance and real estate business. She attended school in Stockton, California and entered the College of the Pacific as a music major. At age fifteen she eloped with a nineteen-year-old boy named John Kenneth Carlyle, but the marriage was annulled four months later. While at college she met a small-time bandleader named Stanley Reames whom she married on October 5, 1946. During the summer of 1946 her mother was employed as a receptionist at the Sugar Bowl Ski Lodge in Soda Springs, California. Mrs. Morrison kept a photograph of Janet on her desk. Norma Shearer was vacationing at the lodge and, when she saw the photograph of Janet, she sent it to MGM, her former studio, with a letter recommending that they give the girl a screen test. Since Janet's husband wanted to go to Los Angeles anyway, in order to break into the big band league, Janet left college and went after the screen test.

Janet recalls, "I was simply flabbergasted when they offered me one of those routine starlet contracts, but I was so happy to get that $50 a week. We were living over my aunt's garage and the money was welcome. I knew I couldn't act, but they promised to give me dramatic lessons, and the first picture I tested for was *The Romance of Rosy Ridge* opposite Van Johnson. I'd only had a few lessons and, when they told me I had the part, I said, 'You can't make me do that. You promised to teach me to act.' They were looking for a green, naive, unsophisticated girl for that picture, and they sure found one."

After surviving the ordeal of *Rosy Ridge*, Janet played the luckless Effie who is befriended by Walter Pidgeon in *If Winter Comes* (1947). She was considered sweetly bland enough to be Tom Drake's sweetheart in two pictures: *Hills of Home* (1948) and *Words and Music* (1948). As Greer Garson's niece in *That Forsyte Woman* (1949) she was wooed by the older Robert Young. She was one of the MGM fillies in the remake of *Little Women* (1949). MGM miscast her as the tormented ballerina who became a nun in *The Red Danube* (1949), but RKO used her effectively as the demure war widow who loves Robert Mitchum in *Holiday Affair* (1949). Two years later RKO again borrowed her to brighten the musical *Two Tickets to Broadway*, in the kind of optimistic ingenue role for which she was best suited.

By this point, however, Janet had taken on a new role, as Mrs. Tony Curtis. After this event, the public seemingly did not care what she played in the movies, for all her fans cared about was seeing another day in the superhappy life of Janet and Tony in the fan magazines. Janet had divorced Reames on July 19, 1948, and had met Curtis two years later at a Hollywood party. They eloped to Greenwich, Connecticut on June 4, 1951. After her marriage, MGM put Janet into a costume dud, *Scaramouche* (1952); a mild comedy with Carlton Carpenter, *Fearless Fagan* (1952); and *The Naked Spur* (1953), a James Stewart Western in which she sported an attractively different close-curled hairdo. Paramount had the bright idea of casting Janet and Curtis, a la Douglas Fairbanks and Mary Pickford, in *Houdini* (1953). The film was not much, but it seemed to please the younger filmgoers.

Janet and Curtis were so popular a married couple with the press that their studios (he was under contract to Universal) did not have to waste good scripts on them. The young stars were so eager to please that they took any role that they were offered. One Hollywood columnist said, "They were fearfully ambitious kids, so determined to make it, they were tiresome." Another columnist called them, "over-eager, over-nice, over-everything." Universal used them in *The Black Shield of Falworth* (1954) and her last MGM picture was a dramatic role in *Rogue Cop* (1954). Columbia put her into the kind of picture she should have been fighting for all along, the musical remake of *My Sister Eileen* (1955). There were three more costarring vehicles with Curtis: *The Vikings* (1958), *The Perfect Furlough* (1958), and *Who Was That Lady?* (1960). In the mid-1950s Janet had been the more prestigious member of that acting couple, but she continually sacrificed her career to being Mrs. Curtis. When she had gone on location to Africa to make *Safari* (1956), Curtis had suffered such pangs of self-doubt and inferiority that she agreed not to accept any additional on-location films that did not include him in the package. In the era of runaway filmmaking productions, this was a disastrous career step for Janet who, as a free-lancer, needed all the varied screen exposure she could obtain. It was her erotic-tinged performances in Orson Welles' *Touch Of Evil* (1958) and Alfred Hitchcock's *Psycho* that reminded filmgoers and industry executives that, once out from under all those period costumes and wigs, she could turn in a good performance.

Despite all the saccharine publicity about the perfect young married couple, Janet and Curtis had many battles in their private life and on the sets of the pictures they made together. In 1957 Curtis, suffering from a complex about being Jewish and being cast in films as the male Yvonne DeCarlo, entered analysis upon the suggestion of friend Blake Edwards. The doctor's efforts produced a new Curtis but failed to save the marriage. Janet vacationed without her husband on the Riviera with the Kennedy clan during the summer of 1961, a vacation interrupted by the suicide of her father who had taken an overdose of barbiturates in his real estate office. He had left a note blaming his marital difficulties as the cause for his action. Janet and Curtis split officially in March 1962. A few days later, while staying at the Sherry-Netherland Hotel in New York City, where she was stopping en route to the Mar de Plata Film Festival in Argentina, Janet was found in a coma on the floor of her bathroom. Friends told the reporters the next day that she had accidentally taken some pills and was in satisfactory condition. Their divorce became final on July 17, 1963. As part of the settlement, Janet kept the $200,000 mansion next to Pickfair in Beverly Hills. They had two daughters, Kelly Lee (June 16, 1956) and Jamie Leigh (November 22, 1958). Because her California divorce did not become final until 1963, Janet obtained a quickie Mexican divorce so she could marry stockbroker Robert Brant on September 15, 1962. Since that time she has sold her Beverly Hills home and purchased a smaller one in Benedict Canyon.

After a two-year screen absence, Janet proved most effective as the *non sequitur*-spouting doll of Frank Sinatra in *The Manchurian Candidate* (1962), giving strong indication that she had found a new screen image for herself. Nevertheless, 1963 proved to be a fiasco year for Janet on the screen. Columbia gave her the Chita Rivera role opposite Dick Van Dyke in the film version of *Bye Bye Birdie* (1963). However, during production of this musical, it was decided that the role of the younger and more blatantly sexy Ann-Margret should be enlarged at the expense of Janet's screen time. Then, when Shirley MacLaine refused to star in Hal Wallis' *Wives and Lovers* (1963), Janet had the thankless task of substituting for that hot star in this weak marital comedy. She was cast as the conventional wife of suddenly successful playwright Van Johnson. Martha Hyer, Shelley Winters, and the title tune were the best ingredients in that film. Thereafter, the forty-year-old Janet took what roles she could get on the diminished moviemaking scene, whether as straight lady to Jerry Lewis in *Three on a Couch* (1966), or a bewildered participant in the Spanish-lensed western *Kid Rodelo* (1966), and the Italian-made jewelry heist caper, *Grand Slam* (1968). Along the way, there was a good but secondary role as Paul Newman's wife in *Harper* (1966) and, more recently, a shrill but effective performance as a bitchy divorceé in MGM's *One Is a Lonely Number* (1972). On television the mature Janet has offered good, brittle performances in several telefeatures, including *The Monk* (1969) and *The House on Green Apple Road* (1970), and has preferred to concentrate on her characterization rather than a wrinkle-free countenance.

Janet is a very active member of the Hollywood community, working for numerous charities and civic causes. Her pet charity is SHARE, Share Happiness and Reap Endlessly, an organization with which she has been associated for fifteen years. She has two plaques commemorating her SHARE work and says, "Those are worth more to me than any award for acting ever could be. Working on behalf of retarded children has given me more inner satisfaction than I could ever describe."

JANET LEIGH

The Romance of Rosy Ridge (MGM, 1947)
If Winter Comes (MGM, 1947)
Hills of Home (MGM, 1948)
Words and Music (MGM, 1948)
Act of Violence (MGM, 1948)
Little Women (MGM, 1949)
That Forsyte Woman (MGM, 1949)
The Doctor and the Girl (MGM, 1949)
The Red Danube (MGM, 1949)
Holiday Affair (RKO, 1949)
Strictly Dishonorable (MGM, 1951)
Angels in the Outfield (MGM, 1951)
Two Tickets to Broadway (RKO, 1951)
It's a Big Country (MGM, 1951)
Just This Once (MGM, 1952)
Scaramouche (MGM, 1952)
Fearless Fagan (MGM, 1952)
The Naked Spur (MGM, 1953)
Confidentially Connie (MGM, 1953)
Houdini (Paramount, 1953)
Walking My Baby Back Home (Universal, 1953)
Prince Valiant (20th-Fox, 1954)
Living It Up (Paramount, 1954)
The Black Shield of Falworth (Universal, 1954)
Rogue Cop (MGM, 1954)
Pete Kelly's Blues (WB, 1955)
My Sister Eileen (Columbia, 1955)
Safari (Columbia, 1956)
Jet Pilot (Universal, 1957)
Touch of Evil (Universal, 1958)
The Vikings (UA, 1958)
The Perfect Furlough (Universal, 1958)
Who Was That Lady? (Columbia, 1960)
Psycho (Paramount, 1960)
Pepe (Columbia, 1960)
The Manchurian Candidate (UA, 1962)
Bye Bye Birdie (Columbia, 1963)
Wives and Lovers (Paramount, 1963)

Three on a Couch (Columbia, 1966)
Harper (WB, 1966)
Kid Rodelo (Paramount, 1966)
An American Dream (WB, 1966)
Grand Slam (Paramount, 1968)
Hello Down There (Paramount, 1969)
One Is a Lonely Number (MGM, 1972)
The Night of the Lepus (MGM, 1972)

With Selena Royle in *The Romance of Rosy Ridge* (1947)

441

With Peter Lawford in *Just This Once* (1952)

With Ezio Pinza and Millard Mitchell in *Strictly Dishonorable* (1951)

With Steve Forrest and Robert Taylor in *Rogue Cop* (1954)

442

Myrna Loy

Few recall that it was Myrna Loy who was named Queen of the Movies in 1937 when Clark Gable was officially tagged the King. Those titles were bestowed as the result of a public poll conducted by the N.Y. *Daily News'* Ed Sullivan. The reason for Myrna's popularity was the success of *The Thin Man* (1934) in which she and William Powell played the memorable Nick and Nora Charles: sophisticated, intelligent, witty marrieds who got into endless screwball situations, playing detectives. Likewise, few remember the nearly seventy films, both silents and talkies, in which Myrna appeared as either the vamp or some exotic Oriental before *The Thin Man* breakthrough. Indeed, Myrna's apprenticeship is one of the longest in film history. However, once *The Thin Man* series established her as the very American, comic lady of virtue with the satin-growl voice, she enjoyed a reign as MGM's and Hollywood's "Perfect Wife" for over a decade.

Of Welsh ancestry, Myrna Williams was born in Helena, Montana on August 2, 1905. She considered herself an ugly duckling as a child: "I've never quite gotten over it, freckled face, slant eyes, and red hair—being redheaded isolates you." Her father was a cattleman and a member of the Montana legislature. When he died in the flu epidemic of 1918, mother and daughter moved to Los Angeles where Myrna attended a private school until the money ran out. She then enrolled in the public Venice High School where one of her teachers thought her attractive enough to use her as a model for a statue named "Aspiration." That statue still stands in the schoolyard in what is now a slum.

Myrna had studied dancing as a child and, after graduating from high school, she got a job in the chorus line at Grauman's Chinese Theatre. Despite her piano leg gams, she was noticed by photographer Henry Waxman and was able to earn a few extra dollars posing for him. Rudolph Valentino (whom Myrna recalls as a "dear, sweet, simple, very kind man") and his wife, Natasha Rambova, were looking for a girl for their upcoming film *Cobra* (1925). They asked Myrna to test for the part after seeing the Waxman photographs of her. The inexperienced actress says the test was "awful" and she did not get the part, but a casting director saw it and suggested her to director Fred Niblo as the Madonna in *Ben Hur* (1926). Metro and Niblo wanted a "name" and gave

443

the part to Betty Bronson, relegating Myrna to a small role as a vamp. Before that feature was released, Myrna was briefly seen on screen as a chorine, along with newcomer Joan Crawford, in Metro's *Pretty Ladies* (1925).

It was director Lowell Sherman who obtained a five-year contract for Myrna at Warner Brothers where, without any star buildup, she played a succession of bad girls, other women, and Orientals. That Eastern stereotyped casting came as a result of her almond-shaped eyes and began with a little film called *Crimson City* (1928) in which she played a Chinese girl who narrowly escapes a slave ring. This image was firmly set the following year when she played the exotic native girl Azuri in *The Desert Song*. "I became known as an American girl gone native in an Easterly direction."

When her Warners' contract expired and she was let go, Samuel Goldwyn used her as Joyce Lanyon in his excellent *Arrowsmith* (1931), and then she signed with Fox for a year. Irving Thalberg saw her as Thomas Meighan's mistress in *Skyline* (1931) and put her under an MGM contract. She was Marie Dressler's spoiled daughter in *Emma* (1932), a witty countess in Paramount's *Love Me Tonight* (1932) with Jeanette MacDonald and Maurice Chevalier, and then did her last Oriental role, playing Boris Karloff's daughter in *The Mask of Fu Manchu* (1932). Thalberg loaned her to RKO to play Coco in John Barrymore's *Topaze* (1933), which took sharp advantage of her comedy flair and Thalberg began to think of his red-haired actress in a new light. He put her in *Manhattan Melodrama* (1934) with Clark Gable and William Powell and gave her some sparkling dialogue by Joseph L. Mankiewicz. (Supposedly Myrna was the favorite actress of Public Enemy John Dillinger, and on the night of July 22, 1934 Dillinger was shot down outside a Chicago theatre by FBI agents after going to see this film.)

Manhattan Melodrama was directed by MGM's famous "one-take" director, W. S. Van Dyke, and after seeing Myrna and Powell together, he persuaded a disinterested Louis B. Mayer to allow him to use these two stars in *The Thin Man*, a comedy–mystery script derived from Dashiell Hammett's detective novel of the same name. Mayer considered both stars "heavies" and, when Van Dyke mentioned comedy, said "no." Van Dyke convinced Mayer he could bring the picture in within three weeks and on that condition Mayer conceded. The picture was a tremendous hit, establishing Myrna and Powell as one of the all-time favorite screen teams, and opened up an entirely new career for the veteran Myrna. Mayer, in one of his typical reversals, now exclaimed to Myrna, "You will always be a lady." And she was just that, in a series of entertaining pictures; *Whipsaw* (1935), *Wife vs. Secretary* (1936), *The Great Ziegfeld* (1936) (as Billie Burke), *Libeled Lady* (1936), *Test Pilot* (1938), *Too Hot to Handle* (1938), and five more as Nora Charles. One of her few duds of the period was her role as Katie O'Shea in the costume entry *Parnell* (1937), starring Clark Gable.

By the time the U. S. was in the Second World War, Myrna became actively involved in politics and finally ended her contract with MGM in 1944. She devoted much of her time to the Red Cross and the beginnings of the

United Nations. After the war she returned to the screen, playing the mother in Samuel Goldwyn's prize-winning war effort, *The Best Years of Our Lives* (1946), which proved to be the apotheosis of her career and reestablished her at the boxoffice. A few charming comedies followed: *The Bachelor and the Bobby Soxer* (1947) with Cary Grant, and *Mr. Blanding Builds His Dream House* (1948) with Grant and Melvyn Douglas. Republic tried to make an arty picture of John Steinbeck's *The Red Pony* (1949) with Myrna as the mother. Twentieth Century-Fox's *Cheaper by the Dozen* (1950) was a big success, but Myrna was billed *third* as Clifton Webb's wife, and she repeated this assignment sans Webb in the sequel, *Belles on Their Toes* (1952). By now, she had moved to Washington, D. C. with her fourth husband, Howland Sargeant, one of Dean Acheson's State Department assistants, and continued to work for public causes. She organized a group to fight McCarthyism, was a U. S. representative to UNESCO, and campaigned with Eleanor Roosevelt for Adlai Stevenson. In 1968 she campaigned for Eugene McCarthy and is now actively involved as a member of the National Committee against Discrimination in Housing.

She has been divorced from Sargeant since 1960 and presently resides in a New York East Side penthouse, being a frequent attendee at Broadway opening nights. (Her previous marriages were to producer Arthur Hornblow, Jr., John Hertz, Jr. of Hertz Rent-A-Car, and writer Gene Markey). She has made only four films in the past fifteen years: playing the alcoholic wife of Robert Ryan in *Lonelyhearts* (1958), the alcoholic mother of Paul Newman in *From the Terrace* (1960), Doris Day's chic Billie Burkelike aunt in *Midnight Lace* (1960), and the wife of Charles Boyer in *The April Fools* (1969). Each was a relatively small assignment. She says she is willing to work but does not want to play ax murderesses or any more alcoholics, and that is the reason for her two lengthy theatricals tours: *Barefoot in the Park* (for which she received Chicago's Sara Siddons Award) and *Dear Love* based on the Elizabeth Barrett–Robert Browning letters. In the early 1960s she had made summer stock tours in *The Marriage-Go-Round* with Claude Dauphin and then starred in the tryout of James Kirkwood's *There Must Be a Pony*. Her most recent professional appearances have been in *Death Takes a Holiday* with Melvyn Douglas and *Do Not Fold, Spindle or Mutilate* with Helen Hayes and Sylvia Sidney, both ABC telefeatures, in the September 1972 opening segment of Peter Falk's *Columb* video series, and as a woman judge in the telefeature pilot *Indict and Convict*.

She finally made her Broadway stage debut in a revival of Clare Luce's *The Women,* which opened in January 1973. When MGM had produced its first film version of the acerbic social comedy in 1939, Myrna was one of the few MGM female stars not to participate in the luminary-clustered production.

Myrna remains today as, at the peak of her cinema queen career, extremely level-headed. Although strong drama has never been her forte, her sophisticated comedy performances in 1930s MGM pictures are still amazingly fresh when viewed in retrospect today.

In a rare recent interview Myrna offered her viewpoint of the so-called "fabulous forties": "They were horrible. When you think of looking back, some of those years that seem so nice now were quite miserable. We were building up to the McCarthy era then. About 1946–47, you could feel this cold wind blowing into Hollywood from the East, chopping the city into factions. There was a clash between the liberals and conservatives. All you had to do was know someone of questionable political persuasion and you were labeled a Commie. There were perhaps six or seven hard-core Communists in Hollywood then, and they were not very dangerous people. But at that time a terror had seized the whole country, and in Hollywood, the terror was that the Communists would take over. So the right wing organized. They engaged in a witch hunt. If you were a staunch Democrat like me and were politically involved, and a friend of Eleanor Roosevelt's, as I was, you were labeled a Commie sympathizer. The people who organized the witch hunt were afraid, suspicious of any kind of intellectualism, much like Mr. Agnew today, with his references to 'effete snobs.' Slurs were made about me in the trades. I finally sued *The Hollywood Reporter* for $1 million. Yet I don't think the witch hunt affected my career, although there's no way of knowing. I was very powerful in Hollywood then, and once I took a stand, I stuck to it. But actresses like Marsha Hunt and Jean Muir—the slurs hurt them thoroughly and their careers suffered. I guess the forties were good to me in a way. *The Best Years of Our Lives* was good and I avoided going to jail. But when you think of those years now with all that fond nostalgia, that sweetness and light, you must admit it wasn't all that. Quite, quite horrible."

MYRNA LOY

Pretty Ladies (MGM, 1925)
Ben Hur (MGM, 1926)
Cave Man (WB, 1926)
The Gilded Highway (WB, 1926)
Across the Pacific (WB, 1926)
Why Girls Go Back Home (WB, 1926)
Don Juan (WB, 1926)
The Exquisite Sinner (MGM, 1926)
So This Is Paris? (WB, 1926)
Finger Prints (WB, 1927)
Ham and Eggs at the Front (WB, 1927)
Bitter Apples (WB, 1927)
The Heart of Maryland (WB, 1927)
The Jazz Singer (WB, 1927)
If I Were Single (WB, 1927)
The Climbers (WB, 1927)
Simple Sis (WB, 1927)
A Sailor's Sweetheart (WB, 1927)
The Girl from Chicago (WB, 1927)

What Price Beauty (Pathé, 1928)
Beware of Married Men (WB, 1928)
Turn Back the Hours (Gotham, 1928)
Crimson City (WB, 1928)
Pay as you Enter (WB, 1928)
State Street Sadie (WB, 1928)
Midnight Taxi (WB, 1928)
Noah's Ark (WB, 1929)
Fancy Baggage (WB, 1929)
The Desert Song (WB, 1929)
Black Watch (Fox, 1929)
The Squall (FN, 1929)
Hardboiled Rose (WB, 1929)
Evidence (WB, 1929)
The Show of Shows (WB, 1929)
The Great Divide (FN, 1930)
Cameo Kirby (Fox, 1930)
Isle of Escape (WB, 1930)
Under a Texas Moon (WB, 1930)

Cock O' The Walk (Sono Art-World Wide, 1930)
Bride of the Regiment (FN, 1930)
Last of the Duanes (Fox, 1930)
The Truth about Youth (FN, 1930)
Renegades (Fox, 1930)
Rogue of the Rio Grande (Sono Art-World Wide, 1930)
The Devil to Pay (UA, 1930)
Naughty Flirt (FN, 1931)
Body and Soul (Fox, 1931)
A Connecticut Yankee (Fox, 1931)
Hush Money (Fox, 1931)
Transatlantic (Fox, 1931)
Rebound (RKO-Pathé, 1931)
Skyline (Fox, 1931)
Consolation Marriage (RKO, 1931)
Arrowsmith (UA, 1931)
Emma (MGM, 1932)
The Wet Parade (MGM, 1932)
Vanity Fair (Hollywood Exchange, 1932)
The Woman in Room 13 (Fox, 1932)
New Morals for Old (MGM, 1932)
Love Me Tonight (Paramount, 1932)
Thirteen Women (RKO, 1932)
The Mask of Fu Manchu (MGM, 1932)
The Animal Kingdom (RKO, 1932)
Topaze (RKO, 1933)
The Barbarian (MGM, 1933)
The Prizefighter and the Lady (MGM, 1933)
When Ladies Meet (MGM, 1933)
Penthouse (MGM, 1933)
Night Flight (MGM, 1933)
Men in White (MGM, 1934)
Manhattan Melodrama (MGM, 1934)
The Thin Man (MGM, 1934)
Stamboul Quest (MGM, 1934)
Evelyn Prentice (MGM, 1934)
Broadway Bill (Columbia, 1934)
Wings in the Dark (Paramount, 1935)

Whipsaw (MGM, 1935)
Wife vs. Secretary (MGM, 1936)
Petticoat Fever (MGM, 1936)
The Great Ziegfeld (MGM, 1936)
To Mary—with Love (20th-Fox, 1936)
Libeled Lady (MGM, 1936)
After the Thin Man (MGM, 1936)
Parnell (MGM, 1937)
Double Wedding (MGM, 1937)
Man-Proof (MGM, 1938)
Test Pilot (MGM, 1938)
Too Hot to Handle (MGM, 1938)
Lucky Night (MGM, 1939)
The Rains Came (20th-Fox, 1939)
Another Thin Man (MGM, 1939)
I Love You Again (MGM, 1940)
Third Finger, Left Hand (MGM, 1940)
Love Crazy (MGM, 1941)
Shadow of the Thin Man (MGM, 1941)
The Thin Man Goes Home (MGM, 1944)
So Goes My Love (Universal, 1946)
The Best Years of Our Lives (RKO, 1946)
The Bachelor and the Bobby Soxer (RKO, 1947)
Song of the Thin Man (MGM, 1947)
The Senator Was Indiscreet (Universal, 1947)*
Mr. Blandings Builds His Dream House (Selznick, 1948)
The Red Pony (Republic, 1949)
Cheaper by the Dozen (20th-Fox, 1950)
If This Be Sin (UA, 1950)
Belles on Their Toes (20th-Fox, 1952)
The Ambassador's Daughter (UA, 1956)
Lonelyhearts (UA, 1958)
From the Terrace (20th-Fox, 1960)
Midnight Lace (Universal, 1960)
The April Fools (National General, 1969)

*Guest Appearance

With (standing) Pat Flaherty, Charlie Williams, Huey White, William Powell, Ben Taggart, and Harry Tenbrook in *The Thin Man* (1934)

With George Brent and Otto Fries in *Stamboul Quest* (1934)

With Una Merkel in *Evelyn Prentice* (1934)

With Gloria Holden in *Wife vs. Secretary* (1936)

With Walter Connolly and William Powell in
Libeled Lady (1936)

With Sidney Toler in *Double Wedding* (1937

With Robert Taylor in *Lucky Night* (1939)

With William Powell in *The Thin Man Goes Home* (1944)

451

Keye Luke

Screen typecasting dies hard and, nearly forty years after the fact, Keye Luke is still best remembered for his portrayal of Charlie Chan's Number One son. But for MGM in the mid-1940s, he served another function. When they decided their long-running *Dr. Kildare* series had to make token acknowledgment of World War II, Luke was hired to essay Dr. Lee Wong How, a patriotic Chinese who would willingly give up his residency under Dr. Gillespie at Blair General Hospital to serve his homeland in the battle against Japan.

Actually, Keye Luke was the only member of his family (three brothers, two sisters) born in China, when his San Francisco-based parents were on a pleasure trip to Canton on June 18, 1904. Three months later they returned to California, where the father owned an Oriental art store. Luke planned to attend Yale University, but his father died and the family relocated in Seattle where he matriculated at the University of Washington and studied architecture and design. After graduation he became a commercial artist in Seattle, specializing in theatrical advertisements. Later he was persuaded to relocate to Hollywood where he was made an advertising artist at RKO. One day the studio was in need of a Chinese actor who spoke perfect English. Luke volunteered and made his screen debut in a RKO short subject. He decided acting was the career for him.

It was in MGM's *The Painted Veil* (1934) that Luke made his feature film debut in a small role as a Chinese doctor. After being Peter Lorre's operating room assistant in *Mad Love* (1935), Luke began his long association with Fox's Charlie Chan series, playing the helpful but inexperienced Number One son Lee. *Charlie Chan in Paris* (1935) was the seventh of the Warner Oland-starred entries. Luke proved so effective as the enthusiastic ("gee Pop!") offspring that he became an integral part of the proceedings thereafter. By the time Oland died in 1938, Luke's Fox contract had expired and Victor Sen Yung was brought in as Number Two son to accompany the new Chan (Sidney Toler) on his escapades. Luke would return to his old role for the final two installments of the Chan series to date, both cheaply produced by Monogram Pictures in 1948–1949 with Roland Winters as the Oriental detective.

With the advent of World War II, Luke found himself usually cast as an Allied-loyal Chinese, as in *The Good Earth* (1937) and *A Yank on the Burma Road* (1942), although occasionally he would follow in the footsteps of Richard Loo and Philip Ahn and would portray a sinister Axis agent, as in *Across the Pacific* (1942). Having costarred as Kato to Gordon Jones' lead in Universal's serial, *The Green Hornet* (1940), Luke found a whole new action career and played in four additional Universal chapter thrillers, including *Secret Agent X-9* (1945).

But it was MGM who offered Luke his meatiest screen role in the studio's long-running *Dr. Kildare* series. Luke told the authors of this book that it was he who suggested to producer Carey Wilson "that a Chinese–American interne would be a good friendship image on the screen." Thus Dr. Lee Wong How made his entry into the medico series, commencing with *Dr. Gillespie's New Assistant* (1942) and for four additional installments. Granted that he was a non-Caucasian, Luke's character was still treated in a rather second-class manner by the scripts, but technically he was on the same level as Van Johnson and Richard Quine in vying for the post of becoming Dr. Gillespie's (Lionel Barrymore) protégé, now that Dr. Kildare (Lew Ayres) had departed from the studio. As part of his MGM term contract, he was used in other studio products, including *Salute to the Marines* (1943). In this Wallace Beery picture he portrayed a former boxing champion who was now in the military service. Luke himself had long been a boxing enthusiast and "had picked up many points about the sport. I managed to get some of them into the character and it paid off ... ." Ironically, when MGM was casting its big-budgeted *Dragon Seed* (1944), Luke tested with most of the players assembled for the production. However, he was not used because it was thought his authentic Oriental looks would make the Caucasian actors appear even more artificial in their slant-eyed makeup.

In the late 1940s Luke toured the country with a club act in which he did impersonations of Ronald Colman, Peter Lorre, *et al.* By the 1950s his film career had dissipated, but a three-year run on Broadway as Father Wong in Rodgers–Hammerstein's musical, *The Flower Drum Song* (1958), renewed professional interest in his career. Unfortunately, he was not used in the film version of this hit show. The 1960s found him in occasional small film roles such as the elderly professor friend of Gregory Peck in *The Chairman* (1969) and the field commander of the enemy force in *Noon Sunday* (1971). More so of late, he has been showing up on television in episodes of such series as *Adam-12*. In the telefeature *Kung Fu* (1972), starring David Carradine, he played "Po," the blind monk. Luke says he is particularly fond of this assignment because the "role contained elements of spiritual wisdom and philosophy which I could project in my dialogue." Since then he has been hired to play the Prime Minister in the teleseries *Anna and the King of Siam* which topcasts Yul Brynner and Samantha Eggar. Strangest of all, he has now graduated to playing Charlie Chan, providing the voice for the Oriental sleuth in the new Saturday morning animated cartoon video series *The Amazing*

Chan and The Chan Clan.

Luke wed Ethel Davis on April 25, 1942 and is the stepfather to her two children by a previous marriage. He still continues with his art work, particularly pen and ink drawings, and frequently lectures on Oriental art, as well as recording LP albums of classic literature. His occasional late night television talk show appearances display his erudition to advantage. To this day he still autographs photographs, "Key Luke, #1 Son, Charlie Chan."

KEYE LUKE

The Painted Veil (MGM, 1934)
Charlie Chan in Paris (Fox, 1935)
Oil for the Lamps of China (WB, 1935)
Shanghai (Paramount, 1935)
Mad Love (MGM, 1935)
Charlie Chan in Shanghai (Fox, 1935)
King of Burlesoue (Fox, 1935)
Here's to Romance (Fox, 1935)
Charlie Chan at the Circus (20th-Fox, 1936)
Charlie Chan at the Race Track (20th-Fox, 1936)
Charlie Chan at the Opera (20th-Fox, 1936)
Anything Goes (Paramount, 1936)
The Good Earth (MGM, 1937)
Charlie Chan at the Olympics (20th-Fox, 1937)
Charlie Chan on Broadway (20th-Fox, 1937)
Charlie Chan at Monte Carlo (20th-Fox, 1937)
Mr. Moto's Gamble (20th-Fox, 1938)
International Settlement (20th-Fox, 1938)
Disputed Passage (Paramount, 1939)
Barricade (20th-Fox, 1939)
Phantom of Chinatown (Monogram, 1940)
No, No Nanette (RKO, 1940)
Sued for Libel (RKO, 1940)
The Green Hornet (Serial: Universal, 1940)
The Green Hornet Strikes Again (Serial: Universal, 1940)
They Met in Bombay (MGM, 1941)
The Gang's All Here (Monogram, 1941)
Let's Go Collegiate (Monogram, 1941)
Bowery Blitzkrieg (Monogram, 1941)
Burma Convoy (Universal, 1941)
No Hands on the Clock (Paramount, 1941)
Mr. and Mrs. North (MGM, 1941)
A Yank on the Burma Road (MGM, 1942)
Invisible Agent (Universal, 1942)
Somewhere I'll Find You (MGM, 1942)

Mexican Spitfire's Elephant (RKO, 1942)
North To the Klondike (Universal, 1942)
Spy Ship (WB, 1942)
Across the Pacific (WB, 1942)
A Tragedy at Midnight (Republic, 1942)
The Falcon's Brother (RKO, 1942)
Destination Unknown (Universal, 1942)
Dr. Gillespie's New Assistant (MGM, 1942)
Adventures of Smilin' Jack (Serial: Universal, 1943)
Dr. Gillespie's Criminal Case (MGM, 1943)
Salute to the Marines (MGM, 1943)
Three Men in White (MGM, 1944)
Andy Hardy's Blonde Trouble (MGM, 1944)
Between Two Women (MGM, 1945)
First Yank into Tokyo (RKO, 1945)
How Do You Do? (PRC, 1945)
Tokyo Rose (Paramount, 1945)
Secret Agent X-9 (Serial: Universal, 1945)
Lost City of the Jungle (Serial: Universal, 1946)
Dark Delusion (MGM, 1947)
Sleep My Love (UA, 1948)
Waterfront at Midnight (Paramount, 1948)
The Feathered Serpent (Monogram, 1948)
Sky Dragon (Monogram, 1949)
Young Man with a Horn (WB, 1950)
The World for Ransom (AA, 1954)
The Bamboo Prison (Columbia, 1954)
Hell's Half Acre (Republic, 1954)
Around the World in 80 Days (UA, 1956)
Battle Hell (DCA, 1957)
Nobody's Perfect (Universal, 1968)
The Chairman (20th-Fox, 1969)
The Hawaiians (UA, 1970)
Noon Sunday (Crown International, 1971)

With Wallace Beery in *Salute to the Marines* (1943)

Jeanette MacDonald

Perhaps no MGM female star of the 1930s kindled such affectionate devotion in her fans as did singing luminary Jeanette MacDonald. She had displayed her sizable abilities as an operetta vocalist and dispenser of wit at Paramount earlier in the decade. However, it was at Metro that she blossomed into her full cinema glory. Louis B. Mayer had his own conception of a humanized prima donna and remolded Jeanette's screen image accordingly. Fortuitously for her, the results were in total accord with filmgoers' ideas on the subject. It is likely Jeanette would have obtained her lofty studio and public status with or without her frequent MGM costar Nelson Eddy. More so than her genre rival Irene Dunne, she possessed a vast amount of marketable charm which allowed her to make the stickiest of confectionary vehicles palatable to the public. With her bewitching smile, the twinkle in her eyes, and her abundant reddish blonde hair, Jeanette was a surprisingly understated bundle of hard-sell entertainment, whether vocalizing a song, dabbling in light drama, or, more especially, performing in her forte, tongue-in-cheek comedy.

She was born in Philadelphia, on June 18th, the daughter of a contractor. The year of her birth was most likely 1901, but most sources put it at 1907. She was of Scottish, Irish, and English ancestry, of which she once said, "I've been told I have an Irish temper, I know I have Scottish thrift, and, like the English, I love a good show." Jeanette was the third daughter born to Daniel and Anne M. (Wright) MacDonald. Her oldest sister, Elsie,* would later run a dance school in Philadelphia, and her next older sister, Blossom, would become best known to the public as Marie Blake, an MGM character actress (especially well known as Sally, the switchboard operator in the *Dr. Kildare* series) and later as Blossom Rock, who played Granny on *The Addams Family* teleseries. Like her sisters, Jeanette early in life displayed show business talents, and her education was geared accordingly. At an early age she was capable of memorizing opera arias but more often performed popular songs in tandem with her sister Blossom. When the latter went to New York to become a chorus girl, Jeanette followed and in 1920 landed a post in the chorus of *The Demi-Tasse Revue*. Her abilities as a singer and light dancer soon won her better parts in *A Fantastic Fricasee* (1922), *The Magic Ring* (1923), and *Tip Toes* (1925). Then in 1925 the Broadway Shuberts signed her to

*Elsie died in November 1971

456

a contract, and she starred in *Bubbling Over* (1926), *Yes, Yes Yvette* (1927), *Sunny Days* (1928), *Angela* (1928), and *Boom Boom* (1929).

Jeanette had tested for Paramount in 1928 at the insistence of star Richard Dix who thought she would be excellent as his costar in a new picture he was preparing. The studio did not give her the role, particularly since the Shuberts would not release her from their contract. Thus it was not until a year later when director Ernst Lubitsch, needing a leading lady for Maurice Chevalier's *The Love Parade* (1929), looked at Jeanette's screen test and chose her for the part. Even by today's standards, *The Love Parade* remains a sophisticated musical sex farce, with Jeanette as the glamorous queen of Sylvania who is anxious to find a husband, more to satisfy her rampant romantic needs than to appease her stolid advisors who insist she find a prince consort for diplomatic reasons. That same year Jeannete made her first RCA Victor recordings, singing "Dream Lover" and "March of The Grenadiers" from the film. The Rudolph Friml operetta, *The Vagabond King* (1930), filmed in two-tone color, followed, and then Lubitsch used her again in *Monte Carlo* (1930). If Jack Buchanan was a trifle fey as the count posing as a hairdresser, Jeanette demonstrated a growing awareness of her screen potential, dominating the action with her burgeoning flair for ladylike risquéness. But the musical movie cycle had taken a fast decline in popularity, and Paramount dropped her. In 1931 a French newspaper reported that she had been killed in an automobile accident, and when she was unable to squelch the rumor, she decided to make a singing tour of European capitals, appearing at the Empire in Paris and the Dominion in London, as well as others.

At this point Lubitsch persuaded the Paramount regime to sign Jeanette for two more musicals with Maurice Chevalier, *One Hour with You* (1932) and *Love Me Tonight* (1932). Jeanette always credited Lubitsch with developing her screen personality and said of the "boudoir diplomat," "He could suggest more with a closed door than all the hay-rolling you see openly on the screen nowadays, and yet he never offended." When these two Paramount musicals failed to consolidate Jeanette's cinema standing, she went to Europe, ostensibly to vacation, but in reality to seek screen offers. She was set to star with Herbert Marshall in *The Queen's Affair* (1933), but production difficulties occurred, and producer Herbert Wilcox's wife Anna Neagle took over as star of that film as well as leading the cast in a followup, *Bitter Sweet* (1933), originally planned for Jeanette. Meanwhile, Jeanette went to the Riviera. Also in France at the time were Irving Thalberg and his wife, Norma Shearer. When Jeanette loaned Shearer the services of her hairdresser–chauffeur, they became fast friends. Thalberg was attempting to obtain a roster of stars in an effort to become an independent producer after his rift with Louis B. Mayer, and offered Jeanette a contract. But Mayer, never far behind available talent, had seen her and had signed Jeanette to a contract first, for two pictures.

A musical version of Moss Hart's *I Married an Angel* was to be her initial vehicle, but that play was shelved when the Will Hays office rejected this script about an angel who loses her virtue via a mortal man. So MGM had her debut in the inauspicious *The Cat and the Fiddle* (1934) opposite the declining studio star, Ramon Novarro. If Warner Brothers could make a packet of money from proletarian, kaleidoscopic musicals such as *42nd Street* (1933) and *Gold Diggers of 1933* (1933), Metro reasoned that it could do equally well with a string of higher-toned operettas. Thalberg prepared Franz Lehar's operetta *The Merry Widow* (1934) as a starring vehicle for Maurice Chevalier and Grace Moore. When billing conflicts ensued, the studio replaced Moore with Jeanette, which pleased director Ernst Lubitsch but brought frowns to the face of boulevardier Chevalier.

MGM was sufficiently satisfied with the results of *The Merry Widow* to place Jeanette under a five-year contract. Mayer cajoled Jeanette into starring in the frothy *Naughty Marietta* (1935), which she had rejected on several past occasions. Mayer, in one of his famous "scenes," called her into his executive suite, acted out the story for her, told her to put more schmaltz into her singing and, on bended knee, sang "Eli, Eli." Legend has it that Jeanette witnessed that display of "sincerity" with tears in her eyes and agreed to appear in the film. Her costar was a blond baritone by the name of Nelson Eddy, and the picture was the first of eight that they made together and also made motion picture history of sorts. While Metro was readying an appropriate second script for the duo, Jeanette starred in a story she herself had chosen and built into a property, under the condition that Clark Gable would costar with her. Gable's first response was, "She's a prima donna. I just sit there while she sings. None of that stuff for me." Mayer's power of persuasion convinced Gable he should star in that "stuff" and the result was one of the great all-time popular pictures, *San Francisco* (1936), and one of Gable's best roles. More importantly for MGM, it grossed a whopping $4 million.

MGM spared no expense, or so it seemed, on the next MacDonald–Eddy outing, *Maytime* (1937), in which an elderly Jeanette recounts the story of her romantic past to convince two young lovers that they should marry at any cost. The musical had both Jeanette and Eddy singing "Will You Remember (Sweetheart)?"—one of the team's most enduring trademark numbers. This was her favorite film. As she explained to film historian DeWitt Bodeen: "There was, too, the satisfaction of working with Robert Z. Leonard, not only one of the ablest all-around directors but one who, being a singer himself, was deft and sympathetic in his handling of the musical phases of the story. He didn't believe in the iron-handed technique, but preferred that the actors follow their own instincts at first, and redo a scene only when they felt ideas different from their own would improve a performance. Leonard always kept us pliable and spontaneous. Once he relieved a period of tension by arranging for me to find, to my horror, a strange man asleep on my couch when I went to my dressing room—a man who, on closer inspection, turned out to be a dummy."

MGM tested Jeanette's solo boxoffice strength by starring her without Eddy in *The Firefly* (1937). Her costar was Allan Jones, a personable studio performer who had become stultified under the shadow of the emerged Eddy. The duo worked well together, playing Napoleonic era spies, and the highlight of the film for many was Jones' rendition of "The Donkey Serenade." As was her habit, Jeanette dubbed her own voice in the foreign versions of her films, to which Mayer took objection. When the independent Jeanette went over Mayer's head to Nicholas Schenck in New York, for permission to do so, Mayer never forgave her. After that Jeanette said she could see her status at MGM diminish even though she was still big boxoffice star. More to the point was that Jeanette, like the similarly self-willed Myrna Loy, did not cotton to Mayer's amorous advances. If Mayer thought Jeanette was playing coy in a ladylike manner, he was finally convinced of her stand when she wed screen actor Gene Raymond on June 17, 1937, reputed to be the biggest Hollywood wedding since that of Vilma Banky and Rod La Rocque a decade before.

To please the public, Jeanette and Eddy were teamed again in *The Girl of the Golden West* (1938), the least bearable and enduring of their joint screen work, followed by the studio's first new process color film *Sweethearts* (1938). *Sweethearts* was a modern operetta of a battling stage singing couple, but it was really Jeanette's next film, *Broadway Serenade* (1939),which took her away from her stance of costume musicals and presented her as a most contemporary song and dance lady who almost loses composer Lew Ayres because of her successful career. If one overlooks the garish Busby Berkeley-staged finale and the contrived story line, this film proves that Jeanette was very capable of handling up-to-date material. Unfortunately, MGM never capitalized on her abilities as a light comedienne and returned her to more frou-frou with Nelson Eddy. *New Moon* (1940) and *Bitter Sweet* (1940) contained too much *déjà vu* and, by the time of the offbeat *I Married an Angel* (1942), it was decided the team had run its course. The studio reasoned it was far less expensive and much easier to dash off a new Mickey Rooney–Judy Garland backstage tale than to mount a MacDonald–Eddy vehicle, and in the tense World War II days, the public accepted the substitution readily enough.

Along the way, Jeanette starred with her husband Gene Raymond in a new version of *Smilin' Through* (1941), saccharine but sincere, and ended her studio stay with the very modestly budgeted entry *Cairo* (1942). Ground out as a program filler by W. S. Van Dyke, *Cairo* is a spoof of spy films and contains the best of Jeanette's unrepressed screen moments. Whether mocking her own camp reputation, dating from *San Francisco*, or her clarion ability to hit a high C, she glided through the film in full control of all the comic moments.

During World War II, Jeanette was a frequent U.S.O. entertainer. Having aspirations for grand opera, she took singing lessons from veteran opera diva Lotte Lehmann. Jeanette made her opera debut in Montreal in 1943, singing *Romeo and Juliet* with Ezio Pinza, and again with Pinza, sang in *Faust* with the Chicago Civic Opera Company in 1944. She gave recitals at Hollywood Bowl, Lewisohn Stadium, and Carnegie Hall, and appeared in stock productions of Noel Coward's *Bitter Sweet*, and Rodgers and Hammerstein's *The King and I*, always to packed audiences. All through these

459

years, the most frequent question put to Jeanette was: "Will you and Eddy ever reteam again?" Her answer was always a polite no. Whatever her personal opinions were of Eddy as a perfomer, she kept them to herself and friends. There had been production plans in 1943 for the duo to appear in a RKO operetta entitled *East Wind*, but that came to naught. In the late 1940s MGM producer Joe Pasternak persuaded Jeanette to return to Metro to play the vivacious mother of three who weds Jose Iturbi in *Three Daring Daughters* (1948), and also in the following year to play a widowed concert performer in the color picture *The Sun Comes Up*, which featured Lassie and studio child personality Claude Jarman, Jr. As cinema writer DeWitt Bodeen aptly analyzed, "Ironically enough, there is more of the real-life Jeanette MacDonald in this final performance than in any of her biggest boxoffice successes."

One of Jeanette's last professional appearances was in 1957, at the funeral of her former boss, Louis B. Mayer, where she sang "Ah, Sweet Mystery of Life." The same year she and Eddy were reteamed on an RCA Victor LP, highlighting their biggest screen song successes. In the last years of her life, Jeanette suffered from a heart ailment. She underwent an arterial transplant in 1963 at the Methodist Hospital in Houston, Texas. She returned to Houston in 1965, planning to undergo open heart surgery, but before the operation could be performed, she died on January 14th. Newspapers reported that on that afternoon she had awakened to find her husband standing beside her. She looked up and said, "I love you." "I love you, too," he replied. With that, she smiled and died. At her funeral, Raymond had recordings of her singing "Ah, Sweet Mystery Of Life" and "Ave Maria" played to the large hysterical crowd that had gathered outside the funeral chapel in Forest Lawn Cemetery.

Jeanette's cinema star reputation has endured and even grown, a phenomenon due to MGM's past policy of reissuing the MacDonald–Eddy operettas to theatres, and also because of the frequent television showing of their features. A very strong Jeanette MacDonald fan club still exists, devoted to preserving her legend. The group meets annually to reshow her films, exchange tidbits of newly discovered data on her level-headed and decorous life, and to share with ardent attendee Gene Raymond sweet moments of memory of the woman who was Jeanette MacDonald.

JEANETTE MACDONALD

The Love Parade (Paramount, 1929)
The Vagabond King (Paramount, 1930)
Monte Carlo (Paramount, 1930)
Let's Go Native (Paramount, 1930)
The Lottery Bride (UA, 1930)
Oh, For a Man (Fox, 1930)
Don't Bet on Women (Fox, 1931)

Annabelle's Affairs (Fox, 1931)
One Hour with You (Paramount, 1932)
Love Me Tonight (Paramount, 1932)
The Cat and the Fiddle (MGM, 1934)
The Merry Widow (MGM, 1934)
Naughty Marietta (MGM, 1935)
Rose Marie (MGM, 1936)

With Ramon Novarro and Leonid Kinskey in *The Cat and the Fiddle* (1934)

With Morgan Wallace and Frank Sheridan in *The Merry Widow* (1934)

With Nelson Eddy in *Rose Marie* (1936)

San Francisco (MGM, 1936)
Maytime (MGM, 1937)
The Firefly (MGM, 1937)
Girl of the Golden West (MGM, 1938)
Sweethearts (MGM, 1938)
Broadway Serenade (MGM, 1939)
New Moon (MGM, 1940)
Bitter Sweet (MGM, 1940)
Smilin' Through (MGM, 1941)
I Married an Angel (MGM, 1942)
Cairo (MGM, 1942)
Follow the Boys (Universal, 1944)
Three Daring Daughters (MGM, 1948)
The Sun Comes Up (MGM, 1948)

With Nelson Eddy in *Maytime* (1937)

With Allan Jones and Warren William in *The Firefly* (1937)

With Buddy Ebsen in *Girl of the Golden West* (1938)

With Nelson Eddy (photograph) and Fay Holden in *Sweethearts* (1938)

With Nelson Eddy, Binnie Barnes, Reginald Owen, and Douglass Dumbrille in *I Married An Angel* (1942)

Marjorie Main

Incongruous as it may seem, it was Marjorie Main, a refined, teetotaling daughter of a conservative minister, who carved a unique niche in screen history, playing a series of raucous hoydenish women. These portraits were distinguished from those of Minerva Urecal and Hope Emerson by a winning inner glow or a burning hatred, depending whether the picture was a comedy or drama. Walking about the set with a section-boss stride and whining with a shrill nasal twang, Marjorie became so popular that in 1946 the 96th Division of the United States Army named her its Occupation Girl. Her greatest popularity was due to her Wallace Beery costarring vehicles at MGM and to the series of Ma and Pa Kettle entries which she made at Universal after her Oscar-nomination performance as the uncouth Ma to Percy Kilbride's indolent Pa in *The Egg and I* (1947). The Kettle pictures were the climax to Marjorie's screen career which had found her at MGM being touted as the successor to Marie Dressler. She never fit such a pat niche. She was herself unique and that was sufficient.

Marjorie was born Mary Tomlinson on February 24, 1890 near Acton, Indiana, where her father was a minister in the Church of Christ. Throughout her schooling she had been interested in dramatics because it gave her an opportunity to express herself. When she finally decided to pursue an acting career, she joined the Chatauqua Theatre Circuit performing Shakespeare and Dickens. She changed her name to save her family any embarrassment and decided upon Main because it was easy to remember. Stock work and vaudeville appearances followed, and once she even played the Palace in New York in a sketch with W. C. Fields.

In 1921 she married Dr. Stanley LeFevre Krebs, a psychologist–lecturer, and for a number of years organized her life around his extensive lecture tours. When they settled in New York, she took to the Broadway stage appearing in *Burlesque* (1927) with Barbara Stanwyck, and playing Mae West's mother in *The Wicked Age*. (She is actually only three years older than the legendary Miss West). She received good notices playing in Jerome Kern's *Music in the Air*, which was the first of three plays in which she appeared in both the Broadway and screen versions. *Dead End* and *The Women* were the other two.

465

Marjorie's film debut took place in 1932 in Universal's *A House Divided* in an unbilled bit while waiting for *Music in the Air* to be filmed with Gloria Swanson. A few more bit parts followed and, when *Music in the Air* was released by Fox in 1934, Marjorie's maid role had become almost a silent cameo with most of her scenes cut out.

Her husband died in 1935 and the grieving Marjorie turned to stage work for therapy and a source of livelihood. In the stage production of *Dead End*, she gave a very memorable performance as the mother of a punk gangster. She was equally as good as the blasé hotelkeeper in the stage version of *The Women*. When Samuel Goldwyn purchased *Dead End* (1937) for the screen, he had Marjorie repeat her role. In one unforgettable scene she slaps the face of her no-good son, Humphrey Bogart, and screams, "Ya dirty yella dog!" Goldwyn used her again as the mother of *Stella Dallas* (1937) which starred Barbara Stanwyck, and Marjorie became one of the busiest character women in the cinema. Many of her picture roles during this period were repeats of the slum mother she had played in *Dead End*, but several, made at MGM, allowed her to exploit her talents for comedy: *Test Pilot* (1938), *Too Hot to Handle* (1938), and *The Women* (1939). She had an excellent death scene at Republic in *Dark Command* (1940) in which she essayed the sacrificing backwoods mother of outlaw Walter Pidgeon.

Since the death of Marie Dressler in 1934, MGM had been vainly looking for her successor and a compatible costar for the assorted screen scamps Wallace Beery continued to make both famous and lucrative for the studio. Not only Beery but the MGM brass as well were delighted when Marjorie's performance in *Wyoming* (1940) proved she was the right one. The studio promptly gave her a seven-year contract which would later be renewed for another seven years. Marjorie enjoyed her MGM association, and she and Beery became a popular team, sharing such vehicles as *Barnacle Bill* (1941), *Jackass Mail* (1942), *Rationing*, and *Big Jack* (1949), the latter being Beery's final film before his death. Although the two players had tremendous rapport onscreen, they never socialized together off screen, for Marjorie was a stay-at-home, little inclined to participate in the Hollywood nightlife.

While playing hearty and salty characters opposite Beery, she also did a variety of acerbic domestics as in such films as *A Woman's Face* (1941), *Meet Me in St. Louis* (1944), *The Harvey Girls* (1946), and, later, *Summer Stock* (1950). After playing the rural wonder, Ma Kettle, in *The Egg and I* on loan to Universal, she was not keen on the idea of building it into a series, and agreed only after MGM strongly insisted. Before the first of the series was finished, she began to enjoy the part and "believe" in the role that established her as a household word for the next nine years.

In 1954 she went from MGM, who had been earning a hefty profit on loaning her services, to Universal, and, when Percy Kilbride tired of the Kettle series, she went on to appear in two more by herself. After a splendid performance as the rough-and-tumble farm wife in *Friendly Persuasion* (1956), Marjorie retired from the screen. Now in her eighties she lives unpretentiously in retirement doing her own cooking and domestic work (she rode the bus to work during many of her MGM years). She recalls her years with the studio and Louis B. Mayer with much affection, although she is not wont to grant interviews or to discuss such topics as her disenchantment with working with Norma Shearer. Every Thanksgiving day, she still makes a public appearance as a celebrity member of Hollywood's Santa Claus Lane Parade.

MARJORIE MAIN

A House Divided (Universal, 1932)*
Hot Saturday (Paramount, 1932)
Take a Chance (Paramount, 1933)
Crime Without Passion (Paramount, 1934)
Music in the Air (Fox, 1934)
Love in a Bungalow (Universal, 1937)
Dead End (UA, 1937)
Stella Dallas (UA, 1937)
The Man Who Cried Wolf (Universal, 1937
The Wrong Road (Republic, 1937)
The Shadow (Columbia, 1937)
Boy of the Streets (Monogram, 1937)
City Girl (20th-Fox, 1937)
Penitentiary (Columbia, 1938)
King of the Newsboys (Republic, 1938)
Test Pilot (MGM, 1938)

Prison Farm (Paramount, 1938)
Romance of the Limberlost (Monogram, 1938)
Little Tough Guy (Universal, 1938)
Under the Big Top (Monogram, 1938)
Too Hot to Handle (MGM, 1938)
Girls' School (Columbia, 1938)
There Goes My Heart (UA, 1938)
Three Comrades (MGM, 1938)
Lucky Night (MGM, 1939)
They Shall Have Music (UA, 1939)
Angels Wash Their Faces (WB, 1939)
The Women (MGM, 1939)
Another Thin Man (MGM, 1939)
Two Thoroughbreds (RKO, 1939)
I Take This Woman (MGM, 1940)
Women Without Names (Paramount, 1940)

With Wallace Beery in *Jackass Mail* (1942)

Dark Command (Republic, 1940)
Turnabout (UA, 1940)
Susan and God (MGM, 1940)
The Captain Is a Lady (MGM, 1940)
Wyoming (MGM, 1940)
The Wild Man of Borneo (MGM, 1941)
The Trial of Mary Dugan (MGM, 1941)
A Woman's Face (MGM, 1941)
Barnacle Bill (MGM, 1941)
The Shepherd of the Hills (Paramount, 1941)
Honky Tonk (MGM, 1941)
The Bugle Sounds (MGM, 1941)
We Were Dancing (MGM, 1942)
The Affairs of Martha (MGM, 1942)
Jackass Mail (MGM, 1942)
Tish (MGM, 1942)
Tennessee Johnson (MGM, 1942)
Woman of the Town (UA, 1943)
Heaven Can Wait (20th-Fox, 1943)
Johnny Come Lately (UA, 1943)
Rationing (MGM, 1944)
Gentle Annie (MGM, 1944)
Meet Me in St. Louis (MGM, 1944)
Murder He Says (Paramount, 1945)
The Harvey Girls (MGM, 1946)
Bad Bascomb (MGM, 1946)
Undercurrent (MGM, 1946)
The Show-Off (MGM, 1946)
The Egg and I (Universal, 1947)
The Wistful Widow of Wagon Gap (Universal, 1947)

Feudin', Fussin' and A-Fightin' (Universal, 1948)
Ma and Pa Kettle (Universal, 1949)
Big Jack (MGM, 1949)
Ma and Pa Kettle Go to Town (Universal, 1950)
Summer Stock (MGM, 1950)
Mrs. O'Malley and Mr. Malone (MGM, 1950)
Ma and Pa Kettle Back on the Farm (Universal, 1951)
The Law and the Lady (MGM, 1951)
Mr. Imperium (MGM, 1951)
It's a Big Country (MGM, 1951)
The Belle of New York (MGM, 1952)
Ma and Pa Kettle at the Fair (Universal, 1952)
Ma and Pa Kettle on Vacation (Universal, 1953)
Fast Company (MGM, 1953)
The Long, Long Trailer (MGM, 1954)
Rose Marie (MGM, 1954)
Ma and Pa Kettle at Home (Universal, 1954)
Ricochet Romance (Universal, 1954)
Ma and Pa Kettle at Waikiki (Universal, 1955)
The Kettles in the Ozarks (Universal, 1956)
Friendly Persuasion (AA, 1956)
The Kettles on Old MacDonald's Farm (Universal, 1957)

*Unbilled appearance

With Keefe Brasselle in *It's a Big Country* (1951)

The Marx Brothers

The "mad" Marx Brothers, those joyously irreverent, supremely illogical zanies who bounced raucously through their lunatic comedies, are today the revered objects of an ever-growing cult, far more appreciated (and commercialized) than at the time during which they made their prime feature films in the 1930s. It was Irving Thalberg, a man many accused of having no sense of humor, who brought the comedy team to MGM in 1935 after their five-picture stay at Paramount. They made five films at Metro, two of which are their finest: *A Night at the Opera* (1935) and *A Day at the Races* (1937). Those were the two features which Thalberg personally supervised before his premature death.

There were five Marx Brothers, born in New York City of German–Jewish ancestry. Chico was born Leonard on March 22, 1891, married three times, had one daughter, and died on October 11, 1961. Harpo was born Adolph Arthur on November 23, 1893, married once, had four adopted children, and died on September 28, 1964. Groucho was born Julius Henry on October 2, 1895, and has three children. His three wives were: Ruth Johnson (1920–1942), Catherine Gorcey (1945–1951), and Eden Hartford (1954–1970). Zeppo was born Herbert on February 25, 1901, married once and has one child. The fifth brother, Gummo, was born Milton, but did not appear with his brothers in motion pictures. He decided to open a talent agency in Hollywood instead.

The Marx Brothers' father was an unsuccessful tailor in the Yorkville section of Manhattan and was known locally as "misfit Marx." It was the dynamic mother of the brood, the former Minnie Schoenberg, who set the five youngsters on their way to a vaudeville career. Her parents had been itinerant entertainers in Germany and her brother was the well-known Al Shean of the popular Gallagher and Shean comedy team. (Shean himself worked frequently at MGM in the late 1930s, playing the much same type of old vaudevillian as fellow MGM-ite Charles Winninger would essay.) Minnie helped Al get settled into the American show business scene and then did the same for her sons, first as singles, then as a group. By 1914 they were evolving their comedy act. According to Groucho they acquired their stage nicknames at a poker game, but it was their own talent, polished by their uncle's suggestions, which caused them to make a name for themselves on the vaudeville circuit. On May 19, 1924 they opened on Broadway in a comedy entitled *I'll Say She Is*. The title of that show was enough to stimulate interest, but the brothers increased the pleasure of the audience. The following year they consolidated their professional reputation with *The Coconuts*, which ran for a season and then was taken on tour. They returned to Broadway in 1928 with *Animal Crackers*, which, in typical Marxian fashion, had been whipped into some sort of frenetic shape by an arduous road tour during which routines were tested, added, and deleted, according to a consensus of audience reaction.

Harpo had made his film debut in a 1925 Richard Dix feature, *Too Many Kisses* and, circa 1926, the team had filmed a silent comedy, *Humorisk*, at a Fort Lee, New Jersey, studio. This movie, which was made in a two-week period at a cost of $6,000 raised by a friend of the Marxes, was never released. It was while playing in *Animal Crackers* that Paramount contracted with them to film *The Coconuts* (1929) at their Astoria, Long Island studio. The filmed results, featuring Margaret Dumont, Mary Eaton, and Kay Francis, were not very cinematic in style, but nonetheless, the movie preserved their stage success. Much more felicitious was Paramount's rendition of *Animal Crackers* (1930). That studio then signed them to a three-picture contract at $75,000 per film, and the group took off for Hollywood, effectively ending their Broadway career. Paramount put them into *Monkey Business* (1931), *Horse Feathers* (1932), and *Duck Soup* (1933). The last was their craziest picture, but it was a boxoffice flop and Paramount offered them nothing more.

Zeppo dropped off the team, and now there were only three: Chico, Harpo, and Groucho. With nothing in the offing, Groucho took off for a summer stock engagement of *Twentieth Century* in Skowhegan, Maine, leaving Chico to handle any pending business matters. The inventive brother soon was approached by Irving Thalberg who said he wanted the team to make some pictures at MGM, and that he would prove that Louis B. Mayer's belief that they were washed up was premature. He offered the boys a salary contract plus fifteen percent of the gross on their films.

It was Thalberg's tactic to insert some romance into the zany Marx Brothers' plotline, maintaining that the men in the audience liked them as a team, but the women did not. In *A Night at the Opera* (1935), the romance was provided by Kitty Carlisle and Allan Jones. In *A Day at the Races* (1937) the love interest was between Jones and Maureen O'Sullivan. As with their past pictures, the brothers underwent an extensive vaudeville tour prior to filming, to work out the new routines sandwiched into their sparse plotline.

Thalberg died before *Races* was released and no one at MGM seemed to care what the team did next. Groucho later said, "After Thalberg's death, my interest in movies waned; I continued to appear in them, but my heart was in the Highlands. The fun had gone out of picture making." The three brothers went over to RKO for one picture, *Room Service* (1938), a successful Broadway show that RKO had purchased for them at the cost of $225,000. Three more Marx Brothers' pictures were made at MGM, each one more

With (front row): Margaret Dumont, Kitty Carlisle, Allan Jones, Robert Emmett O'Connor, Purnell Pratt; (second row): William Gould (police officer), Phillips Smalley (behind Chico Marx), George Irving, Selmer Jackson, and Wilbur Mack (partially hidden by Harpo Marx) in *A Night at the Opera* (1935)

pedestrian than the previous: *At the Circus* (1939), *Go West* (1940), and *The Big Store* (1941). Then, in total disillusionment, they decided to retire. The three brothers did reunite for two faltering comeback vehicles: *A Night in Casablanca* (1946), and *Love Happy* (1949), but they finally decided to call it quits.

Groucho has appeared in several motion pictures on his own, the last being Otto Preminger's big flop, *Skidoo* (1968), and he went on to a long stint on television with a quiz show called *You Bet Your Life* where he was able to ad lib his famous insults to the delight of the audience and the embarrassment of his guests. He often appeared in summer stock in the vehicle *Time Out for Elizabeth*. In retirement for several years, he turned up in the spring of 1972 at New York's Carnegie Hall, at age 77, with an evening of quips, memories, insults, and general chatter to an SRO audience. The same week he was equally "tuned on" as guest host of the Off-Broadway Theatre's Obie Awards. Then it was off to the Cannes Film Festival to pick up a special prize, where he and Gina Lollobrigida were the high spots of an otherwise dull celebration of the cinema.

THE MARX BROTHERS

With Chico, Groucho, Harpo, Zeppo:
The Coconuts (Paramount, 1929)
Animal Crackers (Paramount, 1930)
Monkey Business (Paramount, 1931)
Duck Soup (Paramount, 1932)
Horse Feathers (Paramount, 1933)
With Chico, Groucho, Harpo:
A Night at the Opera (MGM, 1935)
Your for the Asking (Paramount, 1936)
A Day at the Races (MGM, 1937)
Room Service (RKO, 1938)
At the Circus (MGM, 1939)
Go West (MGM, 1940)
The Big Store (MGM, 1941)
A Night in Casablanca (UA, 1946)

Love Happy (UA, 1949)
The Story of Mankind (WB, 1957)
With Harpo:
Too Many Kisses (Paramount, 1925)
Stage Door Canteen (UA, 1943)
With Groucho:
Copacabana (UA, 1947)
Mr. Music (Paramount, 1950)
Double Dynamite (RKO, 1951)
A Girl in Every Port (RKO, 1952)
Will Success Spoil Rock Hunter? (20th-Fox, 1957)*
Skidoo (Paramount, 1968)

*Unbilled appearance

472

With Diana Lewis and John Carroll in *Go West* (1940)

With Douglass Dumbrille in *The Big Store* (1941)

Marilyn Maxwell

Marilyn Maxwell was the singing blonde who bounced her way through a series of forgettable film roles with a breezy manner that was one part Joan Blondell's "Good Joe" and one part Mae West's vamp. Her publicity proclaimed that her figure equaled Jane Russell's, but her sex appeal was less vulgar and her personality more likeable than that of the buxom brunette's. Marilyn was the first female star to entertain American troops in Korea. Traveling with Bob Hope's show, she wore a tight sweater and sang "I Want to Love You." One group of admirers named her the movie star with the most luscious lips and Marilyn herself once said that when the fellas whistled, "I felt like whistling back."

She was born August 3, 1922 in Clarinda, Iowa and christened with the theatrical name Marvel Marilyn Maxwell. Her parents were divorced while she was still a small child and Marilyn traveled with her mother, who played the piano accompaniment for dancer Ruth St. Denis. Marilyn later said that it was her mother who pushed her into a musical career. ("She tried to fulfill her ambitions through me."). At the age of three she did a butterfly dance at the Brandeis Theatre in Omaha, Nebraska under the auspices of Miss St. Denis. She went to high school in Ft. Wayne, Indiana, where her brother owned a radio station. Marilyn had taken singing lessons as a child and persuaded her brother to allow her to sing on one of his broadcasts. He did, and band leader Amos Astot hired her as a vocalist at $35 a week. She was then sixteen. She got a better offer from Buddy Rogers and was vocalist for him for a year. During that time she met Rogers' wife, Mary Pickford, who took a liking to the songstress and arranged a screen test for her. Nothing came of it, however, and Marilyn took a job as vocalist with Ted Weems' band, sharing the singing chores with Perry Como and Mary Lee. Weems was so enthusiastic about Marilyn's potentials that he suggested she study at the Pasadena Playhouse.

Marilyn joined the Playhouse, sang on the radio, made a screen test at Paramount and one at MGM. While on tour with the *Camel Caravan*, entertaining servicemen, MGM offered her a contract. Louis B. Mayer insisted she change the "Marvel" part of her name and the new contractee decided to employ her middle name of Marilyn. She debuted in the uneventful World War II Navy saga *Stand by for Action* (1942) and then was given small roles as a blonde glamor girl in *DuBarry Was a Lady, Presenting Lily Mars*, and *Salute to the Marines*, all 1943 releases. She had a more important part in *Dr. Gillespie's Criminal Case* (1943), in which she played social worker Ruth Edley, who actively chases after Dr. Van Johnson through the corridors of Blair General Hospital. This role she would play to greater advantage in two later series entries, *Three Men in White* (1944) and *Between Two Women* (1945). Meanwhile, as the vocalist with the Kay Kyser band in *Swing Fever* (1943), she elicited her first critical comment from the N.Y. *Times* which referred to her as a "routine blonde warbler."

Marilyn certainly did not get much showcasing opportunity at MGM. She was the singing vaudeville sidekick of Abbott and Costello in *Lost in a Harem* (1944), the understanding wife of braggart Red Skelton in *The Show-Off* (1946), and became a Navy nurse in *High Barbaree* (1947). The best screen role of her career was as the plunky cabaret girl in *Summer Holiday* (1948). The film's highlight occurs when Marilyn, dressed in scarlet-toned clothes and lips to match, sings the "Weary Blues" number and vampishly tries to seduce an inebriated Mickey Rooney. Unfortunately, the picture had been held up in release for two years by an indifferent MGM, so Marilyn's standout performance meant little to studio executives when it did get bookings. She fared much better when loaned to United Artists to play Kirk Douglas' no-good sweetheart in *Champion* (1949), and then back at MGM, she was notable as the bubble dancer who inhabits convention hotels in *Key to the City* (1950), which starred Clark Gable and Loretta Young.

Key to the City ended Marilyn's MGM contract. She went on a Korean tour with Bob Hope, and played in two pictures with him, *The Lemon Drop Kid* (1951) and *Off Limits* (1953), in each case providing serviceable sexual allure but little distinctive zest to her performances. She had a Jane Russell-type vamp role in *East of Sumatra* (1953), and was James Mason's girl friend in *Forever, Darling* (1956). The latter film was made at MGM with Lucille Ball and Desi Arnaz. Her good friend Bob Hope came to her professional rescue by offering her the part of the "other woman" in *Critic's Choice* (1963) which costarred Hope with Lucille Ball. The following year Marilyn joined the unofficial league of has-been players by performing in A. C. Lyles' *Stage to Thunder Rock* (1964) as the prostitute daughter of Lon Chaney, Jr. Her remaining feature film appearances were one embarrassment after another: a would-be teenie-bopper picture, *The Lively Set* (1964); another A. C. Lyles' mini-Western, *Arizona Bushwhackers* (1968); a guest performer along with Leo G. Carroll and Pedro Gonzales-Gonzales in *From Nashville with Music* (1969), and one of the myriad of quickly seen former name personalities in the disastrous *The Phynx* (1970).

During the 1940s and 1950s Marilyn was a popular radio player doing comedy and songs, and also appearing in nightclubs, including New York's famed Latin Quarter. Later she was seen on many television shows, particularly the comedy programs starring Red Skelton and Bob Hope. In 1955 she, Dan Dailey, and Jack Oakie did a video version of the Broadway show *Burlesque*, and in 1961 she played Gracie, the proprietress of the roadside café in the teleseries, *Bus Stop*. She called the series the high spot of her career when she signed the contract but, as the show progressed, her part became smaller and smaller. She left after only thirteen episodes. During her MGM days, Marilyn had starred in a musical play, *Nellie Blye*, which failed to reach Broadway, but later in her career she appeared successfully in stock versions of *Bells Are Ringing*. In 1967, at one of the lower points in her career, she starred in a burlesque show as a stripper in Queens, New York. When reporters asked her if she felt it was a comedown, Marilyn valiantly said: "No, it's fun!" But it was not quite what one expected or hoped for this blonde actress who had said much earlier in life: "I'd like my career to be like Ginger Rogers'. Straight dramatic roles alternating with musical comedy ones. I'm willing to work very hard to attain that." Four years later Marilyn would portray an aging stripper in an episode of TV's *O'Hara, U. S. Treasury*.

In 1944 Marilyn wed MGM actor John Conte in The Little Church Around the Corner in New York City. They were divorced two years later. On January 1, 1949 she married Beverly Hills restaurateur Anders McIntyre, but the marriage ended in divorce the next year because she stated that he drank too much. On November 21, 1954, she wed writer–producer Jerome Davis, and their son, Matthew Paul, was born on April 28, 1956. She divorced Davis on December 21, 1960. Marilyn had always been a fun-loving woman and enjoyed going to parties. On many such occasions her escort was actor Rock Hudson. Marilyn had known him since 1953. Reporters kept pestering her to reveal whether there were marriage plans, but all she would say was, "He's the very, very best friend I ever had. I adore him and he adores me. But it's just friendship."

On March 20, 1972 her son Matthew came home from school and found Marilyn dead in the bathroom of their home, having succumbed to high blood pressure and a pulmonary ailment. Hudson looked after her son during the ensuing funeral arrangements.

During the last decade and a half of her life Marilyn had been in professional limbo, never realizing the sparkling promise she demonstrated in the early 1940s. Damon Runyon once said of her: "She's one of those girls who set a guy's pulse to racing by the merest glance in his direction." Even dubbed the female Errol Flynn because of her sexy, friendly nature, she always remained an "almost" personality. True fame just seemed not to be her life's game.

MARILYN MAXWELL

Stand By for Action (MGM, 1942)
Dubarry Was a Lady (MGM, 1943)
Presenting Lily Mars (MGM, 1943)
Thousands Cheer (MGM, 1943)
Dr. Gillespie's Criminal Case (MGM, 1943)
Salute to the Marines (MGM, 1943)
Swing Fever (MGM, 1943)
Pilot No. 5 (MGM, 1943)
Best Foot Forward (MGM, 1943)
Three Men in White (MGM, 1944)

Lost in a Harem (MGM, 1944)
Between Two Women (MGM, 1945)
The Show-Off (MGM, 1946)
High Barbaree (MGM, 1947)
Summer Holiday (MGM, 1948)
Race Street (RKO, 1948)
Champion (UA, 1949)
Key to the City (MGM, 1950)
Outside the Wall (Universal, 1950)
The Lemon Drop Kid (Paramount, 1951)
New Mexico (UA, 1951)
Off Limits (Paramount, 1953)

East of Sumatra (Universal, 1953)
Paris Model (Columbia, 1953)
New York Confidential (WB, 1955)
Forever, Darling (MGM, 1956)
Rock-A-Bye Baby (Paramount, 1958)
Critic's Choice (WB, 1963)
Stage to Thunder Rock (Paramount, 1964)
The Lively Set (Universal, 1964)
Arizona Bushwhackers (Paramount, 1968)
From Nashville with Music (Bradford, 1969)
The Phynx (WB, 1970)

With Jacqueline White and Marjorie Main in *The Show-Off* (1946)

Lauritz Melchior

MGM producer Joe Pasternak knew just what the public could be made to buy in movie musicals, and he was very much on key with heroic tenor Lauritz Melchior who appeared in four of his Metro releases between 1945 and 1848. Melchior may have been a congenial gargantuan (6' 4", 250 pounds) whom one film critic described as Sophie Tucker in a suit, but he was the "greatest Wagnerian tenor of his time." Most importantly for Metro's purposes, he had a fine sense of perspective about his longhair status. He was fifty-five when he made his film debut, and no one, least of all himself, thought he would play romantic leads. Rather he was happy to be on tap as a comic tenor. He was as intrigued by Hollywood's glitter as MGM was in milking his prestigious reputation. The only slightly bewildered party to this commercial union was the filmgoing public who were amazed, but entertained, at viewing the renowned tenor having a grand old time "acting" and singing in screen tandem with Esther Williams, Jimmy Durante, Xavier Cugat, Kathryn Grayson, Ethel Smith, and Jane Powell.

Lauritz Lebrecht Hommel Melchior was born March 20, 1890 in Copenhagen where his father and grandfather conducted a voice school. He was a boy soprano in the church choir and clerked at a music publishing house. During these years he applied himself assiduously to his musical studies, finally winning a contract with the Copenhagen Royal Opera. He made his operatic debut there in 1913 as a baritone playing in *I Pagliacci* and made in 1918 was first heard in a tenor role. From 1921–1924 he studied in Germany and London and then made his mark singing Wagnerian roles. He made his U.S. debut at the Metropolitan Opera in 1926, performing *Tannhauser*. By this time his first wife Inger Nathansen had died (he had two children by her, one of whom, Ib, is a television writer–director in the United States) and he had wed German film actress Maria Hacker (she died in 1963).

Besides performing his wealth of Metropolitan roles over the years, Melchior enjoyed appearing as a concert performer and guesting on radio shows. When asked how he kept up the grueling pace, he replied, "I never strain. I always sing with the interest, never use my principal." In 1943, during a joking singing commercial for an imaginary "Pasternak's Pretzels" on Fred Allen's radio show, producer Pasternak heard Melchior in this comic stint and, noting the tenor's success at contracasting, induced him to sign a MGM contract.

Melchior was introduced on the screen in no less than an Esther Williams vehicle, *Thrill of a Romance* (1945). He played a jolly cupid with diet trouble. When the cameras were not focused on the Sierra Nevada scenery, Esther's swimming, or Van Johnson's smiling, Melchior worked in a Serenade by Franz Schubert and a rendition of "Please Don't Say No."

The next year he was seen in *Two Sisters from Boston* (1946) as the temperamental Metropolitan Opera tenor, Olaf Olstrom. One scene finds Melchior performing *Lohengrin*, when suddenly from the chorus line up pops Kathryn Grayson to duet on his aria (the plot demands she prove to her Massachusetts relatives in the audience that she has made good in the opera field, although she is really earning her money as a popular songstress in Jimmy Durante's Bowery saloon). Operatic sequences from Liszt and Mendelssohn were also woven into the musical.

Melchior supported Esther Williams again in *This Time for Keeps* (1947), playing the doting dad of Johnnie Johnston, the onscreen ex-G.I. who prefers swing music and Williams to an opera career. When Xavier Cugat was not conducting Latin rhythms or Jimmy Durante not murdering "I Found The Lost Chord," Melchior performed "La Donna e Mobile" from Verdi's *Rigoletto*, an excerpt from *Otello*, "M'Appari" from *Martha*, and Cole Porter's "You'd Be So Easy to Love."

His final MGM release was *Luxury Liner* (1948), in which he was an opera tenor headed for a South American tour aboard a ship skippered by George Brent and plagued by Brent's stowaway daughter Jane Powell. Melchior did snatches from *Aida* and sang a robust Danish drinking song in an obvious spoof of his beer-drinking reputation. However, the surprise rendition of this musical was "I've Got You Under My Skin" by former classical performer Marina Koshetz.

Melchior had been quite delighted with his film fling, but the Metropolitan Opera's new manager, Rudolf Bing, was decidedly not so pleased, and the tenor did not, or, as some have it, was not asked to renew his Metropolitan contract. Melchior blithely turned to guest performing on television and in 1953 returned to the screen in Paramount's *The Stars Are Singing*. He was jovial Poldi who shelters refugee Anna Maria Alberghetti in his Greenwich Village apartment. Among his show business neighbors who hide the girl from the immigration authorites was Rosemary Clooney who sang "Come On-a My House," among other musical numbers. Melchior performed "Vesti la Giubba" from *I Pagliacci* and the popular song "Because." The film was not successful and Melchior returned to television guesting. His singing beer commercial was quite popular in the late 1950s. In 1963 he gave a Carnegie Hall concert marking the fiftieth anniversary of his operatic debut. In 1964 he had wed video producer Mary Markan. They were divorced two years later.

In 1972 Melchior was the recipient of the Deutschen Schallplatternpreises, Germany's highest award for recordings, for the year 1971, for a two-LP album: *Melchior: The Wagner Tenor of the Century*, EMI's reissue of single recordings cut between 1926 and 1935.

Melchior, very erect, tall, and imposing in appearance, with a white beard, mustache, and hair, was still fond of a good time and a good witticism. When asked where he resided, he replied, "Everywhere there is something to eat and drink." Then in a more serious vein, he added, "I live in California on top of a mountain in a house called the Viking. I have five and a half acres there, a garden, and a swimming pool where I can throw people I don't like." He was very much involved with the furtherance of the Wagnerian opera tradition and created a foundation to develop heldentenors who, like Melchior did at his peak, could tackle the great heroic opera roles. He died March 18, 1973, following an emergency gall bladder operation.

LAURITZ MELCHIOR

Thrill of a Romance (MGM, 1945)
Two Sisters from Boston (MGM, 1946)
This Time for Keeps (MGM, 1947)

Luxury Liner (MGM, 1948)
The Stars Are Singing (Paramount, 1953)

With Ray Goulding, Esther Williams, Van Johnson, and Ethel Griffies in *Thrill of a Romance* (1945)

Una Merkel

MGM's greatest stock company void in the 1930s was its lack of wisecracking dames of the Joan Blondell or Natalie Moorhead variety. This deficiency was particularly taxing when it came to casting contract supporting players to interact with star Jean Harlow in her latest screen vehicle. There was the choice of tough Clark Gable or rugged Spencer Tracy as Harlow's rowdy *vis-à-vis*, but there was a definite need for a smart-mouthed gal to bridge the gap between the blonde bombshell's blatant vulgarity and the blander film environment in which she was placed. Such an actress was Una Merkel, who joined MGM in 1931, just as unintentional rhinestones-in-the-rough studio contractees such as Anita Page and Dorothy Jordan were on the way out. Una could dish out jaundiced fast talk as well as any of Warner Brothers' most experienced stable of oncamera gold diggers. But, luckily for tender MGM's sake, she had the saving grace of displaying a "good Joe" quality that shone through her brittle outer guise. Such contrasting personality facets made Una, the girl with the intriguing nasal Southern drawl, a very versatile contract performer.

Una was born in Covington, Kentucky on December 10, 1903, the daughter of Arnold and Bessie (Phares) Merkel. Her father was a traveling salesman. After public school she attended the Girls Annex in Philadelphia and then decided to try for a stage career in New York. She studied at the Alviene Dance School, and supported herself by modeling for *True Story* magazine. She found time to teach Sunday School at a local Congregational Church, with one of her young pupils being Bette Davis. Una did extra work in *Way Down East* (1920) with Lillian Gish and *The White Rose* (1923) starring Mae Marsh, both of which were filmed at D. W. Griffith's Mamaroneck facilities.

The following year Una had the female lead as a lame girl in *The Fifth Horseman* (1924). Because of her great resemblance to silent screen star Lillian Gish, she was hired to be in Charles Ray's *World Shadows* (*c.* 1924), but the production ran out of money and was not completed. She also answered an advertisement for actors to perform in Lee DeForest's new talking picture experiment, and was in the early sound short subject, *Love's Old Sweet Song* (1924).

She made her Broadway debut in *Two by Two* (1925) with a small role. When that closed rather quickly she took over an assignment in *Pigs* (1925). In 1927 she was in *Coquette* with Helen Hayes, and toured with the show for two years.

When Griffith was making tests for *Abraham Lincoln* (1930), to be released by United Artists, Una auditioned and was selected to play Mary Todd. When she reached the studio on the West Coast, Griffith decided to have her play Ann Rutledge instead. Una remained under contract for a year to United Artists, where she played the heroine in the spine chiller *The Bat Whispers* (1930), and then was loaned out to Fox for four films, including Jeanette MacDonald's *Don't Bet on Women* (1931) in which she was an ingenuous southern girl. It was her first screen comedy role. At First National she was cast as the secretary Effie in the original *The Maltese Falcon* (1931).

Fox agreed to keep her under contract when her option period came due, but Una refused to re-sign because the scheduled raise had been cancelled. She went to MGM to test for *Private Lives* (1931) and signed a seven-year featured player's agreement with them, content to receive $50 weekly more than the original escalated United Artists-Fox contract had stipulated. In *Private Lives* she was Robert Montgomery's new wife, and in *Red-Headed Woman* (1932) she and Leila Hyams were snappy pals of stenographer Jean Harlow. In 1932 she and aviator designer Ronald L. Burla were married. They were divorced in 1945.

Una had thirteen 1933 releases. One of her best-recalled prototype roles was as the saucy chorine Lorraine Fleming in *42nd Street* at Warner Brother's. She was the sweetie of stage manager George E. Stone and sang stanzas of "Shuffle off to Buffalo" with chorus partner Ginger Rogers. In Metro's *Whistling in the Dark*, she was the girl friend of mystery writer Ernest Truex, and was one of the beauty shop girls in *Beauty for Sale*. In *Bombshell*, she performed as Miss Mac with movie star Jean Harlow.

Una continued to be used in a wide variety of parts through the end of her MGM contract in 1937. She was loaned to United Artists to be Charles Butterworth's troubled bride in *Bulldog Drummond Strikes Back* (1934), was Harold Lloyd's sweetheart in Fox's *The Cat's Paw* (1934), and at Metro was the regal queen to George Barbier's sovereign in *The Merry Widow* (1934). (She also showed up in MGM's 1952 remake as Lana Turner's traveling campanion–domestic.) She was Toots Timmons in *Murder in the Fleet* (1935), Jean Harlow's harried married sister in *Riffraff* (1935), the secretary Kitty Corbett in *Broadway Melody of 1936* (1935), and Sid Silvers' girl in *Born to Dance* (1936). In the latter film he sang "You'd Be So Easy to Love" to her. For Metro's short subject division she made the two-reel color short *How to Stuff a Goose* (1936). She completed her MGM contract with *Saratoga* (1937), playing Fritzi Kiffmeyer, wife of Frank Morgan and racing track pal of Clark Gable.

In the late 1930s Una was on the radio series *Texaco Star Theatre* and, as a free-lance performer, had the athletic role of Lilybelle Callahan, wife of

Mischa Auer in *Destry Rides Again* (1939). In this film, she was the one who engaged in the drag-out brawl with Marlene Dietrich in the Last Chance Saloon. In *The Bank Dick* (1940) she played W. C. Fields' daughter, and then was Dorothy Lamour's stage partner in *The Road to Zanzibar* (1941) her last youthful role in a major studio picture. By 1944 she was working at Monogram in *Sweethearts of the U. S. A.* and appearing in Columbia's short subject, *To Heir is Human*, with Harry Langdon.

Una returned to Broadway in 1943 to succeed Ethel Owen in *Three's a Family* and later that year went on a U.S.O. tour with Gary Cooper to New Guinea. In the early 1950s, she did *Summer and Smoke* (as Mrs. Winemiller) and *Come Back, Little Sheba*, both at the La Jolla Theatre. She was on Broadway in *The Remarkable Mr. Pennypacker* (1953) and won a Tony Award for her performance in *The Ponder Heart* (1956). After the pre-Broadway washout of *Listen to the Mocking-bird* (1958), the following year she played Walter Pidgeon's wife in *Take Me Along*, the musical version of *Ah, Wilderness!* She shared one song with Pidgeon in this hit show.

During the 1950s she was usually cast in secretarial roles, looking much like a mature Nydia Westman. As contrast she was a nun in *With a Song in My Heart* (1952), the rural lady Marjorie Main matches with "cousin" Arthur Hunnicutt in *The Kettles in the Ozarks* (1956) and Debbie Reynolds' mother in *The Mating Game* (1959) at MGM.

Una's favorite film role was the one she wanted the most, playing the demented Mrs. Winemiller, the mother of spinster Geraldine Page in *Summer and Smoke* (1961). Una was Oscar-nominated for her performance, but lost out to Rita Moreno who won the best supporting actress award for *West Side Story*.

After two Walt Disney features and some television (she had been in the 1958 *Aladdin* special on CBS), she played Cecil Kellaway's well-dressed wife in Elvis Presley's *Spinout* (1966) made for MGM. It is her last screen work to date.

Asked if she minded playing an assortment of mostly featured roles in pictures, Una recently said, "I liked a variety. I was glad to do anything when the part was good. I didn't care what I was supposed to be."

UNA MERKEL

Way Down East (UA, 1920)
The White Rose (UA, 1923)
The Fifth Horseman (E. M. MacMahon, 1924)
Abraham Lincoln (UA, 1930)
The Eyes of the World (UA, 1930)
The Bat Whispers (UA, 1930)
Command Performance (Tiffany, 1931)
Don't Bet on Women (Fox, 1931)
Six Cylinder Love (Fox, 1931)
Daddy Long Legs (Fox, 1931)
The Maltese Falcon (WB, 1931)

The Bargain (FN, 1931)
Wicked (Fox, 1931)
Private Lives (MGM, 1931)
Secret Witness (Columbia, 1931)
She Wanted a Millionaire (Fox, 1932)
Impatient Maiden (Universal, 1932)
Man Wanted (WB, 1932)
Huddle (MGM, 1932)
Red-Headed Woman (MGM, 1932)
They Call It Sin (FN, 1932)
The Secret of Madame Blanche (MGM, 1933)

Whistling in the Dark (MGM, 1933)
Clear All Wires (MGM, 1933)
42nd Street (WB, 1933)
Men Are Such Fools (RKO, 1933)
Reunion in Vienna (MGM, 1933)
Midnight Mary (MGM, 1933)
Her First Mate (Universal, 1933)
Beauty for Sale (MGM, 1933)
Broadway to Hollywood (MGM, 1933)
Bombshell (MGM, 1933)
Day of Reckoning (MGM, 1933)
Women in His Life (MGM, 1933)
This Side of Heaven (MGM, 1934)
Murder in the Private Car (MGM, 1934)
Paris Interlude (MGM, 1934)
Bulldog Drummond Strikes Back (UA, 1934)
The Cat's Paw (Fox, 1934)
Have a Heart (MGM, 1934)
The Merry Widow (MGM, 1934)
Evelyn Prentice (MGM, 1934)
Biography of a Bachelor Girl (MGM, 1935)
The Night Is Young (MGM, 1935)
One New York Night (MGM, 1935)
Baby Face Harrington (MGM, 1935)
Murder in the Fleet (MGM, 1935)
Broadway Melody of 1936 (MGM, 1935)
It's in the Air (MGM, 1935)
Riffraff (MGM, 1935)
Speed (MGM, 1936)
We Went to College (MGM, 1936)
Born to Dance (MGM, 1936)
Don't Tell the Wife (RKO, 1937)
Good Old Soak (MGM, 1937)
Saratoga (MGM, 1937)
True Confession (Paramount, 1937)
Checkers (20th-Fox, 1938)
Four Girls in White (MGM, 1939)
Some Like It Hot (Paramount, 1939)

On Borrowed Time (MGM, 1939)
Destry Rides Again (Universal, 1939)
Comin' Round the Mountain (Paramount, 1940)
Sandy Gets Her Man (Universal, 1940)
The Bank Dick (Universal, 1940)
Double Date (Universal, 1941)
The Road to Zanzibar (Paramount, 1941)
Cracked Nuts (Universal, 1941)
The Mad Doctor of Market Street (Universal, 1942)
Twin Beds (UA, 1942)
This Is the Army (WB, 1943)
Sweethearts of the U. S. A. (Monogram, 1944)
It's a Joke, Son (Eagle–Lion, 1947)
The Man from Texas (Eagle–Lion, 1948)
The Bride Goes Wild (MGM, 1948)
Kill the Umpire (Columbia, 1950)
My Blue Heaven (20th-Fox, 1950)
Emergency Wedding (Columbia, 1950)
Rich, Young and Pretty (MGM, 1951)
A Millionaire for Christy (20th-Fox, 1951)
Golden Girl (20th-Fox, 1951)
With a Song in My Heart (20th-Fox, 1952)
The Merry Widow (MGM, 1952)
I Love Melvin (MGM, 1953)
The Kentuckian (UA, 1955)
The Kettles in the Ozarks (Universal, 1956)
Bundle of Joy (RKO, 1956)
The Fuzzy Pink Nightgown (UA, 1957)
The Girl Most Likely (Universal, 1957)
The Mating Game (MGM, 1959)
The Parent Trap (BV, 1961)
Summer and Smoke (Paramount, 1961)
Summer Magic (BV, 1963)
A Tiger Walks (BV, 1964)
Spinout (MGM, 1966)

With George Barbier and Maurice Chevalier in *The Merry Widow* (1934)

Ann Miller

With her heart-shaped face, her toothpaste smile, and her long, white-thighed limbs, Ann Miller was the most vigorous of the screen's tap-dancing femmes. She exhibited a robust, friendly eroticism as the cheerleader with the classy chassis and sequined tights, who danced her way through twenty years of movie musicals, but never quite making it in the big-time star category. By the time she landed at MGM midway in her career, the glamor days were in their decline, and while that studio did put her in its postwar big-budget musicals, it seemed that Kathryn Grayson not only did the singing, but ended up with the leading man, leaving second lead Ann with Red Skelton. Then there were a few nonmusical roles in which she played a flip-tongued bitch, and, suddenly, her film career was over. The year was 1956. She still looks great, and that full-cheeked smile still shows up on television in guest spots, specials, and commercials. She had the "biggest thrill of my life" when she became the seventh actress to play *Mame* on Broadway in 1969. She appeared in the show for eight months, had one musical number expanded into a tap-dance routine and had the critics hailing her as the "best of the Mames."

Ann was born Lucille Ann Collier in Chireno, Texas on April 12th. Most sources list the year as 1919; she maintains it was 1925, insisting that as a tall, well-developed preteenager, she added years to her real age in order to obtain jobs to support herself and her mother after her parents were divorced. Her father was a criminal lawyer who once supposedly handled a case involving Bonnie and Clyde. Her mother, Clara, had sent her daughter to dancing school at the age of three as therapy for Ann's childhood case of rickets. The tot was soon doing her "quick-style" dancing numbers before the Rotary and Lions' clubs and even placed first in a Big Brothers' Personality contest. When the Colliers were divorced, Clara Collier set her ambitious sights on Hollywood and a cinema career for her talented daughter. The first six months there were rough, and mother had to hock some of her jewels. Little Lucy Ann finally got a booking as a "specialty" at the Orpheum Theatre in Los Angeles, which eventually led to a booking at the Club Bal Tabarin in San Francisco. Among those in the audience was an ambitious young "blonde" actress named Lucille Ball (who herself had wanted to be a chorus

486

girl on Broadway but kept getting fired) and Benny Rubin, a RKO talent scout. Miss Ball was then under contract to RKO, and she suggested that Rubin arrange a screen test for the new find. He did, and Ann was signed at $150 per week. She had already made her screen debut in Grand National's *The Devil on Horseback* (1936), starring Lili Damita.

Ann's first RKO picture was appropriately *New Faces of 1937* (1937). She had no lines, just a bit of tap-dancing a la Eleanor Powell, then MGM's dancing rage. Following this production there were lines but no dancing in *Stage Door* (1937), but at least she had the opportunity to be in a movie with her idol, Ginger Rogers. RKO gave her a musical break in *Radio City Revels* (1938), which included Milton Berle in the cast. But in a turn about, they allowed her and Lucille Ball to get lost amidst the Marx Brothers' antics in *Room Service* (1938). Then Ann was loaned to Columbia for Frank Capra's *You Can't Take It with You* (1938). The director recalls: "She played Alice's [Jean Arthur's] sister, Essie, the awkward Pavlova; played her with the legs of Marlene, the innocence of Pippa, and the brain of a butterfly that flitted on its toes."

After two more RKO outings, *Tarnished Angel* (1938) and *Having Wonderful Time* (1938), her contract with the studio expired and she departed. Her salary was then $250 per week. She went to New York and won a part in George White's *Scandals of 1939*. It was not regarded as White's best musical revue, but Ann had two specialty numbers, one called the "Mexicongo" which was a nightly show-stopper. Brooks Atkinson referred to it as a "heat-treated dance" and Burns Mantle wrote, "She is a shapely tap dancer with a talent that is exceptional and a pictorial appeal beyond that of many of her tapping sisters."

Broadway producer George Abbott was so impressed with her Mexicongo dance that when he took his own Broadway show, *Too Many Girls*, to Hollywood to direct the film version, he took Ann along. The studio was her old lot, RKO, but this time around her salary had jumped to $3,000 per week. The film's stars were Lucille Ball and Desi Arnaz, the new Latin lover. When the picture was completed, Abbott wished her to go back to Broadway with him and continue with a stage career, but Ann wanted to be in the movies and declined his offer. Thirty years later she would say that if she had accepted Abbott's proposal, "Who knows, maybe I'd be somebody like Mary Martin today."

But she remained in Hollywood where she did two quickies for lowbrow Republic, one with Gene Autry, and then signed a seven-year contract with Columbia. She was kept busy in a string of minor musicals with forgettable plots that were enlivened by her musical numbers. They all made money at the plush World War II boxoffice: *Time Out for Rhythm* (1940), *Go West, Young Lady* (1941), *Reveille with Beverly* (1943), *Carolina Blues* (1944), and *Eadie Was a Lady* (1945).

In 1946, just when Columbia's mogul Harry Cohn, in a moment of pique with his superstar Rita Hayworth, was planning to star Ann in a

Technicolor, big-budget musical, she married Reese Llewellen Milner, the scion of an iron works fortune. Milner suggested she retire. Ann did, and Cohn was enraged. He sued her for $150,000 and won the case. But, in looking back on her career, Ann recalls Cohn as a "fair" man, a reputation which Cohn earned only posthumously from a number of celebrities who have written about their careers.

Later, Ann became pregnant. During her pregnancy however, she fell down a flight of stairs and her baby girl was born dead. Her marriage to Milner quickly ended on the rocks and she decided to resume her career. The still-angry Cohn would not take her back, but MGM had a rotten picture that needed some extra punch to sell it at the declining boxoffice. Since their own Eleanor Powell was now enjoying retirement as Mrs. Glenn Ford, they hired Ann to do the "Dance of Fury," a hot flamenco tap number, with Cyd Charisse and Ricardo Montalban as her onscreen partners. The picture was *The Kissing Bandit* (1948) with Frank Sinatra and Kathryn Grayson. Although Ann terms it the worst film in history, she considers her musical number one of the best things she has ever done. MGM thought so too and signed her to a seven-year contract. Fate gave her a chance just like in the movies. When Cyd Charisse broke her leg and could not appear opposite Fred Astaire in *Easter Parade* (1948), Ann got the part in this prestige musical of a distinctly polished MGM variety. She played the bitchy ballroom dancing partner of Astaire, who in early 1900s New York breaks up their partnership in order to become a Ziegfeld star. Astaire turns, to an unknown Miss Brown (Judy Garland) and make her into his dancing–singing partner. Ann had a flashy number, "Shakin' the Blues Away," beating out her rapid tap steps to a jazzy musical background.

MGM continued to put her in their unique brand of musicals. While they did not promote her as a star ("I never played politics, I never was a party girl, and I never slept with any of the producers"), they did display her zesty dancing abilities in the devastating, cave-woman "Prehistoric Joe" number in *On the Town* (1949). She had her best role as Bianca in Cole Porter's *Kiss Me, Kate!* (1953), where she performed "Why Can't You Behave?," "Always True to You, Darling, in My Fashion," "Tom, Dick or Harry," and the provocative "Too Darn Hot." *Small Town Girl* (1953) gave her a lively Busby Berkeley sequence, "I Gotta Hear the Beat," but *Hit the Deck* (1955) was the last of her musicals, and a thin one at that. She completed her MGM contract the next year with two comedies: *The Opposite Sex* and *The Great American Pastime*. *The Opposite Sex* was a Cinemascope musical rehash of *The Women*, filled with waning marquee names. Ann played the bitchy adventuress which had been handled by Paulette Goddard in the original.

Ann's film career was finished, but she remained an attention-getter. In 1957, at a Hollywood soiree in honor of the Maharajah of Baroda, she, along with Hedy Lamarr, were singled out by the maharajah as the two most beautiful women he had ever seen. She married a second time in 1958. ("I used to fall in love with the best-looking man at a party, and sometimes I wound up marrying him.") The man this time was oil millionaire William Moss, who had been divorced from child actress, Jane Withers. He looked like her first husband, she said, and she refers to the marriage as a "disaster that lasted three years." Again on the rebound, she married a third time, again a millionaire, Arthur Cameron. The marriage was annulled when "he didn't want to give up all those pretty girls."

During the past fifteen years, she has appeared in nightclubs and has served as an unofficial ambassadress at Hilton Hotel opening ceremonies. As she says, "Conrad and I are just good friends. He likes to dance." She appeared on television in guest spots at $7,500 to $10,000 an appearance, and in 1971 starred in what was reputed to be that medium's most expensive commercial, $154,000 for Great American Soups. She danced on top of an eight-foot can of soup with twenty-foot water fountains, a bevy of chorus girls behind her, and a 24-piece orchestra supplying the music. The fadeout shows a sedately aproned Ann in a typical American kitchen with a husband exclaiming: "Why must you make such a big production out of everything!"

This commercial was made when she had her successful return to Broadway in 1969, after thirty years, to star as one of the post-Angela Lansbury *Mames*. She had auditioned for the Las Vegas *Mame* edition, but the part went to Susan Hayward. Determined to get into a musical, she had her agent book her for two weeks in Houston in *Can-Can*. John Bowab, *Mame* associate producer, saw her and was convinced she could handle the role in New York. They tested her for six weeks in Miami to sold-out audiences and standing ovation. And so she came to New York and did the show for eight months in 1969–1970, giving its boxoffice a needed shot in the arm. The show was altered so that the song "That's How Young I Feel" was expanded into a full-length tap-dancing routine, and audiences howled for more. In 1971 she appeared in the telescoped television production of the off-Broadway spoof of movie musicals, *Dames at Sea*. She received better reviews than that show's hot star, Ann-Margret. The summer of 1972 found her playing the stock circuit with Tab Hunter in *Anything Goes*. When the production was rehearsing for its August opening at the Municipal Opera Company in St. Louis, she suffered bruises, abrasions, a slight concussion, and vertigo when a stage boom accidentally hit her, and she was forced to withdraw from the musical. The heart-broken Ann wailed, "I don't know what the future holds for little Annie Miller." She has since completely recovered.

Ann currently lives in a Hollywood mansion with her mother, who is president of the Movie Stars Mothers' Club, and a collection of stuffed animals ("I like happy faces around me.") She does not consider her stardom a thing of the past. "They can't make stars like us anymore. I have the name because of the wonderful years with MGM. That was Mr. Mayer's bag, the family thing. The studio was the family and he was the daddy." She published her autobiography, titled *Miller's High Life* in 1972. The book could well be subtitled *The Look*, she says, in reference to the way people look at stars like Ann when they are Up There. "When my contract was dying at MGM, all of a sudden people sort of brushed me off. Even the headwaiters began to look right past me. But all of a sudden, after my opening night in *Mame,* the reception at the end of the show lasted fifteen minutes. I've been through it three times [Columbia, MGM, and *Mame*], and now once more I see 'The Look.' "

ANN MILLER

The Devil on Horseback (Grand National, 1936)
New Faces of 1937 (RKO, 1937)
Stage Door (RKO, 1937)
Life of the Party (RKO, 1937)
Radio City Revels (RKO, 1938)
Room Service (RKO, 1938)
You Can't Take It with You (Columbia, 1938)
Tarnished Angel (RKO, 1938)
Having Wonderful Time (RKO, 1938)
Too Many Girls (RKO, 1940)
The Hit Parade of 1941 (Republic, 1940)
Melody Ranch (Republic, 1940)
Time out for Rhythm (Columbia, 1941)
Go West, Young Lady (Columbia, 1941)
True to the Army (Paramount, 1942)
Priorities on Parade (Paramount, 1942)
Reveille with Beverly (Columbia, 1943)
What's Buzzin' Cousin? (Columbia, 1943)

Jam Session (Columbia, 1944)
Hey, Rookie (Columbia, 1944)
Carolina Blues (Columbia, 1944)
Eve Knew Her Apples (Columbia, 1945)
Eadie Was a Lady (Columbia, 1945)
Thrill of Brazil (Columbia, 1946)
The Kissing Bandit (MGM, 1948)
Easter Parade (MGM, 1948)
On the Town (MGM, 1949)
Watch the Birdie (MGM, 1950)
Texas Carnival (MGM, 1951)
Two Tickets to Broadway (RKO, 1951)
Lovely to Look at (MGM, 1952)
Kiss Me, Kate! (MGM, 1953)
Small Town Girl (MGM, 1953)
Deep in My Heart (MGM, 1954)
Hit the Deck (MGM, 1955)
The Opposite Sex (MGM, 1956)
The Great American Pastime (MGM, 1956)

With Ron Randall, Kathryn Grayson, and Howard Keel in *Kiss Me, Kate!* (1953)

With Ann Sheridan, Joan Collins, Dolores Gray, Barbara Jo Allen, June Allyson, and Agnes Moorehead in *The Opposite Sex* (1956)

Ricardo Montalban

Ricardo Montalban, like Fernando Lamas, was one of the last actors to be promoted in Hollywood as a Latin Lover. He could sing in a passable manner and do a fairly good dance step. MGM cast him in several of their escapist musicals with Esther Williams. Montalban never liked the "lover" image and was determined to escape it, but his modest acting talents held him back for several years. When his MGM contract was terminated in 1953, he found it rough going for several years. He made some films, all of them second-rate, a successful Broadway show, and numerous roles in that rival medium, television. Finally, at age thirty-five with the flush of youth behind him, his maturity, not his romantic allure, stood him in good professional stead. Like his predecessor, Gilbert Roland, he has remained a familiar character star in both films and television ever since. He was never a mysterious, enigmatic romantic lead like Roland, or even Lamas, but his sincerity as a performer made him equally convincing in such disparate roles as a priest or a heavy.

Ricardo Montalban was born in Mexico City on November 25, 1920 and grew up wanting to be an engineer. When he was nineteen, his family sent him to learn English at Fairfax High School in Hollywood where he was the oldest student. An MGM talent scout saw the handsome 5' 11" teenager and suggested he make a screen test. Montalban told his older brother, Carlos, an actor who was living in New York, and his brother said, "Nothing doing." If he wanted to seriously pursue an acting career he should do so in New York. Montalban took his brother's advice and soon landed small roles in Tallulah Bankhead's *Her Cardboard Lover*, Elsa Maxwell's *Our Betters*, and Ann Sten Nancy's *Private Affair*. While in New York he also made a Soundies short subject, *He's a Latin from Staten Island* (1941), in which he strummed a guitar and sang Al Jolson's hit song "A Latin From Manhattan." When his mother died in 1941, he returned to Mexico and continued his acting career in a number of Spanish-speaking films.

Two of these features, *Santa* and *La Fuga*, both made in 1943, were directed by Norman Foster, the ex-husband of Claudette Colbert, who was now married to Sally Blane, sister of Loretta Young. Foster invited Montalban to dinner one evening and, while discussing Mrs. Foster's famous sister, Foster mentioned the name of their stepsister Georgiana. Montalban reached into his wallet and pulled out a photograph of Georgiana as she had appeared in *The Story of Alexander Graham Bell* (1939). Montalban told the Fosters that he had seen her in that picture and had also seen her later in the Catholic Church she attended in Hollywood. While he had never had the courage to speak to her, he had been in love with her ever since. On October 26, 1944 he and Georgiana were wed, and they are still married today. They have four children: Laura, Mark, Anita, and Victor.

Now a married man with some motion picture experience behind him—he won the equivalent of the Oscar for his Mexican cinema work in 1944—Montalban signed a MGM contract. He made his American film debut playing Esther Williams' twin brother in *Fiesta* (1947). Montalban essayed the aspiring young composer who does not want to become a matador, much to his father's chagrin, and Williams masquerades in the bull ring while Montalban does a dance with Cyd Charisse. He was jilted by Williams in *On an Island with You* (1948) and ended up with Charisse again, this time performing a sensuous Apache dance. In *The Kissing Bandit* (1949), Williams was absent, but he, Charisse, and Ann Miller were rung in as guest artists to perform "The Dance of Fury," while stars Kathryn Grayson and Frank Sinatra were reading the scripts of their next picture and hoping for better things.

Back with Williams again, he was a polo player in *Neptune's Daughter* (1949) and was involved with wetback smuggling on the Texas–Mexican border in *Border Incident* (1949). While his reputation as a Latin Lover earned him a *Life* magazine cover story in 1949, he preferred to make it as an actor and said it was Dick Powell who helped him break the mold by casting him as the boxing champ in *Right Cross* (1950) opposite June Allyson. Although he was the Blackfoot Indian Ironshirt in *Across the Wide Missouri* (1951), his Mexican origin typed him for most of the roles he was given. He concluded his MGM stay with two more insipid lover roles: with Pier Angeli in *Sombrero* (1953) and with Lana Turner in, you guessed it, *Latin Lovers* (1953). He was boosted to the stellar position of being Turner's costar when she and Fernando Lamas ended their romance. MGM had decided not to ask for any further trouble on the set by throwing Turner and Lamas into forced love scenes, so Montalban replaced Lamas.

When MGM failed to renew his contract, Montalban reflected, "That studio spoiled me for eight years. They didn't renew my contract, and I felt completely alone and afraid." He further analyzed, "Television destroyed a way of life in Hollywood, and at first I resented it. For old-line movie people, television killed the red carpet. And yet it's to television that I owe my freedom from the bondage of the Latin Lover roles. Television came along and gave me parts to chew on. It gave me wings as an actor." For the next seven years, he worked regularly in some films, on stage, and in numerous segments of his sister-in-law's video series, *The Loretta Young Show*, frequently appearing as a priest or a policeman dedicated to helping juvenile delinquents.

Occasionally he even played a heavy. He and Gloria DeHaven tried Broadway in a musical version of *Seventh Heaven* in 1955, but it flopped. He had much better luck two years later, playing a black opposite Lena Horne in *Jamaica*. That play opened on October 13, 1957, and while the splendid Lena Horne walked away with the critical notices, Montalban earned a good share of acclaim as a properly virile and sexy musical leading man.

By the time he was thirty-five stardom of the first order obviously had passed him by. He said he just never got that "one" role, but his growth as an actor and his maturity made him suitable for character assignments in which he has given some quite sound performances. He was the haughty Japanese performer, Nakamura, in *Sayonara* (1957), starred in a television version of *Rashomon* in 1960, and gave a dextrous performance as the mobster who uses Shelley Winters in the starkly cruel *Let No Man Write My Epitaph* (1960). He was deft as the Italian officer in Hemingway's *Adventures of a Young Man* (1962), an impoverished grand duke in *Love Is a Ball* (1963), and returned to MGM for *The Money Trap* (1966) and to play a priest in *The Singing Nun* (1966). As the womanizer in *Madame X* (1966) he was the only lifelike character in that waxen sudser. In 1968 he starred in a telefeature pilot of *Joachin Murietta* for Twentieth Century-Fox which was shelved for a while, and the next year essayed the caricature part of the Latin Lover movie star in *Sweet Charity*. In the blatantly artificial *Escape from the Planet Of The Apes* (1971) he offered a welcome sincere performance as the sympathetic circus owner, a part he repeated in the followup *Conquest of the Planet of the Apes* (1972). In the telefeature *Fireball Forward* (1972), a World War II actioner, he was third-billed as a Frenchman. In 1972–73, he toured for twenty-two weeks, playing Don Juan in *Don Juan in Hell* by George Bernard Shaw. The cast included Agnes Moorehead and Paul Henreid, but it was Montalban who got raves from the critics, even though it lasted only two weeks on Broadway.

During the past several years, Montalban has become an avid spokesman for NOSOTROS, an organization whose purpose is to clarify the image of the Spanish-speaking people as depicted in the entertainment arts. He and his wife Georgiana have what is often, and, in this case, truly described as a model marriage. She owns a fashionable boutique in Hollywood, and their daughter Laura works as an assistant to American clothing designer Bill Blass.

Montalban says, "It was all so glamourous at MGM. Now Hollywood is a ghost town." And he adds: "Somehow I've always been able to maintain my income. Sometimes by going to Europe and doing some terrible films. I don't say Italian films are terrible. I just say I have done some terrible Italian films. Sometimes you have to meet an economic deadline. It's like Joe Cotten said, 'It's getting so that nowadays you look at a script with very benign eyes.'"

RICARDO MONTALBAN

El Verdugo de Sevilla (Mexican, 1942)
La Razon de la Culpa (Mexican, 1942)
Cinco Fueron Escogidos (Mexican, 1942)
Santa (Mexican, 1943)
La Fuga (Mexican, 1943)
Fantasia Ranchera (Mexican, 1943)
Cadetes de la Naval (Mexican, 1944)
La Hora de la Verdad (Mexican, 1944)
Nosotros (Mexican, 1944)
Fiesta (MGM, 1947)
On an Island with You (MGM, 1948)
The Kissing Bandit (MGM, 1948)
Neptune's Daughter (MGM, 1949)
Battleground (MGM, 1949)
Border Incident (MGM, 1949)
Mystery Street (MGM, 1950)
Right Cross (MGM, 1950)
Two Weeks with Love (MGM, 1950)
Mark of the Renegade (Universal, 1951)
Across the Wide Missouri (MGM, 1951)
My Man and I (MGM, 1952)
Sombrero (MGM, 1953)
Latin Lovers (MGM, 1953)
The Saracen Blade (Columbia, 1954)
A Life in the Balance (20th-Fox, 1955)

Untouched (Excelsior, 1956)
Three for Jamie Dawn (AA, 1956)
Queen of Babylon (20th-Fox, 1956)
Sayonara (WB, 1957)
Let No Man Write My Epitaph (Columbia, 1960)
Hemingway's Adventures of a Young Man (20th-Fox, 1962)
The Reluctant Saint (Royal Films International, 1962)
Gordon il Pirata Nero (Italian, 1962)
Love Is a Ball (UA, 1963)
Cheyenne Autumn (WB, 1964)
The Money Trap (MGM, 1966)
Madame X (Universal, 1966)
The Singing Nun (MGM, 1966)
Sol Madrid (MGM, 1968)
Sweet Charity (Universal, 1969)
Blue (Paramount, 1969)
The Deserter (Paramount, 1971)
Escape from the Planet of the Apes (20th-Fox, 1971)
Conquest of the Planet of the Apes (20th-Fox, 1972)
The Last Three Days of Pancho Villa (1973)

With Larry Keating, Smoki Whitfield, John Gallaudet, and Wally Maher in *Right Cross* **(1950)**

With Lana Turner and Rita Moreno in *Latin Lovers* (1953)

With Glenn Ford in *The Money Trap* (1966)

Robert Montgomery

It was one of the unfortunate realities of Hollywood's golden era that sagacious actors such as Franchot Tone and Robert Montgomery were atrophied by the studio system which placed them into a screen mold and let them solidify there as long as they were boxoffice assets. Montgomery came to motion pictures and MGM just as the talkies became the rage, and he remained with that studio for seventeen years. Generally he was the debonair (tennis, anyone?) courtier of that studio's great ladies. His occasional light comedy assignments proved him adept at this genre, but MGM gave the best of these farceur roles to William Powell or to Melvyn Douglas. Whenever Montgomery had a meaty dramatic assignment at MGM, it was generally by forcing the issue by a head-on collision with Louis B. Mayer. Early in his association with Montgomery, Mayer discovered that when this actor wanted a salary raise, refused to do a picture, or had some new pet project which he knew was right for him, MGM and Mayer would generally have to come to terms. Like him or not, Montgomery was an upper echelon performer who provided the MGM product with the trademark ingredient of class.

Henry Montgomery, Jr. was born on May 21, 1904, in Beacon, New York, the son of the president of the New York Rubber Company. He was educated in the private School for Boys in Pawling, New York and at fashionable schools abroad. However, when his father died he was forced to give up plans to enter Princeton University and to go to work as a mechanic on the New York, New Haven and Hartford Railroad. He later became a mechanic's mate and deck hand on a Standard Oil tanker where he developed the hobby of writing sea stories. He came to New York's Greenwich Village in the 1920s with aspirations of becoming a writer and made his acting debut, for the money, at $35 a week, playing seven parts (five walkons and two offstage voices) in William Faversham's *The Mask and the Face* (1923). The job lasted three weeks, after which he took up with a Rochester stock company. He came back to Broadway to eke out a bare livelihood as a juvenile lead. In 1928 he made a good impression in a role in Edgar Selwyn's *Possession.*

Samuel Goldwyn heard of Montgomery's stage work and had him screen-tested for the lead role opposite Vilma Banky in *This Is Heaven* (1929). Goldwyn changed his mind after seeing the test, saying Montgomery was too skinny and too young. James Hall got the lead in the Banky production. However, author Selwyn convinced his brother-in-law, Joseph M. Schenck, then a major United Artists producer, to use Montgomery in *Three Live Ghosts* (1929), a comedy featuring Beryl Mercer and Joan Bennett. And it was Schenck's brother, Nicholas Schenck, then at MGM, who induced his studio to sign Montgomery to a five-year contract starting at $500 weekly. Metro first used him in a rah-rah musical called *So This Is College* (1929) in which he was the typical good-looking, sophisticated, energetic, society playboy. His career got a big boost when MGM cast him opposite their prized Norma Shearer in *Their Own Desire* (1930) and *The Divorcee* (1930), and then by playing the disturbed killer in *The Big House* (1930). The studio was so pleased with his performance that he was cast in Garbo's *Inspiration* (1931), but he turned in an embarrassingly bad performance. He righted things a bit by appearing again with Norma Shearer in *Private Lives* (1931). Noel Coward, the author of this play admitted he almost liked this cinematization of his stage vehicle.

Having established himself at MGM, Montgomery walked into Louis B. Mayer's office one day, requesting an increase in salary. He said that when MGM had signed him in New York, he had been verbally promised a raise if he demonstrated his abilities. Mayer called him a "God damn liar," and Montgomery was stunned. He replied, "If you were a younger man, Mr. Mayer, I'd give you a beating." When time for renegotiation of his contract came due in 1934, Montgomery's stock as a contract star had made him a very valuable property. He had not forgotten that unpleasant encounter with Mayer and added $25,000 additional to his basic salary request. He got it!

The salary at least was some reward, because his roles, as Montgomery says, "were a little difficult to tell apart," despite his leading ladies being such eminent contractees as Marion Davies, Anita Page, Madge Evans, and Helen Hayes. He made three films with Hayes: *Another Language* (1933), *Night Flight* (1933) and *Vanessa, Her Love Story* (1935). He says Hayes was his favorite lady. Along the way, there were many roles he refused, including *It Happened One Night* (1934). (He had made a similar picture, *Fugitive Lovers* [1934], which was a boxoffice turkey.) MGM first offered him the Franchot Tone role in *Mutiny on the Bounty* (1935), but again he rejected this potential Oscar-nomination assignment. Montgomery became so truculent with Metro officials about his assignments that he was finally allowed to star in *Night Must Fall* (1937) as a perverse punishment. Studio executives were sure that the film version of a play about a psychotic murderer would flop and bring Montgomery back to his "senses." On the contrary, *Night Must Fall* proved to be a sensible thriller and became a classic of its kind. Montgomery received an Oscar nomination, but lost the award to Spencer Tracy who won for his work in MGM's *Captains Courageous*. It was rumored that Montgomery's unpopularity with studio officials and personnel cost him the Oscar.

Night Must Fall was a favorite film of Montgomery's, as was *Yellow Jack* (1939), in which he played one of five soldiers in the Spanish–American war who volunteers to test a serum against yellow fever. He fought with MGM again, to be cast as the lowbrow gangster who inherits an English title in *The Earl of Chicago* (1940). Then he was again a psychopath in *Rage in Heaven* (1940), but he returned to his usual sophisticated form in Alfred Hitchcock's *Mr. and Mrs Smith* (1941), vying for the spotlight with his onscreen wife Carole Lombard. Harry Cohn of Columbia requested him for the role of the dead prizefighter who returns to earth in another man's body in the fantasy *Here Comes Mr. Jordan* (1941). He received another Oscar nomination, but lost to Gary Cooper who won for *Sergeant York*.

In 1939 Montgomery was elected president of the Screen Actors Guild, having been a member of that actors' union since its beginnings a few years earlier. When mobster Willie Bioff began to infiltrate the motion picture industry through his association with various labor unions, Montgomery asked the Guild's board of directors for $5,000 with which to conduct a secret investigation with the help of private detectives. He turned his findings over to Westbrook Pegler, who won a Pulitzer prize for his series of newspaper articles that sent Bioff to prison in 1941. Montgomery next enlisted as an ambulance driver in the American Field Service and remained in France until the Dunkirk evacuation, whereupon he joined the U. S. Navy, serving in Guadalcanal. He was discharged in 1944 as a lieutenant commander, and received the Bronze Star for meritorious duty as one of the operations officers on the first destroyer to enter Cherbourg.

He returned to films after the war, giving his finest performance as the PT boat lieutenant in *They Were Expendable* (1945). James Agee called it director John Ford's best movie and said Montgomery's "sobering, sincere performance, was the one perfection to turn up in movies during the year." Ford had become ill during the production of *They Were Expendable*, and for three weeks Montgomery took over as director. When Ford saw the final results, he stated he could not tell the difference in their work, which, Montgomery says, is indeed a great compliment. MGM had set Montgomery to be Greer Garson's *vis-à-vis* in *Desire Me* (1947), but Montgomery balked and, after several weeks of production, was replaced by newcomer Richard Hart. The studio allowed him to have complete directorial reins in a low-budgeter, *Lady in the Lake* (1946). Montgomery also starred in this good detective story, told in the first person, with the camera lens serving as the protagonist's eyes. That picture and a narrating chore, *The Secret Land* (1948), completed his long association with MGM.

Montgomery went to Universal to be the star and to direct *Ride the Pink Horse* (1947), an adroit melodramatic thriller that was not popular. He was teamed with Bette Davis in *June Bride* (1948) and, although the comedy was a success, Davis loathed working with him.

Montgomery moved to New York and became the commentator of a radio show dealing in topical current events, *A Citizen's View of the News*. He had long been interested in politics and social reforms, aside from his work at the Screen Actors Guild. In the 1930s he had supported the New Deal. In 1947 he founded the Hollywood Republican Committee to oppose Harry Truman in the presidential race. He had voiced opposition to the tactics of the House Un-American Activities Committee, saying it was better to fight communism within the industry than through a government investigation. In 1952 he became television consultant to President Eisenhower, a position he held until 1960. Montgomery had made a strong impression on the video medium with the *Lucky Strike Theatre* and his own dramatic series, *Robert Montgomery Presents*, which played on NBC from 1950 to 1957. His salary reached $500,000 a year during these halcyon days in television. He was not without complaint or uncritical of the new medium: "Our reputation has suffered abroad because, for thirty years or more, we sent over motion pictures which depicted a phoney, ridiculous idea of life in America. In a sense, television is making the same mistake."

The many-faceted Montgomery had also been involved in Broadway play production for some years. In the 1940s he and Elliott Nugent produced *All in Favor, A Place of Our Own,* and *The Big Two.* Montgomery also directed the latter play. In 1954 he produced *The Desperate Hours,* starring Karl Malden, Nancy Coleman, and Paul Newman. In 1960 he and James Cagney coproduced *The Gallant Hours,* a motion picture starring Cagney and directed by Montgomery.

When the Eisenhower administration ended in 1960, Montgomery, became communications consultant to John D. Rockefeller III, with offices on Manhattan's Fifth Avenue. In addition, he served on the board of directors of several major corporations, including R. H. Macy and Co. and the Milwaukee Telephone Company. In 1968 he wrote a book entitled *An Open Letter from a Television Viewer,* which was a "scathing indictment of the industry for its monopolistic tactics." He accused the networks of double-talk regarding public education television, and said; "If we go down as the age of violence, television can be blamed for it .... If acting standards are low, it's because television has been a sort of giant brainwashing machine for too many people in front of and behind the camera." The following year, after resigning his post with Rockefeller, he was invited to be president of the Repertory Theatre Board of Lincoln Center. He held that position for over a year with no salary.

Montgomery married Elizabeth Bryan Allen on April 14, 1928, by whom he had two children, Elizabeth and Robert, Jr. Their marriage broke up when he moved East in the 1940s, and they were divorced in 1950. That same year he wed New York socialite Elizabeth Grant Harkness, and they live in a fashionable town house on Manhattan's East 72nd Street. His daughter Elizabeth gained celebrity status as the star of the long-running ABC-TV comedy series, *Bewitched.* Montgomery takes great pleasure in discussing her show business success. At the time of her debut in the acting world, he offered one and only one piece of advice: "If you are lucky enough to be a success, by all means enjoy the applause and the adulation of the public, but never, never believe it."

So This Is College (MGM, 1929)
Three Live Ghosts (UA, 1929)
Untamed (MGM, 1929)
The Single Standard (MGM, 1929)
Their Own Desire (MGM, 1930)
Free and Easy (MGM, 1930)
The Divorcee (MGM, 1930)
Big House (MGM, 1930)
Our Blushing Brides (MGM, 1930)
Sins of the Children (MGM, 1930)
Love in the Rough (MGM, 1930)
War Nurse (MGM, 1930)
The Easiest Way (MGM, 1931)
Strangers May Kiss (MGM, 1931)
Inspiration (MGM, 1931)
Shipmates (MGM, 1931)
Man in Possession (MGM, 1931)
Private Lives (MGM, 1931)
Lovers Courageous (MGM, 1932)
But the Flesh Is Weak (MGM, 1932)
Letty Lynton (MGM, 1932)
Blondie of the Follies (MGM, 1932)
Faithless (MGM, 1932)
Hell Below (MGM, 1933)
Made on Broadway (MGM, 1933)
Another Language (MGM, 1933)
When Ladies Meet (MGM, 1933)
Night Flight (MGM, 1933)
Fugitive Lovers (MGM, 1934)
Riptide (MGM, 1934)
Mystery of Mr. X (MGM, 1934)
Hideout (MGM, 1934)

Forsaking All Others (MGM, 1935)
Vanessa, Her Love Story (MGM, 1935)
Biography of a Bachelor Girl (MGM, 1935)
No More Ladies (MGM, 1935)
Petticoat Fever (MGM, 1936)
Trouble for Two (MGM, 1936)
Piccadilly Jim (MGM, 1936)
The Last of Mrs. Cheyney (MGM, 1937)
Night Must Fall (MGM, 1937)
Ever Since Eve (WB, 1937)
Live, Love and Learn (MGM, 1937)
The First Hundred Years (MGM, 1938)
Yellow Jack (MGM, 1938)
Three Loves Has Nancy (MGM, 1938)
Fast and Loose (MGM, 1939)
The Earl of Chicago (MGM, 1940)
Haunted Honeymoon (MGM, 1940)
Rage in Heaven (MGM, 1941)
Mr. and Mrs. Smith (RKO, 1941)
Here Comes Mr. Jordan (Columbia, 1941)
Unfinished Business (Universal, 1941)
They Were Expendable (MGM, 1945)
Lady in the Lake (MGM, 1946)
Ride the Pink Horse (Universal, 1947)
The Saxon Charm (Universal, 1948)
The Secret Land (Narrator: MGM, 1948)
June Bride (WB, 1948)
Once More, My Darling (Universal, 1949)
Eye Witness (Eagle–Lion, 1950)
The Gallant Hours (UA, 1960)*

*Unbilled Appearance

With Madge Evans in *Lovers Courageous* (1932)

With Nora Gregor and Edward Everett Horton in *But the Flesh Is Weak* (1932)

Frank Morgan

Of the several scatterbrained, absent-minded screen-type actors in Hollywood, Frank Morgan was the most successful, plying his stock in trade for four decades of movie work and in 52 MGM pictures between 1933 and 1950. If Metro seemingly did not prize his ability to essay the jittery nincompoop to the same degree that filmgoing audiences loved his rascally characterizations, the studio did provide him with his quintessential cinema role. In Metro's *The Wizard of Oz* (1939), as the flibberty-gibbet Wizard, he played to the hilt his beloved oncamera type: the lovable would-be rogue, a stocky middle-aged man who is perpetually surprised by the scope of his own attempted shenanigans and who vocally sputters his mystification at being outsmarted by nearly everyone in sight, whether it be child, adult, or animal.

He was born Francis Phillip Wuppermann on June 1, 1890 in New York City. He was one of eleven sons of the cofounder of the Angostura-Wuppermann Corporation which marketed bitters used in drinks and cocktails. Morgan was a boy soprano in church and later attended Cornell University. He quit college in 1908, got a job selling toothbrushes and, when that did not provide a substantial income, he reluctantly went to work in his father's burgeoning concerns. But Morgan found the business world a bore and soon went in search of more adventurous undertakings. He found himself employment as a newspaper advertisement solicitor for the Boston *Traveler*, and then tried broncho-busting in the Midwest. Finally, at the suggestion of his older brother Ralph (1882–1956), who was already a stage performer, Frank turned to acting. He debuted at the Lyceum Theatre in New York in *A Woman Killed with Kindness* (1914), and then landed the juvenile lead in the Broadway production of *Mr. Wu* in the same year. Also in 1914, on March 11th, he wed Alma Muller and they had a son George, born in 1916.

After *Mr. Wu*, Morgan appeared in several theatrical tours and then tried his luck in motion pictures. He made the rounds of the New York studios and in 1917 appeared in six features for five companies. He was Anita Stewart's leading man in Vitagraph's *The Girl Philippa*, was in the cast of Madge Kennedy's *Baby Mine* at Goldwyn, and supported John Barrymore in Hiller and Wilk's *Raffles, the Amateur Cracksman*. The next year found him in two Alice Brady vehicles, and in 1919 he made *The Gray Towers Mystery* and

511

The Golden Shower, both for Vitagraph. His film assignments did not bring him instant success, so he continued with his stage work, appearing in *Seventh Heaven* (1922), *Lullaby* (1923), *Gentlemen Prefer Blondes* (1926), and *Rosalie* (1926), in which he played the flabbergasted king to Marilyn Miller's lead. In *Topaze* (1930) he had the lead assignment, playing the bespectacled professor. It proved to be his best theatre role.

Meanwhile, thanks to a contract he signed with Paramount in the mid-1920s, Morgan continued with a sporadic film career. In Gloria Swanson's *Manhandled* (1924) Morgan functioned as the owner of a swank dress shop who hires Swanson to impersonate a Russian countess and give the establishment "class." On loan to First National, Morgan was the unwanted baron husband of Mary Astor in *The Scarlet Saint* (1925). Paramount cast him as a womanizing financier in *Love's Greatest Mistake* (1927), starring Evelyn Brent, and for the same studio he made his sound movie feature debut in *Queen High* (1930) a musical comedy in which a young Ginger Rogers played his niece.

His Paramount contract came to a close when he accepted a role in Fred and Adele Astaire's Broadway show, *The Band Wagon* (1931). But the following year he returned to movies as a free-lancer, appearing in such diverse products as RKO's *Secrets of the French Police* and Lupe Velez's *The Half-Naked Truth*, both for RKO. He was appropriate as the mayor of New York in the recitative-style musical *Hallelujah, I'm a Bum* (1933). That same year he signed an MGM contract and moved permanently to Hollywood. He was cast in Metro's high-toned *Reunion in Vienna* (1933) and the impressively mounted *When Ladies Meet* (1933), starring Ann Harding. Metro cast him as Jean Harlow's lazy but lovable fraud of a dad in *Bombshell* (1933), and in *Broadway to Hollywood* (1933), he and Alice Brady were vaudevillians with Madge Evans as their daughter. Morgan was loaned to United Artists for *The Affairs of Cellini* (1934), and he received an Oscar nomination for playing the indecisive duke of Florence. Back at MGM he was in fine form as the befuddled governor in *Naughty Marietta* (1935). He then turned in a sympathetic performance as Billings, the long-standing show business rival of William Powell in *The Great Ziegfeld* (1936). But he still was most in demand for the role he played best, and seemingly so easily, the confused scamp. RKO borrowed him to play an out-of-sorts mayor in the Technicolor *The Dancing Pirate* (1936) and Twentieth Century -Fox employed him to support Shirley Temple in *Dimples* (1936). While MGM occasionally gave him a lead assignment, such as in the programmer *Beg, Borrow or Steal* (1937) with Florence Rice, or allowed him to re-create one of his stage parts, such as in *Rosalie* (1937), he usually was relegated to leading the supporting cast.

In Jean Harlow's last movie, *Saratoga* (1937), Morgan was a good-natured cad, the sugar-daddy husband of fellow race track enthusiast Una Merkel; and in *Broadway Serenade* (1939) he was the middle-aged playboy producer who finally ditches chorine Virgina Grey to wed Rita Johnson. Along the way, he turned in a straight performance as Parisse in *Port of Seven*

Seas (1938), a role Maurice Chevalier would play in the later remake titled *Fanny*. Originally Shirley Temple was to have been Dorothy and W. C. Fields hopefully cast as the Wizard in *The Wizard of Oz*, but in the end, it was Judy Garland and Morgan. That film gave Morgan international acclaim for his gruff but kindly Wizard.

He hit his stride in the 1940s, at an age when most men would have been slowing down their professional activities. He gave a striking psychological study of the jealous shopkeeper in *The Shop Around the Corner* (1940), starring Margaret Sullavan, and was equally convincing in another serious role, that of the old, non-Aryan German professor in *The Mortal Storm*, again with Sullavan. Unlike fellow veteran player Wallace Beery, who graduated from Grade A MGM vehicles in the 1930s to starring roles in profitable programmers in the 1940s, Morgan was only rarely used to topcast a B film. In such double-bill entries as *Henry Goes Arizona* (1940) or *Hullabaloo* (1941), his presence, as always, benefited the picture but really did not bring in the patrons as hoped. Once there, of course, the audiences would enjoy his smooth demonstration of expert ensemble playing, as in *Wild Man of Borneo* (1941) in which he was a parasitic loafer. For MGM he was extremely valuable as bridge between disparate types of lead players in major vehicles, a function he fulfilled with apparent ease and pleasure. He was a good-natured rival of Clark Gable in *Boom Town* (1940) and played Lana Turner's tippling dad in *Honky Tonk* (1941). In 1942 he received a second Oscar nomination, this time in the supporting category, for his portrayal of the "pirate" in the cinematization of John Steinbeck's *Tortilla Flat*. However, another MGM contractee, Van Heflin, won in that category for his performance in *Johnny Eager*.

Morgan showed up in Hedy Lamarr's *White Cargo* (1942), played a Supreme Court judge in *A Stranger in Town* (1943), and stole the limelight in a sketch in the musical revue *Thousands Cheer* (1943). Whether playing a con artist in *Yolanda and the Thief* (1945) or bolstering the rest of the cast in *Courage of Lassie* (1946), Morgan continued to earn his keep at MGM, in the long sun worth far more than the extravagant sums spent on promoting would-be studio stars who could not carry even a good picture. Of his last MGM pictures, his best role was as Uncle Sid in *Summer Holiday* (1948), the procrastinating suitor of Agnes Moorehead. Wallace Beery had played the Morgan part in the earlier *Ah, Wilderness!* (1935) and Jackie Gleason romped through the role on Broadway in the musical *Take Me Along*.

Morgan had already begun work on *Annie Get Your Gun* (1950) when he died in his sleep on September 18, 1949. He was replaced by Louis Calhern in that picture. *Key to the City*, in which Morgan played the sidekick of mayor Clark Gable, was not released until 1950.

From the mid-1930s onward, Morgan had been a frequent radio performer, having his own show at one point, with Robert Young as the host, headlining the *Kraft Music Hall* summer show, and in 1947 performing his monologues on several of *The Old Gold Show* programs. He was a boating enthusiast, and in 1947 won a race with his yacht, the *Dolphin*, between Los

Angeles and Honolulu. Considered an authority on screen acting, he wrote a 4,500-word treatise on the subject for the *Encyclopaedia Britannica*. His brother Ralph had a long film career, specializing in villain roles but never attained the degree of success that Frank Morgan acquired over his decades in Hollywood.

FRANK MORGAN

The Suspect (Vitagraph, 1916)
The Daring of Diana (Vitagraph, 1917)
Light in the Darkness (Vitagraph, 1917)
A Modern Cinderella (Fox, 1917)
The Girl Philippa (Vitagraph, 1917)
Who's Your Neighbor? (Master, 1917)
A Child of the Wild (Fox, 1917)
Baby Mine (Goldwyn, 1917)
Raffles, the Amateur Cracksman (Hiller And Wilk, 1917)
The Knife (Selig, 1918)
At the Mercy of Men (Selznick, 1918)
Gray Towers of Mystery (Vitagraph, 1919)
The Golden Shower (Vitagraph, 1919)
Manhandled (Paramount, 1924)
Born Rich (FN, 1924)
The Man Who Found Himself (Paramount, 1925)
The Crowded Hour (Paramount, 1925)
The Scarlet Saint (FN, 1925)
Love's Greatest Mistake (Paramount, 1927)
Queen High (Paramount, 1930)
Dangerous Nan McGrew (Paramount, 1930)
Fast and Loose (Paramount, 1930)
Laughter (Paramount, 1930)
Secrets of the French Police (RKO, 1932)
The Half-Naked Truth (RKO, 1932)
Hallelujah, I'm a Bum (UA, 1933)
Luxury Liner (Paramount, 1933)
Billion Dollar Scandal (Paramount, 1933)
Reunion in Vienna (MGM, 1933)
When Ladies Meet (MGM, 1933)
Kiss before the Mirror (Universal, 1933)
The Nuisance (MGM, 1933)
Best of Enemies (Fox, 1933)
Broadway to Hollywood (MGM, 1933)
Bombshell (MGM, 1933)
The Cat and the Fiddle (MGM, 1934)
Sisters under the Skin (Columbia, 1934)
Affairs of Cellini (UA, 1934)
Success at Any Price (RKO, 1934)
A Lost Lady (WB, 1934)
There's Always Tomorrow (Universal, 1934)

Naughty Marietta (MGM, 1935)
The Good Fairy (Universal, 1935)
Enchanted April (RKO, 1935)
Escapade (MGM, 1935)
The Perfect Gentleman (MGM, 1935)
I Live My Life (MGM, 1935)
The Great Ziegfeld (MGM, 1936)
The Dancing Pirate (RKO, 1936)
Trouble for Two (MGM, 1936)
Piccadilly Jim (MGM, 1936)
Dimples (20th-Fox, 1936)
The Last of Mrs. Cheyney (MGM, 1937)
The Emperor's Candlesticks (MGM, 1937)
Saratoga (MGM, 1937)
Beg, Borrow or Steal (MGM, 1937)
Rosalie (MGM, 1937)
Paradise for Three (MGM, 1938)
The Crowd Roars (MGM, 1938)
Port of Seven Seas (MGM, 1938)
Sweethearts (MGM, 1938)
Broadway Serenade (MGM, 1939)
The Wizard of Oz (MGM, 1939)
Balalaika (MGM, 1939)
The Shop Around the Corner (MGM, 1940)
Broadway Melody of 1940 (MGM, 1940)
Henry Goes Arizona (MGM, 1940)
The Mortal Storm (MGM, 1940)
Boom Town (MGM, 1940)
Hullabaloo (MGM, 1940)
The Ghost Comes Home (MGM, 1940)
Honky Tonk (MGM, 1941)
The Vanishing Virginian (MGM, 1941)
Washington Melodrama (MGM, 1941)
Wild Man of Borneo (MGM, 1941)
Keeping Company (MGM, 1941)
Tortilla Flat (MGM, 1942)
White Cargo (MGM, 1942)
A Stranger in Town (MGM, 1943)
The Human Comedy (MGM, 1943)
Thousands Cheer (MGM, 1943)
The White Cliffs of Dover (MGM, 1944)
Casanova Brown (RKO, 1944)
Yolanda and the Thief (MGM, 1945)

With Elsa Lanchester and Nelson Eddy in *Naughty Marietta* (1935)

With Clark Gable, Una Merkel, and Margaret Hamilton in *Saratoga* (1937)

With Jack Haley, Bert Lahr, Judy Garland, and Ray Bolger in *The Wizard of Oz* (1939)

Karen Morley

Some performers are too much a product of their period both in looks and acting style and never rise enough above their flashier competition to become the star personalities they deserve to be. Such was the case with Karen Morley who, within four years (1931–1934) came and went at MGM. Like the similar Ann Dvorak she possessed specialized aristocratic good looks and superior acting abilities, but her supercharged acting intensity never won for her a sufficiently wide enough following to make studio executives give her the necessary big promotion. The fact that Karen had a burgeoning independent nature and failed to play a good game of studio politics when first at MGM counteracted the momentum of her several good performances. Thereafter she continued in the profession until the McCarthy hearings ended her career in the early 1950s. She always gave a solid if often hypertense performance even at the end of her career in the smallest of roles or the dinkiest of film productions.

Karen was born Mabel Linton in Ottumwa, Iowa in 1905, but grew up in Los Angeles. She attended Hollywood High School and then the University of California where she performed in theatricals. She left college to join the Los Angeles Civic Repertory Theatre and appeared in such productions as *Fata Morgana*. She was also an extra in Fox's courtroom melodrama *Thru Different Eyes* (1929), starring Warner Baxter.

According to one popular version of her screen "break," Karen was on the MGM lot, preparing for a screen test. During a shooting break, she grabbed a script of Greta Garbo's forthcoming picture *Inspiration* (1931) and began reading the star's dialogue into a nearby microphone. The impromptu test came to the attention of director Clarence Brown, and he signed her to play the ingenue type role of Liane in *Inspiration*. The assignment set the tone for her screen career. She was the friend of artist's model Garbo, and the girl who commits suicide after her much older lover, Lewis Stone, discards her. MGM gave her a term contract and she was in seven other releases that year, including Metro's *Never the Twain Shall Meet* (as Leslie Howard's jilted society fiancée), *Politics* (as Marie Dressler's daughter and in love with William Bakewell), and *Cuban Love Song* (as Lawrence Tibbett's patient girl friend back home).

MGM obviously had initial faith in the twenty-six-year-old Karen, for she was selected to represent the studio as their WAMPAS Baby Star of 1931. Other winners that year were Joan Blondell, Frances Dee, Sidney Fox, Rochelle Hudson, Anita Louise, and Marion Marsh. Karen was not one to sit around waiting for breaks to happen to her. She was a close runner-up to Irene Dunne for the lead in Universal's *Back Street* (1932), but Dunne had already established a name the year before with the tearjerker chronicle *Cimarron*. Although Karen and MGM studio still photographer George Hurrell were not particularly chummy, he took a particularly seductive photo layout of her in a black negligée, and Karen charged into Irving Thalberg's office to offer the pictures as reason for her being cast as the alluring amour of French duke John Barrymore in *Arsene Lupin* (1932). She was given the role, and also that year played the mercenary American dancer who weds German waiter-turned-wrestler Wallace Beery in *Flesh*. In *Washington Melodrama* she was C. Henry Gordon's paramour and in United Artists's *Scarface* she was well made up as Polly, a Jean Harlow-type, but intelligent, moll who once belonged to Osgood Perkins and now is had by Paul Muni. Energetic Karen told the press: "I know I am not pretty. I cannot make a place for myself on the screen as a beauty. I am not even an exciting person. There is, therefore, only one thing left. I must be an actress. And the more variety I can get, the more they will think of me as a capable actress."

But then everything went awry for Karen. In 1932 she wed director Charles Vidor, with whom she had worked at Fox in *Man about Town* (1932). He also had directed her in MGM's *The Mask of Fu Manchu* (1932) in which Karen is almost hacked to pieces by vengeful Boris Karloff. It did not sit well with the Hollywood community that Karen had nabbed one of the bright young men of the year: It made her seem more self-sufficient than was good for an ingenue being given a slow grooming for the bright future. Both Karen and Anita Page tested for *Red-Headed Woman*, but Jean Harlow got the part. Perhaps Karen's biggest nemesis on the MGM lot was Madge Evans, a special favorite of Thalberg. Both Karen and Anita Page supported Evans in *Are You Listening?* (1932), and several other roles that Karen tested for went to Evans. Karen was reduced to a very supporting role in Garbo's *Mata Hari* (1932). In that romantic spy melodrama, Karen played Carlotta, one of Garbo's fellow spies working in Paris under Lewis Stone's German command. When Karen fails in a mission, she is eliminated by Stone's gimpy-legged henchman, which serves as a lesson to the faltering spy Garbo.

Karen's next role was a poor one and her acting was flat in *Gabriel over the White House* (1933) in which she played the assistant to Franchot Tone, himself the Secretary to the President of the United States (Walter Huston). And in the studio's Class A production *Dinner at Eight* (1933) Karen was relegated to the small role of Mrs. Wayne Talbot, wife of Dr. Edmund Lowe. She is the one who remains civilized even when she discovers her husband has been having an affair with Jean Harlow. Looking sleek and well-coiffed, Karen's waning studio position was all the more evident when compared to the much larger part given to Madge Evans, who played the lovesick Paula Jordan.

After giving birth to a son Michael, Karen was seen in one more MGM release, *Straight Is the Way* (1934) as the romantic interest of East Side Jewish mug Franchot Tone. Finally at liberty, Karen hopscotched about the Hollywood lots. She had two more decent years on the screen. She was the erring wife of criminologist Otto Kruger in *Crime Doctor* (1934) and had the lead opposite Tom Keene in King Vidor's followup to *Hallelujah*, titled *Our Daily Bread* (1934). But even in the latter picture Barbara Pepper had the more showy role as a menace interpolated into the plot. In *Wednesday's Child* (1934) Karen and Edward Arnold are a battling couple with their child, Frankie Thomas, the pawn in the middle.

Then there was Paul Muni's *Black Fury* (1935), in which Karen was one of the victims of the coal mining class war. Her last decent job was playing in support of Merle Oberon and David Niven in *Beloved Enemy* (1936), set during the Irish rebellion of 1921. Then it was downhill, and fast, for Karen. She was the avenging sister of a murdered girl who trails suspect Dr. Warren William in *Outcast* (1937), a film coscripted by Dore Schary, and she had the title role in a minor Republic programmer, *Girl from Scotland Yard* (1937). That same year she and Lew Ayres were relegated to being "new–old" faces in Paramount's *Last Train from Madrid*, and in 1938 Karen was reduced to playing one of Loretta Young's forebears in the brief prologue to *Kentucky*. She returned to MGM for *Pride and Prejudice* (1940) in the minor role of Mrs. Collins.

Karen was off the screen for most of the World War II years, during which time she and Vidor were divorced and she remarried. Although she was forty when she returned to pictures in Republic's murder melodrama, *Jealousy* (1945), *The Nation's* James Agee could report that she still was "extremely attractive." Karen was a forlorn psychotic in *The Unknown* (1946), but dropped to fifth billing in *Framed* (1947) with Glenn Ford. It was four years before she made another film, this time in Joseph Losey's banal remake of *M* (1951) at Columbia. She was tenth-billed as Mrs. Coster, mother of one of the victims of child-killer David Wayne.

In the 1950s rash of the Senate's Un-American Activities Committee hearings, Karen was named by two actors as a fellow traveler of the Communist party. When she was questioned, Karen invoked the Fifth Amendment. After that, she made one more picture, the independently produced Western *Born to the Saddle* (1953), and then dropped completely out of professional sight. But when the Academy of Motion Pictures Arts And Sciences screened *Our Daily Bread* in 1971, Karen was on hand to join with director King Vidor in a seminar discussion of the movie.

KAREN MORLEY

Thru Different Eyes (Fox, 1929)
Inspiration (MGM, 1931)
Strangers May Kiss (MGM, 1931)
Never the Twain Shall Meet (MGM, 1931)
Daybreak (MGM, 1931)
High Stakes (RKO, 1931)
Politics (MGM, 1931)
Cuban Love Song (MGM, 1931)
The Sin of Madelon Claudet (MGM, 1931)
Arsene Lupin (MGM, 1932)
Fast Life (MGM, 1932)
Are You Listening? (MGM, 1932)
Mata Hari (MGM, 1932)
Scarface (UA, 1932)
Man about Town (Fox, 1932)
Washington Masquerade (MGM, 1932)
The Phantom of Crestwood (RKO, 1932)
The Mask of Fu Manchu (MGM, 1932)
Flesh (MGM, 1932)
Gabriel over the White House (MGM, 1933)
Dinner at Eight (MGM, 1933)
Crime Doctor (RKO, 1934)

Straight Is the Way (MGM, 1934)
Our Daily Bread (UA, 1934)
Wednesday's Child (RKO, 1934)
Black Fury (FN, 1935)
$10 Raise (Fox, 1935)
The Healer (Monogram, 1935)
Thunder in the Night (Fox, 1935)
The Littlest Rebel (Fox, 1935)
Devil's Squadron (Columbia, 1936)
Beloved Enemy (UA, 1936)
Outcast (Paramount, 1937)
Girl from Scotland Yard (Republic, 1937)
Last Train from Madrid (Paramount, 1937)
On Such a Night (Paramount, 1937)
Kentucky (20th-Fox, 1938)
Pride and Prejudice (MGM, 1940)
Jealousy (Republic, 1945)
The Unknown (Columbia, 1946)
The 13th Hour (Columbia, 1947)
Framed (Columbia, 1947)
M (Columbia, 1951)
Born to the Saddle (Astor, 1953)

With Boris Karloff, Myrna Loy, Charles Starrett, and Jean Hersholt in *The Mask of Fu Manchu* (1932)

George Murphy

Onscreen George Murphy was the stereotyped bland Irish song-and-dance man, whose serviceable performances made him a useful asset at MGM in the late 1930s and early 1940s, before the younger and more virile Gene Kelly superseded Murphy at the studio. If spectacular movie stardom eluded Murphy, at least he had the satisfaction of joining the echelon of "important" people at MGM from the mid-1940s onward because of his offcamera political and union activities which received the high endorsement of Louis B. Mayer and, for a time, the mogul's successor, Dore Schary. It was Murphy who pioneered the now acceptable custom of actor-turned-political-candidate. For his earnest political ambitions he became the brunt of many "Say-didn't-you-use-to-be-George-Murphy-the-hoofer" jokes. However, he survived that ordeal as he had his low-keyed screen career, with a broad smile and a friendly twinkle of his eyes.

George Lloyd Murphy was born, appropriately enough, on Independence Day in 1902 in New Haven, Connecticut. His father, who died when Murphy was eleven years old, was a track coach and had trained the championship team headed by Jim Thorpe at the 1912 Olympic Games in Stockholm. After his father's death the Murphys moved to Detroit, the home of Mrs. Murphy's parents. In 1917 Murphy enrolled in the University of Detroit High School where his interest was more attuned to sports than academic studies. He ran off to join the Navy at fifteen, but his family had the underage boy brought home. Later he earned a partial sports scholarship to the Peddie School in Hightstown, New Jersey, and thereafter, a full scholarship to the Pawling School in New York. While at the latter institution he won the Chauncey Depew Oratory Award for an impassioned speech he made about Theodore Roosevelt. Graduating from there in 1921, he entered Yale University in the class of 1925. There again, his prime interest was not in academics, but in sports. Odd jobs during the summer helped to subsidize his tuition at Yale. One job found him as a bouncer at the Paramount Dance Hall in Newark, New Jersey, and another as a coal-loader in Portage, Pennsylvania. A combination of his low grades and the ill effects suffered from a coal mine accident forced Murphy to leave Yale during his junior year.

At loose ends, Murphy went to New York in the fall of 1924. While working as a stock market runner for the Bache Company, Murphy decided to make use of his abilities as a natural dancer. He had met Juliette Henkel in Detroit and she had since moved to New York. She was working in show business, using the professional name of Julie Johnson. Murphy prepared a dance duo act for them and they found employment entertaining at cocktail parties, cabarets, and with the George Olsen Band. They made their specialty the Varsity Drag, the hit dance from the Broadway musical, *Good News*. When London producer Herbert Morrison came to New York in 1927 to cast the London company of that show, he happened to see Murphy and Johnson perform their act and hired them for the West End production. By this time (December 28, 1926) Murphy and Johnson had wed.

After *Good News* the couple returned to New York and were hired in 1929 to replace Jack Whiting and Betty Compton in the long-running musical *Hold Everything*, starring Bert Lahr. After eight months on Broadway, they went on tour with the show, which, in turn, was followed by the Broadway revue, *Shoot the Works* (1931). Thereafter, Murphy was hired as a solo to play the smart-alecky press agent in George Gershwin's *Of Thee I Sing* (1931), which ran for 441 performances. Having established himself as a personable Broadway performer, Murphy was then hired to join Tamara and Bob Hope in Jerome Kern's *Roberta* which bowed on Broadway on November 18, 1933. He left that musical the following June to go to Hollywood, having signed a contract with Samuel Goldwyn. Murphy made his screen debut as the song-and-dance man opposite Ann Sothern in *Kid Millions* (1934), which starred Eddie Cantor. Despite Murphy's adequate performance in that picture, Goldwyn did not renew his option, so the Broadway hoofer signed with Columbia Pictures. Murphy would later recall that he and studio head Harry Cohn did not hit it off initially, particularly when the "Black Bull of Gower Street," as the actor called Cohn, wanted to change his name to something with more marquee glitter. Two of Murphy's four Columbia pictures, *Jealousy* (1934) and *I'll Love You Always* (1935) starred Nancy Carroll, Paramount's vivacious ex-star. Murphy was not impressed by Carroll's oncamera tactics, but then the public was not particularly aware of Murphy, beyond his being another second string musical comedy lead.

Murphy was never one to sit idly by, and soon after leaving Columbia, he had negotiated an MGM contract. Metro realized his Irish charm could be developed into a suitable screen image that would bolster lesser vehicles. As such, MGM tossed him into *Women Men Marry* and *London by Night*, two studio programmers of 1937. That same year he was employed in a song-and-dance capacity in the grade A picture *Broadway Melody of 1938* and then was loaned out to Universal for the Alice Faye musical, *You're a Sweetheart* (1937). Already typecast as a Broadway hoofer, Twentieth Century-Fox borrowed Murphy for their Shirley Temple entry, *Little Miss Broadway* (1938), and then Universal recalled him for *Letter of Introduction* (1938). Metro assigned him to a dance spot in *Broadway Melody of 1940* and then as Judy Garland's *vis-à-vis* in the shamrock musical, *Little Nellie Kelly*

(1940). He and Garland worked well in that film and Metro planned to reteam him with Garland in *For Me and My Gal* (1942). But by the time that Busby Berkeley picture went into production, MGM had "discovered" Gene Kelly from Broadway and he was given the vaudevillian heel role, the part originally intended for Murphy. Murphy was recast into the innocuous nice guy part in the film.

Thereafter Murphy continued to populate homelot B films such as *Ringside Maisie* (1941) and *The Arnelo Affair* (1947), or similar programmer fodder on loanout, such as United Artists' *The Powers Girl* (1942) and RKO's *Mayor of 44th Street* (1942), both with Anne Shirley. Occasionally he went "dramatic" as in Metro's war actioner *Bataan* (1943) or jumped into a big picture, such as Warner Brothers' *This Is the Army* (1943). But there was hardly any pattern to his 1940s film career, even though after World War II he esschewed musical comedy (he was now in his mid-forties) for straight assignments: *Battleground* (1949), and, on loan to Columbia, *Walk East on Beacon* (1952).

If Murphy had spent two decades on the screen being seen but not remembered, he did much better offcamera. When he arrived in Hollywood, he was a Democrat, but in 1939, being what he described as a "dormant" Democrat, he switched allegiance to the Republican party and the following year helped to organize the Hollywood Republican Committee to support Wendell Willkie's campaign for the presidency. Among his fellow Republicans were actors Robert Montgomery, Ronald Reagan, and Bob Hope. It just so happened that the biggest Republican in the movie industry was Louis B. Mayer and that factor brought Murphy into much closer contact with his studio boss than ordinarily would have been the case. Their joint political work gave Murphy much more status on the MGM lot and to the Hollywood community at large, which had previously considered him just another personable hoofer.

Besides his political work, Murphy thrived on civic activities, being one of the first members of The Screen Actors' Guild, as well as serving as its vice president from 1940 to 1943. He succeeded Robert Montgomery as that organization's president in 1944 and served two terms. He joined with Montgomery in his successful fight against the infiltration of mobsters into the motion picture unions. It was Murphy who, as Guild president, campaigned to have talent agents franchised. During World War II he worked with the Hollywood Victory Committee which arranged for players to entertain servicemen.

After World War II, Murphy turned more and more of his nonscreen activities to politics. He and Montgomery were the guiding lights in founding the new Hollywood Republican Committee in 1947. Murphy was a delegate pledged to Earl Warren's cause in the Republican National Convention in 1948. He was in charge of the entertainment for the 1952 Republican National Convention, a task he also performed in 1956 and 1960.

In 1950 Murphy was awarded an Honorary Oscar by the Academy of

Motion Picture Arts and Sciences for "services in correctly interpreting the film industry to the country at large." The same year his good friend Louis B. Mayer was presented with a special Oscar for his long-standing contributions to the film industry. After Murphy appeared in Metro's programmer, *Talk about a Stranger* (1952), and officially retired from the screen, Mayer kept him under contract as full-time "official ambassador as a liaison between MGM and the unions." Murphy's special MGM contract was the second in that company's history of players' pacts which spread a performer's salary over a period of 52 weeks rather than the usual 40. Garbo's similar agreement had been the first. As Murphy had been a spokesman for the film industry (he was one of those who urged the public "to get more out of life and go to a movie") so was he a touter for MGM product in the mid-1950s. For several weeks of the studio's abortive self-promotional video series, he was the program's host. Murphy resigned from MGM in 1958 when he clashed headlong with outspoken Democrat Dore Schary, who had been helming the studio since Mayer's ouster in 1951. Dore and his executives tried to associate Murphy with Mayer's 1957 attempted studio coup, and Murphy walked out in a pique. Desi Arnaz and Lucille Ball hired Murphy as vice president in charge of public relations for their television company, Desilu, where he stayed for two years. In 1960 he became a director and corporate vice president of the Technicolor Corporation.

Murphy got his first taste of national politics when vice president Richard M. Nixon supported him for the chairmanship of the Republican National Convention, a post he held from October 1953 to August 1954. A decade later he announced his candidacy for U. S. Senator from California, opposing John F. Kennedy's former White House press secretary, Pierre Salinger. During the campaign the Democratic Senator, Clair Engle died, and California governor Pat Brown appointed Salinger to fill out the remainder of Engle's term. Despite this tactic, Murphy won the campaign and was sworn in on January 4, 1965 as a member of the 89th Congress. Murphy had an operation in 1966 on his vocal cord for a growth the doctors suspected of malignancy. The operation was successful, except that it left the ex-actor with a raspy speaking voice, which Murphy likens to the trademark growl of Andy Devine. When Murphy ran for a second senatorial term, he lost due largely to unproved but suspicious business dealings he had while Senator.

In 1970 Murphy wrote his autobiography, *Say ... Didn't You Use to Be George Murphy?*, a mildly anecdotal account of his life, more bland than perceptive, which was really the same quality that detracted from so many of his movie performances. He and his wife of 47 years live on Rodeo Drive in Beverly Hills and have two children, Dennis Michael and Melissa Elaine. Looking back on his multifaceted career, Murphy is much more satisfied with his political activities than with his easygoing screen years. As one film reporter summarized: "Where actors generally are regarded as oblivious to public affairs and professional dancers are supposed to be prey to enlarged hearts, Murphy happily is characterized rather by an enlarged civic consciousness."

GEORGE MURPHY

Kid Millions (UA, 1934)
Jealousy (Columbia, 1934)
I'll Love You Always (Columbia, 1935)
After the Dance (Columbia, 1935)
Public Menace (Columbia, 1935)
Woman Trap (Paramount, 1936)
Top of the Town (Universal, 1937)
Women Men Marry (MGM, 1937)
London by Night (MGM, 1937)
Broadway Melody of 1938 (MGM, 1937)
You're a Sweetheart (Universal, 1937)
Little Miss Broadway (20th-Fox, 1938)
Letter of Introduction (Universal, 1938)
Hold That Co-Ed (Universal, 1938)
Risky Business (Universal, 1939)
Broadway Melody of 1940 (MGM, 1940)
Two Girls on Broadway (MGM, 1940)
Public Deb No. 1 (20th-Fox, 1940)
Little Nellie Kelly (MGM, 1940)
A Girl, a Guy, and a Gob (RKO, 1941)
Tom, Dick and Harry (RKO, 1941)
Ringside Maisie (MGM, 1941)

Rise and Shine (20th-Fox, 1941)
Mayor of 44th Street (RKO, 1942)
For Me and My Gal (MGM, 1942)
The Navy Comes Through (RKO, 1942)
The Powers Girl (UA, 1942)
Bataan (MGM, 1943)
This Is the Army (WB, 1943)
Broadway Rhythm (MGM, 1944)
Show Business (RKO, 1944)
Step Lively (RKO, 1944)
Having Wonderful Crime (RKO, 1945)
Up Goes Maisie (MGM, 1946)
The Arnelo Affair (MGM, 1947)
Cynthia (MGM, 1947)
Tenth Avenue Angel (MGM, 1948)
The Big City (MGM, 1948)
Border Incident (MGM, 1949)
Battleground (MGM, 1949)
No Questions Asked (MGM, 1951)
It's a Big Country (MGM, 1951)
Walk East on Beacon (Columbia, 1952)
Talk about a Stranger (MGM, 1952)

With Rita Johnson in *London by Night* (1937)

With Mary Astor in *Cynthia* (1947)

Margaret O'Brien

Margaret O'Brien was one of the most talented of the cinema child stars but, unfortunately, she was considered just that: a star and not a child actress. She was not a carbon copy of Twentieth Century-Fox's boxoffice bonanza Shirley Temple, certainly not a little Miss Show Biz. Whenever Margaret's screen scripts were not overwhelmingly sentimental, she revealed a naturalness, a reality, and a pathos that set her apart from other child players. Such performances made her characters endearingly human. She began her acting career at the age of four under contract to MGM. But because she was somewhat of a phenomenon, being an actress and not just a performing tot, scripts that showed her to good advantage were difficult to come by. Nevertheless, the studio did find several good roles for her: *Journey for Margaret* (1942), *Meet Me in St. Louis* (1944), and *Our Vines Have Tender Grapes* (1945). She received a special little Oscar and placed among the top moneymakers of 1945 and 1946. William Randolph Hearst adored her and saw all her pictures. When Louis B. Mayer asked her one year what she wanted most for Christmas, the unpretentious youngster said: "Lassie."

She was born Angela Maxine O'Brien on January 15, 1937 in Los Angeles. Her father, who had been a circus rider, died four months before she was born. It was her mother Gladys who decided that the dark-haired child should be trained as a circus rider like her father. Gladys was of Spanish ancestry and had been a flamenco dancer. Her sister Marisao had sung with Xavier Cugat's band. But by the age of three, Maxine, as she was then called, had gravitated into the field of modeling and often was used for magazine cover shots. It was one such pose which brought her to the attention of MGM, and the child was hired for a tiny bit in *Babes on Broadway* (1941) as one of the tenement children brought in to help with the big benefit show. Gladys decided then and there that the movies were more glamorous than the circus and maneuvered for her daughter to be tested for *Journey for Margaret* (1942). As the pigtailed impoverished war orphan, the child was so convincing in her audition that she easily won the role. The girl's reaction to the plum assignment was, "I knew I'd get it. I prayed for it." The film, which featured Robert Young and Laraine Day, launched this little girl to stardom. The N.Y. *Times* said her portrayal could hardly be called a performance because it was "too taut and true." MGM signed her to a seven-year contract, and her name was legally changed to Margaret O'Brien.

MGM cast her in a small role in *Dr. Gillespie's Criminal Case* (1943) and series star Lionel Barrymore exclaimed. "She's the only actress besides Ethel who's made me take out my handkerchief in thirty years." There was another small role in *Thousands Cheer* (1943), really only a comedy skit in which she has an unending passion for ice cream which leads Red Skelton into a vomiting spasm. Then she was starred in *Lost Angel* (1943) as the foundling who is adopted by a group of psychologists, but had relatively minor roles in *Madame Curie* (1943) and in *Jane Eyre* (1944) made on loan to Twentieth Century-Fox. *The Canterville Ghost* (1944) played on her waiflike Irish appeal, but it was the role of Tootie in *Meet Me in St. Louis* which presented the child with the best part of her career. Her singing of "Drunk Last Night," doing the cakewalk with Judy Garland, and her spooky Halloween adventure in that excellent screen musical caused James Agee to call Margaret: "incredibly vivid and eloquent—almost as hypnotizing as Garbo." The public agreed, as did the Academy of Motion Picture Arts and Sciences, which presented her with a special Oscar. The following year she gave another fine performance as the daughter of Norwegian farmer Edward G. Robinson in *Our Vines Have Tender Grapes*. By now she was at her peak of popularity.

The excellence of those two scripts made it difficult for MGM to find suitable projects for her. They tried, but they never came up with anything matching their former triumphs. *Bad Bascomb* (1946) had her tearfully pitted against mugging Wallace Beery, and *Big City* (1948) found her adopted by a Jewish cantor, Danny Thomas, an Irish Catholic cop, George Murphy, and a Protestant minister, Robert Preston. It was more than enough to tax the most patient audience. She was then cast as Beth in the remake of *Little Women* (1949) but many people found her performance too dewy-eyed for the part. When she and her mother refused to go to Disney where she was to play in *Alice in Wonderland*, then being planned as a live-action feature, MGM suspended her. Her salary at the time was $2,500 a week, far above that received by her studio successor, Gigi Perreau.

In 1949 her mother remarried. Margaret's new father was bandleader Don Sylvio. At the wedding ceremony the twelve-year-old Margaret refused to kiss her stepfather who later said that she ruined her mother's wedding night by throwing a tantrum. In 1950 Margaret appeared on tour with Buddy Rogers' orchestra doing recitations which included Beth's death scene from *Little Women* and a prayer for peace. She went to Columbia for *Her First Romance* (1951), a summer camp story in which she received her first screen kiss. Columbia and Margaret learned the hard way that no one seemed to care about the awkward teenager. She retired from the screen and made her stage debut in Clare Booth Luce's *Child of the Morning* in Springfield, Massachusetts, and later appeared in another stock company with *Kiss and Tell*. She made numerous ingenue appearances on television and finally, in 1955, was graduated from high school. The same year she said that her MGM experiences had been wonderful and that she was grateful to her mother for handling her career so well. By a court order, part of her earnings were set aside in U. S. Savings Bonds until she was at least twenty-one. The amount has been variously reported as being anything from $200,000 to $1,000,000.

In 1956 Margaret starred in *Glory,* a bland horse-racing picture for declining RKO, and in 1958 she played in the television version of *Little Women,* repeating the same role she had done a decade before on screen. Having reached the age of twenty-one, she was shown on the cover of *Life* magazine as a grownup and sexy young lady, which only resulted in making many readers realize how old they were getting. On August 28 that year her mother died of a heart attack and the following year, on August 8th, Margaret married commercial artist Harold Robert Allen. She remained active on television and made one more motion picture appearance, playing Eileen Heckart's virtuous daughter in the Western spoof *Heller in Pink Tights* (1960).

She spent much of her time working in touring and summer stock companies of Broadway hits: *Gigi, Under the Yum-Yum Tree, Sunday in New York, A Shot in the Dark, A Thousand Clowns,* and *Barefoot in the Park.* When her stage career alienated her husband, they were divorced in 1969, after which, being of Spanish heritage, she went to live in Peru. She became the hostess of a Spanish-speaking daily television soap opera and made a trio of low budget films, including a horror feature called *Diabolical Wedding* (1971) and *Annabelle Lee* (1972).

For a time she was engaged to Peruvian producer Julio Tijer. When her business manager embezzled $75,000 of her earnings in 1971, Margaret returned to live in Hollywood; a matronly ingenue in search of a new career. Like Shirley Temple, Jackie Coogan, and Jackie Cooper, the public prefers to remember the great child actors at the peak of their tiny-tot triumphs, and only reluctantly accepts them in their alien adult guises.

Margaret popped up in the news again in mid-1972 when she was hired to play the overweight wife of a business executive on an episode of television's *Marcus Welby, M. D.* It was the first time she and series star Robert Young had professionally worked together since 1945. The public found it hard to believe that the once-child star was now thirty-five years old and overweight. "It's true," Margaret admitted. "I've been having some emotional problems over a lawsuit involving misuse of funds I earned as a child. When I get upset, I eat."

MARGARET O'BRIEN

Babes on Broadway (MGM, 1941)	Thousands Cheer (MGM, 1943)
Journey for Margaret (MGM, 1942)	Lost Angel (MGM, 1943)
Dr. Gillespie's Criminal Case (MGM, 1943)	Madame Curie (MGM, 1943)

Jane Eyre (20th-Fox, 1944)
The Canterville Ghost (MGM, 1944)
Meet Me in St. Louis (MGM, 1944)
Music for Millions (MGM, 1944)
Our Vines Have Tender Grapes (MGM, 1945)
Bad Bascomb (MGM, 1946)
Three Wise Fools (MGM, 1946)
The Unfinished Dance (MGM, 1947)
Tenth Avenue Angel (MGM, 1947)

The Big City (MGM, 1948)
Little Women (MGM, 1949)
The Secret Garden (MGM, 1949)
Her First Romance (Columbia, 1951)
Glory (RKO, 1956)
Heller in Pink Tights (Paramount, 1960)
Diabolical Wedding (Ellman Enterprises, 1971)
Annabelle Lee (Ellman Enterprises, 1972)

With Keenan Wynn in *Lost Angel* (1943)

With Robert Young in *The Canterville Ghost* (1944)

With Jimmy Durante in *Music for Millions* (1944)

In *The Unfinished Dance* (1947)

Virginia O'Brien

In Hollywood of the 1940s, specialty performers tended to appear and disappear with remarkable regularity, usually falling back into the medium whence they came. Few are as well remembered or as highly regarded as Virginia O'Brien, who sparkled in fifteen of Metro's productions from 1940 to 1947. Her gimmick was an attention-grabbing deadpan singing style in which she would remain almost sphinxlike while warbling a tune, usually about a man she did not want to lose. Were this gambit her only talent, Miss Red Hot Frozen Face, as some fan magazines called her, might well have paled with her public long before she and MGM separated company. But she was that rare item: a comedienne who was a looker (5' 6 1/2", dark brown hair). In addition, her deep voice was extremely pleasant in its mock delivery. In the occasional screen role in which she had an actual characterization to portray, she displayed an increasingly superior sense of comic timing. Had she had more faith in her overall cinema potentials, she might well have moved out of her guest appearance category into that of a regular second-line star.

Virginia was born April 18, 1922 in Los Angeles, where her father was captain of detectives of the police department. One uncle was postmaster of the city for twelve years and another uncle was screen director Lloyd Bacon. As a child she showed little interest in dramatics, but did study dancing. After graduating from North Hollywood High School she intended working for her father as a secretary, but her stage debut changed all such plans. For this debut she appeared with the Los Angeles Assistance League Players in *Meet the People* (1939). She claims that opening-night jitters caused her to freeze onstage and sing with her body immobile and face frozen. The audience, including Louis B. Mayer, howled with laughter, and Mayer signed her to a MGM contract. The studio gave their permission for her to leave *Meet the People*, which went to Broadway, in order to make her New York stage debut in *Keep off the Grass* (1940). This latter show toplined Jimmy Durante, Jane Froman, and Ray Bolger. As the N.Y. *Times'* Brooks Atkinson noted, "... [Virginia] convulses the audience by removing the ecstasy from high-pressure music." She remained with the revue for eight months.

Back in California, she made an inauspicious screen debut, playing a bit role as a wiseacre manicurist in *Hullabaloo* (1940), which starred Frank

Morgan. She then was lost in the Walter Pidgeon–Nick Carter detective entry, *Sky Murder* (1941), and was just one of the girls employed in the Marx Brothers' *The Big Store* (1941) in which she at least joined in the ensemble number, "Sing While You Sell." She was billed as herself in *Ringside Maisie* (1941) and sang "Your Words and My Music" in her third 1941 release, *Lady Be Good*. Resembling a combination of an older Virginia Weidler and a contemporary Noel Neill in this film, Virginia was cast as dimwit Red Skelton's gal, a quiet female who had a constant yen for food, whether it be a double T-bone steak or a banana.

By the time of Metro's unmemorable *Panama Hattie* (1942), also made with Ann Sothern and Red Skelton, Virginia had loosened up her screen delivery to give a needed variety to her deadpan crooning. She chirped the comic "Fresh as a Daisy" and the saucy "At the Savoy," the latter thought by contemporary standards to be a bit too suggestive. As Ginny, the girl of acid remarks in *Dubarry Was a Lady* (1943), she did "Salome." In *Thousands Cheer* (1943) she was part of the singing trio of Gloria DeHaven, June Allyson, and Virginia O'Brien, performing "In a Little Spanish Town," and made another splash with her frozen-muscle song delivery. She had a specialty number in *Two Girls and a Sailor* (1944), doing "Take It Easy," and appeared in the movie edition of *Meet the People* (1944). As Woodpecker Peg, the deadpan welder, she sang "Say That We're Sweethearts Again," in the big shipyard rally show scene. On radio Virginia was heard on the "Blue Ribbon Town" comedy–variety show (1943) with Groucho Marx and Kenny Baker.

Meanwhile Virginia in 1942 wed actor Kirk Alyn, who later was to become quasifamous as the motion picture Superman. They had a daughter, Teresa, and the couple would divorce in 1955.

Virginia's potentially richest screen year was 1946, but circumstances proved otherwise. In *Ziegfeld Follies* she was glamorously gowned and concluded the lavish "Bring on the Beautiful Girls" number, begun by Fred Astaire, with a parody, "Bring on the Beautiful Men," sung while she rode on a merry-go-round horse, frozen to her seat. She had never looked better in pictures than in this grandly mounted production scene. She then played one of *The Harvey Girls* who comes to New Mexico to be a waitress, but despairs of finding love in "The Wild, Wild West," a number sung while she is shoeing a horse. Because of her obvious pregnancy, her love scenes with coplayer Ray Bolger were eliminated from the filming schedule, and Virginia finally emerged in that picture no more than a specialty performer. She was barely used in Red Skelton's *The Show-Off* which showcased more curvaceous Marilyn Maxwell. The studio announced in the production publicity for *Till the Clouds Roll By* that Virginia would sing "Life upon the Wicked Stage," but in the final print of this plush movie musical, all she vocalized was "A Fine Romance," sans any man. This song was performed in conjunction with the *Show Boat* sequence in the film, in which she was Ellie, the same minor part Marge Champion would have in Metro's 1951 version of this musical.

Virginia's final MGM picture was *Merton of the Movies*, released in

1947. She was second-billed as the Hollywood stunt girl who befriends bumbling Red Skelton, her seemingly perennial MGM *vis-à-vis*. However, her sympathetic role was overshadowed by Gloria Grahame's eyecatching performance as a witless beauty. It was another eight years before Virginia returned to the silver screen, in Universal's *Francis in the Navy* (1955). This series entry had Donald O'Connor in a dual role and Virginia was thirteenth-billed in a small assignment. The following year her old MGM teammate Ann Sothern hired Virginia for a guest part in a *Private Secretary* episode ("The Reunion").

Club dates only followed, and then she wed building contractor Harry B. White. She is the mother of four children. Her eldest daughter, Terri, has an all-girl singing group. Virginia's sister, Mary, had a brief film career at Universal, appearing in such features as *Larceny with Music* (1943).

In the late 1960s a mature but still striking Virginia returned to show business, performing in *Merton of the Movies* at the Hollywood Masquers Club. Still on the go in 1972, she toured with Rudy Vallee in the short-lived nostalgia revue, *The Big Show of 1928*. When that entertainment package fizzled, she joined another revue in mid-1972, *The Big Show of 1936*, which featured such other former show business celebrities as Sally Rand, the Ink Spots, Cass Daley, and Allan Jones.

VIRGINIA O'BRIEN

Hullabaloo (MGM, 1940)
Sky Murder (MGM, 1940)
The Big Store (MGM, 1941)
Ringside Maisie (MGM, 1941)
Lady Be Good (MGM, 1941)
Ship Ahoy (MGM, 1942)
Panama Hattie (MGM, 1942)
Du Barry Was a Lady (MGM, 1943)
Thousands Cheer (MGM, 1943)

Two Girls and a Sailor (MGM, 1944)
Meet the People (MGM, 1944)
Ziegfeld Follies (MGM, 1946)
The Harvey Girls (MGM, 1946)
The Show-Off (MGM, 1946)
Till the Clouds Roll By (MGM, 1946)
Merton of the Movies (MGM, 1947)
Francis in the Navy (Universal, 1955)

With Red Skelton in *Panama Hattie* (1942)

Maureen O'Sullivan

Generally, when the name Maureen O'Sullivan is mentioned today, it conjures up two immediate show business connotations: (1) Tarzan's idyllic onscreen jungle mate and (2) Mia Farrow's mother. But both references ignore the fact that Maureen, with her wistful, piquant beauty and quiet sincerity, was MGM's favorite second-string ingenue in the studio's 1930s quality films and a lead in several of their B products during that decade.

As Irish as her name, Maureen was born Maureen Paul O'Sullivan on May 17, 1911 in Boyle, County Roscommon, Ireland. She was sent to school at the Convent of the Sacred Heart at Roehampton, near London, England. Although her classmate Vivien Leigh had already decided on a theatre career, nine-year-old Maureen was bent on becoming a pilot. As a youngster she recalls she was not much of a movie fan, although she remembers that: "I did once trade a $6 fountain pen for a picture of Rudolph Valentino." Later, Maureen attended school in Paris and then returned to Ireland to be with her family. She was attending one of the final dinner-dances of the yearly Dublin International Horse Show in 1930, where she caught the eye of director Frank Borzage, who was in Ireland filming location shots for Fox's *Song O' My Heart* (1930), starring John McCormack of opera fame. Borzage had the waiter send her a note: "If you are interested in being in a film, please come to my office tomorrow at 11 A.M. [Signed] Frank Borzage." Maureen later told the director she was not sure her father, a major in the Connaught Rangers, would approve. However, he did, and Maureen, accompanied by her mother, came to Hollywood to pursue a film career. Maureen recalls the whole episode as a fluke, but she jumped at the chance to spread her wings. "Boy, did I fly!"

Fox put Maureen under a short-term contract, and she appeared in such studio products as the fantasy *Just Imagine* (1930), and Will Rogers' *A Connecticut Yankee* (1931). However, after completing *Skyline*, Maureen left the studio, wisely comprehending that Fox's production head Winifred Shean was much more interested in promoting colleen star Janet Gaynor than in focusing his attention on the future of any newcomer. Maureen next signed a long-term contract with MGM and 1932 proved to be her most prolific year on the screen: nine films in release, made at four different studios. She was among those supporting Charles Laughton in the melodramatic *Payment*

537

Deferred, and in MGM's all-star *Strange Interlude* she played Madeline, the fiancée of Norma Shearer's illegitimate son. But it was her role as the refined Jane Porter in *Tarzan the Ape Man* that established Maureen's niche in screen history and made her a valuable asset to Metro. It was Irving Thalberg who decided that her dark-haired, delicate but curvaceous beauty would be the perfect complement to Johnny Weissmuller, already selected to play Edgar Rice Burroughs' immortal jungle hero. In this adventure film, directed by W. S. Van Dyke, who had helmed the studio's profitable *Trader Horn*, Maureen was fourth-billed as the British girl who comes to Africa to join her father, C. Aubrey Smith, and his partner, Neil Hamilton, on a trek to the legendary elephant burial grounds in search of ivory. It is not long before Tarzan comes upon the safari, spots the feminine beauty of Maureen, and whisks her away to his tree home.

The public of all ages was generally enthralled with this escapist entertainment and MGM set about making several followups, all to feature the team of Weissmuller and Maureen, with Cheetah the monkey for comic relief, and later Johnny Sheffield as Boy. The early Tarzan films had Jane projected as a beautiful, sensuous girl with a touch of sophistication, barely costumed in provocative strips of leather. Maureen later recalled, "Everybody cared about the Tarzan pictures and we all gave our best. They weren't quickies—it often took a year to make one—but sometimes we were doing three at a time." By 1936 the Will Hays Office began sending MGM directives about the scanty costumes and the use of animals in dangerous scenes, and soon the series became just another job. Besides, Maureen, who did not consider herself a lofty *artist* but had great respect for her profession, was more than miffed to become the subject of "Me Tarzan. You Jane" jokes. (The actual line in the Ivor Novello screenplay for *Tarzan the Ape Man* was "Tarzan–Jane.")

Meanwhile, she was utilized as one of MGM's loveliest ingenues in a variety of studio products: Robert Young's sweetheart in *Tugboat Annie* (1932), the heroine who seeks William Powell's help in *The Thin Man* (1934), as Henrietta Barrett, the most rebellious of Charles Laughton's children in *The Barretts of Wimpole Street* (1934), hapless Dora in *David Copperfield* (1935), virginal Kitty in *Anna Karenina* (1935), Allan Jones' love interest in the Marx Brothers' *A Day at the Races* (1937), Robert Taylor's nominal *vis-à-vis* in two 1938 releases, *A Yank at Oxford** and *The Crowd Roars*. Finally, in *Port of Seven Seas* (1938), she was the Gallic dockside waif in a picture forgotten because the French original of the story was done as a screen trilogy by Marcel Pagnol and later converted into a musical and new movie, titled *Fanny*. In *Pride and Prejudice* (1940) she was Elizabeth Bennett, and also supported Ann Sothern in *Maisie Was a Lady* (1941).

By the time of *Tarzan's New York Adventure* (1942), the sixth of the MGM series, Maureen had long tired of her professional career and preferred

---

*One of the film's scripters, F. Scott Fitzgerald, professed a great romantic admiration for Maureen, and at her request rewrote her part in the film to have substance and novelty.

to concentrate on her family life. On September 12, 1936, she had married John Farrow, a talented young Australian writer who was a junior scripter and part-time director on the aborted first version of *Tarzan Escapes* (1936), which was refilmed to appease the studio heads. Farrow soon became one of Hollywood's noted producer–director–writers. He received the New York Film Critics' award as best director for *Wake Island* (1942) and the Academy Award for the screenplay of Michael Todd's *Around the World in Eighty Days* (1956). The Farrows had seven children: Michael, Patrick, Maria (Mia), John, Prudence, Theresa (Tisa), and Stephanie. Their marriage was considered a Hollywood oddity. One friend said, "They stayed married to each other. They kept having babies. They went to church. John, in addition to producing important films, wrote serious books, among them a history of the papacy, a life of Sir Thomas More, the English saint, and an English–Tahitian dictionary. It was all very odd in film circles." Because of Maureen's frequent pregnancies, she often had to be photographed in the Tarzan entries from the waist up, or discreetly hidden behind oversized jugs and other props. When producer Sol Lesser took over the Tarzan series to be produced at RKO, Maureen rejected his offer to join Weissmuller and Sheffield who had moved over to that studio to continue the jungle entries. (In the first two RKO Tarzan pictures, Jane would be omitted from the storyline, written out of the script as being on vacation in England.)

Having completed *Tarzan's New York Adventure*, in which she wore a contemporary wardrobe, Maureen asked to be released from her MGM contract. Her husband Farrow had been discharged from the Navy with typhus and Maureen wanted to care for him personally. She remained a housewife for six years. Then when Farrow was directing Paramount's suspenser *The Big Clock* (1948), he persuaded Maureen to accept a featured role. Two years later she appeared again in one of her husband's films, RKO's *Where Danger Lives* (1950), but her part was gratuitous and basically she was unbelievable as Robert Mitchum's patient girl friend. Nor were her remaining 1950s features any better. During the middle 1950s she hostessed a syndicated television series, *Irish Heritage*, but spent most of her time nursing Mia, who had suffered a bout with polio. Then in 1958 her oldest son, Michael, was killed in an airplane crash while taking flying lessons.

By 1960 Maureen was convinced that she was permanently retired. However, fellow Irish actor Pat O'Brien talked her into opening in Chicago in the summer stock play called *Roomful of Roses* in 1961. A second stock venture the next year was so successful that producer George Abbott decided to mount it for Broadway. At first the play, which costarred Maureen with Paul Ford, was entitled *Cradle Will Rock*, but for the Broadway debut the title was changed to *Never Too Late*. It opened in November 1962, and was a smash hit. Maureen played a middle-aged wife who becomes pregnant and must cope with her new state of being. Two months after the opening, Maureen's husband died of a heart attack. "This was my moment of struggle — to decide which way my life should go. If we moved to a small town in California, I could manage financially without working and be home with the children. But I wondered whether I would have enough to give them when they came home at the end of the day and asked, 'Mommy, what's new, what's happened?' and all I would be able to say would be, 'Nothing much. The refrigerator broke down.' It sounded as if it might turn into a dreary life for all of us. Staying alone at home, I would not be able to lead them into the worlds of writing and music and art which John had shared with them. I decided finally to stay with the play and with my career."

Following *Never Too Late*, Maureen signed as the *Today* girl on NBC television, but soon tired of it, saying she got a crook in her neck looking from Hugh Downs to Jack Lescoulie and back again, with nothing much else to do. Warners cast both Paul Ford and Maureen in the film version of *Never Too Late*. The next year she appeared in another long-run play, the dramatic *The Subject Was Roses*. She also appeared in summer stock in *Barefoot in the Park* in 1969, and the next year was Mrs. Grant in the limited Broadway engagement of *The Front Page*. She played Amanda in *The Glass Menagerie* at Brandeis University in 1971, and the same year starred in a short-lived Broadway revival of *Charley's Aunt*. One of her first video appearances in America had been on a Fred Astaire segment of *Alcoa Presents*, having already played on television in England and Spain. In 1972 she joined with Douglas Fairbanks, Jr. and Ross Martin to costar with Rosalind Russell in *Crooked Hearts*, an *ABC Movie of the Week*. She returned to the footlights in *No Sex Please, We're British*, a comedy import from London, which arrived on Broadway in early 1973 after a west coast road tour.

Today Maureen is an executive director of Wediquette International, a bridal consulting service, and continues to make occasional professional appearances. She is an outspoken woman who thoroughly believes a mother should "let go" of her children, and that if youths wish to indulge in such experiences as marijuana it is their decision. (Both her sons have been arrested for possession of marijuana.) In 1966 Maureen denied marriage rumors that linked her with a 23-year-old rabbinical student, Henri Sobell. During all of the hullabaloo over daughter Mia's romance and marriage to Frank Sinatra, Maureen was heard to quip, "At his age, he should marry me!"

MAUREEN O'SULLIVAN

Song O'My Heart (Fox, 1930)
So This Is London (Fox, 1930)
Just Imagine (Fox, 1930)
Princess and the Plumber (Fox, 1930)
A Connecticut Yankee (Fox, 1931)
Skyline (Fox, 1931)
Tarzan the Ape Man (MGM, 1932)
The Silver Lining (Patrician, 1932)

Big Shot (RKO, 1932)
Information Kid (Universal, 1932)
Strange Interlude (MGM, 1932)
Skyscraper Souls (MGM, 1932)
Payment Deferred (MGM, 1932)
Okay America! (Universal, 1932)
Fast Companions (Universal, 1932)
Robber's Roost (Fox, 1933)

Cohens and Kellys in Trouble (Universal, 1933)
Tugboat Annie (MGM, 1933)
Stage Mother (MGM, 1933)
Tarzan and His Mate (MGM, 1934)
The Thin Man (MGM, 1934)
The Barretts of Wimpole Street (MGM, 1934)
Hideout (MGM, 1934)
West Point of the Air (MGM, 1935)
David Copperfield (MGM, 1935)
Cardinal Richelieu (UA, 1935)
The Flame Within (MGM, 1935)
Anna Karenina (MGM, 1935)
Woman Wanted (MGM, 1935)
The Bishop Misbehaves (MGM, 1935)
Tarzan Escapes (MGM, 1936)
The Voice of Bugle Ann (MGM, 1936)
The Devil-Doll (MGM, 1936)
A Day at the Races (MGM, 1937)
Between Two Women (MGM, 1937)
The Emperor's Candlesticks (MGM, 1937)
My Dear Miss Aldrich (MGM, 1937)
A Yank at Oxford (MGM, 1938)

Hold That Kiss (MGM, 1938)
Port of Seven Seas (MGM, 1938)
The Crowd Roars (MGM, 1938)
Spring Madness (MGM, 1938)
Let Us Live (Columbia, 1939)
Tarzan Finds a Son (MGM, 1939)
Pride and Prejudice (MGM, 1940)
Sporting Blood (MGM, 1940)
Tarzan's Secret Treasure (MGM, 1941)
Maisie Was a Lady (MGM, 1941)
Tarzan's New York Adventure (MGM, 1942)
The Big Clock (Paramount, 1948)
Where Danger Lives (RKO, 1950)
Bonzo Goes to College (Universal, 1952)
All I Desire (Universal, 1953)
Mission Over Korea (Columbia, 1953)
Duffy of San Quentin (WB, 1954)
The Steel Cage (UA, 1954)
The Tall T (Columbia, 1957)
Wild Heritage (Universal, 1958)
Never Too Late (WB, 1965)
The Phynx (WB, 1970)

With Dudley Digges and Norman Foster in *The Bishop Misbehaves* (1935)

541

With Ruth Hussey in *Spring Madness* (1938)

With Johnny Weissmuller and Johnny Sheffield in *Tarzan Finds a Son* (1939)

Reginald Owen

Along with C. Aubrey Smith, Nigel Bruce, and Edmund Gwenn, Reginald Owen proved to be the most regularly seen British "type" onscreen during the 1930s and 1940s. More so than his compatriots, Owen had the ability by adept use of makeup to disguise himself sufficiently to play scores of contrasting characterizations besides his usual movie stereotype roles. As such, he was a vital asset to MGM who used him on the average of five films a year, generally in substantial supporting parts. It was the continual reappearance of performers like Owen in scores of pictures over the years that gave a studio, like MGM, its particular flavor. Owen consistently contributed solidarity, versatility, and credibility in his gallery of movie roles.

He was born John Reginald Owen on August 5, 1887 in Wheathampstead, Herts, twenty-five miles outside of London. He was the son of Joseph and Francis (Bedford) Owen. His father was a furniture manufacturer. Owen was educated at the City of London School and, because he had demonstrated an avid interest in an acting career, he went on to study at Sir Herbert Tree's Academy of Dramatic Arts. There he appeared in such plays as *The Last of the Dandies*. In 1905 he made his professional debut at His Majesty's Theatre in London in a production of *The Tempest*. Thereafter he has not been idle in show business. He played Mr. Darling in *Peter Pan* (1908), Sir Andrew Aguecheek in *Twelfth Night* (1910), Messala in *Ben Hur* (1912) and a lead in *Our Betters* (1923). It was in that same year that Owen first came to America, to replace Philip Merivale as Prince Albert in the Chicago production of *The Swan.* Once in the United States, Owen decided to remain there and was soon performing on Broadway. His most notable success was as Cardinal Richelieu in *The Three Musketeers* (1928), produced by his good friend Florenz Ziegfeld. In 1930 Owen starred in a production of his own play, *Jack's Up*, in which he essayed a dual role. The show closed after a Providence, Rhode Island engagement.

Owen had made his film bow in 1916 in the British *A Place in the Sun*, released in the U. S. in 1919. Before coming to America in the mid-1920s, he made three other features, including the French-lensed *Phroso* (1923). In 1921 a movie version of *Where the Rainbow Ends* was released, based on the popular children's play Owen had written in collaboration with Mrs. Clifford Mills.

When the first film version of *The Letter* (1929) was made with Jeanne Eagels at Paramount's Long Island studios, Owen was featured as her husband. He came to Hollywood in 1930 and was put to work in MGM's *The Man in Possession* (1931) playing Robert Montgomery's older brother in this v-e-r-r-y British-flavored picture. Owen recently said that he believed it was he who first changed the stock screen stereotype of an Englishman to a more realistic facsimile, and soon became so popular in such assignments that he developed a whole new concept of the Anglo-Saxon type. One of his more intriguing assignments in his early Hollywood years was playing Sherlock Holmes in *A Study in Scarlet* (1933). Directed by Robert Florey he wrote the dialogue for the economy production, which went on to become a very profitable release and a mainstay of early-day television. Because he had played Dr. Watson in Fox's *Sherlock Holmes* the year before, Owen has the distinction of being the only actor to have played onscreen both Conan Doyle's sleuth and the bumbling doctor associate.

Meanwhile, Owen continued with his British man-on-the-screen, playing an ignoble lord in Robert Montgomery's *Lovers Courageous* (1932), and an eccentric classical scholar in *The Narrow Corner* (1933). In George Arliss' *Voltaire* (1933), he was King Louis XIV, and the next year in *Madame Dubarry*, he portrayed King Louis V. The first of his three acting assignments with Greta Garbo was *Queen Christina* (1933) in which he was cast as Prince Charles of Sweden, the popular hero the queen was supposed to wed. Owen considered Garbo his favorite screen actress: "There was a sensitivity about her, like the strings of a violin—an absolutely magical woman."

By 1934 Owen had wed for a second time, this time to Billey Edise. He had previously married Lydia Bilbrooke in 1908, and they had divorced in 1923. When his second wife died in 1956, he remarried later that same year to Mrs. Barbara Haveman.

In 1935 Owen settled into a long-term MGM contract which would be renewed continually until he left the studio in 1953. He proved quite versatile: as Stryver in *A Tale of Two Cities* (1935), Jeanette MacDonald's business manager in *Rose Marie* (1936), as William Powell's manager in *The Great Ziegfeld* (1936), and one of Robert Young's Tyrolean leisure set in *The Bride Wore Red* (1937). Lionel Barrymore had been scheduled to play Scrooge in MGM's *A Christmas Carol* (1938), but his crippling arthritic condition prevented him from doing so. Owen, who had been slated to play the ghost of Christopher Marley, was moved into the lead assignment, with Barrymore coaching him in the role. It remains one of the actor's most distinguished and best recalled film parts.

Owen's better roles in the late 1930s and 1940s were done away from MGM. In *The Real Glory* (1939), he was the commanding officer who becomes a barking martinet to conceal his growing blindness. He was a doddering Oxford don in Jack Benny's *Charley's Aunt* (1941), Charles Laughton's gentleman's gentleman in *Captain Kidd* (1945), the Duke of Malmunster in *Kitty* (1945), and the repressed husband of Judith Anderson in *The Diary of a*

Chambermaid (1946). MGM was still using him for the bumbling English type as in *If Winter Comes* (1947). In *The Miniver Story* (1950) he repeated his role of Mr. Foley from *Mrs. Miniver* (1942). His last MGM release was in the weak Red Skelton vehicle *The Great Diamond Robbery* (1953). He made seven pictures since 1962. He was a crochety hospital patient who terrifies the staff in *Tammy and the Doctor* (1963), and a butler in Rosalind Russell's *Rosie!* (1968). Walt Disney's company used him as an eccentric retired British admiral in *Mary Poppins* (1964) and as a stiff-upper-lipped militia leader in *Bedknobs and Broomsticks* (1971).

Owen had returned to Broadway in 1950 to appear in *Affairs of State,* his first New York play since 1932, and Preston Sturges' *Child of Manhattan.* In 1955–56 he participated as a member of the repertory group sponsored by the Moral Rearmament Group and in 1960 he was in the tryout of *Goodwill Ambassador* which closed out of town. At the age of eighty-four he returned to Broadway in 1972 in the revival of *A Funny Thing Happened on the Way to the Forum,* playing the role of Erronius, handled by Raymond Walburn in the original New York production. As the aging, incurably credulous neighbor, Owen was reported by Variety as "believable, vital, and line-perfect."

On November 5, 1972, Reginald Owen died of a heart attack at the age of eighty-five. He had been convalescing from a recent stroke at his stepson's home in Boise, Idaho.

Death prevented Owen from completing his newly-begun memoirs, which could have told readers a great deal about the history and the personalities of twentieth century theatre and cinema pictures. Owen was no stranger to writing, having written a number of books published several decades ago and authored two plays; he also co-wrote the screenplay to MGM's *Stablemates* (1938).

It was ironic that only a short time ago Owen was the very model of his philosophy that immense vitality is prerequisite to professional longevity. The very chipper gentleman had said, in a recent interview, regarding the deaths of most of his actor contemporaries, "It doesn't bother me. I'm surprised I'm still alive. But I'll never retire. I plan to be around for a while, and I shall always be doing something."

REGINALD OWEN

Sally in Our Alley (Turner, 1916)
A Place in the Sun (Triangle, 1919)
The Grass Orphan (Ideal, 1923)
Phroso (French, 1923)
The Letter (Paramount, 1929)
Platinum Blonde (Columbia, 1931)
The Man in Possession (MGM, 1931)
A Woman Commands (RKO, 1932)
Lovers Courageous (MGM, 1932)
Sherlock Holmes (Fox, 1932)

The Man Called Back (Tiffany, 1932)
Downstairs (MGM, 1932)
The Big Brain (RKO, 1933)
Double Harness (RKO, 1933)
A Study in Scarlet (World Wide, 1933)
The Narrow Corner (WB, 1933)
Voltaire (WB, 1933)
Queen Christina (MGM, 1933)
Nana (UA, 1934)
Stingaree (RKO, 1934)

With Joan Crawford, Franchot Tone, and Mona Barrie in *Love on the Run* (1936)

With Henrietta Crosman and E. E. Clive in *Personal Property* (1937)

Of Human Bondage (RKO, 1934)
The Human Side (Universal, 1934)
The House of Rothschild (UA, 1934)
Countess of Monte Cristo (Universal, 1934)
Here Is My Heart (Paramount, 1934)
Fashions of 1934 (WB, 1934)
Mandalay (WB, 1934)
Madame Dubarry (WB, 1934)
Where Sinners Meet (RKO, 1934)
Music in the Air (Fox, 1934)
Enchanted April (RKO, 1935)
Anna Karenina (MGM, 1935)
The Bishop Misbehaves (MGM, 1935)
Escapade (MGM, 1935)
A Tale of Two Cities (MGM, 1935)
The Good Fairy (Universal, 1935)
Call of the Wild (UA, 1935)
Petticoat Fever (MGM, 1936)
Rose Marie (MGM, 1936)
Yours for the Asking (Paramount, 1936)
Adventure in Manhattan (Columbia, 1936)
The Girl on the Front Page (Universal, 1936)
Love on the Run (MGM, 1936)
Trouble for Two (MGM, 1936)
The Great Ziegfeld (MGM, 1936)
Conquest (MGM, 1937)
Rosalie (MGM, 1937)
The Bride Wore Red (MGM, 1937)
Madame X (MGM, 1937)
Personal Property (MGM, 1937)
Dangerous Number (MGM, 1937)
Kidnapped (20th-Fox, 1938)
The Girl Downstairs (MGM, 1938)
A Chirstmas Carol (MGM, 1938)
Everybody Sing (MGM, 1938)
Paradise for Three (MGM, 1938)
Three Loves Has Nancy (MGM, 1938)
Vacation from Love (MGM, 1938)
Fast and Loose (MGM, 1939)
Hotel Imperial (Paramount, 1939)
Bridal Suite (MGM, 1939)
The Real Glory (UA, 1939)
Remember? (MGM, 1939)
Hullabaloo (MGM, 1940)
Pride and Prejudice (MGM, 1940)
The Earl of Chicago (MGM, 1940)
Florian (MGM, 1940)
Free and Easy (MGM, 1941)
Blonde Inspiration (MGM, 1941)
Tarzan's Secret Treasure (MGM, 1941)
A Woman's Face (MGM, 1941)
They Met in Bombay (MGM, 1941)

Lady Be Good (MGM, 1941)
Charley's Aunt (20th-Fox, 1941)
Random Harvest (MGM, 1942)
We Were Dancing (MGM, 1942)
I Married an Angel (MGM, 1942)
Pierre of the Plains (MGM, 1942)
Somewhere I'll Find You (MGM, 1942)
Cairo (MGM, 1942)
White Cargo (MGM, 1942)
Reunion in France (MGM, 1942)
Woman of the Year (MGM, 1942)
Mrs. Miniver (MGM, 1942)
Assignment in Britanny (MGM, 1943)
Madame Curie (MGM, 1943)
Three Hearts for Julia (MGM, 1943)
Above Suspicion (MGM, 1943)
Salute to the Marines (MGM, 1943)
The Canterville Ghost (MGM, 1944)
National Velvet (MGM, 1944)
Captain Kidd (UA, 1945)
She Went to the Races (MGM, 1945)
The Valley of Decision (MGM, 1945)
The Sailor Takes a Wife (MGM, 1945)
Kitty (Paramount, 1945)
Monsieur Beaucaire (Paramount, 1946)
The Diary of a Chambermaid (UA, 1946)
Cluny Brown (20th-Fox, 1946)
Thunder in the Valley (20th-Fox, 1947)
The Imperfect Lady (Paramount, 1947)
Green Dolphin Street (MGM, 1947)
If Winter Comes (MGM, 1947)
The Pirate (MGM, 1948)
Julia Misbehaves (MGM, 1948)
Hills of Home (MGM, 1948)
Piccadilly Incident (MGM, 1948)
The Three Musketeers (MGM, 1948)
The Secret Garden (MGM, 1949)
Challenge to Lassie (MGM, 1949)
Kim (MGM, 1950)
Ground for Marriage (MGM, 1950)
The Miniver Story (MGM, 1950)
The Great Diamond Robbery (MGM, 1953)
Red Garters (Paramount, 1954)
Five Weeks in a Balloon (20th-Fox, 1962)
Tammy and the Doctor (Universal, 1963)
The Thrill of It All (Universal, 1963)
Voice of the Hurricane (Selected Pictures, 1964)
Mary Poppins (BV, 1964)
Rosie! (Universal, 1968)
Bedknobs and Broomsticks (BV, 1971)

Cecilia Parker

"Cecilia Parker."

"Oh, you mean the British actor."

"No, not Cecil Parker. Cecilia Parker, the Canadian-born actress."

"Who?"

"Mickey Rooney's older sister in the *Andy Hardy* series!"

"Oh."

Such is the fate of blonde, athletic Cecilia, who had made over two dozen features in Hollywood, many of them as a Western heroine, before she found herself cast by MGM in *A Family Affair* (1937). Thereafter, she was used almost exclusively by the studio to function as part of the background for the Andy Hardy series along with Fay Holden as Ma Hardy and Sara Haden as Aunt Milly.

Cecilia was born in Fort William, Ontario, Canada on April 26, 1905, the daughter of a British army officer. During World War I the family lived in England, and when they returned to America, settled in the Los Angeles area. Cecilia attended Immaculate Heart Convent in Hollywood and Hollywood High School. She then went to the Toronto Academy of Music, planning a career in grand opera. However, during her years in Hollywood she had already worked in motion pictures as an extra, and in 1931 was signed by Fox for a series of features.

She was fleetingly seen in Fox's *Women of All Nations* (1931) which had Victor McLaglen and Edmund Lowe continue their *What Price Glory?* camaraderie escapades. But shortly after she found her cinema forte by playing the second fiddle to cowboy stars and their horses. Being a decent equestrienne, she appeared opposite George O'Brien in *The Rainbow Trail* (1932) and *Mystery Ranch* (1932). At Columbia she did *Unknown Valley* (1933) with Buck Jones, and for Monogram made *Riders of Destiny* (1933) with John Wayne. Since she was known as an actress who could take the rough and tumble of horse opera filmmaking, she was cast by Mascot studios as Clyde Beatty's *vis-à-vis*.

Cecilia first broke out of this Western-action film rut with her assignment as Greta Garbo's sister in MGM's *The Painted Veil* (1934). She returned to Metro a year later to appear in Eugene O'Neill's *Ah, Wilderness!*

548

(1935) playing Muriel, the sweetheart of Lionel Barrymore's older son, Eric Linden. After playing the homesick coquette friend of Jeanette MacDonald in *Naughty Marietta* (1935), Metro reunited Cecilia with Linden in *Old Hutch* (1936), primarily a Wallace Beery vehicle. Then poverty row production company Grand National hired the two players for three more costarring pictures: *In His Steps* (1936), *Girl Loves Boy* (1937), and *Sweetheart of the Navy* (1937). They might have become the forerunners of Warners' more potent love team Priscilla Lane and Jeffrey Lynn, but Grand National was in no financial position to publicize this new type of "screen magic" to any noticeable or effective degree.

Meanwhile Cecilia made another Western with George O'Brien, *Hollywood Cowboy* (1937), and then was cast in *A Family Affair* as Marion Hardy, one of Lionel Barrymore's and Spring Byington's three offspring, along with older, married sister Julie Hayden and younger brother Mickey Rooney. Of course, this entry had Eric Linden as Cecilia's sweetheart. When MGM decided to make a full-fledged series of the Hardy family adventures, Barrymore and Byington were replaced with Lewis Stone and Fay Holden, and Hayden was dropped from the story line. In the new format Cecilia was now Rooney's nineteen-year-old sister. She was actually twenty-eight at the time. In *You're Only Young Once* (1938) Cecilia had a good share of the screen time, since the story revolved about a summer romance when the Hardys vacation in Santa Catalina. In *Out West with the Hardys* (1938) she learns the hard way that her cowboy idol, Gordon Jones, is not the man for her; and in *The Hardys Ride High* (1939) she falls victim to nouveau-riche airs when the middle-class family suddenly become legatees to a large fortune.

In 1938 Cecilia wed actor Robert Baldwin and they had two sons and a daughter. For a spell, Cecilia's sister Linda had a MGM contract.

MGM finally cast her in a nonseries entry, the programmer *Burn 'Em Up O'Connor* (1939) with Dennis O'Keefe, and then on loanout to PRC, she, Gale Storm, and Janet Shaw played the title roles in *Gambling Daughters* (1941). Because of her pregnancy she was absent from *Andy Hardy's Private Secretary* (1941) and *Life Begins For Andy Hardy* (1941), but she was used to support Van Heflin and Patricia Dane in *Grand Central Murder* (1942), and was one of the less conspicuous of S. Z. Sakall's daughters in *Seven Sweethearts* (1942). With *Andy Hardy's Double Life* (1942), Cecilia's MGM contract expired and she retired from the screen.

When Mickey Rooney resurrected his old series in *Andy Hardy Comes Home* (1958), fifty-three-year-old Cecilia, already a grandmother, was again on tap as Marion, looking far less than her actual age. It has been her last professional work to date.

With Mickey Rooney in *Out West with the Hardys* (1938)

CECILIA PARKER

Women of All Nations (Fox, 1931)
Young as You Feel (Fox, 1931)
The Rainbow Trail (Fox, 1932)
Mystery Ranch (Fox, 1932)
Tombstone Canyon (World-Wide, 1932)
Unknown Valley (Columbia, 1933)
Rainbow Ranch (Monogram, 1933)
The Fugitive (Monogram, 1933)
Riders of Destiny (Monogram, 1933)
Damaged Lives (Weldon Pictures, 1933)
Secret Sinners (Mayfair, 1933)
Gun Justice (Universal, 1934)
Trail Drive (Universal, 1934)
The Man Trailer (Columbia, 1934)
Lost Jungle (Serial and Feature: Mascot, 1934)
I Hate Women (Goldsmith, 1934)
The Painted Veil (MGM, 1934)
Here Is My Heart (Paramount, 1934)
Enter Madame (Paramount, 1935)
High School Girl (Better Films, 1935)
Ah, Wilderness! (MGM, 1935)
Naughty Marietta (MGM, 1935)
Three Live Ghosts (MGM, 1935)
The Mine with the Iron Door (Columbia, 1936)

Below the Deadline (Chesterfield, 1936)
Old Hutch (MGM, 1936)
In His Steps (Grand National, 1936)
Girl Loves Boy (Grand National, 1937)
A Family Affair (MGM, 1937)
Hollywood Cowboy (RKO, 1937)
Sweetheart of the Navy (Grand National, 1937)
Judge Hardy's Children (MGM, 1938)
You're Only Young Once (MGM, 1938)
Love Finds Andy Hardy (MGM, 1938)
Out West with the Hardys (MGM, 1938)
Burn 'Em Up O'Connor (MGM, 1939)
The Hardys Ride High (MGM, 1939)
Andy Hardy Gets Spring Fever (MGM, 1939)
Judge Hardy and Son (MGM, 1939)
Andy Hardy Meets Debutante (MGM, 1940)
Gambling Daughters (PRC, 1941)
The Courtship of Andy Hardy (MGM, 1942)
Grand Central Murder (MGM, 1942)
Seven Sweethearts (MGM, 1942)
Andy Hardy's Double Life (MGM, 1942)
Andy Hardy Comes Home (MGM, 1958)

Jean Parker

Jean Parker was one of the many "sweet young things" fed into the MGM factory system of the early 1930s. Professionally untrained, she was merely required to blush attractively on cue and to dab coyly with a handkerchief at her large moist eyes, as she sashayed from one cardboard role to another. Given the usual high mortality rate of professional survival in the cinema, it was surprising that she lasted for another decade in movies after MGM dropped her, mostly as a leading lady of B films. This slow decline was even more a pity in that she belatedly developed comic talents along the line of Jean Arthur and that they went unused by filmmakers. She had passed her ingenue prime before many discovered her true screen potentials.

Jean was born Lois Mae Greene on August 11, 1915, though some sources say 1912. Her actual birthplace is Butte, Montana, but as she recently said, "I thought Deer Lodge sounded more romantic for my studio biography." When she was eight months old the family moved to Pasadena, California, where she grew up. While attending the local John Muir High School, where she played in the school orchestra, she and other students were invited to enter an art poster competition celebrating the upcoming 1932 Olympics Games to be held in Los Angeles. As a winner of this competition, Jean was invited to be one of the models decorating the floats in the Pasadena Tournament of Roses. A more important result of the contest was that her photo appeared in the Los Angeles *Times*, where Louis B. Mayer's secretary, Ida Koverman, spotted it and had her auditioned. Jean recalls: "MGM put me in a Jean Harlow dress and curled my hair for my screen test."

Metro signed her to a term contract. After a bit part in Jackie Cooper's *Divorce in the Family* (1932), she had a slightly larger role as the little Duchess Maria in *Rasputin and the Empress* (1932). For a nonexperienced actress she made a sizable number (seven) of films in 1933, each role largely dependent on her radiant youthful looks. She was Phillips Holmes' girl in *The Secret of Madame Blanche*, Danitza in the Serbian-set *Storm at Daybreak*, May Robson's demure daughter in Columbia's *Lady for a Day*, and the angelic Beth who dies in RKO's *Little Women*. The latter was her favorite screen role. Jean received the largest amount of her publicity that year for starring in Columbia's *What Price Innocence?* It was a "daring" exposé, denouncing parents who fail to offer their children proper sex education. As Minna Gombell's daughter, Jean played the unsuspecting miss who is seduced by a beau and then, in a moment of panic, kills herself. During the release of this film Jean was graduated from high school.

Metro's *Lazy River* (1934) set in the Louisiana bayou country, established the general tone for Jean's special screen type: the home-bred rural girl who blends well with rare nature settings. This characterization she repeated to better advantage in the well-remembered wildlife picture, *Sequoia* (1934). She and Russell Hardie had the leads in that film, in reality, but both played support to the film study of the friendship of a puma and a deer in the California mountains. Among her other 1934 pictures were stock assignments as the daughter of bank president Lewis Stone in *You Can't Buy Everything*. In Paramount's *Limehouse Blues* she was the object of George Raft's affection. Regarding her role as a "livin'-in girl," she now says: "I didn't even know what the term, 'livin'-in' meant." She was the pert second female lead to Marion Davies in Metro's *Operator 13* and the same to Loretta Young in Fox's *Caravan*. Jean had to fight hard with Metro to win that loanout assignment. She concluded her Metro stay with the heroine's role in *Murder in the Fleet* (1935).

By 1935 Jean had established a degree of screen popularity, more from the quantity than the quality of her cinema efforts, and was selected to play Eugene Pallette's daughter and Robert Donat's love object in *The Ghost Goes West* (1936). During the London filming of this picture, there was much news in the gossip columns of a romance between Jean and the then-married Donat. This film was the last true peak in her film career, and she was still in her early twenties! It was also in 1936 that she wed New York newsman George MacDonald. They were divorced in 1940, and she then married radio commentator Douglas Dawson in 1941. After they were divorced, she wed Los Angeles insurance broker Curtis Brottier in 1944. That marriage lasted longer than her previous ones, a total of five years. After her divorce from Brottier, she and actor Robert Lowery married in 1951. They had a son, Robert, Jr., and the couple were divorced in 1957.

Jean reverted to backwoods tales with Monogram's *Romance of the Limberlost* (1938) and Columbia's *Romance of the Redwoods* (1939). She then played the girl in *Zenobia* (1939), which paired declining screen comedians Oliver Hardy and Harry Langdon. Later in the same year Jean enacted the flirtatious femme in Stan Laurel and Oliver Hardy's *The Flying Deuces*. For a time it seemed she might buck her descending screen status by winning the role of Melanie in *Gone with the Wind*, but the part went to Olivia de Havilland. Thereafter Jean habitually decorated cheaply made products such as Republic's *She Married a Cop* (1939) and Paramount's Western, *Knights of the Range* (1940) with Russell Hayden. *Beyond Tomorrow* (1940), an above-average B film, had her playing opposite Richard Carlson. The picture has long been a standard item for Christmas season telecasting.

At this juncture Jean associated herself professionally with William

Pine and William Thomas, who headed an economy feature unit at Paramount. Their pictures extended Jean's screen career throughout the early 1940s. From *Power Dive* (1941) through *One Body Too Many* (1944) she appeared in eleven of their productions, as a part of their stock company which included Buster Crabbe, Richard Arlen, and Chester Morris. She would later blame this "overexposure" for ending her screen value. Meanwhile, for other studios, she was the heart's desire of Parisian murderer John Carradine in *Bluebeard* (1944), and played an amateur sleuth in *Detective Kitty O'Day* (1944). She also made a followup to the latter, titled *The Adventures of Kitty O'Day* (1945).

Despite the low production quality of her post-MGM screen work, Jean had acquired an increasingly better command of acting technique and even ventured into summer stock, starring in *Candlelight, Guest in the House*, and *Berkeley Square*. She also did a vaudeville tour with an act that combined skits, songs, and a can-can dance. Her Broadway debut was in the short-lasting *Loco* (1946), followed by a tour of *Dream Girl* later that year. She had hoped to star in the West Coast company of the Elmer Rice play, but the choice role went to Lucille Ball. Then Jean was teamed with Bert Lahr in the 1948 revival of *Burlesque*, and during the next year joined with Lon Chaney, Jr. in the road company version of *Born Yesterday*. At one point both she and Lucille Ball were strong contenders for the lead in Columbia's screen version of that comedy, but the role finally went to Judy Holliday. Nevertheless, Garson Kanin, author of *Born Yesterday*, made it known he thought Jean the best of all the stage Billie Dawns! Had Jean stuck to stage work, her career might have taken a significant upswing.

She returned to pictures in 1950, but she had to be content playing the brief role of the seasoned tough frontier town woman Molly in *The Gunfighter*. Thereafter, she found it increasingly difficult to obtain screen parts. When she did, it was as the typecast hard-boiled broad, as in *Those Redheads from Seattle* (1953), produced by her 1940s employers, Pine–Thomas. In Edward G. Robinson's low budget *Black Tuesday* (1954) she went the Mary Beth Hughes acting route and played a mature moll. Between her role in *The Parson and the Outlaw* (1957) and a small part in the inexpensive Western, *Apache Uprising* (1966), there were a few television appearances, but not much.

Jean currently lives in Eagle Rock, near Pasadena, with her son Robert, Jr. who is attending Santa Barbara University. She is eager for acting work, but there are few assignments available for a nearly sixty-year-old ingenue.

JEAN PARKER

Divorce in the Family (MGM, 1932)
Rasputin and the Empress (MGM, 1932)
Secret of Madame Blanche (MGM, 1933)
Gabriel over the White House (MGM, 1933)
Made on Broadway (MGM, 1933)

Storm at Daybreak (MGM, 1933)
What Price Innocence (Columbia, 1933)
Lady for a Day (Columbia, 1933)
Little Women (RKO, 1933)
Lazy River (MGM, 1934)

You Can't Buy Everything (MGM, 1934)
Two Alone (RKO, 1934)
Operator 13 (MGM, 1934)
Sequoia (MGM, 1934)
A Wicked Woman (MGM, 1934)
Caravan (Fox, 1934)
Have a Heart (MGM, 1934)
Limehouse Blues (Paramount, 1934)
Princess O'Hara (Universal, 1935)
Murder in the Fleet (MGM, 1935)
The Ghost Goes West (UA, 1936)
The Farmer in the Dell (RKO, 1936)
The Texas Rangers (Paramount, 1936)
The Barrier (Paramount, 1937)
Life Begins with Love (Columbia, 1937)
Penitentiary (Columbia, 1938)
Romance of the Limberlost (Monogram, 1938)
The Arkansas Traveler (Paramount, 1938)
Zenobia (UA, 1939)
Romance of the Redwoods (Columbia, 1939)
She Married a Cop (Republic, 1939)
Flight at Midnight (Republic, 1939)
Parents on Trial (Columbia, 1939)
The Flying Deuces (RKO, 1939)
Son of the Navy (Monogram, 1940)
Knights of the Range (Paramount, 1940)
Beyond Tomorrow (RKO, 1940)
The Roar of the Press (Monogram, 1941)
Power Dive (Paramount, 1941)
Flying Blind (Paramount, 1941)
The Pittsburgh Kid (Republic, 1941)

No Hands on the Clock (Paramount, 1941)
Torpedo Boat (Paramount, 1942)
The Girl from Alaska (Republic, 1942)
Hi, Neighbor (Republic, 1942)
Hello, Annapolis (Columbia, 1942)
I Live on Danger (Paramount, 1942)
Tomorrow We Live (PRC, 1942)
Wrecking Crew (Paramount, 1942)
The Traitor Within (Republic, 1942)
Alaska Highway (Paramount, 1943)
Minesweeper (Paramount, 1943)
The Deerslayer (Republic, 1943)
High Explosive (Paramount, 1943)
The Navy Way (Paramount, 1944)
Detective Kitty O'Day (Monogram, 1944)
The Lady in the Death House (PRC, 1944)
Oh, What a Night! (Monogram, 1944)
Dead Man's Eyes (Universal, 1944)
Bluebeard (PRC, 1944)
One Body Too Many (Paramount, 1944)
The Adventures of Kitty O'Day (Monogram, 1945)
The Gunfighter (20th-Fox, 1950)
Toughest Man in Arizona (Republic, 1952)
Those Redheads from Seattle (Paramount, 1953)
Black Tuesday (UA, 1954)
A Lawless Street (Columbia, 1955)
The Parson and the Outlaw (Columbia, 1957)
Apache Uprising (Paramount, 1966)

With Marion Davies in *Operator 13* (1934)

Susan Peters

More so than the equally tragedy-struck Suzan Ball at Twentieth Century-Fox, Susan Peters was definitely a star in the making. Had she not been crippled in 1944 at the age of twenty-two, she would have become a major MGM player. She possessed a young but strong face and the ability to project unwavering sincerity in even the sloppiest of roles dished out to her in her Metro buildup period.

Susan was born Suzanne Carnahan in Spokane, Washington on July 3, 1921. When her father, a construction engineer, was killed in a car crash, Susan was sent at the age of seven to Los Angeles to live with her grandmother, then a leading dermatologist. Susan thought of becoming a physician herself for a while, but she became intrigued with the theatre while at the Flintridge Sacred Heart School and at Hollywood High. During summer vacation she was an elevator operator, wrap girl, and salesgirl at a local department store, but upon graduation from school enrolled at Max Reinhardt's School of Dramatic Arts in Hollywood. While performing in a showcase production of *Holiday*, she was spotted by a talent scout, tested, and signed to a Warner Brothers' contract.

She and Warners got off to a bad start when their publicity department handed her a new screen name, Sharon O'Keefe. She objected and insisted upon sticking with her real name. She was twenty-fourth-billed as Charlotte in Errol Flynn's *Santa Fe Trail* (1940) and was equally lost in such pictures as *Money and the Woman* (1940) with Brenda Marshall, and George Brent's *The Man Who Talked Too Much* (1940). She tested unsuccessfuly for *Kings' Row* (1941) and lost out to Warners' own Joan Leslie for a prize part in Gary Cooper's *Sergeant York* (1941), repeatedly being told by the casting-department she looked too young onscreen. MGM borrowed her for *Susan and God* (1940), in which she played one of the young girls surrounding Rita Quigley, Joan Crawford's onscreen daughter. At the time director George Cukor informed Susan: "You'll be all right, Susan, if only you didn't talk through your nose. Your voice doesn't flow. It squeals."

Back at Warners, she was just a "girl" in *Strawberry Blonde* (1941), an autograph hound in *Meet John Doe* (1941), and she endured four more nothing parts, one on loan to RKO, before she had her break in *The Big Shot* (1942).

Here she was fourth-billed as Ruth Carter, the girl friend of Richard Travis, the prison-convicted associate of gangster Humphrey Bogart.

The remaining five of Susan's 1942 releases were made under her new MGM contract, in which she was now billed as Susan Peters. During the initial rounds of interviews, she told the press she gave herself three years to become a star. In *Tish*, one of Marjorie Main's less happy vehicles, Susan was the girl Main wants nephew Lee Bowman to wed. But it develops that Susan has already married Richard Quine. He is killed in the war, and she dies during childbirth. (In real life, Susan and actor-turned-director Quine would marry in November of 1943.) Next, Susan was featured as Greer Garson's fifteen-year-old daughter Kitty in *Random Harvest*, and won an Academy Award nomination. But then it was back to programmers: Stephen McNally's wife in *Dr. Gillespie's New Assistant*, and a Wainright college girl in *Andy Hardy's Double Life* (filmed before her other Metro releases of that year).

Even if MGM were not sure how to manipulate Susan's movie career, she offered full-bodied performances as one of the two sweethearts along with Signe Hasso, of Jean Pierre Aumont in *Assignment in Brittany* (1943). Signe Hasso was the other woman in Aumont's life in this picture. Aumont plays a loyal Frenchman who is substituted for a look-alike pro-Nazi and returns to the latter's hometown. From this film, Susan was tossed into *Young Ideas* (1943), top-billed as Mary Astor's daughter who, along with brother Elliot Reid, disapproves of the man (Herbert Marshall) mama marries. It was a sappy part, more suitable for studio contractee Virginia Weidler. Then in the studio's elaborate paean to America's war ally, she was costarred with Robert Taylor in *Song of Russia* (1943), he being the prominent American symphony conductor who meets solemn Russian girl Susan in Moscow. This was the feature film that caused the studio so much embarrassment during the later McCarthy Red scare hearings.

For her three 1943 performances Susan was named a star of tomorrow, along with Metro's Van Johnson and Philip Dorn and others, such as Warners' Alexis Smith and Gig Young. Susan was off the screen in 1944, but appeared with Lana Turner and Laraine Day in the vapid *Keep Your Powder Dry* in 1945. She was the humble soldier's wife in this glossy but empty account of a trio of contrasting World War II WACS.

Before *Keep Your Powder Dry* was released, Susan suffered a tragedy that marred the remainder of her life. On New Year's Day, 1944, she and her husband were on a hunting trip in San Diego when she accidentally discharged her gun. The bullet lodged in her spine, and as a result of the accident she was permanently paralyzed from the waist down. During her long recovery, MGM retained her on a $100 weekly salary but later settled her contract. For a long period, Susan would be driven almost daily to a parking area just outside the MGM lot to visit with studio friends and to keep in touch with the industry she missed so much.

In 1946 Susan and Quine adopted a son, Timothy, and two years later she divorced Quine. Rumors had it that the marital split was due to her determination not to be a handicap to him. In that same year she made a rather well-publicized film comeback in Columbia's *The Sign of the Ram* (1948). The film was set on the Cornish coast, and she had the tailor-made role of a wheelchair-ridden woman married to Alexander Knox. The plot revolved around her warped efforts to destroy the happiness of her stepchildren. This John Sturges-directed film was unpopular, although James Agee observed in *The Nation*: " ... [she] polishes off a hearty histrionic banquet at her leisure."

Later in 1948, resilient Susan toured the winter stock circuit in *The Glass Menagerie*, followed by yet a longer tour in *The Barretts of Wimpole Street*. She then beat Raymond Burr's *Ironside* to the punch by several years, when she starred in a Philadelphia-based video series, *Miss Susan* (March 1951–December 1951), playing a woman lawyer confined to a wheelchair.

Susan returned to California after completing this series and went into virtual seclusion. She died there on October 23, 1952, at the age of thirty-one. Both the attending physician and friends of the actress stated, as in true movie tradition, that the ultimate cause of Susan's death was her loss of the will to live.

SUSAN PETERS

Santa Fe Trail (WB, 1940)
Money and the Woman (WB, 1940)
The Man Who Talked Too Much (WB, 1940)
Susan and God (MGM, 1940)
Strawberry Blonde (WB, 1941)
Meet John Doe (WB, 1941)
Here Comes Happiness (WB, 1941)
Scattergood Pulls the Strings (RKO, 1941)
Three Sons O'Guns (WB, 1941)
Escape from Crime (WB, 1942)

The Big Shot (WB, 1942)
Tish (MGM, 1942)
Random Harvest (MGM, 1942)
Dr. Gillespie's New Assistant (MGM, 1942)
Andy Hardy's Double Life (MGM, 1942)
Assignment in Brittany (MGM, 1943)
Young Ideas (MGM, 1943)
Song of Russia (MGM, 1943)
Keep Your Powder Dry (MGM, 1945)
The Sign of the Ram (Columbia, 1948)

With Robert Taylor in *Song of Russia* (1943)

Walter Pidgeon

During the 1930s William Powell and Myrna Loy represented MGM's version of the perfect marriage. They were bright, witty, and reveled in a touch of the screwball. Above all, they were fun! By the time the United States was involved in World War II, MGM's perfect marriage changed from just fun to the noble solidarity exemplified by genteel Greer Garson and solid Walter Pidgeon. In this manner Pidgeon gained stardom in a medium in which he had already been plying his trade for fifteen years. He had gained some eminence in the late 1920s as a lead in filmed operettas, thanks to a pleasant baritone voice, and as a dramatic actor in either second leads or starring assignments in B pictures. Finally, with most of MGM's male contingent serving in the war, Pidgeon was promoted to full-fledged stardom in several handsomely mounted romantic dramas starring that gallant personality of personalities, Greer Garson. They became so popular a screen husband–wife team, that Garson was referred to on the MGM lot as the "daytime Mrs. Pidgeon." While these pictures always emphasized Garson, Pidgeon effectively projected his personality: that of the perfect domesticated male, devoted, honorable, and stoic. He has never been an exciting actor, but he is an enduring one, and when he aged beyond romantic leads, he continued to project the same solidarity in top character roles. He is still active professionally today in his late seventies.

Walter David Pidgeon was born on September 23, 1897 in East St. John, New Brunswick, Canada, where his father owned a haberdashery. At nineteen, after one year at the University of New Brunswick, he earned a lieutenant's commission in the Canadian Field Artillery, 65th Battery, but was crushed between two gun carriages and spent seventeen months in the hospital before he was discharged. He moved to Boston in 1919 to be with his childhood sweetheart, Edna Pickles, who was studying art. They married in 1922, but Edna died in childbirth the following year, and Pidgeon's mother raised their daughter Edna Verne. Pidgeon remained in Boston to study singing at the New England Conservatory of Music, because he possessed a potentially sterling singing baritone. He also joined E. E. Clive's Copley Players and made his stage debut with the company in Shaw's *You Can Never Tell*.

While singing at a cocktail party one evening, Pidgeon was heard by Fred Astaire, who was in Boston with his sister Adele, starring in *Lady Be Good.* Astaire arranged for Pidgeon to audition with Arthur Hammerstein and Charles Dillingham in New York. They did not take him on, but stage entertainer Elsie Janis did, making him her leading man in her tour of *At Home* in the United States and England. When he auditioned for Janis, he did so under the name of Walter Verne, after his daughter, but Janis suggested he should stick to Pidgeon, because it was so funny and people would remember it. Pidgeon introduced two songs on that tour which became hits, Irving Berlin's "What'll I Do" and "All Alone." He was also the first to record "What'll I Do" and "Remember" on the Victor label. His first Broadway appearance was also with Janis, a revue called *Puzzles of 1925* and *Variety* said, "Pidgeon looks like an old and stale Abe Lincoln and sings like the graduate of a southern Iowa correspondence school. Who wants vaudeville when it involves that?"

Such a review was hardly encouraging, but Paramount Pictures thought he would be good as the lead in a Constance Talmadge vehicle and he arrived in Hollywood in 1925. The film they gave him was not with Talmadge, and he was not the leading man. *Mannequin* (1926) starred Alice Joyce and Warner Baxter and he had a supporting role as a reporter. Similar supporting roles followed when First National hired him as their house baritone, and cast him in several all-talking, all-singing, all-stagnant Vitaphone operetta: *Bride of the Regiment* (1930), *Viennese Nights* (1930), *Sweet Kitty Belairs* (1930), and *Kiss Me Again* (1931). However, musicals were dead and Pidgeon knew it. He decided to concentrate on dramatic acting. As he later said, "I was almost wrecked by musicals. I was established as a singer at a time when they couldn't give musicals away." (For one of these musicals there was actually a sign in a theatre lobby that read: "Mr. Pidgeon will sing only once in this picture.")

He turned to the theatre and replaced Melvyn Douglas in *No More Ladies* (1934) on Broadway and then played with Tallulah Bankhead in *Something Gay,* which lasted only nine weeks. However, in 1935 he got a substantial role as a gangster in *The Night of January 16,* and the show ran for fifteen months. When it closed, he rejected the lead in Universal's *Showboat,* preferring not to do any more screen musicals. He put himself under contract with film producer Walter Wanger and when that did not pan out satisfactorily, he signed on at Universal. His assignments at this studio were only four unsatisfactory programmers. So in 1937 he was eager to accept an MGM offer to join their stable. At age forty he hardly could have expected that screen stardom was literally around the corner.

MGM initially slapped the 6' 3" actor with a string of second leads. In one year, 1938, he lost Jeanette MacDonald to Nelson Eddy in *The Girl of the Golden West,* Margaret Sullavan to James Stewart in *The Shopworn Angel,* and Myrna Loy to Clark Gable in *Too Hot to Handle. Nick Carter, Master Detective* (1939) was the first of three detective entries he made within a year. In 1941, Twentieth Century-Fox borrowed him for the excellent Fritz Lang suspense picture, *Man Hunt*, and he was so resolutely good as the big game hunter that they used his services again, giving him one of the best roles of his long career as the clergyman, Mr. Gruffydd, in *How Green Was My Valley* (1941). That Oscar-winning picture was directed by John Ford. Pidgeon said at the time: "I'd never known a director like John Ford. My experiences with him on *How Green Was My Valley* force me to conclude that he operates by telepathy. He smokes a pipe constantly—I doubt if he removes it from his mouth except to eat. He certainly doesn't remove it merely to talk. Furthermore, when he speaks, he mumbles. There's no kinder expression for it. I listened intently to his instructions and if five words out of seventy-five were intelligible I considered it a good average. With most directors the results of such obscurity would be hopeless confusion. With Ford, no. You go out on the set and find yourself following orders you haven't heard."

Finally MGM put him in *Blossoms in the Dust* (1941) with Greer Garson, and it was the beginning of cinema stardom for them both. He was a reporter to Rosalind Russell's hyperactive judge in *Design for Scandal* (1941), then returned with Garson for *Mrs. Miniver* (1942), the most popular of their films together. It grossed $5.5 million. While that picture was laden with lachrymose sentiment, and Garson received most of the publicity as well as the Oscar, Pidgeon was correctly understanding in his portrayal of Clem Miniver, and received his first Academy Award nomination. He lost out to James Cagney for *Yankee Doodle Dandy*.

When contract renewal time came up for Pidgeon at MGM, he went to see Louis B. Mayer. According to reports, their lengthy meeting dealt with St. Johns, where Russian immigrant Mayer had spent his childhood. They discussed life there and the people. Eventually the subject of Pidgeon's salary was broached. Pidgeon said: "Louis, I'm going to leave this in your hands. As a hometown boy, I know you'll do right by me." Pidgeon would later inform associates that no price had been mentioned at the meeting but that, when his new contract was prepared, it stipulated a weekly salary almost double what he had expected.

With a stiff upper lip, Pidgeon played a jungle plantation overseer who fends off Tondelayo (Hedy Lamarr) in *White Cargo* (1942). *Madame Curie* (1943), again with Garson, earned him his second Academy Award nomination, and *Mrs. Parkington* (1944), also with Garson, was mainly lush soap opera as only MGM could do it. More typical MGM fare followed: *Weekend at the Waldorf* (1945) (in the John Barrymore *Grand Hotel* role), *The Secret Heart* (1946), *If Winter Comes* (1947), and *Julia Misbehaves* (1949), a silly programmer with Garson. Then he was given the most solid role of his career, the general in *Command Decision* (1948), a fine picture.

By now Pidgeon was in his fifties, and after three more pictures with Garson, the audiences would no longer buy their romantic respectability. Pidgeon's screen career veered naturally to character roles. He was creditable as the Hollywood producer in *The Bad and the Beautiful* (1952), as one of the six vice presidents in *Executive Suite* (1954), and as the American expatriate

With Henry Kolker and Myrna Loy in *Too Hot to Handle* (1938)

With Leo Carrillo and Jack Gardner in *Society Lawyer* (1939)

With Joyce Compton in *Sky Murder* (1940)

563

father of Elizabeth Taylor in *The Last Time I Saw Paris* (1954). In 1956 he was cast as the scientist father of Anne Francis in *Forbidden Planet*, one of MGM's rare excursions into the science fiction genre. After portraying Paul Newman's tradition-bound dad in *The Rack* (1956), he ended his MGM contract and was one of the few actors eligible for pension. Greer Garson was another one. That same year he enjoyed a run on Broadway in *The Happiest Millionaire* as Philadelphia's Anthony J. Drexel Biddle. He toured in this play for another eight months. When Walt Disney later made a musical film of the play, Pidgeon hoped to re-create his stage assignment, but Disney told him he was too old for the part and gave the role to Fred MacMurray. Pidgeon returned to Broadway in 1959 as Nat Miller in *Take Me Along*, a musical version of Eugene O'Neill's *Ah, Wilderness!*, starring Jackie Gleason as Uncle Sid. In 1966 he again appeared on Broadway, playing in a firm, slick manner the Lionel Barrymore role of Oliver Jordan in Tyrone Guthrie's lavish revival of *Dinner at Eight*.

He continues to appear in feature films and telefilms. Despite being over seventy-five, he still looks and acts like . . . Walter Pidgeon. His two best screen assignments in the last decade have been the Senate majority leader in *Advise and Consent* (1962) and Florenz Ziegfeld in *Funny Girl* (1968).

In early 1972 he returned to MGM for the first time in sixteen years, to appear in the feature film *Skyjacked*, in which he plays a Senator. He said, "Believe me, my homecoming was no sentimental affair. There's just not enough of the old gang around. Everybody's gone except for a few old-timers on the technical crews. My favorite lot, number three, has been turned into a housing development. The difference from the old days is fantastic, and very sad.

"In the good old days every star had his own suite at the studio. Every day after work we'd go to someone's suite—Lionel Barrymore's, Gable's, Fred Astaire's, mine—have a couple of belts and hash over how things had gone. It was like a club.

"Now the suites are gone and they work you so darn late you have to go straight home when you finish. In the old days, I never worked past 6. Now they keep you going 11 hours a day."

He lives in a comfortable Bel Air, California mansion and is still wed to Ruth Walker, a nonprofessional whom he married in 1930. While he recalls the MGM years as "the best. I'd like to have them all back again." he admits: "I never watch my old pictures . . . . [If] someone alerts me that they're on, I say, 'I'll have to miss it; it's way past my bedtime.' "

WALTER PIDGEON

Mannequin (Paramount, 1926)	Marriage License (Fox, 1926)
The Outsider (Fox, 1926)	Heart of Salome (Fox, 1927)
Miss Nobody (FN, 1926)	The Girl from Rio (Gotham-Lumas, 1927)
Old Loves and New (FN, 1926)	The Gorilla (FN, 1927)

The Thirteenth Juror (Universal, 1927)
The Gateway of the Moon (Fox, 1928)
Woman Wise (Fox, 1928)
Turn Back the Hours (Gotham, 1928)
Clothes Make the Woman (Tiffany, 1928)
Melody of Love (Universal, 1928)
Her Private Life (FN, 1929)
A Most Immoral Lady (FN, 1929)
Bride of the Regiment (FN, 1930)
Viennese Nights (FN, 1930)
Sweet Kitty Bellairs (FN, 1930)
Show Girl in Hollywood (FN, 1930)*
Kiss Me Again (FN, 1931)
Going Wild (FN, 1931)
The Gorilla (FN, 1931)
Hot Heiress (FN, 1931)
Rockabye (RKO, 1932)
The Kiss Before the Mirror (Universal, 1933)
Journal of a Crime (FN, 1934)
Big Brown Eyes (Paramount, 1936)
Fatal Lady (Paramount, 1936)
Girl Overboard (Universal, 1937)
She's Dangerous (Universal, 1937)
As Good as Married (Universal, 1937)
A Girl with Ideas (Universal, 1937)
Saratoga (MGM, 1937)
My Dear Miss Aldrich (MGM, 1937)
Man-Proof (MGM, 1938)
Girl of the Golden West (MGM, 1938)
The Shopworn Angel (MGM, 1938)
Listen Darling (MGM, 1938)
Too Hot to Handle (MGM, 1938)
Society Lawyer (MGM, 1939)
6000 Enemies (MGM, 1939)
Stronger than Desire (MGM, 1939)
Nick Carter, Master Detective (MGM, 1939)
It's a Date (Universal, 1940)
Dark Command (Republic, 1940)
The House Across the Bay (UA, 1940)
Phantom Raiders (MGM, 1940)
Sky Murder (MGM, 1940)
Flight Command (MGM, 1941)
Man Hunt (20th-Fox, 1941)
How Green Was My Valley (20th-Fox, 1941)
Blossoms in the Dust (MGM, 1941)
Design for Scandal (MGM, 1941)
Mrs. Miniver (MGM, 1942)
White Cargo (MGM, 1942)

Madame Curie (MGM, 1943)
The Youngest Profession (MGM, 1943)
Mrs. Parkington (MGM, 1944)
Weekend at the Waldorf (MGM, 1945)
Holiday in Mexico (MGM, 1946)
The Secret Heart (MGM, 1946)
Cass Timberlane (MGM, 1947)
If Winter Comes (MGM, 1947)
Julia Misbehaves (MGM, 1948)
Command Decision (MGM, 1948)
The Red Danube (MGM, 1949)
That Forsyte Woman (MGM, 1949)
The Miniver Story (MGM, 1950)
Soldiers Three (MGM, 1951)
Calling Bulldog Drummond (MGM, 1951)
The Unknown Man (MGM, 1951)
Quo Vadis (Narrator: MGM, 1951)
The Sellout (MGM, 1952)
Million Dollar Mermaid (MGM, 1952)
The Bad and the Beautiful (MGM, 1952)
Scandal at Scourie (MGM, 1953)
Dream Wife (MGM, 1953)
Executive Suite (MGM, 1954)
Men of the Fighting Lady (MGM, 1954)
The Last Time I Saw Paris (MGM, 1954)
Deep in My Heart (MGM, 1954)
The Glass Slipper (Narrator: MGM, 1955)
Hit the Deck (MGM, 1955)
Forbidden Planet (MGM, 1956)
These Wilder Years (MGM, 1956)
The Rack (MGM, 1956)
Voyage to the Bottom of the Sea (20th-Fox, 1961)
Big Red (BV, 1962)
Advise and Consent (Columbia, 1962)
The Two Colonels (Titanus, 1962)
The Shortest Day (Italian, 1963)
Cosa Nostra, an Arch Enemy of the F.B.I. (WB, 1967)
Warning Shot (Paramount, 1967)
Funny Girl (Columbia, 1968)
Rascal (Narrator: BV, 1969)
The Vatican Affair (20th-Fox, 1969)
Skyjacked (MGM, 1972)
Harry Never Holds (UA, 1973)
The Neptune Factor (20th-Fox, 1973)
Yellow Headed Summer (1974)
*Unbilled appearance.

With Greer Garson and Richard Nichols in *Blossoms in the Dust* (1941)

With Esther Williams, Jesse White, Victor Mature, Paul Bradley, and Charles Watts in *Million Dollar Mermaid* (1952)

With Angela Lansbury, Virginia Keiley, and Rene Ray in *If Winter Comes* (1947)

With James Cagney in *These Wilder Years* (1956)

Eleanor Powell

Despite her fresh look and enthusiasm, the one unique thing about Eleanor Powell's screen personality was her ability to impress in the solo dance. Ruby Keeler was fresher and more enthusiastic but less of a dancer, and Ann Miller, with her high cheekbones, white teeth, and ample thighs, was more feminine. But Eleanor was the best tap dancer of them all and in fact came to motion pictures after being touted as The World's Greatest Feminine Tap and Rhythm Dancer by the Dance Masters of America. She made her cinema debut in Fox's *George White's Scandals* (1935), but Fox did not consider her star material. It was left to MGM to give her the typical glamor treatment of that glossy factory, making her a film name in *Broadway Melody of 1936* (1935). For the next seven years, during which she made only nine more films, she was a boxoffice draw with her rapid, easy tapping technique. She developed many of her routines herself. While these movies partnered her with the best male dancers of the era, Fred Astaire, George Murphy, Buddy Ebsen, and Ray Bolger, she was always most impressive in solo, such as in the "Broadway Rhythm" number in *Broadway Melody of 1936*, with her spangled tuxedo and a top hat, and those long, acrobatically lithe limbs.

She was born Eleanor Torrey Powell on November 21, 1912 in Springfield, Massachusetts. Her parents pushed her into taking dancing lessons as a cure for her bashfulness. The introverted youngster soon forgot her inhibitions while dancing and began appearing in Gus Edwards' children revues in Atlantic City where the Powell family spent their summer holidays. Edwards convinced her parents that she should be allowed to appear in New York City in his revue at the Ritz Grill. Once in Manhattan, Eleanor learned that the dancing craze of the year was tap dancing. Since she had been trained in acrobatics and ballet, she signed for private lessons with Jack Donahue to learn how to tap. Her style—those rapid, effortless successive taps in which her feet seemed to almost never leave the floor—were the result, she says, of having taken her earlier dancing lessons with sand bags tied to her feet.

After mastering the tapping technique, she landed in *Follow Through* (1929) on Broadway. It ran for a year and a half. More shows followed: *Fine and Dandy, Hot Cha* for Ziegfeld, and *George White's Scandals*. She was named the world's best tap dancer. When Fox filmed the *Scandals*, they used her in a

568

guest spot but decided she lacked the appropriate screen luster. However, MGM tested her for the role of the switchboard operator in *Broadway Melody of 1936* (which was ultimately played by Una Merkel), and Louis B. Mayer liked Eleanor well enough to give her the starring role opposite Robert Taylor. The studio gave her brunette hair a reddish tint, capped her teeth, and built several numbers in the film around her. She danced with Buddy Ebsen and his sister Vilma to the tune "Sing before Breakfast," imitated Katharine Hepburn in *Morning Glory*, did a burlesque of a French mademoiselle in a blonde wig, displaying her rapid tap steps without background music; and then performed the "Broadway Rhythm" in the finale.

Eleanor was a whopping success with the public and, as a result, MGM put her under contract. Before she was assigned to another Metro picture, however, she appeared briefly on Broadway in *At Home Abroad*, a show she had been contracted to before signing with the studio. The play starred Beatrice Lillie and Ethel Waters. After her run in the show concluded, she returned to MGM as the star of *Born to Dance* (1936) with James Stewart. The finale of that film had Eleanor dancing to "Swingin' the Jinx Away" aboard a battleship with a multitude of background dancers and sequined cannons in what MGM's musical director Roger Edens termed "an embarrassment of bad taste." The audiences, however, loved it and wanted more Eleanor Powell films. *Broadway Melody of 1938* (1937) had her dance with Ebsen again and George Murphy, but again she was best when she soloed "Your Broadway, My Broadway" in a black tuxedo and top hat. *Rosalie* (1937) cast her opposite Nelson Eddy *sans* Jeanette MacDonald, and she danced to the rhythm of drums with Ray Bolger.

In 1939 *Honolulu* had not only her nimbly dancing aboard ship while skipping rope, but also George Burns and Gracie Allen for welcome comedy relief. *Broadway Melody of 1940* (1940) partnered her with Fred Astaire, but they did not click as a team. Astaire's magnetic and acting panache were too sophisticated for Eleanor's "pleasant" screen personality. Moreover, while they had the excellent "Begin the Beguine" duet dance, Eleanor was always better on the dance floor alone. Two more starring vehicles, *Lady Be Good* (1941) and *Ship Ahoy* (1942) kept her up front, but the next year she was second fiddle to Red Skelton in *I Dood It*. After a guest appearance in *Thousands Cheer* (1943), she left MGM to marry the rising young actor, Glenn Ford.

After that, she made only minor attempts at resuming her film career. She appeared in *Sensations of 1945* (1944) at United Artists, did a stint at the Palladium in London in the late 1940s, and made a guest appearance in MGM's *Duchess of Idaho* (1950). But her real life role of wife and mother (the Fords' son Peter was born in 1945) was more important to her than her career. The fan magazines called their marriage one of Hollywood's happiest, but insiders had known for years that the marriage was kept together only because of Eleanor's religious beliefs. She devoted most of her married years to work for the Presbyterian church, the Boy Scouts of America, and various charities.

She was named Mother of the Year and Woman of the Year by several organizations, delivered an Easter Sunrise Service at the Hollywood Bowl, and for several seasons in the fifties wrote several scripts for the award-winning television Bible series, *Faith of our Children*. She also appeared on many of the episodes.

On Ford's forty-third birthday, May 1, 1959 (Eleanor was forty-seven), she announced her plans for divorce: "I sued on grounds of extreme mental cruelty, and that's exactly what I mean." She claimed that Ford preferred to live like a bachelor and there were rumors of romances with a number of his leading ladies. After the divorce, Eleanor recalled that, when they were first married and he was just starting out in motion pictures, "He had such an inferiority complex, it was sheer hell. When we went out together everybody flocked around me. I couldn't see that they were ignoring him, but he thought they were." At the time she was making $125,000 per picture. Following her divorce, she spent Christmas in Las Vegas with her son, seeing all the nightclub acts. After being introduced from the audience on several evenings, she said that her son Peter began to realize for the first time that his mother had been a "big" star at one time. He began encouraging her to make a comeback.

The once svelte Eleanor now weighed 160 pounds and considered the likelihood of a comeback an impossibility. But Peter became her staunch supporter and taskmaster, and with a regimented diet and workouts with choreographer David Lichine, Eleanor opened in Las Vegas on February 28, 1961, to excellent reviews and with a better figure than she had ever had. She played to equally good reviews at Manhattan's Latin Quarter, delighting audiences who remembered her films. She had proved, to her son and to herself, therefore, that she could do it. But her religious work was of more importance to her than sustaining a second career, and today she is an ordained minister of the Unity Church. When her son recently married, she and Ford happily posed for wedding photographs.

ELEANOR POWELL

With Una Merkel in *Broadway Melody of 1936* (1935)

George White's Scandals (Fox, 1935)
Broadway Melody of 1936 (MGM, 1935)
Born to Dance (MGM, 1936)
Broadway Melody of 1938 (MGM, 1937)
Rosalie (MGM, 1937)
Honolulu (MGM, 1939)
Broadway Melody of 1940 (MGM, 1940)
Lady Be Good (MGM, 1941)
Ship Ahoy (MGM, 1942)
I Dood It (MGM, 1943)
Thousands Cheer (MGM, 1943)
Sensations of 1945 (UA, 1944)
Duchess of Idaho (MGM, 1950)

In *Born to Dance* (1936)

988-166

With George Murphy in *Broadway Melody of 1938* (1937)

With Gracie Allen and Robert Young in *Honolulu* (1939)

With Robert Young and Rose Hobart in *Lady Be Good* (1941)

Jane Powell

Jane Powell was the perky, blonde little singing star whom MGM never allowed to grow up on screen. They used her as their own version of Deanna Durbin, but unfortunately Jane gained stardom just at a time when movie musicals were on the decline. On camera, she was always the daughter of some veteran MGM star, such as Walter Pidgeon, Jeanette MacDonald, or Ann Sothern, and was usually wealthy, frequently in love, and always ready to burst into song at the drop of a baton. She signed with MGM in 1944 when she was fifteen years old, made her first two pictures on loan to another studio, and after what seemed an endless string of adolescent singing heroines, she exclaimed in exasperation: "There I was, going on twenty-seven, with two children and about to have another, and still considered the baby of the Metro lot. I would like an opportunity play more mature roles and especially nonsinging roles." Her last picture was in 1958, and after thirteen more years of nightclubs, road shows, and television, she said, "When you've been a child personality—well, you get classified. And I still am! No one thinks of me for anything but musical comedies and they just aren't being made today. It used to upset me a great deal, but it doesn't any more."

Jane was born Suzanne Burce in Portland, Oregon, on April Fool's Day in 1929. She began her singing career at the age of seven when her vocal teacher introduced her to the manager of Portland radio station KOIN. She continued her singing throughout grammar school, and when her father, a salesman for a baby food company, moved the family to Los Angeles, Jane was one of six amateurs chosen to perform on the radio show, *Hollywood Showcase*. The hostess of the radio show that night was Janet Gaynor, and Jane stood in trepidation at the thought of performing before the illustrious actress. Sing she did, however, an aria from *Carmen*. She was so good she got booked on the Edgar Bergen–Charlie McCarthy show, and was offered a contract by MGM. The little coloratura with the lyric touch and a two and a half octave range from lower B to high E, was informed by telephone that her professional name would be "Jane Powell," and that her first two picture assignments would be on loan to United Artists.

Her debut role was as the rich little movie star runaway who joins a group of young tomato pickers in *Song of the Open Road* (1944). The highlight

574

of this leaden story was the guest star appearance of W. C. Fields who engaged in another session of verbal exchanges with Charlie McCarthy and Edgar Bergen. The N.Y. *Times* thought Jane "a winsome youngster with a prematurely developed rich soprano voice." Also for United Artists Jane appeared in *Delightfully Dangerous* (1945) with Ralph Bellamy and Constance Moore. It was a mild trifle at best.

MGM brought her back to the home lot and first cast her as Walter Pidgeon's daughter in *Holiday in Mexico* (1946), presumptuously billing the teenage celebrity as "your young singing star." Then Jane appeared as Jeanette MacDonald's eldest daughter in *Three Daring Daughters* (1948). In the latter picture she and her sisters express their disapproval of mama having wed José Iturbi. Jane's first "grown-up" role was the typical teenaged daughter of Wallace Beery in the musical comedy, *A Date with Judy* (1948). Jane suspected Beery of hanky-panky with Latin femme fatale Carmen Miranda, sang "It's a Most Unusual Day," and overcame the daydreaming of her flirtatious friend, Elizabeth Taylor. Then Jane was fathered by cruise ship captain George Brent in *Luxury Liner* (1948), mothered by Ann Sothern in the remake of *It's a Date* entitled *Nancy Goes to Reno* (1950), and cast opposite another junior MGM musical star, Ricardo Montalban, in *Two Weeks with Love* (1950). It was in this picture that she performed the ragtime number "Oceana Roll."

The part that boosted Jane to stardom was the singing–dancing lead opposite Fred Astaire in *Royal Wedding* (1951). June Allyson had originally been set for the part, but when she became pregnant, she was replaced by a nervously exhausted Judy Garland. Judy was unable to fulfill the commitment, so MGM gave Jane her big chance. Her dancing was not up to the nimble Astaire's; mostly she tagged along. But tagging along she did like a trouper and sang her songs, including "Too Late Now," with her usual wide-eyed charm. *Rich, Young and Pretty* (1951) gave her a nondancing partner, Vic Damone, and a most glamorous Parisian screen mother, Danielle Darrieux. Jane introduced "Wonder Why" in this picture. *Small Town Girl* (1953), a musicalized remake of a 1930s Janet Gaynor picture, was fun but not up to snuff. MGM loaned her to Warner Brothers for *Three Sailors and a Girl* (1953) in which she played a vivacious tongue-in-cheek vamp. Gordon MacRae, Gene Nelson, and Jack E. Leonard were the gobs of the title.

The best role of Jane's film career, and one of the most exceptional musicals of the 1950s, was *Seven Brides for Seven Brothers* (1954). Jane's costar was Howard Keel, with whom she sang "When You're in Love." She also did a solo ballad, "Wonderful, Wonderful Day." Michael Kidd's ingenious choreography and the barn-raising sequence are two great high points of MGM musical history. After this pinnacle in her career, Jane and Debbie Reynolds were sisters in pursuit of Edmund Purdom and Vic Damone respectively in the mild *Athena* (1954) in which Jane sang "Imagine" and "The Girl Next Door." Jane was one of the guest stars in *Deep in My Heart* (1954) and then appeared in her last MGM musical, *Hit the Deck* (1955), a reworking of the Fred Astaire–Ginger Rogers' *Follow the Fleet*. In *Hit the Deck*, Walter Pidgeon was again Jane's dad.

By the mid-1950s Jane felt completely frustrated by her MGM contract which did not permit television appearances and required her to get front office permission to accept nightclub performing engagements. More important, like all the other Hollywood studios, Metro was cutting down on their production schedules, and there just were not any roles for Jane. It never seemed to occur to the studio heads that they should abandon Jane's present screen image and let her try film dramatics or comedy, genres to which she was much more eminently suited than her long-standing Metro competitor, Kathryn Grayson.

As a result, Jane had to free-lance. She starred in a musical remake of *Tom, Dick And Harry*, titled *The Girl Most Likely* (1957), in which she must decide between Cliff Robertson, Keith Andes, and Tommy Noonan. She then contracted with Universal to appear in her first nonsinging role; the adopted daughter of Hedy Lamarr in *The Female Animal* (1958). The picture was a dud and Jane has never seen the completed version. Likewise, her last picture to date, *Enchanted Island* (1958), based on Herman Melville's South Sea island tale, *Typee*, was a fiasco. Jane says she accepted the part, "because the script was good and I got to die in the end. But they didn't stick to the script and wouldn't let me die. They said my fans wouldn't let me!" Instead, her motion picture career died at this point.

Occasionally Jane had sung in nightclubs throughout her career, and she made an LP recording for Verve Records in 1957, titled "Can't We Be Friends?" She starred in a television production of *Ruggles of Red Gap* with Peter Lawford and Michael Redgrave (1957) and played a beguiling Esther Smith in the video special, *Meet Me in St Louis* (1959), with MGM stalwarts Walter Pidgeon and Myrna Loy as her parents. She has since appeared in a number of television variety shows and played in stock productions of *Oklahoma, The Unsinkable Molly Brown, Carousel, My Fair Lady*, and *Meet Me in St. Louis*. She performed her own club revue called *Just Twenty Plus Me* in Las Vegas and on tour in Australia. Last year she played in an ABC telefeature entitled *Wheeler and Murdock* with Van Johnson and Diane Baker.

On November 5, 1949, after a two-year engagement, Jane wed Geary Anthony Steffen II, a former ice skating partner of Sonja Henie who had become on insurance executive. She and Steffen had two children: Geary Anthony III (1951) and Suzanne Ileen (1952), but their divorce became final on August 6, 1954. One of the reasons for the breakup of their marriage was the romance between Jane and dancer Gene Nelson, which began while they were both employed on *Three Sailors and a Girl* in 1953. The Powell–Nelson romance was a short-lived column headline, and on November 9, 1954, Jane married auto magnate Patrick W. Nerney, the former husband of actress Mona Freeman. She had a daughter Lindsay Averill (1956), by him. She divorced Nerney in 1963, stating he was "possessive and jealous." Two years later, on June 27, while touring in Australia, she married publicity man James

Fitzgerald. In June 1970, on the Mike Douglas afternoon talk show, Jane informed a nationwide audience about her son's drug addiction, saying he had done everything from smoking marijuana, to taking pills, to shooting heroin, and that unfortunately a family is sometimes too close to a problem to be able to see it in its proper perspective.

Jane is a devout Episcopalian, lives in Pacific Palisades with her third husband and children, enjoys being a housewife and cook, and frequently sees her MGM chum Kathryn Grayson. Jane says, "I'd love to make another movie, but it's not my whole life. There was a time when I thought it was. I guess it was the appeal to ego and vanity. But I've gotten over that." And she further adds, "I didn't quit movies. They quit me. I think it happened mostly because I made musical after musical and I got typecast. I never had a chance to prove I was an actress. I really played myself in all my movies, and when musicals began to lose their popularity, studios didn't want to take a chance on my unproven talents as an actress. Also, I never had a great director for the few dramas I did."

JANE POWELL

Song of the Open Road (UA, 1944)
Delightfully Dangerous (UA, 1945)
Holiday in Mexico (MGM, 1946)
Three Daring Daughters (MGM, 1948)
A Date with Judy (MGM, 1948)
Luxury Liner (MGM, 1948)
Nancy Goes to Rio (MGM, 1950)
Two Weeks with Love (MGM, 1950)
Royal Wedding (MGM, 1951)
Rich, Young and Pretty (MGM, 1951)

Small Town Girl (MGM, 1953)
Three Sailors and a Girl (WB, 1953)
Seven Brides for Seven Brothers (MGM, 1954)
Athena (MGM, 1954)
Deep in My Heart (MGM, 1954)
Hit the Deck (MGM, 1955)
The Girl Most Likely (Universal, 1957)
The Female Animal (Universal, 1958)
Enchanted Island (WB, 1958)

With Ricardo Montalban in *Two Weeks with Love* (1950)

With Fred Astaire in *Royal Wedding* (1951)

With Hans Conried, Una Merkel, Hans Dalio, Vic Damone, and Wendell Corey in *Rich, Young and Pretty* (1951)

With Howard Keel in *Seven Brides for Seven Brothers* (1954)

William Powell

William Powell's thirty-three-year film career was one of the longest in film history and divides into three distinct categories: 1922–1929 as a popular con man, gigolo, or villain in silents; 1929–1947, as a leading man where his forte was urbane comedy; 1947–1955, as a character actor. It was during the middle period that he gained stardom and a vast public following, continually demonstrating that he was one of the wittiest, most polished of light comedians on the screen. Over a decade of his prime professional years were spent as one of MGM's major actors, and it was at that studio that he became identified with *The Thin Man* series. Powell was a modest man, and his economic acting style was as impeccable as the well-tailored haberdashery he wore on screen. His emoting was so facile that he was frequently overlooked as the intelligent actor he really was. It was not until his brilliant portrayal of Clarence Day in Warner Brothers' *Life with Father* (1947) that he was taken seriously as an actor, and by that time he was fifty-five years old and nearing the end of his career.

William Horatio Powell was born in Pittsburgh, Pennsylvania on June 29, 1892. When he was nine, his family moved to Kansas City where he attended public school. In a Christmas play in high school, he played Captain Absolute in Sheridan's *The Rivals* and began to think that acting might be more of a rewarding career than law. His father wanted him to be an attorney, and he did in fact enter the University of Kansas in 1911. He quit after a few weeks, took a job as a clerk for the telephone company and ushered evenings at the local opera house. The Powell family had a wealthy relative, William's aunt, who lived in Mercer, Pennsylvania. The aspiring young actor wrote her a 23-page letter explaining at length his desire to be an actor and requesting a loan of $1,400 to be paid back at six percent interest. The aunt replied by giving him half that amount (which he did pay back thirteen years later at full interest), and with that endowment, Powell enrolled in New York's American Academy of Dramatic Art, where his classmates included Edward G. Robinson and Joseph Schildkraut. He got his first professional acting job playing three bit parts in *The Ne'er-Do-Well*. His salary was $40 a week and the play opened on September 2, 1912. It lasted only two weeks, but during the next ten years, Powell established a promising reputation as an actor on Broadway and with stock companies.

In the road company of Bayard Veiller's *Within the Law*, Powell met actress Eileen Wilson, and they were married in 1915. They had a son William David in 1925, but it was an unhappy marriage, and they were eventually divorced in 1931. On Christmas Day in 1917, Powell opened on Broadway in a musical comedy, *Going Up*, and enjoyed a run of a year. Three years later he received considerable recognition in the romantic melodrama, *Spanish Love*, which led to a part in Samuel Goldwyn's film, *Sherlock Holmes* (1922), starring John Barrymore. Powell played the heavy. William Randolph Hearst signed him to play Frances I in the Marion Davies' vehicle, *When Knighthood Was in Flower* (1922) and used him in the non-Davies picture, *Under the Red Robe* (1923), as the Duke of Orleans. Richard Barthelmess hired him for two pictures for his Inspiration Company, and in both he was the heavy. *The Bright Shawl* (1923) was filmed in Cuba, and *Romola* (1924) was made in Italy. In the latter he was the oily villain who marries Lillian Gish and seduces Dorothy Gish, and he was so good as Tito, the Italian, that Paramount offered him a seven-year contract.

They utilized him as the villain in a series of their silent comedy-melodramas, the best of which was *Beau Geste* (1926), where he excelled as the Italian thief who, upon being tortured, commits suicide. In 1929 he made his talkie film debut in *Interference*, playing a philanderer, and his stage-trained voice served him well. It was his second sound feature, *The Canary Murder Case* (1929), that began to establish the 5' 6", 160-pound actor as a debonair sleuth. He played S. S. Van Dine's Philo Vance. Although he thought the character too much a snob, it was a popular picture, and Powell said: "Vance made a mint of money for the studio and he did well by yours truly also." Powell repeated the Vance character in three more Paramount features, *The Greene Murder Case* (1929), *The Benson Murder Case*, (1930) and in a guest spot in *Paramount on Parade* (1930). Then he costarred in the first of five society dramas with Kay Francis, playing a New York gambler in *Street of Chance* (1930). The following year, Paramount cast him opposite a vivacious blonde named Carole Lombard in *Man of the World*, and they were married on June 26, 1931. Powell was known as a private, shy person, quite in contrast to the much younger, gregarious Lombard. While they remained friends until her death, they divorced in 1933. Powell said: "She was ready to spread her wings and marriage enabled her to do it."

In 1931, when his Paramount contract came up for renewal, his agent Myron Selznick, negotiated for a much better deal at Warner Brothers, which resulted in Paramount's Powell, Kay Francis, and Ruth Chatterton, all Selznick clients, transferring their screen services to the Burbank studio. Powell's new contract with Warners gave him $6,000 a week salary and story approval, but his films there were not exceptional, merely much the same as before, including another Philo Vance entry, *The Kennel Murder Case* (1933). The best of the Warner period was *One Way Passage* (1932), a lachrymose but literate romance story with Kay Francis. Once again Powell proved he was the

In *Manhattan Melodrama* (1934)

With Virginia Bruce (on chair) in *The Great Ziegfeld* (1936)

With Melville Cooper, Sara Haden, and Wallis Clark in *The Last of Mrs. Cheyney* (1937)

With Donald Meek, Edgar Kennedy (rear), Florence Rice, Jessie Ralph, and Myrna Loy in *Double Wedding* (1937)

most debonair of the screen's leading men, far outshining the similarly stocky-built Lowell Sherman.

When Warners reduced Powell's salary to $4,000 weekly in a Depression economic cutback, he made the best move of his career, and signed with MGM, where he became one of that studio's most popular and profitable leading men. His first MGM feature was *Manhattan Melodrama* (1934) with Clark Gable and Myrna Loy. W. S. Van Dyke directed that picture and liked what he saw between Powell and Loy and asked Louis B. Mayer to have them paired for *The Thin Man* (1934), a low-budget detective comedy. Mayer told Van Dyke he was "daffy," saying that the two players were essentially "heavies." Van Dyke convinced Mayer that the picture could be done in a few weeks and would not interfere with any other assignment that Mayer might have slated for the two actors. Mayer said yes, and the picture was completed in two weeks. The result was a sparklingly witty comedy which grossed $2 million, was nominated as best picture of the year, earned Powell the first of his Academy Award nominations, and made Powell and Loy the most popular husband–wife team on the screen at the time. Their insouciance, sophisticated wisecracking and wry martini drinking life made them what the Depression era considered "perfectly married." Five more *Thin Mans* followed. In 1936, Powell played Florenz Ziegfeld in the monumental *The Great Ziegfeld* and received a second Academy Award nomination playing opposite his ex-wife Carole Lombard in one of the best of the screwball comedies, Universal's *My Man Godfrey*. Three more pictures that year helped to make 1936 his *annus mirabilis*: *The Ex Mrs. Bradford* with Jean Arthur, *Libeled Lady* with Jean Harlow, and *After the Thin Man* with Loy. Likewise that year, he refused Irving Thalberg's offer to replace John Barrymore as Mercutio in *Romeo and Juliet*. Barrymore's peccadillos were disrupting the production, but Powell said he would not feel right taking over for Barrymore, whom he held in high regard for being so helpful when Powell was a young actor new to films in *Sherlock Holmes* fourteen years earlier. Thalberg thought it over, said that Powell was right, and suffered with Barrymore in the role.

In 1937 tragedy struck Powell when Jean Harlow died on June 7th at age twenty-six. Powell, who was forty-five, and Harlow had found "true love" in a romance at which Hollywood marveled. He was a grief-stricken mourner at her funeral and endowed a crypt at Forest Lawn—The Jean Harlow Room —with space for three bodies—Jean's, her mother's, and ... ! After Harlow's death, Powell went to Europe and for a time was felled by chronic stomach ulcers, and later on in his career, in the early 1940s, he would undergo operations for rectal cancer. He returned to the screen in *Another Thin Man* (1939) and met a twenty-one-year-old MGM ingenue, Diana Lewis. They were married on January 5, 1940, and have remained so ever since. Because of recurring illness, Powell slowed down his working pace to one or two films a year. He did three more in the waning *Thin Man* series, played an astronomer opposite Hedy Lamarr in *The Heavenly Body* (1944), and guested as the celestial Florenz Ziegfeld in *Ziegfeld Follies* (1946).

Powell had repeatedly requested that Mayer purchase the screen rights to *Life with Father*, the long-running Lindsay–Crouse play, but Mayer refused, saying the asking price of $500,000 was too high. Luckily, when Warner Brothers acquired the rights to the play, they borrowed Powell from MGM, and he performed a screen metamorphosis, transforming his voice and appearance into Clarence Day, and brought a new life to the line, "If you think I'm going to stand there and let Dr. Lloyd splash me with water, you're mistaken," in his adamant refusal to be baptized. It was Powell's finest screen achievement, and Bosley Crowther of the N.Y. *Times* said: "He so utterly dominates the picture that even when he is not on screen, his presence is felt." The film grossed $6 million, Powell was voted the New York Film Critics' Award, and received his third Oscar bid. He lost to his good friend, Ronald Colman, for *A Double Life*.

In post–World War II films there was little room for the glib Dapper Dan that Powell still played so well, and he floundered with four unimportant features made on loan for Universal, although the first, *The Senator Was Indiscreet* (1947), slipped by at the boxoffice on the strength of his name and performance. He ended his MGM association by playing Elizabeth Taylor's lawyer–father in *The Girl Who Had Everything* (1953), a remake of *A Free Soul*, with Fernando Lamas cast opposite Taylor. Powell's longevity with the studio entitled him to a pension. He had a supporting part in *How to Marry a Millionaire* (1953), made at Twentieth Century-Fox, in which he was the wealthy Texas oil man, and he made his last movie appearance as Doc, the philosophical ship's medic in *Mister Roberts* (1955) at Warner Brothers.

He retired permanently from the screen and has lived the past years with his wife Diana in Palm Springs. In the 1960s he underwent an additional cancer operation but recovered completely. In the mid-1960s his son William David committed suicide.

Adolph Zukor, past head of Paramount has said that when Powell was under contract to that studio: "He was always modest, good-humored, and a hard worker—invariably one of the best-liked men on the lot." That reputation followed him throughout his career. For years, Powell has made no public appearances, rarely sees even his good friend Myrna Loy, but whenever she plays a theatre performance he sends her a bouquet of flowers, and they talk occasionally on the telephone. In examining his various roles, Powell has been known to say that the Nick Charles character in *The Thin Man* was the one in which he was most himself.

WILLIAM POWELL

Sherlock Holmes (Goldwyn, 1922)
When Knighthood Was in Flower (Paramount, 1922)
Outcast (Paramount, 1922)
The Bright Shawl (Inspiration, 1923)

Under the Red Robe (Cosmopolitan, 1924)
Romola (Inspiration, 1924)
Dangerous Money (Paramount, 1924)
Too Many Kisses (Paramount, 1925)
White Mice (Paramount, 1926)

Faint Perfume (B.P. Schulberg, 1925)
My Lady's Lips (B.P. Schulberg, 1925)
The Beautiful City (Inspiration, 1925)
Sea Horses (Paramount, 1926)
Desert Gold (Paramount, 1926)
The Runaway (Paramount, 1926)
Aloma of the South Seas (Paramount, 1926)
Beau Geste (Paramount, 1926)
Tin Gods (Paramount, 1926)
The Great Gatsby (Paramount, 1926)
New York (Paramount, 1927)
Love's Greatest Mistake (Paramount, 1927)
Special Delivery (Paramount, 1927)
Senorita (Paramount, 1927)
Paid to Love (Fox, 1927)
Time for Love (Paramount, 1927)
Nevada (Paramount, 1927)
She's a Sheik (Paramount, 1927)
Beau Sabreur (Paramount, 1928)
Feel My Pulse (Paramount, 1928)
Partners in Crime (Paramount, 1928)
The Last Command (Paramount, 1928)
The Dragnet (Paramount, 1928)
The Vanishing Pioneer (Paramount, 1928)
Forgotten Faces (Paramount, 1928)
Interference (Paramount, 1929)
The Canary Murder Case (Paramount, 1929)
The Greene Murder Case (Paramount, 1929)
Charming Sinners (Paramount, 1929)
Four Feathers (Paramount, 1929)
Pointed Heels (Paramount, 1929)
The Benson Murder Case (Paramount, 1930)
Paramount on Parade (Paramount, 1930)
Shadow of the Law (Paramount, 1930)
Behind the Makeup (Paramount, 1930)
Street of Chance (Paramount, 1930)
For the Defense (Paramount, 1930)
Man of the World (Paramount, 1931)
Ladies Man (Paramount, 1931)
The Road to Singapore (WB, 1931)
High Pressure (WB, 1932)
Jewel Robbery (WB, 1932)
One Way Passage (WB, 1932)
Lawyer Man (WB, 1932)
Double Harness (RKO, 1933)
Private Detective 62 (WB, 1933)
The Kennel Murder Case (WB, 1933)
Fashions of 1934 (WB, 1934)
The Key (WB, 1934)
Manhattan Melodrama (MGM, 1934)
The Thin Man (MGM, 1934)
Evelyn Prentice (MGM, 1934)
Reckless (MGM, 1935)
Star of Midnight (RKO, 1935)

Escapade (MGM, 1935)
Rendezvous (MGM, 1935)
The Great Ziegfeld (MGM, 1936)
The Ex Mrs. Bradford (RKO, 1936)
My Man Godfrey (Universal, 1936)
Libeled Lady (MGM, 1936)
After the Thin Man (MGM, 1936)
The Last of Mrs. Cheyney (MGM, 1937)
The Emperor's Candlesticks (MGM, 1937)
Double Wedding (MGM, 1937)
The Baroness and the Butler (20th-Fox, 1938)
Another Thin Man (MGM, 1939)
I Love You Again (MGM, 1940)
Love Crazy (MGM, 1941)
Shadow of the Thin Man (MGM, 1941)
Crossroads (MGM, 1942)
The Youngest Profession (MGM, 1943)
The Heavenly Body (MGM, 1944)
The Thin Man Goes Home (MGM, 1944)
Ziegfeld Follies (MGM, 1946)
The Hoodlum Saint (MGM, 1946)
Song of the Thin Man (MGM, 1947)
Life with Father (WB, 1947)
The Senator Was Indiscreet (Universal, 1947)
Mr. Peabody and the Mermaid (Universal, 1948)
Take One False Step (Universal, 1949)
Dancing in the Dark (20th-Fox, 1949)
The Treasure of the Lost Canyon (Universal, 1951)
It's a Big Country (MGM, 1951)
The Girl Who Had Everything (MGM, 1953)
How to Marry a Millionaire (20th-Fox, 1953)
Mister Roberts (WB, 1955)

With Harry Strang in *Love Crazy* (1941)

With Helen Vinson, Myrna Loy, Thomas Dillon, Anita Sharp-Bolster, Donald MacBride, Gloria De Haven, and Bill Hunter in *The Thin Man Goes Home* (1944)

With Elizabeth Taylor and Fernando Lamas in *The Girl Who Had Everything* (1953)

Frances Rafferty

If Frances Rafferty had happened onto the entertainment scene in the 1950s, she undoubtedly would have been playing *the* Elinor Donahue of some *Father Knows Best* type television series. Instead, she was a product of the Hollywood studio system of the 1940s, and appeared in fifteen MGM features, usually as the competent but undistinguished ingenue, before hitting out on her own in post–World War II Hollywood. Frances had the same lip curl and sardonic-edged voice as the later Faye Dunaway, but unfortunately she was part of the movie age where young screen leads mouthed goo, not expletives.

Frances was born in Sioux City, Iowa on June 26, 1922, the daughter of Maxwell A. Rafferty, a personnel expert. She attended Miss Eaton's School in that city. When still a teenager, she moved with her parents and brother Max to Los Angeles. Later she enrolled at the University of California at Los Angeles, planning a premedical course of study. A friend talked her into auditioning for the revival of *The Merry Widow* at the Los Angeles Civic Opera. She was given a chorus job, but was soon advanced to become the understudy to Vera Zorina, the lead. Frances became hooked on show business and worked up a dance act with friend Alexis Smith. The team got to perform in the Hollywood Bowl, but then in a practice session Frances broke her kneecap, and the act split up. She enrolled in Maria Ouspenskaya's acting classes and was a stand-in for Zorina, then acting at Twentieth Century-Fox. Through Ouspenskaya's connections Frances was given an MGM screen test. That audition led nowhere, but a later one made for Fox was seen by MGM executives and Frances was hired by the studio. A proviso of the standard contract required her not to marry until she was twenty-one years of age.

Frances made her film debut in an MGM Miniature short subject, *Blackout* (1942), and followed this bit with what she described as "Walkons, bits, yesses, and noes" in assorted studio features. But in *Girl Crazy* (1943) she was prominently displayed as Marjorie Tait, the debutante-aged daughter of governor Howard Freeman. It is Frances whom Mickey Rooney escorts to his Western college dance, much to the bewilderment of love-crushed Judy Garland. Frances towered over shortie Rooney, which in those days was considered a standard screen gag, guaranteeing laughs.

Her best screen year was 1944. In the superproduction of Pearl Buck's

Dragon Seed, she played Orchid, the wife of Robert Bice and the daughter-in-law of Walter Huston and Aline MacMahon. She shared several scenes with star Katharine Hepburn (playing another of Huston's daughter-in-laws and wife of Turhan Bey). Frances was no more Chinese than most of her coplayers, but she did have a memorable scene when she is overwhelmed and murdered by marauding Japanese soldiers. Later in the year, she was Edward Arnold's daughter in *Mrs. Parkington*, and Ray Collins' daughter in Wallace Beery's *Barbary Coast Gent*.

Her remaining three Metro assignments were undemanding: the sweetheart of suspect Paul Langdon in *The Hidden Eye* (1945), a feckless ingenue in *Bud Abbott and Lou Costello in Hollywood* (1945), one of that comedy team's weakest entries, and Marshall Thompson's love of life in *Bad Bascomb* (1946).

After this film, MGM dropped her option. Sometime later, Frances encountered MGM casting head Billy Grady, who had moved over to CBS-TV, and asked why she had been summarily dismissed. Grady replied, "Because nobody around there really thought you cared one way or another." Frances' reaction to that explanation was typical: "I just thought every part I got was really peachy keen. Apparently they didn't want any of the fun-loving Rovers over there."

On the open job market Frances had leading roles in a string of unclassy productions at the lesser producing companies. She was the girl jilted at the altar by Franchot Tone in *Lost Honeymoon* (1947). In *Adventures of Don Coyote* (1947) she played the harassed ranch owner, and wandered about the murder mystery plot of *Lady at Midnight* (1948) with Richard Denning. She was the wife of bank robber Hugh Beaumont in *Money Madness* (1948), and supported maturing child star Gloria Jean in *An Old Fashioned Girl* (1948).

Frances temporarily retired in 1948 to wed aircraft executive, later TV writer, Tom Baker. Their son Kevin was born in 1950, and daughter Bridget in 1952. Meanwhile, Frances became one of the busiest actresses in television, performing in a myriad of dramatic series in a wide variety of roles.

After two more nondescript film roles, including a twelfthbilled assignment as a hotel guest in the low-budget *The Shanghai Story* (1954), Frances was cast as Ruth Henshaw, daughter of Spring Byington in *December Bride* (premiere: CBS-TV, October 4, 1954). Although most of the action centered on Byington and her next-door neighbor and cohort Hilda (Verna Felton), Frances had her share of small screen time trying to keep her square husband (Dean Miller) from coming unhinged due to the antics of madcap Byington. The show lasted through 1959, a healthy 154 episodes.

Frances' last screen role to date was in the Canadian-filmed *Wings of Chance* (1961), whose plot concerned a small plane that crashes in the northern woods and the subsequent rescue attempt.

Frances' brother Max has attained a nationwide reputation in recent years for his right-wing political views while serving as California's superintendent of public instruction and director of education.

589

Fingers at the Window (MGM, 1942)
Eyes in the Night (MGM, 1942)
The War against Mrs. Hadley (MGM, 1942)
Seven Sweethearts (MGM, 1942)
Dr. Gillespie's Criminal Case (MGM, 1943)
Girl Crazy (MGM, 1943)
Young Ideas (MGM, 1943)
Slightly Dangerous (MGM, 1943)
Thousands Cheer (MGM, 1943)
Dragon Seed (MGM, 1944)
Mrs. Parkington (MGM, 1944)
Barbary Coast Gent (MGM, 1944)
The Hidden Eye (MGM, 1945)

Bud Abbott and Lou Costello in Hollywood
  (MGM, 1945)
Bad Bascomb (MGM, 1946)
Curly (UA, 1947)
Lost Honeymoon (Eagle–Lion, 1947)
Adventures of Don Coyote (UA, 1947)
Lady at Midnight (Eagle–Lion, 1948)
Money Madness (Film Classic, 1948)
An Old Fashioned Girl (Eagle–Lion, 1948)
Rodeo (Monogram, 1952)
The Shanghai Story (Republic, 1954)
Wings of Chance (Universal, 1961)

With Bob Stanton and Bud Abbott in *Bud Abbott and Lou Costello in Hollywood* (1945)

Rags Ragland

MGM made a healthy share of its boxoffice receipts from its comedy players. The broad mugging of Wallace Beery, Marie Dressler, and Marjorie Main, the tandem antics of the Marx Brothers and Laurel and Hardy, and the buffoonery of Red Skelton drew in patrons by the droves. Occasionally the studio indulged itself by hiring a Damon Runyonesque personality, such as boxer Max Baer who played opposite Myrna Loy in *The Lady and the Prizefighter* (1933). But MGM quickly learned that the "Guys And Dolls" type of humor quickly pales if force-fed to the public in large doses. Thus when professional rube Rags Ragland joined the MGM roster in 1941, he was carefully limited in his onscreen time. Unlike the similar free-lancing Slapsie Maxie Rosenbloom and Huntz Hall at other studios, Rags was made to keep his performances in touch with reality. They always had to be filled with human warmth, even if coated in some amusing stupidity.

Ragland was born John Morgan Ragland in Louisville, Kentucky on August 23, 1905, the son of a building superintendent. At the age of fourteen he dropped out of school to start earning a living, first as a newsboy, then a truck driver, and such "careers" as a preliminary events boxer, and even as an assistant movie theatre projectionist. While learning how to be an expert pool player, he gained a reputation as a lowbrow raconteur. When a touring variety show passed through Louisville and lost its second comic on the way, Ragland applied for the vacancy and was accepted. In 1928 he joined Minsky's burlesque circuit, and for several years wore the traditional floppy pants and red nose, performing in an estimated 2,000 sketches, often teamed with fellow comic Phil Silvers. He made his Broadway debut in *Who's Who* (1938), a revue featuring Imogene Coca, and two years later he was hired by producer B. G. DeSylva for the part of the rollicking sailor in Ethel Merman's *Panama Hattie*. Meanwhile he had married, had a son, John, Jr., and was divorced in 1926.

His success in *Panama Hattie* inspired MGM to sign him to a term contract. He was slated to make his screen debut in *Honky Tonk* (1941) as Clark Gable's card shark pal, but the part went to Chill Wills. He was more appropriately introduced to moviegoers in *Ringside Maisie* (1941), in which his fractured English and mug of a face were in realistic surroundings. His second film, *Whistling in the Dark* (1941), cast him as the sidekick of not-so-bright radio detective Red Skelton, and the popular entry led to two followup productions, *Whistling in Dixie* (1942) and *Whistling in Brooklyn* (1943), in which he played similar roles. He had a sizable part and good billing in the screen version of *Panama Hattie* (1942), also with Red Skelton, but was just crude, instead of congenial, flavoring in *Maisie Gets Her Man* (1942), as "Ears" Kofflin.

In *Dubarry Was a Lady* (1943) his role was Charlie in the club scenes and the clumsy Dauphin in the French court dream sequences. A young Zero Mostel proved the unexpected joy of that film. Ragland was at his best in *Girl Crazy* (1943), in which he has a tender scene consoling the love sick postmistress, Judy Garland, who is convinced she has lost the affections of Mickey Rooney forever. In *Meet the People* (1944) he is a war worker who keeps house in his wife's absence. He inherited Nat Pendleton's role as the folksy ambulance driver in the *Dr. Kildare* entry *Three Men in White* (1944), and in *The Canterville Ghost* (1944) he played a raucous G.I. He exuded his personal warmth as a dumb porter and June Allyson's sympathizer in *Her Highness and the Bellboy* (1945), and was an understanding policeman in *Anchors Aweigh* (1945). He played himself in *Bud Abbott and Lou Costello in Hollywood* (1945). In the "drama," *The Hoodlum Saint* (1946), he was a crony of down-and-out lead, William Powell.

Ragland died on August 2, 1946 of uremic poisoning. As an indication of his popularity in the cinema world, MGM's Frank Sinatra sang at his funeral. No one has ever learned where he adopted his nickname of "Rags" though it typified the best of his raucous humor.

RAGS RAGLAND

Ringside Maisie (MGM, 1941)
Whistling in the Dark (MGM, 1941)
Born to Sing (MGM, 1942)
Sunday Punch (MGM, 1942)
Maisie Gets Her Man (MGM, 1942)
Panama Hattie (MGM, 1942)
The War against Mrs. Hadley (MGM, 1942)
Somewhere I'll Find You (MGM, 1942)
Whistling in Dixie (MGM, 1942)
Dubarry Was a Lady (MGM, 1943)

Girl Crazy (MGM, 1943)
Whistling in Brooklyn (MGM, 1943)
Meet the People (MGM, 1944)
Three Men in White (MGM, 1944)
The Canterville Ghost (MGM, 1944)
Her Highness and the Bellboy (MGM, 1945)
Anchors Aweigh (MGM, 1945)
Bud Abbott and Lou Costello in Hollywood (MGM, 1945)
The Hoodlum Saint (MGM, 1946)

With Robert Walker and June Allyson in *Her Highness and the Bellboy* (1945)

Luise Rainer

"For my second and third pictures, I won Academy Awards. Nothing worse could have happened to me." With those words, Luise Rainer took leave of Hollywood, ending one of its oddest and most meteoric careers, proof that Oscar really can be a jinx. Her cinema span consisted of just nine films, eight of which were made in a three-year period at MGM, 1935–1938, during which time she rose to immense critical and boxoffice heights. Possessing a fragile beauty emphasized by lachrymose eyes, the diminuitive Viennese brought a pathos and fey charm to each of her film portrayals, which elicited unprecedented audience sympathy. Almost by default, automatically she was considered a dramatically versatile actress. As a result, this very heady reputation did her in. Today, in retrospect, her acting technique in these films seems more mannered monotony than versatility. Compared to other actresses of more enduring qualities, such as Ingrid Bergman, Luise seems simply not of flesh and blood.

Luise was born in Vienna on January 12, 1910, and early in her childhood prepared for a theatrical career. She worked with Max Reinhardt's Berlin theatre ensemble and appeared in many European theatrical productions such as *An American Tragedy, Six Characters in Search of an Author*, and *Measure for Measure*. In the mid-1930s, an MGM talent scout Bob Ritchie heard of her Garbo-like reputation and stopped her on a Berlin street one day with what she regarded as a corny approach about "testing" her for Hollywood. Eventually she learned he was in earnest and, after a successful screen test, was signed for a contract at the Culver City lot. At first the studio had no suitable role in mind for her, but when Myrna Loy refused to do *Escapade* (1935), Gottfried Reinhardt, Max's son, implored director Robert Z. Leonard to test Luise. Reinhardt had spotted her at a party hosted by Ernst Lubitsch and thought she would be perfect as the Viennese innocent opposite William Powell.

Luise got the part and, early in production, everyone was so pleased with the rushes that costar Powell graciously allowed her name to be given a costarring billing, a gentlemanly gesture rare among actors. It was a notable motion picture debut for Luise, but the picture was passed off critically as synthetic froufrou.

594

Leonard cast her in his next film *The Great Ziegfeld* (1936) as Anna Held, Florenz Ziegfeld's first wife. In this sumptuous, three-hour-long spun-sugar show business biography, Luise's role was a small one, At the end, however, she had an extremely effective and moving telephone scene in which she congratulates Ziegfeld (William Powell) on his forthcoming marriage to Billie Burke (Myrna Loy): "Hello, Flo? ... Yes, this is Anna ... Congratulations! ... I? ... Oh, Oh, wonderful! Never better in my whole life ... It's all so wonderful and I'm *so* happy ... I hope you are happy too. ... " That scene, which has become a classic of its kind, almost ended up on the cutting room floor. Mayer had urged producer Hunt Stromberg to eliminate it because he thought it extraneous to the plotline. Nevertheless, it won Luise her first Oscar in 1936, causing her to beat MGM's own Norma Shearer, nominated for her role in *Romeo and Juliet.*

With an Academy Award and the New York Film Critics Award behind her, Irving Thalberg deemed it wise to cast Luise as O-Lan, the stoic Chinese peasant wife of Paul Muni, in his ambitious cinematization of Pearl Buck's best-seller, *The Good Earth* (1937). Thalberg died before the film was released and, at Mayer's suggestion, the following inscription was carried in the picture's credits:

To the memory of Irving Grant Thalberg,

We dedicate this picture,

His last great achievement.

It was the only time Thalberg's name appeared on the screen.

In a precedent-setting contest Luise was voted a second Oscar in as many years (incredibly defeating Garbo in *Camille*), and the MGM script writers were ordered to come up with "Rainer vehicles" at once. They did, but their haste resulted in five increasingly bad films, and with each one her chances of professional survival rapidly declined. She was a flirtatious spy opposite William Powell in *The Emperor's Candlesticks* (1937), but was swamped by Spencer Tracy's screen presence in *The Big City* (1937), which dealt mostly with taxi-driver Tracy's warfare against crooked industry leaders.

Luise almost negotiated herself off the silver screen by demanding a higher salary and a more impressive treatment in accordance with her star status, but the difficulties were negotiated, and she essayed a Dixie belle who cannot decide between Melvyn Douglas and Robert Young in *The Toy Wife* (1938). The public was not impressed by either her adopted Southern accent or by the cinematic confection itself. Despite the opulence of its production, *The Great Waltz* (1938) was a standard triangular love affair, set in Vienna of old. Luise played the wife of Johann Strauss (Fernand Gravet), who is self-sacrificing about his budding relationship with diva Miliza Korjus. *Dramatic School* (1938) did more to advance the careers of Paulette Goddard and Lana Turner than Luise, whose intense performance as the European actress determined to make good, left audiences overly satiated with her full-force heavy theatrics. (The film and Luise do have their admirers, such as John Baxter in *Hollywood in the Thirties* (1968), who exclaimed, "Her portrait of the

With Roland Got and Charley Grapewin in *The Good Earth* (1937)

With Spencer Tracy in *The Big City* (1937)

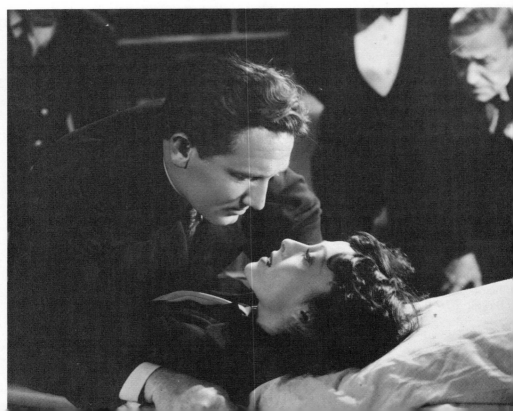

With H. B. Warner and Melvyn Douglas in *The Toy Wife* (1938)

With Melville Cooper in *Dramatic School* (1938)

young actress almost insanely devoted to becoming a star is among the most coherent any performer of the Thirties achieved.")

Luise left Hollywood in 1938, ostensibly to repair her wobbly marriage to playwright Clifford Odets, and in a few months her MGM contract was dissolved. By then the studio had several new European imports on its horizon, including Hedy Lamarr and Greer Garson, and had no further need for the hard-to-cast Oscar winner. She divorced Odets in 1940, and two years later played on Broadway in an undistinguished version of James M. Barrie's *A Kiss for Cinderella*. The next year a film comeback was announced, but the only part she could obtain in Hollywood was in *Hostages* (1943), a mediocre anti-Nazi effort at Paramount. Cast member William Bendix had more effective screen time than she and, with this film, Luise's movie career was finished.

The speculations as to why her career ended so badly are many. Some say that she was indeed not a versatile actress, or that her husband Odets was anti-Hollywood and persuaded her to leave, or that she was just plain too temperamental. One story is still circulated that she did not get along with Mayer, presumably because she would not sit on his lap while discussing contractual arrangements. Her own comments, made some years later, were, "In my day, making films was like working in a factory. You were a piece of machinery with no rights."

Luise now lives in the fashionable Belgravia district of London, and has been married for twenty-six years to American publisher Robert Knittel. They have one daughter. In the past two decades she has made sporadic professional appearances. In 1950 she played on Broadway in Ibsen's *Lady from the Sea*, and the following year received good reviews in a West Coast production of Maxwell Anderson's *Joan of Lorraine*. She performed her telephone monologue scene from *The Great Ziegfeld* on one of Ed Sullivan's television shows, and did *By Candlelight* and *The Seagull* for British television. Her most recent outing was as a French countess on ABC-TV's *Combat* series in 1965, with Ramon Navarro as her husband.

LUISE RAINER

Escapade (MGM, 1935)
The Great Ziegfeld (MGM, 1936)
The Good Earth (MGM, 1937)
The Emperor's Candlesticks (MGM, 1937)
The Big City (MGM, 1937)

The Toy Wife (MGM, 1938)
The Great Waltz (MGM, 1938)
Dramatic School (MGM, 1938)
Hostages (Paramount, 1943)

Donna Reed

Donna Reed spent twenty years in Hollywood films, performing as Miss Average America, the unsophisticated, unspoiled, wholesome screen sweetheart and wife. This was the image of her MGM promoted during her seven unremarkable years with that studio (1941–1948), and also the image she carried with her during her seasons on television playing the wife of a pediatrician in *The Donna Reed Show*. She certainly was not as heroic as Greer Garson, nor as witty as Myrna Loy, and not as lachrymose as June Allyson, but in her economy-size way, she brought warmth, tenderness, and refinement to each of her film portrayals during wartime America. Only once did she play what was an untypical role for her, and for that deviation she received the Academy Award. The role was the prostitute in *From Here to Eternity* (1953). The public and critics raved over the "new" Donna. True, it was a part into which she could sink her teeth, but on closer analysis, her Alma was *not* unlike all her previous movie parts. As director Fred Zinnemann explained: "Alma is not really a professional tramp, but a small-town girl who only wanted to go back and be respectable." It was this underlying awareness of morality that made Donna's performance exceptional. Today Donna has all but retired from acting but is an outspoken, active dove in her fight against the war in Vietnam via an organization called Another Mother for Peace.

Donna Belle Mullenger was born on a farm in Denison, Iowa on January 27, 1921. She regards her beginnings on a farm as "an ideal way to begin life." After graduation from high school, where she was a beauty queen, she went to live with an aunt in Los Angeles to be able to attend Los Angeles City College where she could afford the nominal tuition. When she was elected the Campus Queen in December 1940, her photograph was circulated in the local newspapers, and she began receiving telephone calls from motion picture talent scouts. At college Donna was taking a secretarial course, but she had also become a member of the drama group and appeared in *The Intruder* and *The Happy Journey*. The movies sounded very glamorous to this hard-working country girl.

In June 1941 Donna eagerly signed a MGM contract for $75 a week and made a screen test opposite a rising young leading man, Van Heflin. The studio changed her name to Donna Adams and put her into *Babes on*

Broadway (1941) and *The Getaway* (1941) with Robert Sterling and Heflin. MGM then had second thoughts about the name Adams and changed it to Reed. Donna had not liked Adams but liked Reed even less: "It reminds me of a tall, chic, austere blond that isn't me. It has a cold, forbidding sound." The name stuck, however, and she was put into small roles in three series which MGM used as a training ground for new contract players: *Shadow of the Thin Man* (1941), *Calling Dr. Gillespie* (1942), and *The Courtship of Andy Hardy* (1942). She played the good sister Bess in *The Human Comedy* (1943), was romanced by Richard Carlson in *The Man from Down Under* (1943), and supported the troublesome Robert Walker in *See Here, Private Hargrove* (1944).

Donna was extraordinarily touching as the Army nurse in *They Were Expendable* (1945), a performance which prompted Frank Capra to borrow her for his production of *It's a Wonderful Life* (1946) at RKO. Capra says she was the only actress he wanted to play "the solid, sensible country girl in whose life there could be but one man." Her one man in the film was James Stewart, formerly a top MGM star, and the picture was a break for Donna. She exclaimed, "It's amazing that I could have acted in so many B pictures as I did and then have ended up with *It's a Wonderful Life*. Since then Metro has lined up lots of important roles for me!" There was only a little reality in this remark, because after one more role, as the sister of Lana Turner who grows sad and spiritual in *Green Dolphin Street* (1947), her MGM contract was not renewed. In fact, her contract had two more years to run, but MGM had no parts for her. Except for two minor films at Paramount, both with Alan Ladd, she sat out the remainder of her Metro agreement.

During her MGM tenure, on January 30, 1943 to be exact, Donna had married MGM cosmetic artist William Tuttle. They were divorced in 1945, and the same year she married Tony Owen, a former Chicago newsman turned actor's agent who had worked for the powerful Charles K. Feldman. When Owen accepted a post as executive assistant to Harry Cohn at Columbia Pictures, Cohn put Donna under contract. It was Cohn who suggested Donna for the role of Alma, known as the lofty "Princess" to her sister prostitutes in *From Here to Eternity*. Director Fred Zinnemann had wanted Julie Harris to play Alma, but Cohn regarded that Broadway star as a "child frightener." So Donna was tested on two separate occasions with Aldo Ray, each time with only her profile showing on screen. After several months of indecision, Cohn tacitly had her make a third test, this time with Montgomery Clift, and playing full face the scene where Alma tells Prewitt she wants to live a respectable life. By now Zinnemann had been well exposed to Donna in this role and the third test convinced him that he could work with her. By now he was able to see what director George Sidney described as "her quiet kind of sex." However, Donna's portrayal of Alma was not yet in the bag. During production, Zinnemann kept avoiding closeups of Donna, and each time this occurred she made note of it, as did film editor, William Lyons. Finally Lyons consulted Cohn, and Zinnemann was ordered to shoot the necessary closeups.

Nevertheless, *From Here To Eternity* did not become her entree to success at Columbia. While she was the only Columbia star in the picture, and Cohn touted her performance as "Oscar stuff," the next picture he offered Donna was a low-budget quickie and she refused. Cohn took offense at her refusal and, despite the fact that she later won the Oscar, the only assignments he would give her were Westerns. She asked for her release and Cohn gave it to her.

With no small reason, she refers to her screen career in two parts: Before *Eternity* and After *Eternity*. She made a few more pictures, none exceptional, nothing that would have earned her another crack at the Oscars. Donna reasoned that the Hollywood studio moguls resented the disruption of her sweet girl image by the *Eternity* role, and has stated, "All the Oscar brought me was more bland Goody Two Shoes parts." Then too, she had a reputation for being outspoken about many of the directors on her pictures. She once said, "Most movie directors are a bunch of hackneyed craftsmen. They're scared to death of actors and even more scared of actresses. And they hate women, which is why they make the female characters in their pictures as unpleasant as possible."

In 1958 Donna and her husband formed Todon Productions to produce a teleseries for ABC called *The Donna Reed Show*. She rationalized her TV plunge thus, "One picture a year is hardly enough to keep a career going." The series debuted on September 24, 1958 and, after a slow start in the ratings, became one of the more popular video situation comedies. She played the wife of pediatrician Carl Betz, and the mother of two (later three) children. After completing her eighth season with the series, Donna retired. Her last motion picture appearance for over a decade was a cameo in Columbia's *Pepe* (1960).

In 1967 a woman screenwriter friend of Donna started an organization called Another Mother for Peace, a group of citizens against the Vietnam war. "We don't march or throw rocks; we write letters." The organization's 225,000 membership includes Joanne Woodward, Marlo Thomas, Debbie Reynolds, Betsy Palmer, and Barbara Rush. Donna explained her affiliation: "I love my country but I feel it got off the track. This is my way of helping it find its way back." In 1971 she added to her previous statement: "No American filmmaker has yet made a stand against the war in Vietnam."

On June 10, 1971 Donna and her husband Tony Owen, whom friends describe as a "worldly, check-grabbing extrovert from a well-to-do New Orleans family," were divorced after twenty-six years of marriage and shared a community property settlement of over $3 million. They have four children: two adopted, Penny and Tony, Jr., and two of their own, Timothy and Mary Ann. When prompted, she proves a surprisingly candid and caustic observer of the Hollywood scene. David Susskind, whom she regards as a "conceited blabbermouth," once condescendingly inquired if the bronze Rolls-Royce she drove wasn't "rather — uh, large?" Donna replied, "If you ever get a good series of your own, maybe you'll be able to afford one just like it!" She says,

"Everything they say about Hollywood is true. It's a walled-in city bounded on all sides by arrogance. What's more, the people in Hollywood who make motion pictures simply do not know about people, or, often as not, about making motion pictures." Of her personal experience in films, "Forty pictures I was in, and all I remember is, 'What kind of a bra will you be wearing, honey?' That was always the area of big decision—from the neck to the navel. Even with all the girl-next-door parts I played, there would usually be someone on the set whose job it was to look me up and down and say, 'Is that dress tight enough, baby?' I get so fed up with immature 'sex' and stories about kooky, amoral, sick women. There was a time once when Irene Dunne and Norma Shearer and Greer Garson all played strong, unsick women. But today everything has to be *Butterfield 8*. I'm sick of this kind of misfit role, and I think the public is too."

The Donna of today has suddenly reappeared on television in a new guise, as a spokeswoman for a set of encyclopedias sold through chainstores, and has recently starred in a new film called *Yellow Headed Summer* with Laurence Harvey, Walter Pidgeon and Stuart Whitman.

DONNA REED

Babes on Broadway (MGM, 1941)
The Getaway (MGM, 1941)
The Shadow of the Thin Man (MGM, 1941)
The Bugle Sounds (MGM, 1941)
Calling Dr. Gillespie (MGM, 1942)
The Courtship of Andy Hardy (MGM, 1942)
Mokey (MGM, 1942)
Eyes in the Night (MGM, 1942)
Apache Trail (MGM, 1942)
The Human Comedy (MGM, 1943)
Dr. Gillespie's Criminal Case (MGM, 1943)
Thousands Cheer (MGM, 1943)
The Man from Down Under (MGM, 1943)
See Here, Private Hargrove (MGM, 1944)
Mrs. Parkington (MGM, 1944)
Gentle Annie (MGM, 1944)
The Picture of Dorian Gray (MGM, 1945)
They Were Expendable (MGM, 1945)
Faithful in My Fashion (MGM, 1946)
It's a Wonderful Life (RKO, 1946)
Green Dolphin Street (MGM, 1947)

Beyond Glory (Paramount, 1948)
Chicago Deadline (Paramount, 1949)
Saturday's Hero (Columbia, 1951)
Scandal Sheet (Columbia, 1952)
Hangman's Knot (Columbia, 1952)
Trouble Along the Way (WB, 1953)
Raiders of the Seven Seas (UA, 1953)
The Caddy (Paramount, 1953)
From Here to Eternity (Columbia, 1953)
Gun Fury (Columbia, 1953)
Three Hours to Kill (Columbia, 1954)
They Rode West (Columbia, 1954)
The Last Time I Saw Paris (MGM, 1954)
The Far Horizon (Paramount, 1955)
Ransom! (MGM, 1956)
The Benny Goodman Story (Universal, 1956)
Backlash (Universal, 1956)
Beyond Mombasa (Columbia, 1957)
The Whole Truth (Columbia, 1958)
Pepe (Columbia, 1960)
Yellow Headed Summer (1974)

With Lowell Gilmore in *The Picture of Dorian Gray* (1945)

With Glenn Ford in *Ransom!* (1956)

Debbie Reynolds

The Boop-Boop-A-Boop Girl; The World's Most Famous Girl Scout; Miss Burbank; The All-American Girl. All these sobriquets have described Debbie Reynolds at various stages of her career. Her secret ambition was to be like Lucille Ball. While her professional successes have not come up to that ambition, her life story still reads like a Cinderella tale and makes her the most likely candidate as a modern little Miss Show Biz. She is a nervy, exuberant, indefatigable performer who never had ambitions to be a serious actress. She bounced her way fetchingly through several good MGM musical roles, then proved she had the talent to turn in a good dramatic performance with *The Catered Affair* (1956), for which she was named the best actress in a supporting role by the National Board Of Review. She already had a legion of fans when she married crooner Eddie Fisher in 1955, but the whirlwind of publicity as the wronged wife and mother when Fisher went off with the widow of his best friend, Elizabeth Taylor Todd, caused the public to love her even more. Eventually even Debbie tired of playing overaged screen ingenues, and went after bigger properties in musicals, comedies and dramas. She did not always succeed and today still finds herself best known to the public as a symbol of the days when Hollywood and life were much more carefree.

Mary Frances Reynolds was born on April Fool's Day in 1932 in El Paso, Texas, where her father was a laborer. There was also a brother, Bill, two years older than she, Debbie says, "I was too little to remember the difficult time my family had during the Depression, but I was always impressed by the way Mother and Dad laughed at their struggles. Texas rabbits were never safe from Dad's shotgun. We had rabbit for dinner so many times that my brother Bill still turns green at the thought." The Reynolds moved to Burbank, California when Debbie was eight years old, and her father took a job there as a railroad carpenter for the Southern Pacific line. In school Debbie was a Brownie scout, twirled the baton in school marches, played the French horn, and was a lively tomboy who loved sports. At sixteen she entered the Miss Burbank contest, performing an imitation of Betty Hutton and singing "My Rockin' Horse Ran Away." She was named Miss Burbank of 1948. "I won this contest, and there were two talent scouts there, one from Warners and the other from MGM. They were old friends and they flipped a coin to see which studio would get to interview me. Warners won. They put me under contract at $65 a week, although I'll never know why. About all I could do in the way of talent was be exuberant." Jack Warner changed her name to Debbie. "I don't know why. He probably looked out the window, saw a dog across the street and that was it, Debbie."

Debbie did bits in two Warner films, *June Bride* (1948) and *The Daughter of Rosie O'Grady* (1950), and then, "they dropped me at the end of the year and the talent scout called the man at MGM and said, if they were still interested, I was available. He even took me down there to introduce me." At MGM she was determined to make it, and never stopped working at her lessons in singing, dancing, voice, and drama. Her dancing coach told her: "Miss Reynolds, you're going to make it because you sweat." Debbie's wholesomeness and vivacity impressed the studio executives and they spotlighted her as Helen Kane, The Boop-Boop-A-Boop Girl, in *Three Little Words* (1950) where she mouthed the words to Miss Kane's singing of "I Want to Be Loved by You," and danced with Carleton Carpenter. This role elicited Debbie's first fan mail, and MGM cast her as Jane Powell's sister in *Two Weeks with Love* (1950) and had her sing "Row, Row, Row" and "Aba Daba Honeymoon," again with Carleton Carpenter. Next the studio cast her as the bouncy ingenue in *Singin' in the Rain* (1952) in which she sang a charming duet with Gene Kelly, "You Were Meant for Me." That role was Debbie's stepping stone to star billing in *I Love Melvin* (1953) with Donald O'Connor, where she played a refreshingly cheerful young Broadway actress. Several airy musicals followed, the fan mail poured in, and MGM raised her salary to $3,500 weekly.

In 1954 Debbie became engaged to Eddie Fisher and all America seemed to swoon over their "perfect" romance. Debbie had been photographed with many of filmdom's young leading men and at one time had a crush on Robert Wagner. However, on September 26, 1955, she and Fisher were married at Grossinger's resort in the Catskills. Back at MGM Debbie proved a skillful comedienne in *The Tender Trap* (1955), and surprised audiences as the delicately poignant Bronx girl in *The Catered Affair*. RKO tried to cash in on the Debbie Reynolds–Eddie Fisher union by casting the duo in a musical remake of *Bachelor Mother* titled *Bundle of Joy* (1956). If that film was a fizzle, at least Debbie had her own bundle of joy, when she gave birth to Carrie Frances on October 21, 1956. Shortly afterward, she was loaned to Universal to star as the country lass in *Tammy and the Bachelor* (1957), a gooey entry that spawned several followups, all without Debbie, and contained a title song sung by Debbie that sold over a million copies.

The Fishers took a ten-day European holiday in the summer of 1957 with their good friends, Michael and Elizabeth Taylor Todd. Fisher and Todd were good pals, and Fisher had been his best man when he married Elizabeth on February 2, 1957, while Debbie had been one of the attendants. When the Fishers returned from Europe, they agreed that divorce was inevitable, but they reconciled their differences temporarily. On February 24, 1958, Debbie gave birth to their second child, Todd Emmanuel, named after Mike Todd. Less than a month later, Todd was killed in a plane crash. Fisher rushed to Taylor's side and, before long, the press had labeled Elizabeth as the "husband stealer" and Debbie the "wronged wife." Debbie waived her interlocutory decree so that Fisher could wed Elizabeth in Las Vegas on May 12, 1959. In the meantime Debbie made two pictures with Glenn Ford, *It Started with a Kiss* (1959) and *The Gazebo* (1959). It was hinted that a romance between the two was brewing, but it proved to be merely a friendship in a time of loneliness.

Debbie got out of her MGM contract in 1959, spurred on by the fact that, since her divorce from Fisher, her boxoffice worth had soared tremendously. As she told one interviewer: "I'd never been free before to work where I wanted to." She set out for better roles. As the defeated taxi dancer in *The Rat Race* (1960), she elicited genuine compassion. Then she formed her own company, Harman Productions, to produce several television specials for ABC. The first such special, aired on October 27, 1960, was *A Date with Debbie*. Despite her uncanny imitations of such celebrities as Zsa Zsa Gabor, and her singing, dancing, and clowning, her television career never got off the ground.

On November 25, 1960, she married multimillionaire Harry Karl, owner of over 300 retail shoe stores in fourteen Western states. Karl had been married twice before, once to actress Marie MacDonald and then for several months to Joan Perry Cohn, widow of the Columbia Pictures' head, Harry Cohn. Debbie met Karl at a meeting of the Thalians, a group of Hollywoodites who organized to collect money for the treatment of emotionally disturbed children. For a number of years Debbie has been the president of that charitable organization.

Debbie's screen career in the 1960s has been varied if inauspicious. She managed to hold her own against the sophisticated competition of Fred Astaire and Lilli Palmer in *The Pleasure of His Company* (1961). In MGM's mammoth *How the West Was Won* (1963) she was exuberant as Agnes Moorehead's pioneer daughter, a quality lacking in most of the other guest stars' performances. *My Six Loves* (1963) and the tepid screen version of *Mary, Mary* (1963) proved that Debbie's marquee name could not salvage such comedy flubs. At this point, she had reached a low ebb in her career, and she knew it. When MGM could not borrow Shirley MacLaine for *The Unsinkable Molly Brown* (1964), Debbie waged a year-long campaign to win the part. The deciding factor was her waiving of a profit percentage and an agreement to a flat $200,000 salary. It was her last movie success to date. She wrangled the lead in MGM's *The Singing Nun* (1966), but it was not a successful repeat of *The Sound of Music* formula. She demonstrated that she lacked the finesse of Doris Day in *How Sweet It Is* (1968), which had its own scripting problems. In *What's the Matter with Helen?* (1971), she tiptoed into the *Whatever Happened to Baby Jane?* genre only to have costar Shelley Winters outstrip her in scene-stealing antics. Her most recent movie effort was as the voice of a barnyard spider in Paramount's animated musical feature *Charlotte's Web* (1972), based on the children's classic by E. B. White. She sang four tunes in that film.

Debbie has had more success in the nightclub field, where she still commands a high salary for her Las Vegas appearances. "I'm a ham, an exhibitionist. I've never been nervous about doing anything. The only time I get nervous is when I'm doing a stage appearance and the man is out there talking about me. I just wish he'd say, 'Here she is,' and let me get *on*. I can't stand that awful waiting." Debbie is always *on*. Her husband says, "Every time she opens the refrigerator door and the light goes on, she takes a bow and does 20 minutes." She is also a practical joker. On a television appearance on the *Jack Paar Show* in 1959, she raucously started to remove Paar's clothes on the air. At the Los Angeles opening of the Jim Bailey female impressionist show in April 1972, she returned to her seat at intermission but fell plop on the floor when she misjudged the placement of her chair. Undaunted, she stood up and waved to the onlookers, introduced a few celebrity friends to the audience, did a few cartwheels, and then told everyone to shut up and watch the show.

The Karls live in an old-style Hollywood mansion with round-the-clock guards and three watchdogs. Debbie's family includes her own two children by Fisher and three children of Karl's by his marriage to Marie MacDonald, whom they took to live with them after MacDonald committed suicide in the 1960s. Debbie suffered a miscarriage on June 7, 1963, and she and Karl have no children of their own. Concerning the humiliating publicity surrounding her marital problems in the 1950s, Debbie says: "I have no memories of the past. Elizabeth and I have talked and met each other a number of times since then. In fact, we are old friends because, when we were 17, we were both together in the MGM studio school." Of Fisher, she adds: "He's a welcome guest in my house any time he likes to come."

A television series in 1969 flopped, but Debbie keeps searching for suitable film roles: "I stopped making movies because I don't like taking my clothes off. Maybe it's realism, but in my opinion it's utter filth." In addition to the Thalians organization, Debbie works energetically for the Girl Scouts. As a devoted movie fan and most loyal. She has recently given much of her time and money crusading for the creation of a Hollywood Hall of Fame. She spent $200,000 at the MGM auction in 1970, buying up movie memorabilia. "I want to put back some of the joy I got out of motion pictures. There are many stars who feel as I do. We feel this industry of ours has brought entertainment, education, and enjoyment to millions. It would be a sin to let it die of neglect and apathy."

And to prove that even 1950s style ingenues become nostalgia, Debbie has successfully entered a new medium, the theatre, with the new production of the 1919 musical, *Irene,* costarring Patsy Kelly. The play open on Broadway early in 1973, winning Debbie excellent personal reviews. Miss Show-Biz may have a new career ahead of her.

DEBBIE REYNOLDS

June Bride (WB, 1948)
The Daughter of Rosie O'Grady (WB, 1950)
Three Little Words (MGM, 1950)
Two Weeks with Love (MGM, 1950)
Mr. Imperium (MGM, 1951)
Singin' in the Rain (MGM, 1952)
Skirts Ahoy (MGM, 1952)
I Love Melvin (MGM, 1953)
The Affairs of Dobie Gillis (MGM, 1953)
Give the Girl a Break (MGM, 1953)
Susan Slept Here (RKO, 1954)
Athena (MGM, 1954)
Hit the Deck (MGM, 1955)
The Tender Trap (MGM, 1955)
The Catered Affair (MGM, 1956)
Bundle of Joy (RKO, 1956)
Meet Me in Las Vegas (MGM, 1956)
Tammy and the Bachelor (Universal, 1957)
This Happy Feeling (Universal, 1958)
The Mating Game (MGM, 1959)

Say One for Me (20th-Fox, 1959)
It Started with a Kiss (MGM, 1959)
The Gazebo (MGM, 1959)
The Rat Race (Paramount, 1960)
Pepe (Columbia, 1960)
The Pleasure of His Company (Paramount, 1961)
The Second Time Around (20th-Fox, 1961)
How the West Was Won (MGM, 1963)
My Six Loves (Paramount, 1963)
Mary, Mary (WB, 1963)
The Unsinkable Molly Brown (MGM, 1964)
Goodbye Charlie (20th-Fox, 1964)
The Singing Nun (MGM, 1966)
Divorce American Style (Columbia, 1967)
How Sweet It Is (National General, 1968)
What's the Matter with Helen? (UA, 1971)
Charlotte's Web (Voice Only: Paramount, 1972)

With Lurene Tuttle and Hanley Stafford in *The Affairs of Dobie Gillis* (1953)

With Ernest Borgnine and Bette Davis in *The Catered Affair* (1956)

With Burnell Dietsch, Russ Tamblyn, Frank Reynolds, and Jerry Stabler in *Hit the Deck* (1955)

With Maria Karnilova, Jack Kruschen (bartender), and Harvey Lembeck in *The Unsinkable Molly Brown* (1964)

Ann Richards

Because poised, well-assembled Ann Richards was both talented and Australian-bred, she was agreeably accepted into the 1940s MGM family by Anglophile studio head Louis B. Mayer. She possessed the right physical and emotional attributes to portray admirable quality ladies on the screen. Had not Mayer become so engrossed in furthering the career of Greer Garson in this very same niche, Ann might have remained on the lot well beyond her four pictures and gained the recognition she deserved. Instead she free-lanced, and when this proved fruitless, settled down to enjoy her marriage and her two children, because she had " ... made up my mind to be like the fairy princess who lived happily ever after."

She was born Shirley Ann Richards on December 20, 1919 in Sydney, Australia, the daughter of an American father, who, as a management engineer, had settled in Sydney and wed a New Zealand girl. Upon birth, Ann was registered at the American consulate as a citizen of the U. S. There was also a son, Roderick, who later died in a Japanese prisoner-of-war camp in Borneo during World War II.

As a child, Ann had a strong interest in acting and also studied dancing with Jan Kowsky, former ballet partner of Pavlova. The multitalented girl was also an accomplished water colorist and, later in her life, earned a supplementary income decorating breadboards and salad dishes. She attended Stotts College in Sydney and performed on the side with the amateur Sydney Players Club.

After a brief fling as a secretary–interviewer for a modeling agency, she was spotted by Cinesound, Australia's leading film studio, and put into its talent training course. She was the first actress signed by them to a long-term contract. She made her screen debut in *It Isn't Done* (1937), playing the well-bred daughter of farmer Cecil Kellaway. In the next two years she appeared in five other pictures, including *The Rudd Family* (c. 1938) with Peter Finch, and *100 Thousand Cobbers* (c. 1939) a government-sponsored recruiting film.

With the coming of World War II, the Australian film industry closed shop for the duration of the war, and Ann joined the Celebrity Comedy company, which toured Australia and New Zealand playing shows for the troops in training. Determined to support her family now that her brother was in service, she sailed for America on December 8, 1941, on the last passenger ship to leave Australia until after the war. She visited with a cousin in San Francisco and then, to earn some ready cash, wrote a series of lectures on Australia which she occasionally managed to present in front of women's clubs at $50 per session. One of her Australian film industry friends was writer Carl Dudley. He was then scripting a John Nesbitt *Passing Parade* short for MGM, styled as a plea for civilian aid in the war effort. It was entitled *The Woman in the House* (1942). Ann had meantime been in touch with MGM, who wanted to test her, and she suggested that she would do the short instead, since it required her to play both a young British girl and an old woman. Louis B. Mayer was impressed with her showcase performance and signed her to a contract.

In the typical fashion of casting its new ingenues in either its *Andy Hardy* or *Dr. Kildare* series, Ann found herself fourteenthbilled as nurse Iris Headley in *Dr. Gillespie's New Assistant* (1942), the eleventh in Metro's entries about Blair General Hospital. Unlike contemporary contractree Marilyn Maxwell who, as social worker Ruth Edley, would chase Dr. Van Johnson for three entries, Ann's appearance as a Laraine Day-type nurse was a one-shot deal.

Next she was cast in MGM's upper-case production of *Random Harvest* (1942), teaming the enormously popular Greer Garson with Ronald Colman as the music hall entertainer who befriends a World War I amnesiac. Ann's tiny role as one of Colman's relatives, seen in the Random Hall sequences, was peripheral to the story. According to Ann, if she had arrived on the Metro scene sooner, she undoubtedly would have been cast in the Susan Peters' role of Garson's daughter. She recalls producer Sidney Franklin saying: "You would have been so right for this part, because the girl is supposed to remind Ronald Colman of his earlier love, Greer Garson." The role netted Peters an Oscar nomination. In *Three Hearts for Julia* (1943) a minor marital farce with Ann Sothern and Melvyn Douglas, she had a minuscule part as a member of an all-girl orchestra.

An American Romance (1944) had originally been conceived as a vehicle for Spencer Tracy and possibly Greer Garson. It was an interwoven paean to both the American immigrant and the burgeoning U. S. steel industry. Brian Donlevy was used as a Tracy replacement and, because of Ann's similarity of image to Garson, she was tested and handed the female lead. The King Vidor picture was in production for a year at a cost of $3 million. The studio liked the finished picture, but thought its 135-minute running time excessive. The editing was done without Vidor's supervision, and instead of removing many of the unentertaining technological steel scenes, the chopper excised most of the picture's human elements. Vidor was advised by MGM that the editing had been done in such a way as not to destroy the already completed musical sound track. *An American Romance* was not a success, although Ann, who aged from eighteen to fifty-eight within the film story, was hailed as a new find. Some reviewers compared her to a cross between Garson and Ingrid Bergman.

Unhappy with her MGM experience, Ann obtained her Metro release and was quickly signed by independent producer Hal Wallis, although in the end he proved to be too preoccupied with pushing the career of his contract protégée Lizbeth Scott. Ann was Jennifer Jone's protective friend in Paramount's *Love Letters* (1945), a crusading town editor in Randolph Scott's Western *Badman's Territory* (1946), and the strong-minded wife of pacifist diplomat Robert Young in *The Searching Wind* (1946) starring Sylvia Sidney. As the Washington socialite, Ann's role required her to age from youth to matron, seemingly a stock-in-trade for many of her movie assignments. Her cinema career moved down several notches when she went to Eagle–Lion to play the British wife of amnesiac ex-G.I. Franchot Tone in *Lost Honeymoon* (1947), and for the same company was merely Sylvia Sidney's friend in *Love from a Stranger* (1947). Also for Wallis she was the stern school friend of Barbara Stanwyck in *Sorry, Wrong Number* (1948), the one who first warns the bedridden invalid of Burt Lancaster's true nature. If her movie roles were less than artistically satisfactory, she did enjoy performing in summer stock at the La Jolla Playhouse with Gregory Peck, Dorothy McGuire, and John Hoyt.

Ann married Edmond Angelo on February 4, 1949. A marketing director and a consultant for a space engineering firm, he had previously produced and directed plays on both the East and West Coast. In 1952 he produced and directed the film *Breakdown* which starred his wife as the wealthy girl friend of boxer William Bishop. It had minor programmer release by Realart.

She has three children: Christopher Edmond (December 19, 1949), Mark Richards (March 14, 1951), and Juliet Marion (May 20, 1959). The Angelos now live in W. C. Fields' former Beverly Hills home. In her spare time she writes poetry. A book of her verse, *The Grieving Senses*, appeared in 1971. Alone and with her husband she has performed several concert readings and dramatic presentations, including *Helen of Troy*, a verse play she wrote. She has also recorded the works of many modern poets for CBS radio to be broadcast in the U. S. and abroad.

As she recently told film historian Doug McClelland of her domestic life: "I am now enjoying the most rewarding of experiences, and have no desire to do anything more."

ANN RICHARDS

It Isn't Done (Cinesound, 1937)
Tall Timber (Cinesound, c. 1937)
Lovers and Luggers (Cinesound, c. 1938)
The Rudd Family (Australian, c. 1938)
Come up Smiling (Australian, c. 1938)
100 Thousand Cobbers (Australian, c. 1939)

Dr. Gillespie's New Assistant (MGM, 1942)
Random Harvest (MGM, 1942)
Three Hearts for Julia (MGM, 1943)
An American Romance (MGM, 1944)
Love Letters (Paramount, 1945)
Badman's Territory (RKO, 1946)

The Searching Wind (Paramount, 1946)   Sorry, Wrong Number (Paramount, 1948)
Lost Honeymoon (Eagle–Lion, 1947)   Breakdown (Realart, 1952)
Love from a Stranger (Eagle–Lion, 1947)

With Jack George, Brian Donlevy, and Mary McLeod in *An American Romance* (1944)

Mickey Rooney

Child stars used to be exceedingly popular with American movie audiences. Between 1935 and 1938 Shirley Temple was the Number One money-making luminary in films, but she was pushed out of the top spot in 1939 by MGM's multitalented vaudevillian, Mickey Rooney, the celluloid Napoleon. This pint-sized (5' 3") trooper was perfectly equipped to guide a rash of MGM's family-oriented pictures to boxoffice success. Whether as the ultimate teenager in the Andy Hardy series or in tandem with Judy Garland in some boisterous musicals, Rooney never failed his studio mentor, Louis B. Mayer. He could sing, dance, play the drums, clown, or cause the audience to weep at his onscreen predicaments. Because of his persistent youthful looks, he remained a popular movie "teenager" well into the 1940s. He ended his sixteen-year association with MGM in 1949, at which point he was earning a $5,000 weekly salary. But by the next year, when he was thirty years of age, he was a show business has-been. Ever since, he has been on an occupational see-saw, bouncing up and down with successes and failures in the various entertainment media. Through it all, he has remained a powerhouse of unbridled energy, whose talents have yet to be properly corralled and channeled.

If there is a living proof to that well worn cliché "born-in-a-trunk" it is Mickey Rooney. He was born Joe Yule, Jr. on September 23, 1920 in a theatrical boarding house at 57 Willoughby Street in Brooklyn, New York. His parents, Joe and Nellie Yule, worked as a vaudeville team. At the ripe age of fifteen months, little Mickey crawled into the orchestra pit during his parents' onstage routine and started pounding on the drums. This bit of theatrical upstaging was kept in their act, with the youngster now dressed in a tuxedo. Not long after, he graduated to singing songs such as "Pal O' My Cradle Days." Songs led to jokes, and soon he was an integral part of the act, saying, "Ladies and gentlemen, I'm going to sing. I'm going to dance. I want to spend my whole life entertaining you, and I'm going to start right now."

In the mid-1920s, Joe and Nellie Yule separated, and Nellie headed for Hollywood with her son. She had read that Hal Roach was looking for new child actors. She never got to see Roach, but she did get her son an audition for the movie version of the Toonerville Trolley series by Fontaine Fox. Cast in the series, now called the *Mickey McGuire* series, Rooney's hair was dyed dark to make him look more like the cartoon original of the brash, tough kid. He played this character in nearly fifty short subjects for producer Larry Darmour. He had already appeared in a short subject, *Not to Be Trusted* (1926), in which he played a midget. The series did not make Rooney the hot property that Jackie Coogan had been, but it did lead to some feature film work, which started with Colleen Moore's *Orchids and Ermine* (1927). Since legalities prevented the boy from using the name Mickey McGuire professionally, he became known as Mickey Rooney instead and Universal used him in several features in 1932.

David O. Selznick brought him to MGM in 1933, the year the *McGuire* series ended, to play Clark Gable as a child in *Manhattan Melodrama* (1934). At first Metro employed him only on a week-to-week basis, but the studio soon regarded him sufficiently well to sign him to a long-term contract. Warner Brothers borrowed him to play Puck in the screen version of *A Midsummer Night's Dream* (1935), a role he had played on the stage at the Hollywood Palladium in 1933. MGM suddenly realized it had a hot property on its hands and negotiated a new contract with Rooney which would escalate his $500 weekly salary to $750, with subsequent automatic raises to $2,500 with bonuses.

Metro cast Rooney as the kid brother in *Ah, Wilderness!* (1935), and his way to stardom was assured. He was then showcased opposite MGM's little English gentleman, Freddie Bartholomew, in three pictures: *Little Lord Fauntleroy* (1936) on loanout to United Artists, *The Devil Is a Sissy* (1936), and *Captains Courageous* (1937). Rooney's impishness was the highlight of each of these pictures. Nobody expected great shakes from a programmer entitled *A Family Affair* (1937), based on a wholesome Broadway play called *Skidding*. It featured Rooney as awkward adolescent Andy Hardy. In fact, young Frankie Thomas had originally been chosen for the juvenile lead in this B picture. But the public's fancy was captured by the lighthearted domestic comedy and Louis B. Mayer astutely built the property into a $25 million gross before the series petered out in 1946 after fourteen additional entries. (Rooney and MGM would attempt to resurrect the 1940s kitsch in *Andy Hardy Comes Home* [1958], but neither the performers nor the public were up to the nostalgic gooiness.) The *Andy Hardy* series earned a special Oscar in 1942 for its all-American wholesomeness and was obviously, a major Metro asset. Because of this, Mayer never allowed his production staff to tamper with its basic format. It was fine to use the series as a testing ground for new MGM female contractees, but simplicity and homey virtues were the constant guidelines. When one pundit on the MGM lot suggested that Mayer might combine the *Andy Hardy* series with the studio's popular *Dr. Kildare* entries by having Rooney contact a social disease and seek Dr. Lew Ayres' medical advice, the publicly moral Mayer almost had a seizure of apoplexy.

Not only was Rooney busy with the *Andy Hardy* series, but he and Judy Garland became a favorite MGM musical comedy team. They were first paired in *Thoroughbreds Don't Cry* (1937), then Judy played sweet Betsy Booth in three of the *Andy Hardy* pictures. Rooney's climb to stardom gained additional impetus with *Boys' Town* (1938). He and Garland were reunited in *Babes in Arms* (1939), for which, at age nineteen, he was Oscar-nominated. His competition were veterans such as Clark Gable, Laurence Olivier, James Stewart, and Robert Donat. Donat won for his performance in *Goodbye, Mr. Chips*, but the Academy bestowed a special miniature Oscar upon Rooney for "his significant contribution in bringing to the screen the spirit and per-sonifcation of youth, and as a juvenile player setting a high standard of ability and achievement." He was now Number One at the boxoffice and he let no one forget it on or off the lot. To demonstrate that his well-demonstrated versatility had a few unseen twists, he offered a fantastic impression of Carmen Miranda in *Babes on Broadway* (1941). In addition, his role of Homer in William Saroyan's *The Human Comedy* (1943) was so emotionally on-key that he received another Oscar nomination. Meanwhile, Mayer, who would do most anything to keep Rooney happy, had continued to keep the boy's father under a stock acting contract.

After starring in one of his most popular pictures, *National Velvet* (1944), Rooney joined the Army and returned to play Andy Hardy again after his discharge, in *Love Laughs at Andy Hardy* (1946). But post–World War II America wanted new types of entertainment, and a twenty-six-year-old Rooney capering about as a post-adolescent was not exactly the right approach. He proved he could handle adult roles satisfactorily when kept under careful directorial check in *Killer McCoy* (1947), but, given his freedom, he would mug unmercifully, as when playing composer Lorenz Hart in the musical biography *Words and Music* (1948). That truly artistic turkey was released the same year as *Summer Holiday*, a Rouben Mamoulian musical that Metro had produced in 1946. Neither film did much to endear Rooney to the filmgoing public.

When Rooney, through his own producing company and his personal business manager, attempted to persuade Louis B. Mayer to allow him to do a radio series based on Andy Hardy, he and Mayer came to the parting of the ways, and he was finished at MGM. Rooney later admitted he had been an overgrown, swellheaded "star" at the time and found his free-lancing over the next several years a struggle. Finally, with his performance in a war film, *The Bold and the Brave* (1956), he gained good notices and received an Academy Award nomination for best supporting actor. But the Oscar went to Anthony Quinn for *Lust for Life*. Nevertheless, Rooney had found a niche as a seasoned character performer, in which his plump, balding figure was not at odds with his once young lead image. The following year he made a big splash in television as the bitter comic in *Playhouse 90*'s *The Comedian* for which he was Emmy-nominated. Since that time, he has worked steadily in television, motion pictures, and stock, including the pre-Broadway flop *W. C.*, based on the life of W. C. Fields. His best performance to date has been in *Requiem for a Heavyweight* (1962) as Anthony Quinn's fight manager.

With Lionel Barrymore in *Ah, Wilderness!* (1935)

With Elizabeth Risdon in *The Adventures of Huckleberry Finn* (1939)

With Diana Lewis, and Pat Flaherty in *Andy Hardy Meets Debutante* (1940)

With June Allyson in *Girl Crazy* (1943)

Rooney's marital history is a track record that makes most Hollywoodites look like Pollyanna, and is one of the major reasons, along with professional mismanagement, for his various financial setbacks during the 1950s and 1960s. His first marital venture was with MGM starlet Ava Gardner, on January 10, 1942. To the public it looked like young love, but one Hollywood wag styled it a marriage of convenience on Ava's part for Rooney's chauffeured limousine. At any rate, they divorced after sixteen months. He wed Betty Jane Rase, a former Miss Birmingham, in September 1944. They had two sons, Mickey, Jr. and Timothy. They separated in 1947 and were divorced two years later, with Rooney making a cash settlement of $160,000 on her. On June 3, 1949 he married actress Martha Vickers. They had a son named Theodore, and were divorced in 1951. The following year, on November 18th, he married Elaine Mannken. She received her divorce from him on May 18, 1959, and on the same day, he married Miss Muscle Beach of Santa Monica, Barbara Ann Thomasen, fifteen years his junior. Four months later, the first of their four children, Kelly Ann, was born, and Rooney announced they had actually been secretly married since December 1958. Their subsequent children were Kerry, Kyle, and Kimny Sue. In 1962 Rooney claimed bankruptcy, saying he had made and spent $12 million during his career, and only began to see the black side of his accounting ledger four years later. His marital life seemed to have found peacefulness, at least in the eyes of the public. However, Rooney filed for divorce from Barbara and named a young Yugoslavian actor named Milos Milocevic as correspondent in his suit. A reconciliation ensued, with Barbara promising not to see the young actor again. But on February 1, 1966, while Rooney was ill in the hospital suffering from a fever he had contracted in Manila while filming *Ambush Bay* (1966), Milocevic shot Barbara to death in Rooney's Brentwood home, and then took his own life with the same gun. Nine months later, on September 10th, Rooney married Margaret Lang, a friend of his deceased wife, but the union lasted only a few months. On May 27th, 1969 he married for the seventh time, to a secretary, Carolyn Hockett.

Rooney still continues in the entertainment field, unabated. He is a trouper, and his work schedule is nonstop. There are television guest appearances, motion pictures, and nightclub acts. He is presently involved in the production–writing–direction of feature films, and is planning a series of pictures with comedian Marty Allen, styled in the pattern of the Abbott and Costello comedies. Rooney wrote his autobiography, *i.e.*, in 1965, and there are numerous business ventures to which he lends his name: talent schools for child actors, resort hotels, etc. In 1970, when his former studio, MGM, was going through another of its financial doldrums, he offered to make them twenty pictures for $20 million, claiming that he had all the professional experience they needed for such a task. For better or for worse, MGM refused the offer, a fact which most likely would not stem the flow of activity from the ebullient Mickey Rooney.

Recently, when seeking the custody of four of his children by a former, now deceased wife, Mickey was asked in a Santa Monica, California court if he had a bad temper. "Yes, but I curbed it through Christ," adding that he had become a member of the Science Of Mind Church. "I now live a Christian life," he said.

MICKEY ROONEY

Orchids and Ermine (FN, 1927)
Information Kid (Universal, 1932)
Fast Companions (Universal, 1932)
My Pal the King (Universal, 1932)
Beast of the City (MGM, 1932)
Sin's Pay Day (Mayfair, 1932)
The Big Cage (Universal, 1933)
The Life of Jimmy Dolan (WB, 1933)
Broadway to Hollywood (MGM, 1933)
The Big Chance (Arthur Greenblatt, 1933)
The Chief (MGM, 1933)
The World Changes (FN, 1933)
Lost Jungle (Serial: Mascot, 1934)
Beloved (Universal, 1934)
I Like It That Way (Universal, 1934)
Love Birds (Universal, 1934)
Manhattan Melodrama (MGM, 1934)
Chained (MGM, 1934)
Hide-Out (MGM, 1934)
Upper World (WB, 1934)
Half a Sinner (Universal, 1934)
Blind Date (Columbia, 1934)
Death on the Diamond (MGM, 1934)
County Chairman (Fox, 1935)
The Healer (Monogram, 1935)
A Midsummer Night's Dream (WB, 1935)
Reckless (MGM, 1935)
Ah, Wilderness! (MGM, 1935)
Riff Raff (MGM, 1935)
Little Lord Fauntleroy (UA, 1936)
The Devil Is a Sissy (MGM, 1936)
Down the Stretch (WB, 1936)
Captains Courageous (MGM, 1937)
A Family Affair (MGM, 1937)
The Hoosier Schoolboy (Monogram, 1937)
Slave Ship (20th-Fox, 1937)
Thoroughbreds Don't Cry (MGM, 1937)
Live, Love and Learn (MGM, 1937)
Love Is a Headache (MGM, 1938)
Judge Hardy's Children (MGM, 1938)
You're Only Young Once (MGM, 1938)
Hold That Kiss (MGM, 1938)
Lord Jeff (MGM, 1938)
Love Finds Andy Hardy (MGM, 1938)

Boys' Town (MGM, 1938)
Out West with the Hardys (MGM, 1938)
Stablemates (MGM, 1938)
The Adventures of Huckleberry Finn (MGM, 1939)
The Hardys Ride High (MGM, 1939)
Andy Hardy Gets Spring Fever (MGM, 1939)
Babes in Arms (MGM, 1939)
Judge Hardy and Son (MGM, 1939)
Young Tom Edison (MGM, 1940)
Strike up the Band (MGM, 1940)
Andy Hardy Meets Debutante (MGM, 1940)
Andy Hardy's Private Secretary (MGM, 1940)
Men of Boys' Town (MGM, 1941)
Life Begins for Andy Hardy (MGM, 1941)
Babes on Broadway (MGM, 1941)
The Courtship of Andy Hardy (MGM, 1942)
A Yank at Eton (MGM, 1942)
Andy Hardy's Double Life (MGM, 1942)
The Human Comedy (MGM, 1943)
Girl Crazy (MGM, 1943)
Thousands Cheer (MGM, 1943)
Andy Hardy's Blonde Trouble (MGM, 1944)
National Velvet (MGM, 1944)
Love Laughs at Andy Hardy (MGM, 1946)
Killer McCoy (MGM, 1947)
Summer Holiday (MGM, 1948)
Words and Music (MGM, 1948)
The Big Wheel (UA, 1949)
Quicksand (UA, 1950)
The Fireball (20th-Fox, 1950)
He's a Cockeyed Wonder (Columbia, 1950)
My Outlaw Brother (Eagle–Lion, 1951)
The Strip (MGM, 1951)
Sound Off (Columbia, 1952)
Off Limits (Paramount, 1953)
A Slight Case of Larceny (MGM, 1953)
Drive a Crooked Road (Columbia, 1954)
The Atomic Kid (Republic, 1954)
The Bridges at Toko-Ri (Paramount, 1954)
The Twinkle in God's Eye (Republic, 1955)
The Bold and the Brave (RKO, 1956)
Francis in the Haunted House (Universal, 1956)

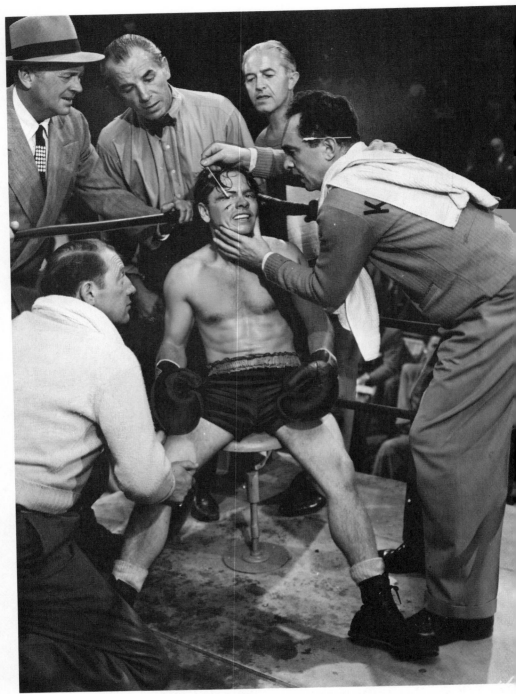

With James Dunn and Sam Levene in *Killer McCoy* (1947)

With Frank Ferguson (seated, behind and to the left of Mickey Rooney) in *Andy Hardy Comes Home* (1958)

In *Platinum High School* (1960)

Selena Royle

From MGM's point of view, Selena Royle was a good bet: a middle-aged former leading lady from the stage, who could handle in an extremely competent manner a string of "mother" assignments in a wide variety of guises, both on the home lot and elsewhere. Audiences, on the other hand, were generally unaware of Selena's screen presence because she blended so well into the film story at hand, conveying her "relative's" assignment so convincingly that seldom was she remembered by her viewers. And for Selena it was a relatively easy, if frustrating way of life. Unfortunately, there was hardly a meaty assignment among her roles to make her Hollywood years memorable. But then characters players were not supposed to be seen or heard, but were just to fill in the gaps while the stars were offcamera.

Selena was born November 6, 1904 in New York City, the daughter of playwright Edwin Milton Royle (he wrote *The Squaw Man*) and actress Selena Fetter. She was educated at the Low and Heywood School in Stamford, Connecticut, and then studied at the American Academy of Dramatic Arts. In 1921 she made her stage debut in one of that school's productions, *Lancelot and Elaine*, in which she played Queen Guinevere. The following year she was on Broadway in *Peer Gynt* with Joseph Schildkraut and Edward G. Robinson, and also appeared for the Theatre Guild in *Her Temporary Husband* (1923). In the mid-1920s she worked as the leading lady of William Wright's Stock Company in Grand Rapids, Michigan. Her coplayers included such future luminaries as Spencer Tracy and Pat O'Brien. In 1926 Selena was signed for a starring role in George M. Cohan's new Broadway show, *Yellow*, and it was she who convinced Cohan to hire her good friend Tracy for a secondary male part in the play. (Years later in Hollywood, Tracy kidded Selena: " ... if it hadn't been for you, I would probably be driving a truck and happy.") She was on Broadway in *Heat Wave* (1931), toured with George M. Cohan in *Confidential Service* (1932), played with Walter Abel and Spring Byington in *When Ladies Meet* (1932), and had a part in *Merrily We Roll Along* (1934).

In 1932, Selena married actor Earle Larimore (they were divorced in the early 1940s), and together they became much in demand on Broadway, despite the fact that their starring vehicle, Eugene O'Neill's *Days Without End* (1934), was not successful. By the end of the decade, Selena was expending

625

more of her professional efforts on radio rather than theatre. She was heard on such soap operas as *Kate Hopkins: Angel of Mercy* (a show coscripted by Gertrude Berg), had the title role in *Woman of Courage*, and, in the 1940s, she was on *Betty and Bob*.

She had made her first motion picture in 1932, *The Misleading Lady* which starred Claudette Colbert and was shot at Paramount's Astoria, Long Island studio. She had the secondary role as the spouse of Curtiss Cooksey. It was her only picture for more than a decade. She claimed to be "too busy for the movies." But then, being at loose ends in 1943, she made a cameo appearance in *Stage Door Canteen* (1943), sharing scenes with Katharine Hepburn. Then she decided to try Hollywood where, the following year, she had the movie part of her career in Twentieth Century-Fox's *The Sullivans*, one of that studio's best sentimental tributes to the American spirit on the World War II homefront. Selena portrayed the real-life Mrs. Sullivan whose five sons were killed at once in combat in the South Pacific during the war. Bearing a striking resemblance to the mature Ann Harding, Selena conveyed all the proper emotions of motherly love and found a niche for herself in 1940s Hollywood.

MGM hired Selena, but strictly on a character actress basis. After years as a leading stage performer, she was miffed by the Hollywood social structure and, being an outspoken person, made no bones about her dissatisfaction. In particular, she was annoyed by the attitude of her once good friend Tracy: "I was quite hurt at first, for I had expected Spence and Louise to ask me to dinner, and of course they never did. I realized eventually that it wasn't anything about *me*; it was just the way things were with everybody."

In *Mrs. Parkington* (1944), Selena played Mattie Trousen, the companion–maid of matriarch Greer Garson, and was Scott McKay's mother in Spencer Tracy's *Thirty Seconds Over Tokyo* (1944). In the programmer *Main Street after Dark* (1944), an expansion from Metro's *Crime Doesn't Pay* short subject series, Selena was the hardened con artist mother of Audrey Totter and Dan Duryea. In *This Man's Navy* (1945) Selena was Tom Drake's widowed mother who eventually weds chief pilot Wallace Beery.

But that, unfortunately, was the end of Selena's professional growth in Hollywood. Thereafter, Selena settled down in a cinematic rut, cast as everybody's mother, aunt, or companion. In 1946 she shepherded *The Harvey Girls* to their New Mexico home; was Mama Leckie, the wife of Hume Cronyn and Jessica Tandy's mother, in *The Green Years*; was Glenn Ford's mama in Columbia's *Gallant Journey*; was the mother of Elizabeth Taylor in *Courage of Lassie*; was loaned to RKO for a similar chore in *Till the End of Time*, where her son was legless army veteran Bill Williams; had marine sergeant Van Johnson as a son in *No Leave, No Love*; and was the mother of Cole Porter (Cary Grant) in Warner Brothers' *Night and Day*. Selena almost made a speedy exit from the latter picture, as she became ill after the first day of shooting on her scenes, but she recovered before a replacement could be found.

The following years saw more of the same stereotyped parts in smaller doses. She was the patient wife of unreconstructed Southerner Thomas Mitchell in *The Romance of Rosy Ridge* (1947); the spouse of crooked district attorney Otto Kruger in *Smart Woman* (1948); and mothered a brood in *Summer Holiday* (1948). She played a Back Bay Bostonite with Anne Baxter for a daughter in *You Were Meant for Me* (1948); was Wallace Beery's sweet wife and Jane Powell's mother in *A Date with Judy* (1948); played an aunt in Republic's *Moonrise* (1948); and was Ingrid Bergman's peasant mama in *Joan Of Arc* (1948).

Offscreen Selena wed French-born actor George Renevant in 1948, and oncamera was the wife of radio show sponsor S. Z. Sakall in *My Dream Is Yours* (1949). For a change of pace, she was a juvenile court judge in Audie Murphy's *Bad Boy* (1949), but she was again a sensible and observant creature, an aunt this time, in *The Heiress* (1949). In her last MGM picture, *The Big Hangover* (1950), she was the wife of "uncle" Edgar Buchanan. Later that year she was Charles Bickford's wife in *Branded*; played a down-and-out socialite hired to give Joan Crawford some polish in *The Damned Don't Cry* (1950); was the fearful mother of Shelley Winters in *He Ran All the Way* (1951); and in *Come Fill the Cup* (1951) was the jittery mother of alcoholic Gig Young.

But by 1951 outspoken Selena found herself *persona non grata* on the Hollywood scene. The studios were undergoing a severe economic depression and trying to recuperate from the Communist witch hunt. No one seemingly wanted to add to their production problems by having to deal with a nondiplomatic character player. So it was two years before Selena obtained another film assignment, and that in the quickie science fiction entry, *Robot Monster* (1953) with George Nader. Her last movie to date was in the programmer *Murder Is My Beat* (1955), in which she was onscreen briefly as the wife of supposedly dead man Roy Gordon. The following year she made one of her rare television appearances, playing with Ethel Barrymore on the *Ethel Barrymore Theatre*, in the episode *The Daughter of Mars*.

For nearly twenty years, Selena has resided in Guadalejara where she is regarded as the "Doyenne" of the Mexican city. She has written a cookbook entitled *A Gringa's Guide to Mexican Cooking*.

SELENA ROYLE

The Misleading Lady (Paramount, 1932)
Stage Door Canteen (UA, 1943)
The Sullivans (20th-Fox, 1944)
Mrs. Parkington (MGM, 1944)
Thirty Seconds over Tokyo (MGM, 1944)
Main Street after Dark (MGM, 1944)
This Man's Navy (MGM, 1945)
The Harvey Girls (MGM, 1946)
The Green Years (MGM, 1946)

Courage of Lassie (MGM, 1946)
Gallant Journey (Columbia, 1946)
Till the End of Time (RKO, 1946)
No Leave, No Love (MGM, 1946)
Night and Day (WB, 1946)
The Romance of Rosy Ridge (MGM, 1947)
Wild Harvest (Paramount, 1947)
Cass Timberlane (MGM, 1947)
Smart Woman (AA, 1948)

Summer Holiday (MGM, 1948)
You Were Meant for Me (20th-Fox, 1948)
A Date with Judy (MGM, 1948)
Moonrise (Republic, 1948)
Joan of Arc (RKO, 1948)
My Dream Is Yours (WB, 1949)
Bad Boy (AA, 1949)
You're My Everything (20th-Fox, 1949)

The Heiress (Paramount, 1949)
The Big Hangover (MGM, 1950)
Branded (Paramount, 1950)
The Damned Don't Cry (WB, 1950)
He Ran All the Way (UA, 1951)
Come Fill the Cup (WB, 1951)
Robot Monster (Astor, 1953)
Murder Is My Beat (AA, 1955)

With Hume Cronyn in *Main Street After Dark* (1944)

Rosalind Russell

After witnessing Rosalind Russell's contagious spirit and spunk in Broadway's *Wonderful Town* (1953), drama critic Brooks Atkinson is said to have proposed her as a likely candidate for the presidency of the United States, a not inappropriate accolade for the screen's favorite "boss lady." In picture after picture, whether as a newspaper reporter, an insurance executive, a psychiatrist, or a college dean, Rosalind was the determined female bucking a man's world by using masculine tactics. All of this woman's lib proselytizing was accomplished by a brittle screwball comedy panache and boundless efficient energy. Always in the last reel, however, the man-tailored suits and horned-rimmed glasses would be replaced by more feminine garb, just in time to give her that touch of romance.

Rosalind was one of the last stars-in-the-making to be groomed by Irving Thalberg. She was initially thought of as a carbon-copy Myrna Loy and was to be used as insurance if Loy should rebel at studio policy. But before long, Rosalind proved herself a more robust if less accomplished comedienne than Loy, and she went along her individual merry way. Just as she began to hit her stride after seven years with Metro, she chose not to renew her contract. Whatever Rosalind's pretentions were to match Norma Shearer or Joan Crawford in the glamorous drama sweepstakes, MGM and the public preferred her a la *The Women* (1939) and *The Feminine Touch* (1941). Her post-MGM period found her in sharp form in *My Sister Eileen* (1942) and *Auntie Mame* (1958), but faltering badly when she ventured into heavy melodrama or attempted to expand her limited acting range.

Rosalind Russell was born in Waterbury, Connecticut on June 4, 1908 (she says 1912), the middle of seven children in an Irish Catholic family. Her father was a lawyer of note and she was named at his suggestion after the S. S. *Rosalind*. Educated in Catholic schools, she convinced her mother she should be allowed to enter the American Academy of Dramatic Art in New York City, ostensibly to learn how to teach acting. After graduation she set out traveling with stock companies, had some brief exposure on Broadway, and was offered a screen test by Universal.

The astute Rosalind stated she preferred to make the test in California, not New York, and the studio obliged, tested her and offered her a

$400-a-week contract. Simultaneously she tested at MGM and, when that studio made her a more lucrative offer, she walked into Carl Laemmle, Jr.'s office at Universal, wearing her worst-fitting garments, bemoaned her mistake in coming to Hollywood and asked out of her contract. Laemmle sympathetically agreed to do as she asked, whereupon the actress raced over to MGM and signed on for seven years. The year was 1934, and her first role was as the other woman in *Evelyn Prentice*, starring Myrna Loy. For several years thereafter, Rosalind was used as a tacit threat to Loy. Each time Loy refused a script, her reason usually being more money, Rosalind would be called up front and offered a starring part, but Loy always managed to settle her differences in the nick of time, and Rosalind would again be the second lead: to Joan Crawford in *Forsaking All Others* (1934), to Maureen O'Sullivan in *West Point of the Air* (1935), and to Jean Harlow in *Reckless* (1935) and *China Seas* (1935). She was not appropriately cast as the femme fatale. Having showed a flair for comedy in *The Casino Murder Case* (1935), Louis B. Mayer gave her a Loy reject, *Rendezvous* (1935), a spy–comedy lead opposite William Powell.

Then director Dorothy Arzner requested her for the part of *Craig's Wife* (1936) at Columbia, and while she was too youthful for the role, she acquitted herself admirably. In the memorable *Night Must Fall* (1937), she was the spinster who is infatuated with axe murderer Robert Montgomery, and in *The Citadel* (1938), filmed on location in England, she was the steadfast wife of physician Robert Donat. Knowing she was right for comedy, Rosalind set out determinedly to win the role of Sylvia Fowler, the bitch of all time, in Claire Luce's *The Women*. She tested five times for the part for director George Cukor, and for the last test, when Cukor urged her to "play her as a freak," Rosalind burlesqued the character, and he gave her the role. The result was that Rosalind became the high point of that film in playing the flamboyant predator, and she has been grateful to Cukor ever since.

Having established comedy as her forte, she was loaned by MGM to Columbia for the best role of her career, Hildy Johnson, the competitive newspaper reporter in *His Girl Friday* (1940), from the Ben Hecht–Charles MacArthur play–film *The Front Page*. One legend has it that director Howard Hawks was stuck with Rosalind after Jean Arthur, Claudette Colbert, Janet Gaynor, and Irene Dunne turned the script down, and another says Hawks had screen writer Charles Lederer prepare the part with Rosalind in mind. Whichever is correct, this role is the apotheosis of her "boss lady" roles. While making this picture, costar Cary Grant introduced her to his house guest, Frederick Brisson, an actor's agent and the son of Danish actor Carl Brisson. Rosalind and he were married October 25, 1941 and, since that time, Brisson has been the major influence on her career. It was he who urged her not to renew her MGM contract, and she followed his advice and free-lanced.

She did the excellent *My Sister Eileen* for Columbia, playing the zany older sister, and received an Academy Award nomination for her work in this film. This picture was part of her five-year nonexclusive pact with the

Columbia studio. She was one of the few female performers who had no difficulty in getting along with irascible Harry Cohn. She starred in RKO's *Flight for Freedom* (1943) an attempt by Hollywood to make a happy love story out of the mysterious disappearance of aviatrix Amelia Earhart. She was off the screen for a year due to the birth of her son Lance in 1943, but returned in Warners' *Roughly Speaking* (1945), a marathon chronicle of an emancipated but feminine woman. Her paycheck for that endeavor was $200,000.

A preview of the future Rosalind could be seen in the heavy-handed tribute to *Sister Kenny* (1946). Rosalind had met Sister Elizabeth Kenny through her work with charities, and proposed the film project herself. The film accomplished its purpose by earning Rosalind a second Oscar nomination, but it was poorly received by the public who did not fancy a two-hour paean to the saintly woman who fought for a polio cure. This overly dramatic portrayal was followed by *The Guilt of Janet Ames* (1947) which is best likened to a joyless *Lady in the Dark. Mourning Becomes Electra* (1947) was a major RKO undertaking of O'Neill's elusive play and one of film history's most interesting flops. Rosalind was completely out of her depth as Lavinia, but received another nomination, as one observer stated, "presumably due to her courage."

The Velvet Touch (1948) was produced by her independent company and was the most plausible of her late 1940s work. She played a Broadway star who murders in a fit of rage, but finds she cannot live with her conscience. Two more production line comedies for Columbia followed, and then it was two years before the modestly budgeted *Never Wave at a Wac* (1952) appeared. She had audience-tested this weak farce in a television version previously.

Well into her forties, Rosalind understood that Hollywood had enough of its own problems without trying to find proper roles for a mature star, so she returned to the stage. A tour of *Bell, Book and Candle* in 1951 inspired her to undertake Broadway in 1953 with a musical called *Wonderful Town*, based on *My Sister Eileen.* Her comedy talents *and* her husky singing voice were hailed by the critics, and she was voted a Tony Award.

She returned to Hollywood to appear in the little-seen musical *The Girl Rush* (1955). Then she accepted the character role of the frustrated schoolteacher in *Picnic* (1955). Columbia, afraid that the public might think Rosalind was attempting the part of the young heroine, played by Harry Cohn's protégée Kim Novak, stressed the special billing of "costarring Rosalind Russell as Rosemary." When Oscar time came around, Rosalind objected to being considered in the supporting actress category and ended up with no nomination at all.

She spent the next three years in the role for which she is most likely to be remembered, *Auntie Mame*, with nearly two years on Broadway, (1955–1957) and the screen version in 1958, which earned her a fourth Oscar bid.

Since that time she and her husband have purchased star-vehicle properties for her, usually proven Broadway successes, but they have repeatedly proven wrong for *her*. Her acting had become simply a series of postured mannerisms in such films as *A Majority Of One* (1961) (Gertrude Berg was the stage lead); *Five Finger Exercise* (1962) (Jessica Tandy played it onstage); *Gypsy* (1962) (Ethel Merman starred in the role onstage), *Oh Dad, Poor Dad, Mama's Hung You in the Closet and I'm Feeling So Sad* (1967) (Jo Van Fleet onstage); and *Rosie!* (1968) (Ruth Gordon performed on stage). Director Ida Lupino made *The Trouble with Angels* (1966) saccharine enough film fare so that Rosalind could repeat her mother superior role in the sequel, *Where Angels Go...Trouble Follows* (1968). Her last film to date, *Mrs. Pollifax—Spy* (1971) was a sufficiently cute enough production for a half-hour television episode but could not endure such a full-blown production or Rosalind's participation in all facets of the film's making. (Under the name of C. A. McKnight she wrote the screenplay to Esther Williams' *The Unguarded Moment* (1956), one of the few occasions when she has acknowledged her script routing or rewriting endeavors.)

Everyone assumed she would star in the Broadway version of *Coco*, a property owned by her husband, but the opinionated Mlle. Chanel objected The most recent project she and Brisson have announced is a musical play based on the life of evangelist Aimee Semple McPherson.

Rosiland returned to television on November 18, 1972 (ABC) in a tele-feature, *Crooked Hearts,* in which she starred as a con artist.

Recently, when asked about her Metro years, Rosalind stated: "MGM in those days was constructed like something that was going to hit the beaches on D-Day. There was a first wave of top stars, then a second wave to replace them in case they got difficult. I was in the second line of defense, behind Myrna Loy.

"I finally got in the first line by loanouts. MGM wouldn't loan the top stars, but I was able to get outside pictures like *His Girl Friday* and *Craig's Wife.* I was annoyed at the time because I was never consulted. But the exposure was great for me."

Despite her very painful bouts with arthritis, Rosalind has refused to slow down in keeping with her advancing years. She enjoys hobnobbing with Frank Sinatra's social set and still searches for a property to bring that elusive Oscar to her mantle. As part of the presentations of the 1972 Academy Awards, she received the Jean Hersholt Humanitarian Award for her contributions to charity. Of her unending acting pursuits, she says, "Success is a public affair. Failure is a private funeral."

ROSALIND RUSSELL

Evelyn Prentice (MGM, 1934)
The President Vanishes (Paramount, 1934)
Forsaking All Others (MGM, 1934)
West Point of the Air (MGM, 1935)
Casino Murder Case (MGM, 1935)
Reckless (MGM, 1935)
China Seas (MGM, 1935)
Rendezvous (MGM, 1935)

The Night Is Young (MGM, 1935)
It Had to Happen (20th-Fox, 1936)
Under Two Flags (20th-Fox, 1936)
Trouble for Two (MGM, 1936)
Craig's Wife (Columbia, 1936)
Night Must Fall (MGM, 1937)
Live, Love and Learn (MGM, 1937)
Man-Proof (MGM, 1938)

The Citadel (MGM, 1938)
Four's a Crowd (WB, 1938)
Fast and Loose (MGM, 1939)
The Women (MGM, 1939)
His Girl Friday (Columbia, 1940)
No Time for Comedy (WB, 1940)
Hired Wife (Universal, 1940)
This Thing Called Love (Columbia, 1941)
They Met in Bombay (MGM, 1941)
The Feminine Touch (MGM, 1941)
Design for Scandal (MGM, 1941)
Take a Letter, Darling (Paramount, 1942)
My Sister Eileen (Columbia, 1942)
Flight for Freedom (RKO, 1943)
What a Woman! (Columbia, 1943)
Roughly Speaking (WB, 1945)
She Wouldn't Say Yes (Columbia, 1945)
Sister Kenny (RKO, 1946)
The Guilt of Janet Ames (Columbia, 1947)
Mourning Becomes Electra (RKO, 1947)
The Velvet Touch (RKO, 1948)
Tell It to the Judge (Columbia, 1949)
A Woman of Distinction (Columbia, 1950)
Never Wave at a Wac (RKO, 1952)
The Girl Rush (Paramount, 1955)

With Soo Yong in *China Seas* (1935)

Picnic (Columbia, 1955)
Auntie Mame (WB, 1958)
A Majority of One (WB, 1961)
Five Finger Exercise (Columbia, 1962)
Gypsy (WB, 1962)
The Trouble with Angels (Columbia, 1966)
Oh Dad, Poor Dad, Mama's Hung You in the Closet and I'm Feeling So Sad (Paramount, 1967)
Where Angels Go ... Trouble Follows (Columbia, 1968)
Rosie! (Universal, 1968)
Mrs. Pollifax—Spy (UA, 1971)

With Myrna Loy, John Miljan, Leonard Penn, and Joyce Compton in *Man-Proof* (1938)

With Robert Montgomery in *Fast and Loose* (1939)

With Norma Shearer in *The Women* (1939)

Ann Rutherford

Like that other Rutherford, actress Margaret, Ann Rutherford is best known as a spunky gal with no pretensions that her screen career is great art. She spent seven of her sixteen moviemaking years at MGM, mainly emoting as Polly Benedict, Mickey Rooney's ever-faithful true love in the *Andy Hardy* series. She eventually tired of "being" Carvel's most loyal booster of Andy Hardy and moved away from MGM to tackle adult roles, though not very successfully. Her ingenue screen performances are remembered for their spirit if not their versatility, and her capacity to make audiences like her screen larking is still enjoyed today.

Ann was born in Toronto, Ontario, Canada on November 2, 1917. Her father, John Defferin Rutherford, had been a Metropolitan Opera singer. Her mother, Lucille Mansfield, a cousin of actor Richard Mansfield, was a former silent screen actress. When Ann was four, the Rutherfords took her and her sister to live in San Francisco. A local stock company there required children for their production of *Mrs. Wiggs of the Cabbage Patch*. Ann auditioned and was hired for the first of many such assignments in that city and later in Los Angeles when the family relocated there. When Ann was eleven, she began performing on assorted radio shows and soon was so versatile that she was often heard performing in roles as diverse as a baby or an old woman. Years later, Ann would return to that medium to replace Penny Singleton as radio's Blondie.

In 1934, a talent agent saw Ann's photograph in the newspaper and happened to hear her on radio. She was taken to Mascot Pictures (soon to become Republic) for a screen test. She lied and said she was eighteen. A few years later MGM's publicity department reversed the process and readjusted her birth year to 1924. Mascot hired Ann and, while she made films in the daytime, she would attend school at night. That same year, Ann's sister, using the professional name of Judith Arlen, was selected as a WAMPAS baby star and made her film debut. When Ann was later contracted to MGM, Judith would join that studio's talent roster, but soon retired to become a housewife. She died in 1968.

At Mascot/Republic, Ann became a knockabout heroine, following in the footsteps of Betsy King Ross and Dorothy Gulliver. She was topbilled in her first film, *Waterfront Lady* (1935), in which she tames Frank Albertson. In the twelve-chapter serial, *The Fighting Marines* (1935), she adorned the background while Grant Withers and Adrian Morris did battle with the mysterious enemy known as the Tiger Shark. She was Gene Autry's leading lady in *Melody Trail* and *The Singing Vagabond*, both made in 1935, and again played the female lead in Autry's *Comin' Round the Mountain* (1936) and *Public Cowboy No. One* (1937). She supported John Wayne in *The Lawless Nineties, The Oregon Trail,* and *The Lonely Trail,* all released in 1936.

By the time Ann's Mascot Republic contract expired in late 1936, she had signed on at MGM for $300 a week. Her salary would escalate to $1,250 before she left. She was quickly used for tiny assignments in Joan Crawford's *The Bride Wore Red,* Madge Evans' *Espionage,* and Rosalind Russell's *Live, Love and Learn,* all in 1937. In the following year Ann blossomed to the full extent that Metro demanded of her professionally. She was James Stewart's sweetheart Annie Hawks in *Of Human Hearts* (1938), and then was selected to replace Margaret Marquis as Polly Benedict in the reshuffled lineup for the *Andy Hardy* series. At 5' 3-1/2", Ann was still taller than star Mickey Rooney. According to the scripters' concept, that fact made Rooney more vulnerable and the romance between Ann's Polly and Rooney's Andy more humorous.

In the twelve *Andy Hardy* entries in which she appeared, Ann usually took a back seat to the likes of Lana Turner in *Love Finds Andy Hardy* (1938), of Virginia Grey in *Andy Hardy Rides High* (1939), of Helen Gilbert in *Andy Hardy Gets Spring Fever* (1939), of June Preisser in *Judge Hardy and Son* (1939), of Diana Lewis in *Andy Hardy Meets Debutante* (1940), of Kathryn Grayson in *Andy Hardy's Private Secretary* (1941), and of Esther Williams in *Andy Hardy's Double Life* (1942). However, unlike Judy Garland who, as Betsy Booth, suffered unrequited love for Rooney in three segments, Ann could be sure that, by the conclusion of each picture, she would have the humbled Mickey back at bay, reaffirming his adolescent love for her.

Meanwhile, Metro employed Ann as the Ghost of Christmas Past—a role traditionally played by males — in *A Christmas Carol* (1938), as an actress student in *Dramatic School* (1938), as a support to Florence Rice in *Four Girls in White* (1939), and as a collegiate in two Lana Turner films, *These Glamour Girls* and *Dancing Co-Ed,* both in 1939. Then she was allowed to be seen briefly as Vivien Leigh's sister Careen O'Hara in *Gone with the Wind* (1939), and was one of the lesser daughters in *Pride and Prejudice* (1940). She played third fiddle to Wallace Beery and Leo Carrillo in *Wyoming* (1940), with Bobs Watson as her relative. As Billie Burke's daughter in *The Ghost Comes Home* (1940), she was just as surprised as mother when head of the household Frank Morgan, long thought dead, reappears on the scene. After playing another nice young lady to MGM contractee John Shelton in *Keeping Company* (1941), she got her first adult role as Carol Lambert, who competes with Virginia Grey for the affection of radio detective Red Skelton in *Whistling in the Dark* (1941). Then she was loaned to Universal to replace Miriam Hopkins in *Badlands of*

Dakota (1941). All these non-Andy Hardy roles were deliberately nondescript assignments, engineered not to harm her valuable virginal Polly Benedict image. Ann was so popular in this screen guise that on one publicity trek to the East Coast in 1939, Rutherford, New Jersey was prompted to hold a special celebration for her.

By the end of 1941, Ann wanted to get out of the Polly Benedict syndrome and resigned from MGM. She then tried her luck at Twentieth Century-Fox, where she had three unrewarding adult roles. But there were no hard feelings between Metro and Ann, and she returned to Culver City on special assignment to appear with Red Skelton in the followup entries, *Whistling in Dixie* (1942) and *Whistling in Brooklyn* (1943).

In 1942, Ann had wed David May, a Los Angeles department store executive, and the following year she gave birth to a daughter, Gloria. Ann and David May were divorced in 1953, and in the same year she wed television producer William Dozier.

The remainder of the 1940s saw Ann's film career going downhill. She was way down in the cast list of two mild Republic whodunits, *Murder in the Music Hall* (1945) and *The Madonna's Secret* (1946). She played Florence Bates' daughter in *The Secret Life of Walter Mitty* (1947), and one of Errol Flynn's lesser romances in *Adventures of Don Juan* (1948), the film which finally broke her good-girl screen image. In *Operation Haylift* (1950) she merely supported Bill Williams and Jane Nigh.

In the 1950s Ann was occasionally on television, playing very middle-aged roles as on *Climax's Public Pigeon No. 1* (1956) with her old MGM costar, Red Skelton, on *Kraft Playhouse's Success* (1957), and opposite Andy Griffith in *The Male Animal* (1958) on *Playhouse 90*. When Mickey Rooney packaged *Andy Hardy Comes Home* (1958), he requested Ann to appear in the new entry, but her salary demand was too high, and she was dropped from the programmer's casting.

Ann was absent from the entertainment world through much of the 1960s, until late in the decade, when she appeared in the "Love and the Positive Man" segment of ABC-TV's *Love, American Style*. The same year she recorded for MGM Records the LP album, "The Adventures of Raggedy Ann."

Regarding her present housewife status, Ann has said: "It's titillating to do an occasional film, but really, I don't need it. Oh, I suppose, if you were a Helen Hayes, it might mean something if you left the business. You'd be depriving the show world of something. I'm depriving that world of nothing." But just for the fun of it, she was talked into returning to MGM for a cameo in *They Only Kill Their Masters* (1972).

When Ann returned to MGM in the summer of 1972 to film her cameo assignment, preparations were already underway to tear down Lot Number Two, which held the famed Andy Hardy-Carvel Street sets. Recalling her apprentice years at MGM brought tears to Ann's eyes: "It was exciting, stimulating. Just to come into the commisary boggled your mind. Just to stick your head out of a stage door and look up and down the street. Just to see Lionel Barrymore walking down the street dressed like a pirate or Wallace Beery dressed like a slob. Greta Garbo, with her retinue, everyone trailing after her, the hairdressers twittering about, her makeup man flapping the powder puff, someone carrying the train ... "

ANN RUTHERFORD

Waterfront Lady (Mascot, 1935)
The Fighting Marines (Serial: Mascot, 1935)
Melody Trail (Republic, 1935)
The Singing Vagabond (Republic, 1935)
The Lawless Nineties (Republic, 1936)
Doughnuts and Society (Mascot, 1936)
The Harvester (Republic, 1936)
Comin' Round the Mountain (Republic, 1936)
Down to the Sea (Republic, 1936)
The Oregon Trail (Republic, 1936)
The Lonely Trail (Republic, 1936)
The Bride Wore Red (MGM, 1937)
Public Cowboy No. One (Republic, 1937)
Espionage (MGM, 1937)
Live, Love and Learn (MGM, 1937)
Of Human Hearts (MGM, 1938)
You're Only Young Once (MGM, 1938)
Judge Hardy's Children (MGM, 1938)
Love Finds Andy Hardy (MGM, 1938)
A Christmas Carol (MGM, 1938)
Dramatic School (MGM, 1938)
Out West with the Hardys (MGM, 1938)
Four Girls in White (MGM, 1939)
The Hardys Ride High (MGM, 1939)
Andy Hardy Gets Spring Fever (MGM, 1939)
These Glamour Girls (MGM, 1939)
Dancing Co-Ed (MGM, 1939)
Judge Hardy and Son (MGM, 1939)

Gone with the Wind (MGM, 1939)
Pride and Prejudice (MGM, 1940)
Andy Hardy Meets Debutante (MGM, 1940)
Wyoming (MGM, 1940)
The Ghost Comes Home (MGM, 1940)
Keeping Company (MGM, 1941)
Andy Hardy's Private Secretary (MGM, 1941)
Washington Melodrama (MGM, 1941)
Whistling in the Dark (MGM, 1941)
Life Begins for Andy Hardy (MGM, 1941)
Badlands of Dakota (Universal, 1941)
The Courtship of Andy Hardy (MGM, 1942)
This Time for Keeps (MGM, 1942)
Orchestra Wives (20th-Fox, 1942)
Whistling in Dixie (MGM, 1942)
Andy Hardy's Double Life (MGM, 1942)
Whistling in Brooklyn (MGM, 1943)
Happy Land (20th-Fox, 1943)
Bermuda Mystery (20th-Fox, 1944)
Two O'Clock Courage (RKO, 1945)
Bedside Manner (UA, 1945)
Murder in the Music Hall (Republic, 1946)
The Madonna's Secret (Republic, 1946)
Inside Job (Universal, 1946)
The Secret Life of Walter Mitty (RKO, 1947)
Adventures of Don Juan (WB, 1948)
Operation Haylift (Lippert, 1950)
They Only Kill Their Masters (MGM, 1972)

With Mickey Rooney and William Orr in *The Hardys Ride High* (1939)

Norma Shearer

If any one personality gave MGM class during its golden age it was the ultrachic Norma Shearer. Between 1923 and her self-imposed retirement in 1942, she made forty films at the studio, emerging from the dewy-eyed heroine of *The Student Prince* (1927) into the amoral ultrasophisticate of *A Free Soul* (1931), and finally into the canonized first lady of the screen in a trio of classic roles: *The Barretts of Wimpole Street* (1934), *Romeo and Juliet* (1936), and *Marie Antoinette* (1938). She was far from a supreme technician, and despite her patrician bearing, she was not really a cinema beauty. But her sharpened aristocratic air was so compelling to many filmgoers that, with a good deal of direction from the MGM publicity department, she was accepted as the epitome of natural high breeding and the final word in feminine sophistication. It was a lofty position to which many aspired, of which the most notable example was MGM rival Joan Crawford. Two other female stars were required to "assume" this status: Greer Garson and Deborah Kerr, each with less success as MGM declined in the 1940s and the world acquired new values.

While Irving Thalberg's influence on his wife's career can hardly be overestimated, it has been filmdom's conjecture for years, by those who know her, anyway, that Edith Norma Shearer would, by her own accord, most likely still have become Queen of the MGM lot, for she was indeed an ambitious young lady. Born into comfortable means in Montreal (August 10, 1900), she won a beauty contest at fourteen which encouraged her mother's desire for Norma to have a theatrical career. When the Depression of 1920 depleted the family finances, her mother packed Norma and her sister Athole (later Mrs. Howard Hawks) off to New York City. Florenz Ziegfeld did not think Norma's legs good enough for the *Follies*, but undaunted, her mother helped Norma attain work as a motion picture extra, in such films as *The Flapper* (1920) and D. W. Griffith's *Way Down East* (1920). Norma went on to a small role in *The Stealers* (1920) and Herbert Brenon paid her $25 per day to do a part in *The Sign on the Door* (1921).

Twenty-one-year-old Irving G. Thalberg saw her in *The Stealers* while he was working as assistant to Carl Laemmle at Universal. When Thalberg joined forces with Louis B. Mayer in 1923, he remembered Norma and gave her a five-year contract at $110 a week. He suggested her for the lead in *Fir*

640

National's *The Wanters* (1923), but deferred to director John M. Stahl and allowed his unknown quantity to be cast in a smaller role. He followed this part by immediately giving her the leading role as the flapper in *Pleasure Mad* (1923) for Mayer's own company. Mayer sensed her inexperience at an early stage in the shooting and advised the overzealous Thalberg accordingly. Thalberg in turn urged his protégée to buckle down, and buckle down she did. In rapid succession Thalberg kept her working on his screen in largely mediocre parts to give her sufficient film experience. Their personal relationship culminated in marriage in 1927 when Thalberg suggested she retire.

With her appetite newly whetted with the magic of motion pictures Norma not only refused, but began to complain to her husband about wanting better roles. He conceded, and she made a successful talking debut in *The Trial of Mary Dugan* (1929) as a knowing showgirl innocently convicted of murder. Four pictures later, she received an Academy Award as the vengeful wife of a philandering husband in *The Divorcee* (1930). She came off second best to Marie Dressler in *Let Us Be Gay* (1930) and likewise to Lionel Barrymore in *A Free Soul* (1931), but in each case she was the heavily promoted commodity that drew in the audiences. She suffered a little better fate in Noel Coward's *Private Lives* (1931) with Robert Montgomery, which was a lively if not believable swank comedy. In the innovative but bland version of O'Neill's *Strange Interlude* (1932) she was again teamed with boxoffice magician Clark Gable. This time she gave birth to his illegitimate child and suffered nobly for reels thereafter.

Unlike lesser MGM stars Joan Crawford and Myrna Loy, who continued to grind out pictures throughout the 1930s, Norma followed the lead of Greta Garbo in making rare screen appearances. She did not want her public to tire of her, and being the wife of Hollywood's wunderkind had its own demanding duties on the social scene. Thus after her saintly appearance in *Smilin' Through* (1932), she was off the screen until 1934 when *Riptide* presented her as Herbert Marshall's straying wife who prefers the caresses of Robert Montgomery. Since Thalberg thrived on prestige productions, he saw no reason why Norma should not grace a select number of such films, and insisted that she was best for *The Barretts of Wimpole Street* (1934). She herself was not thoroughly convinced that the part of Elizabeth Barrett Browning was suitable for her, but when it became evident that William Randolph Hearst was busy persuading Mayer to accept Marion Davies as Elizabeth, she relented. The theatrical sincerity of her performance in the romantic lead appealed to her public and critics, so Norma shrewdly persuaded her husband that Shakespeare's Juliet should be her next role. Actually, she had "attempted" Juliet to John Gilbert's Romeo in the balcony scene extract used for *The Hollywood Revue of 1929* (1929).

All the MGM stops were pulled out for this glamorously mounted production of *Romeo and Juliet* (1936), and while Norma's Juliet (she was then thirty-six years old) raised a few eyebrows, most of the critics and a segment of the moviegoing public (it was not a boxoffice success) thought they were really

In *He Who Gets Slapped* (1924)

th Johnny Mack Brown in *Lady of Chance*
928)

With Tyrrell Davis, Hedda Hopper, Raymond
Hackett, and Sally Eilers in *Let Us Be Gay*
(1930)

With Robert Montgomery, Irene Rich, Bess Flowers (rear), Neil Hamilton, Hale Hamilton, and
Conchita Montenegro in *Strangers May Kiss* (1931)

seeing Shakespeare. She received her fifth Oscar nomination for this film. In retrospect, the film is banal except for John Barrymore's splendid Mercutio and Norma exuded more unpleasing mannerisms than in *The Barretts*. *Romeo and Juliet* premiered in New York City on August 20, 1936 and, twenty days later, Irving Thalberg was dead of pneumonia at the age of thirty-seven. (At the time, he and Mayer had been feuding, and he had planned to splinter off into independent production, taking many stars with him.)

The widowed Norma immediately expressed her desire to retire, but the MGM powers did not wish to lose such a valuable commodity ($400,000 of studio money was already tied up in preparations for *Marie Antoinette*) and demanded the settling of Thalberg's estate be contingent upon her continued contractual involvement with the studio. That involvement was a six-picture contract at $150,000 per picture, the first to be, of course, *Marie Antoinette* Thalberg's meticulous eye for script-doctoring was missing from *Marie Antoinette*, and Norma had a hard time keeping afloat amidst the posh surroundings. Although as the chronicle picture progressed toward the Queen's untimely end, Norma improved, and her regal courage as she goes to meet her doom is memorable. There was talk that Mayer tried to sabotage the production by trying to force Norma to sell her MGM stock.

At about this time, David O. Selznick offered her the role of Scarlett O'Hara but, when the public overwhelmingly objected to this casting, both Norma and Selznick mentioned nothing further on the subject. She was grandly dramatic in *Idiot's Delight* (1939), in the role originally conceived by Lynn Fontanne. However, since she was either required or opted on her own to carbon copy the Fontanne stage performance, most of the screen notices went to Clark Gable as the jovial but seedy traveling hoofer. Her noble womanliness was displayed to good advantage in George Cukor's *The Women* (1939). *Escape* (1940), with Robert Taylor, was improbable melodrama set in Nazi Europe. Of *We Were Dancing* (1942) and *Her Cardboard Lover* (1942), Norma has been quoted as saying, "On those two, nobody but myself was trying to do me in." Simultaneously, she turned down the opportunity to star in *Mrs. Miniver* (1942), and retired from the screen.

Later in 1942 Norma, who had two children by Thalberg, Irving, Jr. and Katharine, wed Sun Valley, Idaho, ski instructor Martin Arouge, some ten years her junior. Before they married, he waived all community property rights to Norma's fortune. Whether traveling in Europe or in the United States with her husband, Norma remained out of the limelight whenever possible, eschewing public appearances, interviews, and photographs. When Universal filmed *Man of a Thousand Faces* (1957) and asked Norma's permission to have an actor portray Thalberg, she not only agreed but picked out Bob Evans, a young New York clothing manufacturer, to essay the role. Since then Evans has become more famous as the production head of Paramount Pictures. In recent years Norma has been quite ill, and she has been hospitalized on a

With Robert Montgomery in *Private Lives* (1931)

645

number of occasions. Her older brother Douglas, for a long time head of MGM's sound and technical development departments, died on January 5, 1971.

NORMA SHEARER

The Flapper (Selznick, 1920)
The Restless Sex (Paramount, 1920)
Way Down East (UA, 1920)
The Stealers (Robertson-Cole, 1920)
The Sign on the Door (FN, 1921)
The Devil's Partner (Iroquois, 1922)
Channing of the Northwest (Selznick, 1922)
The Bootleggers (FBO, 1922)
The Man Who Paid (Producers Security, 1922)
A Clouded Name (Play Company, 1923)
The Wanters (FN, 1923)
Pleasure Mad (Mayer Company, 1923)
Lucretia Lombard (WB, 1923)
Man and Wife (Arrow, 1923)
Broadway after Dark (WB, 1924)
Trail of the Law (Oscar Apfel, 1924)
Blue Waters (New Brunswick, 1924)
The Wolf Man (Fox, 1924)
Empty Hands (Paramount, 1924)
Broken Barriers (Metro-Goldwyn, 1924)
He Who Gets Slapped (Metro-Goldwyn, 1924)
The Snob (Metro-Goldwyn, 1924)
Married Flirts (Metro-Goldwyn, 1924)
Lady of the Night (Metro-Goldwyn, 1925)
Waking up the Town (UA, 1925)
Pretty Ladies (Metro-Goldwyn, 1925)
A Slave of Fashion (Metro-Goldwyn, 1925)
Excuse Me (Metro-Goldwyn, 1925)
The Tower of Lies (Metro-Goldwyn, 1925)
His Secretary (Metro-Goldwyn, 1925)

The Devil's Circus (Metro-Goldwyn, 1926)
The Waning Sex (Metro-Goldwyn, 1926)
Upstage (Metro-Goldwyn, 1926)
The Demi-Bride (MGM, 1927)
After Midnight (MGM, 1927)
The Student Prince (MGM, 1927)
The Latest from Paris (MGM, 1928)
The Actress (MGM, 1928)
Lady of Chance (MGM, 1928)
The Trial of Mary Dugan (MGM, 1929)
The Last of Mrs. Cheyney (MGM, 1929)
The Hollywood Revue of 1929 (MGM, 1929)
Their Own Desire (MGM, 1930)
The Divorcee (MGM, 1930)
Let Us Be Gay (MGM, 1930)
Strangers May Kiss (MGM, 1931)
A Free Soul (MGM, 1931)
Private Lives (MGM, 1931)
Strange Interlude (MGM, 1932)
Smilin' Through (MGM, 1932)
Riptide (MGM, 1934)
The Barretts of Wimpole Street (MGM, 1934)
Romeo and Juliet (MGM, 1936)
Marie Antoinette (MGM, 1938)
Idiot's Delight (MGM, 1939)
The Women (MGM, 1939)
Escape (MGM, 1940)
We Were Dancing (MGM, 1942)
Her Cardboard Lover (MGM, 1942)

With Robert A'Dair, Charles Requa, and Herbert Marshall in *Riptide* (1934)

With Leslie Howard in *Romeo and Juliet* (1936)

With Tyrone Power in *Marie Antoinette* (1938)

Frank Sinatra

Frank Sinatra—the skinny Italian crooner from Hoboken, New Jersey, who looked like an elongated breadstick and went on to become Mr. Swoon, Mr. Cool, and The Chairman of the Board—once quipped, "If it hadn't been for my interest in music, I'd probably have ended in a life of crime." He is the one popular singer responsible for making an art out of popular singing. His career began with ten successful years as a nightclub performer and a star of musical motion pictures. He was under MGM contract from 1944 to 1949, but by 1952 he was washed up in show business. The following year he scored one of the most spectacular comebacks in motion pictures by winning the Oscar for his performance in *From Here to Eternity*. The 1960s found him a cool swinger and, in the 1970s, some of the very people who would not have given him a job voted to award Sinatra a special Oscar for his humanitarianism.

Francis Albert Sinatra was born on December 12, 1915 in Hoboken, the only child of Martin Anthony Sinatra and Natalie (Garvanati) Sinatra, both of Italian ancestry. Mr. Sinatra had been a professional boxer at one time, but later opened a tavern in Hoboken, where his wife worked as a barmaid. She tired of that work, however, and became a trained practical nurse, later drifting into local politics. It was probably through her influence that her husband was appointed to the post of city fire captain. Sinatra was plucky even as a youngster, and was known in the neighborhood as "Slacksy" because of his trademarked "well-dressed" look. He displayed a talent for singing at an early age and, by the time he was in Demarest High School, he was singing for school dances and at political gatherings. He quit high school in order to concentrate on his vocal career, but his mother urged him to take a job on the *Jersey Journal*, where he rose from truck loader to copyboy and then to sometime sportswriter. But Sinatra's heart was not in the work, and he quit. He later recalled, "I disappointed Pop again terrifically when I decided to quit that job and make a go of it singing. I went through the toughest period of my life when making that particular break, because I had actually been doing quite well in the newspaper job."

Against his father's protests that singing was for sissies, he set out in earnest for a career as a vocalist. In 1937 he won first prize on the *Major Bowes*

Amateur Radio Hour singing "Night and Day" and, in 1939, he got his first important singing spot as a vocalist with the Harry James band at $65 a week. Then Tommy Dorsey hired him as his band vocalist for $100 weekly, and Sinatra remained with his organization for two years before deciding to make it on his own. Sinatra appeared with Benny Goodman at New York's famed Paramount Theatre on New Year's Eve in 1942, and the screaming bobby-soxers in the audience set a precedent which would follow the crooner throughout the 1940s. Of his enthusiastic fans, Sinatra once said, "Psychologists tried to go into the reason with all sorts of deep theories. I could have told them why. Perfectly simple: It was the war years and there was a great loneliness, and I was the boy in every corner drugstore, the boy who'd gone off drafted to the war. That's all."

By this time, Sinatra, who had displayed a penchant for getting into public brawls and making his own fight headlines, had made his film debut as the vocalist for Dorsey's band in Paramount's *Las Vegas Nights* (1941) singing "I'll Never Smile Again." The little musical had a very mild impact on the public. After appearing in MGM's *Ship Ahoy* (1942), again as part of Tommy Dorsey's orchestra, and in Columbia's *Reveille with Beverly* (1943) as a guest vocalist, RKO Studios signed him to a seven-year contract. *Higher and Higher* (1943) and *Step Lively* (1944), two unmemorable musicals, were the results of his stay there, after which Louis B. Mayer decided he wanted this crooner, who made the ladies swoon, to work at MGM. So he bought out Sinatra's RKO contract and starred him with Gene Kelly in *Anchors Aweigh* (1945). The film proved a popular success and all but obscured the fact that the same year Sinatra had starred in a ten-minute short for RKO titled *The House I Live In*. This study on tolerance, directed by Mervyn LeRoy, won a special Academy Award that year.

After singing "Ol' Man River" in the star-studded *Till the Clouds Roll By* (1946), Sinatra was showcased in *It Happened in Brooklyn* (1947) as the no-family G.I. who is diverted from his love of Brooklyn Bridge by teacher Kathryn Grayson and then by nurse Gloria Grahame. Anxious to prove himself as a serious actor, Sinatra urged MGM to loan him to RKO for *The Miracle of the Bells* (1948) in which he played Father Paul, the little mining town priest. If that picture excited no boxoffice heat, his next for MGM, *The Kissing Bandit* (1948), was the low point of his film career. But Metro's *Take Me Out to the Ball Game* (1949) and *On the Town* (1949), both with Gene Kelly, were felicitous assignments and displayed Sinatra's musical comedy talents to good advantage. At this point, Sinatra and Louis B. Mayer came to loggerheads. For some reason, Sinatra thought the studio was not doing right by him, and Mayer was firm in his dictate that the crooner had better keep his offcamera life much more private. Thus, with several years still to go on his MGM agreement, Sinatra and the studio negotiated a settlement.

By 1950 it seemed that Sinatra's pull with the ladies in the audience has paled, possibly because they now had their own men back home from the war. It looked as if his career was over, as was his first marriage. He had wed a childhood girl friend named Nancy Barbato on February 4, 1939, and they had three children: Nancy (1940), Frank, Jr. (1944), and Christine (1948). They separated on Valentine's Day, 1950 and were divorced on October 29, 1951, with Nancy receiving custody of the children and one-third of his earnings. Sinatra calls Nancy a noble woman, and they have remained close friends since the divorce. Eight days after his divorce, on November 7th, Sinatra married MGM's love goddess, Ava Gardner, a union that was noisy and temperamental, to say the least. She once threw a diamond ring he had given her out the window of a New York hotel during an argument. Needless to say, it was never retrieved. Sinatra's career was at its nadir and he was "Mr. Ava Gardner." It did not sit well with him. He accompanied Ava to Africa, where she was making *Mogambo* with Clark Gable and Grace Kelly. Gable urged Sinatra to go after the role of Angelo Maggio in *From Here to Eternity*. Ava provided the air fare and Sinatra flew to Hollywood, where he and his agent campaigned for the role, even though Columbia's Harry Cohn had announced that he wanted Eli Wallach for the part. Sinatra countered, "I'm no actor, but I know this guy. I went to school with him. I've been beaten up by him. I might have been Maggio." Cohn tested Sinatra, and the singer flew back to Africa to be with Ava, who had suffered a miscarriage. Columbia cabled him that he been chosen for the Maggio part, and his salary would be $8,000.

A year later, after winning the best supporting actor's Oscar for *From Here to Eternity*, Sinatra would be back on top and earning huge salaries for his multimedia work. Sinatra and Ava separated on October 27, 1953, but she did not get around to picking up the final divorce until 1957. The two have likewise remained close friends, and there have been recurrent rumors of remarriage. Sinatra's life style changed dramatically after *Eternity*, particularly after he won another Oscar nomination, this time as best actor, for his portrayal of the drug addict in Otto Preminger's *The Man with the Golden Arm* (1955). These two dramatic successes for the singing Sinatra set the pace for his "star" years, in both musical and nonmusical vehicles: *Guys and Dolls* (1955), in which he was miscast as Nathan Detroit to Marlon Brando's Sky Masterson; *High Society* (1956), in which he played in support to Bing Crosby, his one-time idol and competitor for being Number One radio crooner; and *Pal Joey* (1957), his ultimate performance as a good-natured heel. Along the way, there had been several boxoffice bombs: the would-be melodrama *Suddenly* (1954), the inept Western *Johnny Concho* (1956), and the costume adventure tale, *The Pride and the Passion* (1957), which not even the trio of stars—Sinatra, Sophia Loren, and Cary Grant—could salvage. If Sinatra had been dramatically uncertain of his playboy doctor's role in *Not as a Stranger* (1954), he was aggressively arrogant as the intended sympathetic American lieutenant in *Kings Go Forth* (1958).

By the time *Some Came Running* (1958) was made at MGM, Sinatra had settled into an acting pattern that contained nine parts the star and an occasional one part characterization, depending upon how he felt that day when he got on the set. This methodology worked well for him in the cinema production of James Jones' unwieldy novel, *Some Came Running*, which remains a generally engrossing film, due in a large part to the sympathetic performance of Shirley MacLaine as a crude but lovable whore and Martha Hyer as a near-frigid teacher, the two women who vie for returning G.I. Sinatra.

As the fabled leader of Hollywood's Rat Pack, Sinatra combined business with pleasure by starring with his troupe of play pals in a series of unsatisfactory pictures: *Never So Few* (1959), *Ocean's Eleven* (1960), *Sergeants Three* (1962), *Four for Texas* (1963), and *Robin and the 7 Hoods* (1964). Along the way, he directed and starred in a conventional World War II actioner, *None But the Brave*, and lent boxoffice support to an unfunny marriage comedy, *Marriage on the Rocks* (1965), with a most unprim Deborah Kerr. Sinatra tried to repeat the success of his role in *The Manchurian Candidate* (1962) by producing and starring in *The Naked Runner* (1967), which emerged only as an unconvincing spy story. He was a flip private detective in *Tony Rome* (1967) and its followup, *Lady in Cement* (1968), but much more in key as the earnest Manhattan police detective in *The Detective* (1968). *The Hollywood Reporter* rightly tagged Sinatra's latest opus, *Dirty Dingus Magee* (1970), as "the most tasteless, witless, and fatuous spoof on Western conventions yet to have been filmed."

Throughout the 1950s and 1960s, Sinatra continued to be a champ in the recording field, particularly when he was associated with musician Nelson Riddle. His mid-1950s TV series for ABC, in which he hosted a musical revue-type program, flopped, but he was at the top of his professional form when he starred in a few highly touted video specials in the late 1960s. He continued to make record-breaking nightclub appearances, particularly in Las Vegas until his summer 1970 engagement at Caesar's Palace, during which he had a much publicized altercation with a casino pit supervisor, and walked out of his engagement in a headline-gathering huff. Since then, he has remained virtually in retirement, having cancelled out of a starring role in *Dirty Harry* (1971) due to a hand injury, and dropping negotiations with Alan Jay Lerner in mid-1972 to star in a musical version of *The Little Prince* for Paramount. He announced his retirement from show business in 1971 and made his last public appearances at the 50th Anniversary benefit show of the Motion Picture and Television Relief Fund. At the 1971 Oscar show, he was the recipient of the Jean Hersholt Humanitarian Award. When presenting the award to Sinatra, Gregory Peck concluded with the remark that Sinatra is "undeniably the titleholder in the soft-touch department."

Over the past decades, the public has continued to follow his much-reported private life, revolving around the Rat Pack, his political alignment with the Kennedys, his rumored association with the underworld, and his continual fist fights along the way. On July 17, 1966 he wed Mia Farrow, the twenty-one-year-old daughter of actress Maureen O'Sullivan. Their courtship, wedding, and bitter divorce was constantly headline gossip.

652

At the time of his marriage to the skinny ex-star of television's *Peyton Place*, Ava Gardner was heard to quip, "I always knew Frank would end up sleeping with a boy!" In 1971 the immensely wealthy swinger donated $800,000 toward the establishment of the Martin Anthony Sinatra Hospital in Palm Springs, California, in memory of his father who had died two years earlier. A controversial man and a very private individual, Sinatra seems to have mellowed with the years. As one friend said, "He is not a new man; simply one with some of the old resentments stripped away."

FRANK SINATRA

Las Vegas Nights (Paramount, 1941)
Ship Ahoy (MGM, 1942)
Reveille with Beverly (Columbia, 1943)
Higher and Higher (RKO, 1943)
Step Lively (RKO, 1944)
Anchors Aweigh (MGM, 1945)
Till the Clouds Roll By (MGM, 1946)
It Happened in Brooklyn (MGM, 1947)
The Miracle of the Bells (RKO, 1948)
The Kissing Bandit (MGM, 1948)
Take Me Out to the Ball Game (MGM, 1949)
On the Town (MGM, 1949)
Double Dynamite (RKO, 1951)
Meet Danny Wilson (Universal, 1951)
From Here to Eternity (Columbia, 1953)
Suddenly (UA, 1954)
Young at Heart (WB, 1955)
Not as a Stranger (UA, 1955)
The Tender Trap (MGM, 1955)
Guys and Dolls (MGM, 1955)
The Man with the Golden Arm (UA, 1955)
Meet Me in Las Vegas (MGM, 1956)*
Johnny Concho (UA, 1956)
High Society (MGM, 1956)
Around the World in 80 Days (UA, 1956)
The Pride and the Passion (UA, 1957)
The Joker Is Wild (Paramount, 1957)
Pal Joey (Columbia, 1957)
Kings Go Forth (UA, 1958)

Some Came Running (MGM, 1958)
A Hole in the Head (UA, 1959)
Never So Few (MGM, 1959)
Can-Can (20th-Fox, 1960)
Ocean's Eleven (WB, 1960)
Pepe (Columbia, 1960)
The Devil at 4 O'Clock (Columbia, 1961)
Sergeants Three (UA, 1962)
The Road to Hong Kong (UA, 1962)*
The Manchurian Candidate (UA, 1962)
Come Blow Your Horn (Paramount, 1963)
The List of Adrian Messenger (Universal, 1963)
Four for Texas (WB, 1963)
Robin and the Seven Hoods (WB, 1964)
None But the Brave (WB, 1965)
Von Ryan's Express (20th-Fox, 1965)
Marriage on the Rocks (WB, 1965)
Cast a Giant Shadow (UA, 1966)
The Oscar (Embassy, 1966)
Assault on a Queen (Paramount, 1967)
The Naked Runner (WB, 1967)
Tony Rome (20th-Fox, 1967)
The Detective (20th-Fox, 1968)
Lady in Cement (20th-Fox, 1968)
Dirty Dingus Magee (MGM, 1970)

*Unbilled appearance

With Henry Mirelez and Clinton Sundberg in *The Kissing Bandit* (1948)

With Betty Garrett, Gene Kelly, Alice Pearce, Jules Munshin, and Ann Miller in *On the Town* (1949)

With Betty Lou Keim in *Some Came Running* (1958)

With Michele Carey in *Dirty Dingus Magee* (1970)

Red Skelton

Often when a highbrow film critic found himself, to his own chagrin, actually enjoying a Red Skelton movie, the next day, he tried to justify his uninhibited pleasure, by describing Skelton's mayhem routines as Chaplinesque. But as a more knowledgeable reviewer opined: "That is nonsense. The only similarity to Chaplin is the absence or paucity of dialogue." In any case, Skelton, with his violently expressive face, his mastery of the pratfall, a boisterous ad-libbing, and a broad pantomimic facility created a strong following for his comic artistry. For fourteen years he plied his trade at MGM, specializing in a genre of onscreen antics as removed from the gloss of Lana Turner vehicles as were the programmers churned out by fellow studio star Wallace Beery.

Richard Bernard Skelton was born in Vincennes, Indiana on July 18, 1913. His father, who died when Skelton was two months old, had been a clown with the Hagenback Wallace Circus. During his childhood Skelton recalls that his family (he had three older brothers) lived in an attic, and he went to work because the family was hungry. At seven, he was a newspaper boy, and at ten he worked part time in the receiving section of a department store. It was there that he met a character named "Doctor" Reynolds Lewis who was passing through town with his traveling medicine show. Lewis hired the precocious youngster, already known as "Red," for a weekly salary of $10. When the show was ready to move on, Skelton quit school and went with it. He was paid $15 a week, and one of his routines was to play a blackface "mammy" singer. He stayed with the show for two years and then joined the John Lawrence Stock Company. But that job did not last long, because the audience laughed at his efforts to deliver dramatic dialogue convincingly. After a time with the Clarence Stout Minstrels, he was hired to perform comedy skits aboard the *Cotton Blossom*, an Ohio and Missouri River showboat, and then spent a short time with the circus in which his father had worked.

By the time he was fifteen, he was a veteran traveler, and he joined up with the burlesque circuit. "Really, burlesque was clean as a whistle. We burlesqued Broadway hits." While playing the Gaiety Theatre in Kansas City, he met the fifteen-year-old daughter of an undertaker, Edna Stillwell, who was an usher in the theatre. Edna was a walkathon enthusiast, and when Skelton emceed a walkathon in which she had entered, they decided to team up, traveling from city to city on the freak event craze. In the summer of 1931 he borrowed two dollars from her, bought a marriage license and married her. They joined the vaudeville circuit as a team, with Edna writing their material and, at the same time, tutoring him in a correspondence course to help him earn a high school diploma. He received a diploma in 1938. The determined young couple got a 26-week booking at Loew's Montreal Theatre, and it was there that Skelton devised his famous doughnut dunking routine, the pantomime specialty which became his trademark. Later in his career, this routine gave him the dubious distinction of being president of the National Dunkers Association. Skelton made his New York vaudeville debut at the Paramount Theatre in July 1937, and on the following August 12, he debuted on radio on the Rudy Vallee show and clicked with his audience.

He was becoming a "name" by now and, in the summer of 1938, he emceed the kickoff for President Roosevelt's infantile paralysis program at the Capitol Theatre in Washington, D. C. As a result, he landed a featured role as the overenthusiastic Catskills Mountains summer camp entertainer in RKO's *Having Wonderful Time* (1938). That picture starred Ginger Rogers, and Skelton performed his dunking routine. He and his wife wrote a lavish musical revue, *Paris in Swing*, and toured it to record-breaking turnouts. However, the production costs were so high that they lost $5,000 on the venture. He made a few Vitaphone shorts in New York during 1939. Then, an offer of a lead in Jerome Kern's comic opera, *Gentleman Unafraid*, turned sour and the show closed out of town. MGM then offered him a contract, and Skelton's career took a solvent turn.

At first MGM was not sure whether Skelton would prove to be just a featured specialty performer a la Rags Ragland, or whether he had sufficient comic resources to sustain an entire picture. Thus he was given a rather straight part as a naval lieutenant in *Flight Command* (1940), a B+ feature with Robert Taylor and Ruth Hussey, and then was tested in two *Dr. Kildare* entries, *The People vs. Dr. Kildare* and *Dr. Kildare's Wedding Day*, both 1941, playing the orderly Vernon Briggs. Briggs was a well-meaning dimwit who frequented the corridors of Blair General Hospital much as dumb-type comedians Nat Pendleton and Rags Ragland also did in the series. In Metro's modest adaptation of *Lady Be Good* (1941), Skelton had Virginia O'Brien as his tagalong girlfriend, but he was still subsidiary to the main plot. It was his fourth studio picture of the year which gave him his first lead, *Whistling in The Dark*, a loose remake of a 1930s Ernest Truex comedy. In a role similar to Bob Hope's part in Paramount's *The Ghost Breakers* (1940), Skelton was cast as "The Fox," a radio detective who finds he must "live" through one of his own stories. The picture was inexpensively produced, but proved exceedingly popular with World War II audiences, who thrived on the slapstick antics of such comics as Abbott and Costello and Olsen and Johnson. It made Skelton a star, and MGM put him into two sequels: *Whistling in Dixie* (1942) and

Whistling in Brooklyn (1943). Meanwhile, he had become a regular on radio's *Avalon Time*, and did a vaudeville tour with his wife and Lupe Velez.

Skelton was given more rein for his comedy in his extended bits in both Eleanor Powell's *Ship Ahoy* (1942), which had Skelton again paired with Virginia O'Brien, and Ann Sothern's *Panama Hattie* (1943), which spent an overgenerous amount of screen time following the capers of gobs Skelton, Rags Ragland, and Ben Blue. The studio built Ethel Merman's theatrical success, *Dubarry Was a Lady* (1943), into a Red Skelton screen farce with Lucille Ball (their styles being too different, they did not blend well together), and gave him his best picture to date, *I Dood It* (1943), in which he was topfeatured over Eleanor Powell. By this time his *Red Skelton's Scrapbook of Satire* was the third most popular show on radio, behind Bob Hope and Fibber McGee and Molly. In a test, his radio show was clocked, and it was reported he got a laugh every eleven seconds.

Bathing Beauty (1944) had him play a songwriter who enters a girls' school to be near his wife, Esther Williams, and has one of the funniest sequences in his career in which he appears in tutu and ballet shoes and satirizes a ballerina. *The Show-Off* (1946) was an aborted attempt at pathos and beyond Skelton's range. *The Fuller Brush Man* (1948), made on loanout to Columbia, gave his broad comedy too much rein, but the audiences liked it. Buster Keaton, who was being wasted by MGM as a "comedy consultant" with no real authority, took a liking to Skelton and requested Louis B. Mayer to let him " ... take Skelton and work as a small company within Metro—do our own stories, our gags, our production, our directing. Use your resources but do it our way—the way I did my best pictures. I'll guarantee you hits. I won't take a cent of salary until they have proved themselves at the boxoffice." Regrettably, Mayer refused to give Keaton any such authority, but Keaton did influence Skelton and helped him work on several of his routines. One such idea appeared in *A Southern Yankee* (1948) in the hilarious scene in which Skelton is required to pass through the lines of both the Blue and the Gray. Wearing a uniform with one side blue and one side gray, and carrying a Union flag and a Confederate flag, Skelton marches across no man's land. Both sides stop shooting when they see their own uniform.

In *Neptune's Daughter* (1949), Skelton played a stable boy who is mistaken by Betty Garrett as a polo player. He and Garrett performed a classic burlesque of the song, "Baby, It's Cold Outside." Both of them, with Arlene Dahl and Ricardo Montalban, performed the same version at the Academy Awards ceremony that year. The song was named the best of that year.

Watch the Birdie (1950) was a remake of Keaton's classic *The Cameraman* (1928), and *Texas Carnival* (1951), in which Skelton and Esther Williams played an impoverished carnival team mistaken for millionaires, had the comic pursued by gold digger Ann Miller. She delivers some fast lines and some even faster taps to a nonplused Skelton. Skelton's attempt at pathos became bathos in *The Clown* (1952). But it did not matter because by the time it was generally released, his MGM contract had expired, and he was firmly entrenched in television. His last starring feature, *Public Pigeon No. 1* (1957), had been much funnier as a television comedy hour, and his last film appearance was in a guest spot in *Those Magnificent Men in Their Flying Machines* (1965), playing the Neanderthal Man who attempts to be a flying bird. It was one of the few delightful moments in that otherwise tedious picture.

Skelton's own television show debuted for CBS on September 22, 1953, and it was in this medium he gained his greatest popularity, outsurviving all other comedians in the rating wars for a record number of seasons through the early 1970s. He created a group of inimitable comic characters that appealed to his mass audiences: Clem Kaddidlehopper, Cauliflower McPugg, Willie Lump Lump, San Fernando Red, Cookie the Gob, the Mean Widdle Kid, Sheriff Deadeye, and Freddie the Freeloader. In his own words, "characters who remind the audience of someone they know." In 1956 he appeared in a dramatic role on *Playhouse 90*, in the production *The Big Slide*.

He divorced Edna Stilwell in 1943 (she later married director Frank Borzage), but she remained his business manager for many years. He credits her with increasing his salary from $50 a week to $7,500. She was also one of the few successful lady gag writers in radio. During World War II, Skelton served in the Army as a private ("I was the only celebrity who went in *and* came out a private"), and performed in some 3,800 shows for servicemen. While still in the Army, he married a former photographer's model, Georgia Maureen Davis (March 1945) and they had two children, Valentina Maris (1947) and Richard (1948). Their marriage was not ideal, but for some time their differences were allayed by their concern over the health of their son. On May 10, 1958, just a few days before his tenth birthday, the child died of leukemia. Skelton was grief-stricken and threw himself into a frenzy of work, making numerous nightclub appearances in addition to his regular television shows. In 1966, while Skelton was performing in a Las Vegas club, his wife was upstairs in their hotel suite, where a gunshot sent a bullet through her left chest. The papers said it was her own gun, that it had gone off accidentally. She was reported in satisfactory condition the following day. On August 4, 1971, the Skeltons separated, and were divorced the following November, citing irreconcilable differences. At the same time, columns reported that Skelton was dating a younger woman.

The limber-legged, rubber-faced comedian has kept his nonprofessional life very private, and one of the few "facts" is that he spends as many as nine hours a day watching television. He is a very wealthy man, makes few public appearances, and, after the demise of his video series, appears to be "unofficially" retired. However, in April 1972 he seemed to have changed his mind and performed his club act at the Hilton International Hotel in Las Vegas. He still bills himself professionally with that understatement, "One of America's Clowns."

With Virginia O'Brien and Eleanor Powell in *Ship Ahoy* (1942)

With Charles Dingle, Pierre Watkin, and Minor Watson in *A Southern Yankee* (1948)

RED SKELTON

Having Wonderful Time (RKO, 1938)
Flight Command (MGM, 1940)
The People vs. Dr. Kildare (MGM, 1941)
Lady Be Good (MGM, 1941)
Whistling in the Dark (MGM, 1941)
Dr. Kildare's Wedding Day (MGM, 1941)
Ship Ahoy (MGM, 1942)
Maisie Gets Her Man (MGM, 1942)
Panama Hattie (MGM, 1942)
Whistling in Dixie (MGM, 1942)
Dubarry Was a Lady (MGM, 1943)
I Dood It (MGM, 1943)
Whistling in Brooklyn (MGM, 1943)
Thousands Cheer (MGM, 1943)
Bathing Beauty (MGM, 1944)
Ziegfeld Follies (MGM, 1946)
The Show-Off (MGM, 1946)
Merton of the Movies (MGM, 1947)
The Fuller Brush Man (Columbia, 1948)
A Southern Yankee (MGM, 1948)

Neptune's Daughter (MGM, 1949)
The Yellow Cab Man (MGM, 1950)
The Fuller Brush Girl (Columbia, 1950)*
Three Little Words (MGM, 1950)
Duchess of Idaho (MGM, 1950)*
Watch the Birdie (MGM, 1950)
Excuse My Dust (MGM, 1951)
Texas Carnival (MGM, 1951)
Lovely to Look At (MGM, 1952)
The Clown (MGM, 1952)
Half a Hero (MGM, 1953)
The Great Diamond Robbery (MGM, 1953)
Susan Slept Here (RKO, 1954)*
Around the World in 80 Days (UA, 1956)
Public Pigeon No. 1 (Universal, 1957)
Ocean's Eleven (WB, 1960)*
Those Magnificent Men in Their Flying Machines (20th-Fox, 1965)

*Unbilled appearance

With Esther Williams in *Texas Carnival* (1951)

With Tim Considine in *The Clown* (1953)

Ann Sothern

There must have been some satisfaction in being MGM's "Queen Of The Bs," or superstar-in-waiting, because Ann Sothern playing Maisie, the honky-tonk chorine with a heart of spun sugar, stuck it out, traveling to every part of the globe as conceived by the set decorators. The *Maisie* programmer series was one of the favorites of exhibitors. Not only the exhibitors, but the critics and patrons also dug *Maisie*. But by doing so, they also dug a very deep ditch for an actress who at long last has achieved artistic respectability only with the decline of the studio star system. But, as one might say, who needed art when there was so much enjoyment bubbling from this bright comedienne? Though soft and pretty in a blonde way, she had a healthy hardboiled edge that delivered the expected wisecrack to the expected wise guy. Unfortunately, she did not seem to possess the same experienced edge when it came to dealing with the MGM executive suite, and the occasional "class" roles came to her only at long intervals. It would appear that Ann must have fought on more than one occasion to be remembered with satisfaction in *Lady Be Good* (1941), *Panama Hattie* (1942), *Cry Havoc* (1943), and, the best of all her films to date, *A Letter to Three Wives*, made at Twentieth Century-Fox in 1948.

In 1953, when her film career looked like it had ended, and a television series based on her Maisie characterization failed to materialize, she entered that rival medium as the effervescent Susie MacNamara in the series *Private Secretary*. A very popular show, lasting four seasons, it was followed by two more years in which she played a similarly likeable meddler named Katie O'Connor in *The Ann Sothern Show*. The two video series brought her a vast audience and financial security. Since that time, except for several years during which she was ill, she has continued to appear in television and motion pictures, a much plumper version of her blonde chorine in more sharply delineated character parts.

She was born Harriette Lake on January 22, 1909, in Valley City, North Dakota, but says she never saw her birthplace, because her concert singer mother just happened to be passing through, not staying. Her nomadic childhood found her following in her mother's musical footsteps in Iowa, Minnesota, and Michigan, while studying singing and musical composition. She attended the University of Washington in Seattle for three years, then

662

moved to Hollywood where her mother, now retired from the concert circuit, had a job as a diction and vocal coach, teaching actors the new technique of the microphone for that scientific wonder, talking pictures.

As Harriet Lake, she had parts in two pictures: *The Show of Shows* (1929) at Warners (she and her real-life sister were among the "sister acts" in a specialty number), and *Doughboys* (1930) at MGM. At the latter studio, the reddish-haired actress momentarily caught the eye of producer Paul Bern, but he was too busy grooming Jean Harlow for MGM stardom to help her career. So Ann decided to give Broadway a try. Florenz Ziegfeld used her in the chorus of Marilyn Miller's hit, *Smiles*, after which she landed the lead in the Rodgers and Hart satire on Hollywood, *America's Sweetheart* in 1931. *Time* magazine called her a "lovely synthesis, one part Ginger Rogers, one part Ethel Merman." She further enhanced her stage reputation by appearing in the successful tour of George Gershwin's *Of Thee I Sing*, doing the Lois Moran role.

Deciding she was ready to take on movies again, she appeared unbilled, as did Lucille Ball, in United Artists' *Broadway Through a Keyhole* (1933). Then Columbia signed her to a term contract, changing her hair to platinum and her name to Ann Sothern. In 1954, when Columbia's studio mogul Harry Cohn was signing Jack Lemmon to star with Judy Holliday in *It Should Happen to You*, he had an argument over changing Lemmon's name. As the story goes, Cohn said: "Let me tell you a story, young man. Once a girl walked into this office, and she was unknown. I changed her name, and she became a star.""Who was that?"

"Ann Sothern," Cohn said proudly.

"And what was her name before you changed it?"

"Harriet Lake."

"That does it. Harriet Lake is much better. Ann Sothern is the most theatrical name I ever heard. I can see it in lights on Broadway. What would you change my name to? Lemmon asked.

Cohn spelled it out: "L-E-N-N-O-N."

"And how would you pronounce it?"

"Lennon."

"Great! Just like Lenin, the Russian. They'll say I'm a Commie!"

"Hah!" Cohn replied in triumph. "I looked up Lenin, and it's pronounced 'Lay-neen.' "Whether or not that exchange ever took place, Ann *did* have a modest reputation in the theatre before signing with Columbia, and Cohn never *did* exert any effort into making her a "star." He simply assigned her to a string of colorless "Bs," with an occasional loanout that broke the monotony. She and George Murphy were the juveniles in Sam Goldwyn's *Kid Millions* (1934), and she scored as Maurice Chevalier's tempestuous chorine in *Folies Bergere* (1935), both on loan to United Artists.

She left Columbia in 1936. Some reports say she was dropped along with a number of other young players during one of Cohn's economy squeezes, while others stated that she asked out. In either case, she signed a

663

With Dean Jagger, Ivan Miller, and Robert Young in *Dangerous Number* (1937)

With Robert Young in *Maisie* (1939)

With Ian Hunter in *Dulcy* (1940)

With Fely Franquelli (standing), Diana Lewis, Heather Angel, Frances Gifford, Connie Gilchrist, Marsha Hunt, Joan Blondell, Gloria Grafton (standing), and Ella Raines in *Cry Havoc* (1943)

seven-year contract with RKO. She had worked at RKO the year before, where she starred with Gene Raymond in a fun, but strictly second-rate musical, *Hooray for Love*. RKO likewise used her in only B pictures. Thinking she and Raymond were a good screen match, RKO paired her with him in two of these "Bs." Ann liked neither Raymond nor her roles and fought to be released from her contract. RKO conceded her point, and Walter Wanger cast her as the Sadie Thompsonlike tart in *Trade Winds* (1938), a second lead to Wanger's then wife, Joan Bennett. Ann walked away with the picture, and MGM signed her to play in *Maisie* (1939). MGM had planned a series around the Maisie character for Jean Harlow, but had shelved the project after Harlow's untimely death.

Their choice of Ann was a good one and, when Maisie hit the screen, the public's response was immediately enthusiastic. The series ran into nine more entries, taking Ann literally around the world while playing the saucy, scatterbrained but ever resourceful Maisie Ravier, a hard-luck actress in *Congo Maisie* (1940), *Gold Rush Maisie* (1940), *Maisie Was a Lady* (1941), *Ringside Maisie* (1941), *Maisie Gets Her Man* (1942), *Swing Shift Maisie* (1943), *Maisie Goes to Reno* (1944), *Up Goes Maisie* (1946), and *Undercover Maisie* (1947). The series was so popular that fan mail addressed to "Maisie, U. S. A." reached Ann in her MGM dressing room. The series was also a training ground for many of MGM's young leading men—Red Skelton, Lew Ayres, George Murphy, and John Hodiak. While the scripts were often quite wobbly, Ann always delivered them with a requisite punch. Critics kept bemoaning the fact that the talented comedienne had such lousy material with which to work, but MGM officials rarely looked beyond the boxoffice receipts. Only infrequently did they give her a script into which she could sink her teeth. They loaned her to Warners to play the wisecracking moll of Edward G. Robinson in *Brother Orchid* (1940), and then gave her the lead in *Lady Be Good* (1941). One of the plum roles they threw to her was the Ethel Merman part in Cole Porter's *Panama Hattie*. Much of the Broadway score was missing, however, and there was an overdose of the Red Skelton–Rags Ragland visual comedy bits. Ann was excellent in *Cry Havoc* (1943) as the no-nonsense but warmhearted ex-waitress, one of the American nurses at Bataan, but the picture belonged to star Margaret Sullavan and Ann came across too much like coplayer Joan Blondell. Her MGM contract expired with *Undercover Maisie* and shortly thereafter she was felled by hepatitis.

After her recuperation, she went to Warners to costar with Dennis Morgan and Jack Carson in *April Showers* (1948), and should have received more acclaim than she did. After a guest stint in MGM's musical biography of Rodgers and Hart, *Words and Music* (1948), she got the best role of her career, the dissatisfied wife of Kirk Douglas in *A Letter to Three Wives* (1948), Joseph L. Mankiewicz's perceptive dissection of three doomed marriages. She did two more pictures for MGM in 1950, playing Jane Powell's blossoming mother in *Nancy Goes to Reno* and portraying a vindictive murderess in *Shadow on the Wall*.

When her recurring hepatitis kept her off the screen for three years, she was befriended by actor Richard Egan. Under his influence she converted to Catholicism. Intimates speculated their friendship would result in marriage, but Ann eschewed such a third matrimonial venture. She had married orchestra leader, Roger Pryor, in 1936, but their long-distance marriage had ended in divorce in 1942. The following year she had married socialite, William J. Hart, who was pursuing an acting career at MGM under the name of Robert Sterling. They had a daughter, Patricia, born December 10, 1944. Ann divorced Sterling in 1949, and their daughter is now an actress under the name of Tisha Sterling.

In 1953 she made a motion picture comeback in Fritz Lang's thriller, *The Blue Gardenia*, receiving excellent notices, the only criticism being that she had been off the screen much too long. This was her last film for some years, however, because that same year she embarked upon a television career. She had intended to try the new medium in a series based around her Maisie portrayal, which she had done in radio as well as her ten MGM pictures. When that project fizzled, she chose the role of Susie MacNamara in *Private Secretary*, playing a lovable, meddlesome secretary to boss Don Porter. The series lasted 104 episodes, earned her three Emmy nominations and a fat bankroll. In 1958 she changed the format to *The Ann Sothern Show*, playing a big-city deluxe hotel employee named Katie O'Connor. The show lasted for two seasons.

Illness kept her away from both television and cinema during the early sixties, but when she returned, plumper and fuller of face, she did so via strong character roles. To land the part of the sleazy prostitute in *Lady in a Cage* (1964), she took second billing to Olivia de Havilland and deferred her salary when they could not meet her price. She stated that both billing and salary were part of an ego trip with which she no longer needed to be concerned. This remark seems to indicate that she probably had not thought it important enough to fight for roles earlier in her career when it would have been beneficial to do so, choosing instead to remain, like Joan Blondell at Warner Brothers, a "studio dame."

Her *Lady in a Cage* assignment was a good one, confirming what critics had been saying for years: this lady could act. During the same year she had the meatiest female role in Gore Vidal's political who's who, *The Best Man*, in which she played a loud-mouthed national committeewoman. The next year she was seen as the fat, old drunk in *Sylvia* (1965), a silly melodrama about reformed whores, starring Carrol Baker; and in 1968 she was the friendly madam in *Chubasco*, which starred her long-standing friend Richard Egan.

In addition, Ann was the voice of an antique car in *My Mother, the Car*, a short-lived video series in 1965 which starred Jerry Van Dyke. During 1966–1967, she garnered good reviews in theatre tours of *The Glass Menagerie*, *Gypsy*, and *The Solid Gold Cadillac*. Having long since eschewed her glamor image in favor of salty characterizations, Ann continues to play dramatic character roles on television. One of her most recent outings was an impressive vignette as a seedy alcoholic mother of a murderer in *A Death of Innocence* (1971), a telefeature which included her daughter Tisha in the cast. Ann's one scene with heady character star Shelley Winters left Miss Winters distinctly behind with egg on her face. In April 1973, she signed to appear in a film for Media Cinema, entitled *The Killing Kind,* co-starring John Savage and Ruth Roman.

Not long ago Ann commented to an interviewer: "Sometimes I'll watch an old movie on television, and once in a while one of mine—such as *April Showers*—will come on and I'll watch it. And you know something? I'm always amazed at what a lousy actress I was. I guess in the old days we just got by on glamor

"Hollywood sold its stars on good looks and personality buildups. We weren't really actresses in the true sense. We were just big names—the products of a good publicity department.

"Today's crop of actresses and actors have real talent. Good looks are no longer an essential part of the business."

With Jane Powell in *Nancy Goes to Reno* (1950)

ANN SOTHERN

The Show of Shows (WB, 1929)
Hearts in Exile (WB, 1929)
Hold Everything (WB, 1930)
Doughboys (MGM, 1930)
Broadway Through a Keyhole (UA, 1933)
Let's Fall in Love (Columbia, 1934)
Melody in Spring (Paramount, 1934)
The Party's Over (Columbia, 1934)
Hell Cat (Columbia, 1934)
Blind Date (Columbia, 1934)
Kid Millions (UA, 1934)
Folies Bergere (UA, 1935)
Eight Bells (Columbia, 1935)
Hooray for Love (RKO, 1935)
The Girl Friend (Columbia, 1935)
Grand Exit (Columbia, 1935)
You May Be Next (Columbia, 1936)
Hellship Morgan (Columbia, 1936)
Don't Gamble with Love (Columbia, 1936)
Walking on Air (RKO, 1936)
My American Wife (Paramount, 1936)
The Smartest Girl in Town (RKO, 1936)
Dangerous Number (MGM, 1937)
50 Roads to Town (20th-Fox, 1937)
There Goes My Girl (RKO, 1937)
Super Sleuth (RKO, 1937)
Danger–Love at Work (20th-Fox, 1937)
There Goes the Groom (RKO, 1937)
She's Got Everything (RKO, 1938)
Trade Winds (UA, 1938)
Maisie (MGM, 1939)
Fast and Furious (MGM, 1939)

Elsa Maxwell's Hotel for Women (20th-Fox, 1939)
Joe and Ethel Turp Call on the President (MGM, 1939)
Congo Maisie (MGM, 1940)
Brother Orchid (WB, 1940)
Maisie Was a Lady (MGM, 1941)
Gold Rush Maisie (MGM, 1940)
Dulcy (MGM, 1940)
Ringside Maisie (MGM, 1941)
Lady Be Good (MGM, 1941)
Maisie Gets Her Man (MGM, 1942)
Panama Hattie (MGM, 1942)
Three Hearts for Julia (MGM, 1943)
Swing Shift Maisie (MGM, 1943)
Thousands Cheer (MGM, 1943)
Cry Havoc (MGM, 1943)
Maisie Goes to Reno (MGM, 1944)
Up Goes Maisie (MGM, 1946)
Undercover Maisie (MGM, 1947)
April Showers (WB, 1948)
Words and Music (MGM, 1948)
A Letter to Three Wives (20th-Fox, 1948)
The Judge Steps Out (RKO, 1949)
Nancy Goes to Rio (MGM, 1950)
Shadow on the Wall (MGM, 1950)
The Blue Gardenia (WB, 1953)
Lady in a Cage (Paramount, 1964)
The Best Man (UA, 1964)
Sylvia (Paramount, 1965)
Chubasco (WB-7 Arts, 1968)
The Killing Kind (Media Cinema, 1973)

With Gigi Perreau in *Shadow on the Wall* (1950)

Robert Sterling

Robert Sterling had all the proper physical attributes for cinema glory, being tall (6' 1"), dark, and handsome, with striking blue eyes. He was the nonsinging Robert Goulet of his day. On screen, however, he came across as little more than a conventional second male lead. Only his boyish charm offset his lack of artistic discipline or versatility. He was useful to MGM as a second-string player, generally portraying the city-soft nice guy with a touch of the playboy in him. Unlike the similar Gig Young, Sterling's offhanded acting style never matured with the years.

He was born William John Hart in New Castle, Pennsylvania on November 13, 1917, the son of Walter S. Hart, a professional baseball player with the Chicago Cubs. Sterling attended New Wilmington High School and was graduated from the University of Pittsburgh. He then became a clothing salesman and found himself in Hollywood in 1938. A talent scout spotted him and had him tested at Columbia Pictures for the lead in *Golden Boy* (1939), but director Rouben Mamoulian decided on William Holden. Columbia did hire Sterling on a short-term contract, and within a year he appeared in sixteen studio releases including a bit in *Golden Boy*. In *Blondie Brings Up Baby* (1939) he was appropriately cast as a salesman.

Dropped by Columbia, Sterling returned to New York and floundered about Broadway for several months before returning to California, where he was signed to a Twentieth Century-Fox contract. *Manhattan Heartbeat* (1940) was the remake of *Bad Girl*, a film which had done so much for James Dunn's career, but the new version with Virginia Gilmore opposite Sterling did nothing for either newcomer. *Yesterday's Heroes* (1940) with Jean Rogers was negligible, and his third and final picture for Fox at this time was the *Cisco Kid* programmer, *The Gay Caballero* (1940), featuring Cesar Romero in the title role. Sterling thus had fared little better on the Fox lot than at Columbia. Even his much-publicized romance with Fox star-in-the-making Gene Tierney fizzled when she suddenly wed fashion designer Oleg Cassini.

Sterling moved on to his third studio, MGM, in three years, where at last he found his bland forte. He was the young farmer who helps reform crook-on-the-lam Edward Arnold in *The Penalty* (1941), while in *I'll Wait for You* (1941) he was the farmer turned criminal who is himself regenerated. He was a G-man in *The Getaway* (1941), and as boxer Terry Dolan in *Ringside Maisie* (1941), he loses star Ann Sothern to fight manager George Murphy. However, in real life he and eight-year-older Sothern fell in love and were wed in 1943. They had a daughter Patricia. He played handsome fill-in roles in two A productions in 1941: as Greta Garbo's smooth dance partner in *Two-Faced Woman* and as support to Robert Taylor and Van Heflin in what is Sterling's favorite film, *Johnny Eager*. Sterling's seventh MGM release of 1941 was *Dr. Kildare's Victory*, which found him cast as Dr. Roger Winthrop, who must rely on Lew Ayres' medical and emotional superiority.

If appearing opposite Ann Rutherford in *This Time for Keeps* (1942) was a nothing assignment, he was certainly noticed in the slick *Somewhere I'll Find You* (1942). He and older brother Clark Gable are war correspondents, each in love with Lana Turner. The billing left no doubt that the script would kill off Sterling in battle so Gable could have Turner.

After completing *Somewhere I'll Find You*, Sterling went into the service as an army pilot instructor. After the war, he returned to MGM for one additional film. In *The Secret Heart* (1946), he was the hero son of Claudette Colbert, although most of the screen action focused on emotionally disturbed June Allyson. It was three years before Sterling made another picture, playing the taciturn cowboy in RKO's *Roughshod* (1949). He then had a secondary role as Robert Preston's brother in the Western *The Sundowners* (1950) and the lead with Joan Dixon in the B entry, *Bunco* (1950). MGM used him mainly as animated set dressing in the seventh-billed role of Stephen Baker in *Show Boat* (1951).

By the time *Show Boat* was released, Sterling had divorced Sothern and moved to New York. In 1951 he made his official Broadway debut in the comedy *The Grammery Ghost*, the cast of which also sported Sarah Churchill. During the run of this show he met Anne Jeffries, who was then appearing in *Kiss Me, Kate!* and they were married November 21, 1951. Later on they had two sons.

Sterling returned to Hollywood to support Audie Murphy in the Civil War Western, *Column South* (1953). Then he and Jeffries became an acting husband and wife team. They had appeared on Sherman Billingsley's *Stork Club* television variety show in 1952 and sang "No Two People." There was so much public response to this number that the couple assembled a club act, and later were asked to costar in the television series version of *Topper*, based on Thorne Smith's novels of the charming ghosts (Sterling–Jeffries) who plague upper crust Cosmo Topper (Leo G. Carroll) and his addled wife (Lee Patrick). The series debuted on CBS-TV on October 9, 1953, and went off the air September 30, 1955. In November 1955 the couple starred in the NBC-TV special of Rodgers and Hart's *Dearest Enemy*. In 1958 Sterling and his wife appeared in a short-lasting teleseries, *Love That Jill*, about rival owners of model agencies. Sterling had little better luck with *Ichabod and Me* (1962), in which he was a small-town newspaper editor. In summer stock, the couple performed in such shows as *Bells Are Ringing*.

Sterling returned to Hollywood to join the miscast of *Return to Peyton Place* (1961). Sterling was virtually reduced to yammering in the town meeting sequence with vituperative Mary Astor holding forth in an example of solid acting performance. *Voyage to the Bottom of the Sea* (1961), was a popular kiddie's film and Sterling was appropriately cast as the nuclear submarine captain. Three years later Sterling made his final feature film to date, flashing his Ipana toothpaste playboy smile in Bob Hope's *A Global Affair*.

Since then, Sterling has been professionally inactive, save for a few television guest shots such as an episode of *The Bold Ones* (1971). He is occasionally mentioned in trade papers, but generally in reference to his spouse, Anne Jeffries, who recently starred in a daytime television soap opera, and in the 1972–73 video season on *Delphi File*.

ROBERT STERLING

Blondie Meets the Boss (Columbia, 1939)
Only Angels Have Wings (Columbia, 1939)
Blondie Brings Up Baby (Columbia, 1939)
First Offenders (Columbia, 1939)
Golden Boy (Columbia, 1939)
Good Girls Go to Paris (Columbia, 1939)
The Man They Could Not Hang (Columbia, 1939)
Missing Daughters (Columbia, 1939)
Mr. Smith Goes to Washington (Columbia, 1939)
My Son Is Guilty (Columbia, 1939)
Outside These Walls (Columbia, 1939)

Those High Grey Walls (Columbia, 1939)
A Woman Is the Judge (Columbia, 1939)
Beware Spooks! (Columbia, 1939)
Romance of the Redwoods (Columbia, 1939)
Scandal Sheet (Columbia, 1940)
Manhattan Heartbeat (20th-Fox, 1940)
Yesterday's Heroes (20th-Fox, 1940)
The Gay Caballero (20th-Fox, 1940)
The Penalty (MGM, 1941)
I'll Wait for You (MGM, 1941)
The Getaway (MGM, 1941)
Ringside Maisie (MGM, 1941)
Two Faced Woman (MGM, 1941)
Johnny Eager (MGM, 1941)
Dr. Kildare's Victory (MGM, 1941)
This Time for Keeps (MGM, 1942)
Somewhere I'll Find You (MGM, 1942)
The Secret Heart (MGM, 1946)
Roughshod (RKO, 1949)
The Sundowners (Eagle–Lion, 1950)
Bunco Squad (RKO, 1950)
Show Boat (MGM, 1951)
Column South (Universal, 1953)
Return to Peyton Place (20th-Fox, 1961)
Voyage to the Bottom of the Sea (20th-Fox, 1961)
A Global Affair (MGM, 1964)

With Lew Ayres, Jean Rogers, and Lionel Barrymore in *Dr. Kildare's Victory* (1941)

James Stewart

"Ya either got it, or ya ain't," sings Ethel Merman in *Gypsy*, and for more than thirty-five years critics have been striving beyond the obvious to properly assess the star qualities that have so endeared James Stewart to the public. In his pre-World War II roles, he emphasized the fumbling, baffled characteristics of a humane country bumpkin, who was wont to trip over his long legs and stumble on his oft-times cocky idealism, and who occasionally had to be steered back onto a course of humility, as in *Of Human Hearts* (1938). But more typically he radiated a naive goodness which had to cope with social corruption in its own style as in *Mr. Smith Goes To Washington* (1939) and *Destry Rides Again* (1939). The postwar Stewart was a sturdier sort as his nervousness, hesitant speech and mannerisms gradually relaxed. His maturity presented the portrait of a cool-headed, trustworthy manhood, which helped him function in admirable if laconic style on the western range, as in *Winchester '73* (1950), in the air in *The Spirit Of St. Louis* (1957), or in the courtroom in *Anatomy Of A Murder* (1959). Like Gary Cooper, who also epitomized the man of integrity, Stewart has done his share of screen biographies dealing with beloved Americans: Monty Stratton, Charles Lindbergh, Glenn Miller. This totally American, deeply human integrity also made him one of the best Hitchcock heroes.

Whomever he portrayed or whatever genre he essayed, Stewart seemed to be performing in such an effortless manner that audiences were convinced his performances were completely natural and they liked his work all the more for such a judgment. Throughout the entire Fifties, he was in the top ten at the boxoffice and even today, as a grandfatherly version of what he always was—the *regular* guy—his name on the movie marquee is worth a great deal.

Stewart spent the first seven years of his screen life at MGM, yet it was his loanout assignments to Frank Capra at Columbia in *You Can't Take It With You* (1938) and as *Mr. Smith* which established his cinema niche and gave his home studio the proper perspective on its largely wasted contractee. But a little more than a year after Stewart won his Oscar in MGM's *The Philadelphia Story* (1940), he was off to World War II service and thereafter worked away from the Culver City lot. In the Fifties, Stewart was the first of the big-league stars to make a modern percentage deal on his filmmaking, but it was with Universal and not MGM, who was hungry and smart enough to accept this restructured style of production financing.

James Maitland Stewart was born on May 20, 1908, in Indiana, Pennsylvania, where his father ran a hardware store. An only child, he enrolled in Princeton, his father's alma mater, to study engineering and then switched to architecture. As a member of the Triangle Club at Princeton he met Joshua Logan. Upon graduation he joined Logan's University Players in Falmouth, Massachusetts, a summer theatre group which included Margaret Sullavan and Henry Fonda. In the fall of 1932, Stewart and Fonda took a room in New York City and soon Stewart was appearing in small roles in theatre productions of *Carrie Nation*, S.N. Behrman's *All Good Americans* and *Yellow Jack*.

In a summer theatre production of *Divided By Three*, which starred Judith Anderson, Hedda Hopper was a member of the cast, and when she returned to Hollywood, she advised the MGM casting department about the gangling young actor. The studio signed him to a seven-year contract and cast him as "Shorty," the reporter, in *The Murder Man* (1935) with Spencer Tracy. Stewart recalls: "I was awful. I was all arms and legs." Next he played the heavy, the outlaw brother of Jeanette MacDonald in the popular *Rose Marie* (1936), and the attention this role attracted caused the novice screen actor to tell one interviewer: "Hollywood dishes out too much praise for small things like my role in *Rose Marie*. I won't let it get me, but too much praise can turn a fellow's head if he doesn't watch his step."

While such modesty was good public relations, the praise for Stewart was just beginning. When Margaret Sullavan requested him for the second lead in Universal's *Next Time We Love* (1936), his home lot took note and featured him with Jean Harlow in *Wife vs. Secretary* (1936) and then with Janet Gaynor in *Small Town Girl* (1936). His first lead was a B picture called *Speed* (1936), which cast him as a test driver, opposite Wendy Barrie. Following this role he played one of Joan Crawford's many admirers in *The Gorgeous Hussy* (1936). His real chance came as the lead opposite Eleanor Powell in *Born To Dance* (1936) in which he introduced Cole Porter's "Easy To Love" in an acceptable non-singing voice. After a villain's role in *After The Thin Man* (1936), MGM loaned him to Twentieth Century-Fox for the lead opposite Simone Simon in the poor remake of *Seventh Heaven* (1937).

All of these films provided exposure for the young actor, but none of them captured the essential Stewart. MGM helped correct this temporarily by casting him as the young soldier in *The Shopworn Angel* (1938) with Margaret Sullavan, and then did even better by him on two loanouts in two good comedies. *Vivacious Lady* (1938) at RKO had him play a professor who falls for a show girl (Ginger Rogers), and the infectiously eccentric *You Can't Take It With You* (1938) made a fortune for Columbia's breadwinning director, Frank Capra. After David O. Selznick borrowed him for *Made for Each Other* (1939), a bigger than life drama about the marital vicissitudes of a young couple (Stewart and Carole Lombard), MGM knocked him back one step.

They had Joan Crawford don ice skates, and Stewart and Lew Ayres were made to cavort in a horse's costume in *Ice Follies of 1939* (1939). A madcap comedy, *It's A Wonderful World* (1939), pleased nearly everyone even if it did come late in the screwball genre cycle, and Capra borrowed him again for *Mr. Smith Goes To Washington*. As the naive young senator, Stewart put forth one of the screen's finest performances and won the New York Film Critics Award, but not the Oscar. Then he helped salvage Marlene Dietrich's career at a time when she was considered boxoffice poison by playing the gun-shy sheriff in *Destry Rides Again* (1939) at Universal. MGM gave him and Margaret Sullavan a good comedy in *The Shop Around The Corner* (1940) then considered him important enough for one of their prestige projects: the film version of Philip Barry's *The Philadelphia Story* (1940). On this outing, portraying the cynical reporter, Stewart got his Oscar. However the three films that followed—*Come Live with Me, Pot O'Gold* and *Ziegfeld Girl*— were hardly worthy of his talents and were the last he made under his MGM contract. On March 22, 1941, he became the first leading screen actor to be drafted into the Army, almost over Louis B. Mayer's dead body.

Stewart's MGM contract expired during his term with the service, and to Mayer's chagrin he chose not to renew when he returned to Hollywood. Instead he joined with the short-lived Liberty Films organized by Frank Capra and George Stevens, and starred in their *It's A Wonderful Life* (1946) which earned him another Oscar nomination. *Call Northside 777* (1948), a documentary-style thriller at Twentieth Century-Fox, demonstrated that Stewart could keep up with the advanced realism of post-war Hollywood. If Alfred Hitchcock's *Rope* (1948) proved lethargic, it nonetheless was the passkey to work with a director who would direct some of his best pictures in the Fifties.

Hitchcock's *Rear Window* (1954), *The Man Who Knew Too Much* (1956) and *Vertigo* (1958) each found Stewart as a conscientious but flawed individual, who nearly causes chaos to all concerned. These three films were all hefty boxoffice grossers and cemented Stewart's lofty standing in the film colony's hierarchy. Like Gary Cooper and Henry Fonda and particularly John Wayne, Stewart found the Western an amiable setting to express his artistic concept of Americana, as well as to avoid the embarrassment of screen lovemaking now that he was well into his forties. Along the way there were flops but his name continued to mean boxoffice insurance with the general movie going public.

The Seventies found the financially well-off Stewart tackling other media. He turned to Broadway to co-star with Helen Hayes in a revival of *Harvey* which had been a favorite part of his since the time he replaced stage star Frank Fay in the original production decades before. In 1950 he had filmed the play. Upon returning to the stage, he commented: "I welcomed the change. My wife, Gloria and I found ourselves sitting around Beverly Hills having conversations with our dogs. Hollywood is a little quiet and depressing right now. It's another one of our disaster times." In the fall of 1971, he joined the cavalcade of film stars who had found solvency, if not acclaim, in a television series. In *The Jimmy Stewart Show* he played a bicycle-riding absent-minded college professor. That series lasted one season and he signed to do a second series, for the 1973-74 season, called *Hawkins on Murder*. He will appear in eight ninety-minute shows.

Until he was forty-one, Stewart remained one of Hollywood's most eligible bachelors. Many attribute his offscreen love for Margaret Sullavan for delaying any wedding plans. But in 1949, he married the former Mrs. Gloria Hatrich McLean. They have twin daughters, Kelly and Judy, as well as two sons, Ronald and Mike, from Gloria's former marriage. In June 1969, Ronald, a Marine First Lieutenant, was killed in Viet Nam. Of this tragedy, Stewart says, without bitterness: "I don't think he died in vain. I believe in the cause that he died for. The war has been a trial, and a tremendously difficult thing for the nation. But if there is a tragedy about it, it is the national tragedy that there has been so much sacrifice without a unified nation behind the cause."

In World War II, Stewart had risen from private to full colonel in the Air Force, and thereafter retained his interest in flying and the service. In 1959, the Senate approved Stewart's promotion to Reserve Brigadier General despite the continual vetoes of a Congressional segment headed by Senator Margaret Chase Smith who noted that since his return to civilian life, he had only nine days of training. He remains today as conservative in his politics as he has been in choosing his professional ventures.

The current changes in the film industry are not entirely to Stewart's liking. "I don't want to sound like 'give-me-the-good-old-days,' but to be realistic, the big studios were an ideal way to take pictures because they were a home base for people. When you were under contract, you had a chance to work at your craft all the time. You would have big parts in little pictures and little parts in big pictures. It was exciting, with writers, producers and directors around all the time. But the whole thing became too expensive. It's just a whole different world today." As to assessing his own screen longevity, Stewart says: "I am James Stewart, playing James Stewart. I couldn't mess around doing great characterizations. I play variations of myself. Audiences have come to expect certain things from me and are disappointed if they don't get them."

JAMES STEWART

Murder Man (MGM, 1935)
Rose Marie (MGM, 1936)
Next Time We Love (Universal, 1936)
Wife vs. Secretary (MGM, 1936)
Small Town Girl (MGM, 1936)
Speed (MGM, 1936)
The Gorgeous Hussy (MGM, 1936)
Born to Dance (MGM, 1936)
After the Thin Man (MGM, 1936)

Seventh Heaven (20th-Fox, 1937)
The Last Gangster (MGM, 1937)
Navy Blue and Gold (MGM, 1937)
Of Human Hearts (MGM, 1938)
Vivacious Lady (RKO, 1938)
Shopworn Angel (MGM, 1938)
You Can't Take it With You (Columbia, 1938)
Made for Each Other (UA, 1939)
Ice Follies of 1939 (MGM, 1939)

It's a Wonderful World (MGM, 1939)
Mr. Smith Goes to Washington (Columbia, 1939)
Destry Rides Again (Universal, 1939)
The Shop Around the Corner (MGM, 1940)
The Mortal Storm, (MGM, 1940)
No Time for Comedy (WB, 1940)
The Philadelphia Story (MGM, 1940)
Come Live with Me (MGM, 1941)
Pot O'Gold (UA, 1941)
Ziegfeld Girl (MGM, 1941)
It's a Wonderful Life (RKO, 1946)
Magic Town (RKO, 1947)
Call Northside 777 (20th-Fox, 1948)
On Our Merry Way (UA, 1948)
Rope (WB, 1948)
You Gotta Stay Happy (Universal, 1948)
The Stratton Story (MGM, 1949)
Malaya (MGM, 1949)
Winchester '73 (Universal, 1950)
Broken Arrow (20th-Fox, 1950)
The Jackpot (20th-Fox, 1950)
Harvey (Universal, 1950)
No Highway in the Sky (20th-Fox, 1951)
The Greatest Show on Earth (Paramount, 1952)
Bend of the River (Universal, 1952)
Carbine Williams (MGM, 1952)
The Naked Spur (MGM, 1953)
Thunder Bay (Universal, 1953)
The Glenn Miller Story (Universal, 1954)

Rear Window (Paramount, 1954)
The Far Country (Universal, 1955)
Strategic Air Command (Paramount, 1955)
The Man from Laramie (Columbia, 1955)
The Man Who Knew Too Much (Paramount, 1956)
The Spirit of St. Louis (WB, 1957)
Night Passage (Universal, 1957)
Vertigo (Paramount, 1958)
Bell, Book and Candle (Columbia, 1958)
Anatomy of a Murder (Columbia, 1959)
The FBI Story (WB, 1959)
The Mountain Road (Columbia, 1960)
Two Rode Together (Columbia, 1961)
X-15 (Narration: UA, 1961)
The Man Who Shot Liberty Valence (Paramount, 1962)
Mr. Hobbs Takes a Vacation (20th-Fox, 1962)
How the West Was Won (MGM, 1963)
Take Her, She's Mine (20th-Fox, 1963)
Cheyenne Autumn (WB, 1964)
Dear Brigitte (20th-Fox, 1965)
Shenandoah (Universal, 1965)
Flight of the Phoenix (20th-Fox, 1966)
The Rare Breed (Universal, 1966)
Firecreek (WB-7 Arts, 1968)
Bandolero! (20th-Fox, 1968)
The Cheyenne Social Club (National General, 1970)
Fools' Parade (Columbia, 1971)

With John **Miljan** in *Of Human Hearts* (1938)

With Claudett Colbert in *It's a Wonderful World* (1939)

With Lana Turner in *Ziegfeld Girl* (1941)

In *How the West Was Won* (1962)

Dean Stockwell

In case *Whatever Happened to Baby Jane?* did not make its point about the upbringing of child film stars firmly enough, former child star Dean Stockwell later said about his childhood, "It's a miserable way to bring up a child, though neither my parents nor I recognized it at the time." Metro intended him to be their male Margaret O'Brien, but never found the proper vehicle for him, although in his final picture for the studio, *Kim* (1950), he had the title role. So he muddled along for six years, consistently proving he was less cloying or "dramatic" than such contemporaries as the brothers Hickman, Darryl and Dwayne or Bobby Driscoll, but never having the opportunity to show his mettle as did past Metro moppet players Jackie Cooper and Freddie Bartholomew. Like the post-awkward age Roddy McDowall, Stockwell has found a niche in recent decades playing the perennial young adult. But Stockwell has chosen onscreen and off to be a conscientious rebel and a brooding craftsman. Unfortunately, he picked his adult guise a decade too late, and coming post–James Dean and Marlon Brando, he seems to be merely a weak exponent of the rugged individualist school of performing artists.

Stockwell was born March 5, 1936, in Hollywood, the son of Harry Stockwell, who later sang the role of the prince in Walt Disney's *Snow White and the Seven Dwarfs*, and of Betty Veronica Stockwell, an actress–dancer. Both Dean and his one-year-younger brother Guy were groomed for entertainment careers at an early age. He was educated at Long Island public schools and then at the Martin Milmore School in Boston. He made his stage debut, along with Guy, in the Theatre Guild's short-lived *The Innocent Voyage* (1942). The Richard Hughes novel–play was later filmed by Walt Disney as *A High Wind in Jamaica*. MGM producer Joe Pasternak spotted Stockwell, and he was signed at MGM. Coming to Hollywood, he made his radio debut on such shows as *Death Valley Days* and *Dr. Christian*.

After playing Paulie in *Valley of Decision* (1945), Stockwell had a much larger part in the musical *Anchors Aweigh* (1945) as the nephew of screen-struck Kathryn Grayson. He was eight-year-old Robert Shannon in Metro's sentimental *The Green Years* (1946), with Tom Drake playing the sensitive child as an adult. Next he was loaned to Twentieth Century-Fox to be Peggy Ann Garner's little brother in *Home Sweet Homicide* (1946), a minor romantic murder mystery tale with Randolph Scott. Of his five histrionically untaxing 1947 releases, he was at his lovable best as the boy adopted by punchy prizefighter Wallace Beery in *The Mighty McGurk* and also as Myrna Loy's and William Powell's son in *Song of the Thin Man*. In addition, that year he functioned at Metro in the John Nesbitt *Passing Parade* short *A Really Important Person*, in which he is shown writing a school essay about his dad.

One of the two high-water marks of his juvenile screen career was in RKO's *The Boy with Green Hair* (1948), Joseph Losey's tentative parable about a World War II orphan who becomes a social outcast when his hair turns green. He was another parentless child in Twentieth Century-Fox's *Deep Waters* (1948), this time with a yearning for the open water, and in the same studio's *Down to the Sea in Ships* (1949) he is taught the rudiments of whaling by sailor Richard Widmark on the ship belonging to the youth's grandfather (Lionel Barrymore). Stockwell finally got to work with Metro's maturing juvenile performer Margaret O'Brien in *The Secret Garden* (1949), a period fantasy built about two youths who fantasize over a garden retreat.

In his last year at Metro, Dean appeared in the Joel McCrea Western, *Stars in My Crown* (1950), shared old-fashioned prep school adventures with Darryl Hickman and Scotty Beckett in *The Happy Years* (1950), based on Owen Johnson's *The Lawrenceville School Stories*, and then was cast in Rudyard Kipling's *Kim*, costarring with Errol Flynn. The latter project had been announced in 1938 for Freddie Bartholomew and Robert Taylor, and then again in 1942 for Mickey Rooney. All of Stockwell's scenes, as the young orphaned son of an Irish sergeant in nineteenth-century India, were shot in California. The rambling film was not the success Metro had anticipated.

Away from MGM, the fifteen-year-old Stockwell made one picture at Universal, *Cattle Drive* (1951) with Joel McCrea, and then "retired." He had not been happy with those Metro years: "I had no friends, except for my brother, and I never did what I wanted to do. I had one vacation in nine years. I went fishing." After graduating from Los Angeles' Alexander Hamilton High School at the age of sixteen, he enrolled as George Stockwell at the University of California, but dropped out after one year ("I was unhappy and couldn't get along with people") and bummed around the country. He later came East to study acting, and made a small stir in the trade when, after auditing one class at the Actors' Studio, he walked out.

By the mid-1950s he was a frequent television performer, reunited with Margaret O'Brien on *Front Row Center*'s *Innocent Witness* (1956) and starring in *Victim* (1957) on *U. S. Steel Hour*. The post-adolescent Stockwell, despite acne-scarred features and the maturing of his build, still retained a baby-faced look. He made his film return as the brother of Jeffrey Hunter and Fred MacMurray in *Gun for a Coward* (1957). *The Careless Years* (1957), about rebellious teenagers, was the his first and last film made under a 1956 six-year contract with Kirk Douglas' Bryna Productions.

Stockwell returned to New York and obtained the colead with Roddy McDowall in Meyer Levin's play *Compulsion*, based on the Leopold and Loeb thrill killing trial. The later film version (1959) had Stockwell repeating his role of Judd Steiner, and it boasts perhaps the finest acting of the performer's career. This film immediately established him as one of the top younger screen players in Hollywood. (That same year he was Ernest Hemingway's Nick Adams in a television special based on *The Killers*.) Stockwell turned down several film offers that he felt were not up to his standards, but did play the brooding young son of Wendy Hiller and Trevor Howard in *Sons and Lovers* (1960).

Then he was off the screen for two years, during which time he married and divorced film starlet Millie Perkins. Finally he appeared in the marathon screen version of *Long Day's Journey into Night* (1962) as the consumptive would-be writer son of Katharine Hepburn and Ralph Richardson. Contrary to its title, *Rapture* (1965) was only the melancholy tale of a young criminal on the loose who entrances a young girl (Patricia Gozzi). It flopped. During this period, Stockwell's brother Guy was getting far more publicity with his more than competent performances in movies, made under his Universal contract.

In a desire to change his image and/or in need of ready cash, Stockwell was in American International's *Psych-Out* (1968) with another former lofty player, Susan Strasberg. Stockwell was a long-haired hippie dropout—very sensitive, of course—caught in the drugged world of San Francisco's Haight-Ashbury. Since the project was just a carbon copy of many other better films, it effectively ended Stockwell's long-standing battle for artistic integrity. *The Dunwich Horror* (1970), from H. P. Lovecraft's tale, is noteworthy only for being the death knell to Sandra Dee's waning screen career. A motorcycle picture with Stockwell titled *The Loners* was released in 1972.

In the past few years, Stockwell has appeared frequently on television, guesting on such series as *Mannix*, having a supporting role in the telefeature pilot, *The Adventures of Nick Carter* (1972), and, most interestingly, in a video movie with Jane Wyman, *The Failing of Raymond* (1971). Stockwell, already thirty-five, was still playing the disturbed young man, this time an escaped psychopath out to murder his former high school teacher (Wyman). This type of role has become his stock in trade.

Not long ago, Stockwell directed a short film, *Crazy Horse*, a movie about Bruce Conner's filming of *Breakaway*. It was shown on the college campus releasing circuit.

Screen veteran Stockwell now insists: "Acting is my business, my work. I love it, even when I'm miserable."

DEAN STOCKWELL

Valley of Decision (MGM, 1945)
Anchors Aweigh (MGM, 1945)
Bud Abbott and Lou Costello in Hollywood (MGM, 1945)
The Green Years (MGM, 1946)
Home Sweet Homicide (20th-Fox, 1946)
The Mighty McGurk (MGM, 1947)
The Arnelo Affair (MGM, 1947)
Song of the Thin Man (MGM, 1947)
The Romance of Rosy Ridge (MGM, 1947)
Gentleman's Agreement (20th-Fox, 1947)
The Boy with Green Hair (RKO, 1948)
Deep Waters (20th-Fox, 1948)
Down to the Sea in Ships (20th-Fox, 1949)
The Secret Garden (MGM, 1949)
Stars in My Crown (MGM, 1950)

The Happy Years (MGM, 1950)
Kim (MGM, 1950)
Cattle Drive (Universal, 1951)
Gun for a Coward (Universal, 1957)
The Careless Years (UA, 1957)
Compulsion (20th-Fox, 1959)
Sons and Lovers (20th-Fox, 1960)
Long Day's Journey into Night (Embassy, 1962)
Rapture (International Classics, 1965)
Psych-Out (AIP, 1968)
The Dunwich Horror (AIP, 1970)
Ecstasy 70 (Unreleased)
The Loners (Fanfare, 1972)
Another Day at the Races (Picture Corp., 1973)

With Felipe Turich, Robert Douglas, Frank Lackteen, and Mike Tellegan in *Kim* (1950)

Lewis Stone

Lewis Stone was the favorite cinema old-father image for both Louis B. Mayer and MGM, particularly after he made such a hit in the *Andy Hardy* series. This casting tag was a mixed blessing. It assured the veteran performer a berth at that studio as long as he lived, but it also curbed and narrowed his wide scope of acting talents. Stone died during the twenty-ninth year of his association with MGM, having first worked for the studio when it was just formed in 1924. He was a handsome and respected leading man in silents and early talkies, and appeared in more pictures with Greta Garbo than any other actor. However, it was his off-the-cuff performances as the benevolent Judge Hardy which earned him the widest popularity he enjoyed at MGM and which epitomized Mayer's supportive affection.

Stone was born on November 15, 1879 in Worcester, Massachusetts. He left college to serve in the Spanish–American War as an infantry instructor in the grade of lieutenant. After the war he turned to acting and made his stage debut in a stock company in Canada. He came to Broadway in *Side-Tracked* (1900) and later starred in a West Coast production of *The Bird of Paradise*. When that show came to New York, opening on January 8, 1912, both he and Laurette Taylor became established Broadway figures. He interrupted his show business career to serve in World War I as a major in the cavalry. Then he returned to acting, this time in motion pictures.

He had made his screen debut at Essanay in *The Man Who Found Out* (1915), and his 5' 10-3/4" lean figure immediately made him a popular leading man. After the war, he free-lanced, playing in such features as *Man's Desire* (1919) with June Novak, and in Samuel Goldwyn's production of Arnold Bennett's and Edward Knoblock's play *Milestones* (1920). He first worked for the Marcus Loew-owned Metro company in 1922 in *The Prisoner of Zenda*, cast in the dual lead role of Rudolf Rassendyll and King Rudolf, with Alice Terry as Princess Flavia. In *Scaramouche*, another swashbuckling tale for Metro, directed by Rex Ingram, who had directed prisoner, and also starring Ingram's wife Alice Terry, Stone played the Marquis de la Tour d'Azyr, the second male lead to Ramon Novarro. When Metro and Samuel Goldwyn merged their companies to become Metro-Goldwyn in 1924, Stone frequently played in their studio products, such as *Cheaper to Marry* (1925), which was a comedy drama starring Conrad Nagel as Stone's law partner. One of Stone's best-remembered films was made during his tenure at First National studios. Arthur Conan Doyle's *The Lost World* (1925) has long been a staple in filmhistory courses, and the film's expansive use of special effects to create the prehistoric monsters has made the movie a must on the list of home movie collectors. Stone played Sir John Roxton, one of the members of Wallace Beery's expedition to the lost world in the heart of South America. For his performance as Count Pahlen, the friend and advisor to Russia's mad Czar Paul the First (Emil Jannings) in Paramount's *The Patriot* (1928), Stone was nominated for an Oscar. But he lost out in the best actor award to Warner Baxter who won for *In Old Arizona*.

In 1928 Stone, on approaching the age of fifty, rejoined MGM on a full-time acting basis, and made the first of his several films with Greta Garbo. John Gilbert was Garbo's love interest in *A Woman of Affairs* (1929) and Stone was the aristocratic English girl's good friend. In the same year's *Wild Orchids* he was Garbo's much-older husband, and the next year she was his ex-mistress in *Romance*. Meanwhile, like the equally versatile Jean Hersholt, he was filling a much-needed role at MGM by bolstering a variety of studio products in a series of guises. In the gangster melodrama, *The Big House* (1930) he was the warden; in the society drama *Strictly Unconventional* (1930), he appeared to advantage as the ambitious and foppish husband of Catherine Dale Owen; and in *Passion Flower* (1930), he was the Spanish spouse of Kay Francis. As a leading character "star," Stone was occasionally loaned out by MGM when not too busy on the home lot. He made eight features in 1931, including Garbo's *Mata Hari*, in which he was the leader of her spy unit. Of his ten 1932 releases, his most memorable was in the star-laden *Grand Hotel*. As Dr. Otternschlag, the white-haired scarred World War I veteran, Stone was the constant lobby observer who uttered the now-classic line, "Nothing ever happens at the Grand Hotel." Stone was equally at ease portraying an Oriental in *The Son–Daughter* (1932) and Garbo's Scandinavian advisor in *Queen Christina* (1933).

As the decade progressed, Stone continued to exhibit versatility, playing Mr. Wickfield in *David Copperfield* (1935), the seemingly cowardly third officer in *China Seas* (1935), and Cary Grant's affluent father in *Suzy* (1936). He bolstered the hoary thriller, *The Thirteenth Chair* (1937), and in Universal's bloodthirsty tale of revenge, *The Man Who Cried Wolf* (1937), he made this lurid yarn, which starred Claude Rains, much more believable.

Ironically, it was not all this yeoman work which made Stone an essential ingredient to the MGM stock company, but his replacement assignment in the second of the *Andy Hardy* series, *You're Only Young Once* (1937). Lionel Barrymore had been set to repeat his role of Judge Hardy from *A Family Affair* (1937), but a hip injury prevented him from playing in the followup picture. Moreover, Spring Byington, who had played Mrs. Hardy in *A Family Affair* was dropped from the lineup in favor of Fay Holden. Together with Stone the two of them became so identified as Mickey Rooney's parents in *You're Only Young Once*, that no further *Andy Hardy* entry would be considered complete without their presence. Because Stone was so well-liked in the role of the small town judge and patient father, it became impossible to cast him in the variety of roles he had played before. Lewis Stone was Judge Hardy, and that was that.

In 1938 Mayer presented Stone with a pair of silver spurs and said, "If it were not so impractical to close the studio down, every one of the thousands on the lot would be here to pay their tribute of affection to Lewis Stone. It is difficult to say what is his greatest attribute—his character of Americanism or his artistry. But I do say he is a credit to his profession, and it is significant that such a man has become the symbol of fatherhood in America as Judge Hardy. It is fitting that he should be the one to do such a perfect interpretation—and that every boy in America should envy Mickey Rooney that he has such a father in his professional life."

Stone never considered retiring, and after the *Hardy* series' demise in 1946, he was to be seen in other prime studio products, ranging from drama, *State of the Union* (1948), to more stately roles in swashbucklers such as the remakes of *Scaramouche* (1952) and *The Prisoner of Zenda* (1952). In his last years at the studio, Stone would work only twelve weeks a year at MGM, but, at Mayer's insistence, he was paid for a full forty. When questioned whether he didn't think himself too old to continue in his craft, he would reply, "Why? And miss all this."

On September 12, 1953, Stone chased three teenagers across his front lawn when he found them breaking up his lawn furniture. He collapsed and died on the lawn with his wife sobbing over him. He was then 73 years old. His widow was the former Hazel Elizabeth Wolf. He had been married twice previously: to Mary Langham and to Florence Pryor, and he had two daughters. He left an estate of $150,000.

When Mickey Rooney and MGM revived Andy Hary in *Andy Hardy Comes Home* (1958), Stone's absence was sorely missed. As the camera panned beyond Fay Holden as Mrs. Hardy to a portrait of the "judge" over the fireplace, audiences everywhere fondly recalled all the fireside chats he and Mickey Rooney had shared in those innocent, long-gone days of the 1930s and 1940s.

LEWIS STONE

The Man Who Found Out (Essanay, 1915)
The Havoc (Essanay, 1916)
Honor's Altar (Triangle, 1916)
According to the Code (Essanay, 1916)
Inside of the Lines (Pyramid-World, 1918)
Man's Desire (Robertson-Cole, 1919)
Man of Bronze (World, 1919)
Milestones (Goldwyn, 1920)

Nomads of the North (FN, 1920)
Held by the Enemy (Paramount, 1920)
The River's End (FN, 1920)
The Child Thou Gavest Me (GN, 1921)
The Concert (Goldwyn, 1921)
The Golden Snare (FN, 1921)
Beau Revel (Paramount, 1921)
Don't Neglect Your Wife (Goldwyn, 1921)

Pilgrims of the Night (Associated Producers, 1921)

The Dangerous Age (FN, 1922)

The Rosary (FN, 1922)

A Fool There Was (Fox, 1922)

The Prisoner of Zenda (Metro, 1922)

Trifling Women (Metro, 1922)

The World's Applause (Paramount, 1923)

You Can't Fool Your Wife (Paramount, 1923)

Scaramouche (Metro, 1923)

The Stranger (Paramount, 1924)

Cytherea (FN, 1924)

Why Men Leave Home (FN, 1924)

Husbands and Lovers (Rimax, 1924)

Inez from Hollywood (FN, 1924)

Cheaper to Marry (Metro-Goldwyn, 1925)

The Talker (FN, 1925)

Confessions of a Queen (Metro-Goldwyn, 1925)

Fine Clothes (FN, 1925)

The Lady Who Lied (FN, 1925)

The Lost World (FN, 1925)

What Fools Men (FN, 1925)

The Girl from Montmartre (FN, 1926)

Midnight Lovers (FN, 1926)

Old Loves and New (FN, 1926)

Too Much Money (FN, 1926)

Don Juan's Three Nights (FN, 1926)

The Blonde Saint (FN, 1926)

An Affair of the Follies (FN, 1927)

Lonesome Ladies (FN, 1927)

The Notorious Lady (FN, 1927)

The Private Life of Helen of Troy (FN, 1927)

The Prince of Headwaiters (FN, 1927)

The Foreign Legion (Universal, 1928)

The Patriot (Paramount, 1928)

Freedom of the Press (Universal, 1928)

A Woman of Affairs (MGM, 1929)

Madame X (MGM, 1929)

The Trial of Mary Dugan (MGM, 1929)

Their Own Desire (MGM, 1930)

Strictly Unconventional (MGM, 1930)

The Big House (MGM, 1930)

Romance (MGM, 1930)

Father's Son (WB, 1930)

The Office Wife (WB, 1930)

Passion Flower (MGM, 1930)

My Past (WB, 1931)

Inspiration (MGM, 1931)

The Secret Six (MGM, 1931)

Always Goodbye (Fox, 1931)

Phantom of Paris (MGM, 1931)

The Bargain (WB, 1931)

The Sin of Madelon Claudet (MGM, 1931)

Mata Hari (MGM, 1931)

Grand Hotel (MGM, 1932)

The Wet Parade (MGM, 1932)

Night Court (MGM, 1932)

Letty Lynton (MGM, 1932)

New Morals for Old (MGM, 1932)

Unashamed (MGM, 1932)

Divorce in the Family (MGM, 1932)

Red-Headed Woman (MGM, 1932)

Mask of Fu Manchu (MGM, 1932)

The Son–Daughter (MGM, 1932)

The White Sister (MGM, 1933)

Men Must Fight (MGM, 1933)

Looking Forward (MGM, 1933)

Bureau of Missing Persons (WB, 1933)

Queen Christina (MGM, 1933)

You Can't Buy Everything (MGM, 1934)

Mystery of Mr. X (MGM, 1934)

Treasure Island (MGM, 1934)

Girl from Missouri (MGM, 1934)

Vanessa, Her Love Story (MGM, 1935)

West Point of the Air (MGM, 1935)

David Copperfield (MGM, 1935)

Public Hero Number One (MGM, 1935)

China Seas (MGM, 1935)

Woman Wanted (MGM, 1935)

Shipmates Forever (WB, 1935)

Small Town Girl (MGM, 1936)

The Three Godfathers (MGM, 1936)

The Unguarded Hour (MGM, 1936)

Sworn Enemy (MGM, 1936)

Suzy (MGM, 1936)

Don't Turn 'Em Loose (RKO, 1936)

Outcast (Paramount, 1937)

The Thirteenth Chair (MGM, 1937)

The Man Who Cried Wolf (Universal, 1937)

You're Only Young Once (MGM, 1937)

Bad Man of Brimstone (MGM, 1938)

Judge Hardy's Children (MGM, 1938)

Stolen Heaven (Paramount, 1938)

Yellow Jack (MGM, 1938)

The Chaser (MGM, 1938)

Love Finds Andy Hardy (MGM, 1938)

Out West with the Hardys (MGM, 1938)

Ice Follies of 1939 (MGM, 1939)

The Hardys Ride High (MGM, 1939)

Andy Hardy Gets Spring Fever (MGM, 1939)

Joe and Ethel Turp Call on the President (MGM, 1939)

Sporting Blood (MGM, 1940)

Life Begins for Andy Hardy (MGM, 1941)

Andy Hardy's Private Secretary (MGM, 1941)

The Bugle Sounds (MGM, 1941)

The Courtship of Andy Hardy (MGM, 1942)

Andy Hardy's Double Life (MGM, 1942)
Andy Hardy's Blonde Trouble (MGM, 1944)
The Hoodlum Saint (MGM, 1946)
Three Wise Fools (MGM, 1946)
Love Laughs at Andy Hardy (MGM, 1946)
State of the Union (MGM, 1948)
The Sun Comes Up (MGM, 1949)
Any Number Can Play (MGM, 1949)
Stars in My Crown (MGM, 1950)
Key to the City (MGM, 1950)
Grounds for Marriage (MGM, 1950)

Night into Morning (MGM, 1951)
Angels in the Outfield (MGM, 1951)
Bannerline (MGM, 1951)
I's a Big Country (MGM, 1951)
The Unknown Man (MGM, 1951)
Just This Once (MGM, 1952)
Scaramouche (MGM, 1952)
Talk about a Stranger (MGM, 1952)
The Prisoner of Zenda (MGM, 1952)
All the Brothers Were Valiant (MGM, 1953)

With Norma Shearer in *The Trial of Mary Dugan* (1929)

687

With Sara Haden, Fay Holden, Cecilia Parker, and Mickey Rooney in *You're Only Young Once* (1937)

With Ann Sothern and William Gargan in *Joe and Ethel Turp Call on the President* (1939)

Margaret Sullavan

The name Margaret Sullavan means very little to anyone under forty, partly because the bulk of her movie work was in filmed soap opera too soupy for modern tastes, and partly because she was not a dedicated actress, hated making motion pictures, and would not play ball with the Hollywood studio system. She was both admirable and exasperating. Above all, she was a willful, ambitious, feminine, honest, and warm actress whose talents were largely untapped by her second-rate tragic heroine screen assignments. She died from an overdose of sleeping pills when she could no longer cope with the almost total loss of her hearing. She slid into the whole acting business in a youthful rebellion against her Victorian childhood, and, not being equipped with the actor's ego, indeed suffering under an intense lack of confidence, she was determined to do her damnedest to succeed. While struggling to attain her professional goals, she was also struggling to find herself as a woman, a wife, and a mother, and her embarrassing directness earned her a reputation as one of the most temperamental of actresses. Despite all this internal conflict, Margaret turned in some enchantingly beautiful performances that, as one critic said, "fit in somewhere between the two Hepburns, Katharine and Audrey." She appeared in only sixteen motion pictures. During her marriage to agent Leland Hayward, he arranged a contract with MGM for her to make six pictures for that studio. Three of them contain her best cinema work.

Margaret Brooke Sullavan was born in Norfolk, Virginia on May 16, 1911. Her family traced their ancestry to pre-Revolutionary stock, and she was educated in private schools. When she announced her desire to be an actress, her straitlaced parents were appalled. Years later, she said, "Like most people, I wanted to break away from home, move out of town. The theatre seemed like an easy and glamorous way to do it. My parents would never have allowed me to come to New York and go into the theatre, so I did it in a roundabout way." She persuaded her parents to allow her to enroll in the Denishawn School of Dance in Boston, (founded by Ruth St. Denis and Ted Shawn), but after three weeks she transferred to E. E. Clive's Copley Theatre Dramatic School and worked in the Harvard Cooperative Bookstore at $18 a week. Clive, later a successful character actor in Hollywood, has recalled, "She had an instinctive grace, a voice that promised depths to be explored, and an earnestness surprising in a little Southern girl the Harvard boys were eager to make a belle of the ball." She was all of seventeen years old.

Through her Harvard acquaintances, she joined the University Players, which included Henry Fonda, James Stewart, Joshua Logan, Myron McCormick, Kent Smith, Mildred Natwick, and Barbara O'Neil. She painted sets, played ingenues, and stooged for Fonda's mad magician act in a local nightclub. The University Players performed in Falmouth, Massachusetts during the summers and wintered in Baltimore. Margaret and Fonda starred in *Coquette, Holiday, The Constant Nymph, Mary Rose*, and *A Kiss for Cinderella*. In addition to her work with the players, Margaret struck out for Broadway on her own. A tour of Preston Sturges' *Strictly Dishonorable* took her to her hometown and, when her family witnessed the scene where she removes her clothes, they considered her "lost" to the theatre.

Her Broadway debut was on May 20, 1931, playing a sixteen-year-old rebellious heiress in *A Modern Virgin*, and critics likened her appearance and husky voice to Ethel Barrymore's. The play lasted for only 33 performances, but the Shubert Brothers contracted her for five years. After the play closed, she went to Baltimore with the University Players to play opposite Fonda in *The Ghost Train*. On Christmas Day 1931 she and Fonda were married in the Kernan Hotel. The courtship of these two young actors had been a stormy one with several rip-roaring fights, and their marital bliss lasted only two months. They were divorced but still remained friends for many years.

Margaret's stage work for the Shuberts, though receiving good notices, turned out to be a series of flops — *If Love Were All, Happy Landing, Chrysalis, Bad Manners*. The girl could act, and when she replaced Marguerite Churchill as the society girl in *Dinner at Eight* in 1933, Hollywood director John M. Stahl saw her and offered Margaret the starring part in *Only Yesterday* (1933), a script that both Claudette Colbert and Irene Dunne had rejected. She accepted, but contracted with Universal only on her own terms: $1,200 weekly, three years, nonexclusive, and approval rights. Universal recognized her talents but also that she was not the usual Hollywood beauty. For that reason, they changed a few things cosmetically: "A mole was removed; so were her eyebrows; her medium-brown hair was dyed blonde; a shield was put over a front tooth that was short; the top lipstick line on her upper lip was raised to reduce the distance between her nose and her mouth; and because the right side of her jaw was lower than the left, and her mouth drooped to the right, the corners of her mouth were heightened with lipstick and her right eyebrow line was raised."

When Margaret saw her first film rushes, she offered to buy out her contract, but Universal declined her offer. Done in the style of *Madame X, Only Yesterday* was a weeper, but the critics adored this wisp of an actress, and it was boxoffice success. Still skeptical, Margaret said, "Acting in the movies is just like ditch-digging. Perhaps I'll get used to the bizarre, elaborate theatricalism called Hollywood, but I cannot guarantee it." Her part in the anti-Fascist *Little Man, What Now?* (1934) was better and critics treated it

MARGARET SULLAVAN

The Shining Hour (MGM, 1938)
The Shop Around the Corner (MGM, 1940)
The Mortal Storm (MGM, 1940)
So Ends Our Night (UA, 1941)
Back Street (Universal, 1941)
Appointment for Love (Universal, 1941)
Cry Havoc (MGM, 1943)
No Sad Songs for Me (Columbia, 1950)

...garet was still suspect and told *Photoplay*: "I still hate ... And I don't like Hollywood any better. I detest the limelight favorably...plicity, and in Hollywood the only thing that matters is the ... of fame. If Hollywood will let me alone to find my way without ... me and rushing me into things, I probably will change my feelings ...ut it. But at present Hollywood seems utterly horrible and interfering and consuming. Which is why I want to leave it as soon as I am able."

Her third picture was the Ferenc Molnar whimsey, *The Good Fairy* (1935), with Herbert Marshall, and her self-distrust made work on the production tedious. Director William Wyler suffered the tantrums in silence until finally in front of the whole crew he said: "Now you listen, and don't interrupt! You've made work on this picture last twelve weeks instead of seven, and you've all but demoralized me. This is the end. You're going to enter left, stand on that chalk mark, and twist that vicious pan of yours into the semblance of a human face and drench this scene with pathos. And you're not going to underplay or suffer silently by gritting your teeth. You're going to *cry*—get it? Bawl! And like it!" She walked off the set; he took her to dinner. They were married November 11, 1934, and were divorced on March 13, 1936. (Some say she married Wyler to escape the persistent attention of Broadway producer Jed Harris.)

Paramount borrowed her for the Civil War-set period piece *So Red the Rose* (1935), which does not hold up well today. Then Universal borrowed James Stewart from MGM to play opposite her in *Next Time We Love* (1936). She was the actress and he the struggling young reporter in this tearjerker, and the film established her preeminence in this genre. She went back to Paramount to star with her ex-husband, Fonda, in a slightly screwball comedy, *The Moon's Our Home* (1936), which was concerned with a world famous actress who weds a celebrated explorer-writer, neither realizing just who the other is. As the spoiled heiress–screen star, Margaret was praised for her ability in creating a sprightly and arresting characterization outside of her usual maudlin forte. That same studio asked her to replace their fading queen, Marlene Dietrich, in *I Loved a Soldier*. Dietrich had walked out of that production after a total of $900,000 had been expended on the project. The costar was Charles Boyer. Margaret began filming, but fell over a light cable and broke her arm. The beleaguered project was eventually passed on to Isa Miranda and Ray Milland and released as *Hotel Imperial* (1939).

After her fall, Margaret returned to New York and scored a personal triumph playing the theatre actress who scorns films in the George S. Kaufman–Edna Ferber play, *Stage Door*. That play opened on October 22, 1936, and the following March 13, she married her New York agent, Leland Hayward. In July their daughter Brooke was born. Hayward convinced his wife to sign a six-picture deal with MGM. Her first film for this studio was the well-mounted edition of Erich Maria Remarque's *Three Comrades* (1938), dealing with post World War I Germany and the rise of Nazism, intertwined with the love tale of Robert Taylor and his tubercular wife Margaret. She

691

received an Academy Award nomination and the Ne~~~~
Award. The N.Y. *Times* extolled, "The word admirable is ~~~~
statement. Her performance is almost unendurably lovely." *The S~~~~
Angel (1938) cast her as playboy Walter Pidgeon's spoiled property wh~~~~
for yokel army private James Stewart. In her third release of th~~~~
Margaret took second billing to the queen of MGM melodram~~~~
Crawford, in *The Shining Hour*, an intriguing acting exercise that ~~~~
congeal into the desired weepy woman's picture. During this ~~~~
self-sacrifice and selfishness, Margaret is ready to give up her husba~~~~
Young) to sister-in-law Crawford who is wed to Melvyn Douglas, ~~~~
conflagration brings Young to his senses. Later, Margaret, ~~~~
bandages, save for her expressive eyes, forgives her erring husba~~~~

Margaret gave birth to a second daughter, Bridget, in 19~~~~
made two more MGM pictures. She was "utterly beguiling" ~~~~
Around the Corner (1940), playing the salesgirl in a novelty sho~~~~
who falls in love with the head clerk James Stewart. In *The M~~~~
fourth feature with Stewart and the third of her Metro films t~~~~
Frank Borzage, she was the idealistic daughter of a non-~~~~
Frank Morgan, who, with Stewart, fights the sweep of Nazis~~~~
went to United Artists to play the Jewish refugee in *So Ends~~~~
based on Erich Maria Remarque's *Flotsam*; and termina~~~~
commitment by performing in two very popular soap ~~~~
(1941) and *Appointment for Love* (1941), both with Char~~~~
birth to her third child, William, in 1942, and finished ~~~~
deal by playing the heroic nurse in *Cry Havoc* (1943). ~~~~

In 1943 she gave her best Broadway performanc~~~~
Turtle. She stayed with that play for one year, but it ra~~~~
divorced Hayward in 1947, and made her final motio~~~~
No Sad Songs for Me (1950), a tearjerker about a ~~~~
cancer. As on so many previous occasions, she ga~~~~
performance in a mediocre script. She wed British i~~~~
in 1950, and retired to Connecticut for two year~~~~
career, it was on the the stage in *The Deep Blue S~~~~
She had done some television, *The Storm* (1948), ~~~~
gained a reputation for undependabillity, parti~~~~
Pilot in 1956, suffering from nervous exhaustion and co~~~~
sanatorium.

Margaret remained inactive for three years, then signed to do a play
called *Sweet Love Remembered*, featuring her University Players' cohort Kent
Smith. That play opened in New Haven, Connecticut on December 28, 1959,
and she received good notices, but the play did not. On New Year's Day,
Margaret was found unconscious in her room in New Haven's Taft Hotel, and
died before she reached the New Haven Grace Hospital. The cause was an

692

With James Stewart and Walter Pidgeon in *The Shopworn An~~~~

With Grace Hayle in *The Shop around the Corner* (~~~~

With James Stewart and Maria Ouspenskaya in *The Mortal Storm* (1940)

Elizabeth Taylor

Elizabeth Taylor, the mid–twentieth century's most beautiful woman and the world's most famous and highest paid actress, is seemingly the last of the great glamor stars to emerge from that dream factory, Hollywood. Today, her life style and boxoffice is rivaled only by that of Italy's Sophia Loren. Although Elizabeth's feature films during the past five years have been artistic duds, she is still that mysterious commodity—a cinema queen—with the public still gobbling up every newspaper and magazine tidbit about the exploits of her and her actor husband, Richard Burton. During her union with Conrad "Nicky" Hilton, the first of her several husbands, she remarked that she had the body of a woman and the emotions of a child. It has been just her womanly vulnerability that has made her so exploitable by the press and so constantly in the public eye. Each step, from her state of being, as she described herself, "a shy girl with a big inferiority complex" through maturity, as well as each marriage, each *faux pas*, each child, each illness — all has been public domain and detailed to a meticulous degree *ad absurdum* by the press.

Elizabeth Rosemond Taylor was born on February 27, 1932 in London, the daughter of an American art dealer, Howard Taylor, whose wife, Sara Warmbraten, a native of Kansas, had been an actress under the stage name of Sara Sothern. Mr. Taylor's business kept his family in London, where Elizabeth was sent to the Vaccani Dancing Academy, whose students also included Britain's Royal Family. At age three, Elizabeth performed in a dance recital before Princesses Elizabeth and Margaret. Later, Elizabeth attended the private Bryon House school. In 1939, confronted by the ensuing war, her father sent her and her mother to California, where she was enrolled in the Hawthorne School in Beverly Hills. She was an exquisitely beautiful child, and family friends were always suggesting that the girl should be in movies. At one time it was suggested that Elizabeth be tested for the role of Scarlett O'Hara's daughter, Bonnie, in *Gone with the Wind*, since she resembled Vivien Leigh so much. Elizabeth's mother liked the idea of her daughter being a child movie star, but Mr. Taylor objected. Finally, Mrs. Taylor won out, and Elizabeth was tested by Universal Pictures.

That studio cast her in *There's One Born Every Minute* (1942) opposite ex–"Our Gang" star Carl "Alfalfa" Switzer, thinking Elizabeth might prove to be another Deanna Durbin. But after that initial film, they offered her no further assignments and allowed her option to lapse. But fate came to the "rescue." As a wartime Civil Defense air raid warden, Mr. Taylor struck up a conversation with MGM executive Sam Marx one day. The result was a screen test for Elizabeth at MGM and her being cast as the little English girl in *Lassie Come Home* (1943). Her role in that picture was small, but the critics noticed her, and she was put under a long-term contract. Metro loaned her to Twentieth Century-Fox as Helen, the child who dies of pneumonia in *Jane Eyre* (1944), and then cast her back on the home lot as the girl friend of young Roddy McDowall in *The White Cliffs of Dover* (1944). (Her part is cut out of the prints shown on television today.) The next year, Metro cast the thirteen-year-old Elizabeth as Velvet Brown in *National Velvet* (1945). This movie transformed the rapturously beautiful child into a star.

Elizabeth left the Hawthorne School and took lessons at the MGM studio school and from private tutors. As part of the MGM "Family" she recalls the yearly celebration of Louis B. Mayer's birthday on the huge Stage Thirty. "All we kids would stand and sing 'Happy Birthday.'" "Then" remembers Elizabeth, "he would address the assemblage with, 'You must think of me as your father. You must come to me, any of you, with any of your problems no matter how slight they might seem to you, because you are all my children.'" Elizabeth's mother took him up on that invitation when she heard that her daughter was about to be cast in a dancing–singing role in a picture to be called *Sally in Her Alley*. Fourteen-year-old Elizabeth and her mother went to Mayer's executive suite to verify the rumor, and if it were true, to plead for time for proper training. Elizabeth, who has described Mayer as a dwarf with a big nose, recollected the scene:

Mayer: "You're so goddamned stupid [i.e., Mrs. Taylor] you wouldn't know what day of the week it is. Don't meddle in my affairs! Don't tell me how to make motion pictures! I took you out of the gutter!"

Elizabeth (yelling): "Don't you dare speak to my mother like that! You and your studio can both go to hell!"

Elizabeth ran out of the office, while the more practical Mrs. Taylor contritely remained behind to smooth things out. The picture was never made, and Elizabeth vowed she would never enter his office again, a promise she faithfully kept.

As Elizabeth blossomed into womanhood, she never suffered any gawky adolescent stage as did fading MGM child star Margaret O'Brien. Elizabeth played her first adult role opposite Robert Taylor in *The Conspirator* (1950). Although she was playing mature girls on the screen, MGM still treated her as a brainless adolescent and, consequently devised studio-endorsed "romances" for her. She protested to little avail. She did become engaged to William Pawly, Jr., son of a former ambassador to Brazil and Peru, but she broke the engagement when he insisted she give up her career. One week before her eighteenth birthday, Elizabeth became engaged to Conrad "Nicky" Hilton. MGM's publicity force went to work. Luckily for them, she

697

With Roddy McDowall in *The White Cliffs of Dover* (1944)

With Jackie "Butch" Jenkins in *National Velvet* (1944)

With Lassie and Frank Morgan in *Courage of Lassie* (1946)

With Margaret O'Brien, Janet Leigh, and June Allyson in *Little Women* (1949)

was propitiously starred in *Father of the Bride* (1950) at the time. However, the marriage lasted a brief two weeks. Elizabeth commented, "I really thought in those days that just because I became a wife, or just because I reached twenty-one, something would automatically happen to me inside. I was always wanting to be older, trying all the superficial things of being sophisticated. But I did have moments of self-revelation. After the wedding I said something about being an emotional child inside the body of a woman, and the press picked it up. Recently I read where I didn't say it at all, that it came out of a press agent's mouth. You want to meet whoever said that and give them a knuckle sandwich. That was my first sexual experience. And I hadn't been adequately prepared for it. I had always had a very strict and proper upbringing, and absolutely necessary it was, living the existence I did. I was really quite a prude. The irony is that the morality I learned at home required marriage. I couldn't just have an affair. So I got married all those times, and now I'm accused of being a scarlet woman. I've only slept with the men I've been married to. How many women can make that claim?"

After her divorce from Hilton, Metro loaned her to Paramount to play the society girl in George Stevens' *A Place in the Sun* (1951). For the first time, critics became aware of more than her face. While in England playing Rebecca the Jewess in *Ivanhoe* (1952), Elizabeth met British actor Michael Wilding, proposed to him, and married him on February 21, 1952 in Caxton Hall. She returned to Hollywood a radiant bride and became the mother of two sons, Michael Howard (born on January 6, 1953) and Christopher Edward (born on his mother's birthday in 1955). During her marriage to Wilding, Elizabeth begged MGM to loan her to Warner Brothers — to play the questing wife in George Stevens' *Giant* (1957). By the time the picture was finished, her marriage to Wilding was ending, and she obtained a divorce on January 30, 1957. She stated at the time, "I'm afraid in those last few years I gave him rather a rough time. Sort of henpecked him and probably wasn't mature enough for him. It wasn't that we had anything to fight over. We just weren't happy." Three days later she wed showman Michael Todd. The day she had announced her separation from Wilding, Todd, who had met her earlier at MGM, informed Elizabeth, "Don't horse around. You're going to marry me!" While she was in Kentucky filming *Raintree County* (1956), he courted via telephone, met her on weekends and overwhelmed her with a 25-karat diamond. He called her Lizzie Schwartzkopf. At their wedding, Mexican comedian Cantinflas and Todd's pal, Eddie Fisher, shared honors as best men. Fisher's wife at the time, Debbie Reynolds, was a matron of honor. Elizabeth bore Todd a daughter, Elizabeth (Liza) Frances, on August 6, 1957. The following March, Todd took off for New York City in his private plane named "The Lucky Liz," to accept the Showman of the Year Award from the National Association of Theatre Owners, for his movie *Around the World in 80 Days* (1956). Elizabeth stayed behind due to a virus infection. The plane crashed and Todd and the other three passengers were killed. Elizabeth says that on the morning of Todd's death, her doctor, Rex Kannamer, and Todd's

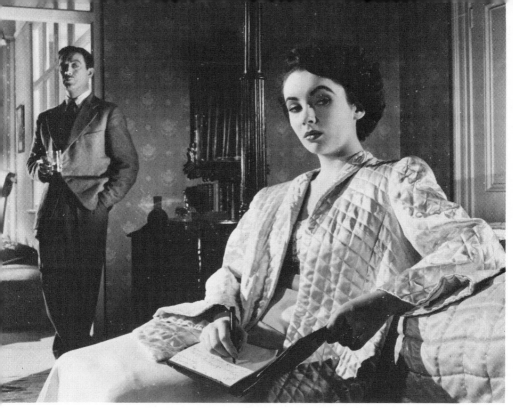

With Robert Taylor in *Conspirator* (1950)

With Van Johnson and Walter Pidgeon in *The Last Time I Saw Paris* (1954)

secretary, Richard Hanley, awakened her at eight-thirty. She sat up in bed and screamed, "No!" They answered, "Yes!" and she knew, before they told her, that Todd was dead.

The man to come to Elizabeth's aid during her grief was Eddie Fisher. The blatant publicity that ensued was the nadir of her career. They were married on May 12, 1959 in a Jewish ceremony in Las Vegas. Elizabeth, who had been studying Judaism during her marriage to Todd, had converted to that religion the previous March. They adopted a crippled child, named Maria, in Germany in 1960. Despite her dubious personal publicity, her career was in top form. She received her second and third Academy Award nominations for *Cat on a Hot Tin Roof* (1959) and *Suddenly, Last Summer* (1959). (The first had been for *Raintree County*.) Elizabeth was obviously top boxoffice draw. While Todd was alive, he made a verbal agreement with MGM that *Cat on a Hot Tin Roof* would be the last of her contractual obligations to the studio. Elizabeth was then offered a precedent-setting $1 million bid to star in *Cleopatra*, but MGM refused to acknowledge the gentlemen's agreement with Todd. They forced her to make *Butterfield 8* (1960) before she moved out and made *Cleopatra*. A vehement and reluctant Elizabeth complied, calling the MGM picture a piece of s——t. Immediately upon its completion, she went to London to star in *Cleopatra* with Stephen Boyd as Mark Anthony and Peter Finch as Caesar. She contracted pneumonia, nearly died, and in one of Hollywood's inexplicably predictable reversals, was awarded the Oscar for *Butterfield 8* on a sympathy vote. Still weak from her hospitalization, she accepted the award in person. Later she explained, "The reason I got the Oscar was that I had come within a breath of dying of pneumonia only a few months before. Nevertheless, I was filled with gratitude when I got it, for it meant being considered an actress and not a movie star. My eyes were wet and my throat awfully tight. But it was the wrong picture. Any of my three previous nominations was more deserving. I knew it was a sympathy award, but I was still proud to get it."

When *Cleopatra* resumed production, now in Rome, the cast changes included Rex Harrison as Caesar and Richard Burton as Mark Antony. Fisher accompanied Elizabeth to Rome but in a very short time it was evident there was a romance on the set between her and Burton. Her marriage was in a shambles, and one story reported Elizabeth coming home to their villa after a day of filming, walking into a room to find Eddie singing, so she screamed, "For Christ's sake, Eddie, knock it off!" She later said, "The marriage was clearly a mistake. We both tried very hard, but the marriage was untenable for both of us." The Taylor–Burton relationship, with both parties married, was the most notorious love affair of the century. *Cleopatra* was released as a $20 million-plus roadshow bomb in 1963. The following spring, Elizabeth and Burton were married in Montreal, Canada, where Burton was appearing in a stage production of *Hamlet*.

Two years later, with Burton as costar, an overweight, deglamorized Elizabeth gave a *tour de force* performance as Martha in *Who's Afraid of*

With Paul Newman in *Cat on a Hot Tin Roof* (1958)

Virginia Woolf? (1966) and received her second Oscar. Since that time, her film work, with or without Burton, has left much to be desired. Still, in the recent *X Y and Zee* (1972), the plump, forty-year-old Elizabeth revealed a sizable bag of acting tricks that might one day place her in the same league with the mature Bette Davis.

If the Taylor–Burton movie outings have not been boxoffice blockbusters, their marriage has remained intact. Burton, with his inimitable charm and caustic wit, describes his celebrated wife thus, "I can hardly say she's the most beautiful creature I've ever seen. She's a pretty girl and has wonderful eyes. But she has a double chin, an overdeveloped chest, and she's rather short in the leg. There isn't an inch of her body that isn't covered with scars. She's had more operations than a charwoman. And she's always talking about them, too." Elizabeth herself says that, to her, Ava Gardner is a beautiful woman.

Elizabeth gives all appearances of being happy both as a wife and mother. With homes in Ireland, Mexico, Switzerland, London, Rome, a yacht named *The Laizma*, a brood of children and animals, as well as the diamonds (including the Krupp gem), the Burtons are regarded by their intimates as "just simple folk" indeed. When her son, Michael, who prefers the life of a commune to the $75,000 London home purchased for him as a wedding present, made Elizabeth a grandmother in 1972, no one was more pleased than the forty-year-old Elizabeth herself.

When Elizabeth and Burton pooled their talents in motion pictures and especially after *Virginia Woolf*, not a few observers speculated that the screen had a new Lynne Fontanne and Alfred Lunt. What has come to pass is hardly Lunt and Fontanne, but Elizabeth has learned from Richard's intellectuality. On the other hand, Burton has seemingly learned from Elizabeth's professional knowledge of the film medium.

Elizabeth says, "Richard and Elizabeth as actors and celebrities are going into semiretirement in a few years — I much sooner than Richard. Once you're up there on that last rung, your head splitting in two, you can only go down. I don't want to be pushed off. I want to walk down with all the dignity I can summon — and not with crutches. I think Richard eventually will give up acting to become a serious writer."

ELIZABETH TAYLOR

There's One Born Every Minute (Universal, 1942)
Lassie Come Home (MGM, 1943)
Jane Eyre (20th-Fox, 1944)
The White Cliffs of Dover (MGM, 1944)
National Velvet (MGM, 1944)
Courage of Lassie (MGM, 1946)
Cynthia (MGM, 1947)
Life with Father (WB, 1947)
A Date with Judy (MGM, 1948)
Julia Misbehaves (MGM, 1948)
Little Women (MGM, 1949)
Conspirator (MGM, 1950)
The Big Hangover (MGM, 1950)
Father of the Bride (MGM, 1950)
Father's Little Dividend (MGM, 1951)
A Place in the Sun (Paramount, 1951)
Quo Vadis (MGM, 1951)*
Ivanhoe (MGM, 1952)
Love Is Better Than Ever (MGM, 1952)

The Girl Who Had Everything (MGM, 1953)
Rhapsody (MGM, 1954)
Elephant Walk (Paramount, 1954)
Beau Brummel (MGM, 1954)
The Last Time I Saw Paris (MGM, 1954)
Giant (WB, 1956)
Raintree County (MGM, 1957)
Cat on a Hot Tin Roof (MGM, 1958)
Suddenly, Last Summer (Columbia, 1959)
Scent of Mystery (Michael Todd, Jr., 1960)
Butterfield 8 (MGM, 1960)
Cleopatra (20th-Fox, 1963)
The V.I.P.'s (MGM, 1963)
The Sandpiper (MGM, 1965)
Who's Afraid of Virginia Woolf? (WB, 1966)

The Taming of the Shrew (Columbia, 1967)
Reflections in a Golden Eye (WB-7 Arts, 1967)
The Comedians (MGM, 1967)
Dr. Faustus (Columbia, 1968)
Boom (Universal, 1968)
Anne of the Thousand Days (Universal, 1969)
The Only Game in Town (20th-Fox, 1970)
X Y & Zee (Columbia, 1972)
Hammersmith is Out (Cinerama, 1972)
Under Milkwood (Altura, 1972)
Night Watch (Avco-Embassy, 1973)
Divorce His, Divorce Hers (1973)
Ash Wednesday (Paramount, 1974)

*Unbilled appearance

With Richard Burton in *The Sandpiper* (1965)

Robert Taylor

"But I thought they were one and the same!" exclaimed one irreverent movie fan after gazing upon a magnificently posed photograph of Robert Taylor and Hedy Lamarr. And indeed, that glossy black and white patina was indicative of Taylor's early Hollywood image—more masculine than Tyrone Power, more enigmatic than Errol Flynn—but little more than something beautifully decorative to be looked at in awe. Nevertheless, lengthy cinema careers such as Taylor's are seldom built solely upon looks. He did begin his career as a vapid foil for Hollywood's most glamorous leading ladies, from the stereotyped playboy–bad boy of *Magnificent Obsession* (1935) to the ineffectual love child of *Camille* (1936). But in the late 1930s MGM added some blood and guts to his ladies' man image with *A Yank at Oxford* (1938), *The Crowd Roars* (1938), and *Billy the Kid* (1941). After returning to films from his World War II service and finding his masculine beauty on the wane, he proceeded quite respectably as an assertive figure in the postwar screen product, bringing ladies *and* gentlemen into the theatres to weep and applaud for him, a not-to-be-taken-lightly feat. Most critics regarded him as just another somnambulistic actor of the Alan Ladd–Kim Novak school, but while Taylor's histrionic talents were limited, he did offer in his mature years a portrait of the steadfast hero possessed of strength, modesty, and honor.

Taylor's MGM tenure was the second longest in that company's history —twenty-five years*—and of MGM and Louis B. Mayer, Taylor stated in 1964: "Some writers have implied that Mayer was tyrannical and abusive, and a male prima donna who outacted his actors. As I knew him, he was kind, fatherly, understanding, and protective. He gave me picture assignments up to the level that my abilities could sustain at the time, and was always there when I had problems. I just wish today's young actors had a studio and boss like I had. It groomed us carefully, kept us busy in picture after picture, thus giving us exposure, and made us stars. My memories of 'L.B.' will always be pleasant, and my days at MGM are my happiest period professionally."

Robert Taylor was born Spangler Arlington Brugh in Filley, Nebraska on August 5, 1911. His father became a doctor late in life and assumed that his son would follow the same profession. However, Taylor took to playing the

*Lewis Stone was associated with MGM for twenty-nine years.

'cello and public speaking in high school and was encouraged by his mother to pursue these interests at Doane College. He later transferred to Pomona College in Claremont, California, and while there, for reasons he could not remember, participated in drama productions of *Camille*, *The Importance of Being Earnest*, and *M'Lord the Duke*. After seeing him as Captain Stanhope in *Journey's End*, MGM's casting director Ben Piazza offered him free acting lessons, but Taylor refused, saying they would interfere with his studies.

Upon graduation in 1933, he did a screen test for Samuel Goldwyn which proved fruitless, and then signed a seven-year contract with MGM starting at $35 weekly. Ida Koverman, Mayer's chief factotum, suggested he use "Robert Taylor" as his screen name, and the studio, which was seeking a new drawing-room dandy to join the ranks of Robert Montgomery, William Powell, *et al.*, began grooming him for stardom. He made his screen debut on loan to Fox for a small assignment in Will Rogers' *Handy Andy* (1934), and then again on loan to Universal for a B picture entitled *There's Always Tomorrow* (1934). The public first took note of Taylor, not in his initial MGM feature *Wicked Woman* (1934) starring Mady Christians, but in the leadoff entry of a new Leo the Lion two-reeler series, *Crime Does Not Pay*. In *Buried Loot* (1935), Taylor was the embezzling bank employee. This was followed by an interne's role in *Society Doctor* (1935), which resulted in Taylor's fan mail increasing and induced the studio to raise his salary to $50 weekly. It was now inevitable that his employers should promote him as a new romantic lead.

He played the glib theatrical producer who sings and dances in *The Broadway Melody of 1936* (1935), and then played the part that made him a big-time star: the playboy in *Magnificent Obsession* (1935). This film role was on loan to Universal, and star Irene Dunne recalls, "I remember sitting with John Stahl looking at some film of Robert Taylor before *Magnificent Obsession* started shooting. Anyone who knew Stahl knows he made all decisions. But I like to recall that I did tell him I thought Bob entirely right for the part. And it was pleasant working with Bob Taylor. He always assumed his full share of responsibility."

Taylor's four 1936 releases cast him opposite four of Hollywood's brightest stars, established him as Number Four at the boxoffice, and gave substantiation to the studio's publicity campaign which hailed him as "the nation's most admired matinee idol since the late Rudolph Valentino." The pictures themselves were not substantial, but they were popular: *Small Town Girl* with Janet Gaynor; *Private Number* with Loretta Young; *His Brother's Wife* with Barbara Stanwyck; and that incredible bit of specious history, *The Gorgeous Hussy* with Joan Crawford. Despite the furor of his sudden stardom, Loretta Young remembers the Taylor of that time as being "a surprisingly normal person, neither fussed nor conceited."

No one knows how Greta Garbo reacted to Taylor being cast opposite her in *Camille* (1937), but he reached the apogee of his glamor period playing the lovesick Armand and moved up to Number Three at the boxoffice, which made him a more commercial if less prestigious asset to MGM than the

With Jean Hersholt in *His Brother's Wife* (1936)

With Robert Wildhack, Judy Garland, Sophie Tucker, and Eleanor Powell in *Broadway Melody of 1938* (1937)

With Vivien Leigh in *Waterloo Bridge* (1940)

With Eddie Dunn, Frank Conlan, Gene Lockhart, Dick Curtis, and Ted Adams in *Billy the Kid* (1941)

Swedish star. Mayer became uneasy about promoting Taylor singularly as a ladies' man and decided upon a he-man tactic. The actor himself was perturbed at the pretty-boy epithets tossed his way, such as the question of whether his eye lashes were longer than Garbo's in *Camille*, so he soon grew a moustache to give pronounced masculinity to his countenance.

After a frivolous comedy called *Personal Property* (1937), in which he seemed at a loss in coping with unbridled costar Jean Harlow, and a loanout to Twentieth Century-Fox for *This Is My Affair* (1937) to exploit the public's awareness of Taylor's personal interest in Barbara Stanwyck, Mayer cast him as the football hero in *A Yank at Oxford* opposite Vivien Leigh. Taylor then played an idealistic veteran in *Three Comrades* (1938) with Margaret Sullavan, and to further toughen his image, the studio cast him as the boxer in *The Crowd Roars*. He returned to being the "face" in *Lucky Night* (1939) and *Lady of the Tropics* (1939) with Hedy Lamarr. Then he was cast in his favorite film, *Waterloo Bridge* (1940), with Vivien Leigh. Taylor considers it his favorite "because it came at a time when I didn't think I was a good actor. When I saw the picture, I was surprised—along with everybody else." He was not right as *Billy the Kid*, but MGM's competitors were also promoting such simplistic folklore to good advantage with he-man images for Errol Flynn (*The Sea Hawk*) and Tyrone Power (*Jesse James*). Taylor likewise was wrong as the gangland boss in *Johnny Eager* (1942).

He had the dubious distinction of being Norma Shearer's *vis-à-vis* in her cinema swan song, *Her Cardboard Lover* (1942). They had played much better together in the earlier anti-Nazi romancer *Escape* (1940). He then appeared in a trio of wartime propaganda films, the most embarrassing being *Song of Russia* (1944) which would be raked over the coals in the 1950s McCarthy Communist threat hearings. At the finish of these films, Taylor enlisted in the Navy, where he became a flying instructor, and during his military stint he directed seventeen training films and narrated *The Fighting Lady*, the Oscar-winning documentary about life on U. S. warships.

MGM reserved its returning-hero campaign for Clark Gable, and Taylor was slipped quietly into several serviceable dramas, the most interesting of which, from the point of his maturing acting ability, was as the American Indian in *Devil's Doorway* (1950) who returns from the Civil War to find he must fight again to regain what is rightfully his. *Quo Vadis* (1951), the first of the postwar epics, gave Taylor a new burst of screen popularity and utility. As the commander of the Roman legion who finds new values in life through meeting and loving Deborah Kerr, he gave the rambling spectacle some semblance of unity. MGM wisely cast him in *Ivanhoe* (1952), a much better spectacle than *Quo Vadis*, and then as the pilot who led America's atomic bomb expedition over Japan in *Above and Beyond* (1952). Two lesser spectacles followed: *Knights of the Round Table* (1953), the studio's first Cinemascope production, and *Quentin Durward* (1955).

Taylor's last films at MGM were programmers, mostly Westerns in which his advancing age could be played down tactfully. He accepted these assignments unflinchingly: "My metabolism doesn't lend itself to the Davis–Cagney brand of high-pressure careering. I stayed with one studio for 20 years, took what they gave me to do, did my work. While I wasn't happy with everything, I scored pretty well.'" In 1959 he made a minor thriller called *The House of Seven Hawks*, and ended his association with equally declining MGM. His neighbor in the San Fernando Valley, Dick Powell, talked him into entering television, and he performed in his own series, *The Detectives*, for three seasons, later playing host–narrator–actor for another video series, *Death Valley Days*. Most of the films he made in the 1960s were unimportant, several being low budgeters made in Europe and shunted off to television, and one would-be horror yarn, *The Night Walker* (1965), costarred him with his ex-wife, Barbara Stanwyck. (They had wed in 1939 and divorced in 1952, when she listened to rumors that he had played around while on Italian location for *Quo Vadis* and thereafter.)

Taylor died of cancer on June 8, 1969, leaving his widow, German actress Ursula Thiess, and two children. Taylor was always modest and self-effacing when discussing his career: "I was a punk kid from Nebraska who's had an awful lot of the world's good things dumped in his lap."

ROBERT TAYLOR

Handy Andy (Fox, 1934)
There's Always Tomorrow (Universal, 1934)
A Wicked Woman (MGM, 1934)
Society Doctor (MGM, 1935)
West Point of the Air (MGM, 1935)
Times Square Lady (MGM, 1935)
Murder in the Fleet (MGM, 1935)
Broadway Melody of 1936 (MGM, 1935)
Magnificent Obsession (Universal, 1935)
Small Town Girl (MGM, 1936)
Private Number (20th-Fox, 1936)
His Brother's Wife (MGM, 1936)
The Gorgeous Hussy (MGM, 1936)
Camille (MGM, 1937)
Personal Property (MGM, 1937)
This is My Affair (20th-Fox, 1937)
Broadway Melody of 1938 (MGM, 1937)
A Yank at Oxford (MGM, 1938)
Three Comrades (MGM, 1938)
The Crowd Roars (MGM, 1938)
Stand Up and Fight (MGM, 1939)
Lucky Night (MGM, 1939)
Lady of the Tropics (MGM, 1939)
Remember? (MGM, 1939)
Waterloo Bridge (MGM, 1940)
Escape (MGM, 1940)
Flight Command (MGM, 1940)
Billy the Kid (MGM, 1941)

When Ladies Meet (MGM, 1941)
Johnny Eager (MGM, 1942)
Her Cardboard Lover (MGM, 1942)
Stand by for Action (MGM, 1943)
The Youngest Profession (MGM, 1943)
Bataan (MGM, 1943)
Song of Russia (MGM, 1943)
Undercurrent (MGM, 1946)
The High Wall (MGM, 1947)
The Secret Land (Narrator: MGM, 1948)
The Bribe (MGM, 1949)
Ambush (MGM, 1949)
Devil's Doorway (MGM, 1950)
Conspirator (MGM, 1950)
Quo Vadis (MGM, 1951)
Westward the Women (MGM, 1951)
Ivanhoe (MGM, 1952)
Above and Beyond (MGM, 1952)
I Love Melvin (MGM, 1953)
Ride, Vaquero! (MGM, 1953)
All the Brothers Were Valiant (MGM, 1953)
Knights of the Round Table (MGM, 1953)
Valley of the Kings (MGM, 1954)
Rogue Cop (MGM, 1954)
Many Rivers to Cross (MGM, 1955)
Quentin Durward (MGM, 1955)
The Last Hunt (MGM, 1956)
D-Day, The Sixth of June (20th-Fox, 1956)

With Audrey Totter in *The High Wall* (1947)

712

With James Mitchell in *Devil's Doorway* (1950)

With Kay Kendall in *Quentin Durward* (1955)

Phyllis Thaxter

While definitely not in the same league with star Margaret Sullavan, Phyllis Thaxter did have the same capacity to effectively portray dewy-eyed and tearful women in tearjerkers. For a while in the mid-1940s, she rivaled another MGM player, June Allyson, as the all-American crying lovely, but the latter proved more versatile, ambitious, and enduring. Today Phyllis is best remembered for having successfully overcome a bout with polio when thirty-one and for eighteen years having been the wife of James T. Aubrey. Aubrey is MGM's executive vice president and apparently was Jacqueline Susann's model for Robin Stone in her best-selling novel, *The Love Machine*.

Phyllis was born November 20, 1921 in Portland, Maine, one of the four children born to Maine Supreme Court Justice Sidney Thaxter and his wife, a former actress with Ben Greet's Shakespeare Company in New York. Phyllis was educated both at St. Genevieve School in Montreal and at Portland's Deering High School. She left home at the age of seventeen to play in stock at the Ogunquit Playhouse in Maine where Laurette Taylor was one of the guest stars, and then worked in repertory in Montreal. She moved to New York and earned a walk-on in *What a Life!* (1939), the Henry Aldrich play. In the Alfred Lunt–Lynn Fontanne drama, *There Shall Be No Night* (1940), she played the maid and understudied the ingenue. Next she won the understudy role to Dorothy McGuire in *Claudia* (1940), later playing the part on Broadway and on the road in Chicago and San Francisco. When David O. Selznick was screen testing for his pending film version of this comedy, he auditioned Phyllis, but eventually selected McGuire for the title role, while giving another would-be movie Claudia, Jennifer Jones, a term contract. At about the time Phyllis tested for Selznick, she also tested for MGM, but nothing was forthcoming for her efforts.

While *Claudia* was playing in San Francisco, MGM, who had momentarily thought of casting her in *Kismet* (1944) in a subsidiary role, suddenly paged Phyllis for a part in *Thirty Seconds over Tokyo* (1944), the story of Lt. Colonel James Doolittle's (Spencer Tracy) U. S. bombing raid over Japan. Producer Sam Zimbalist was hard-pressed to find a spunky, but clean-cut girl to play Ellen Lawson, Van Johnson's wife in the film. He had seen Phyllis' previous screen test and decided on her. As Johnson's courageous

714

spouse, she attracted audience and critical attention and was given a contract. She was then cast as the lead in Arch Oboler's *Bewitched* (1945), a melodrama of a girl with a double personality. James Agee in *The Nation* thought her performance in that film was full of "sensitiveness and charm." In the lush *Weekend at the Waldorf* (1945) she was the nervous, tearful bride-to-be.

In 1944 Phyllis had married Aubrey, then a TV time salesman in Los Angeles, and the following year she gave birth to a daughter, Schuyler. She was back on the screen in *The Sea of Grass* (1947) as the patient but teary daughter of Spencer Tracy and Katharine Hepburn. By the film's finale, she successfully reunites her parents after the death of her half-brother (Robert Walker). She was a wholesome type in *Living in a Big Way* (1947), but this Gene Kelly picture had former model Marie "The Body" McDonald in the main eye-catching lead role. Phyllis was loaned to Columbia for crippled Susan Peters' comeback picture *The Sign of the Ram* (1948), and emoted as the tearful mother of Margaret O'Brien in the hastily distributed *Tenth Avenue Angel* (1948). In RKO's range war Western, *Blood on the Moon* (1948) she had the second female lead to Barbara Bel Geddes by playing Tom Tully's daughter who loves Robert Preston. Her fourth film of the year, and her last under her MGM contract, was in Fred Zinnemann's *Act of Violence* (1948) which found her as the faithful moll of disturbed killer Robert Ryan.

Phyllis had said near the start of her MGM years: "What is mine will come to me; I believe in Fate." Nevertheless, the pickings had been slim for her at Metro. She was not seen in pictures again until 1950, when she supported Barbara Stanwyck and John Lund in *No Man of Her Own*, a turgid Cornell Woolrich tale. Then she signed a contract with Warner Brothers. Her asking price was not prohibitive and, like the physically similar but more neglected Phyllis Avery, she was known to be competent in a quiet way. Phyllis was John Garfield's worn but stimulating wife in *The Breaking Point* (1950), the heroine of Randolph Scott's *Fort Worth* (1951), the patient wife of Indian athlete Burt Lancaster in *Jim Thorpe—All American* (1951), the tolerant spouse of alcoholic Gig Young in *Come Fill the Cup* (1951), the understanding wife of professor Ronald Reagan in *She's Working Her Way Through College* (1952), and Gary Cooper's better half in *Springfield Rifle* (1952). In what proved to be her final Warners' picture, she was one of the stalwart French partisans in the World War II actioner, *Operation Secret* (1952).

While visiting her family in Portland in 1952, Phyllis contracted a form of infantile paralysis. Luckily, her recovery was rapid and in January 1953, she gave birth to a son, James W. Aubrey. But the ailment and the pregnancy caused a termination of her studio contract, and it was not until *Women's Prison* (1955) that she was onscreen again, this time as a high-strung matron. Two years later she was the terrified wife of clergyman George Nader in *Man Afraid*, he being hunted by the father of a boy he had killed in self-defense.

By the late 1950s Aubrey had become a CBS-TV executive and, when he moved to New York, Phyllis and the children went with him. Geographically her movie career was finished, and she was now past the ingenue years. She did an occasional guesting role on television, such as *Alfred Hitchcock Presents, The Twilight Zone, Wagon Train,* but nothing else. In 1961 she returned to Broadway as Art Carney's wife in the hit comedy *Take Her, She's Mine.* The next year she did *Time Out for Ginger* in summer stock opposite Carney.

In 1962 she and Aubrey divorced, and she wed Gilbert Lea, owner and president of Tower Publishing Company (he had three children by a previous marriage). Phyllis' last film to date was in the New York-lensed Peter Sellers comedy *The World of Henry Orient* (1964). She played a rather sophisticated New York matron, the mother of Merrie Spaeth who offers much-needed understanding to Tom Bosley, the father of her daughter's best friend.

She and Lea now live in Cumberland Foreside, Maine, where she is a very civic-minded resident. Occasionally she travels to Hollywood for television guesting, such as in recent episodes of *Medical Center, The F.B.I.,* and a telefeature with Richard Kiley, *Incident in San Francisco* (1971). Her daughter Schuyler has been under contract to Universal and had a feature role in James Coburn's *The Carey Treatment* (1972), released by MGM.

PHYLLIS THAXTER

Thirty Seconds over Tokyo (MGM, 1944)
Bewitched (MGM, 1945)
Weekend at the Waldorf (MGM, 1945)
The Sea of Grass (MGM, 1947)
Living in a Big Way (MGM, 1947)
The Sign of the Ram (Columbia, 1948)
Tenth Avenue Angel (MGM, 1948)
Blood on the Moon (RKO, 1948)
Act of Violence (MGM, 1948)
No Man of Her Own (Paramount, 1950)
The Breaking Point (WB, 1950)
Fort Worth (WB, 1951)
Jim Thorpe—All American (WB, 1951)
Come Fill the Cup (WB, 1951)
She's Working Her Way Through College (WB, 1952)
Springfield Rifle (WB, 1952)
Operation Secret (WB, 1952)
Women's Prison (Columbia, 1955)
Man Afraid (Universal, 1957)
The World of Henry Orient (UA, 1964)

With Margaret O'Brien in *Tenth Avenue Angel* (1948)

Marshall Thompson

Like Robert Stack, lanky Marshall Thompson never gained any degree of mass popularity until he starred in a television series in his middle age, by which time he had developed a sufficiently interesting screen personality. Throughout the 1940s, Thompson was generally cast by MGM as the amiable, well-meaning lad whose most distinguishing characteristic was his 6' 1" height. His bland boyish appeal was put to less effective use than Universal's Robert Paige (who could also sing) or Warner's Robert Hutton, but then MGM had Van Johnson, Robert Walker, and, to a lesser extent, Tom Drake, to handle the bulk of its wholesome-category film assignments.

James Marshall Thompson was born on November 27, 1925 in Peoria, Illinois, and was named after his ancestor, the famed U. S. Supreme Court justice. His mother was a concert singer and musician, while his father was a dentist. Because of Dr. Thompson's poor health, the family moved to Westwood, California, where the young Thompson grew up. During summer vacations, he found himself punching cows on a ranch, and, at the age of fourteen, participating in rodeos. At one point, he became so interested in religion, he thought of becoming a clergyman. He wrote a play, *Faith*, which was produced by the local Westwood Players. While in high school, he played in an amateur production of *Our Town*, as editor Webb, which led to a screen test. Nothing came of it until he had already begun a course of study at Occidental College, whereupon Universal offered him $350 weekly to play in Gloria Jean's *Reckless Age* (1944). Thompson decided to make film acting a full-time career and dropped out of college.

He was cast as one of the U. S. Air Force crew shot down in a Tokyo raid in Twentieth Century-Fox's *The Purple Heart* (1944). It was actor–director Richard Whorf who saw Thompson's performance in *Reckless Age* and had him brought to MGM to play the nice guy engaged to manhunting waitress Gloria Grahame in *Blonde Fever* (1944). For two years he functioned in perfunctory assignments that demanded no effort and brought him no particular notice: an ensign in *They Were Expendable* (1945); as part of the insipid romantic relief (opposite Frances Rafferty) in Wallace Beery's *Bad Bascomb* (1946); and Marilyn Maxwell's brother in *The Show-Off* (1946).

Then, because of his known compatability with animals, Thompson

717

was assigned the lead in the Cinecolor-lensed *Gallant Bess* (1946), in which he was an orphan of seventeen whose pet horse dies while he is in boot camp. While in the South Pacific as a Seebee, he finds another horse who is a dead ringer for the lost animal. *Gallant Bess* was no *National Velvet* or *My Friend Flicka* and it did not launch his career into star status, so it was back to serviceman roles for Thompson: a sergeant in *Homecoming* (1948), a captain in *Command Decision* (1949).

With the changeover in the Metro regime in the late 1940s, there were shotgun attempts to breathe some fire into the careers of several stock contract players. Thomspon was knocked out of his stereotype by being handed the lead of the modest *Dial 1119* (1950). He played the youth who escapes from a mental institution and is bent on killing the police psychiatrist (Sam Levene) who had had him committed. The offbeat casting worked to a degree, and Thompson was quite effective as the baby-faced, cold, and dispassionate killer. This role led to several similar assignments. He was the Georgia-born West Pointer who plans to shoot Abraham Lincoln in *The Tall Target* (1951), his last MGM film under his contract, and then as the young athlete led down the primrose path in Realart's *The Basketball Fix* (1951). In *My Six Convicts* (1952) he was an alcoholic ball player taking a rap for a girl.

By this time, Thompson had married actress Barbara Long (in 1948) and they had a daughter, Janet, born in 1951. He took a flyer on Broadway, costarring with Janet Blair in *A Girl Can Tell* (1953), but the show closed within three weeks. It was back again to second male leads: a lieutenant in *Battle Taxi* (1955), one of the G.I.s in Audie Murphy's *To Hell and Back* (1955), the human combatant to *The Fiend without a Face* (1957), and also to *It! The Terror from Beyond Space* (1958). He took to the air in *First Man into Space* (1959) at MGM, and also in *Flight of the Lost Balloon* (1961).

There was nothing particularly remarkable about Thompson's "Sonn" Sonnenberg, in *A Yank In Viet-Nam* (1964), but the movie was one of the few pro–Vietnam War films made by Americans during the decade. Thompson not only starred in the on-location project, but also directed and coproduced the venture.

Throughout the 1950s, Marshall had been a frequent if inconspicuous television performer in such costarring roles as with Joanne Dru in *The Blackwell Story* (1957) on *Playhouse 90*. In 1960 he played the young man with a French bride (Annie Farge) in the video series *Angel*. This series almost made the grade, unlike the previous year's *World of Giants* series. That one lasted a brief thirteen episodes, and had the gimmick of Thompson as a government espionage agent only six inches tall.

In the early 1960s Thompson had joined the staff of Ivan Tors productions, directing several shorts on animal life. When Tors produced the animal comedy *Clarence, the Cross-Eyed Lion* (1964) for MGM release, Thompson was cast as Dr. Marsh Tracy of the animal study center in Africa. Nevertheless, the real stars were Clarence and Judy the Chimp. The feature did well in the family market, and two years later the story premise reemerged as a

CBS color series, *Daktari*, which lasted through eighty-nine episodes, finally going off the air in 1969. Cheryl Miller played Thompson's daughter. The following year, Thompson was host–narrator of *Jambo*, a live-action series also produced by Tors. It dealt mostly with stories of animal and sea life and was quite unsuccessful. During this period Thompson directed several episodes of the *Daktari* series as well as Tors' *Flipper*. He went to Switzerland in mid-1972 to star with Jack Mullaney in *All About George*, a German-financed syndicated comedy teleseries.

His last feature to date was *Around the World Under the Sea* (1966), a Tors production thrown together for Metro release, and geared to take advantage of the home-screen popularity of four television favorites: Thompson (*Daktari*), David McCallum (*The Man from U.N.C.L.E.*), Brian Kelly (*Flipper*), and Lloyd Bridges (*Sea Hunt*). Shirley "Goldfinger" Eaton was aboard the film's submarine for decoration.

Thompson and his family live in Pacific Palisades, California. Like his unassuming, unpretentious onscreen image, he has been wont to tell the press: "I'm not a person who revels in self-glorification."

MARSHALL THOMPSON

Reckless Age (Universal, 1944)
The Purple Heart (20th-Fox, 1944)
Blonde Fever (MGM, 1944)
Valley of Decision (MGM, 1945)
The Clock (MGM, 1945)
Twice Blessed (MGM, 1945)
They Were Expendable (MGM, 1945)
Bad Bascomb (MGM, 1946)
The Show-Off (MGM, 1946)
The Cockeyed Miracle (MGM, 1946)
Gallant Bess (MGM, 1946)
The Secret Heart (MGM, 1946)
The Romance of Rosy Ridge (MGM, 1947)
Homecoming (MGM, 1948)
B.F.'s Daughter (MGM, 1948)
Words and Music (MGM, 1948)
Command Decision (MGM, 1948)
Roseanna McCoy (RKO, 1949)
Battleground (MGM, 1949)
Devil's Doorway (MGM, 1950)
Mystery Street (MGM, 1950)
Dial 1119 (MGM, 1950)

The Tall Target (MGM, 1951)
The Basketball Fix (Realart, 1951)
My Six Convicts (Columbia, 1952)
The Rose Bowl Story (Monogram, 1952)
The Caddy (Paramount, 1953)
Port of Hell (AA, 1954)
Battle Taxi (UA, 1955)
Cult of the Cobra (Universal, 1955)
Crashout (Filmmakers, 1955)
To Hell and Back (Universal, 1955)
Good Morning Miss Dove (20th-Fox, 1955)
La Grande Caccia (Italian, 1956)
Lure of the Swamp (20th-Fox, 1957)
Fiend without a Face (MGM, 1957)
It! The Terror from Beyond Space (UA, 1958)
The Secret Man (Producers Associated, 1958)
First Man into Space (MGM, 1959)
Flight of the Lost Balloon (Woolner, 1961)
No Man Is an Island (Universal, 1962)
A Yank in Viet-Nam (AA, 1964)
Clarence, the Cross-Eyed Lion (MGM, 1964)
Around the World Under the Sea (MGM, 1966)

With Paula Raymond, Ruby Dee, Dick Powell, Adolphe Menjou, Florence Bates, and Percy Helton in *The Tall Target* (1951)

Lawrence Tibbett

With the advent of talking pictures, Hollywood again embarked on commercializing the novelty of presenting distinguished opera stars in sound pictures. Baritone John Charles Thomas made a few Vitaphone shorts in 1927, and John McCormack, "the world's greatest tenor," made *Song O' My Heart* (1930) for Fox. But in the craze to capitalize on high-class musical screen entertainment, it remained for MGM to corral two of the Metropolitan Opera's brightest young stars. The studio failed dismally from the start with Grace Moore, but with Lawrence Tibbett, billed as the "first American baritone in talking pictures," it achieved initial success in a big way. The studio discovered that this outstanding singer with agile eyebrows was considered surprisingly romantic and dashing by the filmgoing public who flocked to *Rogue Song* (1930). Unfortunately, none of Tibbett's three succeeding Metro productions matched the verve of Paramount's Maurice Chevalier–Jeanette MacDonald operettas, and the singing star floundered in badly conceived roles that yearned to humanize his oversized stage presence.

Tibbett was born in Bakersfield, California on November 16, 1896. His father was a local deputy sheriff, who was killed while capturing a bandit when Tibbett was seven. By the time he graduated from Manual Arts High School in Los Angeles, Tibbett was convinced he wanted an opera career. He had already appeared in school productions and sung with glee clubs. After serving in the Navy in World War I, he returned to Los Angeles and earned a living singing in churches and movie theatres (including vocalizing a prologue to a Charlie Ray picture at Grauman's Chinese Theatre), while taking voice lessons from Joseph Dupuy and Basil Ruysdael. He then came to New York to study with Frank La Forge. Tibbett was rejected on his first Metropolitan Opera audition, but on a second try was signed to a year's contract and thereafter was kept on provisionally because he waived a pay raise. (Tibbett's surname originally had only one final "t," but the opera's printer misspelled his name on a Metropolitan program and the new lettering stuck.) By this time, he had wed Grace Mackay Smith (in 1919), and they had twin sons, Lawrence and Richard. The couple were divorced in 1931 and he then married Jane Maston Bugard, the daughter of a New York banker. They had one son, Michael.

721

Tibbett's operatic debut at the Metropolitan came in November 1923, when he played a monk in *Boris Godunov*. Small roles followed, but in 1925 he achieved overnight success. At the last minute, he was called in to take over the role of Ford in Verdi's *Falstaff*, and was so impressive in the part that he received an unheard-of fifteen-minute ovation. Thereafter, because of the unusual size and flexibility of his voice, Tibbett was called upon to inaugurate several important operas into the Metropolitan's repertory, including *L'Heure Espagnole*, *The King's Henchman*, *Peter Ibbetson*, *Simon Boccanegra*, *The Emperor Jones*, and *Merry Mount*.

MGM hired Tibbett in 1929 at a hefty salary and immediately cast him in the Technicolor *Rogue Song*, an adaptation of Franz Lehar's operetta *Gypsy Love*, directed by Lionel Barrymore. Tibbett played a singing Russian bandit in pre-Soviet days who falls in love with princess Catherine Dale Owen. He sang the Herbert Stothart–Clifford Grey–Franz Lehar score with a "vigorous, vibrant, and distinctive personality" (N.Y. *Herald Tribune*). The picture premiered at New York's Astor Theatre and played a six-month engagement there. For his performance, Tibbett was Oscar-nominated.

Since Grace Moore had flopped in the Jenny Lind story, *A Lady's Morals* (1930), it was decided to team her with Tibbett in *New Moon* (1930). In this version of the Sigmund Romberg operetta, which differs radically in locale and plot from the later Jeanette MacDonald–Nelson Eddy edition, Tibbett was a Russian lieutenant entranced with princess Moore. The film concluded at the Ft. Davaz outpost with a supposedly killed Tibbett riding back to his love, serenading her with "Lover Come Back to Me." The picture had mediocre boxoffice results.

MGM concluded that Tibbett had to be restructured into a new screen image, that of a more conventional, down-to-earth romantic lead. Thus in *The Prodigal* (1931) (a. k. a. *The Southerner*), he is the ne'er-do-well son of a Dixie family who tramps about with Roland Young and Cliff Edwards. He sings Oscar Strauss' "Life Is a Dream," Vincent Youmans' "Without a Song," and snatches of "Home Sweet Home." The public did not buy it.

The Prodigal at least had some dignity, but *Cuban Love Song* (1931) was a flagrant example of studio desperation, churned out in a hurry by W. S. Van Dyke. The plotline had Tibbett joining the Marines, along with Ernest Torrence and Jimmy Durante and, while based in Havana, he is beguiled by the tempestuous peanut vendor Lupe Velez. He eventually returns to the States and to his true love, Karen Morley, but not before he has sung "The Peanut Vendor," "The Cuban Love Song," and "Tramps at Sea."

Both Tibbett and MGM called it quits, and he returned to the Metropolitan Opera where the music critics noted his cinema sojourn had greatly improved his stage presence. After Grace Moore made a terrific film comeback in Columbia's *One Night of Love* (1934) and created a dramatic new stir for operatic subjects, Tibbett was imported back to Hollywood to star in Fox's costly *Metropolitan* (1935). It was a conventional backstage tale, but this time set at the famed opera house, with Tibbett adoring singing ingenue

Virginia Bruce, but having to be more than congenial to man-chasing prima donna Alice Brady. In his rise from spear carrier to soloist, he performs the Prologue to *Pagliacci*, the song "De Glory Road," the love duet from *Faust* (with Bruce), and an aria from *The Barber of Seville*. In a noteworthy departure from his past films, he was allowed to render complete arias rather than the typical snatches. The picture died at the boxoffice. Studio head Darryl F. Zanuck wanted to settle Tibbett's $200,000 contract, but the opera star refused. So he was forced into a B picture *Under Your Spell* (1936), directed by Otto Preminger and costarring Wendy Barrie as a socialite determined to have Tibbett sing at one of her swank parties. The picture came and went, as did its male star.

Tibbett had first performed on radio in 1922 and later helped to found the American Federation of Radio Artists. There was a great stir in 1945 by both camps of music when Tibbett was hired as a replacement for Frank Sinatra on radio's *Your Hit Parade*, but he proved a great success in his seven-month stint.

His last appearance at the Metropolitan was on March 24, 1950, as Prince Ivan in Mussorgky's *Khovantchina*. Like Lauritz Melchior, he came into conflict with the Opera House's new director, Rudolf Bing, by refusing to give up his non-Metropolitan professional activities. Later that year, Tibbett appeared in the Broadway musical play, *The Barrier*, which closed after four performances. In 1956 he replaced the ailing Ezio Pinza in the musical *Fanny*.

Tibbett was the first opera singer to receive the gold medal of the American Academy of Arts and Letters for excellence in stage diction, and in 1937 received the Letteris et Artibus medal from the King of Sweden.

He died July 15, 1960, following brain surgery, mourned by his many fans. Although his films are rarely shown today, reissue of his old recordings still sell well.

LAWRENCE TIBBETT

Rogue Song (MGM, 1930)
New Moon (MGM, 1930)
The Prodigal (MGM, 1931)
Cuban Love Song (MGM, 1931)
Metropolitan (Fox, 1935)
Under Your Spell (20th-Fox, 1936)

With Kate Price and Catherine Dale Owen in
Rogue Song (1930)

Franchot Tone

The very kind of man that Franchot Tone was in real life—the handsome, wealthy, intelligent, aristocratic partygoer—typed him in motion pictures and prevented him from becoming the serious, versatile actor to which he aspired. As film historian David Shipman comments: "In the '30's, nine out of every ten heroes had stepped out of the Social Register." This observation aptly applied to Tone, and during the first part of his cinema career, under contract to MGM, he was promoted chiefly as the epitome of the successful, cultivated, tuxedoed gentleman. Occasionally a meaningful assignment came along, such as *The Lives of a Bengal Lancer* (1935), his favorite part, and *Mutiny on the Bounty* (1935), but they were the exceptions. Tone had come to films from the Broadway stage, and throughout his forty-two-year acting career, he frequently returned to the stage, and later television, to act in quality roles. Some of them were the touchstones for very fine performances. Nonetheless, he is chiefly remembered for those five years at MGM during the 1930s where he brought suavity and elan to some of that studio's classiest productions.

Stanislas Pascal Franchot Tone was born in Niagara Falls, New York on February 27, 1905, the son of the president of the Carborundum Company. He was educated in private schools, graduated from Cornell University (where he was president of the drama club) with a Phi Beta Kappa key in 1927, and spent a summer at the University of Rennes in Paris. Returning to the States, he joined the McGarry Players, a theatre stock company in Buffalo. In 1928 he became associated with the New Playwrights Company in Greenwich Village, making an inauspicious debut in *The Belt*. Then he was cast by Guthrie McClintic as Katharine Cornell's son in *The Age of Innocence* (1929). The next year he became a member of the Theatre Guild, where he appeared in *Red Dust* (1929), *Meteor* (1929), *Hotel Universe* (1930), and as Curly in *Green Grow the Lilacs* (1931), the predecessor to *Oklahoma*! Later he was one of the founding members of the Group Theatre where he performed in *The House of Connelly* (1931), *Night over Taos* (1932), and *A Thousand Summers* (1932) with Jane Cowl. Tone always said that it was the Group Theatre and Lee Strasberg who taught him about real acting.

In 1932, while appearing in the theatre in the evenings, he accepted a role in *The Wiser Sex*, starring Claudette Colbert, filmed at Paramount's Astoria, Long Island studio. Several months later, while playing in the Group Theatre's production of *Success Story*, he was offered a five-year MGM contract, and he accepted. At the time he had a reputable standing in the New York theatre circles as Stark Young attested: "Mr. Tone is one of the best of the young actors in the New York theatre and the most promising in his chances of development. He does not have to go to Hollywood to get a good role; many roles in the theatre are open to him. And for the same reason he doesn't have to stay in Hollywood when he gets there."

He made seven pictures for MGM in 1933. None of them were meaty roles, and they immediately typed him as a slick, well-groomed stuffed shirt. He was Walter Huston's secretary in *Gabriel over the White House* and Joan Crawford's brother in *Today We Live*. He was the carefree playboy who lost Crawford to Clark Gable in *Dancing Lady*, allowed Lee Tracy to win Jean Harlow in *Bombshell*, and did three leads opposite Maureen O'Sullivan in *Stage Mother*, Miriam Hopkins in *The Stranger Returns*, and Loretta Young in *Midnight Mary*. By the last picture, Tone balked and asked Irving Thalberg to abrogate his studio contract. Thalberg and Louis B. Mayer were not seeing eye to eye on many things, and Thalberg wrote to Nicholas Schenck in New York, listing some of his grievances with the MGM executive policies. For one thing, he requested that he be given the right to control Tone's screen career for a while. The Schenck–Mayer–Thalberg line of communication was such that Tone's interests were lost in the shuffle, and he continued to take what they dished out to him.

He was Joan Crawford's lead in *Sadie McKee* (1934), and then was put in his two best pictures more by accident than design. He was loaned to Paramount for *The Lives of a Bengal Lancer*, a popular man's movie in which he and Gary Cooper played the two brother British officers. When Robert Montgomery refused to appear in Metro's *Mutiny on the Bounty*, the studio gave Tone the role of the British gentleman who goes to sea, and he earned an Oscar nomination for his performance as Byam. Nevertheless, it was back to stuffed shirt roles, two of the best of which were the architect in Bette Davis' *Dangerous* (1935) at Warner Brothers, and the World War I soldier turned gangster in *They Gave Him a Gun* (1937).

In October 1935 Tone married MGM's most ambitious young actress, Joan Crawford. After divorcing Douglas Fairbanks, and thinking better of pursuing a romance with a married Clark Gable, she had found herself attracted to this intelligent, handsome New York "actor." Their individual careers prevented the marriage from working, particularly when Crawford's cinema standing outshone Tone's and made him the brunt of endless "Mr. Joan Crawford" tags. They were divorced in 1939, but remained close friends for the remainder of Tone's life.

For the duration of his contract, Tone continued to be MGM's gentleman in residence. After appearing on loan to RKO for the period comedy *Quality Street* (1937) with Katharine Hepburn, and playing opposite

Margaret Sullavan and Robert Young in the sensitive *Three Comrades* (1938), he terminated his studio association by starring with Ann Sothern in *Fast and Furious* (1939).

He returned to the New York stage, possibly a bit wiser from his Hollywood years, but nonetheless shaken, and friends recall he was drinking heavily at the time, although it did not seem to impair his stage work. He went into the Group Theatre's *The Gentle People* (1939) with Sylvia Sidney, but it flopped. One of his best theatre roles was the American newspaperman in Hemingway's *The Fifth Column* (1940) for which he received excellent notices. In 1941 he married blonde starlet Jean Wallace (*nee* Wallasek) and they had two sons: Pascal Franchot and Thomas Jefferson Tone. Their marriage was a troublesome one, ending in 1948 in divorce and a bitter court fight over custody of the boys. Tone claimed Wallace was friends with gigolo Johnny Stompanato (later to gain notoriety as one of Lana Turner's boyfriends) and he was given custody of the boys. She later regained custody, but they went to court again in 1958, she appearing with her new husband, Cornel Wilde, and fighting Tone over what school Pascal should attend. Tone won this round, and the boy went to the Hill School, which Tone had attended as a child.

Throughout the 1940s, Tone had a spotty film career, playing second fiddle to Deanna Durbin in *Nice Girl?* (1941), *His Butler's Sister* (1943), and *Because of Him* (1946). He was a bland nice guy to Veronica Lake's spy in *The Hour before the Dawn* (1944), and then was reduced to second male leads in *Every Girl Should Be Married* (1948) and *Here Comes the Groom* (1951). He did have the lead as the ambitious assistant District Attorney in the minor *Jigsaw* (1949), in which his ex-wife Jean Wallace had a role, and then was among those involved in Burgess Meredith's Paris-lensed misfire, *The Man on the Eiffel Tower* (1949).

In 1951 he appeared in some very unpleasant headlines over a romance with starlet Barbara Payton, when he was beaten senseless on September 14th by ex-boxer Tom Neal, who claimed Payton was engaged to both of them. Extensive plastic surgery was required on Tone's face, but undaunted, he married her. They were divorced the following year.

The theatre now took precedence in his career, with television a close second. Onstage he appeared in Edward Chodorov's *Oh Men, Oh Women* (1953), played in a revival of William Saroyan's *The Time of Your Life* (1955), was Astroff in an off-Broadway production of *Uncle Vanya* (1956), and starred in the television version of *The Little Foxes* (1956) opposite an unconvincing Greer Garson as Regina. He gave the best performance of his career as the lost alcoholic in Eugene O'Neill's *A Moon for the Misbegotten* (1957); and the next year there was Pirandello's *The Rules of the Game* and a television version of *Twelve Angry Men*. In 1959 he was divorced from his fourth wife, actress Dolores Dorn-Heft. He had met her in the cast of *Uncle Vanya* and they had been secretly married in 1956, but it was not made public until two years later.

Tone returned to films in excellent form in *Advise and Consent* (1962), playing the sickly president of the United States who dies in office. He appeared in a revival of O'Neill's *Strange Interlude* on Broadway in 1963, and made his last motion picture appearances as the nightclub owner in the arty *Mickey One* (1965) and the ambassador in *The High Commissioner* (1968). The next year he was too ill to star with Jennifer Jones in a City Center revival of *The Country Girl*, and when he arrived to see the opening night performance, he stepped feebly out of his limousine, walking very slowly with a cane. He sported a gray beard that did not hide his aging face, exchanged hellos with columnist Sheilah Graham, collected his single ticket from the boxoffice window, and walked slowly into the theatre.

In 1967, he and Jean Dalrymple purchased the Theatre Four on West 55th Street to use for experimental play productions. The one show in which Tone appeared there was *Beyond Desire*, a static "play with music" about Felix Mendelssohn. Tone, as Mendelssohn's friend Karl Klingemann, narrated from the side of the stage. His feet were so swollen and numb that he barely could make his exits and entrances with the aid of his cane. Only the melifluous voice was evocative of the Franchot Tone of the movies.

On September 18, 1968, he died of lung cancer. He had lived in a town house on Manhattan's East 62nd Street and kept a summer home in Point Comfort, Canada, where Joan Crawford visited him during his illness. His estate of one-quarter to one-half million dollars was left to his two sons. Just before his death he had acquired the film rights to Jean Renoir's biography, *My Father, Renoir*, as a possible starring vehicle for himself. One theatre friend recalled Tone as a dashing cafe society sophisticate, and another aptly said, "He was tall, wealthy, witty, intelligent, and gracefully handsome, a perfect matinee idol of the time."

FRANCHOT TONE

The Wiser Sex (Paramount, 1932)
Gabriel over the White House (MGM, 1933)
Dancing Lady (MGM, 1933)
Today We Live (MGM, 1933)
Stage Mother (MGM, 1933)
Bombshell (MGM, 1933)
The Stranger's Return (MGM, 1933)
Midnight Mary (MGM, 1933)
Moulin Rouge (UA, 1934)
The World Moves On (Fox, 1934)
Straight Is the Way (MGM, 1934)
Gentlemen Are Born (WB, 1934)
The Girl from Missouri (MGM, 1934)
Sadie McKee (MGM, 1934)
Lives of a Bengal Lancer (Paramount, 1935)
Mutiny on the Bounty (MGM, 1935)
Reckless (MGM, 1935)
No More Ladies (MGM, 1935)
Dangerous (WB, 1935)

One New York Night (MGM, 1935)
Suzy (MGM, 1936)
Exclusive Story (MGM, 1936)
Love on the Run (MGM, 1936)
The King Steps Out (Columbia, 1936)
The Unguarded Hour (MGM, 1936)
The Gorgeous Hussy (MGM, 1936)
Between Two Women (MGM, 1937)
The Bride Wore Red (MGM, 1937)
They Gave Him a Gun (MGM, 1937)
Quality Street (RKO, 1937)
Three Comrades (MGM, 1938)
Man-Proof (MGM, 1938)
Love Is a Headache (MGM, 1938)
The Girl Downstairs (MGM, 1938)
Three Loves Has Nancy (MGM, 1938)
Thunder Afloat (MGM, 1939)
Fast and Furious (MGM, 1939)
Trail of the Vigilantes (Universal, 1940)

With Dudley Digges and Clark Gable in *Mutiny on the Bounty* (1935)

With Robert Montgomery and Joan Crawford in *No More Ladies* (1935)

Nice Girl? (Universal, 1941)
This Woman Is Mine (Universal, 1941)
She Knew All the Answers (Columbia, 1941)
The Wife Takes a Flyer (Columbia, 1942)
Star Spangled Rhythm (Paramount, 1942)
His Butler's Sister (Universal, 1943)
Pilot No. 5 (MGM, 1943)
True to Life (Paramount, 1943)
Five Graves to Cairo (Paramount, 1943)
The Hour Before the Dawn (Paramount, 1944)
Phantom Lady (Universal, 1944)
Dark Waters (UA, 1944)
That Night with You (Universal, 1945)
Because of Him (Universal, 1946)
Honeymoon (RKO, 1947)
Lost Honeymoon (Eagle–Lion, 1947)
Her Husband's Affairs (Columbia, 1947)
Every Girl Should Be Married (RKO, 1948)
I Love Trouble (Columbia, 1948)
Jigsaw (UA, 1949)
The Man on the Eiffel Tower (RKO, 1949)
Without Honor (UA, 1949)
Here Comes the Groom (Paramount, 1951)
Uncle Vanya (Continental Distributing, 1958)
Advise and Consent (Columbia, 1962)

La Bonne Soupe (International Classics, 1964)
In Harm's Way (Paramount, 1965)
Mickey One (Columbia, 1965)
The High Commissioner (Cinerama, 1968)

With Cary Grant in *Suzy* (1936)

With Virginia Bruce in *Between Two Women* (1937)

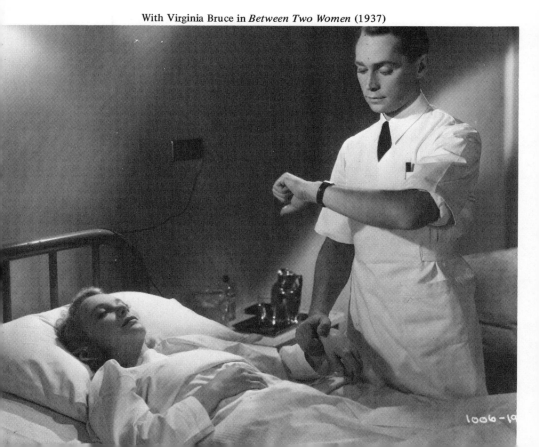

Audrey Totter

Actresses who can play hard-boiled dames in a convincing manner have long been in demand in Hollywood, but they rarely rise to cinema stardom. After all, crime cannot be shown to be too successful on the screen, even in present day motion picture–television productions. Audrey Totter is one of the best examples of such an actress. She went from the ranks of radio soap opera in New York to become MGM's bad girl ingenue of the mid-1940s. She was touted both as another Carole Lombard and a new Jean Harlow but, in front of the camera, she portrayed her own special brand of brittle, florid meanness. Like Veronica Lake and Gloria Grahame, who have the same facial structure and have stalked through the same type of roles, Audrey did not age very well, a major factor in the briefness of her sporadic post-1955 career.

Audrey was born in Joliet, Illinois on December 20, 1918. Her parents were of Swedish–Austrian descent, and she was the eldest of five children. At the age of seven, she became fascinated with a traveling circus playing in Joliet and tried to run away and join the show. Later, as a teenager, she was the bass fiddle player in her high school orchestra, and during summers, she appeared in stock and little theatre productions. After graduation, she went to Chicago and won the lead opposite Ian Keith in *The Copperhead* (1938) and spent the following year with his repertory group, leading to a tour in *My Sister Eileen*. Meanwhile, she became active in Chicago's burgeoning radio soap opera field (*Road of Life, Ma Perkins, Bright Horizon*) and later moved to New York where she became known as "the girl with a thousand voices," heard on such shows as *The Chamber Music Society of Lower Basin Street, Stage Door Canteen*, and *The Kid*.

While in New York Audrey had tested for Warner Brothers and for Twentieth Century-Fox, but without any tangible results. However, she did a screen test for Metro through the good services of MGM test director Al Altman, and they hired her on a seven-year contract. Arriving in Hollywood, she said, "I'm wedded to MGM, I hope. At any rate, engaged! I trust that they'll do right by me." She debuted in *Main Street after Dark* (1944) as Selena Royle's' daughter who rolls servicemen. Then she was the throaty offscreen voice in *Bewitched* (1945). Because of the subsequent rash of screen roles in which her hair and accent differed from picture to picture, she began referring

730

to herself as "the feminine Lon Chaney of the MGM lot." She was a Viennese chanteuse in *Dangerous Partners* (1945), a Rumanian siren in *The Sailor Takes a Wife* (1945), and a clawing cat in the Lucille Ball lion-tamer number of *Ziegfeld Follies* (1946). After receiving good notices as the waitress pickup of John Garfield in *The Postman Always Rings Twice* (1946), she had her first honest-to-goodness ingenue role in *The Cockeyed Miracle* (1946).

Her MGM high spot came when star–director Robert Montgomery cast her as the editor of the detective magazine in *Lady in the Lake* (1946). The film's gimmick was the offscreen voice of Montgomery used as a subjective commentary of the onscreen activity. Because her radio work was well known, Montgomery assumed she would be at ease acting with the inanimate microphone, which she was, to great effect. In the remaining years of her MGM contract she had showy roles in a series of low-key melodramas, many done away from the studio: the grasping relative of Joan Caulfield in Warners' *The Unsuspected* (1947), the police psychiatrist drawn to murder suspect Robert Taylor in *The High Wall* (1947), the club singer gal of Broadway big shot Robert Montgomery in Universal's *The Saxon Charm* (1948), and the reluctant mother who blithely leaves her child in Jane Wyman's care in RKO's *The Blue Veil* (1951). On the home lot, she played such roles as Alexis Smith's parasitic sister who has a yen for brother-in-law Clark Gable in *Any Number Can Play* (1949), a jealous murderess in *Tension* (1949), and a roadhouse chanteuse in *The Sellout* (1951), the picture that concluded her studio tenure.

Now at liberty, she made two Korean USO tours in the early 1950s and, about this time, wed Dr. Leo Fred, chief physician at the Los Angeles Veteran's Hospital. They had a daughter, Mary Elizabeth Ann, born in 1954. From 1951 to 1954, Audrey was the star of the *Meet Millie* comedy series on CBS radio.

Her 1950s features were very low budget fare: a gun moll in the 3-D *Man in the Dark* (1953), Brian Donlevy's wife in the post–Civil War Western *The Woman They Almost Lynched* (1953), the pregnant wife of Warren Stevens in *Women's Prison* (1955), and a Russian nurse in *Jet Attack* (1958). During this decade she was a guest star on several television anthology series and in 1958 she become one of three costars, along with George Montgomery and John Smith, in the Western series *Cimarron City*. However, she dropped out as the boardinghouse keeper because she said, "I don't want to play background leads." But in 1962 she was the employer of butler Stanley Holloway in the *Our Man Higgins* series, and later in the 1960s showed up on *Bonanza* and *Run for Your Life*, as well as playing a drunk murderess in the pilot telefeature *The Outsider* (1967).

Audrey has only made three films in recent years. She was seen briefly as a whore in *The Carpetbaggers* (1964). Then, in the Electronovision version of *Harlow* (1965), she was Paul Bern's (Hurd Hatfield) mistress, and, finally, in *Chubasco* (1968), a much middle-aged Audrey had a few scenes as Susan Strasberg's mother. In 1972 Audrey came out of a self-imposed, four-year retirement to take the recurring role of Nurse Wilcox on the *Medical Center* series. It was old friend Frank Glicksman, executive producer of the series, who lured Audrey back to work. "He suggested I'd be just right for the role of Nurse Wilcox, who's the kind of hard-boiled, tender-hearted type I love to play."

AUDREY TOTTER

Main Street after Dark (MGM, 1944)
Bewitched (Voice only: MGM, 1945)
Dangerous Partners (MGM, 1945)
Her Highness and the Bellboy (MGM, 1945)
The Sailor Takes a Wife (MGM, 1945)
Adventure (MGM, 1945)
The Hidden Eye (MGM, 1945)
The Secret Heart (Voice only: MGM, 1946)
The Ziegfeld Follies (MGM, 1946)
The Postman Always Rings Twice (MGM, 1946)
The Cockeyed Miracle (MGM, 1946)
Lady in the Lake (MGM, 1946)
The Beginning or the End (MGM, 1947)
The Unsuspected (WB, 1947)
The High Wall (MGM, 1947)
Tenth Avenue Angel (MGM, 1948)
The Saxon Charm (Universal, 1948)
The Set-Up (RKO, 1949)
Alias Nick Beal (Paramount, 1949)
Any Number Can Play (MGM, 1949)
Tension (MGM, 1949)

Under the Gun (Universal, 1950)
The Blue Veil (RKO, 1951)
FBI Girl (Lippert, 1951)
The Sellout (MGM, 1951)
Assignment—Paris (Columbia, 1952)
My Pal Gus (20th-Fox, 1952)
The Woman They Almost Lynched (Republic, 1953)
Man in the Dark (Columbia, 1953)
Cruisin' Down the River (Columbia, 1953)
Mission over Korea (Columbia, 1953)
Champ for a Day (Republic, 1953)
Massacre Canyon (Columbia, 1954)
A Bullet for Joey (UA, 1955)
Women's Prison (Columbia, 1955)
The Vanishing American (Republic, 1955)
Ghost Diver (20th-Fox, 1957)
Jet Attack (AIP, 1958)
Man or Gun (Republic, 1958)
The Carpetbaggers (Paramount, 1964)
Harlow (Magna, 1965)
Chubasco (WB-7 Arts, 1968)

With Lloyd Gough in *Tension* (1949)

Spencer Tracy

Spencer Tracy once told superstar Bette Davis that he did not know a damned thing about acting; but his Hollywood colleagues, assorted critics and some of the moviegoing public referred to the ultrapopular screen player as "the actor's actor."

The rationale for such heady admiration is quite simple: Tracy was the finest natural actor of the American sound cinema. What Tracy offered as characterization was a combination of masculine personality and seemingly total sincerity. In the bulk of his cinema work, he demonstrated an impressive truthfulness of character which appeared steeped in infinite wisdom and compassion for his fellow man. Tracy's acting technique was effortless and without the nervous mannerisms that were the hallmark of so many other individualistic stars. Tracy's one dominant identifying professional trait was his look of total concentration. He was Daniel in the lion's den; be it surrounded by women, children, or natural disaster, his solidarity quieted down all outside forces.

Spencer Bonaventure Tracy was born in Milwaukee, Wisconsin on April 5, 1900, the second son of John Edward and Carrie (Brown) Tracy. His Irish Catholic father was a sales manager for a trucking outfit, and the last thing he expected his son to be was an actor. So did Spencer. At seventeen he enlisted in the Navy with his boyhood pal, William J. "Pat" O'Brien. Later he attended Ripon College in Wisconsin, toying with the idea of eventually becoming a plastic surgeon. But after joining the college debating team, appearing in a school production of Clyde Fitch's *The Truth*, and being encouraged by two professors, he embarked for New York in 1922, to audition for and hopefully enroll at the American Academy of Dramatic Arts. Once accepted, he delved wholeheartedly into his chosen profession. While at the AADA, Tracy obtained first a walkon and then a speaking part in the Theatre Guild's production of Karel Capek's *R.U.R.* and, upon graduation, continued to seek theatrical employment.

Tracy landed on Broadway in a short-lived Ethel Barrymore comedy titled *A Royal Fandango* (1923). After more tough years in stock and on the road, Tracy returned to Broadway, thanks to actress Selena Royle, who had been assigned the lead in a new George M. Cohan play, *Yellow* (1926). When one of the secondary males was fired, she suggested Tracy for the replacement. There were more non-Broadway acting chores before he finally hit pay dirt playing the murderous "Killer" Mears in *The Last Mile* (1930), which established him as that legitimate season's good baddie.

During the run of *The Last Mile*, Tracy made several talking short subjects for Vitaphone and four unsuccessful screen tests for major studios. But it was director John Ford who saw Tracy's stage performance and persuaded Fox Pictures' executive head, Winfield Sheehan, to sign him for *Up the River* (1930), a prison comedy which was also Humphrey Bogart's feature film debut. With the success of *Up the River*, Fox contracted with Tracy for a five-year agreement at more than $1,000 weekly. His second picture for the studio, *Quick Millions* (1931), was not the hit anticipated, but typecast him as a gangster. It was with great difficulty that he persuaded studio heads to allow him to perform in other film genres, for Tracy had become to Fox what George Bancroft was to Paramount, Edward G. Robinson to Warners, and Wallace Beery to MGM.

When James Cagney was feuding with Warners, that studio borrowed Tracy to play the lead in *20,000 Years in Sing Sing* (1933), opposite Bette Davis. This prison melodrama consolidated Tracy's screen reputation, which was further enhanced by his performance in Fox's *The Power and the Glory* (1933), of which *The Nation's* William Troy, reported: "Spencer Tracy's railroad president is one of the fullest characterizations ever achieved on the screen."

By 1934 Fox had extended Tracy's screen contract through 1937, calling for his making four pictures a year and to receive sizable pay increases. Loan assignments to other studios could be negotiated only with Tracy's consent. Warner Baxter was increasingly that studio's top boxoffice draw, and if Tracy followed close behind in screen popularity, he certainly won no awards with Fox executives. His drinking bouts, stubborn behavior, and know-it-all attitude were a constant problem both on and off the sets. But when he worked, there was no doubt he was worth the trouble.

Having done so well on loanout to Columbia for the Frank Borzage production, *A Man's Castle* (1933), Tracy was amenable to moving over to MGM to star in a picturization of George Kelly's *The Show-Off* (1934), which garnered Tracy distinguished reviews and paved the way for his later joining that studio. He admired the professionalism on the Culver City lot and was impressed by MGM's brilliant young producer, Irving G. Thalberg, who took a great interest in Tracy's career and the possibility of a future working relationship.

By 1935 Tracy was rebelling more and more at Fox. He refused to appear in *Helldorado* (1935) and was replaced by Richard Arlen. After dropping out of *Marie Galante* (1935), in which Edmund Lowe was substituted, Tracy changed his mind, was reinstated to the cast, and he paid for the retakes of the already filmed sequences with Lowe. After a well-publicized drinking bout in Yuma, Arizona, in which Tracy was arrested, Fox decided to discipline their bad boy by shoving him into a supporting role as the heavy in *The Farmer Takes a Wife* (1935), starring the studio's own Janet Gaynor and newcomer Henry Fonda. Tracy refused to be humbled, and Fox fired him on April 8, 1935. His last release for the studio under his contract appeared in July 1935, a remake of the silent, *Dante's Inferno*, in which he played a fairground entrepreneur opposite Claire Trevor.

On the same day he left Fox, Tracy was in negotiation with MGM for a contract, although paternal studio head Louis B. Mayer was not keen about taking on Fox's hard-to-manage actor (MGM had similar problems with Wallace Beery). Besides, no executive thought Tracy had sex appeal. However, Thalberg saw in Tracy a chance to add a prestige actor to their roster. Tracy certainly was not in keeping with the typical MGM star. He couldn't play sophisticated drawing-room comedy like William Powell, Robert Montgomery, or even Clark Gable to a lesser degree; nor could he play the roughneck, lovable scamp like Wallace Beery or Lionel Barrymore. He was not only a new type for MGM but for the industry: a rather squat leading man with a penchant for portraying the rugged individualist, albeit a crook or self-made honest man.

After appearing in a quickie melodrama, *The Murder Man* (1935), which featured a new Broadway find, James Stewart, Tracy was put in top support of studio luminary Jean Harlow in *Riffraff* (1936), where he had to make an unsavory character sympathetic. It was in the cops-and-robbers yarn, *Whipsaw* (1936), that Tracy first shared costarring billing over the title, here with leading lady Myrna Loy. Tracy proved Thalberg's prediction correct by his splendid emoting in two 1936 productions: as the innocent victim of a kidnaping charge in Fritz Lang's antimob study, *Fury*, and as the embattled priest in the blockbuster, *San Francisco*, with Jeanette MacDonald and Clark Gable. For this characterization, Tracy received the first of his nine Oscar nominations, still a record for a male performer.

The next two years saw Tracy become the only actor to win an Academy Award two years in succession: for his salty portrayal of the Portuguese fisherman in Victor Fleming's *Captains Courageous* (1937) (Tracy's favorite role); and as the crusading Father Flanagan in *Boys' Town* (1938). Thereafter, Tracy received MGM's full preferential treatment.

The studio had refused to lend him to Fox in 1937, for John Ford's *The Plough and the Stars*, fearful it would flop and damage the actor's boxoffice luster, but two years later he was loaned to that company to essay the role of the dedicated American reporter, Henry M. Stanley, who searches in the jungle for the long-lost missionary, Dr. David Livingstone (played by Cedric Hardwicke) in *Stanley and Livingstone* (1939). In exchange for Tracy's services, Fox's Tyrone Power was shipped to Culver City to play opposite Norma Shearer in *Marie Antoinette*. After adventuring with Hedy Lamarr in *I Take This Woman* (1940), which had gone through so many scene retakes it was jokingly referred to as *I Retake This Woman*, Tracy finally had the opportunity of demonstrating his ability to project the American pioneer spirit in the

With Myrna Loy in *Whipsaw* (1935)

With Jean Harlow in *Libeled Lady* (1936)

With Sara Haden, Roy Gordon, Frank Morgan, and Howard Hickman in *Boom Town* (1940)

With Robert Young and Truman Bradley in *Northwest Passage* (1940)

With Addison Richards, Henry O'Neill, Mary ash, Mickey Rooney, and Darryl Hickman in *en of Boys Town* (1941)

With Signe Hasso in *The Seventh Cross* (1944)

cinematization of Kenneth Roberts' mammoth *Northwest Passage* (1940). He was content enough to emote in *Edison, The Man* (1940), a sequel to that year's *Young Tom Edison* featuring Mickey Rooney, and to play second fiddle to Clark Gable in the wildcat oil saga, *Boom Town* (1940). He even willingly agreed to perform again as courageous Father Flanagan in *Men of Boys Town* (1941). But he fought hard against starring in MGM's unthinking remake of *Dr. Jekyll and Mr. Hyde* (1941), which emerged as glossy junk and garnered Tracy bad reviews. Then came preproduction work on *The Yearling*, a project which became so bogged down in internal problems that it was abandoned, to be restarted years later with Gregory Peck.

It was screenwriter–director Garson Kanin who was responsible for linking together the screen's oddest team casting in years, that of Tracy and Katharine Hepburn. Before she made her Broadway comeback in *The Philadelphia Story* and the MGM screen version of that play (1940), she had been branded boxoffice poison. Supposedly, at their first meeting, Hepburn said, "I fear I may be too tall for you, Mr. Tracy." He replied to the haughty actress, "Don't worry, Miss Hepburn, I'll cut you down to my size." The seemingly disparate types worked so well in *Woman of the Year* (1942) that they appeared in a total of nine films together over the next twenty-five years. His strong quiet way blended well with her volatile superiority, making them a charming give-and-take duo.

After starring in the sentimental version of John Steinbeck's *Tortilla Flat* (1942), Tracy was reunited with Hepburn in the cynical *Keeper of the Flame* (1943). Of his trio of patriotic movies made during World War II, his performance in *The Seventh Cross* (1944) as the resourceful concentration camp escapee was by far the most full-bodied, but did not generate the popularity of his assignment opposite Irene Dunne in the fantasy, *A Guy Named Joe* (1943), or his special guest appearance in *Thirty Seconds over Tokyo* (1944) as the stalwart Lt. Colonel Doolittle. Tracy had been too old to serve in World War II, but his matureness provided the right note for his screen portrayals as, said the MGM publicity releases, "the perfect actor."

After playing the dedicated inventor who weds widowed Katharine Hepburn for convenience in *Without Love* (1945), Tracy satisfied a long-building hankering to return to the stage. His choice was the unfortunate *The Rugged Path* (1945) by Robert E. Sherwood, which proved to be a philosophical marathon rather than entertainment. The production was not a success, and despite respectful reviews, Tracy was badly shaken by the return to live acting, and he was talked out of quitting the show before it reached Broadway only by Katharine Hepburn's insistence that he finish what he started.

The Sea of Grass (1947) revealed a graying Tracy as a cattle baron in a sprawling adaptation of Conrad Richter's novel that was artistically and commercially unsatisfying. Far more financially viable was the flaccid screen version of Sinclair Lewis' *Cass Timberlane* (1947), which found judge Tracy wedding Lana Turner, "a nice girl from the wrong side of the tracks." Tracy and Hepburn continued to be boxoffice in the movie edition of the Pulitzer Prize-winning *State of the Union* (1948), and the Garson Kanin-scripted *Adam's Rib* (1949) which George Cukor directed. That comedy dealt with husband and wife attorneys who find themselves battling one another in court over accused murderess Judy Holliday. Tracy ended the decade with the arty *Edward, My Son* (1949), filmed in Britain.

The 1950s began with the specious *Malaya* (1950), but much better was *Father of the Bride* (1950), with Tracy and Elizabeth Taylor in the title roles. It proved the comedy hit of the year and spawned the sequel, *Father's Little Dividend* (1951). After the seamy *People Against O'Hara* (1951), in which Tracy played a drunken ex-criminal attorney, he had much better screen luck with director George Cukor in *Pat and Mike* (1952), playing the sports promoter linked with a physical education instructor (Katharine Hepburn). One of the dullest big-budgeted productions under the Dore Schary regime at MGM was *Plymouth Adventure* (1952), a lacklustre retelling of the Mayflower's voyage to the New World. Many critics labeled it a "Thanksgiving Turkey." By the time of *The Actress* (1953), based on the reminiscences of actress Ruth Gordon, Tracy had moved gracefully and finally into pleasant middle-aged roles, far outside the realm of standardized leading man assignments still captured by such contemporaries as Clark Gable and Gary Cooper. Tracy was indeed impressive in *Bad Day at Black Rock* (1955), in which he played a one-armed veteran searching for the Japanese-American father of a war hero. He won the Cannes Film Festival's prize for that portrayal, then began work on his sixty-ninth feature, a Western titled, *Tribute to a Badman* (1956). However, arguments ensued between Tracy and the film's director, Robert Wise, and when attempts to arbitrate the differences between these two men were thwarted, MGM officials quietly fired Tracy (James Cagney replaced him); but not so quietly that the impact was not felt by a Hollywood already shaken by the demise of the star system.

With his MGM contract terminated, Tracy moved to Paramount and played the mountain guide in the pedestrian *The Mountain* (1956), and rejoined Katharine Hepburn, at Twentieth Century-Fox, in the spiritless rendition of the Broadway comedy, *The Desk Set* (1957). It was the dedicated Tracy who gave his all to the virtual solo vehicle, *The Old Man and the Sea* (1958), a static version of Hemingway's story, which was so tedious that the public stayed away in droves, unintrigued by Tracy's brilliant characterization as the elderly fisherman. It was a far more lively Tracy who bolstered *The Last Hurrah* (1959), a flavorful account of the last campaign of an old-guard Boston politician.

During the last years of his life (he died of a heart attack on June 10, 1967) Tracy appeared in only ten films because of recurring ill health. His association with producer–director Stanley Kramer represented the bulk of Tracy's remaining screen career. They had a mutual respect for one another that often caused Tracy to perform in specious vehicles. *Inherit the Wind* (1960) was an unfelicitous adaptation of the Scopes Monkey Trial play which had been a significant Broadway showcase for Paul Muni. Tracy's performance as Clarence Darrow did not attract sufficient boxoffice interest; and the tawdry *The Devil at Four O'Clock* (1961) had Tracy performing as an alcoholic priest. Tracy was again a judge in the roadshow *Judgment at Nuremberg* (1961), then made a complete change of professional pace in Kramer's frantic comedy fest, *It's a Mad, Mad, Mad, Mad World* (1963), which found a considerably aged Tracy as an old and disillusioned police captain who herds off the greedy culprits who have been after Jimmy Durante's buried fortune, only to grab the loot himself. This Cinerama picture may have been crude in execution, but it pleased the public and netted over $23 million in release.

After more than three years of semiretirement, Tracy returned to the screen in *Guess Who's Coming to Dinner?* (1967). Both Stanley Kramer and costar Katharine Hepburn hoped the project would revive Tracy's dying zest for life. The movie was a slick, commercial approach to the touchy miscegenation issue, which found too-good-to-be-true Sidney Poitier as the intellectual black man. The fact that Tracy died two weeks after production was completed added a sentimental touch to the film and generated greater interest in its initial release. Tracy was awarded a posthumous Academy Award nomination.

With Tracy dead, many of his Hollywood associates began publicizing their past relationships with him, and the general public finally became aware of the man's personal life which had been conducted with an obsessive discretion. He had married actress Louise Treadwell in 1923, when they were both fledgling stock players. They remained married until his death, although they lived separately most of the last decades of his life. Tracy fathered two children: John and Louise. His son, John, was born deaf and it proved a tragedy which Tracy could never reconcile. His wife devoted her life to the care of the child and later founded the John Tracy Clinic, acknowledged to be one of the world's finest medical centers for the deaf.

While filming *A Man's Castle* at Columbia in 1933, Tracy's romantic attachment to his costar, Loretta Young, became a subject of much Hollywood gossip, until finally Miss Young made a dignified public statement to the effect that since both she and Tracy were Catholics and could never properly marry, they had aggreed not to see one another socially again.

From the time of their first professional meeting in the early 1940s until his death, Tracy and Katharine Hepburn remained extremely close friends and traveling companions. It was in a small guest house on the estate of Miss Hepburn's friend and director, George Cukor, that Tracy spent the last meandering years in Hollywood.

In his life, he was often quoted as saying, "All an actor owes the public is a good performance." Tracy, the iconoclast, gave that public more than his share.

SPENCER TRACY

Up the River (Fox, 1930)
Quick Millions (Fox, 1931)
Six Cylinder Love (Fox, 1931)
She Wanted a Millionaire (Fox, 1932)
Sky Devils (UA, 1932)
Disorderly Conduct (Fox, 1932)
Young America (Fox, 1932)
Society Girl (Fox, 1932)
Painted Woman (Fox, 1932)
Me and My Gal (Fox, 1932)
20,000 Years in Sing Sing (WB, 1932)
Face in the Sky (Fox, 1933)
Shanghai Madness (Fox, 1933)
The Power and the Glory (Fox, 1933)
The Mad Game (Fox, 1933)
A Man's Castle (Columbia, 1933)
Looking for Trouble (UA, 1934)
The Show-Off (MGM, 1934)
Bottoms Up (Fox, 1934)
Now I'll Tell (Fox, 1934)
Marie Galante (Fox, 1934)
It's a Small World (Fox, 1935)
Murder Man (MGM, 1935)
Dante's Inferno (Fox, 1935)
Whipsaw (MGM, 1935)
Riffraff (MGM, 1936)
Fury (MGM, 1936)
San Francisco (MGM, 1936)
Libeled Lady (MGM, 1936)
They Gave Him a Gun (MGM, 1937)
Captains Courageous (MGM, 1937)
Big City (MGM, 1937)
Mannequin (MGM, 1938)
Test Pilot (MGM, 1938)
Boys' Town (MGM, 1938)
Stanley and Livingstone (20th-Fox, 1939)
I Take This Woman (MGM, 1940)

Northwest Passage (MGM, 1940)
Edison, the Man (MGM, 1940)
Boom Town (MGM, 1940)
Men of Boys Town (MGM, 1941)
Dr. Jekyll and Mr. Hyde (MGM, 1941)
Woman of the Year (MGM, 1942)
Tortilla Flat (MGM, 1942)
Keeper of the Flame (MGM, 1942)
A Guy Named Joe (MGM, 1943)
The Seventh Cross (MGM, 1944)
Thirty Seconds over Tokyo (MGM, 1944)
Without Love (MGM, 1945)
The Sea of Grass (MGM, 1947)
Cass Timberlane (MGM, 1947)
State of the Union (MGM, 1948)
Edward, My Son (MGM, 1949)
Adam's Rib (MGM, 1949)
Malaya (MGM, 1950)
Father of the Bride (MGM, 1950)
Father's Little Dividend (MGM, 1951)
The People Against O'Hara (MGM, 1951)
Pat and Mike (MGM, 1952)
Plymouth Adventure (MGM, 1952)
The Actress (MGM, 1953)
Broken Lance (20th-Fox, 1954)
Bad Day at Black Rock (MGM, 1955)
The Mountain (Paramount, 1956)
Desk Set (20th-Fox, 1957)
The Old Man and the Sea (WB, 1958)
The Last Hurrah (Columbia, 1958)
Inherit the Wind (UA, 1960)
The Devil at Four O'Clock (Columbia, 1961)
Judgment at Nuremberg (UA, 1961)
It's a Mad, Mad, Mad, Mad World (UA, 1963)
Guess Who's Coming to Dinner (Columbia, 1967)

With Moroni Olsen, Billie Burke, and Joan Bennett in *Father of the Bride* (1950)

With Ernest Borgnine, in *Bad Day at Black Rock* (1954)

Lana Turner

Among the sundry studio molds manufactured by the MGM publicity wheels was the first "Sweater Girl": Lana Turner. This gimmick made a star of the girl who started her professional career on a drugstore seat. "You acted badly; you moved clumsily; but the point is every eye in the audience was on you," says Kirk Douglas to Lana Turner in *The Bad and the Beautiful* (1952). Academy Award scripter Charles Schnee had pinpointed the essence of Lana's silver screen stardom in one crisp sentence.

Starting out in adolescent roles, Lana was the pinup delight of the MGM lot during the World War II years, when she firmly entrenched herself in stardom with several war-theme boxoffice hits. The postwar period thrust her into womanly prominence with MGM's realization of James M. Cain's thriller, *The Postman Always Rings Twice* (1947). Excepting the aforementioned *The Bad and the Beautiful*, most of her features began to go sour with the public, even though she managed to bedazzle with more and more glamour. Several dubbed musicals and historical potboilers aided her in the plastic "I am a Movie Star" image via the roles and costuming; but despite those few bad years during the fifties, Lana is one of the few gorgeous stars who has physically matured gracefully on the screen, albeit in highly improbable, yet moneymaking soap operas.

Always the "Movie Star," she had never been credited with assets on the histrionic side of the ledger. Since her professional discovery, many classically proportioned rumps have warmed the seats of Hollywood drugstores, but hers is the only one which won the hearts of the public. Those hearts have pumped persistently over thirty years and have even been given some nice stimulation in the form of seven marriages: Artie Shaw; Stephen Crane; (by whom she had a daughter, Cheryl); Bob Topping; Lex Barker; Fred May; Robert Eaton; Donald Dante; one murder; and assorted scandals. Her private peccadilloes have always overlapped with and been inseparable from the Lana Turner screen personality. As one observant photographer opined: "Lana Turner is MGM's most compleat studio product." Not the most introspective of film celebrities, Lana was nonetheless known to say on one occasion: "My life has been a series of emergencies." And indeed it has!

Julia Jean Mildred Frances Turner was born in Wallace, Idaho on

February 8, 1920, where her father, an inveterate gambler, was temporarily working in the mines. When the nomadic family moved back to San Francisco, her father was fatally blackjacked two weeks before Christmas in 1930. Her mother was forced to work in a beauty parlor and little Judy, as she was called, was farmed out to what proved cruel foster parents. Later, mother and daughter were reunited and moved to Los Angeles where the auburn-haired Judy attended Hollywood High School. Studio publicity pap maintains that the young girl had wanted to become a nun but changed her mind when she found she would have to cut off all her hair. Then she toyed with the idea of becoming a dress designer (later, while attending the MGM studio school, she usually doodled with fashion layouts rather than paying heed to her studies). Despite the obvious public relations, such dreams would not be unlikely for a teenager sipping a Coke in a drugstore in the thirties, and that was just how Billy Wilkerson of *The Hollywood Reporter* found her in January, 1936, in one of the most famous discovery stories in Hollywood mythology. Wilkerson, so impressed with the nubile adolescent that he uttered the famous tag line, "How'd you like to be in pictures?", sent her to the Zeppo Marx Agency, where, after refusals by David O. Selnick, RKO, and Twentieth Century-Fox, agent Henry Willson (later discoverer of Rock Hudson, Tab Hunter, etc.) brought her to director, Mervyn LeRoy at Warner Brothers.

LeRoy liked her looks but not her name, so the precocious teenager became "Lana," as in lah-de-da, not lady. LeRoy signed her at $50 a week and gave her a small but pivotal part in his sociological drama, *They Won't Forget* (1937), showing her in a tight skirt and tighter sweater, sitting at a drugstore counter and then walking sensuously down the street. "I was one of those photogenic accidents. I was a 15-year old kid (she was really 17) with a bosom and a backside strolling across the screen for less than a minute." That short walk caught the eye of every red-blooded male who saw the picture and, while her character was killed off in the first reel, the film's title proved prophetic. (Forgotten by all concerned was that Lana had actually made her screen debut in a crowd scene in United Artists' *A Star Is Born* [1937].)

Warners used her in a few more bits, but studio head Jack Warner failed to see what everyone else did. He informed LeRoy: "She hasn't got it; she's just a kid." And so LeRoy took her with him when he moved to MGM in 1938.

As a juvenile at Metro, Lana was appropriately cast in the studio's wholesome family series, *The Hardy Family*, in the entry titled *Love Finds Andy Hardy* (1938), which also featured Judy Garland and Ann Rutherford, as well as the series' young star, Mickey Rooney. The critics liked Lana better than Judy as one of Mickey's sweethearts, although they conceded she was a bit too glamourous for a teenager. A few more juvenile roles followed, and she was starred in two campus-oriented programmers: *These Glamour Girls* (1939) and *Dancing Co-Ed* (1939), and moved to young adult assignments in *Two Girls on Broadway* (1940) and *We Who Are Young* (1940). While these were just perfunctory assignments, they were screen exposure, and the studio continued to pound out its Sweater Girl publicity, and the fan mail kept pouring in.

Lana furthered her spotty education at the MGM studio school where, "I spent most of my time fending off learning and fending off Mickey Rooney." She became so caught up with playing the Movie Star role that she was tagged the "Night Club Queen" before she was twenty-one. One observer recalls: "The only thing real to her was the camera and, while she partied almost nightly, she was never late for her early morning studio call." This remained true throughout her career, and she is one of the most popular of actresses with veteran Hollywood crewmen.

With the timing just right, MGM cast her as the showgirl who turns bad in *Ziegfeld Girl* (1941) with Judy Garland and Hedy Lamarr, and gave her lines such as "What's there about me that makes you think I can understand French?" She called it "a once-in-a-lifetime role," and the public agreed. Moviegoers overlooked the fact that she was miscast in *Dr. Jekyll and Mr. Hyde* (1941) (costar Ingrid Bergman had requested she be given the bad girl role and the nice English young lady assignment fell to Lana) and was overwhelmed by the screen chemistry between her and Clark Gable in the Western, *Honky Tonk* (1941). Carole Lombard, Gable's wife, cognizant of her husband's preference for blondes, the color of Lana's once auburn locks, and of Lana's already established reputation for seducing her leading men, walked into MGM mogul Louis B. Mayer's office with the ultimatum that it would be "hands off" for Miss Turner, or she would see to it that Mr. Gable did not show up for work. The film was completed without incident, and Gable and Turner became good friends, going on to make three more pictures together.

Lana was Robert Taylor's gun moll in *Johnny Eager* (1941) and teamed with Gable again in *Somewhere I'll Find You* (1942). Her other wartime pictures were topical if unimportant, and MGM's remake of *Grand Hotel*, the glossy *Weekend at the Waldorf* (1945), was a healthy moneymaker. The best performance of her career was in *The Postman Always Rings Twice* (1947). This thriller was typical of the forties with its brittle plot and high-key lighting. Lana, with platinum hair and antiseptic white costumes, was at the height of her frigid sexuality and perfectly cast as Cecil Kellaway's soulless wife who induces John Garfield to murder her elderly husband. Boxoffice success continued with *Green Dolphin Street* (1947) and *Cass Timberlane* (1947), but *Homecoming* (1948) was less popular than her earlier two with Gable. She was totally out of her depth as the evil Lady DeWinter in *The Three Musketeers* (1948) (in the role studio character star Angela Lansbury wanted but was denied so she could enact the cardboard Queen Anne); then Lana was off the screen for a year for her third marriage. When she returned to MGM in George Cukor's *A Life of Her Own* (1950), about the pitfalls of a modeling career in New York, it was a flop, and her career at a standstill. MGM had not persevered in molding its $4,000 weekly star for "Joan Crawford scripts," as they had once intended, and all they had left was a glamour star in an age of declining production and more emphasis on realism than sparkling chicness. What to do? What to do was to put her in musicals. There glamour was guaranteed, and her voice could always be dubbed. *Mr. Imperium* (1951), which the studio's grand lady, Greer Garson, had refused, and a remake of *The Merry Widow* (1952) were the two musicals, but they were not the commercial answer. A brief respite was the role of the alcoholic actress in *The Bad and the Beautiful* (1952). While she did not excite too many critics, this was a popular film about Hollywood taking a sharp inventory of itself, and it remains a favorite Lana Turner role.

However, Lana's career was still in trouble, and she did not have the power to fight for better roles with the studio executives. The reason—after fourteen years with MGM, she was making a nifty salary, but she was also spending every bit of it and could not afford costly suspensions. So Lana renewed her contract at a time when many stars were leaving the studio, and she took what roles they gave her—*Latin Lovers* (1953) opposite Ricardo Montalban; *Betrayed* (1954), a weak espionage yarn with Gable; and the juvenile Biblical spectacle, *The Prodigal* (1955), whose love priestess set was constructed over the old Esther Williams permanent swimming pool ensemble. About this flop, Lana quipped, "It played two weeks in Pomona. It shoulda played Disneyland."

Much better was her junior femme fatale role opposite John Wayne in *The Sea Chase* (1955), her first loanout in fifteen years at MGM. Then it was to Twentieth Century-Fox for a Cinemascope–color remake of *The Rains Came*, now enlarged to *The Rains of Ranchipur* (1955) with an uncertain Lana playing Myrna Loy's old role, and making unconvincing love to Richard Burton, a Brahmin doctor. Her MGM career ended in a fizzle with a little disaster called *Diane* (1955), and the studio said goodbye to Lana after an eighteen-year association. Like other middle-aged, high-priced commodities, she, at thirty-five years old, was a luxury the studio could not and did not want to afford.

Lana was off the screen for two years, and many thought her career finished, when producer Jerry Wald had the foresight to cast her as Constance MacKenzie in his Twentieth Century-Fox production of *Peyton Place* (1957), a film which proved that an intelligent script can be derived from a vulgar novel; and Lana's colleagues were so impressed they nominated her for an Academy Award. Immediately a top moneymaker, (it grossed $11.5 million), the feature received an added boxoffice impetus when on the evening of Good Friday of 1958, Lana's paramour of fifteen months (gangster and gigolo Johnny Stompanato) was stabbed to death in Lana's pink-carpeted boudoir by her fifteen-year-old daughter, Cheryl, after what was described as a lengthy argument in which Stompanato threatened to scar Lana's face. The headlines that followed and the courtroom drama with defense attorney Jerry Geisler read as interestingly as the plot of *Peyton Place*. During the height of the scandal, which would be turned into a fictional account by Harold Robbins and a subsequent movie with Susan Hayward titled *Where Love Has Gone* (1964), two other Turner pictures were issued. *The Lady Takes a Flyer* (1958) was a vapid programmer with Jeff Chandler, and the British-lensed *Another*

Time, Another Place (1958) with Sean Connery did very little business.

The following year, Lana joined forces with producer Ross Hunter, and starred in the sudsy remake of Claudette Colbert's *Imitation of Life*. While the critics screamed "bathos," Lana, sharing in a percentage of the profits set up to give her a $150,000 annuity for life, listened only to the sound of the shekels pouring into the boxoffice. This was just what she needed and more was to follow: an elaborate murder mystery, *Portrait in Black* (1960); and *By Love Possessed* (1961), an almost unrecognizable and turgid rendering of James Gould Cozzen's fine novel—each was over-produced, overacted, and resembled nothing living.

Another low period followed with her playing straight lady to a too-mature Bob Hope in MGM's *Bachelor in Paradise* (1961) in which her bossa nova drunk scene was her one high spot; and a pedestrian comedy with Dean Martin, *Who's Got the Action?* (1962). It was three years before she returned to the screen in the much-troubled ladies' picture, *Love Has Many Faces* (1965), which provided more male cheesecake via Hugh O'Brian and Cliff Robertson than medium gauzed shots of Lana in a changing wardrobe. The public did not buy it at all. Lana and Ross Hunter had hoped to remake *Dark Angel*, but when legal complications prevented it, they settled for doing the fifth version of the evergreen tearjerker, *Madame X* (1966). While most women in the audience were reaching for a third handkerchief, the indomitable critic, Pauline Kael, wrote quite accurately, "She's not *Madame X*; she's brand X; she's not an actress, she's a commodity."

With a forced deaf ear to all criticism, Lana goes on. After a few nervous guest appearances on video variety shows, she accepted the lead in an expensive to-top-it-all television series, *The Survivors*, a 1970 outing that died in the rating games and proved that the public will not always buy hogwash. That same year, her last feature to date, the Mexican-lensed *The Big Cube*, was released. In New York it played the bottom half of double bills on 42nd Street.

There was a good deal of amazement when it was announced that Lana would make her stage debut in the light comedy, *Forty Carats* where, if not dazzled by the lady's histrionics (she was really quite good), audiences in the summer of 1971 were dazzled by her seemingly endless wardrobe.

Film roles have been increasingly scarce in recent years for the once sex goddess, but it seem that viewers have not seen the last of Lana Turner. "I've got an awful lot of money. I'm not working because I need money. I'm doing it because I need activity. Oh, God, I need activity." Her most recent activity has been the endorsement of a chain of franchised health spas for women, in which she will be director and stockholder. The name: The Lana Turner Mini-Spas. Adela Rogers St. Johns, always an astute Hollywood observer, says, "Look, let's not get mixed up about the *real* Lana Turner. The *real* Lana Turner is Lana Turner. She was always a movie star and loved it. Her personal life and her movie star life *are one*."

LANA TURNER

A Star Is Born (UA, 1937)
They Won't Forget (WB, 1937)
The Great Garrick (WB, 1937)
The Adventures of Marco Polo (UA, 1938)
Four's a Crowd (WB, 1938)
Love Finds Andy Hardy (MGM, 1938)
Rich Man, Poor Girl (MGM, 1938)
Dramatic School (MGM, 1938)
Calling Dr. Kildare (MGM, 1939)
These Glamour Girls (MGM, 1939)
Dancing Co-Ed (MGM, 1939)
Two Girls on Broadway (MGM, 1940)
We Who Are Young (MGM, 1940)
Ziegfeld Girl (MGM, 1941)
Dr. Jekyll And Mr. Hyde (MGM, 1941)
Honky Tonk (MGM, 1941)
Johnny Eager (MGM, 1941)
Somewhere I'll Find You (MGM, 1942)
The Youngest Profession (MGM, 1943)
Slightly Dangerous (MGM, 1943)
Dubarry Was a Lady (MGM, 1943)
Marriage Is a Private Affair (MGM, 1944)
Keep Your Powder Dry (MGM, 1945)
Weekend at the Waldorf (MGM, 1945)
The Postman Always Rings Twice (MGM, 1946)
Green Dolphin Street (MGM, 1947)

Cass Timberlane (MGM, 1947)
Homecoming (MGM, 1948)
The Three Musketeers (MGM, 1948)
A Life of Her Own (MGM, 1950)
Mr. Imperium (MGM, 1951)
The Merry Widow (MGM, 1952)
The Bad and the Beautiful (MGM, 1952)
Latin Lovers (MGM, 1953)
Flame and the Flesh (MGM, 1954)
Betrayed (MGM, 1954)
The Prodigal (MGM, 1955)
The Sea Chase (WB, 1955)
The Rains of Ranchipur (20th-Fox, 1955)
Diane (MGM, 1955)
Peyton Place (20th-Fox, 1957)
The Lady Takes a Flyer (Universal, 1958)
Another Time, Another Place (Paramount, 1958)
Imitation of Life (Universal, 1959)
Portrait in Black (Universal, 1960)
By Love Possessed (UA, 1961)
Bachelor in Paradise (MGM, 1961)
Who's Got the Action? (Paramount, 1962)
Love Has Many Faces (Columbia, 1965)
Madame X (Universal, 1966)
The Big Cube (WB, 1969)

With Cecilia Parker, Mickey Rooney, and Ann Rutherford in *Love Finds Andy Hardy* (1938)

In *Ziegfeld Girl* (1941)

With Clark Gable in *Honky Tonk* (1941)

With Cecil Kellaway and John Garfield in *The Postman Always Rings Twice* (1946)

With Ann Dvorak in *A Life of Her Own* (1950)

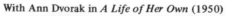

th Kirk Douglas in *The Bad and the Beautiful* (1952)

With Victor Mature in *Betrayed* (1954)

With Bob Hope in *Bachelor in Paradise* (1961)

Robert Walker

Of the screen rebels who have since passed away—Humphrey Bogart, James Dean, John Garfield—Robert Walker is the one major antihero who has not been resurrected into cultdom. (The late Montgomery Clift is still in a transitional status.) MGM had no difficulty in promoting Walker as the nice loser since, at an early age, the actor had accepted life's reversals as the ultimate conclusion and finalized it as an alcoholic. He served his purpose to the studio as the clean-cut "lost generation" symbol of the World War II era, emoting in comedy, melodrama, Westerns, and period pieces with that wateryeyed look that indicated he could calmly accept any and all adversities that the scriptwriters had worked into the scenarios.

"From childhood, I found myself up against mental walls," Walker told columnist Hedda Hopper. "The maladjustments of that age grew and branched out all over the place. I was always trying to make an escape from life." Born in Salt Lake City, Utah, in 1919, Robert Hudson Walker's first maladjustment was his parents' separation while he was still young. The resultant anxieties marred his school years with bad behavior and expulsion. Finally, his maternal aunt, Hortense McQuarrie Odlum (widow of financier Floyd B. Odlum and president of Bonwit Teller from 1934 to 1938), offered to pay his tuition to the San Diego Army and Navy Academy at Carlsbad-by-the-Sea, California. She convinced the headmaster that young Walker needed to find some activity which would demand his interest and build his confidence.

That activity turned out to be the lead in a school play which led to his being awarded the prize for best acting in a contest held at the Pasadena Playhouse. Encouraged, his aunt offered further financial support, and Walker enrolled at the American Academy of Dramatic Art in 1938. He was cast in a production of *The Barretts of Wimpole Street* at the AADA and quickly proceeded to fall in love with his Elizabeth, played by Phyllis Isley, whose later screen name was Jennifer Jones. Walker quit the school in order to make enough money for them to be married, but things were not so easy. After a short-lived job on a freighter, he returned to New York City, and she also quit the AADA to seek employment. At first the only work they could obtain was at Paul Gilmore's Cherry Lane Theatre in Greenwich Village, where they

752

earned fifty cents per performance.

Finally, she was offered a radio job in Tulsa, Oklahoma and managed to have Walker hired with her. After thirteen weeks there they were married (January 2, 1939), and with a blue convertible supplied by her parents, they honeymooned in Hollywood, seeking work in motion pictures. She got two parts at Republic, and Walker managed to secure three bits, one in United Artists's *Winter Carnival* (1939) and two at MGM, in *These Glamour Girls* (1939) and *Dancing Co-Ed* (1939). The couple were screen-tested by Paramount, but nothing materialized, and they returned to Manhattan. She went to work as a millinery model for the Powers Agency and Walker sought radio assignments, soon landing a regular post as Tad Smith on CBS' *Myrt and Marge*. In 1941 she auditioned in New York for David O. Selznick's screen version of *Claudia* (1943), and, after giving what she considered a bad reading, went into hysterics. Selznick witnessed this display and was curiously impressed. While he did not give her the part, he did put her under contract and sent her to study acting with Sanford Meisner. A year later he tested her again and accepted her for the lead in *The Song of Bernadette* (1943). Through his association with MGM (Selznick at the time was married to Louis B. Mayer's daughter, Irene), he obtained a contract for Walker at that studio.

For Walker's first role, MGM assigned him as the shy, young sailor who died in *Bataan* (1943), then wrongly cast him as a scientist in *Madame Curie* (1943). However, he hit his stride in his next film, *See Here, Private Hargrove*, displaying a charming insouciance as the cub reporter who is drafted into the Army. Being of slight build, he gave the characterization a put-upon sad sack presence, a quality which MGM's budding star Van Johnson was too hale and hearty to convey.

While Walker could begin to feel optimistic about his career, he was unable to be so about his personal life. His wife's career had been spectacularly launched with *Song of Bernadette*, and their marriage broke up because of her all-encompassing relationship with Selznick. Walker turned to drinking as his escape, disappearing several days at a time and once being arrested on a hit and run charge. With a logic that seemed only reasonable in Hollywood, he agreed to appear opposite his estranged wife in Selznick's paean to the war front at home, *Since You Went Away* (1944). Walker played the young soldier who, after flunking out of West Point, is killed at Salerno. The public readily identified with the martyrdom.

After a perfunctory role as the corporal in *Thirty Seconds over Tokyo* (1944), MGM gave him his finest part, in *The Clock* (1945), that of the soldier who meets and marries Judy Garland in New York during a forty-eight-hour pass.

Over the next three years, the turmoil of his personal life resulted in the deterioration of his screen career and his studio assignments were the visible results of its lack of confidence in him. Walker told Hedda Hopper, "The breakup with Jennifer gave me an excuse for amplifying my troubles. When I had a few drinks, I got to thinking about Poor Me and the broken home and all the et ceteras." In *Till the Clouds Roll By* (1946), where he played Jerome Kern, and in *Song of Love* (1947) where he was Johannes Brahms, the super productions allowed for no in-depth characterizations on his part. And while the role of the rebellious son of Katharine Hepburn in *The Sea of Grass* (1947) was interesting, the film did not click. He impulsively married director John Ford's daughter Barbara for a brief eight weeks; and, when arrested for drunk driving a short time later, Dore Schary, the new head of MGM, arranged for him to be admitted to the Menninger Clinic.

When Walker returned to the Culver City lot a year later he was quickly put to work in two skimmed-milk-type comedies *Please Believe Me* (1950) with Deborah Kerr and *The Skipper Surprised His Wife* (1950) opposite Warner Brothers' ex-ingenue, Joan Leslie. In the Western *Vengeance Valley* (1951) Walker did show some spunk as the slimy skunk, but Burt Lancaster as his more stable brother held the film together. MGM was happy to loan Walker to Warner Brothers for Alfred Hitchcock's *Strangers on a Train* (1951). He had the attention-getting role of the homosexual psychopath who enters into a pact with tennis player Farley Granger to commit murder. The film contained the best acting either performer ever did on the screen.

Walker's last screen part was as the Communist in Paramount's Red-baiting *My Son John* (1952). Although the major scenes had been completed, Walker did not live to finish it. It is said that outtakes from *Strangers on a Train* were spliced into the new picture to fill out the running time. He died (August 28, 1951) while two physicians tried to revive him with sodium amytol after a drinking bout. His ex-wife, the then Mrs. David O. Selznick, and his two sons, Robert, Jr. and Michael, did not attend the funeral. His two sons are currently pursuing acting careers of their own.

ROBERT WALKER

Winter Carnival (UA, 1939)
These Glamour Girls (MGM, 1939)
Dancing Co-Ed (MGM, 1939)
Bataan (MGM, 1943)

Madame Curie (MGM, 1943)
See Here, Private Hargrove (MGM, 1944)
Since You Went Away (UA, 1944)
Thirty Seconds over Tokyo (MGM, 1944)
The Clock (MGM, 1945)
Her Highness and the Bellboy (MGM, 1945)
What Next, Corporal Hargrove? (MGM, 1945)
The Sailor Takes a Wife (MGM, 1945)
Till the Clouds Roll By (MGM, 1946)
The Sea of Grass (MGM, 1947)
The Beginning or the End (MGM, 1947)
Song of Love (MGM, 1947)
One Touch of Venus (Universal, 1948)
Please Believe Me (MGM, 1950)
The Skipper Surprised His Wife (MGM, 1950)
Vengeance Valley (MGM, 1951)
Strangers on a Train (WB, 1951)
My Son John (Paramount, 1952)

With Judy Garland in *The Clock* (1945)

With Crane Whitley, William Hall, and Keenan Wynn in *What Next, Private Hargrove* (1945)

With Reginald Owen, June Allyson, and Audrey Totter in *The Sailor Takes a Wife* (1945)

With Warner Anderson in *The Beginning or the End* (1947)

Virginia Weidler

By the time Virginia Weidler joined MGM in 1938, she was a well-known juvenile screen personality. With her braided black hair, plain oval face, and funny pushing stride, she was never considered just cute in movie terms. For a time Paramount had groomed her as a moppet rival to Twentieth Century-Fox's Jane Withers. However, that studio never gave Virginia sufficient lead screen vehicles, and she was wilting on the professional vine when MGM hired her. She certainly was a more appealing performer than Warner Brothers' Sybil Jason or the free-lancing Edith Fellowes, but somehow Virginia was never at the right studio at the proper career time. She was a seasoned eleven years old when she joined Metro. By then she was too mature to inspire much audience laughter or tears as precocious Margaret O'Brien would soon do for MGM. And because she had such a slight musical comedy forte the roles available for her at MGM were singularly unrewarding. Above all, she could hardly compete with Judy Garland.

Virginia was born in Eagle Rock, California on March 21, 1927. Her mother was former German grand opera singer Margaret Theres Louisa. Her father, Alfred Weidler, was an architect. There were also three older brothers and two sisters. Virginia almost made her acting debut in John Barrymore's *Moby Dick* (1930), but her assigned screen scene required the tiny tot to remove her dress in front of the camera. She refused and was replaced. However, she did have a bit in Warner Baxter's *Surrender* (1931). A few years later she happened to be visiting one of her brothers who was acting in a RKO film. It developed that the youngster hired to play Constance Bennett's five-year-old niece in *After Tonight* (1933) had not arrived on the set on time. When it was learned that Virginia knew a smattering of French, she was given the role. Then, because her mother had taught her some German, she was hired for the West Coast stage production of *Autumn Crocus* with Francis Lederer, a romantic drama set in the Austrian Tyrol.

After such incidental film assignments as MGM's *Stamboul Quest* (1934), Virginia was cast as Europena, one of Pauline Lord's five children in *Mrs. Wiggs of the Cabbage Patch* (1934). Although W. C. Fields and Zasu Pitts were the comic highlights of this Paramount release, Virginia was sufficiently impressive in the picture to be signed to a studio contract. That film's director,

Norman Taurog, went on record as saying about the "charmingly homely" juvenile: "Virginia's case is hopeless. All she can do is act!"

Virginia quickly found her cinema forte as a rural type in two Gene Stratton Porter stories, *Laddie* and *Freckles*, both produced by RKO in 1935. Tom Brown had the lead in *Freckles*, set in the Indiana backwoods, but little Virginia did not go unnoticed. The N.Y. *Times* cited her as a "pocket-size edition of the machine-gunning Jane Withers." Because she excelled at mimicry, Virginia did an onscreen parody of Shirley Temple in *Freckles* that was right on the mark. In *Peter Ibbetson* (1935) Virginia played Ann Harding as a child, sharing scenes with Dickie Moore (he being Gary Cooper as a youngster).

It was in Paramount's sticky *Girl of the Ozarks* (1936) that Virginia had her first screen lead. She was cast as the poor white trash who is "adopted" by local newspaper publisher Leif Erikson. In Gary Cooper's *Souls at Sea* (1937) it was ship's passenger Virginia who accidentally knocked over a lamp and caused the vessel *William Brown* to go up in flames, while in *The Outcasts of Poker Flat* (1937) Virginia was seen as the "Luck of Roaring Camp." By 1938 it was evident that Paramount had no real star plans for Virginia. In *Scandal Street* the focus was on small town newcomer Louise Campbell, who has been fearfully maligned by her new neighbors. Virginia was just an impish moppet participating in local events such as dance lessons and the yearly recital. In her last Paramount picture, *Men with Wings* (1938), Virginia was merely seen in the introductory scenes playing Louise Campbell as a child. The studio had decided that eleven-year-old Virginia had outgrown her professional usefulness.

But other studios felt Virginia had additional screen life. At MGM she and Mickey Rooney were two waifs adopted by actress Gladys George in *Love Is a Headache* (1938). Later that year Virginia again proved her capacity to steal scenes from master craftsman Rooney in *Out West with the Hardys*, by using a lasso as an effective upstaging prop. MGM put her under contract, but loaned her out for most of 1939. She was in RKO's *The Spellbinder* with Lee Tracy as a shyster lawyer, and was one of John Barrymore's children in *The Great Man Votes*. She supported Gloria Jean in Universal's *The Under-Pup*. In Columbia's *The Lone Wolf Spy Hunt* she was cast as Warren William's precocious child who helps her sleuth dad capture an espionage ring operating in Washington, D. C. Back at Metro she was cast as Norma Shearer's daughter in *The Women*.

Virginia settled in at MGM in 1940 with the lead in *Bad Little Angel*. The story was set in the 1870s, and she was a runaway orphan who has a completely unshakable belief in God. Again she was another orphan, this time out West, in *Henry Goes Arizona* (1940), starring Frank Morgan as a blowhard vaudeville performer. She was one of Mary Nash's more outspoken children in *Gold Rush Maisie* (1940). However, her two attention-grabbing assignments that year were Mickey Rooney's imaginative sister in *Young Tom Edison* and the yo-yo bouncing younger sister of Katharine Hepburn in *The Philadelphia*

Story. For Warners she played Charles Boyer's eldest child in *All This and Heaven Too*, and *Parents Magazine* named Virginia the outstanding juvenile star of 1940.

Whatever value MGM attached to Virginia's presence in its products, her value diminished when awkward teenager Shirley Temple signed a Metro contract. MGM obviously had the full intention of promoting her into the same league as the studio's prized Mickey Rooney and Judy Garland. *Kathleen* (1941) had been purchased as a vehicle for Virginia, but when Temple refused to play Wallace Beery's sappy daughter in the programmer *Barnacle Bill* (1941), Virginia was saddled with that unrewarding assignment, while Temple was assigned to *Kathleen*, which turned out none too well anyway. That same year Virginia was in the lesser production *I'll Wait for You*, playing the daughter of Henry Travers and Fay Holden. However, most of the screen action focused on "sister" Marsha Hunt and her romance with former gangster Robert Sterling. By this point Virginia succumbed to the Baby Jane syndrome and took voice lessons from MGM coach Al Siegel. In *Babes on Broadway* (1941) she had a few opportunities to join in song and to dance a jitterbug. As head of the charity drive to get the tenement kids to the country in this Busby Berkeley musical, she had some screen time, but the picture was mainly a showcase for the diversified antics of Mickey Rooney and Judy Garland.

Virginia was then reteamed with young tap dancer Ray MacDonald who had shown promise in *Babes on Broadway*. They were costarred in *Born to Sing* (1942), but the show business yarn was a minor league effort and sorely required the presence of Rooney and Garland for whom it had originally been concocted. Virginia and MacDonald sang the ballad "Lovely Nights," but no cinematic sparks flew. *The Youngest Profession* (1943) was MGM's last effort to bolster Virginia's screen career. The story was originally planned for Judy Garland and then Kathryn Grayson, but each of these stars had matured too obviously before the film could be put into production. Virginia was seen as the young Miss Fixit, a girl with a penchant for collecting stars' autographs and for solving dad's domestic problems. The film played Radio City Music Hall, but it was the novelty presence onscreen of Lana Turner, Walter Pidgeon, Greer Garson, Robert Taylor, and William Powell which sold this slim vehicle. In *Best Foot Forward* (1943) Lucille Ball was the movie star who comes to a small town school dance on a publicity lark. Her presence causes Virginia to lose her date. Virginia appeared in this musical with an unbecoming upsweep hairdo. The film's snappiest lines went to Nancy Walker, while June Allyson and Gloria DeHaven provided the musical highlights.

By the time *Best Foot Forward* was released, Virginia was on a vaudeville tour doing a song-and-dance turn. She sang in her husky voice "What Do They Think I Am—a Baby?" and did a parody of Virginia O'Brien's deadpan style rendition of "Rock-a-Bye Baby." After that promotion tour, Virginia and MGM ended their contractual ties, because she claimed that she wanted time to try Broadway. She did make her stage debut in *The Rich Full Life*, which opened at the John Golden Theatre on November 10, 1945. She played the daughter of a distraught Judith Evelyn. The show closed after 27 performances. Soon afterward, Virginia retired from show business. She later married and had two sons.

Little was heard of Virginia until July 1, 1968, when at the age of forty she died of a heart attack. She was so forgotten in show business circles that her obituary went unreported in most newspapers.

VIRGINIA WEIDLER

Surrender (Fox, 1931)
After Tonight (RKO, 1933)
Long Lost Father (RKO, 1934)
Stamboul Quest (MGM, 1934)
Mrs. Wiggs of the Cabbage Patch (Paramount, 1934)
Laddie (RKO, 1935)
Freckles (RKO, 1935)
Big Broadcast of 1936 (Paramount, 1935)
Peter Ibbetson (Paramount, 1935)
Timothy's Quest (Paramount, 1936)
Trouble for Two (MGM, 1936)
Girl of the Ozarks (Paramount, 1936)
Big Broadcast of 1937 (Paramount, 1936)
Maid of Salem (Paramount, 1937)
The Outcasts of Poker Flat (RKO, 1937)
Souls at Sea (Paramount, 1937)
Scandal Street (Paramount, 1938)
Love Is a Headache (MGM, 1938)
Mother Carey's Chickens (RKO, 1938)
Men with Wings (Paramount, 1938)
Too Hot to Handle (MGM, 1938)
Out West with the Hardys (MGM, 1938)
The Great Man Votes (RKO, 1939)
The Under-Pup (Universal, 1939)
Fixer Dugan (RKO, 1939)
The Rookie Cop (RKO, 1939)
The Spellbinder (RKO, 1939)
The Women (MGM, 1939)
The Lone Wolf Spy Hunt (Columbia, 1939)
Bad Little Angel (MGM, 1940)
Henry Goes Arizona (MGM, 1940)
Young Tom Edison (MGM, 1940)

With Ann Sothern in *Gold Rush Maisie* (1940)

All This and Heaven Too (WB, 1940)
Gold Rush Maisie (MGM, 1940)
The Philadelphia Story (MGM, 1940)
I'll Wait for You (MGM, 1941)
Barnacle Bill (MGM, 1941)
Keeping Company (MGM, 1941)
Babes on Broadway (MGM, 1941)
This Time for Keeps (MGM, 1942)
Born to Sing (MGM, 1942)
The Affairs of Martha (MGM, 1942)
The Youngest Profession (MGM, 1943)
Best Foot Forward (MGM, 1943)

Johnny Weissmuller

There have been over a dozen screen Tarzans, but the public invariably associates Johnny Weissmuller with the cinema jungle man characterization. He lasted the longest with the role (1932–1948), possibly because he looked like what the public imagined Edgar Rice Burrough's hero to be, with his leonine head and formidable athletic physique. Besides, Weissmuller made his jungle man a likable, strong and simple popular hero.

Peter John Weissmuller was born in Windber, Pennsylvania on June 2, 1904 and was educated at the University of Chicago. He reputedly took up swimming at án early age because he was a physically weak child. He became a member of the Illinois Athletic Club and gained an unprecedented, record-breaking reputation as the world's best swimmer. He thrived on competition, the teamwork involved, and the exultation of winning. In the course of the 1924 and the 1928 Olympics, he won five gold medals, a record that was not equaled until 1968. He established 67 world records, won 52 national championships, achievements which brought him international popularity as a sports star. He traveled with professional swimming and water shows, appeared in a series of Grantland Rice short subjects, and made his motion picture feature film debut as an Adonis figure, clad in a fig leaf, in *Glorifying the American Girl* at Paramount.

MGM had experienced great success with an African-lensed jungle tale, *Trader Horn* (1931), and studio head Louis B. Mayer ordered his wunderkind Irving Thalberg to come up with a similar followup vehicle. Thalberg optioned two of Edgar Rice Burroughs' Tarzan stories and the search for an appropriate lead was started. Director W. S. Van Dyke stated, "What I want is a man who is young, strong, well-built, reasonably attractive, but not necessarily handsome, and a competent actor." Among those considered were Charles Bickford, Johnny Mack Brown, Clark Gable, Joel McCrea, and Tom Tyler. MGM had almost settled on Herman Brix (later Bruce Bennett) for the assignment, but the all-American football star and Olympic shotput champion broke his shoulder while working on a Paramount film. Therefore, when Cyril Hume, working on the adaptation of *Tarzan the Ape Man*, noticed Weissmuller swimming in a Hollywood hotel pool, he suggested Weissmuller for the assignment. The swimmer was agreeable to the project, but he had a prior contract with the BVD company to publicize their swimwear and underwear products. Part of the agreement which released Weissmuller to MGM required that several of Metro's stars had to pose in BVD swimwear. Among those who were later used by BVD were Joan Crawford, Jean Harlow, and Marie Dressler, a full gamut of the MGM female star roster.

MGM's contract with Weissmuller started him at $500 weekly with escalation clauses up to $2,000 and more. The studio billed him as "the only man in Hollywood who's natural in the flesh and can act without clothes." Recalling his early Tarzan work, Weissmuller has said, "I went to the back lot at MGM, they gave me a G string and said, 'Can you climb a tree? Can you pick up a girl?' I could do all that, and I did all my own swinging because I had been a YMCA champion on the rings." As he did that swinging, he emitted a bloodcurdling clarion call, "aaaaaeeeeeoooooo!"

The first MGM entry was *Tarzan the Ape Man* (1932), and it contained some on-location photography, the only Metro Tarzan picture to do so. With the success of this picture, MGM withdrew all its caution about accepting the swimmer into its family of stars and, as a true member of the studio stable, he was required to make personal appearances and to toe the line with his private life, even so far as divorcing his second wife, singer Bobbie Arnst. Reportedly, the studio paid her $10,000 to become the ex-Mrs.Weissmuller. Not long after, Weissmuller met sometime Metro player Lupe Velez and the disparate couple wed in 1933 and went through five years of a stormy marriage and headlines, before they finally divorced in 1938.

Although other Hollywood producers in the 1930s churned out Tarzanlike features, Metro's and Weissmuller's versions were the big boxoffice attractions. As the decade wore on, the Metro Tarzan pictures became more geared for children. Thus it was with some shock that MGM executives viewed the third Weissmuller entry, *The Capture of Tarzan*, which had been completed in late 1935. It was decided that there were just too many horrific episodes in the film, and the picture was reshot and retitled *Tarzan Escapes* (1936). When Maureen O'Sullivan demanded the studio withdraw her from the jungle series, the entry *Tarzan in Exile* had her killed off, with an orphaned boy (Johnny Sheffield) on hand to be Tarzan's new companion in adventure. However, public reaction was so strong to the untimely demise of Jane that the picture had to have a new ending shot which allowed O'Sullivan to live, and the revised version, *Tarzan Finds a Son* (1939), was released to an appeased public.

In ten years MGM had used Weissmuller only in four Tarzan features, afraid to damage his screen image. But once into the 1940s, MGM began losing interest in the series, particularly since its foreign market was nearly cut off, a source which originally had contributed nearly half of the series' profits. Thus Weissmuller was tossed into two Tarzan entries within a year. With *Tarzan's New York Adventure* (1942), Metro had used up all its optioned Edgar Rice Burroughs–Tarzan film rights, and they decided to drop the property. Weissmuller's studio option was allowed to drop, and he moved over to RKO where producer Sol Lesser had reestablished his Tarzan headquarters. The swimmer made five more Tarzan pictures before it was decided that he was getting too old and heavy to be swinging from the vines anymore. With *Tarzan and the Mermaids* (1948) Lesser announced that, by mutual agreement, he and Weissmuller had parted company.

During the 1940s Weissmuller had made only two non-Tarzan appearances—a guest spot in *Stage Door Canteen* and a low-budget Paramount picture, *Swamp Fire* (1946). With the latter film he hoped to prove he could be more than just a screen Tarzan, but the public was indifferent to the mediocre product and to Weissmuller's haphazard characterization. But quickie-film producer Sam Katzman perceived there was still boxoffice life left in Weissmuller, and offered the beefy ex-Tarzan a percentage of the gross to star in a new series, *Jungle Jim,* based on Alex Raymond's comic strip. Between 1948 and 1955 Weissmuller stalled through sixteen of these programmers, all photographed hastily on Columbia's backlot. Unlike the early MGM Tarzan films, none of these entries boasted quality scripts, direction, photography, or supporting casts. Weissmuller then moved into television production with a Jungle Jim series, which was equally profitable for the ex-MGM star. After a twelve-year absence from oncamera appearances, he returned to the screen for a brief spot with Maureen O'Sullivan in the abortive *The Phynx* (1970).

In the 1960s the city of Ft. Lauderdale, Florida invited Weissmuller to come to that city as spokesman for, and first honorary member of, their Swimming Pool Hall of Fame. Since that time he has made Ft. Lauderdale his home and base for his many business enterprises. He heads the Johnny Weissmuller Swimming Pool Company, and is a partner in a franchising business called Johnny Weissmuller's Jungle Hut, Inc., which licenses such diverse ventures as Johnny Weissmuller Natural Food Stores, Safari: Hut Gift Shops, and Ungawa Club Lounges.

Weissmuller has been married and divorced five times: Camilla Louier, Bobbie Arnst, Lupe Velez, Beryle Scott, and Allene Gates. He was wed to Miss Gates from 1948 to 1962, and they had three children, Wendy, John, and Heidi. John, Jr. made a brief splash as an actor in *Andy Hardy Comes Home* (1958).

The Tarzan and Jungle Jim movies, despite recent protests about the pictures' racial aspersions, are perennial television movie fare, and have netted him $200,000 annually (particularly from the Jungle Jim entries). He still receives some 200 letters a week from new young fans, from such diverse locales as Hong Kong and Rumania. He wrote a none-too-lucid autobiography in 1967 entitled *Water, World and Weissmuller.* He seems to have forgotten a fourth "W": Wives!

With Herbert Mundin and Maureen O'Sullivan in *Tarzan Escapes* (1936)

JOHNNY WEISSMULLER

Glorifying the American Girl (Paramount, 1929)

Tarzan the Ape Man (MGM, 1932)

Tarzan and His Mate (MGM, 1934)

Tarzan Escapes (MGM, 1936)

Tarzan Finds a Son (MGM, 1939)

Tarzan's Secret Treasure (MGM, 1941)

Tarzan's New York Adventure (MGM, 1942)

Tarzan Triumphs (RKO, 1943)

Stage Door Canteen (UA, 1943)

With Cheta, Johnny Sheffield, and Maureen O'Sullivan in *Tarzan's Secret Treasure* (1941)

Tarzan's Desert Mystery (RKO, 1943)

Tarzan and the Amazons (RKO, 1945)

Tarzan and the Leopard Women (RKO, 1946)

Swamp Fire (Paramount, 1946)

Tarzan and the Huntress (RKO, 1947)

Tarzan and the Mermaids (RKO, 1948)

Jungle Jim (Columbia, 1948)

The Lost Tribe (Columbia, 1949)

Captive Girl (Columbia, 1950)

Mark of the Gorilla (Columbia, 1950)

Pygmy Island (Columbia, 1950)

Fury of the Congo (Columbia, 1951)

Jungle Manhunt (Columbia, 1951)

Jungle Jim and the Forbidden Land (Columbia, 1952)

Voodoo Tiger (Columbia, 1952)

Savage Mutiny (Columbia, 1953)

Valley of the Headhunters (Columbia, 1953)

Killer Ape (Columbia, 1953)

Jungle Man-Eaters (Columbia, 1954)

Cannibal Attack (Columbia, 1954)

Jungle Moon Men (Columbia, 1955)

Devil Goddess (Columbia, 1955)

The Phynx (WB, 1970)

James Whitmore

When a solidly talented performer is at best attractively homely—and this was years before the virile ugliness of Charles Bronson types became popular—it is difficult to lift a film career beyond character roles. But to have the additional burden of being branded a new edition of an already established screen star at the same studio is professionally disastrous. MGM viewed James Whitmore as the 1950s answer to its cantankerous screen veteran, Spencer Tracy, and for two years sought to groom Whitmore into this image, particularly emphasizing his rugged homely qualities. The graft did not take and, by 1954, Whitmore was out on his own, fending for craggy character roles in a wide variety of undistinguished pictures.

James Allen Whitmore, Jr. was born in White Plains, N.Y. on April 1, 1921, but grew up in Buffalo where his father was chairman of that city's Park Commission (a post he held until he was eighty-two). Whitmore graduated from the private Choate School and then went to Yale University where he was cofounder of the school's radio station. Just before graduation he joined the Marines and received his degree while in boot camp. After leaving the service he toured with the USO in *The Milky Way* (1946) and the following year worked in stock at the Petersboro Players in New Hampshire. That fall he studied at the American Theatre Wing in Manhattan, where he was spotted in a class play by Flora Roberts, then secretary to producer Kermit Bloomgarden. She suggested him for an audition in her employer's new show, *Command Decision* (1947), and he made his Broadway debut as Sgt. Harold Evans. For his performance he received the Tony Awards' best newcomer medal, and also won a Donaldson award. (In MGM's film version of *Command Decision*, Van Johnson had Whitmore's role.) Also in 1947, Whitmore wed Nancy Mygatt and they had three sons: James (1948), Stephen (1950), and Daniel (1952).

On the basis of *Command Decision*, Whitmore received several Hollywood offers. For his screen debut he was cast as the low comedy foil–assistant of tax detective Glenn Ford in Columbia's *The Undercover Man* (1949). That same year he appeared in the first of his Metro features. He was the veteran topkick in Dore Schary's *Battleground*. Whitmore was Oscar-nominated but lost in the best supporting actor's category to Dean Jagger who won for his role in another war picture, *Twelve O'Clock High.*

Metro employed Whitmore in five 1950 releases. After playing a bodyguard stooge in *Please Believe Me*, he was Sterling Hayden's punk sidekick in *The Asphalt Jungle*, and then was sandwiched into the Western *The Outriders.* Then he starred in the bizarre, uncommercial modern miracle parable, *The Next Voice You Hear.* As Joe Smith, American, he played the embittered father who believes God is the voice broadcasting on radio. The propaganda film was not successful, nor did his next picture do what the studio hoped. He was teamed with the "equally unglamorous" Marjorie Main in *Mrs. O'Malley and Mr. Malone.* He played a harebrained Chicago lawyer involved in a train murder caper with radio prize winner Main. It was to be the pilot for a film series, but the studio failed to give it a proper budget, and the film disappeared on the double bill market.

In *It's a Big Country* (1951) he was in the train sketch with William Powell, and then had an uncredited spot in Clark Gable's *Across the Wide Missouri.* Metro lost interest in Whitmore after this, assigning him to what were virtual character roles: the top sergeant to Mario Lanza in *Because You're Mine* (1952), a hobo pearl gatherer in *All the Brothers Were Valiant* (1953), a jovial hood in *Kiss Me Kate!* (1953), and as backup to Red Skelton in the mediocre *The Great Diamond Robbery* (1953), Whitmore's final MGM picture.

Still in his early thirties, Whitmore was forced into accepting character parts on a free-lance basis: an army sergeant in the Cinemascope Western *The Command* (1954), a New Mexico state trooper in the science fiction *Them* (1954), Sgt. Mac in *Battle Cry* (1955), Alan Ladd's pal and superior officer in *The McConnell Story* (1955), and Tyrone Power's good old friend and band manager in *The Eddy Duchin Story* (1956). His role as a convict who forces orphan Sal Mineo to help him escape in *The Young Don't Cry* (1957) had some meat to it, but the picture itself was flat.

Throughout the 1950s Whitmore participated in stage work, particularly at the La Jolla Summer Theatre in such plays as *The Rainmaker* (1954) and *The Skin of Our Teeth* (1957). He did *The Summer of the 17th Doll* (1958) in stock, and was on Broadway in *Winesburg, Ohio* (1959) with Dorothy McGuire.

He has frequently guested on television shows, but had always refused to star in any series (he turned down *Gunsmoke*). Then in 1960 he was topcast as the impassioned attorney in *The Law and Mr. Jones*, which struggled through most of one season, was cancelled, and then briefly reprieved due to audience writeins. Nine years later he was costarred in the quick-loser *My Friend Tony*, portraying a criminologist.

Whitmore's recent film career has been spotty at best. He was the ulcer-weary Federal agent in Dean Martin's *Who Was That Lady?* (1960), and turned up as the white writer who turns himself negroid in *Black Like Me* (1964). He was a numbskull cavalry captain in *Waterhole 3* (1967) and disguised behind a simian costume as the president of the assembly in *Planet of the Apes* (1968). He was the chief police inspector in *Madigan* (1968), a knife-wielding member in *Guns of the Magnificent Seven* (1969), and was Admiral Halsey in *Tora! Tora! Tora!* (1970).

The stage has proven to be Whitmore's solace. He performed with Barbara Barrie in a concert-reading version of Walt Whitman's *Leaves of Grass* in the mid-1960s, performed in the premiere of Evan Hunter's *Conjuror* (1969) at Ann Arbor, and then embarked on a road tour of the one-man show, *Will Rogers' U.S.A.* An abbreviated version of this well-received production was televised in March 1972. A two-record LP set of this Whitmore vehicle, has also been marketed.

Already in his fifties, Whitmore again ventured into the lucrative teleseries field. For the 1972–1973 season he starred in *Temperatures Rising,* cast as a con man doctor working with a young intern, black actor Cleavon Little, in a hospital setting. It was not the artistic challenge Whitmore has always sought, but this video venture insured his standing as a well-known character performer—that is until the show's producers decided to replace him in the 1973-74 season with veteran antic man Paul Lynde. Such are the ups and downs of show business.

JAMES WHITMORE

The Undercover Man (Columbia, 1949)
Battleground (MGM, 1949)
Please Believe Me (MGM, 1950)
The Asphalt Jungle (MGM, 1950)
The Outriders (MGM, 1950)
The Next Voice You Hear (MGM, 1950)
Mrs. O'Malley and Mr. Malone (MGM, 1950)
It's a Big Country (MGM, 1951)
Across the Wide Missouri (MGM, 1951)*
Shadow in the Sky (MGM, 1951)
Because You're Mine (MGM, 1952)
Above and Beyond (MGM, 1952)
Kiss Me, Kate! (MGM, 1953)
The Girl Who Had Everything (MGM, 1953)
All the Brothers Were Valiant (MGM, 1953)
The Great Diamond Robbery (MGM, 1953)
The Command (WB, 1954)
Them (WB, 1954)
Battle Cry (WB, 1955)
The McConnell Story (WB, 1955)
The Last Frontier (Columbia, 1955)

Oklahoma! (Magna, 1956)
Crime in the Streets (AA, 1956)
The Eddy Duchin Story (Columbia, 1956)
The Young Don't Cry (Columbia, 1957)
The Deep Six (WB, 1958)
The Restless Years (Universal, 1958)
Face of Fire (AA, 1959)
Who Was That Lady? (Columbia, 1960)
Black Like Me (Continental, 1964)
Chuka (Paramount, 1967)
Waterhole 3 (Paramount, 1967)
Nobody's Perfect (Universal, 1968)
Planet of the Apes (20th-Fox, 1968)
Madigan (Universal, 1968)
The Split (MGM, 1968)
Guns of the Magnificent Seven (UA, 1969)
Tora! Tora! Tora! (20th-Fox, 1970)
Chato's Land (UA, 1972)
The Harrad Experiment (Cinema Arts, 1973)
Calling Crime Command (Italian, 1974)

*Uncredited

With Nancy Davis and Gary Gray in *The Next Voice You Hear* (1950)

Dame May Whitty

If anyone set an established dignified British tone for MGM films made during World War II, it was Dame May Whitty. Anglophilic Louis B. Mayer thrived on the authentic English air she brought to his productions. Dame May was past seventy years of age when she made the first of her twenty-six features, but she quickly demonstrated in her quiet way that she was a very resourceful actress (everything that the more forceful Mary Forbes in early 1930s films had not been). As the British counterpart to or combination of Lucile Watson, Elizabeth Patterson, Jane Darwell, and Edna May Oliver, Dame May was much in demand as a featured player because she could immediately set the mood for audiences with just a quick oncamera appearance.

Dame May Whitty was born in Liverpool, England on June 19, 1865, the daughter of British journalist Alfred Whitty. She was educated privately and made her stage bow at the age of sixteen in the chorus of *The Mountain Sylph* at the Court Theatre in Liverpool. Her London stage debut was in 1882 in *Boccacio*. She was already a seasoned performer when she wed actor Ben Webster in 1892 (they had a daughter Margaret, born in 1905) and in 1895 first came to the United States on tour with Sir Henry Irving and his company. For her philanthropic services during World War I she was made a Dame in 1918, the third actress to that date to receive the Order of the British Empire. (Years later, when she was in a Broadway play, the elderly stage door keeper threatened to knock down a visitor who had the audacity to call "our Miss Whitty a dame.") She was busy on both sides of the Atlantic throughout the 1920s and, in 1932, was on Broadway with Herbert Marshall and Edna Best in *There's Always Juliet*. When she was offered a costarring role in Emlyn Williams' new play *Night Must Fall* (1935), she very reluctantly accepted the part: "It's just a thriller and won't run, and the part is an old beast in a wheelchair, but I'd better do it." The play was a great success in England and was restaged on Broadway with both Dame May and Williams re-creating their roles to equal acclaim.

Robert Montgomery had requested MGM to purchase *Night Must Fall* as a screen vehicle for him. MGM offered Dame May a contract to come to Hollywood, but she was most reluctant to tread into the uncertain world of

768

filmmaking. In fact, she had booked passage back to England on the liner *Queen Mary* when the Broadway version closed, and the studio's agent had to run on and off the ocean vessel, communicating Dame May's latest demands to studio officials via an onshore pay phone. Finally, she was persuaded and did go to Hollywood, and won an Oscar nomination for playing the stupid old lady who allows psychopathic killer Montgomery to charm his way into her household. That same year she was the old medium in *The Thirteenth Chair* (done later on television with Ethel Barrymore) and was Napoleon's (Charles Boyer) mother in *Conquest*, all for MGM.

After appearing as the motherly aunt to fickle Joan Bennett in *I Met My Love Again* (1938), Dame May had her finest screen role in Alfred Hitchcock's British-filmed thriller, *The Lady Vanishes* (1938). She was charming old Miss Froy who mysteriously disappears on a train, while bound home for England. It develops that she is a British counterespionage agent, and it takes most of the picture's 97 minutes for Margaret Lockwood and Michael Redgrave to rescue her. The concluding scene, set in a Scotland Yard office, contains one of the screen's rarest moments of magic. Lockwood and Redgrave rush into an inspector's office where Dame May has just delivered the secret coded message to the authorities (a few bars of a folk song which she plays on the piano). The young couple enter and are just as surprised as the audience to see Dame May alive and well. The old lady rises from the piano bench with a look of pure joy radiating from her eyes. It is a look every bit as exquisite as the closeup of the ocean-traveling Greta Garbo at the conclusion of *Queen Christina*.

Approaching her seventy-fifth birthday, Dame May was asked if she thought of retiring: "Quit? Only the aged and infirm quit, and I am neither. So long as I can do my bit, I'll keep right on doing it."

Dame May continued to add her British presence to a rash of pictures: as the acidulous old aunt in the remake of *A Bill of Divorcement* (1940), Joan Fontaine's mother in *Suspicion* (1941), and Lady Stackhouse, the grandmother of air cadet John Sutton in the Technicolor production, *Thunder Birds* (1942). (She spent most of her few onscreen moments in that minipicture riding to the hounds and writing letters to Winston Churchill, all manufactured to show Sutton's very, very British upbringing.) In MGM's overenthusiastic paean to England, democracy, and mother love, *Mrs. Miniver* (1942), Dame May was Lady Beldon, the lofty grandmother of Teresa Wright and the imperious competitor of stationmaster Henry Travers in the village's yearly flower competition. She was again Oscar-nominated, but lost to Teresa Wright in the best supporting actress category.

With World War II at its height in 1943, Dame May was at the peak of her film productivity, with seven releases for four different studios that year: ranging from such trivia, as Lana Turner's *Slightly Dangerous*, in which Dame May played an old nurse named Baba, to such altruistic productions as *Stage Door Canteen* and *Forever and a Day*. She was a dowager in *Flesh and Fantasy* and in *The Constant Nymph*, but turned in a subtly shaded comic performance as Tyrone Power's patrician grandmother who approves of Anne Baxter in *Crash Dive*. In the highly commercial *Lassie Come Home* she was the more down-to-earth Dolly, with her real husband Ben Webster playing her onscreen spouse; and in *Madame Curie* she was Walter Pidgeon's mother who dies of cancer.

In *The White Cliffs of Dover* (1944) she essayed the loving old governess Nanny, while, in contrast, she played the wealthy, garrulous Thornton Square neighbor of Ingrid Bergman in *Gaslight* (1944).

Dame May had returned to Broadway in 1941 to appear in *The Trojan Women* and in 1945 costarred with Eva Le Gallienne, playing the wheelchair-ridden lady in *Therese*. It was directed by Dame May's daughter Margaret who had gained a sizable stage reputation herself, particularly with the plays of Shakespeare. Dame May's sole 1945 picture was *My Name Is Julia Ross*, a neat little thriller, with Dame May and her screen son George Macready attempting to manipulate the life of secretary Nina Foch for devious ends. In the much-delayed release of *Devotion* (1946) Dame May was the attentive aunt of the Brontë girls (Olivia de Havilland, Nancy Coleman, and Ida Lupino). But her yearly production quota bounced back with three 1947 films: the role of the retired equestrian star grandmother of Esther Williams in *This Time for Keeps*, the wise mother superior in *Green Dolphin Street*, and the made-to-order role of the elderly villager from Penny Green, England who takes Janet Leigh into her home as a companion when her son is drafted into World War II in *If Winter Comes*. Hers was only a small part in Columbia's *The Sign of the Ram* (1948). She and Alexander Knox were among those coping with the machinations of wheelchair-bound Susan Peters. Dame May's last picture was the fantasy, *The Return of October* (1948), in which she was cast as Aunt Martha to Terry Moore's lead.

In January, 1948 Metro had assigned Dame May to a principal role in *Julia Misbehaves* (1948), but she became ill and had to be replaced by Lucile Watson. Dame May died on May 29, 1948 at the age of eighty-two. (Her husband had died in 1947.) Instead of flowers being sent to the funeral, her will requested that CARE packages be sent to England. C. Aubrey Smith, Edmund Gwenn, Herbert Marshall, Boris Karloff, Brian Aherne, Alexander Knox, and John Van Druten were among the Hollywood British colony friends who spoke words of tribute at the funeral.

In 1969, Dame May's daughter (who died in 1972) published her autobiographical account, *The Same Only Different,* tracing the stage careers of her parents and herself with her typical sense of humor and modesty. Dame May once summed up her long acting years as a bit of "variety and sandwiches."

DAME MAY WHITTY

With Robert Montgomery and Rosalind Russel in *Night Must Fall* (1937)

Night Must Fall (MGM, 1937)
The Thirteenth Chair (MGM, 1937)
Conquest (MGM, 1937)
I Met My Love Again (UA, 1938)
The Lady Vanishes (Gaumont–British, 1938)

Raffles (UA, 1940)
A Bill of Divorcement (RKO, 1940)
One Night in Lisbon (Paramount, 1941)
Suspicion (RKO, 1941)
Mrs. Miniver (MGM, 1942)
Thunder Birds (20th-Fox, 1942)
Slightly Dangerous (MGM, 1943)
Forever and a Day (RKO, 1943)
Crash Dive (20th-Fox, 1943)
The Constant Nymph (WB, 1943)
Lassie Come Home (MGM, 1943)
Madame Curie (MGM, 1943)
Stage Door Canteen (UA, 1943)
The White Cliffs of Dover (MGM, 1944)
Gaslight (MGM, 1944)
My Name Is Julia Ross (Columbia, 1945)
Devotion (WB, 1946)
This Time for Keeps (MGM, 1947)
Green Dolphin Street (MGM, 1947)
If Winter Comes (MGM, 1947)
The Sign of the Ram (Columbia, 1948)
The Return of October (Columbia, 1948)

With Ingrid Bergman in *Gaslight* (1944)

Esther Williams

Esther Williams was to MGM what Sonja Henie had been to Twentieth Century-Fox—an athletically talented woman who for a virtual decade brought countless filmgoers to theatres. With her eighteen apple-pie-on-water escapist motion pictures, she racked up some $80 million at the boxoffice between 1944 and 1955. Where Henie had glided across the ice and was surrounded by romantic leading men, MGM took their statuesque champion swimmer and put her into a tank of heated water, decorated it a la Hollywood baroque, lighted it, and had her perform aquatic ballets to Busby Berkeley routines. No one ever pretended she was an actress, least of all Esther: "I can't act, I can't sing, I can't dance. My pictures are put together out of scraps they find in the producer's wastebasket." But her swimming technique was as fascinating to watch as Fred Astaire's dance routines. And just to make sure that audiences did not become restless with Esther's H_2O virtuosity, her pictures were decked out in Technicolor, beautiful offbeat resort backdrops, and a variety of guest supporting performers, ranging from Jimmy Durante and Lauritz Melchior to the bands of Tommy Dorsey and Xavier Cugat.

Esther was born in the Inglewood suburb of Los Angeles on August 8, 1921, and her mother said she could swim before she could walk. Esther's mother was a member of the Inglewood Board of Education and helped raise funds for that neighborhood school's swimming pool. It was there that Esther, at the age of eight, got her first job, counting towels. (After counting each one hundred towels, she was allowed to swim free of charge in the pool for one hour.) Her swimming lessons preempted all other childhood interests and, as a part of the audience at the 1932 Olympics in Los Angeles, she set her sights on becoming a member of that Olympic team. She won several local swimming championships and, after earning the Pacific Coast Championship, she was signed for the Olympics, to be held in Finland in 1940.

She practiced diligently at the Los Angeles Athletic Club with Olympic champion Aileen Allen, only to have her dream shattered when World War II erupted and the Olympics were cancelled. Dejected, she turned to college for a while, attending the University of Southern California. While there, the attentions of a premedical student, Leonard Kovner, interested her, more than any of her academic studies. She quit school to take a job as a stock clerk and part-time model at the I. Magnin retail store. Entrepreneur Billy Rose saw her and offered her a $40 weekly contract to replace Eleanor Holm in his San Francisco Aquacade. The shrewd Esther countered with a proposal that Billy costar her with that show's Johnny Weissmuller and pay her $150 a week. Rose agreed, and it was at the Aquacade that MGM executives got their first look at their future swimming star. Thinking they could use Esther in much the same way Twentieth Century-Fox had exploited Sonja Henie, they offered her a screen test. But Esther turned them down, and quit the Aquacade to become Mrs. Leonard Kovner.

MGM persisted, and about a year later she agreed to test. In October 1941 she signed a contract and looked forward to swimming again. However, the first role the studio offered her was a straight lead opposite Clark Gable in *Somewhere I'll Find You* (1942). Gable liked her and agreed to Esther being in the picture. To most starlets this would have been like dying and going to that big movie screen up there in the sky, but Esther had her head together and said, "I am a swimmer, not an actress." So Lana Turner got the part, which had been planned for her all along. MGM had been piqued at Turner for running off to marry Stephen Crane, and they dangled this role in front of her as an enticement to return to the fold.

Thus Esther's screen debut was in *Andy Hardy's Double Life* (1942). She did get to swim and received her first screen kiss from Mickey Rooney. Scenes from this pictures would be interpolated into a flashback in *Andy Hardy Comes Home* (1958). Her next role, however, was a nonswimming one, as the girl friend of Van Johnson, in the very popular *A Guy Named Joe* (1943), starring Spencer Tracy and Irene Dunne. This was the first of five pictures she would do with Johnson, and when this film was rereleased to theatres in 1955, she and Johnson received star billing in the advertisements.

After a proper publicity buildup, as only MGM could afford to do, Esther was soon a pinup favorite with the G.I.s, and advanced to full-fledged stardom in the color production, *Bathing Beauty* (1944), with Red Skelton and Ethel Smith. She was showcased in a John Murray Anderson water spectacle in that film. Her underwater ballet in *Ziegfeld Follies* (1946) was directed in 1945 by Vincente Minnelli, and the same year she was starred with Van Johnson in *Thrill of a Romance* (1945) as, of course, a swimming instructor at a resort who falls for recuperating serviceman Johnson. This Joe Pasternak production had the further distinction of introducing Metropolitan Opera star Lauritz Melchior to the public.

Then MGM foolishly put her into another straight role, as a newspaper gal enamored of a journalist who has become a con artist, William Powell in *The Hoodlum Saint* (1946). The film was an artistic mistake for all concerned. A much better role followed in *Easy to Wed* (1946), a remake of Jean Harlow's *Libeled Lady*. Esther played the heiress, but this time in water, and she was surrounded by Van Johnson, Lucille Ball, Keenan Wynn, Latin music, and Ethel Smith at the organ. Like *Thrill of a Romance*, it grossed $4.5 million in receipts. After a guest stint in *Till the Clouds Roll By* (1946), Metro gave her above-the-title billing in *Fiesta* (1947), where a rather confused plot had her and Ricardo Montalban as twins. To add to the confusion, Montalban wants to be a composer instead of a bullfighter, and Esther masquerades as a matador to cover up for him. Just to keep things alive, there was some Aaron Copland music, a fiery dance by Montalban and Cyd Charisse, and Esther, as usual, swimming.

There followed a series of films which spotlighted Esther's swimming and placed her Number Eight in the top moneymakers of 1949. She cavorted with Johnnie Johnston in Wisconsin in *This Time For Keeps* (1947); was a movie star on location in Hawaii and chased by Peter Lawford in *On An Island With You* (1948); preferred Gene Kelly to Frank Sinatra in the nostalgic, bustle-era *Take Me Out to the Ball Game* (1949); and was a bathing suit designer who finds romance in South America in *Neptune's Daughter* (1949).

Esther was doing very nicely indeed at the boxoffice, and even the new Dore Schary regime at MGM was not about to tamper with the formula glitter that held her pictures together. *Duchess of Idaho* (1950) reunited her with Van Johnson at Sun Valley. If *Pagan Love Song* (1950), which teamed her with Howard Keel on Tahiti, was below par, *Texas Carnival* (1951), also with Keel and with Red Skelton, was just as empty. The reduced production budgets on these two entries showed badly. Esther had a guest star cameo in *Callaway Went Thataway* (1951), and in *Skirts Ahoy* (1952), she, Vivian Blaine, and Joan Evans were three WACS with romantic problems.

Million Dollar Mermaid (1952) returned Esther to her best form and to the general splendor, if not *joie de vivre*, of her 1940s pictures. She was professional swimmer Annette Kellerman who finds Victor Mature most attractive, but makes screen time to participate in two Busby Berkeley-staged Hippodrome extravaganzas, in the water, of course. *Dangerous When Wet* (1953) found Esther as a midwestern miss determined to swim the English channel, and Fernando Lamas as her leading man. MGM trouped Esther and company to Cypress Garden, Florida, for location filming on *Easy to Love* (1953), with Van Johnson and Tony Martin vying for Esther's affection. To further whet the appetites of its viewers, a climactic scene has Esther leading one hundred water skiers through the paces, and smiling every splash of the way.

It was two years before Esther made another picture at MGM, *Jupiter's Darling* (1955), and it proved her final one for the studio. Based on Robert Sherwood's *Road to Rome*, the film portrayed Esther as a Roman lass engaged to George Sanders. Nevertheless, she finds time to flirt with Hannibal (Howard Keel) and prevent him from sacking Rome. George Sidney gave the Cinemascope color production a lavish treatment, but improper studio exploitation of the project and changing public tastes made the film a boxoffice misfire. At age thirty-four, Esther and MGM parted company, she being one of the last holdovers from the lot's 1940s musical film days. Her

With Van Johnson in *Easy to Wed* (1946)

With Richard Lane, Tom Dugan, Dick Wessel, Gene Kelly, Jules Munshin, and Gordon Jones in *Take Me Out to the Ball Game* (1949).

In *Pagan Love Song* (1950)

In *Easy to Love* (1953)

permanent swimming pool set at Metro was quickly converted to a Biblical temple for a Lana Turner vehicle, *The Prodigal* (1955).

Esther turned up at Universal the following year in *The Unguarded Moment* (1956), playing a threatened schoolteacher. The script was based on a story by Rosalind Russell, who had initially written the project for herself. The picture flopped, and Esther's declining status on the Hollywood scene dropped further.* In 1957 Esther's second marriage ended. She had married Benjamin Gage in 1945, a year after divorcing Kovner. Gage, a former radio announcer, was "the only one I could find tall enough for me," and was the man responsible for investing her money carefully into various business ventures: service stations, metal products, a restaurant, and a swimming pool construction firm. Their divorce became final in 1958, and Esther received custody of their three children, Benjamin, Kimball, and Susan.

After the breakup of her marriage, Esther went to Rome to do *Raw Wind in Eden* (1958) with Jeff Chandler. The picture did not click, but the two costars did, and their names were linked in the romance columns for months. Three years later, she returned to Europe and costarred with Fernando Lamas in *The Big Show* (1961). This circus yarn had Esther as a rich American wooed by Cliff Robertson. She took one brief dip in the water. Esther remained in Europe and did another picture with Lamas, *The Magic Fountain* (1961). Made in Spain, it never had U. S. release.

In 1967 Esther traveled to Ft. Lauderdale, Florida to be named to the Swimming Pool Hall of Fame, and her escort was again Lamas. It was announced they had been married in Europe. The dates vary: some sources say 1963, some 1967. At any rate, on December 31, 1969, they were married again in Hollywood at the Founders Church of Religious Sciences. They now live in Santa Monica and are preparing a joint nightclub act.

During the 1960s Esther appeared in several aqua spectaculars on television, and recently did a swimming cereal commercial for Kellogg. Because of video revivals of her films and her well-exploited pool company, her name still has a ring of familiarity to the new generation of filmgoers.

*Esther did not fare much better when she made her dramatic debut on television, starring in *Lux Video Theatre's The Armed Venus* (1957).

ESTHER WILLIAMS

Andy Hardy's Double Life (MGM, 1942)
A Guy Named Joe (MGM, 1943)
Bathing Beauty (MGM, 1944)
Thrill of a Romance (MGM, 1945)
The Hoodlum Saint (MGM, 1946)
Ziegfeld Follies (MGM, 1946)
Easy to Wed (MGM, 1946)
Till the Clouds Roll By (MGM, 1946)
Fiesta (MGM, 1947)
This Time for Keeps (MGM, 1947)

On an Island with You (MGM, 1948)
Take Me Out to the Ball Game (MGM, 1949)
Neptune's Daughter (MGM, 1949)
Duchess of Idaho (MGM, 1950)
Pagan Love Song (MGM, 1950)
Texas Carnival (MGM, 1951)
Callaway Went Thataway (MGM, 1951)
Skirts Ahoy (MGM, 1952)
Million Dollar Mermaid (MGM, 1952)
Dangerous When Wet (MGM, 1953)

Easy to Love (MGM, 1953) Raw Wind in Eden (Universal, 1958)
Jupiter's Darling (MGM, 1955) The Big Show (20th-Fox, 1961)
The Unguarded Moment (Universal, 1956) The Magic Fountain (Spanish, 1961)

In *Jupiter's Darling* (1955)

Keenan Wynn

"I was always the actor with 'and' above his name in the credits, never the star and never the featured player. A contract player like me could make two or three pictures simultaneously, going from set to set as the shooting schedule demanded: a headwaiter here; cowhand's sidekick there; crook; cop; playboy; lush. Directors wanted us around to handle the dialogue between love scenes in their pictures, the word that moved the plot along. The list of star names who had trouble getting words out was a long, long one." So stated Keenan Wynn in his autobiography, *Ed Wynn's Son*, in 1959. Wynn has spent over thirty years being one of Hollywood's most underrated actors. He was too homely to be a conventional leading man and too insecure for many years to fight for better screen roles. Although he is one of the finest character actors in the business, most of his ninety-odd film roles have been so inconsequential that he has never once been nominated for an Academy Award.

Francis Xavier Aloysius Keenan Wynn was born into a show business family on July 27, 1916 in New York City. His maternal grandfather was the stage and silent films Shakespearean tragedian, Frank Keenan. His mother, Hilda Keenan, was an actress, and his father was the inimitable "Perfect Fool," Ed Wynn. His childhood was a pampered, spoiled one. His father was worth $3 million by the time Keenan was nine years old, and Wynn said for years he regarded himself as a poor little rich boy. He felt he would never get out from under the shadow of his dominating father. He was educated at St. Johns Military Academy. By the time he was seventeen, he had the attention-getting reputation for recklessly racing cars, motorcycles, and speedboats. He took up acting early, straight acting like his grandfather, *not* comedy like his father. He made his official professional debut with the Lakewood Players in Maine in *Accent on Youth*. Then, he did some radio bits on *Five Star Final* and *True Detective*.

In 1937, Wynn got paid $40 weekly for playing two small roles in Broadway's *Hitch Your Wagon*. On opening night a friend of Wynn's brought two guests backstage. One was Tom Lewis who was to later marry Loretta Young. The other was an actress named Eve Abbott. When Wynn and Eve began talking, it became apparent that he was struggling to find a "direction" for his career. Eve soon became his stage "mother," coach, and advisor. After

Wagon, he took a job as stage manager for a tour of *Room Service* by George Abbott (no relation to Eve), but this post left him yearning for an acting assignment. Eve advised him to quit, saying she could get him an audition with Guthrie McClintic. She kept her promise, and he got a gutsy role in *The Star Wagon*. More plays, mostly flops, followed, and there was some radio work including Orson Welles' *Mercury Theatre on the Air*. Again he spent his summer with the Lakewood Players. On September 30, 1938, he and Eve were married.

There were more secondary parts in more plays: *One for the Money*; *Two for the Show; The More the Merrier*; and *Johnny on a Spot*. A son, Edmund, was born on April 27, 1941. Meanwhile, Wynn made two screen tests in New York for Twentieth Century-Fox, with Eve appearing with him. Eve called her friend Tyrone Power. He in turn had his agent Nat Goldstone urge Darryl F. Zanuck to consider Wynn for a studio contract. Zanuck declined and Goldstone got Billy Grady of MGM to test Wynn. He tested with Esther Williams and asked for $750 as his weekly salary. Grady said the love scenes in the test were lousy and the best Metro could offer was $300. Wynn had already been making $500 a week on Broadway, but he accepted the offer, since he wanted to try his hand in motion pictures. He had already been in one MGM picture, *Chained* (1934), where, as a seventeen-year-old speedboat enthusiast, his father allowed him to be Joan Crawford's double in the opening scene of that film in which she had to drive a boat.

Under his contract he became a MGM jack of all trades. He debuted in *Somewhere I'll Find You* (1942) and played the comic mobster in *Lost Angel* (1943). He was a soldier pal of Robert Walker in *See Here, Private Hargrove* (1944) as well as in the followup, *What Next, Corporal Hargrove?* (1945). When Wynn played Lucille Ball's *vis-à-vis* in *Without Love* (1945) James Agee said, "I have a hard time breaking myself of the idea that Keenan Wynn is the best actor in Hollywood, rather than just a very good one indeed." In *The Clock* (1946) Wynn's alcoholic cadenza was brilliant, as was his telephone routine in *Ziegfeld Follies* (1946). Probably his best screen role was the newspaper editor in *Easy to Wed* (1946), an excellent musical remake of *Libeled Lady* with Esther Williams, Van Johnson, and Lucille Ball. Wynn played the role Spencer Tracy had performed in the original. But no matter how well Wynn performed in an MGM product, or on an occasional loanout, he could not seem to rise above his supporting actor status. Louis B. Mayer and he were never friends, but the former realized how valuable Wynn was for comedy relief in the studio product, and kept him working in picture after picture.

Keenan and Eve had a second son, Tracy, born in 1945. However, their marriage had become more friendship than marital bliss. It was she who negotiated with Mayer for Wynn's salary increases, which rose to $2,500 weekly. In 1946 their marriage ended in divorce in one of Hollywood's most curious marital triangles. The third party of this triangle was Van Johnson, Wynn's closest friend. They had met when they were both working in various George Abbott shows on Broadway. The Wynns had welcomed bachelor

Johnson into their home when he came to Hollywood. Wynn said: "I must have been born to be a bachelor. I never noticed the new drapes or wallpaper or even Eve's new dress, but Van did. I hated shopping trips and I used to ask Van to go along with Evie." Wynn's father was so confused by the ultrafriendly threesome that upon returning to New York from visiting with his son in California, he told a friend, "I can't keep them straight. Evie loves Keenan. Keenan loves Evie. Van loves Evie. Evie loves Van. Van loves Keenan. Keenan loves Van." Later, when the divorce was more imminent, Ed Wynn further complained, "Tonight Keenan and Evie are out together. Tomorrow he's going to put her on a train for Sun Valley to get a divorce." Keenan did give her power of attorney for a quickie Mexican divorce, and the next day, January 25, 1947, she married Johnson. Wynn babysat with their two boys while she went on her honeymoon. Deciding he was not really a bachelor at heart, Wynn married Betty Jane Butler, a twenty-seven-year-old model on January 11, 1949. They separated three years later and divorced on June 29, 1953. Betty Jane stated that he was too friendly with his ex-wife, Evie.

Wynn was reluctant to sign a long-term renewal to his MGM contract and decided to commit himself to only one more year. He did three films, but finding it dangerous to give up a regular and safe job, he signed for another five years. His status at the studio, however, remained unchanged. They liked him in his place and that was just where they continued to keep him. One of his better 1950s roles was on loan out to Twentieth Century-Fox for *Phone Call from a Stranger* (1952), in which he played Bette Davis' faithful husband.

After finally leaving MGM in 1954, he appeared on television in one of the *U.S. Steel Hour's* best segments, *The Rack*, after which José Ferrer offered him the role of the money-grabbing, venal promoter in *The Great Man*, released by United Artists in 1957. Wynn's father, Ed, now in his declining years as clown, was given a small role in the film as the radio station owner. Although father and son had no scenes together, the younger Wynn provided great encouragement to the nervous, elderly comic. Before that picture was released, *Playhouse 90* cast father and son together in stronger roles and scenes together in *Requiem for a Heavyweight*. Ed played the tragic, ex-pugilist trainer and Keenan was seen as the ruthless fight manager. By now, Keenan was married for a third time, on January 8, 1954, to Sharley Jean Hudson. They have two children, Hilda and Edwynna.*

In 1959 Wynn starred in a teleseries, *The Trouble Shooters*, and during

*In recent years Wynn has suffered from tinnitus, a ringing in the ear that blocks out exterior sound. "You know," says Wynn, "how your ears ring for a minute or so after an explosion? Well, I have that for 24 hours a day, with a high-pitched 'Shhh' in one ear and a lower 'Hsss' in the other.

"Through all that noise in my ear, I can't pick up what people are saying at all. It just comes through as babbling.

"But this has been very good for my acting, because I can't depend on a person's voice to convey his lines to me. I have to watch his lips. This calls for a lot of concentration. And the fact that I'm so concentrated while acting makes my eyes much more expressive. And that's what gives my performances the unique quality that people comment on."

the last decade has continued to be one of the most steadily employed actors in both motion pictures and television. Two of his characterizations that seem to occur more and more often are a high-pressure military officer or a grizzled, white-haired Western type. Directors seem disinclined to temper Wynn's hard-sell performances, often allowing him to chomp all the scenery in sight, as in *Viva Max!* (1969) or *Pretty Maidens All in a Row* (1971). But then subtlety was never Wynn's forte.

Keenan's father died in 1966 at the age of eighty. Ed Wynn had been Jewish and his wife Hilda was a Catholic and raised Keenan in that faith. He says that out of these religious differences grew an antagonism which for a number of years put a great strain on the family relationship. Keenan claims that today he is out from under the shadow of his illustrious father but, as an individual in his own right, he is still proud of his family's heritage in show business.

KEENAN WYNN

Chained (MGM, 1934)
Somewhere I'll Find You (MGM, 1942)
Northwest Rangers (MGM, 1942)
For Me and My Gal (MGM, 1942)
Lost Angel (MGM, 1943)
See Here, Private Hargrove (MGM, 1944)
Since You Went Away (UA, 1944)
Marriage Is a Private Affair (MGM, 1944)
Without Love (MGM, 1945)
The Clock (MGM, 1945)
Between Two Women (MGM, 1945)
Weekend at the Waldorf (MGM, 1945)
What Next, Corporal Hargrove? (MGM, 1945)
Ziegfeld Follies (MGM, 1946)
Easy to Wed (MGM, 1946)
The Thrill of Brazil (Columbia, 1946)
No Leave, No Love (MGM, 1946)
The Cockeyed Miracle (MGM, 1946)
The Hucksters (MGM, 1947)
Song of the Thin Man (MGM, 1947)
B. F.'s Daughter (MGM, 1948)
The Three Musketeers (MGM, 1948)
My Dear Secretary (UA, 1948)
Neptune's Daughter (MGM, 1949)
That Midnight Kiss (MGM, 1949)
Love That Brute (20th-Fox, 1950)
Annie Get Your Gun (MGM, 1950)
Three Little Words (MGM, 1950)
Royal Wedding (MGM, 1951)
Angels in the Outfield (MGM, 1951)
Kind Lady (MGM, 1951)
Texas Carnival (MGM, 1951)

It's a Big Country (MGM, 1951)
Phone Call from a Stranger (20th-Fox, 1952)
The Belle of New York (MGM, 1952)
Fearless Fagan (MGM, 1952)
Sky Full of Moon (MGM, 1952)
Desperate Search (MGM, 1952)
Holiday for Sinners (MGM, 1952)
Battle Circus (MGM, 1953)
Code Two (MGM, 1953)
All the Brothers Were Valiant (MGM, 1953)
Kiss Me, Kate! (MGM, 1953)
The Long, Long Trailer (MGM, 1954)
Men of the Fighting Lady (MGM, 1954)
Tennessee Champ (MGM, 1954)
The Marauders (MGM, 1955)
The Glass Slipper (MGM, 1955)
Running Wild (Universal, 1955)
Shack-Out on 101 (AA, 1955)
The Man in the Gray Flannel Suit (20th-Fox, 1956)
Johnny Concho (UA, 1956)
The Naked Hills (AA, 1956)
The Great Man (UA, 1957)
Don't Go Near the Water (MGM, 1957)
Joe Butterfly (Universal, 1957)
The Fuzzy Pink Nightgown (UA, 1957)
The Deep Six (WB, 1958)
A Time to Love and a Time to Die (Universal, 1958)
The Perfect Furlough (Universal, 1958)
A Hole in the Head (UA, 1959)
That Kind of Woman (Paramount, 1959)

The Crowded Sky (WB, 1960)
The Absent-Minded Professor (BV, 1961)
King of the Roaring 20's—The Story of Arnold Rothstein (AA, 1961)
Pattern for Plunder (Herts Lion International, 1963)
Son of Flubber (BV, 1963)
Man in the Middle (20th-Fox, 1964)
Dr. Strangelove (Columbia, 1964)
Honeymoon Hotel (MGM, 1964)
Stage to Thunder Rock (Paramount, 1964)
The Patsy (Paramount, 1964)
Bikini Beach (AIP, 1964)
The Americanization of Emily (MGM, 1964)
Nightmare in the Sun (Zodiac, 1964)
The Great Race (WB, 1965)
Promise Her Anything (Paramount, 1966)
Stagecoach (20th-Fox, 1966)
Around the World Under the Sea (MGM, 1966)
Night of the Grizzly (Paramount, 1966)
Warning Shot (Paramount, 1967)
Run Like a Thief (Feature Film Corp. o America, 1967)
Point Blank (MGM, 1967)

Welcome to Hard Times (MGM, 1967)
The War Wagon (Universal, 1967)
Finian's Rainbow (WB-7 Arts, 1968)
Blood Holiday (Cinegai-Jolly, 1968)
Smith! (BV, 1969)
MacKenna's Gold (Columbia, 1969)
Viva Max! (Commonwealth United, 1969)
The Monitors (Commonwealth United, 1969)
80 Steps to Jonah (WB, 1969)
Once upon a Time . . . In the West (Paramount, 1969)
Loving (Columbia, 1970)
The Animals (Levitt-Pickman, 1971)
B. J. Lang Presents (Maron Films, 1971)
Pretty Maidens All in a Row (MGM, 1971)
Longest Hunt (Heritage, 1972)
Snowball Express (BV, 1972)
Cancel My Reservation (WB, 1972)
Wild in the Sky (AIP, 1972)
The Artist (Gross National, 1973)
Chateau Bon Vivant (BV, 1973)
The Longest Hunt (Heritage, 1973)
Panhandle 38 (Italian, 1973)
The Further Adventures of the Love Bug (BV, 1973)

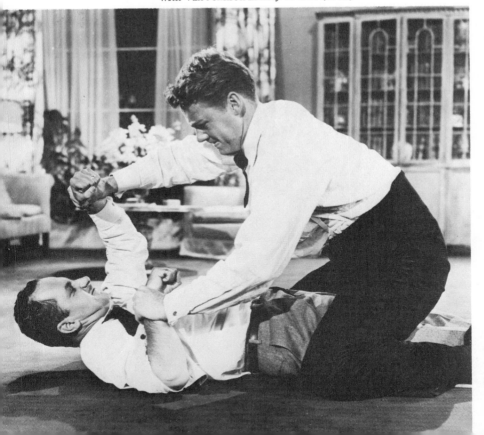

With Van Johnson in *Easy to Wed* (1946)

With Van Johnson, Pat Kirkwood, and Katherine Booth in *No Leave, No Love* (1946)

With James Garner in *The Americanization of Emily* (1964)

Robert Young

Robert Young is best remembered for his portrayal of the kind and amiable pipe-smoking husband–father of the *Father Knows Best* television series and the more current video program, *Marcus Welby, M.D.* His easygoing proficiency as an actor was gained as a result of the fourteen years he spent under contract to MGM. Between 1931 and 1945 he was one of the studio's all-around leading men in what were mostly B pictures. He was never a vibrant star in the Clark Gable or Robert Taylor category, but, at his best, he exuded a dapper masculine charm and a reliable integrity.

He was born Robert George Young in Chicago on February 22, 1907, the fourth of five children of Thomas and Margaret (Fyfe) Young. Less than a year after Young's birth the family moved to Seattle, Washington. When he was ten years old his father, an Irish Protestant carpenter, deserted his family, and the Youngs moved to the seemingly more prosperous Los Angeles. Young recalls working for a living since he began selling newspapers at the age of eight. He remembers himself as being "a pretty dull and humorless fellow when I was a kid." It was while attending Santa Monica's Lincoln High School that his sweetheart, Elizabeth Louise Henderson, suggested he continue with his theatrical dabbling and try for a spot at the Pasadena Community Playhouse after graduation. The shy but handsome teenager found himself embarking upon a career in which he would feel insecure for a long time to come.

Young appeared in more than thirty productions at the Playhouse, while working variously as a bank clerk and a reporter, and even earning a few dollars as an extra with the movies' Keystone Kops. Finally a Playhouse director, character actor Moroni Olson, offered Young the lead in a touring production of *The Ship*. This showcase led to actor-turned-agent Herb Tobias spotting Young in the play and taking him to MGM in 1931, where he was successfully screen-tested and hired at $150 per week. He was immediately loaned to Fox for a small part in *The Black Camel* (1931), one of the *Charlie Chan* features. Young says, "I really owe my first big opportunity to Irving Thalberg's technique of remaking pictures to his satisfaction. I was hired for a bit part as Helen Hayes' son in *The Sin of Madelon Claudet* (1931) and, after shooting was completed, Thalberg kept adding scenes and reshooting so that, by accident, my bit part became a significant role." That picture earned Hayes an Oscar, and the role of the doctor–son catapulted Young into a decade of charming second leads and a few starring parts in B-type pictures.

In those ten years he appeared in nearly sixty films, sometimes working in three at a time. Many of these films starred Hollywood's most glamorous leading ladies: Norma Shearer in *Strange Interlude* (1932), Janet Gaynor in *Carolina* (1934), Loretta Young in *House of Rothschild* (1934), Katharine Hepburn in *Spitfire* (1934), Alice Faye in *Stowaway* (1936), Claudette Colbert in *I Met Him in Paris* (1937), Luise Rainer in *The Emperor's Candlesticks* (1937), and Joan Crawford in *The Bride Wore Red* (1937). In each of these he was suavely competent but never stole the limelight from the female star, which pleased them no end and made him a much-sought-after screen *vis-à-vis*.

Three of Young's better performances were opposite Margaret Sullavan: *Three Comrades* (1938), *The Shining Hour* (1938), and *The Mortal Storm* (1940). Despite solid acting and adequate reviews in these pictures, both critics and public alike were pleasantly surprised with Young's characterization of the dapper, restrained Bostonian, *H. M. Pulham, Esq.* (1941). This was one of Young's few first-rate features and a few more followed: the war correspondent in *Journey for Margaret* (1942), Dorothy McGuire's husband in *Claudia* (1943), its followup *Claudia and David* (1946), and Betty Grable's newspaperman–boyfriend in *Sweet Rosie O'Grady* (1943).

But after *The Canterville Ghost* (1944) Young did not renew his MGM contract, choosing to free-lance instead. At first he did not fare too badly with such romancers as *The Enchanted Cottage* (1945), his favorite film assignment, and *Those Endearing Young Charms* (1945) with Laraine Day. There was also the anti-Semitism expose, *Crossfire* (1947), and a popular marital comedy, *Sitting Pretty* (1948). A number of other movies, such as *Bride for Sale* (1949) and *Secret of the Incas* (1954), were bad. With the decline of good properties in motion pictures, Young turned to radio in 1949, and struck gold with *Father Knows Best*, playing the archetypical American father, Jim Anderson. The series went from radio to television five years later and became one of the most enduring family series in that medium's history, still being shown in syndicated reruns across America. The program ended in 1960, after earning Young two Emmy Awards and making him a wealthy man. A second series, *Window on Main Street* (1961), in which he played a novelist who returns to his hometown, flopped.

Young went into a seven-year retirement in 1962, except for a brief tour of the play *Generation*. He did not return to movies instead of retiring because, as he says, "Films were already changing into what they are today when I became 'available' in '62. The kind of role I was supposedly best suited for—light romantic comedy leads—no longer existed. There wasn't a place for me. ... Feature films, you might say, passed me by." But then in 1969, he returned to television as the mature, humanistic doctor in *Marcus Welby, M.D.* and received another Emmy. That series is still running in the Top Ten, and Young occasionally takes time out from the show to act in such telefeatures as *Vanishing Point* (1971).

Young's success in representing the ideal middle-aged American contrasts with the fact that much of his personal life has been lived behind a smiling face that hid "constant terror." Young says when he began acting, "I thought I was an introvert in a field of extroverts." For nearly thirty years that insecurity was so intense he could not face the day "without a few martinis." Young speaks frankly of his problem of "social drinking" leading to acute alcoholism and the long personal fight, with the help of his wife (he wed Elizabeth Henderson in 1933 and they had four daughters), in overcoming the problem. His wife introduced him to the Science of the Mind philosophy (spiritual metaphysics), and, with that support and the aid of Alcoholics Anonymous, he was able to cure himself. Today, a respected and socially conscious citizen, he frequently holds AA meetings in his home. Furthermore, he says, "I've got enough new lease on life for at least 300 years." He recently was chosen Honorary Chairman of National Health Week and stated when he was selected, "It is a source of satisfaction to know that the theme of the series —the life and work of the contemporary family doctor—is a strong concern of the medical profession."

ROBERT YOUNG

Black Camel (Fox, 1931)
The Sin of Madelon Claudet (MGM, 1931)
Guilty Generation (Columbia, 1931)
Hell Divers (MGM, 1931)
Wet Parade (MGM, 1932)
Strange Interlude (MGM, 1932)
New Morals for Old (MGM, 1932)
Unashamed (MGM, 1932)
The Kid from Spain (UA, 1932)
Today We Live (MGM, 1933)
Hell Below (MGM, 1933)
Men Must Fight (MGM, 1933)
Tugboat Annie (MGM, 1933)
Saturday's Millions (Universal, 1933)
Right to Romance (RKO, 1933)
House of Rothschild (UA, 1934)
Carolina (Fox, 1934)
Cardboard City (Fox, 1934)*
Lazy River (MGM, 1934)
Spitfire (RKO, 1934)
Whom the Gods Destroy (Columbia, 1934)
Paris Interlude (MGM, 1934)
Death on the Diamond (MGM, 1934)
The Band Plays On (MGM, 1934)
West Point of the Air (MGM, 1935)
Vagabond Lady (MGM, 1935)
Calm Yourself (MGM, 1935)
Red Salute (UA, 1935)

The Bride Comes Home (Paramount, 1935)
Remember Last Night? (Universal, 1935)
Secret Agent (Gaumont–British, 1936)
It's Love Again (Gaumont–British, 1936)
Three Wise Guys (MGM, 1936)
Sworn Enemy (MGM, 1936)
The Bride Walks Out (RKO, 1936)
The Longest Night (MGM, 1936)
Stowaway (20th-Fox, 1936)
Dangerous Number (MGM, 1937)
I Met Him in Paris (Paramount, 1937)
The Emperor's Candlesticks (MGM, 1937)
Married Before Breakfast (MGM, 1937)
The Bride Wore Red (MGM, 1937)
Navy Blue and Gold (MGM, 1937)
Paradise for Three (MGM, 1938)
Josette (20th-Fox, 1938)
The Toy Wife (MGM, 1938)
Three Comrades (MGM, 1938)
Rich Man, Poor Girl (MGM, 1938)
The Shining Hour (MGM, 1938)
Honolulu (MGM, 1939)
Bridal Suite (MGM, 1939)
Maisie (MGM, 1939)
Miracles for Sale (MGM, 1939)
Florian (MGM, 1940)
Northwest Passage (MGM, 1940)
The Mortal Storm (MGM, 1940)

Sporting Blood (MGM, 1940)
Dr. Kildare's Crisis (MGM, 1940)
The Trial of Mary Dugan (MGM, 1941)
Western Union (20th-Fox, 1941)
Lady Be Good (MGM, 1941)
Married Bachelor (MGM, 1941)
H. M. Pulham, Esq. (MGM, 1941)
Joe Smith, American (MGM, 1942)
Cairo (MGM, 1942)
Journey for Margaret (MGM, 1942)
Slightly Dangerous (MGM, 1943)
Claudia (20th-Fox, 1943)
Sweet Rosie O'Grady (20th-Fox, 1943)
The Canterville Ghost (MGM, 1944)
Those Endearing Young Charms (RKO, 1945)
The Enchanted Cottage (RKO, 1945)
The Searching Wind (Paramount, 1946)

Lady Luck (RKO, 1946)
Claudia and David (20th-Fox, 1946)
They Won't Believe Me (RKO, 1947)
Crossfire (RKO, 1947)
Relentless (Columbia, 1948)
Sitting Pretty (20th-Fox, 1948)
Adventure in Baltimore (RKO, 1949)
Bride for Sale (RKO, 1949)
That Forsyte Woman (MGM, 1950)
And Baby Makes Three (Columbia, 1950)
Goodbye, My Fancy (WB, 1951)
The Second Woman (UA, 1951)
The Half-Breed (RKO, 1952)
Secret of the Incas (Paramount, 1954)

*Unbilled Appearance.

With Myrna Loy in *New Morals for Old* (1932)

With Madge Evans in *Death on the Diamond* (1934)

789

With Lana Turner in *Rich Man, Poor Girl* (1938)

With Laraine Day and Tom Conway in *The Trial of Mary Dugan* (1941)

The Genesis of Metro-Goldwin-Mayer, Inc.

On April 17, 1924 Marcus Loew, of the distributing company of Loew's Incorporated, announced the formation of Metro-Goldwyn Pictures Corporation, and the California-based company legally came into being the following May 16th. The new industry complex was housed at the Goldwyn Studios which boasted six soundstages on its lot. The merger was Loew's creation and was made up of Metro Pictures Corporation and Goldwyn Pictures.

Metro Pictures was formed in 1915 and acquired in 1920 by Loew's Inc. to supply that distributing company with its own product. Goldwyn Pictures had been formed in 1916–1917 when Samuel Goldfish (later Goldwyn) joined with brothers Edgar and Archibald Selwyn, well-known Broadway producers. The company's motto, *Ars Gratia Artis* ("art for art's sake"), was the brainchild of a young New York advertising man, Howard Dietz, later a Hollywood producer. It was also Dietz who suggested the use of the roaring lion as a company trademark. In 1918 Goldwyn Pictures leased Thomas H. Ince's Triangle Studio in Culver City, California, six miles southwest of Hollywood. By 1922 Goldfish, now legally Goldwyn, departed from the company, maintaining a small share of stock.

Soon after the Metro-Goldwyn Pictures merger, Marcus Loew, Nicholas M. Schenck, and other Loew's Inc. executives saw that further expansion was in order. Overtures were made to Louis B. Mayer, whose small but energetic Louis B. Mayer Productions had successfully produced a series of motion pictures starring Anita Stewart (released through First National) and Mildred Harris (distributed through Loew's own Metro Corporation). Later in 1924 merger agreements were completed, and Metro-Goldwyn-Mayer, Inc. came into legal existence, with Mayer's associates, Irving G. Thalberg and attorney J. Robert Rubin, holding important executive posts in the new organization.

From the beginning of his association with Metro-Goldwyn-Mayer, Mayer held firm to his theory that motion pictures were a business, first and foremost. To make technically superior product was not good enough to gather in revenue; a company needed more. It needed star personalities to emote in its product. Thus the real motto for Mayer and MGM was MORE

791

STARS THAN THERE ARE IN HEAVEN, a phrase created in the company's first year of existence. That motto became MGM's credo and goal.

When Mayer arrived on the MGM scene, the studio was featuring in its product Mae Murray, John Gilbert, Lon Chaney, Ramon Novarro, Antonio Moreno, Norma Shearer, and a newcomer named Joan Crawford who was to be the first official star to be solely discovered and developed by MGM. Mayer and Thalberg soon added other glittering personalities to the roster, including Lillian Gish, Buster Keaton, and Greta Garbo. Before the complete takeover of the motion picture industry by the sound medium, MGM had made its mark as a formidable competitor to the other studios. Their first talking picture was *Alias Jimmy Valentine* (1928), starring the personable smart aleck, William Haines. Their second sound vehicle, *Broadway Melody* (1929), starring Bessie Love, Anita Page, and Charles King, was their first picture to receive the Academy Award. Certainly by 1932 MGM was no longer just another competitor; it was the best equipped studio in the world, and that year six of the top ten moneymaking stars were under MGM contract: Marie Dressler, Joan Crawford, Greta Garbo, Norma Shearer, Wallace Beery, and Clark Gable. In addition to these luminaries, Metro's performer roster included John and Lionel Barrymore, Jackie Cooper, Marion Davies, Madge Evans, Jean Harlow, Helen Hayes, Jean Hersholt, Myrna Loy, Robert Montgomery, Maureen O'Sullivan, Lewis Stone, Franchot Tone, Johnny Weissmuller, and Robert Young. And this was just the beginning!

Thalberg had supervised MGM's major production since joining the studio. Always of frail health, Thalberg was stricken with grief when his studio associate producer Paul Bern committed suicide in September 1932. Thalberg asked to be released from his contract, and Nicholas Schenck, who had risen to the presidency of Loew's Inc. upon the death of Marcus Loew (1927), temporarily appeased Thalberg with a lucrative stock-option deal. This rankled Mayer, and the relationship between Mayer and Thalberg rapidly deteriorated. In December 1932 Thalberg collapsed, and Schenck came to the studio from New York City a second time. At this juncture it was suggested that Mayer's son-in-law, David O. Selznick, be hired from RKO to relieve Thalberg of some of the burden of supervising the studio's output. Selznick was hired, but Thalberg balked at the usurpation of his power. Schenck appeased him by allowing Thalberg to supervise his own production unit at Metro, for which he could produce the kind of literate picture he preferred: *The Barretts of Wimpole Street* (1934), *China Seas, Mutiny on the Bounty, A Night at the Opera* (all 1935), *Romeo and Juliet* (1936), *Camille* (1937), and *The Good Earth* (1937). Thalberg died before the latter picture was completed, and the film's opening credits carried a memorial tribute to the late guiding force of the studio.

Selznick, whose reputation as an artistic producer was second only to Thalberg's, added equal luster to MGM's prestige and assets with *Dinner at Eight, Night Flight, Dancing Lady* (all 1933), *Viva Villa!* (1934), *David Copperfield* and *Anna Karenina* (1935), and *A Tale of Two Cities* (1936). Other

MGM production units released *San Francisco* (1936), *The Great Ziegfeld* (1936), *Boys Town* (1938), and *The Wizard of Oz* (1939). Equally important to the studio's financial welfare were its B production units, started up in 1933 to churn out double-bill movies that ran 60 to 70 minutes. These B films, and especially the popular series programmers (*Andy Hardy, Dr. Kildare, Maisie,* and the more prestigious *Tarzan* and *Thin Man*), served as a training ground for the brightest of MGM's second generation of stars: Judy Garland, Lana Turner, Esther Williams, Kathryn Grayson, Donna Reed, Marilyn Maxwell, Laraine Day, Ava Gardner, and Van Johnson.

If there could have been a replacement for Thalberg at the time of his death (September 14, 1936), the logical choice would have been Selznick. However, Selznick had completed his contractual tieup with the studio and had entered independent production elsewhere (although, through a series of industry manipulations, MGM would initially release his bonanza *Gone with the Wind* (1939) and in 1944 would become its sole owner). Moreover, Mayer was very much enjoying his studio autonomy, and did not wish a replacement. Loew's Inc. did not push the matter at the time, since everything at the Culver City lot was running smoothly, with the Metro factory grinding out an average of one feature a week. Nicholas Schenck did insist, however, over Mayer's objections, that the studio become involved in a production tieup with England, and in 1937 Metro purchased a studio facility at Denham, outside London. The British complex was headed by Michael Balcon, former head of Gaumont–British. The first MGM undertaking at that studio was *A Yank at Oxford* (1938). It was on his trip to that studio in the summer of 1937 that Mayer made two of his most important star discoveries of the 1940s: Greer Garson and Hedy Lamarr. In just two short years the British venture proved highly successful, with the release of such films as *Pygmalion* and *The Citadel* (both 1938), and *Goodbye, Mr. Chips* (1939).

For several years after Thalberg's death, MGM ran smoothly on the momentum that the creative genius had accelerated. But by the end of World War II, something at MGM seemed awry, and it was not just the government's antitrust suits that would separate Loew's theatres from MGM, or the rising threat of commercial television. The problem was a lack of star power. James Stewart had left the lot to serve in World War II and refused to return to Metro when he was discharged. Rosalind Russell had left the studio in 1941 and the following year three of the lot's cinema queens took their leave: Greta Garbo, Norma Shearer, Joan Crawford, and a fourth, Jeanette MacDonald, followed soon after. While Metro had its Garsons, Lamarrs, Rooneys, Garlands, and Gable and Tracy as their stars of the 1940s, during the period 1946–1948, not a single major Academy Award was bestowed upon an MGM release. Production costs were rising to a staggering high and the studio output, normally 52 pictures a year, was decreasing: 24 in 1946, 29 in 1947, 23 in 1948. Finally, it was apparent that a new Thalberg, if such a creature were to be found, was desperately needed to manage the gargantuan Culver City lot, since Mayer, in these days, was more interested in his racing stable than in his star stable.

Mayer immediately broached Selznick to assume the post of command at MGM, but Selznick refused the offer. Mayer then decided to take a chance on a new Hollywood name, Dore Schary. Schary had worked for MGM as a scripter–producer in the late 1930s and early 1940s, later joining David O. Selznick's Vanguard Company and then serving as vice president in charge of production at RKO in 1947–1948, before Howard Hughes grabbed the reins of that studio. On July 1, 1948 Schary signed a contract which made him vice president in charge of production at MGM.Schary—a liberal Democrat and a socially concerned intellectual did not have the same working rapport with the conservative Republican Mayer that Thalberg had. From the start there were major differences between the two men, with Schary increasingly going over Mayer's head to Schenck for final approval on decisions. One of the most bitter points of contention was over the House Un-American Activities Committee, with which Mayer openly sided and Schary violently opposed (at least in theory).

The growing disscusion between Schary and Mayer ruptured in 1951, when the New York-based Loew's executives demanded Mayer's resignation, with Mayer departing on June 22nd and Schary remaining in charge. Schary was not the strong disciplinarian that Mayer had been in his prime, or that even the mercurial Thalberg was. He found himself forced to deal with a faltering studio complex adrift in an industry that was undergoing irrevocable changes far above and beyond the introduction of 3-D and widescreen Cinemascope–stereophonic sound. Television had proven its staying power as a powerful media rival, independent producers were coming into their own, stars were battling for percentage deals, and the studio stock companies were eroding in a time of financial retrenchment. The golden years of the Hollywood system had passed.

In a few short years Schary resigned as company head, Nicholas Schenck was pushed into the nonvital role of Chairman of the Board of Loew's Inc., and Louis B. Mayer, after one final attempt to overtake his former position, died of leukemia in 1957. Meanwhile, like the other once great Hollywood film studios, Metro gradually became a distribution–packaging complex handling the product of independent producers and the diminishing number of studio-originated products.

By 1960 all the old-line big-time Metro stars had long since departed, retired, or died, and the studio was angling for the likes of such potential contractees as Connie Francis, Yvette Mimieux, Paula Prentiss, Jim Hutton, and George Hamilton, all of whom graced the dismally inferior but successful Metro entry *Where The Boys Are* (1960). In the 1960s MGM continued to make more money from the sale of its own pictures to television, selling off real estate, and producing such video series as *Dr. Kildare* and *The Man from U.N.C.L.E.* By the middle of the decade MGM's "more stars than there are in the heavens" would be reduced to one major contract player, Chad Everett.

After a series of new MGM presidents and changes of the executive board, Las Vegas financier, Kirk Kerkorian obtained control of the company in 1969 by buying up 48 percent of the stock. Former CBS-TV executive James Aubrey was hired as the studio's new president. Under the new regime, the British studio was sold, additional Culver City (backlot) real estate was packaged, and in May 1970, there was the famous MGM auction, wherein studio sets and memorabilia were sold to the highest bidder. The days of the movie moguls were over. Now the industry was run by moneymen involved in intricate conglomerate corporate maneuverings. MGM's most recent undertaking has been the planning of the Grand Hotel resort in Las Vegas.

Appendix 1: Capsule Bibliographies of MGM Executives

LOUIS B. MAYER: Born Louis Burt Mayer July 4, 1895 in Minsk, Russia; emigrated to St. John, New Brunswick at age three; was in scrap metal business with father; settled in Boston, purchased several theatres for operas, stage shows, and motion pictures, exhibited D. W. Griffith's *Birth of a Nation*. In 1914 he organized own motion picture distributing company in Boston; in 1918 founded own production company, and in 1924 became vice president in charge of production of the newly formed Metro-Goldwyn-Mayer. Was ousted in 1951. Salary in 1940: $697,048; in 1941: $949,765. Married Margaret Shenberg June 14, 1904; had two daughters Edith (August 13, 1905) and Irene (April 2, 1907); married Lorena Danker in 1948. Died of leukemia October 29, 1957.

Most of Mayer's estate, valued at from $7.5 to $9 million, went to the Louis B. Mayer Foundation. In 1967 $250,000 from that foundation was used to build the Louis B. Mayer Memorial Center at the Motion Picture Country House in Woodland Hills, California, a building which houses a chapel, a theatre, a recreational, and an occupational therapy area.

IRVING G. THALBERG: Born Irving Grant Thalberg May 30, 1899 in Brooklyn; was hired by Universal's Carl Laemmle in 1918 as a clerical assistant, and soon became Laemmle's private secretary; in 1921 became general manager of Universal; in 1922 was first head of a studio to fire a powerful director (Erich Von Stroheim on *Merry-Go-Round*); on February 15, 1923, became vice president in charge of production to the Louis B. Mayer Company, and in 1924 became second vice president and supervisor of production of the newly formed Metro-Goldwyn-Mayer Corporation. Married Norma Shearer on September 29, 1927. Two children: Irving Grant, Jr. (August 25, 1930), Katherine (June 13, 1935). Died September 14, 1936.

DAVID O. SELZNICK: Born David Selznick on May 10, 1902 in Pittsburgh, Pennsylvania, the son of pioneer motion picture promoter-distributor, Lewis J. Selznick; (brother Myron became a powerful Hollywood talent agent); in 1926 hired by MGM as assistant story editor; fired by Thalberg in 1927; in 1928 hired as assistant general manager of Paramount; on March 29,1930 wed Louis B. Mayer's daughter, Irene; had two sons: Lewis Jeffrey (1932) and Daniel Mayer (1936); in 1931 head of production at RKO; resigned 1932; on February 6, 1933 hired by Mayer to head own production unit at MGM, where he prepared, among others: *Dinner at Eight* (1933), *Dancing Lady* (1933), *Viva Villa!* (1934), *David Copperfield* (1935), *Anna Karenina* (1935); resigned from MGM in 1935 to go into independent production; 1939 released *Gone with the Wind* through MGM; in 1949 divorced Irene; on July 13, 1949 married Jennifer Jones by whom he had a daughter, Mary Jennifer (August 12, 1954); died June 22, 1965.

DORE SCHARY: Born Isidore Schary on August 31, 1905 in Newark, New Jersey; theatre and newspaper background led to screen writing; Oscar in 1938 for original story of *Boys' Town*; in 1942 executive producer with Harry Rapf at MGM; resigned in 1943; joined David O. Selznick's Vanguard Company as producer which released through RKO; in 1947–1948 vice president in charge of production at RKO; in 1948–1956, vice president in charge of production at MGM; in 1957 authored and produced stage version of *Sunrise at Campobello*; other play ventures thereafter. He is currently president of Theatre Vision, Inc., a pay-television company. Married Miriam Svet in 1932.

MARCUS LOEW: Born May 8, 1870 in New York City. After spending his early years as a fur salesman, he purchased a share of a penny arcade business from his friend Adolph Zukor in 1903. Under the name of People's Vaudeville, he formed his own arcade and nickelodeon business in 1905. Two years later he acquired the Royal Theatre in Brooklyn, and in 1910 formed Loew's Consolidated Enterprises and began amassing a national theatre chain which became known as Loew's Inc. (incorporated in 1919) with 50 theatres. Instrumental in forming MGM in 1924, and died on September 5, 1927. He had married Caroline Rosenheim on March 4, 1894.

NICHOLAS SCHENCK: Born November 14, 1881 in Rybinks, Russia. Studied pharmacy, but became involved in amusement parks, arcades, nickelodeons, and joined Loew's People's Enterprises, operating the Lyric Theatre, Hoboken, New Jersey. In 1910 became secretary of the newly formed Loew's Consolidated Enterprises, and in 1919 was made vice president and general manager of Loew's Inc. Upon Loew's death in 1927 he became president of Loew's Inc., and remained so until he was eased into the post of Chairman of the Board in 1955. He retired in 1958 and died of a stroke in Miami Beach, March 4, 1969, survived by second wife and three daughters.

Appendix 2: MGM Academy Award Nominations and Winners

The Academy of Motion Picture Arts and Sciences was born out of a conversation between MGM executive Louis B. Mayer, director Fred Niblo, and actor Conrad Nagel. The Academy was officially organized on May 4, 1927, when thirty-six representatives of the Hollywood motion picture industry met to discuss its formation as an organization to improve the artistic quality of motion pictures and to pay recognition to outstanding achievements of the twentieth century's new art form. Douglas Fairbanks, Sr. was named its first president, and the gold-plated statuette was derived from a sketch made by MGM's notable art director, Cedric Gibbons, on the banquet table cloth. The first awards were announced on February 18, 1929 and presented at a banquet held at the Hollywood Roosevelt Hotel on May 16, 1929. Since those unpretentious beginnings, the annual presentation ceremony has become the television spectacular of the year, and the winners are guaranteed a monetary return at the boxoffice.

Periodically, there are honorary or special awards voted by the Academy's Board of Governors. Two of these awards commemorate two MGM alumni—Irving G. Thalberg and Jean Hersholt.

The Irving G. Thalberg Memorial Award was established in 1937 and is voted for "outstanding motion picture production" as the Board deems deserving. The Jean Hersholt Humanitarian Award was established in 1956 and is likewise voted by the Board periodically when it feels there is a deserving recipient.

*DENOTES ACADEMY AWARD WINNERS

1927/28
Direction—King Vidor for *The Crowd*
Writing—(Title writing—not given after this year)
    *Joseph Farnham for *The Fair Co-Ed*
    *Joseph Farnham for *Laugh, Clown, Laugh*
    *Joseph Farnham for *Telling the World*
Artistic Quality of Production (not given after this year)—*The Crowd*

1928/29
Picture—*Broadway Melody
  Holiday Revue
Direction—Lionel Barrymore for Madame X
  Harry Beaumont for Broadway Melody
Actress—Ruth Chatterton for Madame X
  Bessie Love for Broadway Melody
Writing—Achievement—Josephine Lovett for Our Dancing Daughters
  Bess Meredyth for Wonder of Women
Art Direction—*Cedric Gibbons for The Bridge of San Luis Rey
  Cedric Gibbons for Hollywood Revue
Cinematography—George Barnes for Our Dancing Daughters
  *Clyde De Vinna for White Shadows in the South Seas

1929/30
Picture—The Big House
  The Divorcee
Direction—Clarence Brown for Anna Christie
  Clarence Brown for Romance
  Robert Z. Leonard for The Divorcee
  King Vidor for Hallelujah
Actor—Wallace Beery for The Big House
  Lawrence Tibbett for Rogue Song
Actress—Greta Garbo for Anna Christie
  Greta Garbo for Romance
  *Norma Shearer for The Divorcee
  Norma Shearer for Their Own Desire
Writing—Achievement—*Frances Marion for The Big House
  John Meehan for The Divorcee
Cinematography—William Daniels for Anna Christie
Sound Recording—*Douglas Shearer for The Big House

1930/31
Picture—Trader Horn
Direction—Clarence Brown for A Free Soul
Actor—*Lionel Barrymore for A Free Soul
Actress—*Marie Dressler for Min and Bill
  Norma Shearer for A Free Soul
Sound Recording—MGM Sound Department (no specific picture)

1931/32
Picture—The Champ
  *Grand Hotel
Direction—King Vidor for The Champ

799

Actor—*Wallace Beery for *The Champ*
    Alfred Lunt for *The Guardsman*
Actress—Marie Dressler for *Emma*
    Lynn Fontanne for *The Guardsman*
    *Helen Hayes for *The Sin of Madelon Claudet*
Writing—Original Story—*Frances Marion for *The Champ*

1932/33

Picture—*Smilin' Thru*
Writing—Original Story—Frances Marion for *The Prizefighter and
    the Lady*
    Charles MacArthur for *Rasputin and the Empress*
Art Direction—Cedric Gibbons for *When Ladies Meet*
Cinematography—George J. Folsey, Jr. for *Reunion in Vienna*
Assistant Director—*Charles Dorian

1934

Picture—*The Barretts of Wimpole Street*
    The Thin Man
    Viva Villa!
Direction—W. S. Van Dyke for *The Thin Man*
Actor—William Powell for *The Thin Man*
Actress—Norma Shearer for *The Barretts of Wimpole Street*
Writing—Adaptation—Frances Goodrich and Albert Hackett for *The Thin
    Man*
    Ben Hecht for *Viva Villa*!
    Original Story—Mauri Grashin for *Hide Out*
    *Arthur Caesar for *Manhattan Melodrama*
Art Direction—*Cedric Gibbons and Frederic Hope for *The Merry Widow*
Cinematography—George J. Folsey, Jr. for *Operation 13*
Film Editing—*Conrad A. Nervig for *Eskimo*
Sound Recording—Douglas Shearer for *Viva Villa*!
Assistant Director—*John Waters for *Viva Villa*!

1935

Picture—*Broadway Melody of 1936*
    David Copperfield
    Mutiny on the Bounty
    Naughty Marietta
Direction—Frank Lloyd for *Mutiny on the Bounty*
Actor—Clark Gable for *Mutiny on the Bounty*
    Charles Laughton for *Mutiny on the Bounty*
    Franchot Tone for *Mutiny on the Bounty*
Writing—Original Story—Moss Hart for *Broadway Melody of 1936*

Screenplay—Jules Furthman, Talbot Jennings, and Carey Wilson
for *Mutiny on the Bounty*
Film Editing—Robert J. Kern for *David Copperfield*
Margaret Booth for *Mutiny on the Bounty*
Music—Score—Herbert Stothart for *Mutiny on the Bounty*
Sound Recording—*Douglas Shearer for *Naughty Marietta*
Assistant Director—Joseph Newman for *David Copperfield*

1936

Picture—**The Great Ziegfeld*
Libeled Lady
Romeo and Juliet
San Francisco
A Tale of Two Cities
Direction—Robert Z. Leonard for *The Great Ziegfeld*
W. S. Van Dyke for *San Francisco*
Actor—Spencer Tracy for *San Francisco*
Supporting Actor—Basil Rathbone for *Romeo and Juliet*
Actress—*Luise Rainer for *The Great Ziegfeld*
Norma Shearer for *Romeo and Juliet*
Supporting Actress—Beulah Bondi for *The Gorgeous Hussy*
Writing—Original Story—Norman Krasna for *Fury*
William Anthony McGuire for *The Great Ziegfeld*
Robert Hopkins for *San Francisco*
Screenplay—Frances Goodrich and Albert Hackett for *After the
Thin Man*
Art Direction—Cedric Gibbons, Eddie Imazu, and Edwin B. Willis for
The Great Ziegfeld
Cedric Gibbons, Frederic Hope, and Edwin B. Willis for
Romeo and Juliet
Cinematography—George J. Folsey, Jr. for *The Gorgeous Hussy*
Film Editing—William S. Gray for *The Great Ziegfeld*
Conrad A. Nervig for *A Tale of Two Cities*
Music—Song—Harold Adamson and Walter Donaldson for "Did I
Remember?" from *Suzy*
Sound Recording—Elmer A. Raguse for *General Spanky*
*Douglas Shearer for *San Francisco*
Dance Direction—*Seymour Felix for "A Pretty Girl Is Like a Melody"
from *The Great Ziegfeld*
Dave Gould for "Swingin' The Jinx" from *Born to Dance*
Assistant Director—Joseph Newman for *San Francisco*

1937

Picture—*Captains Courageous*
The Good Earth

Direction—Sidney Franklin for *The Good Earth*
Actor—Charles Boyer for *Conquest*
      Robert Montgomery for *Night Must Fall*
      *Spencer Tracy for *Captains Courageous*
Supporting Actor—Roland Young for *Topper*
Actress—Greta Garbo for *Camille*
      *Luise Rainer for *The Good Earth*
Supporting Actress—Dame May Whitty for *Night Must Fall*
Writing—Screenplay—Marc Connelly, John Lee Mahin, and Dale Van Every
      for *Captains Courageous*
Art Direction—Cedric Gibbons and William Horning for *Conquest*
Cinematography—*Karl Freund for *The Good Earth*
Film Editing—Elmo Vernon for *Captains Courageous*
      Basil Wrangell for *The Good Earth*
Music—Score—Herbert Stothart for *Maytime*
      Marvin Hatley for *Way Out West*
Sound Recording—Douglas Shearer for *Maytime*
      Elmer Raguse for *Topper*
Dance Direction—Dave Gould for "All God's Children Got Rhythm" from
      A Day at the Races

1938

Picture—*Boys' Town*
      The Citadel
      Pygmalion
      Test Pilot
Direction—Norman Taurog for *Boys' Town*
      King Vidor for *The Citadel*
Actor—Robert Donat for *The Citadel*
      Leslie Howard for *Pygmalion*
      *Spencer Tracy for *Boys' Town*
Supporting Actor—Robert Morley for *Marie Antoinette*
Actress—Wendy Hiller for *Pygmalion*
      Norma Shearer for *Marie Antoinette*
      Margaret Sullavan for *Three Comrades*
Supporting Actress—Beulah Bondi for *Of Human Hearts*
      Billie Burke for *Merrily We Live*
      Miliza Korjus for *The Great Waltz*
Writing—Adaptation—*Ian Dalrymple, Cecil Lewis, and W. P. Lipscomb for
      Pygmalion
      Original Story—*Eleanore Griffin and Dore Schary for *Boys'
      Town*
      Frank Wead for *Test Pilot*
      Screenplay—John Meehan and Dore Schary for *Boys' Town*
      Ian Dalrymple, Elizabeth Hill, and Frank Wead for

The Citadel
      *George Bernard Shaw for *Pygmalion*
Art Direction—Cedric Gibbons for *Marie Antoinette*
      Charles D. Hall for *Merrily We Live*
Cinematography—*Joseph Ruttenberg for *The Great Waltz*
      Nobert Brodine for *Merrily We Live*
Film Editing—Tom Held for *The Great Waltz*
      Tom Held for *Test Pilot*
Music—Score—Herbert Stothart for *Sweethearts*
      Original Score—Herbert Stothart for *Marie Antoinette*
      Song—Chet Forrest, Bob Wright, and Edward Ward for "Always
      and Always" from *Mannequin*
      Arthur Quenzer and Phil Craig for "Merrily We Live" from
      Merrily We Live.
Sound Recording—Elmer Raguse for *Merrily We Live*
      Douglas Shearer for *Sweethearts*
Honorary—Mickey Rooney
      Oliver Marsh and Allen Davey for color cinematography
      of *Sweethearts*

1939

Picture—*Gone with the Wind*
      Goodbye, Mr. Chips
      Ninotchka
      The Wizard of Oz
Direction—*Victor Fleming for *Gone with the Wind*
      Sam Wood for *Goodbye, Mr. Chips*
Actor—*Robert Donat for *Goodbye, Mr. Chips*
      Clark Gable for *Gone with the Wind*
      Mickey Rooney for *Babes in Arms*
Actress—Greta Garbo for *Ninotchka*
      Greer Garson for *Goodbye, Mr. Chips*
      *Vivien Leigh for *Gone with the Wind*
Supporting Actress—Olivia deHavilland for *Gone with the Wind*
      *Hattie McDaniel for *Gone with the Wind*
Writing—Original Story—Melchior Lengyel for *Ninotchka*
      Screenplay—*Sidney Howard for *Gone with the Wind*
      Eric Maschwitz, R. C. Sheriff, and Claudine West
      for *Goodbye, Mr. Chips.*
      Charles Brackett, Walter Reisch, and Billy Wilder for *Ninotchka*
Art Direction—*Lyle Wheeler for *Gone with the Wind*
      Cedric Gibbons and William A. Horning for *The Wizard
      of Oz*
Cinematography—Color—*Ernest Haller and Ray Rennahan for *Gone with
      the Wind*

Film Editing—*Hal C. Kern and James E. Newcom for *Gone with the Wind*
  Charles Frend for *Goodbye, Mr. Chips*
Music—Score—Roger Edens and George E. Stoll for *Babes in Arms*
  Song—*E. Y. Harburg and Harold Arlen for "Over The Rainbow" from *The Wizard of Oz.*
Sound Recording—Thomas T. Moulton for *Gone with the Wind*
  Douglas Shearer for *Balalaika*
  A. W. Watkins for *Goodbye, Mr. Chips*
Special Effects—John R. Cosgrove, Fred Albin, and Arthur Johns for
  Gone with the Wind
  A. Arnold Gillespie and Douglas Shearer for *The Wizard of Oz*
Honorary—Judy Garland

1940

Picture—*The Philadelphia Story*
Direction—George Cukor for *The Philadelphia Story*
Actor—*James Stewart for *The Philadelphia Story*
Actress—Katharine Hepburn for *The Philadelphia Story*
Supporting Actress—Ruth Hussey for *The Philadelphia Story*
Writing—Original Story—Walter Reisch for *Comrade X*
  Hugo Butler and Dore Schary for *Edison the Man*
  Screenplay—*Donald Ogden Stewart for *The Philadelphia Story*
Art Direction—Black & White—*Cedric Gibbons and Paul Groesse for
  Pride and Prejudice
  Color—Cedric Gibbons and John S. Detlie for *Bitter Sweet*
Cinematography—Black and White—Harold Rosson for *Boom Town*
  Joseph Ruttenberg for *Waterloo Bridge*
  Color—Allen Davey and Oliver T. Marsh for *Bitter Sweet*
  William V. Skall and Sidney Wagner for *Northwest Passage*
Music—Score—George Stoll and Roger Edens for *Strike Up the Band*
  Original Score—Herbert Stothart for *Waterloo Bridge*
  Song—Roger Edens and George Stoll for "Our Love Affair" from
  Strike Up the Band
Sound Recording—*Douglas Shearer for *Strike Up the Band*
Special Effects—A. Arnold Gillespie and Douglas Shearer for *Boom Town*

1941

Picture—*Blossoms in the Dust*
Actress—Greer Garson for *Blossoms in the Dust*
Art Direction—Black and White—Cedric Gibbons, Randall Duell,
  and Edwin B. Willis for *When Ladies Meet*
  Color—*Cedric Gibbons, Urie McCleary, and Edwin B. Willis
  for *Blossoms in the Dust*

Cinematography—Black & White—Karl Freund for *The Chocolate Soldier*
 Joseph Ruttenberg for *Dr. Jekyll and Mr. Hyde*
 Color—William V. Skall and Leonard Smith for *Billy the Kid*
 Karl Freund and W. Howard Greene for *Blossoms in the Dust*
Film Editing—Harld F. Kress for *Dr. Jekyll and Mr. Hyde*
Music—Dramatic Score—Franz Waxman for *Dr. Jekyll and Mr. Hyde*
 Musical Score—Herbert Stothart and Bronislau Kaper for *The Chocolate Soldier*
 Song—*Oscar Hammerstein II and Jerome Kern for "The Last Time I Saw Paris" from *Lady Be Good*
Sound Recording—Douglas Shearer for *The Chocolate Soldier*
Special Effects—A. Arnold Gillespie and Douglas Shearer for *Flight Command*

1942

Picture—*Mrs. Miniver*
 Random Harvest
Direction—Mervyn LeRoy for *Random Harvest*
 *William Wyler for *Mrs. Miniver*
Actor—Ronald Colman for *Random Harvest*
 Walter Pidgeon for *Mrs. Miniver*
Supporting Actor—*Van Heflin for *Johnny Eager*
 Frank Morgan for *Tortilla Flat*
 Henry Travers for *Mrs. Miniver*
Actress—*Greer Garson for *Mrs. Miniver*
 Katharine Hepburn for *Woman of the Year*
Supporting Actress—Susan Peters for *Random Harvest*
 Dame Mae Whitty for *Mrs. Miniver*
 *Teresa Wright for *Mrs. Miniver*
Writing—Original Screenplay—George Oppenheimer for *The War Against Mrs. Hadley*
 *Michael Kanin and Ring Lardner, Jr. for *Woman of the Year*
 Screenplay—*George Froeschel, James Hilton, Claudine West, and Arthur Wimperis for *Mrs. Miniver*
 George Froeschel, Claudine West, and Arthur Wimperis for *Random Harvest*
Art Direction—Cedric Gibbons, Randall Duell, Jack Moore, and Edwin B. Willis for *Random Harvest*
Cinematography—Black & White—*Joseph Ruttenberg for *Mrs. Miniver*
Film Editing—Harold F. Kress for *Mrs. Miniver*
Music—Dramatic Score—Herbert Stothart for *Random Harvest*
 Musical Score—Roger Edens and George Stoll for *For Me and My Gal*

Song—Ralph Freed and Burton Lane for "How about You?" from
Babes on Broadway
Sound Recording—Douglas Shearer for *Mrs. Miniver*
Special Effects—A. Arnold Gillespie, Warren Newcombe, and Douglas
Shearer for *Mrs. Miniver*
Honorary—To MGM for its achievement in representing the American
Way of Life in the production of the *Andy Hardy* series of films.
Irving G. Thalberg Memorial Award — Sidney Franklin, producer of
Random Harvest and *Mrs. Miniver*

1943

Picture—*The Human Comedy*
     Madame Curie
Direction—Clarence Brown for *The Human Comedy*
Actor — Walter Pidgeon for *Madame Curie*
     Mickey Rooney for *The Human Comedy*
Actress—Greer Garson for *Madame Curie*
Writing—Original Story—*William Saroyan for *The Human Comedy*
Art Direction—Black & White—Cedric Gibbons, Paul Groesse, Hugh Hunt,
     and Edwin B. Willis for *Madame Curie*
     Color—Cedric Gibbons, Daniel Cathcart, Jacques Mersereau,
     and Edwin B. Willis for *Thousands Cheer*
Cinematography—Black & White—Harry Stradling for *The Human Comedy*
     Joseph Ruttenberg for *Madame Curie*
     Color—Leonard Smith for *Lassie Come Home*
     George Folsey for *Thousands Cheer*
Music—Dramatic Score—Herbert Stothart for *Madame Curie*
     Musical Score—Herbert Stothart for *Thousands Cheer*
Sound Recording—Douglas Shearer for *Madame Curie*
Special Effects—A. Arnold Gillespie, Donald Jahraus, and Michael Steinore
     for *Stand By for Action*

1944

Picture—*Gaslight*
Actor—Charles Boyer for *Gaslight*
Supporting Actor—Hume Cronyn for *The Seventh Cross*
Actress—*Ingrid Bergman for *Gaslight*
     Greer Garson for *Mrs. Parkington*
Supporting Actress—Angela Lansbury for *Gaslight*
     Aline MacMahon for *Dragon Seed*
     Agnes Moorehead for *Mrs. Parkington*
Writing—Original Story—David Boehm and Chandler Sprague for *A Guy
     Named Joe*
     Original Screenplay—Richard Connel and Gladys Lehman for
     Two Girls and a Sailor

Screenplay—John L. Balderston, Walter Reisch, and John Van
Druten for *Gaslight*
Irving Brecher and Fred F. Finkelhoffe for *Meet
Me in St. Louis*
Art Direction—Black & White—*Cedric Gibbons, William Ferrari,
Paul Huldschinsky and Edwin B. Willis for *Gaslight*
Color—Cedric Gibbons, Daniel B. Cathcart, Richard Pefferle, and
Edwin B. Willis for *Kismet*
Cinematography—Black & White — Sidney Wagner for *Dragon Seed*
Joseph Ruttenberg for *Gaslight*
Harold Rosson and Robert Surtees for *Thirty Seconds over
Tokyo*
George Folsey for *The White Cliffs of Dover*
Color—Charles Rosher for *Kismet*
George Folsey for *Meet Me in St. Louis*
Music—Dramatic Score—Herbert Stothart for *Kismet*
Musical Score—George Stoll for *Meet Me in St. Louis*
Song—Ralph Blane and Hugh Martin for "The Trolley Song" from
Meet Me in St. Louis
Sound Recording—Douglas Shearer for *Kismet*
Special Effects—*A. Arnold Gillespie, Donald Jahraus, Warren Newcombe,
and Douglas Shearer for *Thirty Seconds over Tokyo*
Honorary—Margaret O'Brien

1945

Picture—*Anchors Aweigh*
Direction—Clarence Brown for *National Velvet*
Actor—Gene Kelly for *Anchors Aweigh*
Actress—Greer Garson for *The Valley of Decision*
Supporting Actress—Angela Lansbury for *The Picture of Dorian Gray*
*Anne Revere for *National Velvet*
Writing—Original Screenplay—Myles Connolly for *Music for Millions*
Harry Kurnitz for *What Next, Corporal Hargrove?*
Art Direction—Black & White—Cedric Gibbons, Hans Peters, John
Bonar, Hugh Hunt, and Edwin B. Willis for *The Picture
of Dorian Gray*
Color—Cedric Gibbons, Urie McCleary, Mildred Griffiths, and Edwin
B. Willis for *National Velvet*
Cinematography—Black & White—*Harry Stradling for *The Picture of Dorian
Gray*
Color—Charles Boyle and Robert Planck for *Anchors
Aweigh*
Leonard Smith for *National Velvet*
Film Editing—*Robert J. Kern for *National Velvet*
Music—Dramatic Score—Herbert Stothart for *The Valley of Decision*

Musical Score—*George Stoll for *Anchors Aweigh*
Song—Sammy Cahn and Jule Styne for "I Fall In Love Too Easily"
from *Anchors Aweigh*
Sound Recording—Douglas Shearer for *They Were Expendable*
Special Effects—A. Arnold Gillespie, Donald Jahraus, R. A. MacDonald,
and Michael Steinore for *They Were Expendable*

1946

Picture—*The Yearling*
Direction—Clarence Brown for *The Yearling*
Actor—Gregory Peck for *The Yearling*
Supporting Actor—Charles Coburn for *The Green Years*
Actress—Jane Wyman for *The Yearling*
Writing—Original Story—*Clemence Dane for *Vacation from Marriage*
Art Direction—Color—*Cedric Gibbons, Paul Groesse, and Edwin B. Willis
for *The Yearling*
Cinematography—Black & White—George Folsey for *The Green Years*
Color—*Arthur Arling, Leonard Smith, and Charles
Rosher for *The Yearling*
Film Editing—Harold F. Kress for *The Yearling*
Music—Musical Score—Lennie Hayton for *The Harvey Girls*
Song—*Johnny Mercer and Harry Warren for "On The Atchinson,
Topeka and Santa Fe" from *The Harvey Girls*
Honorary—Claude Jarman, Jr.

1947

Cinematography—Black & White—George Folsey for *Green Dolphin Street*
Film Editing—George White for *Green Dolphin Street*
Music—Musical Score—Johnny Green for *Fiesta*
Song—Ralph Blane, Hugh Martin, and Roger Edens for "Pass That
Peace Pipe" from *Good News*
Sound Recording—*Green Dolphin Street*
Special Effects—*A. Arnold Gillespie, Warren Newcombe, Douglas
Shearer, and Michael Steinore for *Green Dolphin Street*

1948

Direction—Fred Zinnemann for *The Search*
Actor—Montgomery Clift for *The Search*
Writing—Story—*Richard Schweizer and David Wechsler for *The Search*
Screenplay—Richard Schweizer and David Wechsler for *The Search*
Cinematography—Color—Robert Planck for *The Three Musketeers*
Costume Design—Irene for *B. F.'s Daughter*
Music—Musical Score—*Johnny Green and Roger Edens for *Easter Parade*
Lennie Hayton for *The Pirate*
Honorary—Ivan Jandl

808

1949

Picture—*Battleground*
Direction—William Wellman for *Battleground*
Supporting Actor—James Whitmore for *Battleground*
Actress—Deborah Kerr for *Edward, My Son*
Writing—Story—*Douglas Morrow for *The Stratton Story*
      Story & Screenplay—*Robert Pirosh for *Battleground*
Art Direction—Black & White—Cedric Gibbons, Jack Martin Smith,
      Edwin B. Willis, and Richard A. Pefferle for *Madame Bovary*
      Color—*Cedric Gibbons, Paul Groesse, Edwin B. Willis,
      and Jack D. Moore for *Little Women*
Cinematography—Black & White—*Paul C. Vogel for *Battleground*
      Color—Harry Stradling for *The Barkleys Of Broadway*
      Robert Planck and Charles Schoenbaum for *Little Women*
Film Editing—John Dunning for *Battleground*
Music—Musical Score—*Roger Edens and Lennie Hayton for *On the Town*
      Song—*Frank Loesser for "Baby, It's Cold Outside" from
      Neptune's Daughter
Honorary—Fred Astaire
      Jean Hersholt

1950

Picture—*Father of the Bride*
      King Solomon's Mines
Direction—John Huston for *The Asphalt Jungle*
Actor—Louis Calhern for *The Magnificent Yankee*
      Spencer Tracy for *Father of the Bride*
Supporting Actor—Sam Jaffe for *The Asphalt Jungle*
Writing—Story—Leonard Spigelgass for *Mystery Street*
      Screenplay—Benn Maddow and John Huston for *The Asphalt Jungle*
      Frances Goodrich and Albert Hackett for *Father of the Bride*
      Story & Screenplay—Ruth Gordon and Garson Kanin for *Adam's Rib*
Art Direction—Color—Cedric Gibbons, Paul Groesse, Edwin B.
      Willis, and Richard A. Pefferle for *Annie Get Your Gun*
Cinematography—Black & White—Harold Rosson for *The Asphalt Jungle*
      Color—Charles Rosher for *Annie Get Your Gun*
      *Robert Surtees for *King Solomon's Mines*
Film Editing—James E. Newcom for *Annie Get Your Gun*
      *Ralph Winters and Conrad A. Nervig for *King Solomon's Mines*
Costume Design—Black & White—Walter Plunkett for *The Magnificent
      Yankee*
      Color—Walter Plunkett and Valles for *That Forsyte Woman*
Music—Musical Score—*Adolph Deutsch and Roger Edens for *Annie Get
      Your Gun*
      Andre Previn for *Three Little Words*

Song—Sammy Cahn and Nicholas Brodszky for "Be My Love" from *The Toast of New Orleans*
Honorary—George Murphy
    Louis B. Mayer

1951

Picture—**An American in Paris*
    Quo Vadis?
Direction—Vincente Minnelli for *An American in Paris*
Supporting Actor—Leo Genn for *Quo Vadis?*
    Peter Ustinov for *Quo Vadis?*
Writing—Story—Alfred Hayes and Stewart Stern for *Teresa*
    Story & Screenplay—*Alan Jay Lerner for *An American in Paris*
    Robert Pirosh for *Go for Broke!*
Art Direction—Black & White—Cedric Gibbons, Paul Groesse, Edwin B. Willis, and Jack D. Moore for *Too Young to Kiss*
    Color—*Cedric Gibbons and Preston Ames for *An American in Paris*
Cinematography—Color—*Alfred Gilks and John Alton for *An American in Paris*
    Robert Surtees and William V. Skall for *Quo Vadis?*
    Charles Rosher for *Show Boat*
Film Editing—Adrienne Fazan for *An American in Paris*
    Ralph E. Winters for *Quo Vadis?*
Costume Design—Color—*Orry-Kelly, Walter Plunkett, and Irene Sharaff for *An American in Paris*
    Helen Rose and Gile Steele for *The Great Caruso*
    Herschel McCoy for *Quo Vadis?*
Music—Dramatic Score—Miklos Rozsa for *Quo Vadis?*
    Musical Score—*Johnny Green and Saul Chaplin for *An American in Paris*
    Peter Herman Adler and Johnny Green for *The Great Caruso*
    Adolph Deutsch and Conrad Salinger for *Show Boat*
    Song—Bert Kalmar, Harry Ruby, and Oscar Hammerstein II for "A Kiss to Build a Dream On" from *The Strip*
    Alan Jay Lerner and Burton Lane for "Too Late Now" from *Royal Wedding*
    Sammy Cahn and Nicholas Broadszky for "Wonder Why" from *Rich, Young and Pretty*
Sound Recording—*Douglas Shearer for *The Great Caruso*
Honorary—Gene Kelly
Irving G. Thalberg Memorial Award—Arthur Freed

1952

Picture — *Ivanhoe*
Actor—Kirk Douglas for *The Bad and the Beautiful*

Supporting Actress—*Gloria Grahame for *The Bad and the Beautiful*
    Jean Hagen for *Singin' in the Rain*
Writing—Screenplay—*Charles Schnee for *The Bad and the Beautiful*
    Story and Screenplay—Ruth Gordon and Garson Kanin for *Pat and Mike*
Art Direction — Black & White—*Cedric Gibbons, Edward Carfagno, Edwin B. Willis, and Keogh Gleason for *The Bad and the Beautiful*
    Color—Cedric Gibbons, Paul Groesse, Edwin B. Willis, and Arthur Krams for *The Merry Widow*
Cinematography—Black & White—*Robert Surtees for *The Bad and the Beautiful*
    Color—F. A. Young for *Ivanhoe*
    George J. Folsey for *Million Dollar Mermaid*
Costume Design—Black & White—*Helen Rose for *The Bad and the Beautiful*
    Color—Helen Rose and Gile Steele for *The Merry Widow*
Music—Dramatic Score—Miklos Rozsa for *Ivanhoe*
    Musical Score—Lennie Hayton for *Singin' in the Rain*
    Song—Sammy Cahn and Nicholas Broadszky for the title song from *Because You're Mine*
Special Effects—*Plymouth Adventure*

1953

Picture—*Julius Caesar*
Direction—Charles Walters for *Lili*
Actor—Marlon Brando for *Julius Caesar*
Actress—Leslie Caron for *Lili*
    Ava Gardner for *Magambo*
Supporting Actress—Grace Kelly for *Magambo*
    Marjorie Rambeau for *Torch Song*
Writing—Story—Beirne Lay, Jr. for *Above and Beyond*
    Screenplay—Helen Deutsch *for Lili*
    Story & Screenplay—Betty Comden and Adolph Green for *The Band Wagon*
    Sam Rolfe and Harold Jack Bloom for *The Naked Spur*
    Millard Kaufman for *Take the High Ground*
Art Direction—Black & White—*Cedric Gibbons, Edward Carfagno, Edwin B. Willis, and Hugh Hunt for *Julius Caesar*
    Color—Cedric Gibbons, Paul Groesse, Edwin B. Willis, and Arthur Krams for *Lili*
    Cedric Gibbons, Preston Ames, Edward Carfagno, Gabriel Scognamillo, Edwin B. Willis, Keogh Gleason, Arthur Krams, and Jack D. Moore for *The Story of Three Loves*
    Cedric Gibbons, Urie McCleary, Edwin B. Willis, and Jack D. Moore for *Young Bess*

Cinematography—Black & White—Joseph Ruttenberg for *Julius Caesar*
    Color—George Folsey for *All the Brothers Were Valiant*
    Robert Planck for *Lili*
Costume Design—Black & White—Walter Plunkett for *The Actress*
    Helen Rose and Herschel McCoy for *Dream Wife*
    Color—Mary Ann Nyberg for *The Band Wagon*
    Walter Plunkett for *Young Bess*
Music—Dramatic Score—Hugo Friedhofer for *Above and Beyond*
    Miklos Rozsa for *Julius Caesar*
    *Bronislau Kaper for *Lili*
    Musical Score—Adolph Deutsch for *The Band Wagon*
    Andre Previn and Saul Chaplin for *Kiss Me Kate!*
    Song—Leo Robin and Nicholas Brodszky for "My Flaming Heart"
    from *Small Town Girl*
Sound Recording—A. W. Watkins for *Knights of the Round Table*

1954

Picture—*Seven Brides for Seven Brothers*
Supporting Actress—Nina Foch for *Executive Suite*
Writing—Screenplay—Albert Hackett, Frances Goodrich, and Dorothy
    Kingsley for *Seven Brides for Seven Brothers*
Art Direction—Black & White—Cedric Gibbons, Edward Carfagno, Edwin
    B. Willis, and Emile Kuri for *Executive Suite*
    Color—Cedric Gibbons, Preston Ames, Edwin B. Willis,
    and Keogh Gleason for *Brigadoon*
Cinematography—Black & White—George Folsey for *Executive Suite*
    John Seitz for *Rogue Cop*
    Color—George Folsey for *Seven Brides for Seven Brothers*
Film Editing—Ralph E. Winters for *Seven Brides for Seven Brothers*
Costume Design—Black & White—Helen Rose for *Executive Suite*
    Color—Irene Sharaff for *Brigadoon*
Music—Musical Score—*Adolph Deutsch and Saul Chaplin for *Seven Brides*
    for Seven Brothers
Sound Recording—Wesley C. Miller for *Brigadoon*
Honorary—Greta Garbo

1955

Direction—John Sturges for *Bad Day at Black Rock*
Actor—James Cagney for *Love Me or Leave Me*
    Spencer Tracy for *Bad Day at Black Rock*
*Supporting Actor—Arthur Kennedy for *Trial*
Actress—Susan Hayward for *I'll Cry Tomorrow*
    Eleanor Parker for *Interrupted Melody*
Writing—Story—*Daniel Fuchs for *Love Me or Leave Me*
    Screenplay—Millard Kaufman for *Bad Day at Black Rock*

Richard Brooks for *Blackboard Jungle*
Daniel Fuchs and Isobel Lennart for *Love Me or Leave Me*
Story & Screenplay—*William Ludwig and Sonya Levien for
Interrupted Melody
Betty Comden and Adolph Green for *It's
Always Fair Weather*
Art Direction—Black & White—Cedric Gibbons, Randall Duell, Edwin B.
Willis, and Henry Grace for *Blackboard Jungle*
Cedric Gibbons, Malcolm Brown, Edwin B. Willis,
and Hugh B. Hunt for *I'll Cry Tomorrow*
Cinematography—Black & White—Russell Harlan for *Blackboard Jungle*
Arthur E. Arling for *I'll Cry Tomorrow*
Film Editing—Ferris Webster for *Blackboard Jungle*
Costume Design—Black & White—*Helen Rose for *I'll Cry Tomorrow*
Color—Irene Sharaff for *Guys and Dolls*
Helen Rose for *Interrupted Melody*
Music—Musical Score—Jay Blackton and Cyril J. Mockridge for *Guys and
Dolls*
Andre Previn for *It's Always Fair Weather*
Percy Faith and George Stoll for *Love Me or Leave Me.*
Song—Sammy Cahn and Nicholas Brodszky for "I'll Never Stop
Loving You" from *Love Me or Leave Me.*
Sammy Cahn and James Van Heusen for "Love Is the Tender
Trap" from *The Tender Trap*
Sound Recording—Wesley C. Miller for *Love Me or Leave Me*

1956

Actor—Kirk Douglas for *Lust for Life*
Supporting Actor—*Anthony Quinn for *Lust for Life*
Writing—Screenplay—Norman Corwin for *Lust for Life*
Original Screenplay—Andrew L. Stone for *Julie*
Art Direction—Black & White—*Cedric Gibbons, Malcolm F. Brown, Edwin
B. Willis and Keogh Gleason for *Somebody Up There Likes Me.*
Color—Cedric Gibbons, Hans Peters, Preston Ames, Edwin
B. Willis, and Keogh Gleason for *Lust for Life.*
Cinematography—Black & White—*Joseph Ruttenberg for *Somebody Up
There Likes Me*
Film Editing—Albert Akst for *Somebody Up There Likes Me*
Costume Design—Black & White—Helen Rose for *The Power and the Prize*
Music—Musical Score—Johnny Green and Saul Chaplin for *High Society*
George Stoll and Johnny Green for *Meet Me in Las Vegas*
Song—Tom Adair and Leith Stevens for the title song from *Julie*
Cole Porter for "True Love" from *High Society*
Special Effects—A. Arnold Gillespie, Irving Ries, and Wesley C.
Miller for *Forbidden Planet*

1957

Actress—Elizabeth Taylor for *Raintree County*
Writing—Story & Screenplay—*George Wells for *Designing Woman*
Art Direction—William A. Horning and Gene Allen for *Les Girls*
　　　William A. Horning and Urie McCleary for *Raintree County*
Costume Design—Orry-Kelly for *Les Girls*
　　　Walter Plunkett for *Raintree County*
Music—Score—Johnny Green for *Raintree County*
Sound Recording—Wesley C. Miller for *Les Girls*

1958

Picture—*Cat on a Hot Tin Roof*
　　　Gigi
Direction—Richard Brooks for *Cat on a Hot Tin Roof*
　　　*Vincente Minnelli for *Gigi*
Actor—Paul Newman for *Cat on a Hot Tin Roof*
Supporting Actor—Lee J. Cobb for *The Brothers Karamazov*
　　　Arthur Kennedy for *Some Came Running*
Actress—Shirley MacLaine for *Some Came Running*
　　　Elizabeth Taylor for *Cat on a Hot Tin Roof*
Supporting Actress—Martha Hyer for *Some Came Running*
Writing—Screenplay—Richard Brooks and James Poe for *Cat on a Hot Tin Roof*
　　　*Alan Jay Lerner for *Gigi*
　　　Story & Screenplay—Williams Bowers and James Edward Grant for *The Sheepman*
Art Direction—*William A. Horning, Preston Sturges, Henry Grace, and Keogh Gleason for *Gigi*
Cinematography—Color—William Daniels for *Cat on a Hot Tin Roof*
　　　*Joseph Ruttenberg for *Gigi*
Film Editing — *Adrienne Fazan for *Gigi*
Costume Design—*Cecil Beaton for *Gigi*
　　　Walter Plunkett for *Some Came Running*
Music—Musical Score—*Andre Previn for *Gigi*
　　　Song—*Alan Jay Lerner and Frederick Loewe for the title song from *Gigi*
　　　Sammy Cahn and James Van Heusen for "To Love and Be Loved" from *Some Came Running*
Special Effects—*Tom Howard for *Tom Thumb*
　　　A. Arnold Gillespie and Harold Humbrock for *Torpedo Run*

1959

Picture—*Ben Hur*
Direction—*William Wyler for *Ben Hur*
Actor—*Charlton Heston for *Ben Hur*

Supporting Actor—*Hugh Griffith for *Ben Hur*
Writing—Screenplay—Karl Tunberg for *Ben Hur*
  Story and Screenplay—Ernest Lehman for *North by Northwest*
Art Direction — Color—*William A. Horning, Edward Carfagno, and Hugh
  Hunt for *Ben Hur*
    William A. Horning, Robert Boyle, Merrill Pye, Henry
    Grace, and Frank McKelvy for *North by Northwest*
Cinematography—Color—*Robert L. Surtess for *Ben Hur*
Film Editing—*Ralph E. Winters and John D. Dunning for *Ben Hur*
  George Tomasini for *North by Northwest*
Costume Design—Black & White—Helen Rose for *The Gazebo*
  Color—*Elizabeth Haffenden for *Ben Hur*
Music—Dramatic Score—*Miklos Rozsa for *Ben Hur*
Sound Recording—*Franklin E. Milton for *Ben Hur*
  A. W. Watkins for *Libel*
Special Effects—*A. Arnold Gillespie, Robert MacDonald, and Milo
  Lory for *Ben Hur*

1960
Actress—*Elizabeth Taylor for *Butterfield 8*
Art Direction—Color—George W. Davis, Addison Hehr, Henry Grace,
  Hugh Hunt, and Otto Siegel for *Cimarron*
Cinematography—Color—Joseph Ruttenberg and Charles Harten for *Butter-
  field 8*
Music—Musical Score—Andre Previn for *Bells Are Ringing*
Sound Recording—Franklin E. Milton for *Cimarron*
Special Effects—A. J. Lohman for *The Last Voyage*
  *Gene Warren and Tim Baer for *The Time Machine*

1961
Music—Song—Henry Mancini and Mack David for the title song from
  Bachelor in Paradise

1962
Picture—*Mutiny on the Bounty*
Supporting Actor—*Ed Begley for *Sweet Bird of Youth*
Actress—Geraldine Page for *Sweet Bird of Youth*
Supporting Actress—Shirley Knight for *Sweet Bird of Youth*
Writing—Screenplay—Vladimir Nabokov for *Lolita*
Art Direction—Black & White—George W. Davis, Edward Carfagno, Henry
  Grace, and Richard Pefferle for *Period of Adjustment*
    Color—George W. Davis, J. McMillan Johnson, Henry Grace,
    and Hugh Hunt for *Mutiny on the Bounty*
    George W. Davis, Edward Carfagno, Henry Grace,
    and Richard Pefferle for *The Wonderful World of
    The Brothers Grimm*

815

Cinematography—Color—Robert L. Surtees for *Mutiny on the Bounty*
　　　Paul C. Vogel for *The Wonderful World of the
　　　Brothers Grimm*
Film Editing—John McSweeney, Jr. for *Mutiny on the Bounty*
Costume Design—Color—*Mary Wills for *The Wonderful World of the
　　　Brothers Grimm*
Music—Original Score—Bronislau Kaper for *Mutiny on the Bounty*
　　　Adapted Score—Leigh Harline for *The Wonderful World of the Brothers
　　　Grimm*
　　　Song—Bronislau Kaper and Paul Francis Webster for "Follow Me"
　　　from *Mutiny on the Bounty*
Special Effects—A. Arnold Gillespie and Milo Lory for *Mutiny
　　　on the Bounty*

1963

Picture—*How the West Was Won*
Supporting Actor—Nick Adams for *Twilight of Honor*
Supporting Actress—*Margaret Rutherford for *The V.I.P.s*
Writing—Story and Screenplay—Carlo Bernari, Pasquale Festa Campanile,
　　　Massimo Franciosa, and Nanni Loy for *The Four Days of Naples*
　　　*James R. Webb for *How the West Was Won*
Art Direction—Black & White—George W. Davis, Paul Groesse, Henry
　　　Grace, and Hugh Hunt for *Twilight of Honor*
　　　George W. Davis, William Ferrari, Addison Hehr, Henry
　　　Grace, Don Greenwood, Jr., and Jack Mills for *How the
　　　West Was Won*
Cinematography—Color—William H. Daniels, Milton Krasner, Charles
　　　Lang, Jr., and Joseph LaShelle for *How the West Was Won*
Film Editing—*Harold F. Kress for *How the West Was Won*
Costume Design—Color—Walter Plunkett for *How the West Was Won*
Music—Original Score—Alfred Newman and Ken Darby for *How the West
　　　Was Won*
Sound Recording—*Franklin E. Milton for *How the West Was Won*

1964

Actress—Debbie Reynolds for *The Unsinkable Molly Brown*
Supporting Actress—Grayson Hall for *The Night of the Iguana*
Art Direction—Black & White—George W. Davis, Hans Peters, Elliot
　　　Scott, Henry Grace, and Robert R. Benton for *The Americanization of
　　　Emily*
　　　Stephen Grimes for *The Night of the Iguana*
Cinematography—Black & White—Philip H. Lathrop for *The Americanization
　　　of Emily*
　　　Gabriel Figueroa for *The Night of the Iguana*
　　　Color—Daniel L. Fapp for *The Unsinkable Molly Brown*

Costume Design—Black & White—*Dorothy Jeakins for *The Night of the Iguana*

Music—Adapted Score—Robert Armbruster, Leo Arnaud, Jack Elliott, Jack Hayes, Calvin Jackson, and Leo Shuken for *The Unsinkable Molly Brown*

Sound Recording—Franklin E. Milton for *The Unsinkable Molly Brown*

Special Visual Effects—Jim Danforth for *The 7 Faces of Dr. Lao*

Honorary—William Tuttle for makeup achievement on *The 7 Faces of Dr. Lao*

1965

Picture—*Doctor Zhivago*

Direction—David Lean for *Doctor Zhivago*

Supporting Actor—Tom Courtenay for *Doctor Zhivago*

Actress—Elizabeth Hartman for *A Patch of Blue*

Supporting Actress—*Shelley Winters for *A Patch of Blue*

Writing—Screenplay—*Robert Bolt for *Doctor Zhivago*

Art Direction—Black & White—George W. Davis, Urie McCleary, Henry Grace, and Charles S. Thompson for *A Patch of Blue*

Cinematography—Black & White—Robert Burks for *A Patch of Blue*
Color—*Freddie Young for *Doctor Zhivago*

Costume Design—Color—*Phyllis Dalton for *Doctor Zhivago*

Music—Original Score—*Maurice Jarre for *Doctor Zhivago*
Song—*Johnny Mandel and Paul Francis Webster for "The Shadow of Your Smile" from *The Sandpiper*

Sound Recording—Franklin E. Milton for *Doctor Zhivago*

1966

Art Direction—Black & White—George W. Davis, Paul Groesse, Henry Grace, and Hugh Hunt for *Mister Buddwing*

Film Editing—*Fredric Steinkamp, Henry Berman, Stewart Linder, and Frank Santillo for *Grand Prix*

Music—Adapted Score—Harry Sukman for *The Singing Nun*

Sound Recording—*Franklin E. Milton for *Grand Prix*

Sound Effects—*Gordon Daniel for *Grand Prix*

1967

Supporting Actor—John Cassavetes for *The Dirty Dozen*

Film Editing—Michael Luciano for *The Dirty Dozen*

Music—Original Score—Richard Rodney Bennett for *Far from the Madding Crowd*

Sound Recording—*The Dirty Dozen*

Sound Effects—John Poyner for *The Dirty Dozen*

Honorary — Arthur Freed

1968

Direction—Stanley Kubrick for *2001: A Space Odyssey*

Actor—Alan Bates for *The Fixer*
Supporting Actor—*Jack Albertson for *The Subject Was Roses*
Actress—Patricia Neal for *The Subject Was Roses*
Writing—Story & Screenplay—Ira Wallach and Peter Ustinov for *Hot Millions*
> Stanley Kubrick and Arthur C. Clarke for
> *2001: A Space Odyssey*
Art Direction—George W. Davis and Edward Carfagno for *The Shoes of the Fisherman*
> Tony Masters, Harry Lange, and Ernie Archer for *2001: A Space Odyssey*
Cinematography—Daniel L. Fapp for *Ice Station Zebra*
Music—Original Dramatic Score—Alex North for *The Shoes of the Fisherman*
Special Visual Effects—Hal Millar and J. McMillan Johnson for *Ice Station Zebra*
> *Stanley Kubrick for *2001: A Space Odyssey*

1969
Actor—Peter O'Toole for *Goodbye, Mr. Chips*
Music—Musical Score—Leslie Bricusse and John Williams for *Goodbye, Mr. Chips*

1970
Supporting Actor—*John Mills for *Ryan's Daughter*
Actress—Sarah Miles for *Ryan's Daughter*
Cinematography—*Fred A. Young for *Ryan's Daughter*
Sound Recording—Gordon K. McCallum and John Bramall for *Ryan's Daughter*
Honorary—Jean Hersholt Humanitarian Award—Frank Sinatra

1971
Music—Dramatic Score—Isaac Hayes for *Shaft*
> Musical Score—Peter Maxwell Davies and Peter Greenwall
> for *The Boy Friend*
> Song—*Isaac Hayes for the title song from *Shaft*

1972
Actress—Maggie Smith for *Travels With My Aunt*
Art Direction—John Box, Gil Parrondo and Robert W. Laing for *Travels With My Aunt*
Cinematography—Douglas Slocombe for *Travels With My Aunt*
Costume Design—*Anthony Powell for *Travels With My Aunt*
Jean Hersholt Humanitarian Award—Rosalind Russell

Index

831

Lugosi, Bela, 16, 68
Lukas, Paul, 88, 409
Luke, Keye, 452-455
Lullaby, 512
Lund, John, 715
Lundigan, William, 219
Lunt, Alfred, 155, 215, 326, 704, 714
Lupino, Ida, 632, 770
Lust for Life, 617
Luxury Liner, 278, 479, 575
Lydia Bailey, 219
Lydon, Jimmy, 132, 277
Lynde, Paul, 766
Lynn, Diana, 380
Lynn, Jeffrey, 384, 549
Lysistrata, 46

M, 519
Ma and Pa Kettle, (series), 80
Macao, 286
Macbeth, 67, 127, 507
McCambridge, Mercedes, 145
McCarthy, Charlie, 574, 575
McCarty, Mary, 119
McCary, Leo, 47
McClintic, Guthrie, 136, 215, 724, 780
McConnell Story, The, 12, 765
McCormack, John, 537, 721
McCormick, Myron, 690
McCoy, Tim, 141
McCrea, Joel, 42, 136, 165, 374, 680, 760
MacDonald, Jeanette, 42, 63, 85, 86, 201, 202-203, 295, 317, 359, 371, 374, 380, 390, 391, 415, 444, 456-464, 482, 544, 549, 561, 569, 574, 575, 674, 721, 722, 735
McDonald, Marie "The Body," 396, 607, 608, 715
MacDonald, Ray, 758
McDowall, Roddy, 248, 380, 679, 680, 697
McGuire, Dorothy, 37, 613, 714, 765, 786
Machinal, 223
McKay, Scott, 626
McLaglen, Victor, 548
MacLaine, Shirley, 110, 397, 440, 607, 652

MacMahon, Aline, 589
MacMurray, Fred, 18, 208, 244, 374, 380, 564, 680
McNally, Stephen, 557
MacRae, Gordon, 389, 390, 575
Macready, George, 770
Mad Genius, The, 62
Mad Love, 452
Madame Bovary, 129, 334
Madame Curie, 268, 270, 384, 528, 562, 753, 770
Madame Dubarry, 544
Madame X, 68, 302, 494, 690, 746
Made for Each Other, 674
Mademoiselle, 269
Madigan, 766
Madonna of the Seven Moons, 290
Madonna's Secret, The, 637
Madron, 110
Madwoman of Chaillot, The, 343, 419
Magda, 60
Magic Carpet, The, 53
Magic Fountain, The, 777
Magnificent Ambersons, The, 506, 507
Magnificent Obsession, 305, 706, 707
Magnificent Yankee, The, 105, 106
Magnolia Alley, 133
Main, Marjorie, 80, 280, 302, 465-468, 483, 557, 591, 765
Main Street after Dark, 626, 730
Main Street to Broadway, 57, 70, 327
Maisie, 367, 666
Maisie Gets Her Man, 592, 666
Maisie Goes to Reno, 188, 666
Maisie Was a Lady, 42, 380, 538, 666
Major and the Minor, The, 86, 380
Major Barbara, 363, 401
Majority of One, A, 632
Make Mine Music, 204
Make Way for Tomorrow, 47
Malaya, 352, 739
Malden, Karl, 501
Male Animal, The, 17
Maltese Falcon, The, 37, 482
Mame, 53, 417, 419, 420, 486, 489, 490
Mamoulian, Rouben, 177, 237, 617, 670
Man about Town, 518
Man Afraid, 715

855

859

862